Credit Solutions:

Kershman on Advising Secured and Unsecured Creditors

(How to Get Paid in Ontario)

Problems are simply solutions in waiting™

Stanley J. Kershman

B.Admin., LL.B.

CARSWELL
A THOMSON COMPANY

National Library of Canada Cataloguing in Publication Data

Kershman, Stanley J.
Credit solutions: Kershman on advising secured and unsecured creditors: on how to get paid in Ontario

Include index.
ISBN 0-459-26186-X

1. Debtor and creditor — Ontario. 2. Security (Law) — Ontario. I. Title.

KEO317.K47 2001 346.71307'7 C2001-901832-0

CARSWELL
A THOMSON COMPANY

One Corporate Plaza
2075 Kennedy Road
Toronto, Ontario
M1T 3V4

Customer Relations:
Toronto 1-416-609-3800
Elsewhere in Canada/U.S. 1-800-387-5164
Fax 1-416-298-5094

Dedications and Acknowledgments

This book marks the achievement of one of my life goals — to have it published.

This book is dedicated to the memory of several outstanding people.

Firstly, my father, Harry Kershman, of blessed memory. No one could want for a better, more loving and understanding father. I miss him dearly. A soft-spoken man who understood what life was all about and lived by those principles.

Secondly, my friend, Dr. Eric Stulberg, of blessed memory. A fine doctor and family man who was taken from this world at too young an age.

Thirdly, Ben Baylin, of blessed memory. He was a great man with a heart of gold — to his family, his friends, his cub pack and all those who knew him. Again, taken at the prime of his life.

Lastly, Mrs. Naomi Bulka, of blessed memory, who was a woman of great elegance, humility and of rock solid values. After watching her family grow up, she went back to school and worked as a technical writer before illness struck her down in her prime of life.

I acknowledge, with gratitude, the assistance of Percy Ostroff (Doucet, McBride LLP), Sean Cumming (MacDonald, Sager, Manis LLP) and Ross Macfarlane (Mann & Associates), Susan Brown (Fraser, Milner, Casgrain LLP), Douglas Buchmayer (Drache, Burke-Robertson & Buchmayer LLP), Bill Neville (Low, Murchison) and Ken Wright (Soloway, Wright LLP) for reading drafts of chapters and for their helpful suggestions for improvement.

Many thanks to Karen McLaurin and all of the staff of the County of Carleton Law Association for their assistance including Nathalie Leonard and Leslie LeMarquand. In addition, many thanks to the staff at the Ottawa Court House including Ray Culleton, Michelle Denis, Danielle Charlebois, Peggy Bamber, Sheila Labonte, Doreen MacMillan, Sue Treganowan, Diane Muldoon, Jackie Clifford, Audrey Webster, Shairoz Rupani, Shailina Awadia, Arlene Cook, Marie St. Clair, Tim Ginley, Penny Mylonakov, Brian Forrester, Sylvia Lord, Mike Ryndzak, Jean Saikaley, Sandra Davidson and Doreen MacMillan. In addition, thanks to Terry Brown, Land Registrar, and all of the staff at the Ottawa Land Registry/Land Titles Office (No. 4).

Thank you very much to Rachel Francis, Elda Sherman, Patti Bayley Thompson and Marco Acchione at Carswell Thomson Professional Publishing for their continuing and dedicated support in the writing and publishing of this book. Also, a sincere thank you to Rabbi Reuven Bulka, Jeff

Madison, David Dienstock, Colin Rowe, Dona Stethem, Patrick Conway, Jason Babb, Bernie Aron, Patricia den Boer of Powerhouse Communications Group Inc., and Linda Rowe and the staff of Computer Composition.

Many thanks to Yvonne Jeffery Hope, my researcher, without whom this book would never have made it to publication. Her dedication, hours of research and sheer stamina made this book as good as it is.

Many thanks to my legal assistant, Mary Neill, for her computer skills and transforming my chicken scratchings and many revisions into a workable manuscript.

Thank you to my wife Carol, and my children Zev and Kayla, for all of their support and sacrifices that they made while I was writing this book. Special thanks to my mother, Sylvia Kershman, for her many years of love and mentoring, without which, in large measure, I would not be where I am today.

Lastly, I want to thank G-d for providing me with the skill and talent together with the tools to use them effectively in everyday life.

Stanley J. Kershman
Kershman & Kerr
283 McLeod Street
Ottawa, Ontario
K2P 1A1
Tel: (613) 238-1924
fax: (613) 238-4490
email: info@bankruptlaw.com
website: www.bankruptlaw.com

Credit Solutions: Kershman on Secured and Unsecured Creditors

Introduction

The unwillingness or inability of an individual or business to repay their debts can ripple out to affect a wide circle of creditors, both secured and unsecured. Advising such creditors is much like the role of a ship's pilot, who comes on board to navigate the ship through the roughest of waters. Just as the pilot knows how to bring the ship safely to harbour, despite shallow waters and sandbanks, so you must understand how to navigate financial and legal waters to ensure that your client receives the best possible opportunity to recover the debt owed.

Keep in mind that those unpaid debts can take a serious toll on the creditor's own financial situation. You need to assist your client to understand the options available, and the consequences of exercising those options.

This Practice Guide is designed to help you do just that. Like a navigational aid, it can assist you to gather the correct information, analyze the facts, recognize potential problems and guide your client to a satisfactory solution. While it will not address every case that your clients will bring to you, it will provide an overview of the entire process, from when your client first contacts you to when the matter is closed.

Although its primary audience is a legal one, this Practice Guide should also prove useful to other professionals operating in the areas of insolvency and bankruptcy, including:

- Accountants
- Banking Personnel
- Business People
- Credit Managers
- Credit Counsellors
- Debt Collectors
- Legal Assistants and Legal Secretaries
- Paralegals
- Mediators
- Trustees in Bankruptcy and Receivers

TABLE OF CONTENTS

Chapter 3 Collection and Enforcement of the Debt - Unsecured

TABLE OF CASES

FIRST CONTACT WITH THE SECURED OR UNSECURED CREDITOR AND THE INITIAL INTERVIEW

Table of Contents

1.1 THE FIRST CONTACT

In the storm that a financial crisis can bring, a secured creditor has a distinct advantage over an unsecured creditor: the collateral that a secured creditor holds can mitigate what might otherwise be a serious loss, acting as a ship's anchor acts to stabilize the situation. Even in the case of an unsecured creditor, there may be options available that can increase the likelihood of full or partial debt recovery.

In both cases, you should keep in mind that by the time a creditor (secured or unsecured) seeks legal recourse, he or she has likely been dealing with the debtor unsuccessfully for some time. Quick and careful action is therefore necessary to ensure that the creditor's interests are protected as fully as possible.

1.1.1 FIRST TELEPHONE CALL/CONTACT

- Determine the general situation. In particular, ask what the problems are so that you can determine if you have a time limitation or deadline to work with.
- Based on the general situation, and any potential deadlines, determine if there is immediate advice that should be given. If so, make a written note of any recommendations that you provide.
- Recommend an appointment with the client as soon as possible.

1.1.2 ARRANGING THE INITIAL INTERVIEW

- Set sufficient time aside, at a time convenient for both yourself and the creditor, to address the problem.
- Ensure that all relevant documents are brought to the initial interview. See 1.2.2 below for the information you require. *Detailed information is essential for advising a creditor appropriately; do not rely on what the client says, but on what the documentation says.*

1.2 THE INITIAL INTERVIEW

1.2.1 THE AIM OF THE INTERVIEW: INFORMATION, INFORMATION, INFORMATION

- Rely on the relevant documents to provide accurate information, but don't hesitate to ask any questions that the documents give rise to. If the material has not been brought, have it sent by courier, or faxed or e-mailed to the meeting.
- Photocopy the documentation, or request that the file be left, including all notes. *Sometimes, the notes will tell you more than the person advising you.*
- Note all additional information the creditor provides and all advice you give.

1.2.2 INFORMATION TO OBTAIN

(a) General Information about the Creditor

- The creditor's name, and business and personal addresses and contact numbers (phone, fax and e-mail/Internet).
- Background of the situation, including whether the debt was provided on a business or a personal basis, or both.
- Name and contact numbers of accountant.

(b) General Information about the Debtor

- Obtain the debtor's legal name(s), and business and personal addresses and contact numbers (phone, fax and e-mail/Internet). If the debtor is an employee, obtain the particulars of his place of employment. If the debtor does business under more than one entity, ensure you have all appropriate corporate or business names. *Having all applicable names will aid subsequent searches (see Chapter 2).*

- Name and contact numbers of debtor's accountant, financial advisor, lawyer and trustee in bankruptcy, if any.

(c) Financial Information

- Obtain all financial information/documentation regarding your client's security, if any, and the debtor's indebtedness, including:

  - contracts, invoices, statements, etc. regarding the debt;
  - security documents;
  - title documents and mortgages;
  - searches, if any performed to date (see Chapter 2);
  - details of any applicable lawsuits, pending or complete;
  - notice of intention under Section 427 of the *Bank Act*, if applicable;
  - any relevant correspondence; and
  - notes of any conversations.

- Ensure that you have the client's complete history of the debt. *You are looking for evidence that will show the debtor failing to meet liabilities or pay debts as they generally become due, or having liabilities in excess of assets. The evidence may also show the debtor's situation deteriorating over time, which would be another factor to validate your client's concern. This may be important later, both legally and tactically.*

- Is the person attending the interview the same person who oversaw the granting of the debt? Has the same individual been involved on the receivable/collections side of the situation for its duration? *If not, as can be the case where debt collection is a separate corporate function from debt granting, you may wish to interview those originally involved to ensure you have a complete picture of the situation.*

- Obtain as much information as possible regarding the debtor's overall financial situation, including assets and liabilities. Has the debtor made a proposal or declared bankruptcy?

- Obtain as much information as possible regarding other secured and unsecured creditors. Is your client aware of other creditors who may be pressuring the debtor for payment?

- Has your client begun action to collect on the debt or realize on the security?

- What will the impact be on the debtor of calling the debt or realizing the security? *If a debtor is likely to be put out of business if the creditor proceeds, and particularly if the situation is complex, you need to assure yourself that your client has received adequate and independent professional advice. Otherwise, a hasty decision to call the debt can backfire in court, with your client being found by the court in disfavour for trying to shut down the debtor's business without sufficient cause.*

- What is the financial impact on your client of the debtor's failure to satisfy the debt? *This will indicate how quickly action must be taken to alleviate your client's situation.*

- How are relations between your client and the debtor? *To effectively advance your client's interests, it is important to know whether relations between the creditor and debtor have become hostile, or are on relatively cordial terms, and why. If the relations are good, speak to your client about the best person to contact at the debtor's business, or, if the debtor is an individual, where to contact them. Give them a call and see if you can work out a payment arrangement suitable to both the debtor and the client.*

1.2.3 COSTS

Creditors may underestimate the costs of legal action to realize on the security or collect the debt, or may allow the emotion of the situation to override cost concerns.

- Realistically estimate the legal costs required to satisfy the debt. *If it is likely to cost the client $20,000 to obtain $10,000 in recovery, the plan of realization should be reconsidered or modified.*

- Discuss a retainer of fees, or payment schedule, with the client to ensure the client knows when legal costs will become due. *Particularly if your client is likely to be severely affected by non-payment of the debt, there are actions you should take to ensure that you are recompensed for your advice and action. See Chapter 14 for more information about the solicitor as creditor.*

1.2.4 INITIAL ADVICE TO CLIENT

Your advice will be based initially on the information provided in the first interview, including credit reports, information from searches already performed, and what has previously occurred on the file. Do not, however, forget the emotional side of the situation. Does your client wish to sever the relationship with the debtor, or is it important to maintain the relationship for some reason?

- Advise the client as to the options that can be pursued, such as seizure and sale by the sheriff, foreclosure, and accepting a proposal or debt restructuring.

- Advise your client what priority they may have vis-à-vis other creditors.

- Speak to the client about the potential of mediation to find a solution to the problem. Using this approach, a meeting between the creditor and the debtor would be set up, with a third-party neutral as chair. The third-party neutral is especially important if there is concern that the meeting would be hostile, or if the debtor may be intimidated by the creditor. (A neutral mediator levels the playing field between the creditor and debtor, thus encouraging a debtor to attend.) If a satisfactory resolution is realized, much time, expense and aggravation can be saved for your client. Very often, the non-adversarial nature of mediation can also save a long-term relationship between the two parties.

2

SEARCHES

Table of Contents

2.1 SEARCHES: AN ESSENTIAL SOURCE OF INFORMATION

- Your client has likely provided important information about the debtor's financial situation. Performing a variety of searches is the next step in the quest for information about the debtor with whom you are dealing. Searches can reveal details about the debtor's whereabouts, assets, liabilities and general financial situation. From a tactical point of view, the more information you have about the debtor's situation, the better.

- Searches will also confirm whether or not a secured creditor has perfected security. *Technical defects in security documents can, at worst, render the security unenforceable and even result in the debtor's legal action against the creditor for wrongful seizure if the creditor has pursued this route. Defects can also result in a secured creditor's claim becoming subordinate to the claims of other creditors or a trustee in bankruptcy — becoming, in fact, an unsecured claim.*

- Many of the searches described here have fees associated with them, and can take several days, or even longer, to see results. This should be taken into consideration for planning purposes. You can set up your own office to handle the searches, or you can seek the services of an agency that specializes in searches.

2.2 RELEVANT SEARCHES

These are some relevant searches that you may wish to undertake. The specific searches you choose will depend upon the security involved, the debtor, and the information you already have on hand.

2.2.1 CORPORATE SEARCH

- If the debtor is incorporated either provincially or federally, these searches will provide the corporation's correct name, its head office address, the names and addresses of its officers and directors, and whether or not it has been dissolved. *The correct corporate name is essential for many other searches.*

- Conduct a corporate profile search provincially though the Ministry of Consumer and Business Services in Toronto. Along with the corporate search, a Name Search should be requested to find out if there are other names that the corporation uses to conduct business.

- Conduct a corporate profile search federally through Industry Canada's Corporations Branch.

2.2.2 BUSINESS NAME/PARTNERSHIP SEARCH

- All businesses that use a business name must register their name under the *Business Names Act* with the Ministry of Consumer and Business Services in Toronto. Even if the business is incorporated federally, it must register the business name provincially. Conducting this search through the Ministry will indicate the business names of both individuals and partnerships.

2.2.3 REAL ESTATE SEARCH

- These searches will reveal the name of the real estate's owner(s), their address and the property description, plus any mortgages or construction liens that are registered and who they are in favour of, along with their addresses.

- These searches are conducted at Registry/Land Titles Offices throughout Ontario. The offices can be accessed in person, through a search house, or by opening an account with Teranet Land Information Services Inc. in Toronto for computer access from your office. Their web site address is *www.teranet.ca*.

- You can request copies of the relevant documents for your review: these documents can provide you with valuable information about the debtor and/or their assets.

2.2.4 MOTOR VEHICLE SEARCH

- This search shows the vehicles that the debtor owns, and may also provide a current address.

- Conduct this search through the provincial Ministry of Transportation by visiting your local motor vehicle licensing office, sending the appropriate form to Toronto, or setting up a telephone or electric data transfer account with the Ministry.

- Once you know what vehicles the debtor owns, and their vehicle identification numbers, a PPSA search can be conducted to determine if there are liens registered against them.

2.2.5 *PERSONAL PROPERTY SECURITY ACT* (PPSA)

- This search will show which of the debtor's assets are secured under the PPSA, and will confirm whether or not your client's security, if any, has been correctly registered. *This must be carefully reviewed to ensure that the security is perfected: defects have the potential to seriously undermine your client's position.*

- Ontario has a central registry for all securities registered under the PPSA. This registry may be accessed via a telephone call in person at your local Registry/Land Titles Office, through opening an account with the Personal Property Security Registry in Toronto for telephone access from your office, or through an agency via the Internet.

- You can request a verbal, printed or certified printed copy of the search results.

- Four search types can be requested: individual specific (which requires the individual's surname, first name, initial and birthdate); individual non-specific (requires the surname and first name); business debtor (requires the business name); and motor vehicle (requires the vehicle identification number (VIN)).

- In order to obtain the fullest advantage from a PPSA search, you should request the following information:

  - the debtor's full name, including middle initials, and birthdate;
  - a business debtor's full corporate name, including any French version;
  - the debtor's address, including whether any collateral to be secured is located there;
  - the full name and address of any secured party;
  - a description of any collateral that has been secured, including the reason for the security, the principal security amount and the security registration's date of maturity;
  - the makes, model numbers and vehicle identification numbers of any motor vehicles included in the security; and
  - whether the secured party has included a general collateral description on the financing statement.

- The resulting list will tell you which of the debtor's assets have encumbrances against them, and may also provide a current or previous address for the debtor. Additional information about the debtor could be obtained by contacting the creditors who have registered their property under the PPSA.

2.2.6 EXECUTION SEARCH

- Use this search to determine if other creditors have obtained judgments against the debtor.

- Such a judgment usually results in a writ of seizure and sale being filed with the sheriff of the county or district where the debtor does business or holds property; thus, conduct the search in both the sheriff's office and the registry/land titles office of all appropriate counties or districts.

- If the search reveals such a judgment, it can help to indicate the severity of the debtor's financial situation, including the number and attitude of other creditors. Contacting these creditors may provide further information, such as how they've gone about collecting on their debt, and how the debtor has responded.

2.2.7 BANKRUPTCY SEARCH

- Conduct this search to determine if and when the debtor has made an assignment in bankruptcy or made a proposal under the BIA. This search would also reveal the name of the trustee in bankruptcy. Contact the trustee to get particulars of the situation, then review your options based on the particulars of your client's debt. *If your client's debt is included in such an assignment, there may be little point in pursuing a separate legal action against the debtor.*

- The Office of the Superintendent of Bankruptcy, at Industry Canada in Ottawa, handles bankruptcy searches for the entire country, via mail, telephone or Internet links. The phone number for searches is 1-613-941-2863.

2.2.8 CREDIT BUREAU SEARCH

- This search will help you to determine the debtor's financial situation in terms of credit rating, outstanding loans or judgments, and credit card payments.

- Conduct the search at the credit bureau that is local to the debtor's place of business or residence. If you are not a member of this credit bureau (only members can request searches), this information could likely be obtained through your client's bank manager, upon payment of the appropriate fee.

2.2.9 THE *BANK ACT*, (CANADA) SECTION 427 SEARCH

- Use this search to find out if the debtor has given a bank security over its inventory or other assets.

- This search request can be made by mail or in person at the Bank of Canada agency in the province or territory where the debtor does business or resides.

2.2.10 DRIVER'S LICENCE SEARCH

- This search can assist in obtaining the debtor's address information, if necessary.

- Lawyers are authorized to request address information through the Address Request Application form. Having the debtor's previous address or date of birth may be of assistance.

2.2.11 CITY DIRECTORY AND TELEPHONE LISTINGS SEARCHES

- These searches can assist in obtaining address and employer information.

- City Directories, which list names, addresses and telephone numbers, are available through libraries and CD-ROM. A previous address may reveal neighbours or employers who can assist with your enquiries.

2.3 DEALING WITH DEFECTS

- Discovering a defect in the security may affect the advice you give a secured creditor as to realizing on the security. Assess the defect. Is it material enough to allow the debtor or a trustee in bankruptcy to have the security set aside? What action, if any, can be taken to correct the defect?

3

COLLECTION AND ENFORCEMENT OF THE DEBT – UNSECURED

Table of Contents

Note: Unless otherwise noted, Rules referred to in this chapter are the Rules of Civil Procedure.

3.1 COLLECTIONS: CHOOSING YOUR ROUTE

- When acting for a creditor who is attempting to collect a debt, you need to be aware that several initiatives have been undertaken in recent years in an attempt to make the court process more efficient, faster, and less expensive for the parties concerned. All of the initiatives emphasize early settlement of disputes, and introduce timetables that prevent debtors from unduly delaying the process while ensuring that creditors act promptly.
- One of the initiatives is the Ontario-wide introduction of the Simplified Procedure (Rule 76 of the Rules of Civil

Procedure), which streamlines the process of obtaining a judgment against a debtor for amounts $25,000 and under. *Note that as of April 2, 2001, the monetary limit for Small Claims Court has been increased from $6,000.00 to $10,000.00.*

- The advantages of the Simplified Procedure originate in its elimination of examinations for discovery and cross-examinations on affidavits (you instead include names and addresses of potential witnesses in your affidavit of documents), in its mandatory settlement discussions within 60 days of the close of pleadings, and in the ability of the creditor to bring a motion for summary trial or summary judgment after the close of pleadings. This saves both time and expense, and allows you to give your client a good indication of the time and cost involved in pursuing the judgment. *Note that an examination for discovery under Rule 31.03 or 31.10, a cross-examination of a deponent on an affidavit under Rule 39.02, and an examination of a witness on a motion under Rule 39.03 are not permitted in an action under the Simplified Procedure.* Rule 76.05

- The Simplified Procedure applies to actions commenced on or after March 11, 1996. It may be applied to an action commenced before this date, as long as all parties file a consent to its application. Rule 76.01(1)(2). *The Simplified Procedure does not apply to actions under the* Class Proceedings Act, the Construction Lien Act*, Rule 69 (divorce actions) or Rule 70 (family law proceedings).* Rule 76.01

- You must use the Simplified Procedure where the creditor's claim amounts to $25,000 (not including interest and costs) in money, in the value of real or personal property at the start of the action, or in a combination of the two. Rule 76.02(1). *In one case, for example, a $35,000 motor vehicle insurance claim was allowed to proceed under the Simplified Procedure because its deductible was $10,000, which thus brought the claim within the $25,000 limit. Lillie v. Bisson* (1998), 116

O.A.C. 168 (Div. Ct.) affirmed (1999) 46 O.R. (3d) 94 (C.A.)

Practice Tip: There is a new draft Rule 76 currently being circulated that may change the limit for the Simplified Procedure to $50,000.00, remove those cases from case management, and have a type of case management for Rule 76 matters only.

Practice Tip: Note that the burden of proving that the fair market value of the property at the date the action commenced was $25,000 or less lies with the plaintiff: in this case, your client, the creditor. You may wish to consider obtaining two independent appraisals of the property, in order to prove its value. Rule 76.10(7)

- Even if the amount is over the $25,000 limit, you may choose to proceed under the Simplified Procedure. However, the defendant can object to this within their statement of defence. If the defendant so objects, you have the option of proceeding under the Simplified Procedure only if you abandon the amount of the claim that exceeds $25,000. Rule 76.02(2)(4)(5)(6)

- If you do not abandon the excess, the claim proceeds under the Ordinary Procedure. Rule 76.02(7)

- Where there is more than one creditor, and the claim is not a joint claim, the Simplified Procedure must be used if each of the creditors' claims is within the $25,000 limit. Rule 76.02(8). *Wondercard Inc. v. Electric Colourfast Printing Corp.* (1999), 43 O.R. (3d) 799 (Gen. Div.)

- If the debtor makes a counterclaim, crossclaim or third party claim, the original action and the new claim remain under the Simplified Procedure as long as the debtor's claim is within the $25,000 limit, or, if it is above the limit, neither the defendant under the debtor's claim nor the debtor under the original claim objects to the Simplified

Procedure, or the debtor abandons the excess amount. If any of the claims are above the limit and the excess is not abandoned upon the objection of that claim's defendant, both the original action and the debtor's counterclaim fall under the Ordinary Procedure. Rule 76.02(9)(10)

- In addition to the possible application of the Simplified Procedure to the process, certain other streamlining procedures may apply. In Toronto and Ottawa, for example, civil case management rules are in effect that provide additional deadlines and mechanisms designed to settle cases prior to going to trial. Mandatory mediation may also apply to certain proceedings in Toronto and Ottawa, and it is expected to expand over the coming years to include other jurisdictions. *Note that mandatory mediation does apply to actions under the Simplified Procedure, except for actions started in Toronto.*

- Be aware that even when you obtain judgment against a debtor, enforcement proceedings to actually collect the debt can be time-consuming and, particularly if there are other creditors involved, not necessarily successful in paying all, or even part of, the debt. Because of this, you should seriously consider any settlement offers made by the debtor, which include payments, weighing the potential for complete collection against the offer being made, and taking into consideration the debtor's ability to pay. Settlement can be made at any step in the proceeding, before or after judgment. You may wish to accept payments over time, or in one lump sum, or to hold a consent to judgment in return for a series of payments. If settlement is effected after judgment, file a writ of seizure and sale as you would if the settlement had not been made: this gives you notice in case other creditors are enforcing their own judgments against the debtor. Bennett, Frank. *Bennett on Collections.* pp. 33-34.

> **Practice Tip:** If you are settling the matter, based on a consent to judgment, try to negotiate that if there is a default in the payment scheme, that the consent to judgment is for the full amount of the claim, plus interest and costs, less any payments made prior to the date of default. This is more preferable to a consent to judgment for the discounted settlement balance less any payments made.

3.2 COLLECTIONS: SIMPLIFIED PROCEDURE

Note that all other Rules of Civil Procedure apply to the Simplified Procedure unless the Simplified Procedure in Rule 76 states otherwise. Rule 76.01(3)

3.2.1 STATEMENT OF CLAIM

- An action to obtain judgment against a debtor begins with the filing of a Statement of Claim and, if Rule 77 (Case Management) applies, a Notice of Commencement of Proceeding (Form 77A) with the court. Rule 14.03(1)

- Where there is insufficient time to prepare a statement of claim, an action other than a divorce action may be commenced by the issuing of a notice of action (Form 14C) that contains a short statement of the nature of the claim. Rule 14.03(2). *In certain cases a client may not instruct counsel until shortly before the limitation period to issue the claim. In such cases, in order to comply with the limitation time constraints a Notice of Action can be filed.*

- Where a notice of action is used, the plaintiff shall file a statement of claim (Form 14D) within 30 days after the notice of action is issued: no statement of claim can be filed thereafter except with the written consent of the defendant or with leave of the court obtained on notice to the defendant. Rule 14.03(3). *Angelopoulos v. Angelopoulos* (1986), 55 O.R. (2d) 101 (H.C.) , additional reasons at (1986), 55 O.R. (2d) 101 at 110 (H.C.)

- The notice of action is served with the statement of claim. Rule 14.03(4). *It is not served separately from the Statement of Claim.*

- In an action commenced by the issuing of a notice of action, the statement of claim may alter or extend the claim stated in the notice of action. Rule 14.03(5)

- You must note on the statement of claim (Form 14A, 14B or 14 D) or the notice of action (Form 14 C) if the action is being brought under the Simplified Procedure. Rule 76.02(3)

- If the action was commenced under the Ordinary Procedure, but the requirements for using the Simplified Procedure are met, you can amend the statement of claim to continue the action under the Simplified Procedure: state that the action was commenced under the Ordinary Procedure and has been continued under the Simplified Procedure. Rule 76.03(1)(2)

Practice Tip: You should fully evaluate whether or not to commence the action under the Simplified Procedure as early in the process as possible. Regardless of whether you are eventually successful in the action, if you commence under the Ordinary Procedure, and then amend the statement of claim to continue under the Simplified Procedure, your client, regardless of the outcome of the action, must pay, up to the date of the amendment of the claim, the solicitor-client costs of the opposing party that would not have been incurred had you begun the action under the Simplified Procedure. Rule 76.03(5)

- If the action was commenced under the Simplified Procedure, but the requirements for using that procedure were not met, the amended pleading must state that the action was commenced under the Simplified Procedure and continued under the Ordinary Procedure. Rule 76.03(6)(7)

- In one case, the defence objected to the Simplified Procedure, and the action was therefore continued under the Ordinary Procedure. The plaintiff's motion to bring the proceeding back under the Simplified Procedure by abandoning the excess over $25,000 was allowed, subject to the plaintiff delivering an affidavit of documents: the defendant had argued that by reverting to the Simplified Procedure, they lost the right of discovery; however, the court found that it was just to revert in that the defendant's potential exposure at trial had been limited by the plaintiff abandoning the excess. *Stapley v. Intermap Technologies Ltd.*, 34 C.P.C. (4th) 328, [1999] O.J. No. 1411 (Master)

- The statement of claim, as an originating process, must be personally served on the opposite party (in this case, the debtor). All pleadings other than the originating process must be served on every opposite party and every party who delivers a pleading or notice of intention to defend in the main action or a related claim. Rule 16. *The defendant may be an individual, a partnership, a corporation or other entity. The method of service of each type of defendant is different.* Rule 16.02(1)

- Complete the statement of claim as follows:

  - *Title of Proceedings*: identify the court, plaintiff(s) and defendant(s); set out how long the defendant has to defend the action; the documents required to be filed to defend the action; and that failure to do so may result in a judgment. Note how payment or assessment of costs is made if the claim is paid. The date of issuance, name of registrar and address of the court office follow. Indicate if Rule 76 applies.
  - *Prayer for Relief*: set out the amount of the claim as of a certain date; prejudgment interest and postjudgment interest (based on an agreement between the parties or on the *Courts of Justice Act* sections 127 through 130); costs either on a party-party or solicitor-client basis; and any further relief that is appropriate, such as an injunction or certificate of pending litigation.

- *Body of the Claim*: describe who the plaintiff(s) and defendant(s) are, including any business name. Set out the particulars of your claim, giving as full an accounting as possible.
- *Place of Trial*: under Rule 46.02, the trial is to be held at the place named in the statement of claim; however, if the trial is required to be held at another place by statute or the balance of convenience substantially favours another place, either party can bring a motion to change the location.
- *Ending*: set out the law firm name, address and telephone number, the name of the solicitor in charge of the file and their Law Society of Upper Canada registration number.
- *Debt Collection, Part II - Procedure: How To Begin,* pp. II-3 to II-6; Bennett, Frank. *Bennett on Collections*, p. 28

• In drafting your statement of claim (or any other pleading), ensure that you follow these rules:

- Provide a concise statement of the material facts on which you are relying for your claim (note that you do not have to state the evidence by which you will prove those facts). Rule 25.06(1)
- You may raise a point of law in your statement of claim, but conclusions of law may only be pleaded if you also plead the material facts supporting them. Rule 25.06(2)
- You do not need to set out the conditions precedent to your claim: these are implied in your pleadings. (Note, however, that the opposite party who contests a condition precedent must specify that condition and its non-performance or non-occurrence in their pleading.) Rule 25.06(3)
- You may make inconsistent allegations if you make it clear that they are being pleaded in the alternative. If you later want to make an inconsistent allegation or a new ground for your claim, you must make it by way of amending the statement of claim, rather than in a new pleading. Rule 25.06(4)(5)

- Where you allege notice to a person, you simply allege notice as a fact, unless the form or a precise term of the notice is material. Rule 25.06(6)
- Plead the effect of a document or conversation that is material as briefly as possible. You do not need to plead the precise wording unless the words themselves are material. Rule 25.06(7)
- If you are alleging fraud, misrepresentation, breach of trust, malice or intent, include full particulars. You may allege knowledge as a fact without pleading the circumstances from which it is inferred. Rule 25.06(8)
- In your claim for relief, include the nature of the relief claimed. Where you are claiming damages, include the amount claimed for each claimant in respect of each claim. Include the amounts and particulars of special damages to the extent that you know them at the time of making the statement of claim. Notice of any further amounts and particulars must be delivered as soon as you know them, and at the latest, not less than 10 days before trial. Rule 25.06(9)

Practice Tips:

- In drafting your statement of claim, resist the temptation to use **BoldFace**, *Italics*, exclamation marks! or colourful language in an attempt to emphasize your point. *Use italics instead of underlining for names of statutes. Underlining denotes amendments to the pleadings.*
- The value of accurate spelling and good grammar should not be underestimated.
- As a last check, reread your claim, and imagine that you are drafting a statement of defence in response: are there any weak points that could be exploited by an opposite party?

Beaudoin, Robert. *Perilous Pleadings*, p.1-2.

- A vague or poorly drafted statement of claim can result in motions for particulars (Rule 25.10); for striking out all or portions of the statement of claim (Rule 25.11 v. Rule

21.01); for a better affidavit of documents and for better production (Rules 30.06 and 30.08); for answers to questions objected to on discovery; and for amendments to pleadings (Rule 26.01). Beaudoin, Robert. *Perilous Pleadings* p. 4. *This can delay the proceedings, increase the costs to your client and jeopardize the strength of your claim.*

- A poorly drafted statement of claim may also allow the defence to limit the production of documents. *Paddison v. Deloitte Touche, Tohmatsu International* (June 30, 1999), Doc. Ottawa 98-CV-7422 (Ont. Master), Beaudoin, Robert. *Perilous Pleadings*, p. 4.

- The statement of claim must be divided into consecutively-numbered paragraphs. If practical, each allegation should have its own paragraph. Rule 25.02

- Once the statement of claim has been issued, you must serve it within six months. Rule 14.08(1)

- Service must be by personal service or, if required, by alternatives to personal service. Rule 16.01(1), 16.02, 16.03

- If you are having trouble serving the statement of claim, you may apply to the court for an extension or an alternative form of service; however, you should be prepared to show how you have attempted to serve it thus far. Rule 3.02(1)

3.2.2 DISMISSAL BY REGISTRAR

- As long as Rule 77 (Case Management) does not apply to the action, the registrar has the authority to dismiss certain actions as abandoned in Toronto (for actions commenced before January 1, 1998) and in the County of Frontenac and the Territorial District of Timiskaming. Rule 76.05(1)(2)

- If Rule 77 (Case Management) does apply, where no defence has been filed and the proceedings have been disposed of by final order or judgment, the registrar shall, 180 days after the date of issue of the originating process, make an order dismissing the proceedings as abandoned. Rule 77.08. *If an action has been dismissed, and the plaintiff seeks to set aside the dismissal, the test to be applied on the motion is the test for setting aside a default judgment, i.e. whether the motion was made as soon as possible, the circumstances of the default and the merits of the claim. O'Donnell v. Xanthopoulos* (1992), 11 O.R. (3d) 724 (Gen. Div.)

- For actions commenced on or after January 4, 1999, the registrar shall order the action dismissed as abandoned:

  - where no defence has been filed and the action has not been disposed of by final order or judgment, 180 days after the originating process was issued; and
  - where a defence has been filed but the action has not been set down for trial or summary trial, and the action has not been disposed of by final order or judgment, 150 days after the filing of the first defence. Rule 76.05.1(3)(4)(5)

  This applies only to the Municipality of Metropolitan Toronto, County of Frontenac and the Territorial District of Timiskaming.

- For actions commenced before January 4, 1999, the registrar must also provide the parties with 45 days notice of default prior to dismissing the action. Rule 76.05.1(6)(7)

3.2.3 DEFAULT JUDGMENT

(a) Noting in Default

- Where the defendant - in this case, the debtor - does not deliver a statement of defence within the prescribed time, you (as the plaintiff) may, on filing proof of service of the statement of claim, require the registrar to note the defendant in default. Rule 19.01(1)

Practice Tip: You should diarize the file for 20 days after service. If no Notice of Intention to Defendant or no Statement of Defence has been served and filed, immediately note the default in default and obtain default judgment. This will reduce the potential for delays and will please your client to know that you are working the time clock on their behalf.

- You may also require the defendant noted in default where their statement of defence has been struck out, without leave to deliver another, or with leave but the defendant has failed to deliver it within the time allowed. Rule 19.01(2)

- Note that if the plaintiff does not require the defendant to be noted in default, any other defendant who has delivered a statement of defence may, on notice to the plaintiff, ask the court to order the registrar to note the defendant in default. Rule 19.01(3)

Practice Tip: Note that a defendant under disability may not be noted in default without leave of a judge obtained on motion under Rule 7.07. Rule 19.01(4)

- A defendant who has been noted in default is deemed to admit the allegations of fact made in the statement of claim. Rule 19.02(1)(a)

- Once noted in default, the defendant requires either leave of the court or consent from the plaintiff to deliver a statement of defence or take any other step in the action, other than a motion to set aside the noting of default or any judgment obtained through the default. Rule 19.02(1)(b)

- Once a defendant is noted in default, any step in the action that would normally require the defendant's consent no longer requires that consent. Rule 19.02(2)

- In addition, a defendant noted in default is not entitled to notice of any further step in the action, and does not have to be served with any document except in the circumstances provided for in Rule 19.02(3).

- The court may set aside the noting of default. Rule 19.03(1) *Where there has been no undue delay and there has been an intention to defend throughout, a noting in default will be set aside without the necessity of establishing the merits of the case. Axton v. Kent* (1991), 2 O.R. (3d) 797 (Div. Ct.)

- If the plaintiff consents to the defendant delivering a statement of defence, the noting of default is deemed to have been set aside. Rule 19.03(2)

(b) Default Judgment

- Once the debtor has been noted in default, you may then require the registrar to sign judgment against the debtor in respect of a claim for a debt or liquidated demand in money, including interest if you claimed it on the statement of claim (Form 19A); for recovery of possession of land (Form 19B); for the recovery of possession of personal property (Form 19C); or for foreclosure, sale or redemption of a mortgage (Forms 64B to D, G to K and M). Rule 19.04(1)

- To request the default judgment, file with the registrar a requisition for default judgment (Form 19D), with the following information:

    - a statement that the claim comes within the class of cases for which default judgment may properly be signed;
    - a statement as to whether there has been partial payment of the claim, setting out such dates and amounts;
    - a description of how prejudgment interest is calculated if you claimed prejudgment interest in your statement of claim;

- the rate of postjudgment interest if you claimed postjudgment interest in the statement of claim at a rate other than that of the *Courts of Justice Act* section 129; and
- a statement as to whether you wish costs to be fixed by the registrar or assessed.

  Rule 19.04(2)

- On signing default judgment, the registrar fixes the costs under Tariff A to which you are entitled, and includes those costs in the judgment unless the judgment directs a reference or you stated in the requisition that you wished the costs to be assessed. Rule 19.04(6). *If you wish the costs to be assessed, prepare a Bill of Costs and obtain a date and time for the assessment. Contact the court office to see if assessment will result in an inordinate delay in getting the default judgment. If it does delay you, you can get the default judgment for the principal amount and assess the costs at a later date.*

- If you claimed postjudgment interest in the statement of claim at a rate other than that contained in the *Courts of Justice Act* section 129, the default judgment shall provide for interest at the rate you claimed. Rule 19.04(5)

Practice Tip: From a practical perspective, if you are noting a defendant in default, you should also obtain default judgment at the same time or shortly thereafter.

- If the claim has been partially satisfied, the judgment will be for the amount that remains unpaid. Rule 19.04(4)

- If the registrar is uncertain as to the class of case to which the claim belongs, or the amount or rate of interest, they may decline to sign default judgment. In this case, you can move before a judge for judgment under Rule 19.05 or, in the case of a claim for a debt or liquidated demand in money, make a motion to the court for default judgment. Rule 19.04(3)(3.1), 19.05(1)

- Support your motion with affidavit evidence and documentation, if any, if the claim is for unliquidated damages. Rule 19.05(2)

- The judge will then grant judgment, dismiss the action, or order that the action proceed to trial. If the action proceeds to trial, you may bring a motion at the trial for judgment on the statement of claim against a defendant noted in default. Rule 19.05(3)(4)

> **Practice Tip:** In order to succeed on a motion for judgment or at trial, be prepared to show that the facts in the statement of claim entitle you to judgment. (It is not enough that the default automatically deems the facts to be admitted.) Rule 19.06. The facts must support the claim. Remember the obligation under Rule 39.02(6) to make full and fair disclosure. You can also still require an examination for discovery or a Rule 39.03 examination, even though a defendant has been noted in default. Rule 31.04(2)(b)

- A default judgment does not prevent you from proceeding against the same defendant for any other relief. Rule 19.07. You can obtain default proceedings for part of the claim and continue against the same party for the balance of the claim. This will get around the argument of res judicata defence. *You may have a claim with two parts: one for liquidated damages and one for unliquidated damages. You would obtain default judgment on the liquidated damages portion and then proceed to trial or an assessment of the damages for the balance of the claim.*

- A default judgment can be set aside or varied by a judge or the court on such terms as are just. In addition, the court or judge may also set aside the noting of default. Rule 19.08(1)(2)(3)

3.2.4 DEALING WITH A STATEMENT OF DEFENCE

- The defendant must deliver the statement of defence within 20 days after the service of statement of claim if served in Ontario, 40 days if served in Canada or the U.S., and 60 days if served elsewhere. Rule 18.01

- The defendant who intends to defend the action may deliver a notice of intent to defend (Form 18B) within the time limits noted for delivery of a statement of defence. In this case, the defendant will be entitled to a further 10 days to deliver the statement of defence. Rule 18.02(1)(2)

- If Rule 77, Case Management, applies, the defendant files a notice of defence (Form 77B) when a notice of intent to defend, a statement of defence or motion in response to an action is served. Rule 18.03(1)

- Once the time limits have passed, and the defendant has not served and filed either the Notice of Intention to Defend or a Statement of Defence, you may begin the process to have the defendant noted in default; however, note that a defendant may deliver a statement of defence at any time before being noted in default under Rule 19.01. Rule 19.01(5)

- A party is entitled to demand particulars of an allegation contained in the pleading of an opposite party. This means that the debtor can demand particulars of allegations in your statement of claim, and that you can similarly demand particulars of allegations in their defence. Note that where such particulars are demanded, and the party does not supply them within seven days, you can apply to the court to order them supplied within a specified time. Rule 25.10

- Note that all allegations of fact that the debtor does not deny in the defence are deemed admitted, unless the debtor pleads having no knowledge of that fact. Rule 25.07(2)

- In an action for damages, the amount of damages is deemed in dispute unless the defendant specifically admits them. Rule 25.07(6)

- In the defence, the debtor must admit every allegation of fact from the statement of claim that they do not dispute. In addition, if they intend to prove a different version of facts than the one contained in your statement of claim, they must plead that version of the facts. They are also required to plead any matter that they intend to rely on and that might take you by surprise or raise an issue that has not already been raised in your statement. If you alleged an agreement in your claim, the debtor's denial of that agreement is construed only as a denial of the making of the agreement or of the facts from which the agreement may be implied by law; it is not a denial of the agreement's legality or sufficiency in law. Rule 25.07(1)(3)(4)(5)

- If the defence pleads a version of facts that is different from your version of facts, and that you have not already dealt with in your statement of claim, you need to deliver a reply, setting out your version of facts. Rule 25.08(1)

- Note that the defendant can object to the use of the Simplified Procedure in the statement of defence. If this objection is raised, you must consider whether the advantages of the Simplified Procedure outweigh the disadvantages of abandoning the excess over $25,000 and thus keeping the action within the Simplified Procedure.

- If you intend to respond to a defence with any matter that might take the opposite party by surprise, or raise an issue not raised in a your statement of claim, you also need to deliver a reply, setting out that matter. Rule 25.08(2). *Keep in mind that inconsistent or new claims require an amended statement of claim, rather than a new pleading.* Rule 25.06(5)

  You only deliver a reply where required by the above two points. Non-delivery of a reply is deemed to mean a denial of the allegations of fact made by the defendant. Rule 25.08(3)(4)

- If you do deliver a reply, you must admit every allegation of fact in the defence that you do not dispute. Rule 25.09(1)

- You have 10 days after the service of the statement of defence to serve your reply, unless the defendant (the debtor) counterclaims, in which case you have 20 days to reply.

Practice Tip: The court may strike out or expunge all or part of a pleading, such as a defence, with or without leave to amend, on the grounds that it may prejudice or delay the action's fair trial; is scandalous, frivolous or vexatious; or abuses the process of the court. Rule 25.11. If you believe that any of those grounds apply to a debtor's defence, you should apply to the court to have that defence (or a portion of it) struck out. By doing so, you avoid having to deal with those matters in the subsequent hearings or trial. In an extreme case, where the defence was struck out without leave to amend, you would be able to have the defendant noted in default, and seek default judgment.

You can bring a motion before a judge to strike out a pleading in a defence on the basis that it discloses no reasonable defence. It has to be a pleading that is so bad on its face that it will be struck out. Rule 21.01

3.2.5 AFFIDAVIT OF DOCUMENTS

- Within 10 days after the close of pleadings, each party must serve on every other party an affidavit of documents (Form 30A or 30B) disclosing to the full extent of the party's knowledge, information and belief all documents relating to any matter in issue in the action that are or have been in the party's possession, control or power. Rule 30.03(1)

- In addition, each party must include in its affidavit of documents (Form 30A or 30B) a list of the names and addresses of all those who might reasonably be expected to have knowledge of transactions or occurrences at issue, unless the court orders otherwise. Rule 76.04(1)

- In the solicitor's certificate under Rule 30.03(4) (full disclosure in affidavit), you must include a statement that you have explained to the deponent the necessity of complying with the requirement to list all potential witnesses and have explained the type of documents that might be relevant to the proceedings. Rule 76.04(3)

- Those potential witnesses not listed in the original or a supplementary affidavit of documents may not be called as a witness at trial, except with leave of the trial judge. Rule 76.04(2)

3.2.6 SETTLEMENT CONFERENCES

- Pleadings are closed when the plaintiff has delivered a reply to every defence in the action (or the time for delivery of a reply has expired). If the defendant did not deliver a defence in the action, pleadings close once the defendant has been noted in default. Rule 25.05

- Within 60 days after the close of pleadings, the solicitors for the parties must consider, by way of a meeting or telephone call, whether any or all of the issues in the action can be settled. Rule 76.07(1)

3.2.7 SUMMARY JUDGMENT AND SUMMARY TRIAL

(a) Moving for Summary Judgment or Summary Trial

- After the close of pleadings, you may move before a judge, with supporting affidavit material, for summary judgment or summary trial of the action and of any counterclaim, cross-claim or third party claim. Rule 76.06(1)

- Your notice of motion must state that the motion is to be heard or the trial held on a date to be fixed by the registrar not earlier than 50 days after the service of the notice of motion. Rule 76.06(2)

- Immediately after serving your notice of motion and supporting material on the other parties, you must file the notice of motion (but not the supporting material) and proof of service in the court office where the motion will be heard. Rule 76.06(3)

- Where you are requesting a summary trial, the responding party can, within 30 days of your service, serve you and all the other parties with a notice refusing summary trial. Your motion will then proceed as a motion for summary judgment. Rule 76.06(4)

Practice Tip: Where a respondent is refusing a summary trial, and you wish to avoid having your motion proceed for summary judgment, you will need to deliver a notice of abandonment. In this case, your client could be ordered to pay the respondent's costs for the motion, not exceeding $200. Rule 76.06(5)(6)

Your only other option would be to convince the judge that a summary trial is necessary because either the issues cannot be decided without cross-examination, or that to proceed by a summary judgment would be unjust. Rule 76.06(14). Note that this test for summary judgment is under the Simplified Procedure less onerous than that under the Ordinary Procedure. Rule 20.04. Under the Simplified Procedure, the motions judge can make determinations of fact, including determinations of credibility, on a motion for summary judgment. The motions judge must grant judgment unless cross-examination is required, or it would be otherwise unjust. Rule 76.06(14)

Under Rule 20.04, the court must be satisfied that there is no genuine issue for trial. *Newcourt Credit Group Inc. v. Hummel Pharmacy Ltd.* (1998), 38 O.R. (3d) 82, 18 C.P.C. (4th) 319, 113 O.A.C. 389 (Div. Ct.)

- A judge on a motion for judgment under the Simplified Procedure will be guided by the following principles as set out in *Heller v. Labbett Insurance Services Ltd.* (1997), 14 C.P.C. (4th) 282 (Ont. Gen. Div.):

- that the test is lower than on a motion for summary judgment under the Ordinary Procedure;
- that the considerations of justice and fairness are the governing criteria; and
- that the parties must put forward their complete and best defence.

- The responding party must serve you with (but not file) any affidavit material for use on the motion within 30 days after being served with your material. In responding to your affidavit material, the party cannot rest on the mere allegations or denials of your pleadings, but must set out specific facts showing that judgment should not be granted or, in the case of a motion for summary trial, proving their claim or defence. Rule 76.06(8)(9)(10)

Practice Tip: Although an affidavit supporting a motion for summary judgment or trial can be made on information and belief as permitted in Rule 39.01(4), the judge during the hearing for the motion or the trial may draw an adverse inference if a party has failed to provide the evidence of individuals who have personal knowledge of contested facts. Rule 76.06(11). *As a practical matter, information and belief should only be used for uncontentious facts or if no other option is available. A reluctant witness cannot be compelled to give an affidavit, so if their evidence is crucial and cannot be dealt with by way of a request to admit (Rule 51), it is probably safest to proceed with a regular trial. This would avoid the need for an affidavit based on information and belief in a motion for summary trial or summary judgment.*

- As the moving party, you must serve a motion record on all other parties to the motion, and file it, with proof of service, at least five days before the date for the hearing of the motion for summary judgment or for the trial. The motion record must contain, in consecutively numbered pages and in the following order:

- a table of contents describing each document, including exhibits, by its nature and date and, if applicable, exhibit number;
- a copy of the notice of motion;
- a copy of all affidavits served by any party for use on the motion or at the summary trial; and
- a copy of the pleadings, including those relating to any counterclaim, crossclaim or third party claim.

Rule 76.06(12)(13)

- The hearing of the motion or the summary trial takes place in the county where the solicitor's office of any responding party is located or where the responding party who acts in person resides, if they reside in Ontario. Where no responding party resides in Ontario, it takes place in the county where the proceeding was commenced, or where the solicitor's office for any party is located or where any party who acts in person resides. Rule 76.06(15). *Note, however, that if Rule 77 Case Management applies, the motion will have to take place in the county where the proceeding was commenced.* Rule 77.01(5)

- Once you have obtained summary judgment, you can proceed against the same defendant for any other relief. Rule 20.07. *This overcomes the res judicata defence. You may have a claim with two parts: one for liquidated damages and one for unliquidated damages. You would obtain default judgment on the liquidated damages portion and then proceed to trial or an assessment of the damages for the balance of the claim.*

- The court can stay the enforcement of a summary judgment pending the determination of any other issue in the action or associated counterclaims, cross-claims or third party claims. Rule 20.08

- The following types of actions where summary judgment has been permitted include the following:

- ° claim for payment for professional services rendered. Defendant's affidavit evidence consisted of bald obligations without proper supporting evidence. *Heller v. Labbett Insurance Services Ltd. (supra).* No real facts in dispute; and
- ° interpretation of a construction contract. *Bradley-Kelly Construction Ltd. v. Ottawa-Carleton Regional Transit Commission* (1996), 30 O.R. (3d) 301 (Gen. Div.)

(b) Summary Judgment Refused

- Where summary judgment is refused, or granted only in part, the issues that remain in dispute proceed to trial. The court can specify the facts not in dispute, which are then deemed by the trial court to be established, unless that would create an injustice. The court can also define the issues to be tried, and order that the action be placed on a list of cases requiring speedy trial, or set down in the normal course or within a specified time for trial. Rule 20.05(1)(2)

- Where the action is ordered to proceed to trial, the court can order payment into court of all or part of the claim, or of security for costs, and can order the nature and scope of discovery limited to matters not already dealt with on the motion. Rule 20.05(3)

- If a party fails to pay the claim or security into court as ordered, an opposing party may move to dismiss the action, strike out the statement of defence, or make such other order as is just. Rule 20.05(4). *Note that if the statement of defence is struck out, the defendant is deemed noted in default and you can obtain judgment based on the default.* Rule 20.05(5)

(c) Proceeding to Trial

- To set a defended action down for trial, you must serve a notice of readiness for pre-trial conference (Form 76A) on every party to the action and any counterclaim, cross-claim or third party claim, and forthwith file the notice with proof of service. Rule 76.08(1)(2).

- As your client's solicitor, you must also certify in the notice of readiness that a settlement conference took place. Rule 76.08(2)

- The registrar places the action on the appropriate trial list immediately after you file the notice of readiness for pre-trial conference. Rule 76.09

- You must, at least five days before the pre-trial conference, provide the pre-trial conference judge or officer with a copy of your affidavit of documents, or any other material necessary for the conference. A pre-trial conference memorandum is not, however, provided unless all parties consent. Rule 76.07(2). *It has become a practice for counsel to provide a short statement of issues. Some jurisdictions (e.g. Toronto) have practice directions that require the delivery of a statement of issues.*

- The pre-trial conference judge or officer fixes the date for trial. Rule 76.07(3)

- A party who intends to cross-examine the deponent of an affidavit at the summary trial must give notice of that intention to the party who filed the affidavit at least 10 days before the trial date. This allows the parties to arrange for the attendance of the deponent at the trial. Rule 76.06(17). *The deponent should be served with a summons to witness to ensure the deponent's attendance. Failure to attend, after being served with the summons to witness will lead to a bench warrant to issue for the person's arrest.* Summons to Witness, Form 53A or 53C as required, Warrant for Arrest of Defaulting Witness, Form 53B.

- Not less than 10 days before the trial commences, the party who set the action down for trial must serve a trial record as per Rule 48.03 on every party to the action and any counterclaim, cross-claim or third party claim, and must forthwith file the trial record with proof of service. Rule 76.08(3). *This is not required for a summary trial.*

- A summary trial is conducted as follows:

  - the moving party adduces evidence by affidavit;
  - any adverse party may cross-examine on the moving party's affidavits (note that a party must complete all of its cross-examinations within 50 minutes);
  - the moving party has a maximum of 10 minutes to re-examine any cross-examined deponent;
  - the responding party then adduces evidence by affidavit;
  - any adverse party may cross-examine on the responding party's affidavits;
  - the responding party has a maximum of 10 minutes to re-examine any cross-examined deponent;
  - the moving party then, with leave of the trial judge, adduces any proper reply evidence; and
  - after the presentation of evidence, each party has a maximum of 45 minutes to make oral argument;
  - after the summary trial concludes, the judge grants judgment.

    Rule 76.06 (16)(18)

(d) Costs Awarded at Summary Trial for Judgments of $25,000 or Less

- This applies to judgments, exclusive of interest and costs, that amount to $25,000 or less, real or personal property whose fair market value when the action commenced was $25,000 or less, or any combination of such money and property to $25,000 or less. Rule 76.10(1)

- As the plaintiff, your client shall not recover any costs unless the action was commenced under the Simplified Procedure, or unless you can satisfy the court that it was reasonable to have commenced and continued the action under the Ordinary Procedure. This applies even if your client made an offer to settle. It does not apply, however, if you were unable to use the Simplified Procedure due to a defendant's counterclaim, crossclaim or third party claim being above the $25,000 limit. Rule 76.10(2)(3)(4). *Wondercard Inc. v. Electric Colourfast Printing Corp.* (1999), 43 O.R. (3d) 799 (Gen. Div.). *Note that these cost implications are significant, further emphasizing the need to realistically assess the potential of the judgment to exceed $25,000 prior to selecting whether to proceed via the Simplified or Ordinary Procedure.*

- At the trial judge's discretion, the plaintiff can be ordered to pay all or part of the defendant's costs, including solicitor-client costs, in addition to any costs the plaintiff is required to pay under rule 49.10(2) (defendant's offer). Rule 76.10(5)

- If the defendant objected to the use of the Simplified Procedure based on the grounds that the property's fair market value when the action commenced exceeded $25,000, and if the court finds that the value was in fact $25,000 or less, the defendant must pay the plaintiff's solicitor-client costs that would not have been incurred under the Simplified Procedure, unless the court orders otherwise. Rule 76.10(6)

- Note that these cost rules also apply to counterclaims, crossclaims or third party claims. Rule 76.10(8)

3.3 COLLECTIONS: ORDINARY PROCEDURE

3.3.1 STATEMENT OF CLAIM

- As with the Simplified Procedure, you commence an action with a statement of claim. For a detailed discussion, please see section 3.2.1.

3.3.2 DEFAULT JUDGMENT

- Where the debtor files no defence, you can have them noted in default and obtain default judgment. Please see section 3.2.3.

3.3.3 DEALING WITH A STATEMENT OF DEFENCE

- As plaintiff, you have the right to reply to the defendant's statement of defence. Please see section 3.2.4

3.3.4 MOTIONS

(a) General

- Make a motion by way of notice of motion (Form 37A), unless the nature of the motion or the circumstances make a notice of motion unnecessary. Rule 37.01. *Under Rule 77 you do not necessarily need a notice of motion; you can bring a motion by way of Case Management Motion Form.*

- A motion properly made without notice may be made in the county where the proceeding was commenced, where any party resides, or where the solicitor's office of the solicitor of record for any party is located. Rule 37.03(1)

- A motion made on notice must generally be made in the county where the solicitor's office of any responding party is located or where a responding party who acts in person resides. Rule 37.03(2). *Where the motion is made with notice and the respondent does not have a solicitor of record, the motion is returnable in the county where the respondent resides. Cox v. Cox* (1996), 22 R.F.L. (4th) 126 (Ont. Gen. Div.). *The exception is under Rule 77, where motions are all heard in the county where the proceedings were commenced.*

> **Practice Tip:** The definition of "solicitor's office" is set out in Rule 1.03 and means the office of the solicitor of record as set out in the last document filed by him or her.

- Bring your motion to the court (meaning that it will be heard before a master or a judge). If the motion involves the following matters, it can only be heard before a judge:
  - a statute or rule that expressly confers on a judge the power to grant the relief sought;
  - setting aside, varying or amending an order of a judge;
  - abridging or extending a time prescribed by an order that a master could not have made;
  - judgment on consent in favour of or against a party under disability;
  - the liberty of the subject;
  - section 4 or 5 of the *Judicial Review Procedure Act*; or
  - an appeal.

  Rule 37.02(2), 37.04

- Bring any motion that cannot be heard before a master to a judge. Rule 37.02(1), 37.04

- In your notice of motion (Form 37A), include:
  - the precise relief sought;
  - the grounds to be argued, including a reference to any statutory provision or rule that you are relying on; and
  - a list of the documentary evidence that you will use at the hearing of the motion.

  Rule 37.06

- Serve the notice of motion on any person or party who will be affected by the order you are seeking. Rule 37.07(1)

- Where a motion is made on notice, the notice of motion and supplementary materials shall be served on all of the parties at least four days before the date on which the motion is to be heard. Rule 37.07(6)

- Where a motion is made on notice, file the notice of motion with proof of service at least three days before the hearing date in the court office where the motion will be heard. Where service of the notice of motion is not required, file it at or before the hearing. Rule 37.08(1)(2)

- If the nature of the motion or the circumstances render service of the notice of motion impracticable or unnecessary, you may request that the court make an order without notice. Rule 37.07(2). *On motions made without notice, the court will ensure that all of the procedural requirements have been met by the applicant prior to signing the order or judgment. Failure to satisfy all of these requirements may result in the court refusing the order or judgment. Vinski v. Lack* (1987), 61 O.R. (2d) 379 (Master)

> **Practice Tip:** If you must bring a motion on an ex parte basis, ensure that you provide the court with all relevant information. Ensure that if there are any "warts" in your case, you advise the court of them. The judge will then be able to make an informed decision. Failure to do so could lead to the order being set aside and, even worse, your reputation being tarnished in the eyes of the judiciary, which can have a negative effect on your future legal career.

- If the delay necessary to effect service might entail serious consequences, you may request that the court make an interim order without notice. Rule 37.07(3)

- Unless the court orders or the Rules of Civil Procedure provide otherwise, you will need to serve an order that was made without notice on the person or party affected by the order, together with a copy of the notice of motion and all affidavits and other documents used at the hearing of the motion. Rule 37.07(4). *The party affected by the order has the opportunity to move to set aside the order.* Rule 37.14(1)

- Where you make the motion on notice, you need to serve a motion record on every other party to the motion and file it, with proof of service, in the court office where the motion is to be heard, at least three days before the hearing. Note that the court file is not placed before the judge or master hearing the motion unless they request it or a party requisitions it. Rule 37.10(1). *The only documents that will be before the judge or master are the motion records. If you are responding or objecting to a motion made by another party, requisitioning the court file can provide vital information to assist you in your arguments.*

- The motion record must contain, in consecutively numbered pages arranged in the following order,

  - a table of contents describing each document, including each exhibit, by its nature and date and, if applicable, by exhibit number or letter;
  - a copy of the notice of motion;
  - a copy of all affidavits and other material served by any party for use on the motion;
  - a list of all relevant transcripts of evidence in chronological order, but not necessarily the transcripts themselves; and
  - a copy of any other material in the court file that is necessary for the hearing of the motion.

  Rule 37.10(2)

- A responding party who believes that the motion record is incomplete may serve a responding party's motion record on every other party, and file it, with proof of service, at least two days before the hearing. The responding party's motion record contains, in consecutively-numbered pages arranged in the following order:

- ○ a table of contents describing each document, including each exhibit, by its nature and date and, if applicable, by exhibit number or letter; and
- ○ a copy of any material to be used by the responding party on the motion and not included in the motion record.

Rule 37.10(3)

In reality, a respondent should serve a motion record that includes an affidavit responding to the motion made by the applicant. Failure to do so may lead the court to an adverse inference against the respondent.

- Note that as part of your motion record, you may file a notice of motion and any other material served for use on your motion, together with proof of service: there is no need for this material to be filed separately. Rule 37.10(4)

- If you intend to refer to a transcript of evidence at the hearing of the motion, file a copy of the transcript as per Rule 34.18. Rule 37.10(5)

- A party may serve on every other party and file, with proof of service, in the court office where the motion is to be heard, at least two days before the hearing, a factum consisting of a concise statement, without argument, of the facts and law relied on by the party. Rule 37.10(6). *In reality, each party should serve and file a factum.*

(b) Motion for Particulars

> **Practice Tip**: Records for motions need to have a blue backing sheet. The Applicant's factum shall be bound front and back in white covers, and a factum of a respondent or responding party shall be bound front and back in green covers. Failure to have the proper backing sheets on the motion records and factums can result in the court office refusing to accept the documents for filing. Factums of the applicant and the respondent shall be served at least four days before the hearing and filed in the court office where the motion is to be heard at least two days before the hearing. Rule 38.09(1), (3) and (3.2)

- Where a party demands particulars of an allegation in the pleading of an opposite party, and the opposite party fails to supply them within seven days, the court may order particulars to be delivered within a specified time. Rule 25.10

- You should always consider making a motion for particulars if the statement of defence involves fraud, misrepresentation or breach of trust. Similarly, you should expect the defendant to make a motion for particulars if you have alleged these conditions in your statement of claim. *When pleading these types of allegations, the pleadings should contain full particulars so that such motions can be avoided.*

(c) Motion to Strike Out

- The court may strike out or expunge all or part of a pleading or other document, with or without leave to amend, on the ground that the pleading or other document:

  - may prejudice or delay the fair trial of the action;
  - is scandalous, frivolous or vexatious; or
  - abuses the process of the court.

  Rule 25.11

(d) Motion to Determine Issue Before Trial

- Where you believe that a defence raises a question of law that, if determined before trial, could dispose of all or part of the action, substantially shorten the trial, or result in substantial cost savings, you can bring a motion before a judge to have the question of law determined. Rule 21.01(1)(a)

- You may also bring a motion before a judge to strike out a pleading on the grounds that it has no reasonable cause of defence. Rule 21.01(1)(b)

- The defendant may bring a motion before a judge to have your action stayed or dismissed on the grounds that:

  - the court has no jurisdiction over the subject matter of the action;
  - the plaintiff does not have the legal capacity to commence or continue the action or that the defendant does not have the legal capacity to be sued;
  - another proceeding is pending in Ontario or another jurisdiction between the same parties in respect of the same subject matter; or
  - the action is frivolous or vexatious or otherwise abuses the process of the court.

  Rule 21.01(3)

- Whether the above motions are made by you or the defendant, they must be made promptly. If they are not, the court can take the delay into account when awarding costs. Rule 21.02

- These motions require that the moving party serves on every other party to the motion a factum consisting of a concise statement, without argument, of the facts and law relied on by the party, and file it, with proof of service, at least two days before the hearing. Rule 21.03

(e) Motion to Dismiss for Delay

- Any delay on your part in proceedings related to your statement of claim can have serious consequences, including the dismissal of the action. *Therefore, ensure that your office has a good diary system to keep track of and stay on top of your cases. Failure to do so may bring a motion for dismissal and a lot of explaining to do to your client.*

- For example, a defendant who is not in default may move to have an action dismissed for delay where you have failed,

  - to serve the statement of claim on all the defendants within the prescribed time;
  - to have noted in default any defendant who has failed to deliver a statement of defence within 30 days after the default;
  - to set the action down for trial within six months after the close of pleadings; or
  - to move for leave to restore to a trial list an action that has been struck off the trial list, within 30 days after the action was struck off.

  Rule 24.01(1)

3.3.5 SUMMARY JUDGMENT

- After the defendant has delivered a statement of defence or served a notice of motion, you can move, with supporting affidavit material or other evidence, for summary judgment on all or part of your claim. Rule 20.01(1)

- If there is a need for urgency in the summary judgment, you may also move, without notice, for leave to serve a notice of motion for summary judgment together with the statement of claim. Rule 20.01(2)

- Note that a defendant may also move for summary judgment to dismiss all or part of your claim. Rule 20.01(3)

> **Practice Tip**: Although an affidavit supporting a motion for summary judgment can be made on information and belief as permitted in Rule 39.01(4), the judge during the hearing for the motion may draw an adverse inference if a party has failed to provide the evidence of individuals who have personal knowledge of contested facts. Rule 20.02. *You may wish to make a Request to Admit under Rule 51 rather than getting another affidavit for which there would be a right of cross-examination.*

- At least two days before the hearing of the motion, each party must serve on all other parties a factum which consists of a concise statement (without argument) of the facts and law it is relying on, and must also file the factum, along with proof of service. Rule 20.03

- In responding to affidavit or other evidence supporting a motion for summary judgment, a party must set out in its own affidavit or evidence specific facts that show there is a genuine issue for trial. Rule 20.04(1)

- If the court is satisfied that there is no genuine issue for trial with respect to a claim or defence, it grants summary judgment accordingly. Rule 20.04(2). *T1T2 Ltd. Partnerships v. Canada* (Attorney General) (1995), 23 O.R. (3d) 81 (Gen. Div.), additional reasons at (1995), 38 C.P.C. (3d) 167 at 180 (Ont. Gen. Div.), affirmed (1995), 24 O.R. (3d) 546 (C.A.).

- Where the only genuine issue is the amount to which the moving party is entitled, the court can order a trial of that issue, or grant judgment with a reference to determine the amount. Rule 20.04(3)

- Where the only genuine issue is a question of law, a judge may determine the question and grant judgment; if the motion is being heard by a master, it must be adjourned to be heard by a judge. Rule 20.04(4)

- Where the plaintiff is the moving party and claims an accounting, and where the defendant fails to show that there is a preliminary issue to be tried, the court may grant judgment on the claim with a reference to take the accounts. Rule 20.04(5)

> **Practice Tip:** The leading cases dealing with summary judgment are as follows: *Irving Ungerman Ltd. v. Galanis* (1991), 4 O.R. (3d) 545 (C.A.); *Pizza Pizza Ltd. v. Gillespie* (1990), 75 O.R. (2d) 225 (Gen. Div.); and *Ron Miller Realty Ltd. v. Honeywell, Wotherspoon* (1991), 4 O.R. (3d) 492 (Gen. Div.), affirmed (1993), 16 O.R. (3d) 255 (C.A.)

> **Practice Tip:** On a summary judgment motion, the court will take a hard look at the merits of the case in deciding whether the case should be referred to trial. If there are real issues of credibility, the resolution of which is essential to the determination of the facts, the matter will proceed to trial. The motions judge will have to assess the general nature and quality of the evidence supporting the motion made for summary judgment. The test that the court applies is whether the court concludes that the case is so doubtful that it does not deserve consideration at a trial.

- Where summary judgment is refused, or granted only in part, the issues that remain in dispute proceed to trial. The court can specify the facts not in dispute, which are then deemed by the trial court to be established, unless that would create an injustice. The court can also define the issues to be tried, and order that the action be placed on a list of cases requiring speedy trial, or set down in the normal course or within a specified time, for trial. Rule 20.05(1)(2)

- Where the action is ordered to proceed to trial, the court can order payment into court of all or part of the claim or security for costs, and can order the nature and scope of discovery limited to matters not already dealt with on the motion. Rule 20.05(3)

- If a party fails to pay the claim or security into court as ordered, an opposing party may move to dismiss the action, strike out the statement of defence, or make such other order as is just. Rule 20.05(4). Note that if the statement of defence is struck out, the defendant is deemed noted in default. Rule 20.05(5). *Once the defendant is noted in default, the plaintiff can apply for a default judgment without notice.*

- If the motion for summary judgment fails, the court fixes the opposite party's costs of the motion on a solicitor-client basis, and orders the moving party to pay them forthwith, unless the court feels that the motion was reasonable. Rule 20.06(1)

- If the court feels that a party to a motion has acted in bad faith or to delay, the court can fix the costs of the motion on a solicitor-client basis and order them paid forthwith. Rule 20.06(2)

- Once you have obtained summary judgment, you can proceed against the same defendant for any other relief. Rule 20.07

- The court can stay the enforcement of a summary judgment pending the determination of any other issue in the action or associated countering claims. Rule 20.08

3.3.6 AFFIDAVIT OF DOCUMENTS

- Within 10 days after the close of pleadings, each party must serve on every other party an affidavit of documents (Form 30A or 30B) disclosing to the full extent of the party's knowledge, information and belief all documents relating to any matter in issue in the action that are or have been in the party's possession, control or power. Rule 30.03(1)

- In your affidavit, list and describe, in separate schedules, all documents relating to any matter in issue in the action:

   - that are in your possession, control or power and that you do not object to producing;
   - that are or were in your possession, control or power and for which you are claiming privilege, and the grounds for your claim;
   - that were formerly, but are no longer, in your possession, control or power, whether or not you are claiming privilege for them, together with a statement of when and how you lost them and their present location.

   Rule 30.03(2)

- Also include a statement that you have never had possession, control or power over any document relating to any matter in issue in the action other than those listed in your affidavit. Rule 30.03(3)

- As your client's lawyer, you must also certify on the affidavit that you have explained to the deponent the need to make full disclosure of all documents, and what kind of documents are likely to be relevant to any matter at issue in the action. Rule 30.03(4)

- Note that an affidavit of documents is not filed unless it is relevant to an issue on a pending motion or at trial. Rule 30.03(5)

- If you believe that the defence has omitted a relevant document or made an improper claim of privilege in their affidavit of documents, you may apply to the court for an order to:

   - cross-examine on the affidavit of documents;
   - require the service of a further and better affidavit of documents;
   - disclose or produce for inspection the document, or a part of the document, if it is not privileged; and
   - require the inspection of a document for the purpose of determining its relevance or the validity of a claim of privilege.

   Rule 30.06

- If, after you have served your affidavit of documents, you obtain further relevant documents, or you realize that your affidavit is inaccurate or incomplete, immediately serve a supplementary affidavit, explaining how your affidavit of documents needs to be modified, and disclosing any additional documents. Rule 30.07

- A party's failure to disclose a document or produce a document for inspection as required will result, if the document favours the party's case, in the party not being able to use that document at the trial except with leave of the trial judge. If the document does not favour the party's case, the court may make such order as is just. Rule 30.08(1)

- A party's failure to serve an affidavit of documents or produce documents as required can result in the court revoking or suspending the party's right, if any, to initiate or continue an examination for discovery; in the dismissal of the action, if the party is a plaintiff, or in the striking out of a statement of defence, if the party is a defendant; and any other order as is just. Rule 30.08(2)

> **Practice Tip:** The solicitor's obligation to explain the documentary disclosure obligations should always be considered seriously. Failure to disclose a document can be fatal to your client's case. Explain the meaning of "document," give your clients examples and tell them to give you everything that <u>may</u> be relevant, so that you can make the call as to both relevance and privilege. If opposing counsel serves an affidavit of documents that has obvious omissions, bring a motion before examinations for discovery to make the examinations more efficient, with fewer undertakings.

3.3.7 INSPECTION OF DOCUMENTS

- A party who serves on another party a request to inspect documents (Form 30C) is entitled to inspect any document that is not privileged and that was listed in the other party's affidavit of documents. Rule 30.04(1)

- A request to inspect documents may also be used to obtain the inspection of any document that a party referred to in its originating process, pleadings or other affidavit. Rule 30.04(2). *As a practical matter, most solicitors will provide copies of such documents, but a formal request may be necessary in some cases.*

- A party on whom a request to inspect documents is served must immediately inform the party making the request of a date within five days after the service of the request to inspect documents, and of a time between 9:30 a.m. and 4:30 p.m. when the documents may be inspected. The inspection site may be the office of the solicitor of the party served, or some other convenient place. At the stated time and place, the party must make the documents available for inspection. Rule 30.04(3)

- If a document has been produced for inspection, the party inspecting the document is entitled to make a copy of it at their own client's expense. The alternative is that the person having possession or control over the document can make a copy of it, in which case that person will be reimbursed for the cost of making the copy. Rule 30.04(7)

- Unless the parties agree otherwise, all documents listed in a party's affidavit of documents that are not privileged and all documents previously produced for inspection by the party shall, without notice, summons or order, be taken to and produced at:

    - the examination for discovery of or on behalf of the party; and
    - the trial of the action.

    Rule 30.04(4)

- If you have requested an inspection of documents that are not privileged, and the other party has not complied with your request, apply to the court for an order forcing the other party to produce them as required. Rule 30.04(5)

- If the other party has claimed privilege for a document, and you dispute that, you can apply to have the court inspect the document to determine the validity of the claim. Rule 30.04(6)

- If you have been asked to produce a document that would become relevant only after the determination of an issue in the action, and the disclosure of that document beforehand would seriously prejudice your case, you can bring a motion asking the court to grant leave to withhold disclosure until after the issue has been determined. Rule 30.04(8)

> **Practice Tip:** Note that each document over which privilege is claimed must be separately listed and described, including the nature of the privilege, in schedule "B" of the Affidavit of Documents. A "catch-all" statement in schedule "B" will leave you open to a motion for a further and better affidavit of documents, with potential costs consequences.

3.3.8 EXAMINATIONS FOR DISCOVERY

- You have the option of examining a party for discovery either orally or by written questions - but not both, unless you obtain the leave of the court. Generally, where more than one party is entitled to examine, the examination is oral, unless all the parties agree otherwise. Rule 31.02(1)(2)

- You can only examine a party adverse in interest once, unless you obtain leave of the court. Rule 31.03(1). *If the party examined provides undertakings to provide further information and/or documentation, at the end of the examination adjourn it sine die pending the receipt and review of the undertakings. If you need further clarification of this new information, you can require the party to reattend at the examination.*

- Where the party is a corporation, you may examine any officer, director or employee on behalf of the corporation. The corporation can, however, bring a motion to have the court order the examination of a different individual. Where you have examined an officer, director or employee of a corporation, you may not examine any other officer, director or employee of the corporation without leave of the court. Rule 31.03(2)(3)

- Where the party is a partnership or a sole proprietorship using the firm name, you may examine each person who was, or is alleged to have been, a partner or the sole proprietor at a material time. Rule 31.03(4)

- You may also examine an assignor, assignee or trustee in bankruptcy as applicable. Rule 31.03(6)(7)

- The court can limit multiple examinations that it considers would be oppressive, vexatious or unnecessary. Rule 31.03(9)

- A party who seeks to examine your client (the plaintiff), for discovery must deliver a statement of defence and, unless the parties agree otherwise, serve an affidavit of documents before serving you with a notice of examination under Rule 34.04 or written questions under Rule 35.01. Rule 31.04(1)

- To examine the defendant, you may serve a notice of examination under Rule 34.04 or written questions under Rule 35.01 only after the defendant has delivered a statement of defence and, unless the parties agree otherwise, you have served an affidavit of documents, or the defendant has been noted in default. Rule 31.04(2)

- The first party to serve a notice of examination on another party may examine first and may complete the examination before being examined by another party, unless the court orders otherwise. Rule 31.04(3)

- A person examined for discovery shall answer, to the best of their knowledge, information and belief, any proper question relating to any matter in issue in the action, and may not object on the grounds that:

- the information sought is evidence;
- the question constitutes cross-examination, unless the question is directed solely to the credibility of the witness; or
- the question constitutes cross-examination on the affidavit of documents of the party being examined.

  Rule 31.06 (1)

- The following matters may be included in the questions during the examination:
  - the names and addresses of persons who might reasonably be expected to have knowledge of transactions or occurrences in issue in the action, unless the court orders otherwise. Rule 31.06(2);
  - the name, address, findings, opinions and conclusions of an expert engaged on behalf of the party being examined that relate to a matter in issue in the action (but the party being examined need not disclose the information, name and address of the expert where the expert's findings, were made in preparation for contemplated or pending litigation and for no other purpose, and the party being examined undertakes not to call the expert as a witness at the trial). Rule 31.06(3); and
  - the existence and contents of any insurance policy under which an insurer may be liable to satisfy all or part of a judgment in the action or to indemnify or reimburse a party for money paid in satisfaction of all or part of the judgment, thee amount of money available under the policy, and any conditions affecting its availability. Note that the information about the insurance policy is admissible in evidence only if it is relevant to an issue in the action. Rule 31.06(4)(5)

- Where information may become relevant only after the determination of an issue in the action, and the disclosure of the information before the issue is determined would seriously prejudice a party, the court on the party's motion may grant leave to withhold the information until after the issue has been determined. Rule 31.06(6)

- Where a person or party being examined has refused to answer a proper question or to answer a question on the ground of privilege, and has failed to furnish the information in writing not later than 10 days after the action is set down for trial, the party may not introduce the information at trial except with leave of the trial judge. Rule 31.07(1)

- Where a party, or a person examined for discovery on behalf of or in place of a party, has undertaken to answer a question but has failed to furnish the information in writing not later than 10 days after the action is set down for trial and the party may not introduce the information at trial refused on discovery except with leave of the trial judge. Rule 31.07(2)

- Additional sanctions for failing to provide answers or information are contained in Rule 34.15.

- If you realize, after examination, that your client gave an incorrect or incomplete answer during the examination, or the answer is no longer correct and complete, you must immediately provide that information in writing to every other party. The new information is then treated as if it formed part of the original examination; however, any adverse party may require that it be verified by affidavit or further examination. Rule 31.09(1)(2)

- Where a party fails to correct incomplete or inaccurate answers, if the information subsequently discovered is favourable to their case, they may not introduce the information at trial without leave of the trial judge. If the information is not favourable to their case, the court may make such order as it feels is just. Rule 31.09(3)

> **Practice Tip:** Corrections should be made as promptly as possible. It is probably an abuse of process to provide corrections on the eve of trial, and the trial judge will certainly not be impressed. Original answers, even if corrected, can still be read in at trial against a party. *Capital Distributing Co. v. Blakey* (1997), 33 O.R. (3d) 58 (Gen. Div.)

3.3.9 PRE-TRIAL

(a) Setting the Action Down for Trial

- Your statement of claim named the location for the trial as a place in which the court normally sits in the county in which the action was commenced. Where a statute requires an action to be tried in a particular county, you should name a place where the court normally sits in that county. Rule 46.01(1)(2). *It is prima facie improper to name a place for trial that has no connection with either the parties or the cause of action. There must be some rational connection between the facts of the case and the place where the matter is to be tried. Laurin v. Favot* (1996), 28 O.R. (3d) 114 (Gen. Div.)

- The trial will be held at the place set out in the statement of claim unless the court orders otherwise. Rule 46.02 and 46.03. *While the plaintiff has the right to choose the place of trial, the court can change the place of trial if the other party establishes a substantial "preponderance of convenience" in favour of the trial being held in another location. Laurin v. Favot*, supra.

- A party to an action may require that the issues of fact be tried or the damages be assessed, or both, by a jury, by delivering a jury notice (Form 47A) at any time before the close of pleadings, unless section 108 of the *Courts of Justice Act* or another statute requires that the action be tried without a jury. Rule 47.01

- After the close of pleadings, any party to an action or related claim who is not in default and who is ready for trial may set the action and its related claims down for trial. Rule 48.01

> **Practice Tip:** If an undefended action has been set down for trial, the registrar will place it on the trial list forthwith. In the case of a defendant action, it must be placed on the trial list by the registrar 60 days after it was set down for trial, or on the date of filing if all of the parties consent. If a proceeding has not been set down for trial within two years of the close of pleadings, a status notice will be sent to all of the parties.

- Where an action is defended, you may set it down for trial by serving a trial record prepared in accordance with Rule 48.03 on every party to the action or a related claim, and on any third or subsequent party, and immediately filing the trial record with proof of service. Rule 48.02(1)

- If the court has ordered the trial of an undefended action, you may set it down for trial by filing a trial record prepared in accordance with Rule 48.03. Rule 48.02(2)

- Where an action is to be tried at a place other than where it was commenced, the party filing the trial record shall by requisition require the court file, including the trial record, to be sent to the court office at the place of trial. Rule 48.02(5)

- The trial record shall contain, in the following order:

    - a table of contents, describing each document by its nature and date;
    - a copy of any jury notice;
    - a copy of the pleadings, including those relating to any counterclaim or crossclaim;
    - a copy of any financial statement delivered under Rule 69.14 or 70.04 or waiver of financial statements filed under Rule 69.14(3);

  - a copy of any demand or order for particulars of a pleading or financial statement and the particulars delivered in response;
  - a copy of any notice of amounts and particulars of special damages delivered under clause 25.06(9)(b);
  - a copy of any order respecting the trial; and
  - a certificate signed by the solicitor setting the action down, stating:
    - that the record contains the documents required above;
    - that the time for delivery of pleadings has expired;
    - where applicable, that a defendant who has failed to deliver a statement of defence has been noted in default; and
    - where applicable, that judgment has been obtained or that the action has been discontinued or dismissed against a defendant.

    Rule 48.03(1)

- If you are filing the trial record, it is your responsibility to place with the record, before the trial, a copy of:

  - any notice of amounts and particulars of special damages delivered after the filing of the trial record;
  - any order respecting the trial made after the filing of the trial record;
  - any memorandum signed by counsel, or any order made by the court, following a pre-trial conference;
  - any financial statement delivered under Rule 69.14 (14) or 70.04(14) after the filing of the trial record;
  - in an undefended action, any affidavit to be used in evidence; and
  - any report of the Children's Lawyer and supporting affidavit and any dispute of, or waiver of the right to dispute, the report or affidavit.

  Rule 48.03(2)

- Any party who has set an action down for trial and any party who has consented to the action being placed on a trial list shall not initiate or continue any motion or form of discovery without leave of the court. Rule 48.04(1). *You must still, however, comply with undertakings that you gave on an examination for discovery and with rules governing, for example, the requirement to correct incomplete or inaccurate answers.* Rule 48.04(2)

(b) Offers to Settle

- A party to a proceeding may serve on any other party an offer to settle any one or more of the claims in the proceeding on the terms specified in the offer to settle (Form 49A). Rule 49.02(1)

- An offer to settle may be made at any time, but where the offer to settle is made less than seven days before the hearing commences, the costs consequences of refusing the offer do not apply. Rule 49.03

- Where you, as the plaintiff, make an offer to settle at least seven days before the hearing and the defendant does not accept it, and where you obtain a judgment that is as (or more) favourable than your terms of settlement, you are entitled to party-party costs to the date the offer to settle was served and solicitor-client costs from that date, unless the court orders otherwise. Rule 49.10(1)

- Where a defendant makes an offer to settle at least seven days before the hearing, and you do not accept it, and where you obtain a judgment as (or less) favourable than your terms settlement, you are entitled to party-party costs to the date the offer was served and the defendant is entitled to party-party costs from that date, unless the court orders otherwise. Rule 49.10(2)

(c) Pre-Trial Conference

- In an action or application, a judge may, at the request of a party or on their own initiative, direct the solicitors for the parties and the parties as required, to appear before a judge or officer for a pre-trial conference to consider:

  - the possibility of settling of any or all of the issues in the proceeding;
  - the simplification of the issues;
  - the possibility of obtaining admissions that may facilitate the hearing;
  - the question of liability;
  - the amount of damages, where damages are claimed;
  - the estimated duration of the hearing;
  - the advisability of having the court appoint an expert;
  - the advisability of fixing a date for the hearing;
  - the advisability of directing a reference; and
  - any other matter that may assist in the just, most expeditious and least expensive disposition of the proceeding.

  Rule 50.01

- At the conclusion of the conference, counsel may sign a memorandum setting out the results of the conference, and (where the conference is conducted by a judge), the judge may make such order as necessary or advisable with respect to the conduct of the proceeding. The memorandum or order binds the parties unless the judge or officer presiding at the hearing orders otherwise to prevent injustice. A copy of a memorandum or order must be placed with the trial or application record. Rule 50.02(1)(2)

- All documents intended to be used at the hearing that may be of assistance in achieving the purposes of a pre-trial conference, such as medical reports and reports of experts, shall be made available to the pre-trial conference judge or officer. Rule 50.05. *The pre-trial conference date is not to be seen as a cut off date for the production of expert reports. Kungl v. Fallis* (1988), 26 C.P.C. (2d) 102 (Ont. H.C.)

- A party may at any time, by serving a request to admit (Form 51A), request any other party to admit, for the purposes of the proceeding only, the truth of a fact or the authenticity of a document. Where practicable, serve with the request a copy of any document that the request mentions, unless the other party already has it. Rule 51.02(1)(2). *This will significantly speed up the proceeding by streamlining the proof of evidence at trial.*

Practice Tip: Requests to admit are used too infrequently, most probably because busy counsel do not turn their minds to them early in the process. Apart from the costs sanctions of a refusal to admit, there is an obvious tactical advantage to providing facts or documents that an opposing party had previously refused to admit, as the earlier refusal could be used in cross-examination.

- A party on whom a request to admit is served shall respond to it within 20 days after it is served by serving on the requesting party a response to request to admit (Form 51B). Rule 51.03(1). *Striking the matter off the trial list does not mean that the action is dismissed unless the judge specifically orders the action dismissed. If the matter is struck off the trial list, the parties will need to reattend and have the matter set down for trial again. This will needlessly increase your client's expense.*

- If the party does not serve a response, they are deemed to admit the truth of the facts or the authenticity of the documents mentioned in the request to admit. Rule 51.03(2). *It is thus essential to reply to such requests promptly: if you do not, you risk admitting something that may severely undermine your case.*

- Similarly, a party is also deemed to admit the truth of the facts or the authenticity of the documents mentioned in the request, unless the party's response specifically denies the truth or authenticity mentioned in the request, or refuses to admit the truth or authenticity and sets out the reason for the refusal. Rule 51.03(3)

3.3.10 TRIAL

- Where an action is called for trial and all the parties fail to attend, the trial judge may strike the action off the trial list. Rule 52.01(1). *If a matter is struck from the trial list, it can be reinstated after taking the appropriate steps. If the action is dismissed, you will have to bring a motion to reinstate the action.*

- Where an action is called for trial and a party fails to attend, the trial judge may:

  - proceed with the trial in the absence of the party;
  - where the plaintiff attends and the defendant fails to attend, dismiss the counterclaim, if any, and allow the plaintiff to prove the claim;
  - where the defendant attends and the plaintiff fails to attend, dismiss the action and allow the defendant to prove the counterclaim, if any; or
  - make such other order as is just.

  Rule 52.01(2)

- A judge may set aside or vary, on such terms as are just, a judgment obtained against a party who failed to attend at the trial. Rule 52.01(3)

- A judge may postpone or adjourn a trial to such time and place, and on such terms, as are just. Rule 52.02

3.3.11 COSTS

- In exercising its discretion under section 131 of the *Courts of Justice Act* to award costs, the court may consider, in addition to the result in the proceeding and any offer to settle or to contribute made in writing:

  - the amount claimed and the amount recovered in the proceeding;
  - the apportionment of liability;
  - the complexity of the proceeding;
  - the importance of the issues;
  - the conduct of any party that tended to shorten or to lengthen unnecessarily the duration of the proceeding;

- ° whether any step in the proceeding was improper, vexatious or unnecessary or taken through negligence, mistake or excessive caution;
- ° a party's denial of or refusal to admit anything that should have been admitted;
- ° whether it is appropriate to award any costs or more than one set of costs where a party commenced separate proceedings for claims that should have been made in one proceeding, or in defending a proceeding separated unnecessarily from another party in the same interest or defended by a different solicitor; and
- ° any other matter relevant to the question of costs. Rule 57.01(1). *Costs will be awarded in connection with the services of solicitors, students-at-law and law clerks operating under the supervision of a solicitor. Agents are not entitled to costs even though they may have represented successful parties. Garson v. Braithwaite* (1994), 34 C.P.C. (3d) 87 (Ont. Gen. Div.)

- The fact that a party is successful in a proceeding or a step in a proceeding does not prevent the court from awarding costs against the party in a proper case. Rule 57.01(2)

- In awarding costs, the court may fix all or part of the costs with or without reference to the Tariffs, instead of referring them for assessment, and where the costs are not fixed, they may be assessed under Rule 58. Rule 57.01(3)

- The court has the authority to award or refuse costs in respect of a particular issue or part of a proceeding, to award a percentage of assessed costs, or award assessed costs up to or from a particular stage of a proceeding; or to award all or part of the costs on a solicitor and client basis. Rule 57.01(4)

- Where a rule or order provides that a party is entitled to the costs of all or part of a proceeding between party and party and the costs have not been fixed by the court, they shall be assessed in accordance with Rule 58. Rule 58.01

- In assessing costs the assessment officer may consider:

  - the amount involved in the proceeding;
  - the complexity of the proceeding;
  - the importance of the issues;
  - the duration of the hearing;
  - the conduct of any party that tended to shorten or to lengthen unnecessarily the duration of the proceeding;
  - whether any step in the proceeding was improper, vexatious or unnecessary, or taken through negligence, mistake or excessive caution;
  - a party's denial of or refusal to admit anything that should have been admitted; and
  - any other matter relevant to the assessment of costs.

  Rule 58.06(1)

- For further information on the question of costs, see Chapter 13

> **Practice Tip:** On any motion, it is prudent to be ready to speak to costs at the end of the hearing. Bring copies of your dockets and disbursement receipts for opposing counsel and the court.

3.4 COLLECTIONS: DEALING WITH CASE MANAGEMENT

- The goal of establishing the civil case management system under Rule 77 is to reduce unnecessary cost and delay in civil litigation, facilitate early and fair settlements, and to balance the need to bring the matter quickly through the system with the requirement to provide sufficient time that the proceeding is fairly conducted. Rule 77.02. *Key advantages of civil case management include mandatory settlement conferences and the ability to provide your client with a fixed trial date.*

- Rule 77, Civil Case Management, applies to actions and applications commenced in Ottawa, and to actions and applications randomly assigned to case management by the registrar in Toronto. In addition, a case management judge or master may order that a matter be placed under civil case management. Rule 77.01(1), 77.11(1.1)

- Civil case management does not apply to:

  - matters to which the Toronto Family Case Management Rules apply;
  - matters to which Toronto Family Case Management Rule 1.01(1), paragraphs 1 to 4, apply if commenced in Ottawa on or after January 2, 1997;
  - matters placed on the Commercial List established by practice direction in Toronto;
  - mortgage actions;
  - construction liens;
  - bankruptcy and insolvency matters; and
  - class proceedings, unless certification as a class proceeding has been denied.

  Rule 77.01(2)(2.1)

- In the event of a conflict between Rules 1 to 76 and Rule 77, Rule 77 applies. Rule 77.01(3)

- Matters proceed in case management on either the fast track for simpler cases, or the standard track for more complex cases.

- If you begin the case on the fast track, and subsequently realize that you need more time to prepare for the hearing, you may, within certain time limits, bring a motion to have it switched to the standard track. Rule 77.07

- Case management judges and masters have the power to require a hearing, case conference or conference call to deal with any case management matter, including non-compliance with the Rules. Rule 77.11(2). *Case management judges and masters supervise the process, and can be called upon at any time in the process to han-*

dle matters such as motions or failures to abide by timetables.

- Deadlines prescribed in Rules 1 to 76 or in Rule 77 may only be changed by order of a case management judge or master. Rule 77.01(4)

- All hearings on motions under Rule 77 will be held in the county where the proceeding was commenced, unless the court orders otherwise. Rule 77.01(5)

3.4.1 COMMENCING THE PROCEEDING

- When an originating process is issued (such as a statement of claim), the plaintiff files a notice of commencement of proceeding (Form 77A) and serves it with the originating process. Rule 77.06(1)

- Note that under civil case management, only the notice of commencement of proceeding is filed when the originating process is issued; the originating process itself is not filed until a further step (other than a notice of discontinuance) is taken. Rule 77.06(3)(4). *If a statement of claim is not filed and you would like to see it, you can view a copy after payment of the prescribed fee and requisitioning the document. Courts of Justice Act,* s.137(1), Rule 77.06(9)

- On filing the notice of commencement of proceeding, you need to choose either the fast or standard track for the proceeding. To make this decision, take into account: the complexity of the issues of fact or law involved; the likely expense to the parties; the importance to the public of the issues; the number of parties; the amount of intervention likely to be required by the case management judge; and the time required for proper discovery, if applicable, and preparation for trial or hearing. Rule 77.06(5)(6)

- The action proceeds on the track chosen by the plaintiff, unless the court orders otherwise. The court may consider whether to transfer a proceeding between tracks on a party's motion, made before the close of pleadings in the case of an action, or before the 10th day after the first affidavit filed by the respondent in the case of an application. The court will take into account the same considerations as noted above. Rule 77.06(7), 77.07(1)(2)(3)

- However, all actions governed by the Simplified Procedure (Rule 76) proceed on the fast track. Rule 77.06(8)

3.4.2 DISMISSAL OF THE PROCEEDING

- If no defence is filed and the proceeding has not been disposed of by final order or judgment within 180 days after the originating process, the registrar must dismiss the proceedings as abandoned. Rule 77.08. *This highlights the need to maintain an accurate schedule of such deadlines within your office, to ensure that an action is not inadvertently dismissed because of your lack of timely action. The court office will advise you in writing that the proceeding will be dismissed as abandoned on a particular date unless further steps are taken. In the event that the proceedings are abandoned, you can bring a motion to set aside the abandonment of the proceedings. See sections 3.2.2 and 3.2.3.*

3.4.3 DEALING WITH THE DEFENCE

- Once the defendant serves a defence, and serves and files the notice of defence (Form 77B), the proceeding is assigned to a case management judge or team for management. Rule 77.09(1)(3). *Note that the defendant files a notice of defence and not the statement of defence itself unless it is required for a hearing. Rule 77.09(4)*

3.4.4 TIME REQUIREMENTS

- If a party fails to comply with the time requirements established in the Rules, the case management judge or master may convene a case conference for the purposes of creating or amending a timetable, ordering the party to comply with it, and ordering the party to pay costs. Rule 77.10(1)

- If a party fails to comply with a timetable, the case management judge or master may:
  - strike out any document filed by the party;
  - dismiss the party's proceeding or strike out the party's defence;
  - amend the timetable and order the party to comply with it;
  - order the party to pay costs;
  - make any other order that is just.

  Rule 77.10(2)

3.4.5 MOTIONS

- A motion may only be made to a case management judge or master. Before the motion is heard, the moving party must serve a case management motion form (Form 77C) as per Rule 37.07. Rule 77.12(1)(2)

- Depending on the situation, you can make the motion with or without supporting material or a motion record, by actual attendance, conference call, telephone call, fax or in writing. Rule 77.12(2.1). The responding party may serve and submit a case management motion form, but is not required to. Rule 77.12(2.2)

- If the motion is opposed and is to be argued other than in writing, the moving party's solicitor must confirm to the registrar by fax or in writing by 2 p.m. the day before the hearing that the motion is to proceed as scheduled. If this confirmation is not received, the motion will not proceed on that date. Rule 77.12(3)

- The case management judge or master addresses the issue of costs at the end of each motion. Rule 77.12(4)

- Certain motions can also be dealt with by the registrar. You may be dealing with a motion for an order on consent, for example, where all parties have filed their consent (including a statement that no party affected by the order is under a disability), or with a motion where no responding material is filed and the notice of motion or case management motion form states that no party affected by the order is under disability. In these cases, the registrar shall make the order granting the relief sought where the order is for:

- amending a pleading, notice of application or notice of motion;
- adding, deleting or substituting a party;
- removing a solicitor as solicitor of record;
- setting aside the noting of a party in default;
- setting aside a default judgment;
- discharging a certificate of pending litigation;
- security for costs in a specified amount;
- re-attendance of a witness to answer questions on an examination;
- fulfillment of undertakings given on an examination; or
- dismissing a proceeding with or without costs.

Rule 77.12(5)

3.4.6 CASE CONFERENCES

- A case management judge or master may convene a case conference at any time, on his or her own initiative or at a party's request. Rule 77.13(1). *Cases conferences are a reasonably informal way to solve problems that may arise during a case's route through civil case management. They bring the necessary parties together as required, and attempt to resolve issues by consensus if possible, and by order if not.*

- A case management judge or master may direct that the parties, or a representative of the parties who can make decisions and instruct the solicitor, attend the conference personally. Rule 77.13(2)

- At the conference, a case management judge or case management master may: identify the issues and whether or not they are contested; explore methods to resolve the contested issues; if possible, secure the parties' agreement on a specific schedule of events for the proceeding; create a timetable for the proceeding; and review and amend an existing timetable. Rule 77.13(3)

- It is essential that counsel attending the conference have the authority to deal with the matters referred to above, and that they are fully acquainted with the facts and legal issues involved. Rule 77.13(4). *This is not the place for a lawyer with little knowledge of the file to step in. This is an important step and requires the lawyer who has been dealing with the file to attend the case conference.*

- Note that the powers of a case management judge and a master differ. A judge, for example, may: create or amend a timetable for the proceeding; make a procedural order; on consent of the parties, make an order for interlocutory relief; on consent of the parties, refer any issue for alternative dispute resolution; convene a settlement conference; convene a hearing; and give directions. Rule 77.13(5)

- A case management master, however, may: create or amend a timetable for the proceeding; make a procedural order; on consent of the parties make an order within the jurisdiction of a case management master; on consent of the parties refer any issue for alternative dispute resolution; and convene a settlement conference. Rule 77.13(6)

- Note that in an action under the Simplified Procedure (Rule 76), a case conference may be convened only in conjunction with a settlement conference. Rule 77.13(7)

- Case conferences can be dealt with by telephone and by videoconferencing provided that the court deems it appropriate. Rule 1.08

3.4.7 SETTLEMENT CONFERENCE

- The registrar shall, on at least 45 days notice to the parties, schedule a settlement conference to take place as follows:

  - if the proceeding is on the fast track, within 150 days after the first defence is filed;
  - if the proceeding is on the standard track, within 240 days after the first defence is filed.

  Rule 77.14 (1)

- In cases where mandatory mediation is required, the mediation will have taken place within 90 days after the filing of the first defence. If mediation did not resolve all of the issues, the settlement conference provides one further opportunity for resolution prior to proceeding to trial.

- All examinations, production of documents and motions arising out of examinations and production of documents must be completed before the settlement conference date. Rule 77.14(2)

- A case management judge or master may direct the parties, or a representative who can make decisions and instruct the solicitor, to attend all or part of a settlement conference personally with their counsel. Rule 77.14(3). *The reason for requiring the parties to attend is to try to settle all or at least some of the outstanding issues face to face.*

- Except in actions under the Simplified Procedure (Rule 76), the plaintiff shall deliver not later than 10 days before the settlement conference a settlement conference brief, containing all material the plaintiff considers necessary for the settlement conference, and shall certify that all examinations, document production and associated motions have been completed. Rule 77.14(4).

- Except in actions under the Simplified Procedure (Rule 76), every other party shall deliver a settlement conference brief containing any other material the party considers necessary for the settlement conference not later than five days before the conference. Rule 77.14(5)

- In your settlement conference brief, you must include:

  - a concise summary of the facts, including the agreed upon facts and admissions;
  - where necessary, a concise summary of the issues and the law you are relying upon;
  - a list of witnesses and a summary of each witness's evidence;
  - the relevant portions only of transcripts, experts' reports and other evidence that may be adduced at trial; and
  - your pleadings, including any demand or order for particulars of a pleading and the particulars delivered in response.

  Rule 77.14(6)

- At the conference, if a settlement is not reached, a case management judge or master shall assign a trial or hearing date, or refer the parties to a judge responsible for assigning the date. Rule 77.14(7). *This gives you and your client a fixed trial date for which you can then plan accordingly; prior to case management, you would have little idea when your case would be called for trial and it would be placed on a trial list and the matter would be dealt with in assignment court.*

- A trial or application record must be served and filed in accordance with Rule 48.02 or 38.09(1) no later than seven days before the trial or hearing date. Rule 77.14(8)

- A pre-trial conference under the Simplified Procedure (Rule 76.07) is deemed to be a settlement conference for the purpose of civil case management. Rule 77.14(9)

- Settlement conferences can be dealt with by telephone and by videoconferencing provided that the court deems it appropriate. Rule 1.08

3.4.8 TRIAL MANAGEMENT CONFERENCE

- A trial management conference may be held on or following the setting of a trial date, at the request of one of the parties or on the initiative of the trial judge, case management judge or master. Rule 77.15(1)

- A trial management conference form (Form 77D) must be filed by the plaintiff and the defendant no later than 14 days before the trial or four days before the trial management conference, whichever is earlier. Rule 77.15(2)

- At the trial management conference, the trial judge, case management judge or case management master may:

  - canvass with the parties the names of the witnesses intended to be called and the substance of their testimony;
  - explore whether admissions can be made that will facilitate proof of non-contentious matters;
  - explore alternative methods of presentation of evidence, such as the filing of affidavits or reports;
  - explore with counsel expeditious means for the presentation of evidence; and
  - give directions that will facilitate the orderly and expeditious conduct of the trial.

  Rule 77.15(3)

- In an action under the Simplified Procedure (Rule 76), a trial management conference may be convened only in conjunction with a settlement conference. Rule 77.15(4)

3.5 COLLECTIONS: DEALING WITH MANDATORY MEDIATION

- Rule 24.1 established a pilot project for mandatory mediation in case-managed actions, with the goal of reducing costs and delays in litigation, and of facilitating the early and fair resolution of disputes. Although this Rule will be revoked automatically on July 4, 2001, it is expected that mandatory mediation will continue, and may indeed be expanded. Rule 24.1.01, 24.1.17

- Mediation requires a shift away from a focus on "winning the case" towards "finding solutions" - solutions that all the parties involved can agree upon. To assist them in reaching mutually acceptable solutions, mediation employs a neutral third party to help the parties find common ground and to communicate with each other. Rule 24.1.02

- Mandatory mediation currently applies to case-managed actions in the cities of Toronto and Ottawa. Rule 24.1.04(1)

- Mandatory mediation does not apply to:

  - actions under the *Substitute Decisions Act, 1992*, or Part V of the *Succession Law Reform Act*;
  - an action commenced in Toronto and governed by Rule 76 (Simplified Procedure); or
  - an action that was subject to mediation under section 258.6 of the *Insurance Act*, if the mediation was conducted less than a year before the delivery of the first defence in the action.

  Rule 24.1.04(2)

- If your claim involves the *Proceedings Against the Crown Act*, if the notice required by section 7 of that Act has not been served, the Crown is entitled, but not required, to participate in mandatory mediation. Rule 24.1.04(3)

- Mandatory mediation is intended to work with civil case management under Rule 77. Where mediation or the provisions of civil case management do not appear practicable, the parties may seek a case conference for direction as to how to proceed with either mediation or another form of alternative dispute resolution.

3.5.1 INITIATING MEDIATION

- Under Rule 24.1, mediation is initiated either by the parties themselves, or by the mediation coordinator if the parties do not act.

- The court may exempt a party from mandatory mediation, on that party's motion for exemption. Rule 24.1.05

- Within 30 days after the first defence is filed, the parties must choose a mediator, and the plaintiff (in this case, the creditor who has filed the statement of claim) must file with the mediation coordinator a notice (Form 24.1A) stating the mediator's name and the date of the mediation session.

- The mediation must take place within 90 days after the first defence is filed. If a delay is necessary, you may apply to the court for an extension, keeping in mind that in making its decision, the court will take into account the number of parties and complexity of the issues, whether a party intends to bring a motion under Rule 20 (Summary Judgment), Rule 21 (Determination of an Issue Before Trial) or Rule 22 (Special Case), or whether the delay will allow the parties to acquire more information and thus would make the mediation more likely to succeed. Rule 24.1.09(1)(2)

- If the action is on the standard track of civil case management, the mediation may be postponed for up to 60 days if all the parties consent. The consent needs to be filed with the mediation coordinator. Rule 24.1.09(3)

- If the parties do not choose a mediator within the 30-day limit, the mediation coordinator will automatically assign a mediator from the roster list of mediators. Rule 24.1.09(6). *Note that there have been problems caused by parties who are late filing their Notice of Selection of Mediator: by the time the Notice is filed, the mediation coordinator may already have assigned a mediator to the case, and that mediator may have begun working on the case. Thus, once a court-assigned mediator has been assigned, the parties will need to file a motion if they wish to change the mediator to one they themselves have selected; notice of this motion must be served on the court-appointed mediator. Furthermore, if the court finds that the court-assigned mediator incurred time and expense in dealing with the matter, the court can make an order appointing a new mediator conditional on payment of fees or expenses for the court-assigned mediator. Letter of Master Robert Beaudoin to all members of the Bar re: Assignment of Mediators, November 10, 2000; Sunny Bay Investments Inc. v. Carlsbad Paving Inc.* Court File No. 99-CV-010909.

- The assigned mediator then fixes a date for the mediation, and at least 20 days prior, serves on every party a notice (Form 24.1B) stating the place, date and time of the mediation and advising that attendance is mandatory.

3.5.2 PARTICIPANTS IN THE MEDIATION

(a) The Mediator

- A roster of mediators is available from the Mandatory Mediation Office or via the Internet at *www.attorneygeneral.jus.gov.on.ca/manmed.* The local mediation committee selects the mediators who appear on this roster, which is updated monthly. It is from this roster that the mediation coordinator assigns a mediator if the parties have not chosen one themselves (the assignment is made using an electronic random selection process to ensure the system's fairness). Rule 24.1.08(1)

- The parties themselves, however, are not restricted to choosing a mediator from the roster, but - whether the mediator is selected by the parties from the roster or outside it - all the parties must all agree with their selection. Rule 24.1.08(2)

- A number of factors should be considered in selecting a mediator, including their experience in the type of law involved, their familiarity with the civil litigation process and their approach to mediation - plus the mediation location and the hourly fee if the mediation extends past the three-hour timeframe. *It is essential that a mediator understand the legal implications of the solutions discussed by the parties, to ensure that time is not wasted on solutions that could prejudice one or more of the parties.*

> **Practice Tip**: Because the roster mediators have been chosen for their ability to mediate - not necessarily for their background in claims or even the legal system - it is preferable for the parties involved to choose their own mediator, rather than have one assigned by the mediation coordinator. Choosing your own mediator, whether from the roster or not, also fosters a more constructive mediation atmosphere, as the individual who is responsible for conducting the mediation has been agreed to by all of the parties.

- Mediators selected for the local mediation committee's roster must follow a Code of Conduct, which emphasizes such factors as impartiality, confidentiality and the quality of the mediation process, and includes provisions that mediators will act in compliance with the mediation rule, maintain competence, encourage fairness and foster public confidence in the program.

- Any party to a mediation under Rule 24.1 can submit a written complaint about a roster mediator's conduct to the local mediation committee within 60 days after the last mediation session. The committee must then respond to the complaint. Rule 24.1.07(4)

(b) The Parties

- Unless the court orders otherwise, parties must attend the mediation in person, with their legal counsel if they are represented. The attendance of other individuals must be approved by all parties beforehand. Rule 24.1.11(1)

Practice Tip: It can be useful to include someone your client relies upon for moral support - a spouse, friend or colleague, for example - in the mediation session. Their role would be one of passive observer during the mediation, with the possibility of more direct assistance during caucusing. Their attendance can have a positive effect on the mediation through their ability to help your client deal with personal, cultural, emotional or other matters that you as counsel may not even be aware of. Of course, their attendance must not be a surprise: the other designated parties must be notified and must give their consent.

- For the mediation to succeed, it is essential that the parties in attendance have authority to settle the matters in dispute. If a designated party needs someone else's approval of their agreement to settle, they must arrange for that individual to be immediately and continuously available by telephone throughout the mediation session. Rule 24.1.11(2)

- Counsel's attendance at mediation is not sufficient: the designated parties themselves must attend, unless a court order specifies otherwise. Although the court may, at its discretion, direct attendance of a designated party by teleconference, this requires significantly more of the party than simply being available by telephone. *Magalhaes v. Lusitania Portuguese Recreation Club* (August 3, 1999), Doc. Ottawa Court 99-CV-8667 (Ont. Master)

3.5.3 MEDIATION TIME AND LOCATION

- It is essential that the parties meet face to face, in the same room. *In this way, not only the words of the parties can be analyzed, but also their body language and facial expressions, presenting a complete communication picture. A statement that might be perceived as harsh when communicated over the telephone can be perceived as merely firm if the facial expression that accompanies it is seen to be non-threatening.*

- Although having the parties meet in person is clearly preferable, there are some instances that force the mediation to take place via a medium such as teleconferencing. In these cases, a court order must be obtained authorizing the party or parties involved to participate in the mediation via such a medium.

- The mediation location - the courthouse, mediator's office or the offices of counsel for one of the parties, for example - must also be agreeable to all parties. The parties must perceive the location to be neutral, reasonably convenient for all parties, and comfortable: making mediation comfortable also makes it more productive, of course, as it encourages communication between participants. Breakout rooms should be available for caucusing purposes; restrooms and refreshments should be readily accessible; and the room itself should be set up in a non-adversarial layout with all supplies such as flipcharts and pens close at hand.

Practice Tips:

- Find out from the mediator if refreshments such as coffee are available; if they're not, ask how they can be brought in, particularly if you expect the mediation to exceed the initial three hours.
- Ensure you're satisfied with mediation location's neutrality. For example, you don't want your client to be intimidated by walking into an expensively furnished boardroom at an opposing party's legal firm. In this case, the location can send a message before the mediation even begins.
- As at January 1, 2001, mediation facilities are available in both Ottawa and Toronto on a no-cost, first-come-first-served basis. In Ottawa, the Case Conference Room is located on the fifth floor of the Courthouse at 161 Elgin Street, and is available from 8:30 a.m. to 5:00 p.m. Monday to Friday. Call (613) 239-1180 to book. In Toronto, the ADR Centre is on the 8th floor of 77 Grenville Street, and is available from 8:30 a.m. to 6:00 p.m. Monday to Friday. Call (416) 314-1361 to book.

- The mediation lasts up to three hours; however, the parties may continue the session for a longer period if they consent.

3.5.4 PREPARING FOR MEDIATION

- Mediation requires committed effort on the part of both client and counsel prior to the mediation session. Your role as counsel is to work with your client to encourage productive, cooperative discussions during the mediation, and will include:

    - determining and discussing the consequences of proceeding to court and the subsequent implications of either winning or losing the case;
    - estimating the costs of proceeding to trial;
    - analyzing what elements would create the best possible mediated settlement, what elements would be essential for an acceptable mediated settlement, and what elements or solutions your client is prepared to propose;
    - analyzing the other parties' positions and their issues;
    - deciding whether a court precedent needs to be set;
    - factoring in whether publicity or maintaining an ongoing relationship with other parties is an issue; and
    - identifying and understanding the emotional issues that need to be voiced.

- You will also need to assemble all applicable documentation in advance, including the breakdown of financial figures into their constituent parts, on paper. Present this to your client prior to the mediation, to ensure that your client agrees on the figures and issues that are documented. *Waiting until the mediation to present it can create a situation where your client doesn't agree with your figures, requiring you to deal with that issue before you can even begin to deal with the mediation. Not only is this preparation necessary for the mediation to reach a concrete settlement, but it will also prove helpful in case mediation fails and a trial becomes necessary.*

- Another key element in your preparation is preparing your client to speak for themselves, possibly as early as the mediation session's opening statement. The client needs to understand the active and essential role that mediation requires of them. *Your role as counsel during the mediation session itself becomes much more passive than in litigation: you are an observer, a strategist and an advisor on legal areas, protecting your client's interests in the settlement agreement, but keeping in mind that the client's interests and emotions can be as important in mediation as the legal issues of right and wrong.*

- Discuss the settlement options with your client prior to the mediation.

- The client has to be prepared to be an active participant in the process. Talk to your client in depth prior to the mediation, practicing if necessary their opening statements and their responses to statements likely to be made by the other parties.

- All communications at a mediation session - including the mediator's notes and records - are deemed to be without prejudice settlement discussions. This ensures the confidentiality of documents or statements made within the mediation: they can neither be released to the public nor used in court, whether the mediation succeeds or not. *It also means that the mediator cannot be called by a party as a witness at trial.* Rule 24.1.14

- Each designated party to a mediation must prepare Form 24.1C, the statement of issues, and provide it to the mediator and all other parties at least seven days prior to the scheduled mediation session. Rule 24.1.10(1)

- In the statement, the parties briefly identify the facts and the legal issues that are in dispute. In addition, the parties set out their position and their interests, making it clear what they hope to achieve. To assist all parties in preparing for the mediation, copies of all important documentation are to be attached to the statement of issues. Rule 24.1.10(2)(3)

- As the plaintiff, you will need to include a copy of the pleadings with the copy of the statement of issues that you send to the mediator. Rule 24.1.10(4)

Practice Tip: Although the statement of issues requires only the issues in dispute to be listed, you should demonstrate your positive approach to mediation by also identifying the issues that are not in dispute. By establishing common ground before the mediation even begins, you can contribute to an atmosphere of trust and willingness to discuss the issues.

3.5.5 NON-COMPLIANCE

- If the mediation cannot be conducted because a party has not filed a statement of issues, the mediator cancels the session and files with the mediation coordinator a certificate of non-compliance (Form 24.1D). Rule 24.1.10(5)

- If the mediation cannot be conducted because a party fails to attend within the first 30 minutes of the mediation, the mediator cancels the session and files with the mediation coordinator a certificate of non-compliance. Rule 24.1.12

- The mediation coordinator refers the matter to a case management master or judge, who may then convene a case conference under Rule 77.13(1), and may:

  - establish a timetable for the action;
  - strike out any document filed by a party;
  - dismiss the action, if the non-compliant party is a plaintiff, or strike out the statement of defence, if the non-compliant party is a defendant;
  - order a party to pay costs; and
  - make any other order that is just.

  Rule 24.1.13(1)(2)

3.5.6 THE MEDIATION PROCESS

- For a detailed discussion of the mediation process, please see Chapter 5.4.10.

3.5.7 RESULTS

- If some or all of the issues are not settled, and all of the parties consent, the court may order the parties to participate in an additional mediation session, which follows the rules set down for the initial mediation in terms of timing and procedure. Rule 24.1.16(1)(3)

- If the parties agree to solutions for some or all of the issues in dispute, all parties or their lawyers sign a settlement agreement regarding those issues. Rule 24.1.15(3)

- If the agreement settles the action, the defendant files a notice to that effect 10 days after the signing if the agreement is unconditional, and 10 days after the condition is satisfied if the agreement is conditional. Rule 24.1.15(4)

- If the agreement does not completely settle the action, or if no issues were settled, the matter returns to the civil case management process.

- If a party fails to comply with the settlement agreement, any other party to the agreement may bring a motion to a judge for judgment in the terms of the agreement or may continue the action as if there had been no agreement. Rule 24.1.15(5)

Practice Tip: As solicitor for the plaintiff, include a clause of what should happen in the event of default by the defendant. The most expeditious clause would be to include a provision that if the default is not rectified within 10 days after written notification is given, that the Minutes of Settlement acts as a consent to judgment for the outstanding balance claimed in the Statement of Claim plus interest plus costs, less any amounts paid.

3.5.8 COSTS

- The mandatory mediation programs are based on a user-pay system, with the costs divided between the designated parties unless the court or the mediation settlement agreement directs otherwise. For Rule 24.1, the Mediators' Fees Regulation explains who the parties are for purposes of cost division, and what the mediator may charge these parties. (Regulation 451/98)

- These fees cover the mediator for 30 minutes of preparation time for each party and up to three hours of mediation, and they increase with increased numbers of parties. For example, with two parties the maximum fee to be split between the parties is $600 plus GST. For three, the maximum fee increases to $675 plus GST; for four parties, the fee is $750 plus GST; and for five or more parties, the maximum fee is $825 plus GST.

- The mediator should specify before the mediation begins what their fees are for sessions that run beyond the three hours. Generally, the "overtime" fee is calculated on either an hourly basis or a flat fee. If the overtime and its associated fees are agreed upon by all parties, the mediation session will continue past the initial three hours.

> **Practice Tip**: If you and your client are seeking a non-equal division of fees between the designated parties, it should be included in the mediation's settlement agreement.

- Reducing the costs involved in resolving disputes is one of the mandatory mediation program's cornerstones: mediation must be both accessible and affordable. The courts have therefore found that travel expenses such as transportation, accommodation and food costs will not be paid for roster mediators appointed by the court who conduct mediation sessions outside their immediate geographical area. *Riviera Properties Ltd. v. Royal Bank* (October 29, 1999), Doc. Ottawa 99-CV-9976 (Ont. Master)

- It should be noted, of course, that where the designated parties have chosen their own mediator, whether from the roster or not, and agreed to pay the mediator's additional expenses, the mediator is permitted to charge those expenses.

- All other disbursement expenses, whether travel-related or not, must be understood and approved by all parties before the mediation begins.

- Should one or more of the designated parties be unable to pay the mediation fees, the Mediators Fee Regulation of Rule 24.1 notes that this does not increase the fees payable by the other parties. Where the party unable to pay holds a legal aid certificate, the mediator can receive partial compensation, assuming that the mediator is recognized by the Ontario Legal Aid Plan.

- Where the party in financial distress does not hold a legal aid certificate, the mediator provides services to this party *pro bono* as long as the party meets the mandatory mediation program's financial eligibility test. (Further details are available from the mediation coordinator.)

- The mediator may charge cancellation fees in two circumstances: where a designated party has not submitted a statement of issues; and where a party does not show up at the mediation within the session's first thirty minutes. The maximum cancellation fee is the total cost of the mediation that would have been charged according to the Mediators' Fees Regulation, and is borne by the party or parties who caused the cancellation. *Baliotis v. 1093707 Ontario Ltd.* (2000), 44 C.P.C. (4th) 75 (Ont. Master)

- In addition to the cancellation fee, other costs can be awarded, including the counsel fee for the parties who did attend the mediation. *Merrill Lynch Canada Inc. v. Vacation Properties Time Sharing Inc.* (1999), 37 C.P.C. (4th) 317 (Ont. Master)

3.6 ENFORCEMENT: WRIT OF SEIZURE AND SALE

- Your first step in using a writ of seizure and sale to enforce a judgment is to find out whether it is worth pursuing the debtor's assets in this way. You need to determine what assets the debtor owns, where the assets are located, and whether the assets are subject to the claims of any other creditors (such as in the case of a car owned by the debtor, but subject to a security interest registered by a bank who loaned funds to the debtor).

- To determine what assets the debtor owns and whether those assets are subject to other liens, conduct real estate, motor vehicle, *Personal Property Security Act* PPSA), execution, bankruptcy and credit bureau searches. For more information on searches, see Chapter 2.

- Note that there are exemptions to the assets that can be seized, including:

  - property in the hands of a court-appointed receiver. Rule 60.07(14);
  - property exempt under the *Executions Act* section 3, including clothing up to $5,000, household furniture up to $10,000, and tools and chattels used for business up to $10,000. *Executions Act*, s.3; and
  - certain income, such as pension, workers' compensation and employment insurance benefits.

Practice Tip: The *Execution Act* was amended on April 15, 2001. The exemption levels have changed as set out above. In addition, the exemption for farmers is now $25,000.00. A new exemption has been included for motor vehicles up to $5,000.00. *Execution Act*, R.S.O. 1990, c.E-24, s.2

The Regulations under the *Execution Act* also allow the exemption levels to be changed every five years based on the Consumer Price Index for Canada. *Execution Act,* s.35

- A debtor's RRSP can be seized and sold; however, if the RRSP includes an insurance provision, and the beneficiary of that insurance is the debtor's spouse, child, parent or grandchild, the plan is protected from seizure. *Executions Act,* ss.18, 19 and the *Insurance Act* s.196

- Once you have decided that a writ of seizure and sale is appropriate, file with the registrar where the proceeding was commenced a requisition, detailing the date and amount of any payment received since the order was made, the amount owing, and the rate of postjudgment interest. Rule 60.07(1). *If costs are assessed at some point after the order is made, apply to the registrar for an additional writ of seizure and sale to cover the costs.*

Practice Tip: Electronic filing of writs of seizure and sale is available now in some jurisdictions. Rule 60.07(1.1)

Practice Tip: In the event that part of the judgment is paid, a letter should be sent to the sheriff advising them how much of the amount, so that the sheriff's records can reflect the new amount that is outstanding on the judgment.

Practice Tip: If your address or the creditor's address changes after the writ is issued, a new address can be noted on the writ by filing a requisition to that effect with the sheriff. Rule 60.07(12.1)

- If six years have elapsed since the date of the order, or if the order's enforcement was subject to a condition, you need to seek the leave of the court to obtain a writ of seizure and sale. Rule 60.07(2)

- Such an order granting leave expires one year after it was granted; if a writ was not issued within that year, you will need to bring a motion to the court for leave to be granted again. Rule 60.07(3)

- If the order was for the payment of money into court, the writ must state that money realized under the writ must be paid into court. Rule 60.07(4)

- Every writ must also state the name and address of the creditor and the creditor's solicitor. Rule 60.07(12). *If these addresses change after the writ is issued, file with the sheriff a requisition to note the new address on the writ.* Rule 60.07(12.1)

- If the order specifies payment on or after a specified date, the writ cannot be issued until after that date. Rule 60.07(5)

- The writ remains in force for six years. To renew a writ before its expiration, file a request to renew (Form 6E) with the sheriff if the writ is filed with a sheriff, or a requisition to renew the writ with the registrar who issued the writ, as applicable. The writ will remain in force for a further six years from each renewal. Rule 60.07(6)(8)(9). *The procedure with respect to renewing a writ of seizure and sale has been amended in recent years. Previously, the sheriff would mail a notice to the solicitor noted on the writ prior to the expiration advising that the creditor could renew the writ of seizure and sale for a further six year period. The practice now is that the sheriff does* not notify anyone of the expiry of the writ of seizure and sale. It is up to the solicitor and/or the creditor to maintain a filing system by date to ensure that the writ is renewed before it expires. This also offers an opportunity for you to contact your client to see if they require any other services at the same time.

- You may encounter situations where the debtor changes their name after the writ is issued, uses an alias, or varies the spelling of their name. In this case, you should bring a motion (without notice) for an alias writ, seeking a change or variation to the original writ. The court may then order the sheriff to amend the writ by adding the words "now or also known as" followed by the debtor's new or varied name; amend the index of writs accordingly; and send a copy of the amended writ to the land registrar if applicable. Rule 60.07(10)(11)

- Once the writ of seizure and sale has been issued, you must then direct the sheriff to enforce it. To do so, file with the sheriff a copy of the order, along with a direction to enforce (Form 60F), which includes:

    - the date of the order and the amount awarded;
    - the rate of postjudgment interest payable;
    - the costs of enforcement to which the creditor is entitled under Rule 60.19;
    - the date and amount of any payment received since the order;
    - the amount owing, including postjudgment interest; and
    - a direction to the sheriff to enforce the writ for the amount owing, subsequent interest and the sheriff's fees and expenses.

    Rule 60.07(13)

- The writ should be filed with the sheriffs of every county or district in which the debtor has assets that are available for seizure, and the county or district in which the debtor resides. *It is important that you file the writ in counties where the assets are located. If a writ is not filed in the appropriate county, it will not bind the assets held in that county and they could slip through the creditor's hands.*

- If you are seeking the seizure of real property, and the county or district involved uses both the Land Registry and the Land Titles systems, ensure that the sheriff registers the writ under both systems. *Failure to file in both the land registry system and the land titles system may also allow assets to slip by the creditors.*

- If the sheriff refuses to enforce the writ because of uncertainty as to whether it has been properly issued or filed, bring a motion to the court for directions. Rule 60.07(13.1)

- Be prepared to provide the sheriff with a deposit to cover sheriff's fees and the costs of seizing certain assets. (Motor vehicles, for example, require storage and possibly towing charges.)

- You will also need to provide the sheriff with adequate details about the property to enable the identification and seizure of the correct property. For example, a motor vehicle seizure would require a full description of the vehicle with the vehicle identification number, proof of ownership and a certified PPSA search that no liens are outstanding against it. A seizure of land would require a legal description of the property, proof of ownership and information as to the street number, construction, type of house and an appraisal. *Note that the sheriff will only seize the owner's interest in the property, subject to any outstanding encumbrances. Therefore, if the property is subject to encumbrances, it will be less attractive for potential purchasers. If the property is real estate, as long as the encumbrance is low in relation to the value of the property, people should still be interested. If the property is held by the debtor with a co-owner, the real potential buyer will be the co-owner. Third party owners will shy away from purchasing the property because they will not necessarily have any relationship with the co-owner.*

- Once the sheriff has seized the property, the sheriff must then send the creditor and debtor notice of the sale's time and place at least 10 days prior to the sale, and must published notice of the sale in a newspaper of general circulation where the property was seized. Rule 60.07(16)

- Note that you cannot take any action to sell land under a writ of seizure and sale until four months after the writ was filed with the sheriff (or four months after it was re-filed, if it has been withdrawn). The sale itself cannot take place until six months after the writ was filed or re-filed. The creditor and debtor must be notified of the sale's time and place at least 30 days before the sale. Notice of the sale must also be published in *The Ontario Gazette* once at least 30 days prior to the sale, and in a newspaper of general circulation in the locale of the land once a week for two successive weeks, with the last notice to be published between one and three weeks before the sale. It must also be posted at the sheriff's office for at least 30 days before the sale. Rule 60.07(17)(18)(19)

- If the sheriff believes that a more advantageous price could be realized by delaying the sale, they have the power to adjourn the sale, and conduct it on a later date with such further notice as they deem advisable. Rule 60.07(21)

- If a notice of sale of land that is under a writ of seizure and sale is published in *The Ontario Gazette* before the writ expires, the sale may be completed by a sale and transfer of the land after the writ expires. Rule 60.07(22). *If the writ expires, you will need to bring a motion to renew the writ unless you renewed it prior to expiration.*

- If the property or land remains unsold for want of buyers, the sheriff will notify the creditor of the situation and its circumstances. You may then instruct the sheriff in writing to sell the property or land in whatever way will realize the best price, subject to encumbrances, including taxes. Rule 60.07(23)(24)

> **Practice Tip:** A sale of a one-half interest of a piece of property is usually difficult because third parties are not interested in purchasing an interest in a property. They much prefer purchasing a whole property. In such a case, consider an application under the *Partition Act* for partition and sale of the property. Note that if the co-owner is a spouse who has a family living in the property, the courts will be reluctant to grant the application for partition and sale.

- Proceeds realized through the seizure and sale of property or land will be distributed in accordance with the *Creditors' Relief Act*. For further details, see Chapter 6.1.4.

3.7 ENFORCEMENT: GARNISHMENT

- You may also enforce a judgment by garnisheeing debts that are payable to the debtor by other people, such as an employer that must pay wages, salaries or commissions to the debtor, or a bank that holds the debtor's bank accounts or guaranteed investment certificates. Rule 60.08(1)

- If the debt is payable to the debtor and to one or more co-owners, one-half (or a greater or lesser amount specified in an order under Rule 16) may be garnished.

- If six years have elapsed since the date of the order, or if the order's enforcement was subject to a condition, you need to seek the leave of the court to obtain a notice of garnishment. Rule 60.08(2)

- Such an order granting leave expires one year after it was granted; if the garnishment notice was not issued within that year, you will need to bring a motion to the court for leave to be granted again. Rule 60.08(3)

- To obtain a notice of garnishment, file with the registrar where the proceeding was commenced a requisition for garnishment (Form 60G), a copy of the order, any other evidence to establish the amount awarded and the creditor's entitlement, and an affidavit stating:

    - the date and amount of any payment received since the order;
    - the amount owing, including postjudgment interest (and costs of enforcement, such as fees for issuing the notice of garnishment as per Rule 60.19);
    - details of how the amount owing and postjudgment interest are calculated;
    - the debtor's address;
    - the name and address of each person to whom a notice of garnishment is to be sent;
    - that the creditor believes these persons are or will be indebted to the debtor and the grounds for the belief;
    - any known particulars of the debts;

- where a garnishee is not in Ontario, that the debtor is entitled to sue that person in Ontario to recover the debt, and the basis of that entitlement; and
- where a garnishee is not yet indebted to the debtor, the date on which and circumstances under which the debt will arise.

Rule 60.08(4)

- Note that the above affidavit may contain statements of information and belief, if the source of the information and fact of the belief are specified. Rule 60.08(5)

- Once the registrar issues the notice(s) of garnishment, (each notice lists one debtor and one garnishee), you must serve the notice(s) on the debtor, together with a copy of the affidavit, and on the garnishee, with a blank garnishee's statement (Form 60I). Service shall be by ordinary mail, personal service or an alternative to personal service. Rule 60.08(6)(6.1)(7)(8). *If you believe that the debtor is owed money by several parties, you will have to issue and serve separate notices of garnishment to each prospective garnishee.*

- The garnishee must make the payment under the notice of garnishment (less $10 for the cost of making the payment) within 10 days after the notice is served or after the debt becomes payable, whichever is later. Rule 60.08(11). *Such debts payable include a debt that is payable within six years after the notice is served, or on the fulfillment of a condition within that six years. Debts do not include money in an account that was opened after the notice was served, money that was earned from employment that commenced after the notice was served, or money that is payable under an insurance policy entered into after the notice was served.* Rule 60.08(12)(13)

- The garnishee must make the payment to the sheriff (not, for example, directly to the creditor). If payment is made to any other person, the garnishee remains liable to the pay that amount to the sheriff. Rule 60.08(14)(18)

- For the purposes of calculating garnishment amounts, wages do not include any amounts that an employer is required by law to deduct from wages, such as income tax, employment insurance and Canada Pension Plan amounts. *Wages Act* s.7(1). In the case of an income tax demand under section 224(1) of the *Income Tax Act*, the employer should calculate the garnishment without taking into consideration the demand, as it has been found not to be specified by statute, and therefore not exempt under the *Wages Act. Bain v. Rosen [Erie Meat Products Ltd. Garnishee]* (1984), 7 D.L.R. (4th) 505 (Ont. Div. Ct.)

- Payments from an insurance or indemnity plan that are intended to replace income lost because of disability are deemed to be wages. *Wages Act*, s.7(1.1)

- Tips received by wait staff via credit card remittances have been found to be wages. *Jantunen v. Ross* (1991), 85 D.L.R. (4th) 461 (Ont. Div. Ct.)

- The *Wages Act* allows 80 percent of a person's wages to be exempt from garnishment; in the case of the enforcement of an order for support or maintenance in Ontario, however, the exempted amount drops to 50 percent. In addition, a judge can increase or decrease the exemption if they believe it is just to do so, given the nature of the debt, the debtor's financial circumstances and other such issues. *Wages Act,* s.7(2)(3)(4)(5)

- Creditors should note that the assignment of wages to secure payment of a debt is invalid, except in the case of an assignment to a credit union to which the *Credit Unions and Caisse Populaires Act* applies. *Wages Act*, ss.7(7),8

- If the garnishee disputes the garnishment, or pays less than the amount set out in the notice of garnishment due to the debt being co-owned, they must, within 10 days of being served, serve a garnishee's statement (Form 60I) on the creditor and debtor, and file it with the court.

- If you receive a garnishee's statement indicating the debt is co-owned, you must forthwith serve the co-owners with a notice to co-owner (Form 60I.1) and a copy of the garnishee's statement. Rule 60.8(15.1)

- The courts have held that the following assets are not garnishable:

  - the deposit on the last month's rent held by a landlord. *Markle May, Phibbs v. Oliver* (1999), 44 O.R. (3d) 154 (Gen. Div.);
  - a retainer paid to a solicitor. This is not considered to be a debt owing to the client, nor does it belong to the client. *Toronto Dominion Bank v. Cooper, Sandler, West & Skurka* (1996), 139 D.L.R. (4th) 83 (Ont. Gen. Div.), affirmed (1998), 157 D.L.R. (4th) 515 (Ont. Div. Ct.), leave to appeal to C.A. refused (May 21, 1998), Doc. CA M22142 (Ont. C.A.)
  - a G.I.C. held by a bank as security for a letter of credit issued by that bank. *Stratton v. Jantree No. 15 Ltd. Partnership* (1991), 4 C.P.C. (3d) 200 (Ont. Gen. Div.)

- A creditor, debtor, garnishee, co-owner of the debt or any other interested person may bring a motion requesting a garnishment hearing. At the hearing, the court may:

  - where it is alleged that the debt of the garnishee to the debtor has been assigned or encumbered, order the assignee or encumbrancer to appear and state the claim's nature and particulars;
  - determine the rights and liabilities of the garnishee, debtor, co-owner and any assignee or encumbrancer;
  - vary or suspend periodic debts under a notice of garnishment; or
  - determine any other matter in relation a notice of garnishment.

  Rule 60.08(16)

- The court may proceed in a summary manner, unless an issue raised to a master is one of fact or law, in which case it is adjourned to be heard by a judge. Rule 60.08(16)

- If a person who was served with a notice to co-owner wants to dispute the enforcement of the creditor's order, their motion for a garnishment hearing must be brought within 30 days after service of the notice. Rule 60.08(16.2)

- If the garnishee does not make payments as set out in the notice of garnishment, and does not serve and file a garnishee's statement, the creditor may bring a motion, on notice to the garnishee, for an order against the garnishee for payment of the amount the court finds is payable by the garnishee to the debtor, or the amount in the notice, whichever is less. Rule 60.08(17). *On the motion, the garnishee will have to show why it is not liable on the notice of garnishment: for example, it does not owe any money to the debtor. You will need to keep track of files to see if garnishee statements are filed on the time by the garnishee. If not, steps will then have to be taken against the garnishee.*

- The debt is considered discharged when the garnishee has made the payment(s) as set out in the notice of garnishment. Once the amount is paid, the creditor forthwith serves a notice of termination of garnishment (Form 60J) on the garnishee and the sheriff. Rule 60.08(19)(20)

- If the garnishee pays a debt owed to the debtor and one or more co-owners, and no notice of a motion for a garnishment hearing is delivered within the time required, the creditor should within 30 days file with the sheriff proof of service of the notice to co-owner and an affidavit stating that the creditor believes no co-owner of the debt is a person under disability, and the grounds for that belief. If this material is not filed, the sheriff returns the money to the garnishee. Rule 60.08(21)(22)(23)

- It is quite possible that even once the garnishee has paid the amount due under the notice of garnishment, the judgment will not be full satisfied. This may be a result of interest accruing on the unpaid balance between the issuing of the notice of garnishment and the payment, of the distribution of proceeds under the *Creditors' Relief Act* or of the amount collected not satisfying the debt in full. In this case, you may have to issue and serve another notice of garnishment, to cover the amount owing.

- Proceeds realized through the seizure and sale of property or land will be distributed in accordance with the *Creditors' Relief Act*. For further details, see Chapter 6.1.4.

- Garnishment of provincial Crown Employees is commenced under the *Proceedings Against the Crown Act,* R.S.O. 1990, c.P-27.

- A notice of garnishment must be served on the Crown in accordance with Form 1, which is a Statement of Particulars. R.R.O. 1990, Reg. 940

- The notice of garnishment can either be served personally or by mail. If sent by mail, it must be sent to the Chief Financial Officer at the head office of the administrative unit. An administrative unit is defined as a Ministry of the Government of Ontario, a Crown Agency, or the Office of the Assembly under the *Legislative Assemblies Act* (1990), c.L-10. Garnishment proceedings are not restricted solely to Crown employees' wages but also apply to a client of monies owed or accruing by the Crown to debtors for goods and services (i.e. suppliers to the Crown). *Legislative Assemblies Act,* s.21(2)

- Garnishment of Federal Crown employees is commenced under the *Garnishment, Attachment and Pension Diversion Act,* R.S.C. 1985, c.G-2 and amendments thereto.

- To garnishee a Federal Crown employee you must serve the Federal Crown with a "Notice of Intention to Garnishee" in duplicate, together with a copy of the order or judgment on which the garnishment is based. Garnishment and Attachment Regulations, SOR/DORS/97-177

- Garnishment documents may be served upon the Federal Crown by registered mail. Service is deemed effective on the date of receipt of the documents. *Garnishment, Attachment and Pension Diversion Act ss.*7 and 16

- The regulations provide the place, offices and addresses at which service can be effected. Garnishment and Attachment Regulations, SOR/83-212 [am.SOR/84-47] s.4 [am. S.C. 1992 c.1, s.141]

- The creditor must wait 30 days after the notice is given, at which time they may issue a notice of garnishment with the supporting documentation in the usual manner. The garnishee is either named as Her Majesty the Queen in the Right of Canada, or the Crown corporation, as the case may be. *The notice of garnishment must be served by registered mail within 30 days after being issued.*

3.8 ENFORCEMENT: EXAMINATION IN AID OF EXECUTION

- In order to make effective decisions on how to enforce a judgment, you need information regarding the debtor's financial situation and willingness to comply with the judgment order. An examination of the debtor can provide much of this information.

- An oral examination is held before a person assigned by the official examiner, a reporting service agreed on by the parties, or a reporting service named by the examining party. Rule 34.02 (1). *In reality, the execution creditor will usually name the reporting service to be used.*

- A creditor may examine the debtor, asking questions that relate to:

- the reason for nonpayment or nonperformance of the order;
- the debtor's income and property;
- debts owed to and by the debtor;
- any disposal made by the debtor of property, either before or after the order;
- the debtor's past, present and future means of satisfying the order;
- whether the debtor intends to obey the order, and if they have any reason for not obeying it; and
- any other matter pertinent to the order's enforcement.

Rule 60.18(2)

- If the debtor is corporate, you may examine an officer or director of the corporation. If the debtor is a partnership or sole proprietorship, you may examine a partner or the sole proprietor. Rule 60.18(3). *In a partnership situation, examine all of the partners because they are jointly and severally liable.*

- To examine a person, other than the debtor, who has knowledge of matters regarding the debtor's financial situation and intention or ability to satisfy the judgment, you may request that the court order an examination of that person. Rule 60.18(6)(a). *Note that the power of the court extends further, in that an order can be made for the examination of any other person as is just.* Rule 6018(6)(b)

> **Practice Tip:** The motion to examine a person other than the debtor can be made on a without notice basis.

- Unless the court orders otherwise, only one examination of a debtor is allowed per 12-month period in the same proceeding. Rule 60.18(4)

- You will need to serve any party who is to be examined in aid of execution with a notice of examination either personally or by an alternative to personal service. Rule 60.18(7)

- Where the person to be examined resides in Ontario, they must be given at least two days notice of the time and place of the examination, unless the court orders otherwise. Rule 34.05(1), 60.18(7)

- The notice of examination must include the date, time and place of the examination. Unless the court orders otherwise, or the debtor agrees, the examination must take place in the county where the debtor resides. Rule 34.02(1), 34.03

- A person may consent to the examination, and to its time and place, and may choose to dispense with notice. Rule 34.06. *Notwithstanding the fact that the person may consent to the examination, the better practice is to issue and serve a notice of examination in aid of execution so that in the event that the debtor does not appear, you can obtain a certificate of non-attendance and, if necessary, bring a motion for contempt.*

- A person who objects to being examined at the time or place set out in the notice of examination or before an assigned person may make a motion to show that the time, place or person is unsuitable for the proper conduct of the examination. Rule 34.02(2)

- If the debtor has concealed or disposed of property in order to defeat or defraud creditors, the judge may make a contempt order against the debtor. Rule 60.18(5)

- The person to be examined must bring to the examination all documents that are not privileged. Rule 30.04(2), 34.10(1). *Ensure that you include in the notice of examination a list of the documents (such as bank statements) you require the person to bring to the examination.*

- Where a person admits, on an examination, that they have any other document that relates to a matter in issue in the proceeding and is not privileged, they must produce it for inspection by the creditor forthwith, if the person has the document at the examination, and if not, within two days thereafter, unless the court orders otherwise. Rule 34.10(4)

- If the individual fails to appear at the examination, refuses to take an oath or make an affirmation, to answer any proper question, or to produce a document or thing that they are required to produce, the court may:

  - where an objection to a question is held to be improper, order or permit the person being examined to reattend at their own expense and answer the question, in which case the person shall also answer any proper questions arising from the answer; or
  - make such other order as is just.

  Rule 34.15 (1)

- To obtain the required relief, you must bring a motion to the court, asking for an order for such action as compelled attendance or re-attendance, or the production of certain documents.

- Where a person does not comply with such an order, you may then bring a motion for a contempt order against the person. Rule 34.15(2)

- The motion for a contempt order must be made to the judge who made the order that you are now seeking to enforce (for attendance or production, for example). Rule 60.11(1)

- Unless the court orders otherwise, you must serve the notice of motion personally on the person against whom a contempt order is sought, and not by an alternative to personal service. Rule 60.11(2). *It is not permissible to serve the debtor's solicitor of record.*

- A judge may issue a warrant (Form 60K) for the arrest of the person against whom a contempt order is sought where you can satisfy the judge that the person's attendance at the hearing is necessary in the interest of justice and it appears that the person is not likely to attend voluntarily. Rule 60.11(4)

- The contempt order may grant leave to issue a writ of sequestration under Rule 60.09 against the person's property, and include provisions that the person in contempt:

  - be imprisoned for such period and on such terms as are just;
  - be imprisoned if the person fails to comply with a term of the order;
  - pay a fine;
  - do or refrain from doing an act;
  - pay such costs as are just; and
  - comply with any other order that the judge considers necessary.

  Rule 60.11(5)

- Where a corporation is in contempt, the judge may also make an order of contempt against any officer or director of the corporation and may grant leave to issue a writ of sequestration under Rule 60.09 against his or her property. Rule 60.11(6)

- A contempt order for imprisonment may be enforced by the issue of a warrant of committal (Form 60L). Rule 60.11(7)

- On motion, a judge may discharge, set aside, vary or give directions in respect of a contempt order, and may grant such other relief and make such other order as is just. Rule 60.11(8)

3.9 ENFORCEMENT: EQUITABLE EXECUTION

- An order for the payment or recovery of money may be enforced with the appointment of a receiver by equitable execution. Rule 60.02(1)(d)

- Equitable execution should only be requested where the assets cannot be otherwise seized, by seizure and sale or by garnishment.

- Bring a motion in the action in which judgment was obtained, requesting the appointment of the receiver, showing that other methods of enforcement are not available or possible. It is not enough that the other methods would be inconvenient. Support your motion with an affidavit, and serve the motion on the debtor. *Debt Collection*, *Part III: Collecting Judgment*, p. III-23.

- Include in your motion the name of the receiver who has consented to act. The receiver can be the sheriff; however the sheriff may refuse to act. A trustee in bankruptcy is often appointed in the sheriff's place. *Debt Collection, Part III: Collecting Judgment*, p. III-23.

- An order appointing a receiver shall:

  - name the person appointed or refer that issue in accordance with Rule 54;
  - specify the amount and terms of the security, if any, to be furnished by the receiver for the proper performance of the receiver's duties, or refer that issue in accordance with Rule 54;
  - state whether the receiver is also appointed as manager and, if necessary, define the scope of the receiver's managerial powers; and
  - contain such directions and impose such terms as are just.

  Rule 41.03

- In defining the scope of the receiver's duties, the order will provide the asset(s) that they are appointed to realize on, that if the asset is real property, it is subject to encumbrances or execution by the sheriff, and that if the asset is money, it is to be paid into court. *Debt Collection, Part III: Collecting Judgment*, p. III-23.

- A receiver may obtain directions at any time on motion to a judge, unless there has been a reference as to the conduct of the receivership, in which case the motion shall be made to the referee. Rule 41.05

- A receiver may be discharged only by the order of a judge. Rule 41.06
- Proceeds from the realization of the asset by the receiver are distributed under the *Creditors' Relief Act*, which can be found at Chapter 6.1.4.

4

USING SMALL CLAIMS COURT TO YOUR CLIENT'S ADVANTAGE

Table of Contents

Small Claims Court exists to hear civil matters in an atmosphere informal enough that representation by legal counsel is not required - although, of course, litigants can choose to be represented by counsel if they wish. For the secured and unsecured creditor, Small Claims Court provides access to court-ordered judgments and enforcement options without incurring substantial legal costs, and at a pace significantly faster than higher courts.

Small Claims Court in Ontario hears matters that involve a limit of $10,000 (exclusive of interest and costs), a debt that in other courts would normally be considered too small to pursue when compared with the legal costs involved. For claims over $10,000.00 and under $50,000.00 see the Simplified Rules in Chapter 3. It is, therefore, an option well worth discussing with your client, in some cases even when the debt involved is greater than $10,000.

Note: Unless otherwise noted in this chapter, all references are to the Rules of the Small Claims Court.

4.1 WHEN SMALL CLAIMS COURT MAKES SENSE

Matters heard in Small Claims Court involve claims for money owed, claims for damages and claims for the return of personal property. Issues commonly dealt with include failure to make loan payments, unpaid accounts for goods purchased or services rendered, funds owing on a non-sufficient-funds cheque, damage to property and breach of contract.

- Consider Small Claims Court when the debt involved, exclusive of interest and legal costs:
  - totals $10,000 or less;
  - totals more than $10,000, but the likelihood of collecting an amount more than $10,000 is small; or
  - totals more than $10,000, but the projected legal costs for collection would offset any amount collected above $10,000.

- Note that an action cannot be split: e.g., in a claim involving $19,000, you cannot separate it into two claims of $10,000 and $9,000 in order to have both heard in Small Claims Court.

- You can, however, abandon the excess: e.g., in a $19,000 claim, you can choose to file for $10,000 in Small Claims Court and abandon the excess of $9,000. R.6.02. *If, in this case, legal fees to pursue the full claim in a higher court would likely reach $9,000, you might advise your client that Small Claims Court would be faster, less expensive and equally as effective at returning the net monetary amount of $10,000. When you prepare the claim, note that your client has reduced the amount to allow it to be heard in Small Claims Court with the following wording "We waive the excess claim over the limits as set out in the Small Claims Court Rules".*

- Cases in Small Claims Court are decided on the balance of probabilities; therefore, an additional consideration should be whether your client's claim can be proven on that basis.

- Consider limitations: has the limitation period expired for your client's cause of action? Limitation periods vary depending on the type of action, eg. limitation for a personal injury matter is generally 2 years, the limitation period for a debt is generally 6 years.

- Prior to beginning action to file the claim, ensure that a demand letter detailing the amount owed including interest has been sent to the debtor.

4.2 DO YOU NEED TO REPRESENT YOUR CLIENT?

Small Claims Court is specifically designed for litigants to act for themselves. They may also be represented by a qualified agent such as a law student or, indeed, a lawyer.

4.2.1 MAKING THE DECISION

- In advising your client whether or not to be represented in court by legal counsel, consider the following:
    - legal costs;
    - the client's ability and willingness to take the time and effort to represent themselves, including their familiarity with the facts and law regarding their individual case;
    - potential consequences if your client's case fails; and
    - the need for legal counsel to act as an impartial advisor. *If emotions are running high or have the potential to do so, your client may not be the best person to represent themselves either in court or in settlement negotiations.*

4.2.2 YOUR ROLE IF CLIENTS CHOOSE TO REPRESENT THEMSELVES

- Discuss with your client the extent to which they wish you to advise them "behind the scenes" in the matter, and your related costs for doing so.

- Your advice could include any or all of: filing procedures, argument strategies, required documentation, Small Claims Court procedures, court behaviour/etiquette and settlement options.

- Emphasize the potential help available from the Small Claims Court clerk in terms of filing the correct paperwork in the correct location, plus information about scheduling, filing costs, evidence and enforcement.

Practice Tip: Small Claims Court has more than a dozen self-help guides available that explain specific steps in the process, and guide the completion of the forms involved. Although these guides would prove invaluable for a client representing themselves, they also provide excellent information for anyone involved in the process - including legal counsel. The full selection of guides is available at courthouses, or through Access Ontario (1-800-268-8758, or check the Blue Pages of your telephone book under Province of Ontario) and at www.attorneygeneral.jus.gov.on.ca. The Small Claims Court Rules are available at www.publications.gov.on.ca (search for Regulation 258/98) or by calling Publications Ontario at 1-800-668-9938.

4.3 FILING A CLAIM IN SMALL CLAIMS COURT

4.3.1 WHERE TO FILE THE CLAIM

- The claim must be filed:
  - in the territorial division where the cause of action arose;
  - in the territorial division where the defendant (or at least one of the defendants if there are more than one) resides or carries on business; or
  - at the court's place of sitting nearest to where the defendant, or at least one of the defendants, resides or carries on business.
    R.6.01(1)

- The court can order the action to be tried at another location if it is satisfied that the balance of convenience favours that location. R.6.02. *If you wish to submit a request for another location under this rule, you should make it part of the claim.*

- The Small Claims Court clerk can advise you on the appropriate territorial division in which to file a claim. If the trial judge later finds that the location is not appropriate, the action will be transferred to the correct location unless the balance of convenience favours a different one. R.6.03

- If you are filing the claim in a territorial division in which at least one of the defendant neither resides nor does business, consider filing an affidavit with the claim explaining why the claim is properly brought in this particular division. This affidavit will be needed later in the proceedings (before the defendant is noted in default, for example, and in order to close the pleadings): filing the affidavit now speeds up the process later.

4.3.2 HOW TO FILE THE CLAIM

(a) Filing the Claim

Note: the terms "plaintiff" and "defendant" are used throughout this section with reference to the claim filed in Small Claims Court. Plaintiff, of course, refers to the secured or unsecured creditor; defendant refers to the debtor. Once judgment has been obtained, the plaintiff officially becomes the judgment creditor or creditor; the defendant becomes the judgment debtor or debtor.

- Obtain from the clerk a fee schedule for issuing documents.

- File a plaintiff's claim (Form 7A) with the Small Claims Court clerk, including a copy of the claim for each defendant and the filing fee. The claim must include:

    - the full name(s) of all parties, including both plaintiff and defendant(s) and the capacity in which they are suing or are being sued. *Failure to sue the proper entity may require you to start the whole process again, this time with the correct name. Ensure you have the right name as follows (details about searches can be found in Chapter 2):*
        - *If any parties are disabled, you'll need the name of the litigation guardian.*
        - *In dealing with a corporation, a corporate search will show the head office address and the names and addresses of the directors.*

  - *For partnerships, use a Business Names Act search to allow you to name the partnership and all of the partners.*
  - *If the business is unincorporated, a* Business Names Act *search will reveal the owner's name;*

- a specific, detailed explanation of the claim, including the date, place and nature (e.g. secured or unsecured) of the debt incurred;
- the monetary amount of the debt and the relief requested, including costs. *If the debt bears interest at a specified rate, note it; otherwise, the judge may set postjudgment interest. Even if you claim an interest rate for post-judgment interest, the court has the discretion to amend the interest rate for it. In addition, if your client is abandoning the excess over $10,000, it should be noted in the claim;*
- the name, address, phone and fax numbers of the lawyer representing the plaintiff. *If clients are representing themselves, they would include their details, not yours;*
- the address where you believe the defendant can be served; and
- copies of any documents on which the claim is based. *If a document is unavailable, the claim must explain why.*

R.7.01, 7.02.

- The clerk will issue your claim by dating, signing and sealing it, and assigning it a court file number. The defendants' copies will be returned to you for service. R.7.03

Practice Tip: Clients who wish the claim to be dealt with in French (including the pre-trial conference and the hearing) can file the claim in French. They may also file with the clerk a written request for a French hearing any time before the notice of trial has been sent, or request a French hearing at their court appearance.

(b) Serving the Claim

- Previously, the court would employ process servers to serve the claims. This has now been discontinued, and it is up to the plaintiff to serve the claim (and any other of the plaintiff's documents requiring service, such as a notice of motion).

- Personal service, or an appropriate alternative to personal service, is required to serve the claim on the defendant(s). R8.01(1), 8.02, 8.03

> **Practice Tip:** Although it is permissible for the creditor to serve the claim personally on the defendant, the use of a process server should be considered to ensure a verifiable record of service (an endorsed Form 8A, certificate of service, for example, where service is made by the process server). In this way, the defendant cannot later argue that they were not aware of the claim because they were not served properly.

- Service must be effected within six months after the claim was issued; however, the court can extend this deadline, either before or after the six months has elapsed. In order to do so, the plaintiff must bring a motion to extend the time for service. R.8.01(2). *Rule 8.02 explains how to serve the claim on various defendants, including individuals, municipalities, businesses and the Crown.*

- Once the claim has been served on the defendant(s), they have 20 days to file a defence (Form 9A) with the clerk. R.9.01(1)

> **Practice Tip:** Although the Small Claims Court Rules generally state that a party has 20 days to respond to the filing of claims and defences, in practice, the court provides 20 days for filing the defence where the claim was personally served, 25 days where it was served by an alternative to personal service and 40 days where it was served by mail.

(c) Amending the Claim

- The claim can be amended by filing a copy marked "amended" and identifying the changes to the clerk at least 30 days before the trial (unless you bring a motion to the court requesting a shorter time limit). The amended claim must then be served on the parties involved. R.12.01(1)(2)(3)

(d) Filing a Motion

To file a motion, use Form 15A, notice of motion, and Form 15B, an affidavit that explains why you're commencing the motion. If the motion needs to be heard prior to the trial, the court will provide you with a date and time. Serve the notice and affidavit, at least seven days before the motion is to be heard, on every party who has filed a claim or defence. R.15.01. *You may, for example, require motions to extend the time to serve a claim or to obtain an order for substituted service.*

4.4 IF THE CLAIM IS UNDEFENDED

- If the defendant does not file a defence within the time limits, you must file with the clerk an affidavit that the claim was served.

- If the claim was served outside the court's territorial division, you will also need to file either an affidavit for the clerk or evidence before the judge proving that the action was properly brought in the court's territorial division.

- Once the required proof of service is filed, the clerk notes the defendant in default. R.11.01, 18.01

- A defendant who has been noted in default cannot file a defence or take other action in the proceeding, except by bringing a motion to set aside the default, or by obtaining the plaintiff's consent. In addition, the defendant is no longer entitled to notice of any further steps in the proceedings. R. 11.05

- Default judgment can be set aside by the court upon a motion by the defendant, or by the clerk with the written consent of the parties. R.11.06

- To successfully set aside a default judgment, the defendant must bring a motion within a reasonable time after being made aware of the default judgment, and must provide valid reasons why it should be set aside: e.g. being served by mail at an old address.

- For secured and unsecured creditors, you will generally be dealing with debts, or liquidated demands where the money claimed is clear. In this case, the clerk may enter judgment against the defendant. R.11.02

- In the case where the defendant is noted in default and either damages are claimed or the amount claimed is unliquidated, the claim will be listed for assessment before a judge. The plaintiff will have to attend at court and give evidence, and the court will then determine if the amount claimed is correct.

- In the case of solicitor's fees, a judgment can only be entered if the claim is a liquidated amount - one that clearly shows a fixed amount that was agreed upon by the client, or one that clearly shows an hourly amount agreed upon by the client plus the hours worked on the case.

4.5 IF THE CLAIM IS DEFENDED

4.5.1 DEALING WITH THE DEFENCE

(a) Receiving the Defence

- The defendant must file with the clerk a defence, with supporting documents, within 20 days (or the court's allowed period) of being served with the claim. R.9.01(1)

- The clerk will serve the plaintiff with the defendant's defence by mail or fax. R.9.01(1), 8.01(3)

- When you receive the defence, it should include the following information:
  - a reasonably detailed explanation of why the defendant disputes the claim;
  - the defendant's name, address and phone and fax numbers, plus the same information for the defendant's lawyer/agent if applicable; and
  - a copy of any document the defendant is relying upon in the defence. R.9.02(1), 9.02(2)
- If the defence only deals with part of the claim, request that the clerk note the defendant in default and enter judgment for the undefended portion. R.11.02(2)

(b) If Liability is Admitted

- In the defence, a defendant may admit liability for all or part of the debt and propose terms of payment. R.9.03(1)
  - If your client agrees to the proposal, no action is required: the defendant should then make payments direct to your client (or to you in trust) as set out in the proposal. R.9.03(2)(a). If the defendant does not make those payments, you must file with the clerk an affidavit (either by your client or someone in your law firm) that details the failure to meet the terms of the proposal, the amount paid to date and the amount of money remaining to be paid. The clerk will then sign judgment against the defendant who made the payment proposal. R.9.03(2)(b)

> **Practice Tip**: Remember that affidavits can be signed either by the plaintiff or by the plaintiff's agent: i.e., someone in your law firm. Having affidavits prepared and signed within the law firm can often be faster than seeking your client's signature each time an affidavit is required.

  - If your client disagrees with the proposal, you must file with the clerk a request for hearing within 20 days (or the court's allowed time period) of being served. R.9.03(3)

- If liability is admitted in the defence, but no proposal is offered, the clerk also sets a date for a hearing.
- The clerk will serve you and the other parties involved with a notice of hearing, telling you the time, date and place involved. R.9.03(4)
- At the hearing, a referee or other person presiding can order terms of payment by the defendant. R.9.03(5). If the defendant fails to appear at the hearing, default judgment (Form 11A) can be ordered against the defendant for the portion of the plaintiff's claim for which liability was admitted. R.9.03(6). If the defendant does not make payments as ordered, you must file an affidavit by the plaintiff or its agent detailing the default and stating the amount paid and the amount remaining unpaid. R.9.03(7)

4.5.2 DEALING WITH A DEFENDANT'S CLAIM (FORMERLY COUNTERCLAIMS, CROSS CLAIMS AND THIRD PARTY CLAIMS)

- The defendant, when faced with the plaintiff's claim, may in turn make a claim (Form 10A) against the plaintiff and/or against a third party which is related to the plaintiff's claim in some way. R.10.01(1). *The defendant's claim replaces previous rules dealing with counterclaims, third party claims and cross claims.*

- The defendant can file this claim simultaneously with the defence, or at any time prior to trial or a default judgment. R.10.01(2)

- When you are served with the claim, it should contain the following information:

  - names of the parties to the plaintiff's claim and to the defendant's claim and the capacity in which they are being sued or are suing;
  - concise and reasonable detail as to the nature of the claim, including dates and places;
  - amount of the claim and relief requested;

  - the defendant's name, address and telephone and fax numbers, plus the same information for their lawyer/agent, if any;
  - addresses where all parties against whom the defendant is making the claim should be served; and
  - a copy of any document involved, or reasons why such a document is not available.

  R.10.01(4), 10.01(5)

- You must file a defence of a defendant's claim with the clerk on Form 9A within 20 days (or the court's allowed period) after you are served. R.10.03. *Failure to file a defence will result in the defendant obtaining default judgment against the plaintiff (your client) and/or a third party.*

- Prepare to deal with the defendant's claim at the hearing of the plaintiff's claim. If hearing the two claims together will unduly complicate the proceedings or cause undue prejudice to a party, however, consider bringing a motion to have them heard separately. R.10.04

4.5.3 THE PRE-TRIAL CONFERENCE: STREAMLINING THE ACTION

A pre-trial conference is designed to streamline and even resolve the action. In its encouragement of open, frank and confidential discussion of the issues, it echoes the function of mediation. Indeed, in some cases, it leads to settlement of some or all of the issues; in others it at least narrows the issues and consequently contributes to a speedier trial. Even when the action does proceed to a trial, a pre-trial conference can help the parties prepare effectively, ensuring full exchange of any required documentation and full disclosure of relevant facts. R.13.02(1)(2)(3)

- A pre-trial conference can be requested by a party or directed by the court. To request one, file Form 13A with the clerk. R.13.01(1)(2). *A pre-trial conference can be particularly useful if you suspect that the defendant's defence is weak: this fact may become evident to the defendant and their lawyer during the conference, encouraging them to make an offer to settle without the time and expense associated with proceeding to trial.*

Practice Tip: The practice has developed that all documents to be relied upon at the trial are ordered to be produced to the other parties at least 10 days before the pre-trial conference.

- At the pre-trial conference, the judge or individual presiding may make recommendations to the parties in order to assist in the resolution of the action. These may include simplifying the issues, eliminating unsupported claims or defences and making suggestions as to the admission of facts or documents without further proof. R.13.03(1). *Ensure that you have all appropriate documentation prepared for the pre-trial conference, as it is on the basis of that documentation that many of the recommendations, or even orders, will be made.*

- The judge may also make any order regarding the action that the court could make. This includes joining parties, amending or striking out a claim or defence, referring the matter to a referee or awarding costs for failure to attend or inadequate preparation. (If a designated person is conducting the conference, a judge may make an order based on that person's recommendation.)

  R.13.03(2)(3)(4)

- If a party fails to attend a pre-trial conference, the court can impose sanctions, including costs, against the party. Additionally, if a party is so inadequately prepared that they hinder the proceeding, costs can be awarded. In these cases, costs shall not exceed $50 without special circumstances. R.13.01(4)(5)(6). *Although these costs may seem small, it is worth requesting them if the circumstances make the request a reasonable one. Where the defendant's behaviour is particularly troublesome or dishonest, consider requesting costs above $50.*

- At the end of the conference, the individual presiding may prepare and file with the clerk a summary of the issues agreed to and those remaining, relevant evidentiary matters and the schedule of any remaining steps in the proceeding. R.13.03(5)(6)

- The action must be disposed of within 30 days after the pre-trial conference; if it is not, you must request a trial date and pay the prescribed fee required to set the matter down. R.13.01(7)

- Note that unless all of the parties consent in writing, the judge conducting the pre-trial conference will not preside at the actual trial. R.13.04

- If some or all of the issues are settled, it is highly recommended that the parties set out the resolution in a settlement agreement, which they then sign.

> **Practice Tip:** In some jurisdictions, such as Toronto, a judge's approval of the agreement is not required, but in others it is. The advantage of a signed and duly approved settlement agreement is that if the defendant subsequently defaults on the agreed payments, you can file with the clerk an affidavit from the plaintiff requesting judgment on the amount unpaid. Without it, you will have to continue your action and the time and expense to your client will be far greater. The clerk then enters judgment.

4.5.4 SETTLEMENT: THE PREFERRED OPTION

Whether or not a pre-trial conference is involved, an offer to settle can avoid the time and expense of going to trial, an advantage even in the scaled-down system of the Small Claims Court.

- Any party may serve on any other party an offer to settle a claim, at any time before the court disposes of the claim involved. R.14.01, 14.02, 14.03(2). *There are, however, cost consequences to consider that encourage the offer to be made in writing more than seven days prior to the hearing.* R.14.07

- Discuss with your client (the plaintiff) how much it would likely cost to proceed to trial, and how much of the debt the plaintiff can realistically expect to collect as a result of the trial. Taking costs and expectations into account, it may be to your client's advantage to make an offer to settle at a lesser amount than the claim. *Monies paid are better than an uncollectable judgment.*

- In the offer to settle, you can require that the defendant pay the money into court. R.14.05(2). *This option can speed up the collection process, as the defendant can only accept the offer by notifying the plaintiff that the money has been paid into court. However, a more practical option would be to have the monies paid direct to your client or yourself by cash or certified cheque: this avoids the time and expense of having to get the monies paid out of court.*

- Your offer to settle should also deal with costs. *You would at least be entitled to your disbursements up to the date that you served the offer on the defendant.* R.14.05(4)(b)

- To withdraw an offer, serve written notice of the withdrawal at any time before the offer is accepted. R.14.03(1)

- If the defendant serves an offer to settle on your client, again consider costs and expectations of success to determine whether the offer is worth accepting. If your client opts for acceptance, you can require the defendant to pay the money involved into court or direct to you or your client by cash or certified cheque. R.14.05(3)

- If you accept the defendant's offer to settle, and that offer does not deal with costs, you are entitled to your disbursements up to the date you were served with the offer. R.14.05(4)(a)

- If an offer to settle is accepted, and the defendant fails to make the required payments, you have the option of bringing a motion to the court for judgment on the offer's terms, or continuing the proceeding as if no offer to settle had been made. R.14.06. *Whether you seek immediate judgment or continue the proceeding will likely depend once again on the cost of proceeding compared to the probable result. If proceeding will not gain you an advantage over the judgment, then it is not worth pursuing the matter to trial.*

- If an offer to settle is not accepted, the trial judge will not see the offer until the action has been disposed of except for the question of costs. R.14.04

> **Practice Tip:** In the case of your written offer to settle (made more than seven days prior to the hearing and not withdrawn or expired), if you obtain a judgment at least as favourable as your offer, the judge can award up to twice the costs of the action. R.14.07(1). Where you do not accept the defendant's written offer to settle (made more than seven days prior to the hearing and not withdrawn or expired), if you obtain a judgment that was less than or no better than the defendant's offer, the judge can award the defendant up to twice your costs. R.14.07(2). (If your client chooses to represent themselves, the amount awarded would be up to $300 to compensate for inconvenience and expense. R.14.07(3).)

4.5.5 THE TRIAL: GOING ALL THE WAY

(a) Setting a Date

- Once a defence is filed, the matter can only proceed to trial if the plaintiff pays the required fee.

- If there was no pre-trial conference but the defendant filed a defence, the clerk serves a notice on each party who filed a claim or defence, detailing the time and location for the trial.

- Where a pre-trial conference was conducted and the matter is not settled within 30 days after the conference, you need to request a trial date. R.16.01

(b) Preparing Witnesses and Evidence

- For a claim involving repair work, you should obtain at least two estimates for the cost of the work.

- Evidence such as a statement (e.g. an expert's report) or a document (e.g. financial records or bills) made by a witness who is not expected to attend the trial can be entered into evidence. Serve copies of the statement or document on all parties at least 14 days (if served in person) or 19 days (if served by mail) prior to the trial, and include the individual's name and address. The court can then accept the statements; however, if another party wants to cross-examine the witness, that party must serve a summons to witness under Rule 18.03(1), notifying all other parties that they have done so. R.18.02(4). *You must apply to court after 30 days post-trial to get such documentation back, otherwise it will be destroyed.*

- Witnesses may be subpoenaed to attend court if necessary by way of a Summons to Witness. Witnesses must be personally served with the summons prior to the trial, and provided with attendance money. Notice must also be served on all other parties to the action. R.18.03.

- Ensure that witnesses have direct, personal knowledge of the facts or the issues.

- Prepare any witnesses that you plan to call for both your own questioning and for cross-examination.

- Hearsay evidence is permitted at trial, provided that the information is relevant. Whether the evidence is accepted or rejected is at the judge's discretion, as is the weight attributed to it. *Courts of Justice Act,* S.O. 1984, c. 11, s. 80(1)

> **Practice Tip:** Allowing hearsay evidence, even for matters critical to the case, in Small Claims Court helps to reduce costs and time delays that would otherwise be incurred in calling extra witnesses. However, in recognition that such evidence cannot be tested by cross-examination, the judge will likely give it less weight than direct evidence. *Central Burner Service Inc. v. Texaco Can. Inc.* (1989), 36 O.A.C. 239 (Div. Ct.). You may find it practical to submit documents or use witness testimony that constitutes hearsay evidence in order to simplify the process at trial - and, of course, you should be aware that the opposing party may use hearsay evidence that does not provide you with an opportunity for cross-examination. Part of your preparation for trial involves assessing the risk presented by hearsay evidence (i.e., the effect of the judge's decision as to the evidence's weight) in order to decide whether to use it, and how to counter it from the opposing party.

- Prepare your client for cross-examination by the defendant/defendant's lawyer.

- Prepare questions for your cross-examination of the defendant.

- Ensure that you can prove that a legal relationship exists between the plaintiff and defendant - that the defendant is, in fact, liable for the debt - or the loss was incurred as a result of the defendant's action or lack thereof.

- If your client is acting without your representation, ensure that they are prepared for the trial. This should include the following advice:

  - notes can be referred to but not read from, so be familiar with the key points;

  - stick to the subject at hand (tangents are a waste of the court's time and may not be permitted by the judge);
  - remain calm and unemotional;
  - discuss facts, not feelings;
  - don't argue with witnesses ;
  - be prepared for a cross-examination, but don't be nervous: the judge controls the cross-examination to ensure it doesn't become unduly hostile; and
  - keep the final argument concise.

(c) In the Courtroom

- Note that during the trial, the court can strike out or amend all or a portion of a claim or Defence if it:

  - shows no reasonable cause of action or defence;
  - is scandalous, frivolous or vexatious;
  - may prejudice, embarrass or delay fair trial of the action; or
  - otherwise abuses the court's process.

  R.12.02(1)

- If a party fails to attend the trial, the judge has latitude to either proceed with the trial or make any other just order. For example, if you and your client fail to attend, your claim can be dismissed. If the defendant fails to attend, the defence and defendant's claim can be dismissed and judgment awarded in your favour. You should note, however, that if the defence has raised the issue of proper place of trial, the judge shall consider the issue and make a finding. R.17.01. *To avoid the need to reschedule a trial, ensure that you file the claim in the proper territorial division.*

- If a witness is served with a summons to witness, and fails to attend or fails to remain in attendance at the trial, the judge may issue a warrant for the arrest of the witness. Once arrested, the witness will either be detained in custody or be released on terms, and can be ordered to pay costs due to the failure to attend. R.18.03(7)

- Be aware that a defendant who failed to attend the trial can subsequently bring a motion to set aside or vary a judgment against them. R.17.01(4). *Similarly, if you and your client had a valid reason for not attending the trial, you can request a new trial or a variance in a judgment that might have been brought against you in your absence.*

- If necessary, the court can adjourn a trial, often with the payment of costs by the party causing the adjournment to compensate for inconvenience and expenses. R.17.02. *If the defendant fails to attend the trial without valid reasons and thus causes an adjournment, you can request a reasonable amount (such as for preparation, pleading and inconvenience) from the judge. This Rule has also been used by the judge to order the defaulting party to pay such costs in order to have the matter put back on the trial list, and to order fees paid to the court where there was an abuse of the court's time.* (Small Claims Court Revisited*, Voell, p. 5-4*)

> **Practice Tip:** Advise your client to dress neatly and conservatively when attending court. They should not chew gum, wear heavy perfume or clangy jewellery, and if they want to talk while they are waiting for their case to be heard, they should go outside the courtroom.

4.6 AWARDING COSTS

Familiarizing yourself with the cost entitlements of a successful judgment, and ensuring that your client's claim deals with those costs, will maximize the judgment amount and the amount that your client will potentially collect from the defendant.

- The successful party is entitled to have its disbursements (including costs of serving other parties up to $20 per person served) paid by the unsuccessful party, unless the court orders otherwise. These disbursements will be assessed by the clerk in accordance with the Small Claims Court tariff and may be reviewed by the court (particularly if disbursement costs requested are higher than the tariff). R.19.01

- The successful party can also be allowed up to $50 for preparation and filing of pleadings. R.19.03

- If the claim of a successful party exceeds $500, exclusive of interest and costs, and the party was represented by a lawyer, counsel fees may be allowed as follows:

  - for a lawyer, up to $300; or
  - for a student-at-law, up to $150.

  R.19.04

- In the same situation but without legal representation, the court may allow up to $300 for inconvenience and expense if the court feels that the unsuccessful party unduly complicated or prolonged the process. R.19.05

- Although costs are generally not recoverable for motions, the exception is for motions that should not have been brought or opposed, or where the motion was needed due to a party's default. Unless special circumstances exist, costs will not exceed $50. R.15.02

- Costs are also provided for in sections 25, 29 and 131 of The Courts of Justice Act (CJA), which overrides the Small Claims Court Rules if the two are in conflict. *For example, in a case involving the need for numerous experts, costs of more than $17,000 were awarded — well above the Small Claims Court limits. The judge used sections 29 and 131(1) of the CJA, which allow the court to exercise its discretion regarding costs where the case circumstances warrant it. Jones v. LTL Contracting* (July 20, 1995), Doc. Thunder Bay D.94-95, (Ont. Small Cl. Ct.); Small Claims Court Revisited, *p. 5-6.*

4.7 WHEN THE TRIAL IS NOT THE LAST WORD

4.7.1 REQUEST FOR A NEW TRIAL

- Within 30 days of the trial, a party may make a motion to the court for a new trial if the party had a valid reason for not appearing at the trial, a key piece of evidence or a key witness only became available after the trial was concluded, or there was a mathematical error in calculating damages. R.17.04(1)(3)

- In response to the motion, the court can grant a new trial, pronounce the judgment that should have resulted from the trial, or dismiss the motion. R.17.04(2)

4.7.2 APPEALS

- An appeal from a Small Claims Court final order or judgment can only be sought when the claim exceeds $500 (excluding costs).

- Appeals must be requested within 30 days of the final order or judgment being made and must be served on every party involved.

- Appeals must be based on the judge having made an error in law and/or fact. An appeal cannot be filed simply because you are dissatisfied with the judge's decision.

- Appeals proceed outside Small Claims Court to the appropriate Divisional Court: this means that the Rules of Civil Procedure apply, legal costs can be significantly higher, and it is not advisable for clients to attempt the appeal without legal representation.

- To properly transfer the case to the appeal court, you must, within 30 days of filing the notice of appeal, prove that you have ordered transcripts of the Small Claims Court trial. You will be notified when the transcripts have been prepared; within a further 30 days, you must have the record and original exhibits transferred to the Divisional Court Registrar. The cost of transcripts must also be considered as they can be very expensive, especially in lengthy trials. A factum, appeal book and transcript must also be filed with the Divisional Court and given to each opposing party.

- The appeals court may give the judgment that should have been given at the original trial, order a new trial, or dismiss the appeal.

4.8 ENFORCEMENT

Once judgment has been entered against the defendant, the challenge is to collect the monies owing. It is the responsibility of your client, as the judgment creditor, to collect the money owed: the court's judgment is simply a decision, not a guarantee that the creditor will receive the money.

Should the defendant default on voluntary payment of the judgment, you have several options available for enforcement:

- a writ of seizure and sale of personal property;
- a writ of delivery;
- a writ of seizure and sale of land; and
- garnishment. R.20.03

In addition, the court may make a further order as to payment, for example, through a consolidation order or an examination of the defendant.

You can initiate more than one of these processes at the same time, depending on the options that you feel bear the most chance of success.

4.8.1 PREPARING TO ENFORCE

Note: At this point in the proceedings, your client has become the judgment creditor, and the defendant has become the judgment debtor.

(a) The First Steps

- Make it your practice to check regularly with the court to ensure that the debtor is making payments as required. *This applies both pre-enforcement to ensure that enforcement is started as soon as possible after the defendant defaults, and during enforcement proceedings to ensure that consolidation orders and garnishments are being respected.*

- If the defendant fails to pay the judgment as ordered, you must file an affidavit with the clerk requesting a certificate of judgment (Form 20A) and stating the amount still owed. R.20.04(1). *Be sure to calculate and include post-judgment interest: if you don't, your client will not be able to collect it.*

- The certificate of judgment will include the date of the order, the amount awarded, postjudgment interest rate and the amount still owing including interest. R.20.04(2)

- Serve a copy of the judgment on the debtor.

Practice Tip: You can proceed with requesting the certificate of judgment and further action even if the debtor has brought motions to set aside the judgment or request a new trial.

Practice Tip: A variation between the name used on your claim and the name the individual uses may mean that your Writ of Seizure and Sale will not catch the debtor's assets (e.g. Bobby vs. Robert). Bring a motion to amend the Debtor's name to reflect the use of both names. Rules of Civil Procedure R.60.07(10)

(b) Limits to Enforcement Proceedings

- If the debtor has filed an appeal of the decision, there is an automatic stay on enforcement proceedings. Rules of Civil Procedure, R.63.01. *Any funds paid into court by the defendant will not, therefore, be released to the creditor until after the period for an appeal to be filed has passed without such filing.*

- In the case of an order for periodic payments, the only step you can take to enforce the judgment is to have a writ of seizure and sale of land issued, and file it with the sheriff (Enforcement Office). R.20.02(2). Note that an order for periodic payments terminates if the defendant is in default for 21 days. R.20.02(3)

- The court can stay the enforcement of the order, or vary its provisions for payment (if, for example, the defendant's circumstances have changed or if the defendant has been successful in a motion to set aside default judgment). R.20.02(1)

4.8.2 EXAMINATION OF THE DEBTOR OR OTHER PERSON

- If the debtor is in default of an order for payment or in default of payment of a judgment, you can, in the interest of obtaining information about the likelihood of future payment, request an examination of the debtor (or, in the case of a business, a representative of that business). R.20.10(1)

- Individuals you may examine include an officer or director of a corporate debtor, the sole proprietor of a sole proprietorship or partners in a partnership. R.20.10(5)

- File your request for examination with the clerk of the territorial division where the individual resides or carries on business. You must include an affidavit that states:

  - the date and amount of the order;
  - the territorial division where the order was made;
  - the rate of postjudgment interest;
  - the amount of payments received since the order was granted;
  - the total amount now owing including interest; and
  - a certificate of judgment (Form 20A) if the order was made in another territorial division. R.20.10(2)

- The clerk will issue Form 20H, a notice of examination, which you must then serve on the individual.

- Depending on the debtor with whom you are dealing, it may be worthwhile to contact them prior to the date of the examination. If they make a suitable payment arrangement, provide them with a consent to payment to sign when they arrive for the examination. You can then file the consent when the action is called, and should the debtor subsequently not make the payments, you can proceed to enforce the judgment. R.20.10(7)

- During the examination (which is private, unless the court orders otherwise) you may ask questions related to:

  - the reason the debt has not been paid;
  - the debtor's income and property;
  - debts owed to and by the debtor;
  - property disposal by the debtor before and after the order was made;
  - the debtor's present, past and future means to satisfy the order;
  - whether the debtor intends to obey the order or has any reason for not doing so; and
  - any other pertinent matter. R.20.10(4)(6). *See Annex A to Chapter Four for a sample checklist of questions.*

- If the debtor did not sign a written consent, the court may make an order as to payment after the examination, taking into account the debtor's financial situation. R.20.10(7)

- If the person to be examined fails to attend without a reasonable excuse or refuses to answer questions, the court may find them in contempt and order that they attend a contempt hearing. If a contempt hearing is ordered, the creditor must serve the notice of contempt hearing on the debtor. R.20.10(9)(10)

- On failure to attend a contempt hearing, the court may:

  - order the person to attend an examination;
  - make an order as to payment; or

  - order the person to be jailed for a period not exceeding 40 days. R.20.10(11)

4.8.3 WRIT OF SEIZURE AND SALE OF PERSONAL PROPERTY

- File with the clerk an affidavit stating the amount of the judgment still owed and requesting that a writ of seizure and sale of personal property (Form 20C) be issued to the bailiff. R.20.06(1). *Note that assets listed as exempt in Part III of the* Execution Act *cannot be seized.*

- The writ must be completed by the creditor, and must show the name, address and telephone number of the creditor and their lawyer/agent, if any. R.20.06(4)

- Also file with the clerk specific written instructions to take possession of the property.

- If you require a particular piece of the debtor's property to be seized, you must provide specific details to enable the bailiff to properly identify it. You should also conduct a PPSA search (see Chapter 2) to ensure that no liens are registered against it.

  - If you are requesting the seizure and sale of a vehicle, provide description details than include make, model, colour and serial number. Obtain a certified proof of ownership from the provincial Ministry of Transportation and a certified printout from the PPSA registry showing no liens against the vehicle (or, at least, liens for significantly less than the vehicle's value. These documents must be given to the bailiff before action to seize the vehicle can be taken.

- Expect to pay a security deposit of between $1,500 and $2,500 to cover the costs of seizure and sale, such as storage, moving and advertising expenses. These costs are added to the debt to be collected.

- The writ remains in force for six months, and may be renewed before its expiration by filing a renewal request with the clerk. R.20.06(2)(3)

- The bailiff enforces the writ for the amount owing, post-judgment interest and the bailiff's fees and expenses. Personal property seized must be sold at public auction for a reasonable price upon at least 14 days' notice of the time and place of sale to both creditor and debtor. R.20.06(1)(6)

4.8.4 WRIT OF DELIVERY

- Where the judgment orders the debtor to return personal property to the creditor, and the debtor fails to do so, file with the clerk an affidavit stating that the property has not been returned and requesting a writ of delivery. Expect to pay storage costs in advance as for a writ of seizure and sale of property. R.20.05(1)(4)

- The writ of delivery authorizes the seizure of the personal property identified in the judgment. If this property is not available (if the debtor has sold it, for example), file a notice of motion requesting the seizure of other personal property. Once the substitute property has been seized, file a motion requesting disposition of the property. R.20.05(2)(3)

4.8.5 WRIT OF SEIZURE AND SALE OF LAND

- File with the clerk an affidavit stating the amount of the judgment still owed and requesting that a writ of seizure and sale of land (Form 20D) be issued to the sheriff. R.20.07(1). *This writ can only be enforced against real property.*

- The writ has the same force and effect and may be renewed or withdrawn in the same manner as a writ of seizure and sale issued under Rule 60 of the Rules of Civil Procedure. R.20.07(2)

- The writ must show the name and address of both the creditor and the creditor's solicitor. Rules of Civil Procedure, R.60.07(12)

- The writ remains in force for six years from the time it is filed, and may be renewed before its expiration by filing a request to renew (Form 60E) with the sheriff. Rules of Civil Procedure, R.60.07(6)(8)

- You must wait for four months after the writ was filed with the sheriff before taking any step to sell the land involved; in addition, you must wait six months after the writ was filed before holding a sale of the land. Rules of Civil Procedure, R.60.07(17)(18). The writ can only be enforced against lands in that particular sheriff's jurisdiction. In order to have the writ of seizure and sale apply against lands in other jurisdictions, you need to file a writ of seizure and sale in each of the other jurisdictions and pay the appropriate fees.

4.8.6 GARNISHMENT

- You may also seek to enforce a payment order by garnisheeing debts payable to the debtor by someone else, such as an employer or the debtor's bank. R.20.08(1)

> **Practice Tip:** Before a bank will forward monies to the Sheriff's office, it will review its files to see if the debtor owes it any money and if so, will use those monies against its own debts first – the common law right of set-off. If there are no monies available for the garnishment, the bank will advise the Sheriff's office that there are no monies available to satisfy the judgment.

- If the debt owed to the debtor is joint – meaning that the debt is co-owned, such as in the case of a joint bank account - half of the debt owed, or an amount ordered at a garnishment hearing, can be garnished. R.20.08(2)

- File with the clerk in the territorial division where the debtor resides or carries on business an affidavit stating:

  - the date and amount of the order;
  - the territorial division where the order was made;
  - the rate of postjudgment interest;
  - total amount received since the order was made;
  - the amount now owing, including postjudgment interest;
  - names and addresses of each person to whom a notice of garnishment is to be directed;
  - the reasons why those persons are indebted to the debtor;
  - any particulars of those debts, if known; and
  - a certificate of judgment if the order was made in a different territorial division.

  R.20.08(3)

- The clerk will issue a notice of garnishment (Form 20E) for each person so named in the affidavit. You must then serve the notice of garnishment on each of those persons. R.20.08(4)(5)(6)

- If the garnishee disputes the garnishment, they have 10 days after service to file a statement (Form 20F) explaining why. R.20.08(11)

- If the garnishee does not dispute the garnishment, they have 10 days after service or after the debt becomes payable (whichever is later) to pay the clerk the amount shown in the notice of garnishment. If the garnishee is an employer, this amount is subject to section 7 of the Wages Act, which limits the amount that can be deducted from each pay to 20 percent of the net pay. R.20.08(7)(9)

- Ensure that the garnishee is aware that they must pay the clerk: not, for example, the creditor. Any payments not made to the clerk will not be counted against the debt. R.20.08(18)

- Check to see if more than one creditor has issued a notice of garnishment, as any funds received by the clerk under any of the notices will be distributed equally among those creditors. R.20.08(10)

- A garnishment remains effective for 24 months from the date of service. If the amount owed cannot be paid during those 24 months, you must file a new affidavit requesting garnishment for the remaining amount. R.20.08(8)

- If the garnishee does not make payment of the debt, and does not send a garnishee's statement explaining why, you can request from the court an order against the garnishee for payment of the amount set out in the garnishment notice. R.20.08(17)

- A garnishment hearing can be requested by a creditor, debtor, garnishee, co-owner of the debt or any other interested person. At the garnishment hearing, the court may:

  - if it is alleged that the garnishee's debt has been assigned or encumbered, order the assignee or encumbrancer to appear to explain the claim;
  - determine the rights and liabilities of the garnishee, co-owner of the debt, the debtor and any assignee or encumbrancer;
  - vary or suspend periodic garnishment payments; or
  - determine any other garnishment matter involved.

  R.20.08(15)

4.8.7 CONSOLIDATION ORDER

- The debtor may, if they are facing more than one order for payment, make a motion to the court for a consolidation order. This order will list details of the unsatisfied orders for payment against the debtor, and the amounts and timing of payments the debtor must make to the court under the consolidation order. R.20.09(1)(4)

- At the hearing of the motion, you (acting for the creditor) may make submissions as to the amount and timing of payments. R.20.09(6)

- If your client's order against the debtor is obtained after a consolidation order was made, but involves a debt incurred before the consolidation order, you must file with the clerk a certified copy of the order. Your client will then be added to the order, and will share in the distribution. R.20.09(7). *Note that a consolidation order terminates immediately if an order for payment is obtained against the debtor involving a debt incurred after the consolidation order was made.* R.20.09(8)

- Set up a reminder in your calendar to check that payments received by the clerk under a consolidation order are being distributed at least once every six months. R.20.09(12)(13). *Payments will be distributed equally among the creditors listed in the order. While the section says "equally", the funds are usually distributed on a pro rata basis.*

- The only enforcement action you can take against the debtor while the consolidation order is in force is to file with the sheriff a writ of seizure and sale of land. R.20.09(9)

> **Practice Tip:** You should recommend to your client that a writ of seizure and sale of land be filed to ensure that the debtor does not take steps to creditor-proof their property by putting assets beyond the reach of their creditors while the consolidation order is in effect.

- If a debtor is in default under the consolidation order for 21 days, the order terminates immediately: you will be notified of this by mail by the clerk. R.20.09(10)(11). You should be prepared to immediately take further proceedings on your client's behalf, such as garnishment or writ of seizure and sale.

5

COLLECTION FROM DECEASED ESTATES

Table of Contents

Terminology Note: The individual responsible for the deceased person's estate is known as the legal personal representative, or personal representative. This personal representative may also be known as an executor or executrix (where the deceased's will names a personal representative) or an administrator or administratrix (where there is no will or where the will does not name an executor or executrix). You should note that the latest Rules of Civil Procedure updates use the term 'estate trustee' in place of the terms 'executor/executrix,' and 'administrator/administratrix,' but the legislation still refers to the former terms.

5.1 DEALING WITH A DECEASED'S ESTATE

- Collecting a debt from an individual who is deceased is complicated by the requirement to deal with such legislation as the *Estates Act* and the *Estates Administration Act*; however, there are clear procedures to follow in establishing a claim and collecting a debt.

- If a will is available, it may be useful to obtain a copy of it. If a Certificate of Appointment of Estate Trustee has been issued (formerly called "Letters Probate"), you can obtain a copy from the Superior Court of Justice (Estates) on payment of the prescribed fee. *Estates Act*, s.27. If a will has been probated, a copy of it will be contained within the Certificate.

- When a person dies, all of their real and personal property is vested in their personal representative. Before that property is distributed to the beneficiaries, however, it is subject to the payment of the deceased person's debts. *Estates Administration Act*, s.2(1)

- A creditor can bring a proceeding against the executor, administrator or trustee representing the estate without joining the beneficiaries as parties. Rules of Civil Procedure Rule 9.01(1). *There are, however, several exceptions to this rule that require the beneficiaries to be joined as parties, which are as follows:*

  - *the establishment or contesting of the validity of a will;*
  - *the interpretation of a will;*
  - *the removal or replacement of an executor, administrator or trustee;*
  - *an action against an executor, administrator or trustee for fraud or misconduct; or*
  - *or the administration of an estate by the court.*

  Rules of Civil Procedure, Rule 9.01(2)

- In order to act for the deceased's estate, the personal representative applies to the court for a Certificate of Appointment of Estate Trustee. This will not be granted if the will is being contested. If a creditor needs to continue or launch a proceeding against the estate, you should apply to the court for directions; the court can appoint a Litigation Administrator to oversee the litigation. Of course, you will not be able to collect any judgment until the will or any other issues are resolved. *Bennett on Collections* p. 313

- In an estate where there is no personal representative (i.e., no will exists or no estate trustee has been appointed) the court may appoint a Litigation Administrator to represent the estate for the purposes of the proceeding. Rules of Civil Procedure, Rule 9.02(2)

- Because a creditor cannot proceed against a deceased person, but rather must proceed against the estate, if a personal representative is not designated or already appointed by the court, a creditor may need to apply to the court to have one assigned. This situation may arise if the deceased died intestate (without a will), and therefore did not designate a personal representative. *Bennett on Collections* p. 311. *If you are concerned that assets may dissipate due to a delay in the personal representative's designation, you should apply to the court for the appointment on those grounds.*

- If, in error, you have commenced a proceeding against the deceased, the court no longer considers the proceeding a nullity but rather may order the proceedings to be continued as against the executor, administrator or litigation administrator, and the title of the proceedings shall be amended accordingly. Rules of Civil Procedure, Rule 9.03(3)(5). *Previously, if proceedings were commenced against an estate only, it was deemed that the proceedings were a nullity. The remedial provisions were added to ensure that the proceedings would no longer be a nullity. Whitford v. Cardinal* (1988), 56 Alta. L.R. (2d) 302 (Q.B.)

- One of the personal representative's actions is generally to advertise in local newspapers for creditors, thus notifying potential creditors that the individual is deceased, and setting out the deadline for claims against the estate to be filed. Reviewing local newspapers for such advertisements should form part of your regular routine if you are dealing with collecting for creditors. *If you are reviewing newspapers and notice that one of your debtors has passed away, cut out the notice and include it in the file. Wait for approximately one week, then write to the deceased person's address and to any close relatives listed in the death notice to advise of the existence of the debt and request that they contact you to provide you with information as to whether there is a will, and if so, the name of the executor named in the will. Once you get this information, immediately write to that person to give them notice of the existence of the debt. At that point, ask a personal representative to sign an acknowledgment of the debt. You will then have this information on file and can follow up with the personal representative to ensure that payment is made. However, it is just as possible that no such advertisement will be made, or that it will be made much later in the administration of the estate.*

- The personal representative has the discretion to pay or allow any debt based on any evidence that the personal representative considers sufficient without requiring a court action. *Trustee Act, s. 48(1)*

- The personal representative has the same rights and responsibilities involved in disposing of and dealing with the real property of the deceased person as they have with disposing of the personal property of the deceased person. *Estates Administration Act,* s.16

- Where the personal representative is disposing of property in order to pay in whole or in part the deceased's debts, there is no requirement that the heirs to the estate concur with the property's disposal. *Estates Administration Act,* s. 17(1). *There is a requirement to pay the debts prior to disposition of assets to beneficiaries.*

- Unless the will specifies otherwise, the deceased person's debts, funeral and testamentary expenses, and the cost of administration are applicable among the residuary beneficiaries ratably. *Estates Administration Act,* s.5. *If you have an estate with a will that provides for the payment of debts and funeral and testamentary expenses prior to the distribution to the residuary beneficiaries, the debts will be paid as such. If the will does not provide for the payment of these debts, the* Estates Administration Act *provides for them to be paid out of the residue prior to the payment of the residuary beneficiaries. This is to ensure that testator cannot avoid the payment of those debts and expenses to the detriment of the creditors.*

> **Practice Tip:** Financial institutions may pay bills of deceased people, if there are enough funds in the account and if they are provided with a copy of the invoice, a notarial copy of the death certificate, a notarial copy of the will and a direction signed by all of the estate trustees named in the will. (Alternate estate trustees do not need to sign a direction unless the original estate trustees are deceased or unable or unwilling to act as trustees.)

- Priorities of claims are generally as follows: funeral expenses, testamentary and administration costs, the deceased's debts and bequests under the will. *Estates Administration Act,* s. 5

- In the case of an intestacy, or a very poorly drafted will, the legal personal representative of the deceased's estate has three years after the deceased's death to distribute the real property included in the estate to the heirs, before the property becomes vested automatically in those heirs. If the real property cannot be distributed or disposed of within that time frame, the representative must sign and register a caution in the appropriate land registry or land titles office in order for the property to remain vested in the representative. *Estates Administration Act,* s.9(1). *This will prevent the vesting for a period of three years and can be renewed for an additional period of three years.*

- Prior to the expiration of the three years, the personal representative or an heir may apply to the court for the estate to be distributed. *Estates Administration Act,* s.17(5). *If your client is a creditor of the beneficiary, they should be able to apply under section 17(5) for distribution prior to the three years claiming that they are beneficially entitled through the beneficiary to the amount due and owing to them as creditor.*

- Real property that is transferred by the personal representative to an heir continues to be liable for the deceased's debts as long as it is in the heir's possession.

Where it is sold by the heir to a third party, in good faith and for value, the heir is responsible for the deceased's debts to the extent of the sale's proceeds. *Estates Administration Act,* s. 21(2). *If you have obtained a judgment against a deceased while they were alive, ensure that you file a writ of seizure and sale with the Sheriff's Office where the deceased held real estate. In this way, if the personal representative attempts to transfer the property without payment of the judgment, the transfer will become subject to the writ of seizure and sale.*

- An individual who purchased real property, in good faith and for value, from a personal representative or an heir is not liable for any debts or liabilities of the deceased, unless there was a specific charge on the property in the will or unless the purchaser knew of the creditors' claims at the time of purchase. However, where the property has been sold in this way, a creditor in the estate may hold the personal representative and/or the heir responsible for the amount of the debt. *Estates Administration Act,* ss.19, 21(1), 22(1), 23(1) and (2)

- Where the deceased died intestate, no distribution can be made on the estate for one year. Where distribution is made to the heirs, and a creditor's claim is later sued for and recovered, the heirs are responsible for refunding the distribution for their ratable share of the debt and any costs involved in the personal representative's part in the suit. *Estates Administration Act,* s. 26

- If the personal representative, in error, pays a creditor more than they are entitled to, the overpayment does not entitle any other creditor to recover more than they are entitled to if the overpayment had not been made. *Trustee Act,* s. 50(2).

- If the personal representative overpays a creditor, the court may relieve the personal representative in whole or in part from personal liability as to the overpayment if the court is satisfied that the personal representative has acted honestly and reasonably and for the protection or preservation of the assets of the estate. *Trustee Act,* s. 50(3)

- Where the estate has sufficient assets to cover the deceased person's debts, but not to cover all beneficiaries, the estate is still considered solvent and all creditors must be paid in full. *Barrett Estate, Re,* [1996] N.J. No. 54, 11 E.T.R. (2d) 260 (Nfld. T.D.)

5.2 DECEASED'S ESTATE AND INSOLVENCY

5.2.1 DEALING WITH A DEFICIENCY OF ASSETS (INSOLVENCY)

- If the deceased's estate holds insufficient assets to cover all of the deceased's debts (legacies to beneficiaries not being debts), the estate is considered insolvent. *Barrett Estate, Re,* [1996] N.J. No. 54, 11 E.T.R. (2d) 260 (Nfld. T.D.)

- All of the assets from an insolvent estate are applied to pay debts before any gifts can be made. In the event that there are insufficient assets after all of the debts have been paid, the gifts are abated in the following order:

  - Personalty that was not bequeathed;
  - Real estate designated to pay debts;
  - Real estate not designated to pay debts;
  - General legacies; and
  - Specific legacies.

  Armstrong, Anne. *Estate Administration*, p. 3-54

- If no meeting of creditors is held, the personal representative can appoint creditors as inspectors to assist in the realizing and management of the estate. The personal representative must apply to the court to get approval of the appointment of such inspectors, prior to the inspectors taking any role. *Trustee Act,* s. 59(3)

- If there is a deficiency of assets, every creditor who holds security on the estate of the deceased debtor (or who holds security on the estate of a third person from whom the estate of the deceased debtor is only secondarily liable) must place a value on that security. Upon distribution of the assets of the estate, the creditor will receive only their proportionate share of the unsecured portion of the claim after deducting the value of the security. *Trustee Act,* s. 57(1). *This assumes, of course, that the creditor is permitted to realize on their security.*

- The personal representative has the right to require a creditor to value their claim and state whether they hold any security for the claim. *Trustee Act,* s. 57(2)

- If a creditor is asked to value the security and does not do so, the personal representative can apply to the Superior Court of Ontario (Estates) for an order barring the creditor from sharing in the proceeds of the estate if that creditor does not value the claim within a certain period of time. *Trustee Act,* s. 58. *The creditor will have the right to apply to court to extend the time for valuing the security.*

- If the personal representative decides to take over the security, then the creditor will receive its proportionate share of the full amount of the debt. *Trustee Act,* s. 57(1)

- The personal representative can require an assignment of the security held by the creditor. *Trustee Act,* s. 57(2)

- In the event of an assignment, the personal representative has to pay the creditor an advance of 10 percent of the value of the security, with the balance being paid when the personal representative disposes of the security or is able to make the payment from other assets of the estate. *Trustee Act,* s. 57(2).

- In the event that there is a deficiency of assets, debts due to the Crown, to the personal representatives and others are paid proportionately and without any preference or priority. *Trustee Act,* s. 50(1). *Any validly registered liens will take priority to the above noted debts.*

- If the personal representative believes that there will be a deficiency of assets or that the creditors will not receive payment in full, the personal representative can call a meeting of the creditors and set out the financial situation of the estate. The creditors can appoint inspectors to assist the personal representative in the administration of the estate. *Trustee Act*, s. 59(1). *If your client is asked to attend one of these creditors' meetings, recommend that they do so or that you be allowed to attend on their behalf with the proper written authorization. This will give the creditor an opportunity to see what the real situation is and assess the possibility of obtaining a greater return for the creditors. Ask that the personal representative provide the information in writing at the meeting, so that if you see that certain actions (such as those constituting acts of bankruptcy) have been taken either prior to the death of the debtor or by the personal representatives, you will have grounds to bring a petition for a receiving order against the estate.*

- From a creditor's perspective, if creditors who hold ten percent or more of the debts of the estate request a meeting of creditors, the personal representative will be required to call the meeting. *Trustee Act*, s. 59(2). *By a creditor calling a meeting, you are taking control of the situation to assess what the assets and liabilities really are and whether the debts can be paid. If the creditor believes that there will be a deficiency in assets and the estate is insolvent and the creditors cannot agree about the payment of the debts, they can recommend either a formal proposal under the Bankruptcy and Insolvency Act to the creditors or a bankruptcy. Note than an informal payment plan by the debtors of the estate would be more effective to the creditors and provide a greater return than would either a* Bankruptcy and Insolvency Act *(BIA) proposal or bankruptcy.*

Practice Tip: If a property is held as joint tenants, and the creditor files a writ of seizure and sale against a joint tenant who subsequently dies, the property automatically vests in the surviving joint tenant against whom there is no writ of seizure and sale. To ensure that property does not skip through your hands by the death of the debtor, it is strongly urged that you file a petition for a receiving order if the creditor is unable to collect after filing the writ of seizure and sale (see section 5.2.3) The effect of filing the petition is to sever the joint tenancy so that the parties become tenants in common. If the debtor passes away after the date that the petition is issued, the property does not vest in the surviving joint tenant by virtue of the death of the debtor.

Practice Tip: If RRSPs and/or RRIFs are designated to a specific beneficiary that is not the Estate, that specific beneficiary can then notify the institutional holder of the plan about the death of the testator. That institution will then pay the proceeds to the named beneficiary. These funds could easily slip through the estate's fingers because they are not caught by the administration of the estate. The institution can pay out the amount to the specified beneficiary and be exonerated from any liability. Therefore, as a creditor, the first thing you must do is to put all financial institutions on notice that the deceased's estate is insolvent and that the creditors will be looking to the proceeds of the RRSP or the RRIP to assist in the payment of debts. *NB*: If the financial institution is an insurance provider, the aforesaid will not be applicable because the funds are protected pursuant to Section 196 of the *Insurance Act*, R.S.O. 1990, c.I-8

Practice Tip: If a debt is forgiven by the testator/testatrix in a will, that debt is included in the calculation of probate fees. If you forgive it prior to death, it is not included in the calculation for probate fees. *Estates Act*, s.32

- Debts forgiven by the deceased person are not considered assets of an estate. *Watt Re*, [1958] O.W.N. 418 (H.C.); *Barrett Estate, Re* [1996] N.J. No. 54, 11 E.T.R. (2d) 260 (Nfld. T.D). However, if the deceased's estate is bankrupt, the trustee would have the option of collecting the debts payable by the deceased pursuant to the will.

- For further information on dealing with the *Bankruptcy and Insolvency Act* (BIA), see Chapters 9, 10 and 11.

5.2.2 PROPOSALS AND BANKRUPTCY

- The legal personal representative of a deceased debtor may apply to the court for leave to file a proposal. Of course, the deceased debtor's estate must be insolvent in order for leave to be approved. *Piotrowski, Re* (1970), 16 C.B.R. (N.S.) 28 (Ont. S.C.)

- The personal representative of a deceased debtor may also, with the leave of the court, make an assignment into bankruptcy on the estate's behalf. BIA s.49(1). *The personal representative must file a notice of application together with affidavit evidence in the Superior Court of Justice in Bankruptcy and Insolvency, showing that the estate is insolvent. Once the order is obtained, the personal representative will have the capacity to sign the documents required by the trustee in bankruptcy for the estate to file for bankruptcy.*

- If the deceased bankrupt gave evidence to court in a proceeding under the BIA prior to their death, the deposition can be admitted as evidence. BIA, s. 191

- Since the BIA allows the trustee in bankruptcy to examine anyone who reasonably has knowledge of the bankrupt's affairs, this means that the estate trustee of the deceased's estate may be examined. The trustee in bankruptcy does not require a court order to do so. The trustee can ask questions regarding the bankrupt and their dealings and property, and can order the estate trustee to produce any related paperwork or correspondence. BIA, s.163(1); *Jenset (Trustee of), Re* (1986), 61 C.B.R. (N.S.) 189 (Ont. S.C.); *Schroeder, Re* (1965), 8 C.B.R. (N.S.) 156 (Ont. S.C.)

- If the creditor is not satisfied with the examination of the estate trustee, they may apply to the court to conduct their own examination of the estate trustee. BIA, s.163(2). *The creditor's examination must name the specific person who is being examined. It cannot just name "the estate of A.B." R.L. Coolsact of Canada Ltd., Re* (1996), 45 C.B.R. (3d) 30 (Ont. Bktcy.)

- The courts have found that pension benefits are not capable of assignment or alienation during the person's lifetime and thus are not payable to a living bankrupt's estate for the benefit of creditors. After death, they would be paid to the estate trustee for the benefit of the deceased's beneficiaries regardless of the insolvency of the deceased. *Bonus Finance Ltd. v. Smith* (1971), 16 C.B.R. (N.S.) 87 (Ont. H.C.); *Miles Estate (Trustee of) v. Miles* (1997), 35 O.R. (3d) 312 (Gen. Div. [Commercial List])

- In a situation where a bankrupt died, and life insurance benefits were paid out of a policy in which the bankrupt had not designated a beneficiary, the life insurance benefits were considered after-acquired property and thus formed part of the deceased bankrupt's estate for distribution to creditors. It is possible, however, that had a beneficiary been named, section 173 of the *Insurance Act*, R.S.M. 1970, c.140 would have directed the benefits to the named beneficiary, not the creditors. *Kelleher v. Meadows,* [1983] M.J. No. 87, 48 C.B.R. (N.S.) 311

(Q.B.). The *Insurance Act of Ontario* also contains a similar provision. R.S.O. 1990, c.I-8, s.196

5.2.3 RECEIVING ORDERS

- If a debtor against whom a petition for a receiving order has been filed dies while proceedings are ongoing, the proceedings continue as if the debtor were alive. BIA, s. 43(17). *If the debtor has left a will that appoints an executor, service of the petition can be made on the executor. This can be done even prior to the executor making application for a Certificate of Appointment of Estate Trustee. The authority of the executor is derived from the will and not from the Certificate of Appointment of Estate Trustee. Hollowey v. Adams* (1926), 58 O.L.R. 507 (H.C.); *Hanton v. White,* [1956] O.W.N. 775 (Master). *However, the Certificate ensures that the executor is committed to the role - you can't force an executor to act* unless the Certificate has been issued.

- A creditor may file a petition for a receiving order against the estate of a deceased debtor, assuming of course that the debt owed to the creditor is at least $1,000.00, and the debtor committed an act of bankruptcy in the six months immediately preceding the filing of the petition. BIA, ss.43(1) and 44(1)

- Once a petition for a receiving order has been filed against the estate of a deceased debtor, the legal personal representative of that debtor can make no payments out of the estate except for funeral and testamentary expenses until the petition is disposed of. *An argument could be made that probate fees would also be paid prior to the disposition of the petition.* The representative would be personally liable for any payments of other expenses, but would not be liable for payments or actions done in good faith before the petition was served. BIA, s. 44(2)

- In deciding on whether to issue a receiving order, the courts consider such points as whether an act of bankruptcy has occurred, and whether the estate can be more economically managed under a different administration than the BIA, such as the Superior Court of Justice (Estates), which was formerly the Surrogate Court). *Gillingham Estate, Re* (1955), 35 C.B.R. 10 (Ont. S.C.)

- If a petition for a receiving order is successful, the petitioner's costs are paid out of the deceased debtor's estate unless the court orders otherwise. If the estate contains insufficient proceeds to pay the trustee's costs, the court can order the petitioner to pay those costs. BIA s.45(1) and (2). *Before petitioning a deceased debtor's estate, you should examine your potential liability for costs to ensure that it does not cost you more to collect the debt than what the debt is worth.*

5.3 ESTABLISHING A CLAIM AGAINST THE ESTATE

- The person seeking a Certificate of Appointment of Estate Trustee from the court must include in the application a statement of the total value of the deceased's property at the time of death. Such applicant must also pay the necessary fees in accordance with the *Estate Administration Tax Act, 1998.* Any property discovered after the Certificate of Appointment of Estate Trustee with a Will (formerly Letters Probate) or Certificate of Appointment of Estate Trustee without a Will (formerly Letters of Administration) is issued must be reported to the estate registrar. *Estates Act,* s.32(1) and (2)

- Where the deceased person owed money or property to your client, the first step in establishing a claim against the estate is to submit the claim or demand to the estate's personal representative, or to notify the personal representative that a claim or demand will be made. This must be done in writing. If the debt itself is not yet payable, you may make a notice of a claim or demand instead.

- Where the claim is based on a constructive trust, such as a verbal agreement between the deceased debtor and the creditor, corroborative evidence is necessary in order to establish the claim. *Wanechko-Horn v. Orloff Estate,* [1993] A.J. No. 452, 10 Alta. L.R. (3d) 392 (Q.B.)

- A resident of a rest home is responsible for the costs of residing in that rest home. Therefore, the owner of the rest home can make a claim against a deceased resident's estate for payment of any unpaid costs. *Homes for the Aged and Rest Homes Act,* s.23; *Conway, Re,* [1973] 2 O.R. 213 (H.C.)

- The trustee may choose to accept the claim and pay it, or alternatively, may choose to contest it in part or in whole.

- If the personal representative disagrees with the claim or demand, they may serve the claimant with a Notice of Contestation, which details the section of the *Estates Act* under which the claim is contested, the specific portion of the claim being contested, and the grounds on which it is being contested. *Estates Act,* s.44(1). The purpose of this procedure is to force a creditor to file a claim. *This is a summary procedure for the benefit of the executor.*

- Within 30 days of receiving the notice of contestation, the creditor must file with the estate registrar a statement of claim, verified by affidavit and accompanied by the notice of contestation; then, apply to the Superior Court of Justice (Estates) - or the Small Claims Court if the claim is less than $10,000.00 - for an order allowing the claim and determining its amount. *Estates Act,* s.44(2) and (3)

- You may also apply to the Superior Court of Justice (Estates) for permission to file a late claim within three months of receiving the notice of contestation. *Estates Act,* s.44(2) and (3)

- If you do not respond to the notice of contestation within the three-month time limit, the claim is deemed to have been abandoned, and is thus barred forever. *Estates Act,* s.44(2).

- Claims that would be barred by the *Limitations Act* within the three months following the death of an individual are deemed not to be barred until three months after the date of death. *Estates Act,* s.47(2)

- Serve notice of the application hearing at least seven days before the hearing date, on the estate's personal representative, the Children's Lawyer if minors are involved, and to any other persons that the judge directs should be served. *Estates Act,* s.44(4)

- Where the contested claim is less than $800.00, the judge hears the case, including witnesses as necessary, and makes a decision. Where the claim is more than $800.00, and when asked to do so by one of the parties or a party having an interest in the estate, the judge will direct the creditor to bring an action for the recovery or the establishment of the claim, or, where the parties consent to have the trial before the judge, will hear the case, including witnesses, and make a decision. *Estates Act,* s. 44(2), 44(2)(5) and 44(2)(6)

- If the claim is unliquidated, the judge may direct the creditor to bring an action for the recovery or the establishment of the claim, or, where the claim or demand is not currently recoverable, direct the time after which the creditor should proceed. *Estates Act,* s.45(4)

- The Rules of Civil Procedure apply to these proceedings as they relate to examinations and enforcement proceedings and costs, and costs of such proceedings may be awarded by the judge as they see fit. *Estates Act,* s.44(12)

- Where you have established your claim under the *Estates Act*, you must apply to the court for permission to commence enforcement proceedings against the estate. *Estates Act,* s.44(13)

- Where you receive permission to enforce payment of your claim, the order is filed in the Superior Court of

Justice (Estates) and an execution is then issued to the appropriate enforcement office. *Estates Act,* s.44(14)

- If there is no legal personal representative for the estate, and your client wishes to foreclose on a freehold property, the defendants in the action would be the persons entitled to the property or proceeds from the property either through the will's provisions or Part II of the *Succession Law Reform Act. Estates Act,* s. 8.8(1)

5.4 ESTATE MEDIATION

5.4.1 ESTATE MEDIATION: WHY AND WHEN

- Settling estate matters can often be a particularly difficult process, due to the influence of such emotions as loss, sadness, despair, guilt and anger. If you are dealing with such a situation, you need to be prepared to deal with the emotions involved as well as with the legal requirements.

- Alternative dispute resolution techniques can assist with not just the questions of law and justice involved in estate cases, but also the emotions involved. A pilot program currently underway in Ottawa and Toronto is assessing mediation's effectiveness in estate cases by mandating mediation in various circumstances, including:

    - Rule 75.01 (formal proof of testamentary instrument); Rule 75.03 (objection to issuing certificate of appointment); Rule 75.05 (return of certificate of appointment); and Rule 75.08 (claims against an estate);
    - Contested applications to pass accounts under Rule 74.18;
    - The *Succession Law Reform Act* Part V (support of defendants);
    - The *Substitute Decisions Act;*
    - The *Absentees Act, Charities Accounting Act, Estates Act, Trustee Act and Variations of Trusts Act;*

- ° Subrule 14.05(3) if the matter relates to an estate or trust; and
- ° The *Family Law Act* subsection 5(2) (division of net family property on death).

Rule 75.1

- Originally started as a pilot program, Rule 75.1 has been extended.

- Estate mediation requires a shift away from a focus on "winning the case" towards "finding solutions" - solutions that all the parties involved can agree upon.

5.4.2 INITIATING MEDIATION

- Mediation should be initiated when you receive a copy of any one of the following: a Notice of Application; a Statement of Claim; an Application to Pass Accounts; or a Notice of Objection to the issuance of a Certificate of Appointment.

- To initiate mediation under Rule 75.1, make a motion to the court seeking directions for the mediation's conduct within 30 days of the last day for serving a notice of appearance. R. 75.1.05(1) and (2)

- In the case of contested will matters, you can streamline the process by combining this motion with a motion for directions under Rule 75.06 (R. 75.1.05(3)). *In Ottawa, these motions are heard by the case management master, who strongly recommends that counsel agree in advance on the terms to be included in the order for directions.*

- The court may direct a range of issues in the order for directions. Your motion for directions, therefore, must also deal with these issues, including: the matters to be dealt with in mediation; selecting the party having carriage of the mediation; setting a timeframe for mediation; determining the designated parties and how they are to be served; recommending whether notice should be given to parties submitting their rights to the court under rule 75.07.1; dividing costs among the parties; and any other factor that you feel can facilitate the mediation process, such as selecting the mediator. R. 75.1.05(4)

- In choosing to be proactive by submitting the motion for directions, particularly one that considers the above-mentioned factors, you can initiate the mediation on a sound foundation. *Demonstrating your client's willingness to participate in mediation and to approach solution-finding in good faith can provide a constructive atmosphere for the entire mediation, and thereby increase your client's chances of finding a win-win solution to the conflicts involved.*

- Where Rule 75.06 does not apply to an application, you can avoid repeat court appearances by adjourning the application's return using the motion confirmation form and then filing the motion for directions.

- In the case of a contested passing of accounts, bring the motion for directions on the hearing date specified in the notice of application to pass accounts. R. 75.1.05(5). *The normal practice is to adjourn the passing of accounts to allow a motion for directions or to bring a motion for directions prior to the hearing date.*

- Unless the court directs otherwise, the party who has carriage of the mediation is the applicant in the proceedings under which Rule 75.1 applies. Be aware, however, that there is an unresolved debate as to whether a party who has submitted its rights to the court can be the party having carriage of the mediation. In fact, larger issues are in question with respect to these parties, including what their status is, whether they are "parties" and whether they can be "designated parties." *This is still under debate. The issue is not their involvement, but whether they end up having to pay costs. This remains an unresolved issue.*

- You should ensure that the motion for directions designates all the parties whose agreement to settle is required, particularly if the agreement will require some action of them. Otherwise, you may find that one or more of the parties needed to resolve the dispute will not be required to attend the mediation, or that the settlement agreement fails because a party involved in the dispute was not designated, and therefore did not approve the agreement.

5.4.3 EXEMPTIONS FROM MEDIATION

- Only the court can order an exemption from mandatory mediation. The parties may bring a motion for such an order, or the court may make the order based on its own motion. R. 75.1.04

- Grounds for exemption from mediation can include situations where all of the parties consent to a motion requesting the case be exempted from mandatory mediation, and where previous voluntary attempts at mediation have failed to reach a settlement. *Garneau v. Allstate Insurance Company,* Order of Master Beaudoin, August 25, 1999, Ottawa

> **Practice Tip:** If you believe your case should be exempted from mediation, you can include the request for an exemption on your motion for directions. If your case deals with Rule 75.08 (claims brought against an estate), and you are satisfied that the summary procedure laid out in the *Estates Act* and the Rules of Civil Procedure for such cases is adequate, you may wish to request an exemption on that basis.

5.4.4 PARTICIPANTS IN THE MEDIATION

(a) The Mediator

- The parties must choose a mediator within 30 days after the court makes its order for directions. If the parties do not choose a mediator within this timeframe, the party with carriage of the mediation must file a request for the mediation coordinator to assign a mediator (Form 75.1A:

Request for Assignment of Mediator). If no such request is filed, any designated party may file the request. Rule 75.1.07

- A roster of mediators is available from the Mandatory Mediation Office or via the Internet at www.attorneygeneral.jus.gov.on.ca/manmed. The local mediation committee selects the mediators who appear on this roster, which is updated monthly. It is from this roster that the mediation coordinator assigns a mediator if the parties have not chosen one themselves (the assignment is made using an electronic random selection process to ensure the system's fairness).

- The parties themselves, however, are not restricted to choosing a mediator from the roster, but - whether the mediator is selected from the roster or outside it - all the parties must all agree with their selection. R. 75.1.06

- A number of factors should be considered in selecting a mediator, including their experience in estate law and estate mediation, their familiarity with the civil litigation process and their approach to mediation - plus the mediation location and the hourly fee if the mediation extends past the three-hour timeframe. *It is essential that a mediator understand the legal implications of the solutions discussed by the parties, to ensure that time is not wasted on solutions that could prejudice one or more of the parties.*

Practice Tip: Because the roster mediators have been chosen for their ability to mediate - not necessarily for their background in estate matters or even the legal system - it is preferable for the parties involved to choose their own mediator, rather than have one assigned by the mediation coordinator. Choosing your own mediator, whether from the roster or not, also fosters a more constructive mediation atmosphere, as the individual who is responsible for conducting the mediation has been agreed to by all of the parties.

- Mediators selected for the local mediation committee's roster must follow a Code of Conduct, which emphasizes such factors as impartiality, confidentiality and the quality of the mediation process, and includes provisions that mediators will act in compliance with the mediation rule, maintain competence, encourage fairness and foster public confidence in the program.

- Any party to a mediation under Rule 75.1 can submit a written complaint about a roster mediator's conduct to the local mediation committee within 60 days after the last mediation session. The committee must then respond to the complaint.

(b) The Parties

- Designated parties - those whom the order for directions has required to participate in the mediation - must attend the mediation in person, with their legal counsel if they are represented. The attendance of other individuals must be approved by all parties beforehand. Rule 75.1.09(1)

> **Practice Tip:** It can be useful to include someone your client relies upon for moral support - a spouse, friend or colleague, for example - in the mediation session. Their role would be one of passive observer during the mediation, with the possibility of more direct assistance during caucusing. Their attendance can have a positive effect on the mediation through their ability to help your client deal with personal, cultural, emotional or other matters that you as counsel may not even be aware of. Of course, their attendance must not be a surprise: the other designated parties must be notified and must give their consent.

- For the mediation to succeed, it is essential that the parties in attendance have authority to settle the matters in dispute. If a designated party needs someone else's approval of their agreement to settle, they must arrange for that individual to be immediately and continuously available by telephone throughout the mediation session. R. 75.1.09(2)

- Counsel's attendance at mediation is not sufficient: the designated parties themselves must attend, unless a court order specifies otherwise. Although the court may, at its discretion, direct attendance of a designated party by teleconference, this requires significantly more of the party than simply being available by telephone. *Magalhaes v. Lusitania Portuguese Recreation Club* (August 3, 1999), Doc. Ottawa 99-CV-8667 (Ont. Master)

- A person who has submitted their rights to the court under Rule 75.07.1 technically ceases to be a party to the proceedings. However, in the case of mediation, this person must still be served with written notice of the time and location for the mediation, as the settlement agreement will require the approval of that person.

5.4.5 COSTS

- The mandatory mediation programs are based on a user-pay system, with the costs divided between the designated parties unless the court or the mediation settlement agreement directs otherwise. For Rule 75.1, the Mediators' Fees Regulation explains who the parties are for purposes of cost division, and what the mediator may charge these parties.

- These fees cover the mediator for 30 minutes of preparation time for each party and up to three hours of mediation, and they increase with increased numbers of parties. For example, with two parties the maximum fee to be split between the parties is $600 plus GST. For three, the maximum fee increases to $675 plus GST; for four parties, it's $750 plus GST; and for five or more parties, the maximum fee is $825 plus GST.

- The mediator should specify before the mediation begins what their fees are for sessions that run beyond the three hours. Generally, the "overtime" fee is calculated on either an hourly basis or a flat fee. If the overtime and its associated fees are agreed upon by all parties, the mediation session will continue past the initial three hours.

> **Practice Tip**: If you and your client are seeking a non-equal division of fees between the designated parties, you should include it, and your reasons, on the motion for directions. It should also be included in the mediation's settlement agreement.

- Reducing the costs involved in resolving estate disputes is one of the mandatory mediation program's cornerstones: mediation must be both accessible and affordable. The courts have therefore found that travel expenses such as transportation, accommodation and food costs will not be paid for roster mediators appointed by the court who conduct mediation sessions outside their immediate geographical area. *Riviera Properties Ltd. v. Royal Bank* (October 29, 1999), Doc. Ottawa, 99-CV-9976 (Ont. Master)

- It should be noted, of course, that where the designated parties have chosen their own mediator, whether from the roster or not, and agreed to pay the mediator's additional expenses, the mediator is permitted to charge those expenses.

- All other disbursement expenses, whether travel-related or not, must be understood and approved by all parties before the mediation begins.

- Should one or more of the designated parties be unable to pay the mediation fees, the Mediators Fee Regulation of Rule 75.1 notes that this does not increase the fees payable by the other parties. Where the party unable to pay holds a legal aid certificate, the mediator can receive partial compensation, assuming that the mediator is recognized by the Ontario Legal Aid Plan.

- Where the party in financial distress does not hold a legal aid certificate, the mediator provides services to this party *pro bono* as long as the party meets the mandatory mediation program's financial eligibility test. (Further details are available from the mediation coordinator.)

- The mediator may charge cancellation fees in two circumstances: where a designated party has not submitted a statement of issues as per Rule 75.1.08(1); and where a party does not show up at the mediation within the session's first thirty minutes. The maximum cancellation fee is the total cost of the mediation that would have been charged according to the Mediators' Fees Regulation, and is borne by the party or parties who caused the cancellation.

- In addition to the cancellation fee, other costs can be awarded, including the counsel fee for the parties who did attend the mediation. *Merrill Lynch Canada Inc. v. Vacation Properties Time Sharing Inc.* (1999), 37 C.P.C. (4th) 317 (Ont. Master)

5.4.6 MEDIATION TIME AND LOCATION

Where the parties have chosen a mediator themselves, the party with carriage of the mediation will give the order for directions to the mediator. Where a party is requesting that a roster mediator be assigned, a copy of the order for directions must be attached to the request for a mediator, and both forms forwarded to the mediation coordinator, who then passes the order for directions to the assigned mediator. R. 75.1.07

Unless the order for directions contains a date for the mediation, the mediator sets the date and serves every designated party at least 20 days in advance of that date with Form 75.1B: Notice by Mediator, which explains the time, date and place for the mediation. R. 75.1.07(7)

- Generally, only one mediation session is necessary between the parties. The standard session - and the one on which the mediator's fee is based - takes up to three hours, but depending on the case, the parties' preparation and their willingness to discuss the issues in dispute, the session may run into overtime.

- As noted already, if the session is to continue past three hours, the parties must agree to the continuation and to the payment of the mediator's additional fees.

- As Rule 75.1 does not set out a timeline for the mediation process, a timeline should be set out in the order for directions. Should the parties be unable to meet the date set by the mediator, they will have to return to court and have the order for directions amended to obtain an extension.

- A mediation in which a roster mediator has been assigned must take place within the judicial district for which the roster is maintained, unless all the parties agree to a different location. *Royal Bank of Canada v. Karrys* (July 21, 1999), Doc. 99-CV-165461CM (Ont. Master)

- Where the parties all agree to hold the mediation outside the original jurisdiction, the mediation location would, of course, be valid.

- It is essential that the parties meet face to face, in the same room. *In this way, not only the words of the parties can be analyzed, but also their body language and facial expressions, presenting a complete communication picture. A statement that might be perceived as harsh when communicated over the telephone can be perceived as merely firm if the facial expression that accompanies it is seen to be non-threatening.*

- Although having the parties meet in person is clearly preferable, there are some instances that force the mediation to take place via a medium such as teleconferencing. In these cases, a court order must be obtained authorizing the party or parties involved to participate in the mediation via such a medium.

- The mediation location – the courthouse, mediator's office or the offices of counsel for one of the parties, for example – must also be agreeable to all parties. The parties must perceive the location to be neutral, reasonably convenient for all parties, and comfortable: making mediation comfortable also makes it more productive, of course, as it encourages communication between participants. Breakout rooms should be available for caucusing purposes; restrooms and refreshments should be readily accessible; and the room itself should be set up in a non-adversarial layout with all supplies such as flipcharts and pens close at hand.

Practice Tips:

- Find out from the mediator if refreshments such as coffee are available; if they're not, ask how they can be brought in, particularly if you expect the mediation to exceed the initial three hours.
- Ensure you're satisfied with mediation location's neutrality. For example, you don't want your client to be intimidated by walking into an expensively furnished boardroom at an opposing party's legal firm. In this case, the location can send a message before the mediation even begins.
- As at January 1, 2001, mediation facilities are available in both Ottawa and Toronto on a no-cost, first-come-first-served basis. In Ottawa, the Case Conference Room is located on the fifth floor of the Courthouse at 161 Elgin Street, and is available from 8:30 a.m. to 5:00 p.m. Monday to Friday. Call (613) 239-1180 to book. In Toronto, the ADR Centre is on the 8th floor of 77 Grenville Street, and is available from 8:30 a.m. to 6:00 p.m. Monday to Friday. Call (416) 314-1361 to book.

5.4.7 PREPARING FOR MEDIATION

- Mediation requires committed effort on the part of both client and counsel prior to the mediation session. Your role as counsel is to work with your client to encourage productive, cooperative discussions during the mediation, and will include:

  - determining and discussing the consequences of proceeding to court and the subsequent implications of either winning or losing the case;
  - estimating the costs of proceeding to trial;
  - analyzing what elements would create the best possible mediated settlement, what elements would be essential for an acceptable mediated settlement, and what elements or solutions your client is prepared to propose;
  - analyzing the other parties' positions and their issues;
  - deciding whether a court precedent needs to be set;
  - factoring in whether publicity or maintaining an ongoing relationship with other parties is an issue; and
  - identifying and understanding the emotional issues that need to be voiced.

- You will also need to assemble all applicable documentation in advance, including the breakdown of financial figures into their constituent parts, on paper. Present this to your client prior to the mediation, to ensure that your client agrees on the figures and issues that are documented. *Waiting until the mediation to present it can create a situation where your client doesn't agree with your figures, requiring you to deal with that issue before you can even begin to deal with the mediation. Not only is this preparation necessary for the mediation to reach a concrete settlement, but it will also prove helpful in case mediation fails and a trial becomes necessary.*

- Another key element in your preparation is preparing your client to speak for themselves, possibly as early as the mediation session's opening statement. The client needs to understand the active and essential role that mediation requires of them. *Your role as counsel during the mediation session itself becomes much more passive than in litigation: you are an observer, a strategist and an advisor on legal areas, protecting your client's interests in the settlement agreement, but keeping in mind that the client's interests and emotions can be as important in mediation as the legal issues of right and wrong.*

- Discuss the settlement options with your client prior to the mediation.

- The client has to be prepared to be an active participant in the process. Talk to your client in depth prior to the mediation, rehearsing if necessary their opening statements and their responses to statements likely to be made by the other parties.

- All communications at a mediation session - and the mediator's notes and records - are deemed to be without prejudice settlement discussions. This ensures the confidentiality of documents or statements made within the mediation: they can neither be released to the public nor used in court, whether the mediation succeeds or not. *It also means that the mediator cannot be called by a party as a witness at trial.* Rule 75.1.11

- Each designated party to a mediation must prepare Form 75.1C: Statement of Issues, and provide it to the mediator and all other designated parties at least seven days prior to the scheduled mediation session. R. 75.1.08

- In the statement, the parties briefly identify the facts and the legal issues that are in dispute. In addition, the parties set out their position and their interests, making it clear what they hope to achieve. To assist all parties in preparing for the mediation, copies of all important documentation are to be attached to the statement of issues

Practice Tip: Although the statement of issues requires only the issues in dispute to be listed, you should demonstrate your positive approach to mediation by also identifying the issues that are not in dispute. By establishing common ground before the mediation even begins, you can contribute to an atmosphere of trust and willingness to discuss the issues.

5.4.8 NON-COMPLETION OF MEDIATION

(a) Non-Compliance

- The mediator can cancel mandatory mediation sessions in which it is impractical or impossible for mediation to proceed successfully. Generally, there is a clear indication that at least one of the designated parties is not approaching the mediation in good faith, or is unwilling to participate in mediation:

    - **Non-compliance with the order for directions.** If one or more of the parties, or the mediator, does not comply with the court's direction, the matter is referred for further direction as follows: in Ottawa, to the case management master; and in Toronto, to a judge. R. 75.1.05(6)
    - **Non-compliance regarding the statement of issues.** Where a designated party has not provided a statement of issues to the mediator and all other designated parties at least seven days prior to the mediation, thus making the mediation session impractical, the mediator cancels the session, and files Form 75.1D: Certificate of Non-Compliance with the court. R. 75.1.08(4)
    - **Failure to attend the mediation session.** If one or more designated parties do not attend the mediation session within the first 30 minutes of the session, the mediator cancels the session and files Form 75.1D: Certificate of Non-Compliance with the court. R. 75.1.09(3). *If counsel for one of the parties fails to appear, thus rendering the mediation impractical, this has the same effect as if the parties themselves did not appear.*

- After the mediator files a certificate of non-compliance with the court, the party with carriage of the mediation must, within 15 days after the date of the cancelled mediation session, bring a motion for further directions. In Toronto, the motion would be brought before a judge, either the judge who issued the order for directions or any available judge. In Ottawa, the motion is brought before the case management master. R. 75.1.10(1)

- In order to make a decision regarding the case's progress through further mediation attempts or court, the judge or case management master can require the appearance of the designated parties. Based on the affidavit evidence given and the previous circumstances, the judge or case management master has several options to exercise, including establishing a new timetable for mandatory mediation, striking out a document filed by a designated party, ordering a designated party to pay costs, or making any other order that is just and appropriate given the situation. R. 75.1.10(2)

(b) Prior Settlement

- If the parties are able to settle the issues in dispute prior to the scheduled mediation, counsel advises the mediator and the mediation coordinator in writing that this is the case. In addition, the Rules of Civil Procedure require counsel to advise the court of the settlement.

(c) Adjournment

- There may be situations that require an in-progress mandatory mediation session to be adjourned - such as the illness of one of the parties, or the need to seek out further information. The next session must be held within 90 days. If the parties require additional time, they will need to obtain a court order extending the timetable and file the paperwork with the mediation coordinator.

5.4.9 THE MEDIATION PROCESS

Practice Tips:

- Bring to the mediation all documents and files relating to the matter, including auxiliary files that may contain references to the matter. At the time of the mediation, there may not have been discoveries, or possibly a disclosure of documents, so what you think is important may not be what the other parties think is important. You therefore need to have all available information on hand to enable you to deal effectively with changes in direction.

- Ensure that counsel participating in mediation know the file thoroughly; the lawyer who prepares the pleadings should be the counsel at the mediation as well.

(a) Introducing the Process

- This stage basically asks *what are we here to do, and how are we going to do it?* Introductions of all those present at the mediation, and a brief description of their role if necessary, will be followed by ensuring that all present are familiar with the process and conduct of the mediation, including such procedures as caucusing. All parties should also sign a confidentiality agreement at this stage, emphasizing Rule 75.1.11's assertion that information revealed during mediation cannot later be used, for example, to support or oppose a party's position in court.

(b) Identifying the Issues

- This stage goes beyond *What are we here to do?* to *What are we here to resolve?* Each party will make a brief opening statement outlining the highlights of their position and interests. The mediator may re-state issues to ensure that what has been said has also been understood, and may ask questions to clarify certain details. Areas of agreement will be identified, and issues that remain in dispute will be identified and prioritized. An agenda is often set to provide a framework for the balance of the session.

> **Practice Tip:** It can be good strategy to leave crucial points of disagreement, such as the matter of costs, until later in the agenda, when agreements on issues already dealt with will have reinforced a positive atmosphere.

(c) Exploring and Resolving the Issues

- *This stage explores how and why each party feels the way they do.* This is where negotiating begins, as each party tries to demonstrate the merits and reasoning behind their position or interests. The mediator will encourage the free flow of information, manage personalities as necessary, and help identify what is important to the eventual settlement agreement. Parties should be prepared to offer some sort of compromise or movement in their positions, and can expect to caucus (or speak alone) with their counsel or supporters either with or without the mediator's presence.

- Some issues may be too complicated to attack from a "big picture" viewpoint. It may help to break them down into more manageable components, and work on solving those component issues.

- Caucusing with your client can provide a breather or cooling-off period should tempers flare; it can also provide the mediator with areas of possible movement to investigate with the other parties.

- Party impact statements can be effective tools to help the parties express their interests and their emotions. In the statement, the party can explain how the events or issues in dispute have affected them and their families. The opportunity to express these feelings can help the party feel that they've been listened to, and can thus contribute to the potential success of the mediation.

(d) Finalizing the Settlement

- Here, the work of the previous stages is pulled together into a settlement agreement that all designated parties and/or their lawyers will sign. Even if some issues remain unresolved, those that have been resolved should be summarized and committed to via the signed settlement agreement. R. 75.1.12(3)

- The settlement terms agreed upon in the signed agreement must be fulfilled by the parties as if the court had ordered the terms. If a party later fails to comply with the terms, any of the other parties may either make a motion to a judge for judgment in the terms of the agreement, or continue the proceeding as if no agreement had been reached. R. 75.1.12(6)

5.4.10 ESTATE MEDIATION'S RESULTS

Three possible situations can result from mediation, each with their own implications.

(a) All issues are resolved

- All parties and/or their lawyers will sign the settlement agreement. The party with carriage of the mediation must then file notice with the court within 10 days of the mediation session if the agreement is unconditional, and within 10 days of the conditions being fulfilled if the agreement is conditional. R. 75.1.12(4). *Additionally, the mediator must, within 10 days of the mediation session, complete the Mediator's Report and ensure that it is given to the mediation coordinator and the designated parties.* R. 75.1.12(1)

(b) Some issues are resolved

- The parties and/or their lawyers sign a settlement agreement dealing with the issues that were agreed upon.
- If all of the parties *agree to continue the mediation process* on a non-mandatory basis, the mediator files an Interim Report (including a specific date for the next mediation session) to the mediation coordinator within 10 days of the initial mediation session. The timelines for additional sessions must still remain within case management timelines set out in Rule 77; however, with the parties' consent, the court may at any time in the proceeding make an order requiring that they attend an additional mediation session. R. 75.1.13(1)
- If the parties *do not agree to continue mediation*, the unresolved issues proceed based on directions given at Rule 75.06, or based on a motion for directions made as soon as possible under that rule. R. 75.1.12(7). *The mediator must file the Mediator's Report with the mediation coordinator and the parties within 10 days of the mediation session.*

(c) No issues are resolved

- The matter proceeds based on directions given at Rule 75.06, or based on a motion for directions made as soon as possible under that rule. R. 75.1.12(7). *Again, the mediator must file the Mediator's Report with the mediation coordinator and the parties within 10 days of the failed mediation session.*

6

STATUTORY REMEDIES

Table of Contents

A number of statutory remedies can assist creditors to collect amounts due and/or protect creditors' rights in specific cases, such as the sale of a business, or a debtor who has left the province. These remedies can mean the difference between collecting a debt – or at least a portion of it – and writing it off as uncollectable.

> **Practice Tip:** When the word "execution" is used in the CRA, it means writ of seizure and sale.

6.1 CREDITORS' RELIEF ACT

- The *Creditors' Relief Act,* R.S.O. 1990, c. C.45 (CRA) provides a mechanism for proven creditors to pursue payment of debts through execution carried out by the sheriff. The key here is that when a creditor instructs the sheriff to seize an asset of the debtor, once that asset is seized, the sheriff must comply with the provisions of the CRA, not only on behalf of the instructing creditors but on behalf of all of the debtor's creditors who have filed writs of seizure and sale in the sheriff's office. CRA s.3(1). *This means that the sheriff will distribute pro rata any proceeds realized under the attachment among the creditors who have filed writs of seizure and sale or proven their claims.* CRA s.5(11)

6.1.1 FILING THE CLAIM

- There are two ways under which a creditor can be entitled to share under the CRA:
  - by filing an execution with the sheriff; or
  - by obtaining a certificate of proof of claim CRA s.9(1) and s.17

- A creditor who has recovered a judgment in Small Claims Court against the debtor is entitled to use the CRA by delivering to the sheriff a certificate from the Small Claims Court of the amount of the judgment and costs to which that creditor is entitled. CRA s.16. *This certificate will have the same force and effect as if it were a writ of seizure and sale issued by the Ontario Superior Court of Justice.* CRA s.16

- Note that in order to share in any proceeds under the CRA, a creditor must either deliver the execution to the sheriff or prove their claim and obtain a Certificate of Proof of Claim. Creditors who do not follow the CRA's procedures will not be able to share in the distribution of proceeds. *CSI Sporting Goods Canada Inc. v. Colleis Enterprises Ltd.* [1997] S.J. No. 173, 154 Sask. R. 270 (Q.B.); *Swertz v. Polyco Window Manufacturing Ltd.* (October 11, 1994), Doc. Weyburn Q.B. 95/92, [1994] S.J. No. 547 (Q.B.)

- The claim is filed with the registrar of the Ontario Superior Court of Justice by way of Affidavit of Claim in Form 2 detailing the debt and its particulars, by either the creditor or an individual familiar with the facts. CRA s.7(1)(2). *The form is filled out in duplicate.*

- Either before the Affidavit of Claim is filed, or at the same time, a certificate of the sheriff or an affidavit is also filed that details the proceedings already taken against the debtor that entitle the creditor to proceed under the CRA. CRA s.7(2)

- The creditor then serves the debtor, or the debtor's solicitor with a duplicate of the Affidavit in Form 2 as well as the notice to be served in the Affidavit of Claim in Form 3. *The forms shall be personally served if possible; however, a judge may order substitutional service if you can show that personal service is not possible.* CRA s.8(6)

- The creditor also files an affidavit of service with the Form 2 Affidavit of Claim and a copy of the notice in Form 3 with the registrar of the Ontario Superior Court of Justice for the county where the sheriff has the execution that is involved. CRA s.8(5)

6.1.2 WHERE THE CREDITOR'S CLAIM IS DISPUTED

- The debtor or another creditor of the debtor can contest a claim. CRA s.10(1). *The only claim that can be contested is a claim made under CRA s.7(1). If the creditor has obtained a judgment and filed a writ of seizure and sale, it cannot be contested by another creditor. The only recourse would be to the debtor, who could move to set aside the judgment and lift the writ of seizure and sale.*

- If only a portion of the claim is disputed, the creditor has the choice to abandon the disputed portion and claim only the balance. To do this, notify the registrar in writing that the disputed portion is being abandoned. CRA s.9(1)

- In the case of contestation by a debtor, the debtor files an affidavit with the registrar stating that they have a good defence to the claim or to a part of it. The debtor must also serve a copy of the affidavit on the creditor within 10 days of having been served with the notice of claim. The judge may dispense with the requirements to file the affidavit on terms or otherwise. CRA s.10(2)(3). *The purpose behind a creditor "contesting" the validity of another creditor's debt is similar to one or more creditors asking a trustee in bankruptcy to disallow the claim of a particular creditor. One presumes that it is a rare situation where a creditor actually does contest another creditor's claim, but clearly the CRA must have a mechanism to grant status to a creditor to contest in circumstances in which the debt claimed by one creditor may not truly exist or may be exaggerated, for example.*

- Note that if the service address is located outside the Province of Ontario, a judge must set a time for the debtor's response to the claim. CRA s.7(4)

- In the case of contestation by a creditor, the creditor files an affidavit with the registrar stating that they have reason to believe that the debtor does not owe the money. The judge may dispense with the affidavit on terms or otherwise. CRA s.10(4). The creditor may file this affidavit at any time before distribution is made by the sheriff. Once the disputing creditor delivers a notice of contestation to the sheriff, the sheriff immediately notifies the creditor who has filed the certificate of proof of claim that a notice of contestation has been received. CRA s.10(6)

- In either case, the party contesting the claim must serve a notice of contestation, along with a copy of the affidavit if applicable, on the creditor within five days after filing the affidavit or after the judge's order if the affidavit was dispensed with. CRA s.10(5)

- The creditor whose claim is being contested may apply to the judge for an order allowing the claim and determining the amount within eight days of receiving the notice of contestation. The judge may allow an extension of this time; however, if the application is not made within the allowed time, the creditor is deemed to have abandoned the claim. CRA s.12(2). *There are potential cost implications if a creditor abandons a claim. The court can award costs to the debtor or to the creditor who contested the claim.*

- If the contestation is by a creditor, and any other creditor believes that the contestation is not being carried on in good faith, that creditor may apply for an order for permission to intervene in the contestation. CRA s.12(3)

- The judge may determine any question or dispute either in a summary manner, or by directing an action to be brought, to be tried with or without a jury. CRA s.13(1). *If a determination is required, it is usually done by a judge alone.*

- If the court directs the trial of an issue, the procedure to be used will be the same as if an action was commenced. CRA s.13(2)

- Appeals of any decision of a judge under the CRA may be made to the Divisional Court as long as the amount in question is more than $100. CRA s.38

6.1.3 OBTAINING THE CERTIFICATE

- If the debtor does not contest the claim within 10 days after being served (having filed the appropriate documents proving service on the debtor), or if a disputed claim has been decided in favour of the creditor, the creditor applies to the registrar for a certificate (Form 5). CRA s.9(1)

- If a solicitor obtains the certificate on behalf of a client, the solicitor's address must be endorsed upon the certificate; if the creditor obtains the certificate. CRA s.9(4).

- The certificate is then delivered to the sheriff and the creditor is subsequently considered an execution creditor, and is able to share in the distribution of any proceeds as if they had filed an execution with the sheriff. CRA s.9(2)

- Once the sheriff has received the certificate, the sheriff make any further seizures of property as are necessary to fulfill the claim. CRA s.9(5)

- The certificate is also deemed to be an execution for the purposes of interpleader proceedings. CRA s.9(3)
- The certificate remains in force for three years, and may be renewed in the same way as an execution. CRA s.9(6).
- Note that if an execution or certificate expires in the same month during which the sheriff receives a notice of money having been levied or received, the execution or certificate is deemed to be in full force with regard to any money levied or received during that month. CRA s.9(7)

> **Practice Tip:** If the original execution or certificate documents are lost, you can obtain a copy of the applicable entry in the book held by the registrar that details each certificate or execution issued with regard to a claim. The entries are indexed alphabetically under the debtor's name. CRA s.15

- If you have established a claim in one county, you can transfer the same claim to another county by obtaining the certificate in Form 5 from the registrar in the established county, and delivering it to the registrar in the county you wish to establish the claim in. CRA s.17

6.1.4 DISTRIBUTION OF PROCEEDS

(a) General Distribution Matters

- The debtor must pay the monies under attachment to the sheriff either in the county in which the debtor resides, or if the debtor resides outside the province, in the county in which the judgment proceeding commenced. CRA s.3(2)
- There is no priority among execution or garnishment creditors under the Ontario Superior Court of Justice, the Unified Family Court and the Ontario Court (Provincial Division); however, the CRA does not affect the priority of

an execution or garnishment creditor under the Small Claims Court. CRA s.2

> **Practice Tip:** If there is money in Small Claims Court on behalf of a defendant, a Superior Court garnishment can seize the money held in Small Claims Court and have that money shared ratably amongst the Superior Court of Justice creditors. If the Small Claims Court creditor wants to share in the proceeds, such creditor would have to file a writ of seizure and sale.

- In the event that there is a garnishment under a federal tax department writ, check the writ carefully to see if there is a claim for provincial income tax as well. Federal income tax writs that include provincial income tax claims have priority to all other writs. Once those writs have been satisfied, then other federal writs are paid, e.g. GST, Employment Insurance, *Excise Tax Act.* Then, support and maintenance order garnishments are paid, then provincial government writs such as Retail Sales Tax, provincial corporate tax and, finally, the priority is to Superior Court of Justice and Small Claims Court garnishments.

- A further exception to the equality of creditors is made for support or maintenance orders. Regardless of when an enforcement process is issued or served, support or maintenance orders have priority over every other judgment debt for (in the case of periodic payments) the arrears owing at the time of seizure or attachment, or (in the case of a lump sum payment) the amount of the lump sum for spousal support and/or child support. CRA s.4(1). Support or maintenance orders rank equally with each other. CRA s.4(2). *Note that support or maintenance orders have a higher priority ranking than do executions or garnishments in the Ontario Superior Court of Justice and Small Claims Court. Garnishment for support or maintenance orders can be up to 50 percent of net wages, compared to 20 percent of net wages under a Superior Court of Justice garnishment or a Small Claims Court garnishment.*

- Creditors who have executions against goods or lands only, or against goods and lands, share equitably with other creditors, regardless of whether the proceeds were recovered under an execution against goods or lands or both, or under an attaching order. CRA s.5(10)

- Creditors may also be entitled to costs as per the court's tariff. Generally, the creditor under whose execution or garnishment the proceeds have been realized has priority for those costs. A creditor with an attachment order under the *Absconding Debtors Act* whose attachment was made before an execution was delivered to the sheriff will have priority over the execution creditors for the costs of the attachment order. CRA s.5(2),21(1)

- In order to satisfy in whole or in part the executions and claims, the sheriff will access funds belonging to the debtor that are being held by the court. CRA s.23

- If the sheriff cannot find enough goods to satisfy all of the claims, any goods or funds of the debtor that are being held by the Small Claims Court under an execution or attachment can be demanded for distribution among all creditors. CRA s.25. *This section sets out an exception to the general rule that is found in CRA section 2. Execution creditors in the Ontario Superior Court of Justice will have judgments for greater than $10,000.00, whereas any Small Claims Court judgment will be for a lesser amount. Hence, the two sections will work together to provide a check and balance. Where the sheriff is able to locate assets to make a distribution, section 2 should apply: whatever amount has been recovered on behalf of the Small Claims Court creditor should not be touched. This is only fair and reasonable; if it was otherwise, the Small Claims Court creditor would forever have to go to the back of the line because they would not have a claim provable in the Sheriff's office so as to participate in a pro rata distribution. However, where the sheriff cannot find assets to make a distribution, it would be unreason-*

able for those who have suffered the greatest loss to receive nothing while the Small Claims Court creditor receives a large amount of his money back. Accordingly, in those limited circumstances, the amount, net of any Small Claims Court bailiff's costs, are available for distribution pro rata to both Superior Court of Justice judgment creditors and Small Claims Court creditors.

- If the debtor - without any sale by the sheriff - pays all amounts due from executions and claims, or where the executions or certificates are withdrawn from the sheriff, the sheriff does not make the Form 1 entry, and the monies are not distributed pro rata among the creditors. CRA s.20(1)(2)

- If there is only one debt, any payment by the debtor is applied to that debt, and is not entered by the sheriff in Form 1. CRA s.20(3). *If there is only one writ of seizure and sale or certificate, as the case may be, filed with the sheriff's office in respect of a particular debtor, then the sheriff, after passage of the prescribed statutory waiting period, will simply distribute the payment received on account of the debtor to the creditor, net of any exigible costs to be deducted from the amount in recognition of the sheriff's costs in administering the CRA.*

- Monies levied or collected by the sheriff are distributed pro rata among all execution creditors, and among other creditors whose executions or certificates under the CRA were either in the sheriff's hands at the time the money was levied or received or within one month from that date. CRA s.5(2),25(4),26. *The sheriff pays the appropriate sheriff's fees and creditor's costs from the proceeds prior to distribution. The sheriff will hold the funds for a period of 30 days and will advise all of the creditors of the amounts received and the proposed distribution.*

- If further monies are levied or collected by the sheriff within a month of the original monies, those monies are distributed as if they had been received before the original monies. If the monies are levied or collected more than a month after the original, the sheriff makes a new entry in their book, and distributes the proceeds pro rata as of the new entry date. CRA s.5(7)(8)

> **Practice Tip:** If the proceeds for distribution are the result of an order of attachment under the *Absconding Debtors Act*, the one-month period after the entry in the sheriff's book extends to two months. CRA s.5(12)

- If a creditor contests a claim after a certificate has been received by the sheriff, the sheriff retains the amount of the proceeds that would apply to the claim until the contestation is settled, unless a judge orders otherwise. CRA s.12(1)

- Creditors may continue to share pro rata in any subsequent distributions by the sheriff, to the limit of their claims filed previously. CRA s.5(9)

> **Practice Tip:** If you need information about the property of the debtor and the likely proceeds to be realized, ask the sheriff: they are required to answer, without fee, any reasonable verbal question about the property. CRA s.31

(b) Distribution Under Interpleader Proceedings

- If a person has in their possession personal property that is claimed by two or more other persons, the first person can apply for the court for an interpleader order: i.e. an order that allows that person to deposit the property with the court. *This will ensure that the first person no longer has any responsibility and/or obligation for that property.*

- Special rules govern interpleader status as it relates to a sheriff. Rules of Civil Procedure, Rule 43.05

- Money received by the sheriff as a result of a sale of property under an interpleader order is not distributed pro rata among all execution creditors. Instead, if the interpleader proceeding is decided in favour of the creditor(s) who launched it, the money is distributed pro-rata among those creditors. Since they took the risk of contesting the adverse claim, and agreed to share pro rata the related expenses, they also share the proceeds. CRA s.5(3)(4)

- The judge has the jurisdiction to allow creditors who want to become parties to the interpleader proceedings a reasonable time to file their executions or certificates with the sheriff. CRA s.5(6)

- If the judge assigned carriage of the interpleader proceedings to one of the contesting creditors, the costs of the proceedings have a first charge over the creditors' claims on a solicitor and client basis. CRA s.5(5)

(c) Distribution and Garnishments

- Debts that are attached by garnishment in the Small Claims Court, the Superior Court of Justice or the Unified Family Court are not subject to the pro rata distribution among creditors under the CRA unless, before the creditor actually receives payment under the garnishment, an execution is filed against the debtor's property with the sheriff for the county. CRA s.3(3)

> **Practice Tip:** Garnishments by the Federal Crown, e.g. GST, Employment Insurance, Excise Tax Act, take priority over garnishments for spousal or child support (including those under the Family Responsibility Office). CRA s.5 and 26 These, in turn, take precedence over other garnishments, including Provincial Crown garnishments for such things as retail sales tax or Worker's Compensation Board premiums and provincial corporate tax. These, in turn, take precedence over Superior Court of Justice garnishments and Small Claims Court garnishments.

- While garnishments under Federal Crown claims may take priority over spousal and/or child support, under certain circumstances, the Federal Crown may agree to either defer their claim in whole or in part or to share ratably with the support claim.

- On the other hand, if you are the creditor who has launched garnishee proceedings against the debtor, there is an advantage to be gained by filing your own execution or certificate with the sheriff under the CRA. Without such an execution or certificate, the maximum funds you can receive are those under the garnishment proceedings - which, of course, do not always constitute the full amount of the debt. CRA s.3(6)

- Note that once an execution creditor has invoked the CRA, a creditor issuing the garnishment has no priority to then garnishee money paid into court. That garnishor shares ratably with other execution creditors in this case. *Polyco Window Manufacturing Ltd. v. Prudential Assurance Co.,* [1994] S.J. No. 137, [1994] 5 W.W.R. 659 (Q.B.)

- Because of the county-based system for filing executions, you may find that garnishment monies have been paid to a sheriff in a county where no execution has been filed. If an execution has been filed in a different county, however, you may still be able to access the funds in the first county. The sheriff, a creditor or even the debtor can apply to the court to have the garnisheed funds paid to the sheriff of the county in which an execution exists, for distribution among creditors. CRA s.3(4)

(d) Distribution Where Funds Are Insufficient to Meet Claims

- If the proceeds realized by the sheriff cannot pay all the claims, the sheriff prepares and sends to the debtor and to all creditors a list of the creditors entitled to share in the distribution, along with the amounts due to each, broken down by principal, interest and costs. The list also shows the amounts payable to each creditor. CRA s.32(1)(2)

- If you as a creditor have any objection to the distribution as per the list, you must make that objection within eight days of receiving the list by giving a notice in writing to the sheriff that explains the grounds for your objection. In addition, in the next eight days after your notice to the sheriff, you must apply to the judge for an order on the matter, otherwise your objection will be deemed to have been abandoned. CRA s.32(3)(5)(6)(7)

- If you fail to file a notice of contestation within the required time, but still wish your contestation to be heard, be prepared to show the court sufficient and reasonable grounds why you were unable to file the notice. Otherwise, the court is likely to refuse your request. *Swertz v. Polyco Window Manufacturing Ltd.* (October 11, 1994), Doc. Weyburn Q.B. 95/92, [1994] S.J. No. 547 (Q.B.)

- You must also serve the debtor and the creditors, or any creditors whom the judge orders to be served, with the objection in Form 7, and a copy of the appointment for hearing. CRA s.32(8)

- The sheriff shall, in the meantime, distribute any of the monies not in dispute. CRA s.32(4)

- The determination of any matter in dispute can be dealt with the court in a summary manner or by a trial of an issue with or without a jury. CRA s.32(9). *If the matter is dealt with by way of a trial of an issue, it will usually be dealt with by a judge alone. The cost of a jury trial would be prohibitive.*

- Any monies eventually found not due to the objecting creditor will be distributed pro rata among other creditors. CRA s.32(10)

- If the debtor becomes bankrupt after the sheriff has collected funds but before the funds are distributed to creditors, the funds in the sheriff's hands are considered part of the bankrupt's estate, and cannot be distributed under the CRA. *Stormont Chemicals Ltd. (Trustee of) v. Sulquisa,* [1993] O.J. No. 107, 17 C.B.R. (3d) 59 (Gen. Div. [Commercial List]). *If the debtor becomes bankrupt or files a proposal under the* Bankruptcy and Insolvency Act *(BIA) prior to the funds being distributed by the sheriff, the trustee in bankruptcy will serve and file a notice of stay of proceedings under the BIA with the sheriff and will direct the sheriff to pay the funds to the trustee in bankruptcy for the benefit of all of the debtor's creditors. The execution creditors who thought they would have been receiving funds will now be required to file a proof of claim in the bankruptcy and will be able to share ratably with all creditors of the debtor. Together with their proof of claim, they will need to file a copy of the judgment evidencing the debt owing, and a schedule updating the amount inclusive of interest to the date of bankruptcy. Note that the amount that these creditors will be entitled to will in all likelihood be far less than prior to the filing for bankruptcy or a proposal, because there will now be an increased number of creditors entitled to share.*

6.2 ABSCONDING DEBTORS ACT

- The *Absconding Debtors Act,* R.S.O. 1990, c. A.2 (ADA) allows creditors to have the debtor's property seized and sold to satisfy the debt in the case where the debtor has left Ontario with the intent to defraud creditors or avoid being arrested or served with process. ADA s.2(1)

- The debtor's property is seized through an order of attachment. ADA s.2(1)

- In order to use the provisions of the ADA, the attachment order must be made only in a pending action. ADA s.2(2)

6.2.1 OBTAINING THE ORDER OF ATTACHMENT

- To obtain an order of attachment, the creditor first completes an affidavit that includes the following details:

  - that the debtor owes the creditor an amount exceeding $100 (also include the actual amount);
  - the cause of action;
  - that the creditor has good reason to believe the debtor has left Ontario;
  - the debtor's new place of residence (or that the creditor has been unable to obtain information about the new place of residence);
  - that the debtor left with the intent to defraud creditors or to avoid being arrested or served with process; and
  - that the debtor has real or personal property in Ontario that is not exempt from seizure. ADA s. 3

- Two other individuals must also prepare affidavits that include the following statements:

  - they are well acquainted with the debtor; and
  - they believe the debtor has left Ontario with the intent to defraud creditors or to avoid being arrested or served with process. ADA s. 3

- It is essential that the requirements regarding the nature and content of the affidavits, relied upon by the applicant, be followed precisely. Failure to comply with the conditions of the ADA can mean either failure to obtain an order of attachment, or the eventual finding that the order of attachment is a nullity. *McPherson v. Patmore* (1964), 43 D.L.R. (2d) 527 (B.C. S.C.), reversed (1964), 49 W.W.R. 567 (B.C. C.A.)

- The ADA can be a difficult remedy to use, due to the necessity to prove the intent of the debtor to defraud creditors. The creditor must be prepared to show grounds for believing the intent exists; if not, the order for attachment may not be issued. *Big Sky Steel*

Fabrications Inc. v. Northline Well Servicing Ltd. (1983), 18 A.C.W.S. (2d) 181 (Sask. Q.B.)

- To use the ADA, the creditor applies to a judge of the Ontario Superior Court of Justice for an order for the attachment of the debtor's property. ADA s.3. *The order is made on a without notice basis using a motion record, which will include a notice of motion and affidavit evidence.*

- Once the order has been obtained, the creditor serves a copy of it on the debtor. ADA s.4. *If you cannot serve the debtor, you may have to go back to court for further instructions. In order to avoid this situation, in your notice of motion to the court, request such directions about how and where to serve the debtor.*

- The order for the attachment of property of the debtor remains in force for six months. ADA s.5. *If the creditor is unable to attach any of the debtor's property within the six months, the creditor will have to go back to court to extend the time period, and will have to show valid reasons why the order should be extended.*

6.2.2 USING THE ORDER OF ATTACHMENT

- An absconding debtor's property is attached in the same way as it might be seized under execution. The sheriff, with the aid of two substantial freeholders located in the area, must inventory the personal property and return the inventory listing with the order. ADA s.7. *The phrase "substantial freeholders" is a very old phrase. It is suggested that the requirement can be satisfied if two additional people over the age of 18 attend with the sheriff to take the inventory.*

- If the property includes livestock or perishable goods, the sheriff must have them appraised by two competent appraisers. If the creditor wishes to have the goods sold, they must deposit a bond worth double the appraisal to the sheriff on the condition that if the pending action is found in favour of the debtor, proceeds from the sale will be given to the debtor. After the bond is received, the sheriff sells the property at public auction to the highest bidder, giving at least six days' notice of the sale unless the property cannot be held even for that length of time. ADA s.8(1)(2). *If the creditor does not deposit the bond within four days of the sheriff's notification that the property has been seized, the sheriff returns the property. This could leave the creditor open for an action in damages by the debtor.*

- If any perishable goods have been sold by, or garnishments paid into, the Small Claims Court, the sheriff can demand those monies from the Small Claims Court. The costs and disbursements incurred by the Small Claims Court bailiff are a first charge on the proceeds of the property. ADA s.9(1)(2). *This will give the creditor who obtained the order a priority over the Small Claims Court. The sheriff must be instructed by the creditor to seize those monies; it will not be done automatically. If you obtain such an order, conduct a search with the Small Claims Court to see if there are any outstanding garnishment orders or funds being held by the Small Claims Court on account of executions. If so, direct the sheriff to demand those monies from the Small Claims Court.*

- A creditor has three months after the order of attachment is issued to deliver to the sheriff a writ of seizure and sale against the debtor's property. If needed, the creditor can apply to the court for an extension of this time period. If no execution is filed within the applicable time period, the sheriff returns the debtor's property. ADA s.18. *As a practice, once you have obtained the order of attachment, issue and file a writ of seizure and sale whether you have been able to obtain property of the debtor or not. By doing so, you will avoid having to go back to court if you miss the three-month time frame.*

- The sheriff's costs for seizing and taking charge of the debtor's property are paid by the creditor, who is then able to claim them as disbursements in the action. ADA s.10. The costs of the first attachment and its execution have priority over all execution debts and other costs. ADA s.13

- The debtor, or someone acting on their behalf, may file with the court where the first order of attachment was issued a bond with at least two sufficient sureties, with the condition that the appraised value of the property (or the amount necessary to pay the creditors' claims) will be paid into court whenever ordered. The judge may then direct the sheriff to return the debtor's property. The debtor has one month after the property has been attached to file the bond. If the debtor does not file the bond within this time period, the judge can direct the sale of the property. ADA s.12(1)(2)

- If the creditor is aware that the debtor is owed money by another person, or that another person is holding property belonging to the debtor, the creditor should have that person served with notice in writing of the order of attachment. (This can be done either by the sheriff, or by (or on behalf of) the creditor.) If the person then pays the debt or gives the property back to the debtor, and the other property seized by the sheriff is not sufficient to satisfy all claims, that person is liable to the sheriff for the amount of the debt or the value of the property. ADA s.14. *The creditor will likely need to provide the sheriff with a bond with at least two sufficient sureties, in double the amount of the debt or property value, to indemnify the sheriff from costs incurred in prosecuting the action. If, before the sheriff determines whether seized property is sufficient to satisfy the claims, the person is sued by the debtor for the debt or the property, the person can apply for a stay of that proceedings until the sheriff determines whether the other property is needed. For the purposes of this Act, the bond can be obtained from a valid bonding company.*

- If it would be more beneficial for the sheriff to sell the debtor's debts, rather than attempt to collect on them, the sheriff can, with the leave of the court, sell them by public auction. ADA s.15

6.3 RECIPROCAL ENFORCEMENT OF JUDGMENTS ACT

- The *Reciprocal Enforcement of Judgments Act* (REJA) allows creditors who have obtained a judgment in a jurisdiction in Canada, other than in Ontario, to apply in Ontario to enforce the judgment. Similar provincial legislation can also be used, in other provinces, to allow a creditor who has obtained a judgment in Ontario to follow the debtor for enforcement of the judgment if they move to another province.

- Reciprocating provinces include Alberta, British Columbia, Manitoba, New Brunswick, Newfoundland, Nova Scotia, Prince Edward Island, Saskatchewan, the Northwest Territories and the Yukon Territory. REJA Note. *There is no Reciprocal Enforcement of Judgment Act with the Province of Quebec. In order to enforce a judgment from the Province of Quebec, it will be necessary to start an action in Ontario based on the Quebec judgment.*

- A creditor who is seeking security for costs in an action because the other party resides outside Ontario should keep in mind that the courts consider the applicability of the REJA when considering such an order. Where the REJA is applicable, the order for security for costs has been refused. *Greensteel Industries Ltd. v. Binks Manufacturing Co. of Canada* (1982), 131 D.L.R. (3d) 343 (Ont. C.A.). *Even though an order for security for costs may have been refused, it is still important to consider such an order. At the very least, it may dissuade a party from bringing an action, knowing that they may have to post security for costs at some point in the action.* Rules of Civil Procedure, Rule 56

- A creditor who has obtained a judgment in a reciprocating province may apply in Ontario within six years of the judgment date to register the judgment in Ontario. The application may be made to any court in Ontario having jurisdiction over the judgment's subject matter, or to the Ontario Superior Court of Justice. REJA s.2(1)

- If the debtor was not personally served with process in the original action, or did not appear or defend or otherwise submit to the jurisdiction of the original court, the creditor must give the debtor reasonable notice of the application to register the judgment in Ontario. REJA s.2(2). *In all other cases, the application will be made on a without notice basis.*

- The judgment cannot be registered under the REJA if it is shown (by the debtor, for example) that:

  - the original court acted without jurisdiction;
  - the debtor neither carried on business nor resided in the original court's jurisdiction, and did not voluntarily appear or otherwise submit to the proceedings;
  - the debtor was not duly served with the process of the original court and did not appear, despite residing or carrying on business in the original court's jurisdiction;
  - the judgment was obtained by fraud;
  - an appeal is pending, or the debtor is entitled and intends to appeal the judgment;
  - the judgment's cause of action would not have been entertained by the registering court due to public policy or some other similar reason; or
  - the debtor would have a good defence if an action were brought in the original jurisdiction. REJA s.3

- An application has been granted where a New Brunswick creditor applied for an order registering a judgment in Ontario. Because the debtors contested the validity of the writ of summons in a New Brunswick court, they were found to have voluntarily attorned to the jurisdiction of the court. *McCain Foods Ltd. v. Agricultural Publishing* (1979), 103 D.L.R. (3d) 724 (Ont. H.C.), affirmed (1979), 26 O.R. (2d) 758 at 768 (C.A.), leave to appeal refused (1980), 31 N.R. 449n (S.C.C.)

- If the application is approved, the court issues an order for registration of the judgment. REJA s.2(1)

- The creditor registers the judgment by filing with the registrar or clerk of the court an exemplification or a certified copy of the judgment, plus the order for registration. REJA s.2(3)

- When registered, the judgment has the same force and effect as if the judgment had been obtained in the registering court, and that court has the same control and jurisdiction over the judgment as it has over judgments it gives. REJA s.4(a)(b)

- The registering court cannot, however, vary the judgment. *Susin v. Delazzer* (1997), 155 D.L.R. (4th) 170 (N.S. C.A.)

- The costs of registering the judgment are recoverable as if they were sums payable under the judgment. REJA s.4(c)

- If the registration order was made without notice to the debtor, the creditor will give notice of the judgment's registration to the debtor within one month of the registration. The service is in the same manner as the court uses for service of originating process. REJA s.5

- The debtor has one month after receiving notice to apply to the court to set aside the registration. No sale of the debtor's property can be made prior to the expiration of this time. REJA s.5,6

- The debtor can also appeal the registration. Where, for example, a debtor did not live or reside in Ontario, and did not submit to the jurisdiction of the Ontario court proceeding, the registration of the subsequent judgment in New Brunswick was allowed to be appealed. *Sims v. Bower* (1993), 108 D.L.R. (4th) 677 (N.B. C.A.)

- The setting aside of registration of a judgment in Alberta was upheld on appeal where the debtor had moved from British Columbia to Alberta when the original action was commenced. The original proceedings should have taken place in Alberta, where the debtor resided, rather than in British Columbia, where the cause of action accrued. The REJA does not change this point of common law. *Kelowna & District Credit Union v. Perl* (1984), 13 D.L.R. (4th) 756 (Alta. C.A.)

6.4 WAGES ACT

- The *Wages Act,* R.S.O. 1990, c.W.1 (WA) works in two very different ways: firstly, it details the claims and priorities that employees have for wages that should have been paid by a debtor; and secondly, it allows for an employee's wages to be garnished to satisfy judgments obtained against the employee.

6.4.1 EMPLOYEES AS CREDITORS

- Where a debtor has filed for bankruptcy, the assignee must pay, in priority to the claims of ordinary or general creditors, the wages of those who were the debtor's employees in the month prior to the assignment. The priority extends to three months' wages; for any amounts exceeding three months, employees are treated as ordinary or general creditors. WA s.2. *See* Bankruptcy and Insolvency Act, *s.136 for the priorities.*

- Where a sheriff has seized the property of an execution debtor under the *Creditors' Relief Act*, those who were the debtor's employees in the month prior to the seizure are entitled to priority for claims for up to three months' wages; for any amounts exceeding three months, employees share proportionately with other creditors. WA s.3

- Where a sheriff has seized the property of an absconding debtor under the *Absconding Debtors Act*, those who were the debtor's employees in the month prior to the seizure are entitled to priority for claims for up to three months' wages; for any amounts exceeding three months, employees share proportionately with other creditors. WA s.4

- Any individual employed in the month prior to an employer's death has priority over the claims of ordinary or general creditors for wages up to three months. For any residual claim, the employee ranks as an ordinary or general creditor. WA s.5

- Wages that constitute priority claims must be paid to the employees within one month of the estate being given to an individual who is responsible for winding up or distributing the debtor's estate. WA s.6(1)

- If the estate is not sufficient to cover the wage priority claims and the estate's ordinary expenses (which do not include the cost of litigation and other unusual expenses unless the employees agree) the one-month time period for paying the wage claims does not apply. WA s.6(1)(2). If the estate paid the wage claims, and it later turns out that insufficient funds were available to make those payments, the individual in charge of the estate is not liable for the payments if they acted in good faith, and believed on reasonable grounds that the estate's funds would be sufficient. WA s.6(3)

- Employees may join together to pursue claims for wages in any action, suit or proceeding. WA s.6(4)

6.4.2 EMPLOYEES AS DEBTORS

- An individual's wages can be garnished by creditors to enforce payment of judgment debts. Rules of Civil Procedure, Rule 60.08

- To request garnishment, the judgment creditor files with the court a requisition, accompanied by an affidavit detailing the amount outstanding on the judgment (after payments and interest are calculated), the names and addresses of garnishees that are or will become indebted to the debtor (such as employers or banks where the debtor holds accounts) and the particulars of those debts. Rules of Civil Procedure, Rule 60.08(4)

- Once the court issues the Notice of Garnishment, the creditor serves the notice on the garnishee, along with a garnishee's statement in Form 60I.

- The garnishee must then pay direct to the sheriff the amounts eligible to be paid out of its indebtedness to the judgment debtor. If it objects to the amount or disagrees that it owes any debt to the debtor, the garnishee must serve a garnishee's statement on the creditor, explaining why. Rules of Civil Procedure, Rule 60.08(15)

- The Notice of Garnishment is effective for six years from the date of service. *Any wages earned by the employee are subject to the notice of garnishment, even if the employee quits and is subsequently rehired, as long as it is within six years from the date of service of the notice of garnishment.*

- For the purposes of calculating garnishment amounts, wages do not include any amounts that an employer is required by law to deduct from gross wages, such as income tax, employment insurance and Canada Pension Plan amounts. WA s.7(1)

- In the case of an income tax demand under section 224(1) of the *Income Tax Act*, the employer should calculate the garnishment without taking into consideration the demand, as it has been found not to be specified by statute, and therefore not exempt under the *Wages Act*. *Bain v. Rosen* (1984), 7 D.L.R. (4th) 505 (Ont. Div. Ct.)

- Payments from an insurance or indemnity plan that are intended to replace income lost because of disability are deemed to be wages. WA s.7(1.1)

- Tips received by waiters/waitresses via credit card remittances have been found to be wages. *Jantunen v. Ross* (1991), 85 D.L.R. (4th) 461 (Ont. Div. Ct.)

- The *Wages Act* allows 80 percent of a person's wages, after deductions for income tax, employment insurance and Canada Pension Plan, to be exempt from garnishment; in the case of the enforcement of an order for support or maintenance in Ontario, however, the exempted amount drops to 50 percent. In addition, a judge can increase or decrease the exemption if they believe it is just to do so, given the nature of the debt, the debtor's financial circumstances and other such issues. WA s.7(2)(3)(4)(5). *Creditors should review the garnishee's statement to see how much the judgment debtor is earning and consider the earnings of any spouse or significant other of the judgment debtor to see if an application should be made to court to reduce the exemption from 80 percent to a lower figure based on the family's earning capacity.*

- Creditors should note that the assignment of wages to secure payment of a debt is invalid, except in the case of an assignment to a credit union to which the *Credit Unions and Caisse Populaires Act* applies. WA s.7(7),8. *The assignment of wages is 20 percent of the employee's net income, which can be subject to increase or decrease as the court may allow.*

6.5 FRAUDULENT CONVEYANCES ACT

- The *Fraudulent Conveyances Act,* R.S.O. 1990, c. F.29 (FCA) can be used by unsecured creditors to attack suspicious transfers of property by the debtor. If you succeed in setting aside the transfer, the advantage is that there is now more of the debtor's property from which to repay the debt. Be aware, however, that the burden of proof required by the FCA is quite onerous. The provisions for dealing with fraudulent conveyances under the *Bankruptcy and Insolvency Act* (BIA) are less onerous, so if a bankruptcy occurs, the BIA's provisions should be used and the FCA provisions should also be claimed in the alternative. *The courts have held that the language of the FCA is to be given liberal interpretation. Optical Recording Laboratories Inc. v. Digital Recording Corp.,* [1990] O.J. 2311 (C.A.)

- The FCA can also be used in conjunction with the BIA, where, for example, the BIA's stipulation that the transfer took place within three months' of the bankruptcy would prevent you from succeeding under the BIA. Creditors can make use of provincial legislation as long as it does not conflict with federal legislation: in this case, it did not. *Optical Recording Laboratories Inc. v. Digital Recording Corp., supra; Ramgotra v. North American Life Assurance Co.,* [1996] 1 S.C.R. 325 (S.C.C.); *Re: Marathon Music Inc.; R.C.A. Ltd. v. Can. Imperial Bank of Commerce* (1977), 24 C.B.R. (N.S.) 20 (Ont. S.C.)

- The FCA does not include any time limits for when the transfer of property took place.

- If you are a secured creditor, you can use the FCA with respect to any deficiency in your security. *Sun Life Assurance Co. v. Elliott* (1900), 31 S.C.R. 91

- If you are an unsecured creditor, you can use the FCA if you can show that, at the time of the transfer, another creditor existed who remains unpaid and would be able to use the FCA, or that the debtor intended to put all of their assets beyond the reach of their creditors, present and future. Roebuck, Gold. *Fraudulent Conveyances, Preferences and Other Voidable Transactions,* section 3vi; *Gauthier v Wollatt,* [1940] 1 D.L.R. 275 (Ont. H.C.); *Ottawa Wine Vaults Co. v. McGuire* (1913), 48 S.C.R. 44

- A conveyance of real or personal property made by the debtor with the intent to defeat their creditors is considered void as against those creditors, unless the person that the property was transferred to was acting in good faith and without knowledge of the intent to defeat creditors. FCA s.2, 3, 4, 5 and 6

- Even when no creditors exist at the time of the conveyance, a transaction can be set aside if the requisite intent was proven. *Ottawa Wine Vaults Co. v. McGuire,* supra

- To bring an action under the FCA, you must therefore be able to prove that the property was transferred, that there was inadequate consideration involved, and that the debtor intended to defeat their creditors. If valuable consideration was involved in the transfer, you must also prove that both the debtor and the person to whom the property was transferred were acting with the intent to defeat the debtor's creditors.

- Although there is clearly a strong presumption that a conveyance is fraudulent if it results in delaying or defeating creditors, it is only a presumption, and can be rebutted by evidence that establishes an honest purpose in the conveyance. *Mandryk v. Merko* (1971), 19 D.L.R. (3d) 238 (Man. C.A.)

Practice Tip: The onus of proof on the applicant is the onus as required in an ordinary civil case, i.e. proof on the balance of probabilities. *Habel v. Galemar Holdings Ltd.*(1981), 42 C.B.R. (N.S.) 295 (Ont. H.C.)

Once the presumption of fraud has been raised by the applicant, the onus then shifts to the grantee to show that the conveyance was made in good faith and for bona fide consideration to a person who was not a party to the fraud. *633746 Ontario Inc. (Trustee of) v. Salvati* (1990), 79 C.B.R. (N.S.) 72 (Ont. S.C.)

- Note that the property conveyed must have been eligible for seizure or execution in order for the FCA to succeed: after all, even if the property was fraudulently conveyed, it would do a creditor no good to set aside the transaction if the property was covered under the *Execution Act* and therefore not available to the creditor. Similarly, property that the debtor holds in trust for another individual could not be seized, and is therefore not covered under the FCA. McElcheran, Kevin, *Unsecured Creditors' Rights and Remedies*, Ch.13, p. 13-15.

- Suspicious circumstances that warrant further examination or investigation of the property transfer are known as "badges of fraud," and include:

  - a transfer between relatives or friends or related companies;
  - a transfer done in secret;
  - the conveyance of substantially all of the bankrupt's assets;
  - unusual haste in closing;
  - continued enjoyment or use of the asset by the debtor;
  - false statements in the deed that note the price paid by the purchaser;
  - a date of conveyance close to the date that a creditor begins attempting to enforce payment of a debt through legal means;
  - insolvency of the debtor;
  - inadequate consideration.
    Bennett, Frank. *Bennett on Collections*. p. 428-429

- In addition, the following caselaw also shows situations where the intention to defeat creditors was assumed, including:

  - where the transfer renders the debtor unable to meet their liabilities. *Sun Life Assurance Co. v. Elliott* (1900), 31 S.C.R. 91;
  - where a suspicious transfer was made between relatives (here, exact corroborative evidence was required by the court to prove the bona fides of the transaction). *Koop v. Smith* (1915), 51 S.C.R. 554, *Gallop v. Hamlin* (1973), 1 O.R. (2d) 156 (C.A.); *Mutual Trust Co. v. Alidina* (December 15, 2000), Doc. 31-287179, [2000] O.J. No. 4792 (S.C.J. [Commercial List]);
  - where there was a lack of documentation and extremely suspicious circumstances. *PCL Constructors Canada Inc. v. Great Pacific Fire Protection Ltd.,* [2000] B.C.J. No. 744, 3 C.L.R. (3d) 62 (S.C.); and

- where the consideration was merely nominal or entirely inadequate. *Meeker Cedar Products v. Edge* (1968), 12 C.B.R. (N.S.) 49 (B.C. C.A.), affirmed (1968), 12 C.B.R. (N.S.) 60 (note) (S.C.C.).

- Statutory presumptions of intent to defeat creditors in certain circumstances may also apply. In these cases, the debtor would have to show why the transfer was not fraudulent. Examples include:
  - where the debtor receives no money from the person to whom the property was transferred; and
  - where the parties are related in some way and the circumstances are suspicious.
    Bennett, Frank. *Bennett on Collections*. p. 429

- To launch a proceeding under the FCA, apply to the court for an order that the transaction should be declared void and that the asset be reconveyed to the debtor as if it had never been transferred. You should name the debtor and transferees as parties. *If the property is subject to encumbrances, any judgment will be subject to those encumbrances, assuming that the encumbrances are bona fide.*

- If the person who received the property from the debtor has transferred the property to another purchaser, whom you name in your action will depend on whether the subsequent purchaser knew the conveyance was fraudulent. If the purchaser had knowledge of the fraudulent conveyance, you can bring an action against that subsequent purchaser. If not, bring the action against the person to whom the debtor conveyed the property. If you are not sure whether to bring the action against the subsequent purchaser, start with the action against the debtor. The examination for discovery should provide you with information as to whether the subsequent purchaser had knowledge. If so, you can amend the pleadings at that time.

- If the property cannot be recovered from the person to whom the debtor conveyed the property, you can bring an action to recover the value of the property from that person under section 12 of the *Assignment and Preferences Act*, which applies to a fraudulent transfer under the FCA. *Westinghouse Canada Ltd. v. Buchar* (1975), 9 O.R. (2d) 137 (C.A.); *Thomas Flynn & Sons Construction (Toronto) Ltd. v. Laporte,* [1990] O.J. No. 188, 78 C.B.R. (N.S.) 158 (S.C.). *The proper cause of action would be an action on behalf of all creditors, with the proceeds distributed under the* Creditors' Relief Act.

> **Practice Tip:** If the plaintiff has judgment, the statement of claim will name the plaintiff in its own name. If the plaintiff creditor has not obtained judgment, the plaintiff in the statement of claim will be styled "in the (name of the plaintiff creditor) on behalf of the creditors of (transferor).

- Your statement of claim should include the following details:
  - the amount of and reason for the debt;
  - the judgment date and amount (which would include court directions regarding pre- and post-judgment interest);
  - your efforts to collect the debt, including execution attempts;
  - the fact that the debt remains unsatisfied;
  - a description of the property that you believe was fraudulently transferred. *If real estate is involved, a certificate of pending litigation should be filed against the lands. Rules of Civil Procedure, Rule 42*;
  - the individual to whom the debtor transferred the property;
  - any details of the transfer, such as consideration given;
  - the reasons you believe the transfer was fraudulent, such as any badges of fraud;
  - the fact that the transfer reduced the debtor's assets to the creditors' prejudice;

- a request that the transfer be set aside as against you and other creditors; and
- a claim under section 12 of the *Assignment and Preferences Act* (see section 6.6 for further details) to allow you to trace the proceeds of the property in case the property is transferred again.

  Roebuck & Gold, *Fraudulent Conveyances, Preferences and Other Voidable Transactions*, section 2ii

- As part of the relief claimed, it is usual to request the court to sell the assets in question. As the court may not have jurisdiction to grant the relief under the *Fraudulent Conveyances Act,* the better practice would be for the sheriff to seize the assets and sell them pursuant to the provisions of the *Rules of Civil Procedure* and the *Executions Act,* R.S.O. 1990, c. E.24, after the transfer has been set aside. Dowdall, Daniel R. *Extraordinary Remedies,* Law Society of Upper Canada Continuing Education Program, December 9, 1986.

- You can also examine other individuals who might have knowledge of the debtor's financial affairs and transactions, with the leave of the court. Be prepared to show why the examination is necessary, and that you have pursued all other available options for collecting the debt. Rules of Civil Procedure, Rule 60.18(6)(a)(b)

- If the transferee has sold the subject property, you are entitled to have judgment against that transferee for an amount equal to the value of the property.

- Where the proceeds realized from the property exceed the creditors' claims, the surplus belongs to the person who received the property from the debtor. *Ideal Reading Company, Limited v. Holland,* [1907] 2 Ch. 157

- The limitation period to attack a fraudulent conveyance is at least six years and may be up to 20 years. *Perry, Farley & Onyschuk v. Outerbridge Management Ltd.* (2000), 20 C.B.R. (4th) 129 (Ont. S.C.J.) , additional reasons at (2000), 20 C.B.R. (4th) 141 (Ont. S.C.J.), additional reasons at (November 21, 2000), Doc. 21435/91U (Ont. S.C.J.), reversed (May 7, 2001), Doc. CA C34942 (Ont. C.A.)

> **Practice Tip:** In addition to bringing the application, if the transaction was a fraudulent conveyance, consider bringing an interlocutory injunction. You need only satisfy the court that there is a strong indication that the conveyance was fraudulent. *Robert Reiser and Co. v. Nardoni Food Processing Equipment Ltd.* (1977), 25 C.B.R. (N.S.) 162 (H.C.), *Houlden & Morawetz, Bankruptcy and Insolvency Law of Canada*, p.4-30

- If a fraudulent conveyance action has been commenced and there is a subsequent bankruptcy, provided that leave is granted pursuant to section 69(1) of the *Bankruptcy and Insolvency Act* to continue the action, the action will not be affected by virtue of the bankrupt having been given a discharge. *OK Builders Supplies Ltd. v. Weninger* (1983), 50 C.B.R. (N.S.) 295 (B.C. S.C.)

6.6 ASSIGNMENTS AND PREFERENCES ACT

- The *Assignments and Preferences Act,* R.S.O. 1990, c. A.33 (APA) can be used by unsecured creditors to attack the debtor's suspicious transfers of property, and any payments that unfairly favour one creditor over other creditors. If you succeed in overturning the transfer or payments, the advantage is that there is now more of the debtor's property from which to recover your debt. *Be aware, however, that the burden of proof required by the APA is quite onerous, particularly as it requires you to prove that the debtor was insolvent at the time of the transaction and that both the debtor and the creditor had the intent to unjustly prefer or fraudulently convey.*

- The APA also allows a debtor to assign certain assets to a trustee for distribution among their creditors.

- Actions to set aside fraudulent conveyances in particular are often brought under both the APA and the *Fraudulent Conveyances Act* (FCA).

- Actions under the APA may also be combined with actions under the *Bankruptcy and Insolvency Act* (BIA), in order to make use of the differing provisions of each Act. For example:

  - the APA contains no time limit within which the transaction must have taken place, while the BIA restricts transactions to within three months of bankruptcy or within twelve months where the parties are related;
  - the APA requires both creditor and debtor to have the intention to prefer, while the BIA requires only the debtor to have that intention;
  - the APA allows for the doctrine of pressure to be considered as a defence, while the BIA does not; and
  - the APA allows certain exceptions that the BIA does not, including for the payment of money to a creditor or the grant of security for a pre-existing debt. Bennett, Frank. *Bennett on Collections* p. 432-433.

6.6.1 FRAUDULENT CONVEYANCES AND UNJUST PREFERENCES UNDER THE APA

- Transactions that are captured under the APA encompass situations where the debtor is actually insolvent, where they are unable to pay their bills in full, or where they know themselves to be on the eve of insolvency. APA s.4(1)(2). *To prove these circumstances, be prepared to show that the debtor's assets were insufficient to cover the debtor's debts and liabilities at the time of the transaction, or that the debtor had failed to meet their obligations generally as they became due. It may be of assistance to show that the debtor had other debts at the time of the transaction that have not yet been paid, and to make a fresh demand for payment. Rae v. McDonald* (1886), 13 O.R. 352 (C.A.). *Mutual Trust Co. v. Stornelli* (1995), 138 D.L.R. (4th) 316 (Ont. Gen. Div.), additional reasons at (1996), 138 D.L.R. (4th) 316 at 332 (Ont. Gen. Div.), affirmed (1999), 170 D.L.R. (4th) 381 (Ont. C.A.)

- A conveyance of real or personal property that is made by the debtor while in insolvent circumstances, with the intent to defeat their creditors, is considered void as against those creditors, unless the person that the property was transferred to was acting in good faith. APA s.4(1)

- Any transfer of goods or payment made to a creditor by a debtor who is in insolvent circumstances, with the intent to give the creditor an unjust preference over other creditors, is void as against any creditor who is prejudiced by the transaction. APA s.4(2)

- If the unjust preference took place within 60 days prior to an action being brought with respect to that preference, it is a statutory presumption that the debtor had the intent to prefer, whether the debtor made the preference voluntarily or under pressure. APA s.4(3). *This means that the onus is then on the debtor to prove that the transaction did not unjustly prefer one creditor over the others by showing, for example, that the debtor's action was reasonable at the time or that the person to whom the property was transferred had no intent to defraud creditors. D& G Burner Service Inc. (Trustee of) v. Flex-Temp Ltd.* (1987), 63 C.B.R. (N.S.) 27 (Ont. S.C.). *The statutory presumption can be rebutted. Lawson v. McGeoch* (1893), 20 O.A.R. 464 (C.A.)

- Transactions made under certain circumstances are not considered fraudulent conveyances or unjust preferences under the APA, even in cases where they preferred creditors. These circumstances include:

    - where the debtor has made an assignment to the county sheriff (or, with the consent of a majority of creditors holding claims of $100 or more, to an individual resident in Ontario) in order to pay pro rata all of their debts;
    - where the sale or payment was made in good faith in the ordinary course of business to an innocent person;

- where the conveyance or payment was made in good faith in consideration of a present actual payment of money;
- where the conveyance or payment was made in good faith by way of security for a present actual advance of money; or
- where the consideration given in the transaction was of a fair and reasonable relative value.

  APA s. 5(1); *Kisluk v. B.L. Armstrong Co.* (1982), 44 C.B.R. (N.S.) 251 (Ont. S.C.)

- In addition, certain other payments are exempted from the APA, including:
  - wages due to the debtor's employees;
  - a surrender of securities, where the debtor has paid a creditor in return for the creditor giving up their security;
  - an exchange of securities, where one security is substituted in full for another security; and
  - the situation where security is given to a creditor for a pre-existing debt in return for the creditor advancing money to the debtor in the belief that the money will enable the debtor to continue in business and pay their debts in full.

  APA s.5(5)(a)(b)(c)(d)

- Where the debtor has sold goods or property to a purchaser and the consideration for the sale passed from the purchaser to a creditor of the debtor (instead of passing to the debtor), and where such a payment if made directly from the debtor to the creditor would have been a fraudulent conveyance or unjust preference, the sale is void as against the creditor that received the consideration, but valid for the purchaser. APA s.5(2)

- Under the APA, the debtor may be able to use pressure, such as the threat by a creditor of legal action, as a defence: if, for example, the debtor made the conveyance or preference in response to pressure, in the belief that the business would be able to continue, the transaction may be allowed. Bennett, Frank. *Bennett on Collections* p. 432; *Molsons Bank v. Halter* (1890), 18 S.C.R. 88. *The doctrine of pressure cannot be used as a defence within the 60-day statutory presumption period.*

- If the person who received the property from the debtor has transferred the property to another purchaser, whom you name in your action will depend on whether the subsequent purchaser knew of the unjust preference in the conveyance. If so, you can bring the action against the subsequent purchaser. If not, bring the action against the person to whom the debtor conveyed the property. APA s.12(1)

- If the property cannot be recovered from the person to whom the debtor conveyed the property, you can bring an action to recover the value of the property from that person. APA s.12. *Westinghouse Canada Ltd. v. Buchar* (1975), 9 O.R. (2d) 137 (C.A.); *Thomas Flynn & Sons Construction (Toronto) Ltd. v. Laporte,* [1990] O.J. No. 188, 78 C.B.R. (N.S.) 158 (S.C.). *Where there is no assignment for the benefit of creditors, the proper cause of action would be an execution, with the proceeds distributed under the* Creditors' Relief Act *to proven creditors, or, if the property cannot be seized under execution, a class action for the general benefit of creditors. APA s.12(2)(3)*

- In order to bring an action to have a preference successfully overturned under the APA, you must have had a liquidated claim at the time of the conveyance or preference. *G.T. Campbell & Associates Ltd. v. Hugh Carson Co.* (1979), 23 O.R. (2d) 136 (Div. Ct.), affirmed (1979), 7 B.L.R. 84 (Ont. C.A.). *This is because your claim cannot have been prejudiced by the payment of another creditor's claim if your claim did not exist at that time. Alriyatti Ltd. v. O.B. Properties Canada Ltd.* (April 14, 2000), Doc. 99-GD-47342 [2000] O.J. No. 1466 (S.C.J.), additional reasons at (May 1, 2000), Doc. 99-GD-47342

(Ont. S.C.J.), additional reasons at (July 19, 2000), Doc. 99-GD-47342 (Ont. S.C.J.)

- Note that the property conveyed must have been eligible for seizure or execution in order for the APA to succeed: after all, even if the property was fraudulently conveyed, it would do a creditor no good to set aside the transaction if the property was exempt under the *Execution Act* and therefore not available to the creditor. Similarly, property that the debtor holds in trust for another individual could not be seized, and is therefore not covered under the APA. McElcheran, Kevin, *Unsecured Creditors' Rights and Remedies*, Ch.13, p13-15; Gold, Roebuck. *Fraudulent Conveyances, Preferences and Other Voidable Transactions*, section 3.vi

- Suspicious circumstances that warrant further examination or investigation of the property transfer are known as "badges of fraud," and include:

    - a transfer between relatives or friends or related companies;
    - a transfer done in secret;
    - the conveyance of substantially all of the bankrupt's assets;
    - unusual haste in closing;
    - continued enjoyment or use of the asset by the debtor;
    - false statements in the deed that note the price paid by the purchaser;
    - a date of conveyance close to the date that a creditor begins attempting to enforce payment of a debt through legal means;
    - general insolvency of the debtor;
    - an action pending, demand for payment or execution issued; and
    - inadequate consideration.

    Bennett, Frank. *Bennett on Collections*. p. 428-429

- Caselaw also shows situations where the intention to defeat creditors was assumed, including:

  - where the transfer renders the debtor unable to meet their liabilities. *Sun Life Assurance Co. v Elliot* (1900), 31 S.C.R. 91;
  - where a suspicious transfer was made between relatives (here, exact corroborative evidence was required by the court to prove the bona fides of the transaction). *Koop v. Smith* (1915), 51 S.C.R. 554; *Gallop v. Hamlin* (1973), 1 O.R. (2d) 156 (C.A.); *Mutual Trust Co. v. Alidina* (December 15, 2000), Doc. 31-287179, [2000] O.J. No. 4792 (S.C.J. [Commercial List]);
  - where there was a lack of documentation and extremely suspicious circumstances. *PCL Constructors Canada Inc. v. Great Pacific Fire Protection Ltd.,* [2000] B.C.J. No 744 , 3 C.L.R. (3d) 62 (S.C.);
  - where the consideration was merely nominal or entirely inadequate. *Meeker Cedar Products v. Edge* (1968), 12 C.B.R. (N.S.) 49 (B.C. C.A.), affirmed (1968), 12 C.B.R. (N.S.) 60 (note) (S.C.C.);
  - where the conveyance's circumstances were suspicious and badges of fraud were present. *Mutual Trust Co. v. Stornelli*, [1999] O.J. No. 680, (sub nom. *XLO Investments Ltd. v. Hurontario Management Services*) 118 O.A.C. 258 (C.A.)

- To launch an action under the APA, bring it to set aside the transaction on behalf of all creditors. *Westinghouse Canada Ltd. v. Buchar* (1975), 9 O.R. (2d) 137 (C.A.)

- Your statement of claim should include the following details:

  - the amount of and reason for the debt;
  - the judgment date and amount (which would include court direction regarding pre- and post-judgment interest);

  - your efforts to collect the debt, including execution attempts;
  - the fact that the debt remains unsatisfied;
  - a description of the property that you believe was fraudulently transferred;
  - the individual to whom the debtor transferred the property;
  - any details of the transfer, such as consideration given;
  - the reasons you believe the transfer was fraudulent, such as any badges of fraud;
  - the fact that the transfer reduced the debtor's assets to the creditors' prejudice;
  - a request that the transfer be set aside as against you and other creditors;
  - a claim under section 12 of the APA to allow you to trace the proceeds of the property in case the property is transferred again;
  - the grounds on which you believe that the debtor was insolvent at the time of the transaction.

    Roebuck & Gold, *Fraudulent Conveyances, Preferences and Other Voidable Transactions*, section 2ii

- When the order setting aside the transaction is obtained, you can then pursue appropriate enforcement measures, such as filing a writ of seizure and sale or having the sheriff sell the assets, subject to the exemptions set out in the *Executions Act*.

6.7 BULK SALES ACT

- The *Bulk Sales Act*, R.S.O. 1990, c. B.14 (BSA) provides for creditor protection where a business owner wants to sell all or most of the business. The risk is that the sale proceeds will not provide the business with the amount it would need to pay off its creditors.

- The BSA sets out various provisions with respect to creditor treatment during the sale. Failure to follow these provisions will allow a creditor to attack the sale, and potentially have it set aside. BSA s.16(1). *Alternatively, it could require the purchaser of the assets to be personally liable to account to the seller's unpaid creditors to the extent of the value of the property that the purchaser received.*

- The BSA applies to every bulk sale, unless it is carried out by an executor, administrator, guardian under the *Substitute Decisions Act*, a creditor realizing upon security, receiver, assignee or trustee for the benefit of creditors, trustee under the *Bankruptcy and Insolvency Act*, liquidator or official receiver, or a public official acting under judicial process. BSA s.2

- A seller may apply to a judge for exemption from the BSA. The judge may order the exemption if satisfied that the sale is advantageous to the seller and will not impair the seller's ability to pay creditors in full, and may require notice of the application to the seller's creditors. BSA s.3(1)(2). The request for exemption must be in respect of an actual, rather than a proposed, sale. Sale agreements must have been executed by the parties. *Copp Clark Ltd. v. Hunter Rose Co.* (1982), 136 D.L.R. (3d) 767 (Ont. Co. Ct.)

6.7.1 REQUIREMENTS UNDER THE BSA

- The seller must provide the buyer with a statement (verified by affidavit in Form 1) that lists:

  - all unsecured trade creditors, their names and addresses, and the amounts owing or accruing to each; and
  - all secured trade creditors, their names and addresses, the nature of the security and whether the claims are due or, in the event of sale, become due on the sale date.

  BSA s.4(1)(2)

- Once this statement has been delivered, creditors cannot obtain any preference or priority over the stock or the sale proceeds through such avenues as attachment or garnishment. BSA s.5

- As a creditor of the seller, you have the right to demand particulars in writing of the sale in bulk from the seller or the buyer. BSA s.7

> **Practice Tip:** In some cases, your client, in the interests of maintaining a good working relationship with the new owner of the business, may advise you that they will waive the right to be paid from the sale proceeds.

- The sale may be completed once the seller's statement is delivered to the buyer, on the condition that:

  - unsecued trade creditors' claims do not exceed $2,500 and secured trade creditors' claims do not exceed $2,500; or
  - the seller delivers a statement verified by their affidavit showing that the claims of all unsecured and secured trade creditors have been paid in full; or
  - adequate provision has been made for the immediate payment in full of all claims for the unsecured trade creditors and of all claims due before or upon the sale for the secured creditors. BSA s.8(1)

- If the creditors will not be paid in full as a result of the sale, the seller must obtain the consent to sale of 60 percent of the unsecured trade creditors whose claims exceed $50. The consent, in Form 3, must be delivered to the buyer, along with an affidavit confirming that, at least 14 days before the date fixed for the completion of the sale, the seller delivered the following to all of the unsecured and secured trade creditors:

  - a copy of the contract of the sale in bulk;
  - the statement of creditors at BSA s.4(1); and
  - the statement of affairs in Form 4.

BSA s.8(2). *The affidavit must also confirm that the buyer's affairs have not materially changed since Form 4 was completed.*

- A sale under BSA section 8(2) - where the creditors will not be paid in full - also requires that a trustee be appointed, either by either a majority of creditors or a judge. BSA s.9. The trustee in many cases is a trustee in bankruptcy. Courts may consider the appointment of an accountant or a lawyer as the trustee, but will rarely consider the appointment of any other person.

- Within five days of the sale's completion, the buyer must file with the court an affidavit describing the sale's particulars, including the subject matter and the name and address of the trustee, if any. As applicable, the seller's statement and affidavit confirming that all creditors will be paid in full (BSA s.8(1)(b)), any creditors' waivers of immediate payment in full in Form 2, and the consent of sale of the creditors if required must also be filed. BSA s.11(1). The affidavit must be filed in the court offices where the assets are located. If the assets are located in more than one jurisdiction, the affidavit must be filed in each court office where the assets are located.

- If the above affidavit is not filed, a judge may order the buyer to comply, extend the time for compliance, or set aside the need for compliance if one year has passed since the sale and the creditors' claims have been paid in full. BSA s.11(3)

- If the trustee receives notice within 30 days of filing the sale affidavit that a petition for a receiving order against the seller has been filed, the trustee cannot distribute the proceeds of the sale until the petition has been disposed of. If the receiving order is approved, the proceeds are paid to the trustee under the receiving order. BSA s.12(3)

- Otherwise, the trustee distributes the proceeds among the seller's creditors. The methods of proving, contesting, deciding and ranking claims follow the Bankruptcy and Insolvency Act procedures. (The only exception is that nothing in the BSA affects the rights of any municipality under the Assessment Act or Part XXII of the Municipal Act). BSA s.12(1)

- Before making the distribution, the trustee must publish a notice of that distribution in at least two issues of a newspaper in the area where the stock in bulk was located at the time of the sale. Distribution is made no sooner than 14 days after the last notice. BSA s.12(2)

6.7.2 BRINGING AN ACTION TO SET ASIDE A SALE UNDER THE BSA

- If the buyer has filed a *Bulk Sales Act* affidavit, the creditors must commence their action within six months of the filing of the affidavit. If no affidavit has been filed, there is no limitation period within which to object to the sale. BSA 16(2), 17, 19 and *Webber v. Hall* (1921), 56 D.L.R. 253 (N.S. C.A.)

- To attack a sale for non-compliance under the BSA, you must be a creditor of the seller. BSA s.17(1), *Sidaplex-Plastic Suppliers, Inc. v. Elta Group Inc.* (1998) 162 D.L.R. (4th) 367

- An unliquidated claim for damages for negligence or breach of contract has been found not to be a "creditor" within the scope of the BSA. *Pizzolati & Chittaro Manufacturing Co. v. May,* 26 D.L.R. (3d) 274, [1972] 2 O.R. 606 (C.A.)

- In the case of a bankrupt seller, the trustee of the seller's estate may apply to have the sale in bulk set aside. BSA s.17(1)

- Your action must be brought on behalf of all the seller's creditors. *Busuttil v. Diamond Trucks (Toronto) Ltd.,* [1969] 1 O.R. 245 (C.A.)

- In the case where real property has been included in a sale in bulk, there is no right of action if the property was conveyed in good faith for valuable consideration without actual notice of non-compliance with the BSA by the buyer. BSA s.17(2)

- Situations where sales have been set aside under the BSA include:

  - failure of the seller to send notice of the sale to creditors, to publish a notice to creditors, and to obtain the consent to the sale of 60 percent of the creditors where creditors were not to be paid in full. *Sico Inc. v. Lilly Enterprises Ltd.,* [1998] N.J. No. 278, 169 Nfld. & P.E.I.R. 340 (T.D.); and
  - where the buyer failed to demand and receive from the seller a statement of secured and unsecured creditors. *Sidaplex-Plastic Suppliers Inc. v. Elta Group Inc.* (1998), 162 D.L.R. (4th) 367 (C.A.)

- The onus of proving that the BSA was complied with is on the person upholding the sale in bulk (the buyer). BSA s.18

- If you are attacking a sale that has already taken place, and an order setting aside the sale is given, the buyer is personally liable for the value of the stock received. BSA s.16(2), *Sidaplex-Plastic Suppliers Inc. v. Elta Group Inc.* (1998), 162 D.L.R. (4th) 367 (C.A.)

- If you are attacking a sale that is still in progress, and an order preventing the sale is given, you may proceed against the seller to collect your debt: if, for example, you have obtained judgment against the seller, you can proceed to execution. *Thomson & Sons Ltd. v. Nelson (Town),* [1913] 4 W.W.R. 712, 11 D.L.R. 851 (B.C. S.C.)

6.8 MAREVA INJUNCTION

In the Superior Court of Justice, an interlocutory injunction or mandatory order may be granted (or a receiver or receiver-manager may be appointed) where the judge finds it just or convenient to do so. *Courts of Justice Act,* s.101(1)

- The Mareva injunction originated in an English case in 1975: *Mareva Compania Naviera S.A. v. International Bulkcarriers S.A.,* [1980] 1 All E.R. 213 (1975) at p. 215, in which Lord Denning M.R. stated that: "If it appears that the debt is due and owing and there is a danger that the debtor may dispose of his assets so as to defeat it before judgment, the court has jurisdiction in a proper case to grant an interlocutory judgment so as to prevent his disposing of those assets."

- Thus, a Mareva injunction can allow a creditor to ask for the court's assistance in protecting their interests while pursuing judgment against the debtor: for example, to prevent the debtor from disposing of assets in a way that would defraud or prejudice creditors, before the judgment can be obtained.

- To apply for a Mareva injunction, be prepared to meet Lord Denning's five-point test as follows:

  - full and frank disclosure of all matters involved;
  - full and fair particulars of your claim against the debtor, including the amount and the nature of the claim;
  - the grounds for believing that the debtor has assets within the jurisdiction, what those assets are, and where they are located;
  - the grounds for believing that there is a risk that the debtor will remove those assets before judgment; and
  - your undertaking as to damages in case you do not receive judgment.
  - *Mareva Compania Naviera S.A. v. International Bulkcarriers S.A.(1975);* [1980] 1 All E.R. 213 (C.A.); *Canadian Pacific Airlines Ltd. v. Hind* (1981), 122 D.L.R. (3d) 498 (Ont. H.C.); *Chitel v. Rothbart* (1982), 141 D.L.R. (3d) 268 (Ont. C.A.)

- You must convince the court that you have a strong *prima facie* case on the merits, and demonstrate a real danger of disposition of the only assets of the debtor that might satisfy the judgment. *Canadian Pacific Airlines Ltd. v. Hind* (1981), 122 D.L.R. (3d) 498 (Ont. H.C.); *Chitel v. Rothbart* (1982), 141 D.L.R. (3d) 268 (Ont. C.A.)

- Note that the Supreme Court of Canada has found that the lawful removal of assets from one province to another by a federally incorporated company is not a situation in which the extraordinary remedy of an injunction restraining disposition of assets should be granted. The right to enforce judgment across provinces is protected by reciprocal enforcement legislation. *Aetna Financial Services Ltd. v. Feigelman* (1985), 15 D.L.R. (4th) 161 (S.C.C.)

- A Mareva injunction was refused where there was no evidence that the debtor was the kind of person who was likely to remove assets in order to defeat or hinder execution of judgment. *663309 Ontario Inc. v. Bauman* (2000), 190 D.L.R. (4th) 491(Ont. S.C.J.), leave to appeal refused (October 24, 2000), Doc. 646/2000 (Ont. Div. Ct.)

- An injunction was found to be appropriate where grounds for believing that assets were being removed or dissipated included the debtor having withdrawn cash deposits, sold residential real estate, transferred commercial real estate in the United States without consideration, sold mortgage receivables and requested that a term deposit be released a few days prior to its maturity date. *Liberty National Bank & Trust Co. v. Atkin* (1981), 121 D.L.R. (3d) 160 (Ont. H.C.)

6.9 CERTIFICATE OF PENDING LITIGATION

- If you believe that real property may be removed or dissipated, rendering it unavailable to you as a creditor, you may obtain a certificate of pending litigation under section 103(1) of the *Courts of Justice Act*, or under Rules of Civil Procedure, Rule 42.

- A certificate of pending litigation that is issued by the court and registered in the proper land registry office or land titles office provides notice of a proceeding in which an interest in land is in question. *Courts of Justice Act* s.103(1) or Rules of Civil Procedure, Rule 42

> **Practice Tip:** The party bringing the motion should include a claim for the certificate of pending litigation either in the notice of application or the statement of claim, together with the proper legal description of the land in question. The legal description of the land should be checked with the appropriate land registry office/land titles office to ensure that it complies with their requirements and should include a property identifier number (PIN) if any. Rules of Civil Procedure, Rule 42.01(2)

- For entitlement to a certificate of pending litigation, you only need to show that you have an interest in the land that is in question in the proceeding; you do not need to claim an interest in the land directly. *Chilian v. Augdome Corp.* (1991), 78 D.L.R. (4th) 129 (Ont. C.A.). *In the case of 1072456 Ontario Ltd. v. Ernst & Young Inc.* (1997), 10 C.P.C. (4th) 351 (Ont. Master), *the court granted a certificate, although damages and return of a deposit were claimed in the alternative, where there was no doubt that the action was brought to obtain specific performance of an agreement to sell land.*

- A certificate of pending litigation may be registered under the *Land Titles Act* or the *Registry Act. Courts of Justice Act,* s.103(2)

- A party who registers a certificate without a reasonable claim to an interest in the land is liable for any damages sustained as a result of the registration *Courts of Justice Act,* s.103(4)

- The court may order the discharge of the certificate where you claim a sum of money instead of an interest in the land, where you do not have a reasonable claim to the land, if you do not prosecute the proceeding with reasonable diligence, where your interests can be adequately protected by other security, or on any other just ground. *Courts of Justice Act,* s.103(6); *Vulcan*

Packaging Inc. v. Capital Ventures Group Inc. (1989), 63 D.L.R. (4th) 723 (Ont. H.C.), reversed (1990), 71 O.R. (2d) 554 9 R.P.R. (2d) 32 (Ont. C.A.)

- It has been found that lien claims that arise subsequent to the registration of a certificate of pending litigation are subject to the certificate to the limit of the property's value upon registration of the certificate. *Rinaldis v. Landmark Development (North Bay) Ltd.* (1995), 124 D.L.R. (4th) 279 (Ont. Div. Ct.), leave to appeal allowed (July 17, 1995), Doc. CA M15948 (Ont. C.A.)

Practice Tip: If the certificate of pending litigation is obtained without notice, you are obliged to serve the motion record, which includes the notice of motion, affidavit and all documents relied upon at the hearing, to obtain the order. These documents must be served on all parties who have an interest in the property. Rules of Civil Procedure, Rule 42.01(4). Failure to comply with this rule can lead to the court vacating the certificate of pending litigation. *791715 Ontario Inc. v. Robinson* (1989), 72 O.R. (2d) 337 (Master), affirmed (1990), 72 O.R. (2d) 337n (H.C.)

6.10 INTERIM ORDER FOR THE RECOVERY OF PERSONAL PROPERTY

- In an action in which the recovery of possession of personal property is claimed and it is alleged that the property was unlawfully taken from you, or is being unlawfully detained by the defendant, the court may make an interim order for recovery of possession of the property. *Courts of Justice Act*, s.104(1) or Rules of Civil Procedure, Rule 44.

- Note that the person who obtains possession by obtaining or setting aside such an interim order is liable for any loss suffered by the person ultimately found to be entitled to the property. *Courts of Justice Act,* s.104(2)

- Bring a motion for the order, including an affidavit setting out:

  - a description of the property to render it easily identifiable (e.g. the make, model and serial number of a vehicle);
  - the property's value;
  - that you are the owner of the property, or are lawfully entitled to possession;
  - that the property was taken or is being detained unlawfully by the defendant; and
  - the facts and circumstances of the unlawful taking or detention.

  Rules of Civil Procedure, Rule 44.01(1)

- Serve the notice of motion on the defendant, unless you satisfy the court that there is reason to believe the defendant may improperly try to prevent recovery of possession, or that there is other sufficient reason not to serve the notice of motion. Rules of Civil Procedure, Rule 44.01(2)

- Where the motion is made on notice to the defendant, the court may:

  - order you to pay into court security of twice the value of the property or another amount as the court specifies, and direct the sheriff to give you the property;
  - order the defendant to pay into court security at twice the value of the property, or another amount as the court specifies, and direct the property to remain with the defendant; or
  - make such other order as is just.

  Rules of Civil Procedure, Rule 44.03(1)

- Where the motion is made without notice to the defendant, the court may:

  - order you to pay into court security of twice the value of the property, and direct the sheriff to detain the

property for 10 days after service of the interim order on the defendant before giving it to you; or
- make any other such order that is just.

Rules of Civil Procedure, Rule 44.03(2)

> **Practice Tip:** To obtain an order for interim possession, the plaintiff must establish (1) substantial grounds for its claim that its property is being unlawfully detained by the defendant; and (2) that the balance of convenience favors the plaintiff. *Clark Door of Canada Ltd. v. Inline Fiberglass Ltd.* (1996), 45 C.P.C. (3d) 244 (Gen. Div.)

- The court can set aside or stay enforcement of an interim order for the recovery of personal property. Rules of Civil Procedure, Rule 44.05

- The sheriff must report to you what property, or portion of the property, has been recovered, and the reasons for any non-recovery. Rules of Civil Procedure, Rule 44.07(4)

- If the defendant prevents recovery, the court may order the sheriff to take other personal property of the defendant and give it to you or hold it until the defendant surrenders your property. Rules of Civil Procedure, Rule 44.08

> **Practice Tip:** Consider including relief that the police department in the area where the property is located be authorized to attend at the premises with the sheriff.

- The court may also make an interim order for the custody or preservation of any property that is in question or relevant to a proceeding. Where the property is perishable, the court may order its sale in a just manner. Rules of Civil Procedure, Rule 45.01

- Where the right of a party to a specific fund is in question, the court may order the fund to be paid into court or otherwise secured. Rules of Civil Procedure, Rule 45.02

7

RESIDENTIAL POWER OF SALE PROCEEDINGS

Table of Contents

* Author's Note: This chapter deals for the most part with residential power of sale proceedings as opposed to commercial power of sale proceedings.

* The reader must make a distinction between a mortgage in default and a mortgage that has matured. A mortgage that is in default means that the mortgagor has done or omitted to do some act that has placed the mortgage in default. A matured mortgage is a mortgage whose term has matured and has not been extended. If a mortgage has matured, the mortgagor is not entitled to continue to make the monthly payments.

7.1 LAUNCHING POWER OF SALE PROCEEDINGS

7.1.1 DETERMINING THE RIGHT OF POWER OF SALE

- A power of sale basically allows the holder of a mortgage - the mortgagee - a self-help remedy to sell the property in order to realize on their security should the debtor fail to make the required payments on the mortgage.

- Any creditors who hold security with a priority over the mortgagee must be paid out of the sale proceeds before the mortgagee can apply the proceeds to the mortgage.

- When a mortgagor is in default of payments required under a mortgage, the mortgagee may be entitled to launch power of sale proceedings under one of three authorities:

  - Part III of the *Mortgages Act* if the mortgage document includes a provision allowing for the power of sale (a contractual power of sale);
  - Part II of the *Mortgages Act* if the mortgage document includes no such provision and is not one that is secured by bonds or debentures (a statutory power of sale); or
  - The *Land Registration Reform Act* if the mortgage involves property registered under the *Land Titles Act*.

    Mortgages Act, s. 41; *Land Registration Reform Act,* s.7(1)1.v

- When the mortgage is in default, prior to issuing a notice of sale under mortgage, it is usual for the mortgagee, through its solicitor, to send a demand letter, and, if applicable, a *Bankruptcy and Insolvency Act* notice ("BIA section 244 notice") to the mortgagor and guarantor, to notify them of the default and to require that they cure the default within a specific period of time. The usual default is in the payment of principal and/or interest. *Out of an abundance of caution, you may wish to provide the letter of demand and the BIA section 244 notice to the spouse of the mortgagor and the guarantor, if any, to defuse any potential problems in the future.*

- If the mortgagee enforces its security under a power of sale over all or substantially all of the inventory, accounts receivable or other property of an insolvent person, they have to send a section 244 BIA notice. This notice may be applicable in residential situations where the property is a residential rental premises and the secured creditor is attempting to attorn the rents to the property. BIA s.244. *Therefore, the mortgagee should consider serving the BIA s.244 notice at the same time as they serve the demand letter.*

- If there is a contractual provision to sell under the power of sale in the mortgage, the mortgagor must be in default for at least 15 days before the mortgagee can commence power of sale proceedings. *Mortgages Act,* s. 32

- If the power of sale is operating under Part II of the *Mortgages Act* (covering situations where the mortgage contains no contractual provision to sell under power of sale), the mortgage must be in default for at least 15 days, the power of sale must be issued and the notice period must be no less than 45 clear days. The mortgagee may not enter into an agreement of purchase and sale for the property or do anything that may constitute a sale of the mortgage property until three months after the date of the default. *Mortgages Act,* s.24 and 26. *The statutory power of sale under Part II is available where the mortgage is an equitable mortgage, the mortgage specifically provides that the power of sale must be exercised under Part II of the Mortgages Act, or the mortgage does not contain a power of sale and is not a mortgage that is exempt by Section 41 of the Mortgages Act. Dunn and Gray,* Marriott and Dunn Practice in Mortgage Remedies in Ontario *p. 25-4. Under a Part II power of sale, you will have to wait for the 15 days of default, then you will have to issue the 45-day notice under the* Mortgages Act *and you cannot sell until three months after the date of the default.*

Practice Tip: It is very important to ensure that power of sale proceedings are contractually included in the mortgage. This will allow the mortgagee to proceed much earlier than if it had to rely on Part II of the *Mortgages Act.* It can also lessen the possibility of a deficiency, because the mortgagee will not have to wait as long prior to commencing the proceedings.

- The *Mortgages Act* does not require any time limit to elapse to commence power of sale proceedings if the default is on account of insurance premiums. *Mortgages Act,* s. 24

- Power of sale proceedings will be launched by issuing a notice of sale under mortgage. (See section 7.2)

- If the mortgagee prepared the mortgage document, and that document is not clear about the mortgagee's right to institute power of sale proceedings, the court will interpret the situation in favour of the mortgagor. *Boyer v. Fox* (1980), 29 O.R. (2d) 330 at 332 (H.C.). If the default under the mortgage is other than a monetary default, send a "Boyer and Fox" notice; i.e., a letter stating that there is a default and that the mortgagee is accelerating the mortgagor's debt. When this notice is sent, a BIA section 244 notice should also be sent, if applicable.

7.1.2 FARM DEBT MEDIATION

* Author's Note: Since the Farm Debt Mediation Act was enacted in 1997, this section has been included to assist those dealing with this relatively new legislation.

- If the mortgage involves property belonging to a farmer, the *Farm Debt Mediation Act,* S.C. 1997, c.21 must also be complied with. The *Farm Debt Mediation Act* ("FDMA") was proclaimed in force on April 1, 1998. By virtue of the FDMA, s.31, the *Farm Debt Review Act* was repealed in its entirety. Furthermore, the *Farm Debt Mediation Regulations* ("FDMR") S.O.R./98-168 became effective on March 13, 1998 and replaced the regulations made under the *Farm Debt Review Act. Note that "property belonging to a farmer" does not necessarily mean farm property. It could be a cottage owned by a farmer or a condominium owned by a farmer. This distinction is extremely important, because failure to understand it may lead to the non-compliance with the* Farm Debt Mediation Act, *and accordingly may result in your client having to recommence the proceedings, which is both time consuming and costly.*

- The general purpose of the FDMA is to "provide for mediation between insolvent farmers and their creditors." *Farm Debt Mediation Act,* Preamble

- The emphasis of the FDMA is on mediation; however, it does not impose a mandatory obligation where a majority of creditors refuse to participate in the mediation. FDMA s.14(2)(a). *Where a majority of creditors agree to participate in the mediation, any minority creditors who do not wish to participate in the mediation may be forced to participate in or be bound by the mediation.*

- The FDMA is binding on federal and provincial governments. FDMA s.3. *Accordingly, the Crown and Crown agencies such as Canada Business Development Bank (formerly the Federal Business Development Bank) are subject to the Act.*

- A municipality may also be bound by the FDMA where it tries to realize on its tax lien for unpaid municipal taxes. *Lomond (Rural Municipality No. 37) v. Trobert* (1987), 41 D.L.R. (4th) 573 (Sask. C.A.), leave to appeal refused (1988), 87 N.R. 238 (note) (S.C.C.)

- In Ontario, the Farm Debt Mediation Service is located at 174 Stone Road West, Guelph, Ontario, N1G 4T1. Phone: (519) 836-8135 or (800) 265-7288. Fax: (519) 836-3213. Web site: http://www.agr.ca./progser/fdms_e.phtml.

- To be considered a "farmer" within the provisions of the FDMA, the farmer must be "engaged in farming" as set out in the test in *Moyer v. Polsin* (1992), 11 O.R. (3d) 216 (Div. Ct.). *It is extremely important that you review the file to see whether the mortgagor comes within the definition of a farmer under the FDMA. If so, you must comply with the necessary requirements, failing which, your power of sale proceeding may be a nullity.*

- A secured creditor under the FDMA includes (a) any creditor holding a mortgage ... pledge, charge, lien, privilege, priority claim or other security interest on or against the property of the farmer or any part thereof as security for a debt due or accruing due from the farmer, and (b) any bank to which security on the property of the farmer or any part thereof has been given under section 427 of the *Bank Act. FDMA* s.2. *Therefore, if acting for a mortgagee, consider doing a* Bank Act *search to see if there is any security held by a bank under that Act.*

- A secured creditor must give the farmer written notice and advise the farmer that they have the right to make an application under section 5 of the FDMA for a stay of proceedings against the farmer if the secured creditor intends to either:

  - enforce any remedy against the property of a farmer; or
  - commence any proceeding or any action, execution or other proceedings for the recovery of a debt, the realization of any security or the taking of any property of a farmer. FDMA s. 21

- The notice of intention to realize on security is a preprinted form and is a prescribed form. Failure to serve the notice in the prescribed form can be considered a nullity. Therefore, ensure that in a situation where you are dealing with a farmer or a potential farmer, you consider serving the notice to ensure that you have complied with all of the provisions of the FDMA. *Failure to serve the notice may or may not be fatal to the power of sale proceedings. The mortgagor may attack the proceeding based on the fact that no notice was given and this may result in delays or possibly having to start the proceedings over again.*

- Failure to send the notice in the prescribed form has been considered by the courts to be an irregularity that is capable of being cured. *Kerr v. Quigley* (1999), 23 R.P.R. (3d) 95 (Ont. Gen. Div.), affirmed (2000), 29 R.P.R. (3d) 202 (Ont. C.A.). Note that there are no provisions under the FDMA that would allow a farmer to waive the right to receive notice under the FDMA. The FDMA provisions are similar in this respect to those of the former *Farm Debt Review Act,* and to date, there are no reported cases interpreting the provision of waiver of the right to notice. However, the former *Farm Debt Review Act,* section 22 did not contain any provision that prohibited a farmer from waiving the right to notice under it.

Indeed, the leading case in Ontario is *Burgers v. Canadian Imperial Bank of Commerce* (1995), 32 C.B.R. (3d) 64 (Ont. Gen. Div.). In that case, the court held that a farmer to whom a proper notice of intention to realize on security was able to waive his rights under the *Farm Debt Review Act* and enter into an arrangement with the lender.

- Service of the notice of intention to enforce security on an individual farmer may be given:
  - by leaving a copy of the notice with them;
  - by leaving a copy of the notice in a sealed envelope addressed to the farmer with anyone who appears to be an adult at the farmer's place of residence, and on the same day, or on the following day, mailing another copy of the notice to the farmer at that place of residence; or
  - by sending a copy of the notice by priority post, courier or registered mail to the farmer. FDMR s.17(1)

- Service on a farmer who is a corporation, cooperative, partnership or other association is effective if made by:
  - by leaving a copy of the notice with an officer, director, partner or agent of the corporation, cooperative, partnership or other association;
  - by leaving a copy of the notice with a person at any place of business of the farmer who appears to be in control or management of the place of business; or
  - by sending a copy of the notice by priority post, courier or registered mail addressed to the last known address of the head office or principal place of business of the farmer. FDMR s.17(1)

- The giving of the notice under certain of those subsections is deemed to be effective seven business days after the date on which the notice is sent. FDMR s.17(2)

- "Business day" means a day that is not a Saturday or holiday. FDMR s.1(1)

- A farmer has the right to apply for either:

    - a stay of proceedings against all of the farmer's creditors, a review of the farmer's financial situation and mediation between the farmer and the farmer's creditors for the purpose of assisting them to reach a mutually acceptable arrangement; or
    - a review of the farmer's financial affairs and mediation between the farmer and the farmer's secured creditors for the purpose of assisting them to reach a mutually acceptable arrangement. FDMA s. 5

- Once the farmer applies to the administration for a stay of a mortgagee's proceeding, the administrator must decide if the farmer is eligible as an "insolvent farmer." FDMA s.5, 6 and 7.

- In the event that the application is eligible, the administrator will issue a 30-day stay of proceedings against the farmer, which is binding on all of the farmer's creditors. FDMA s.7(1)

- Once the stay of proceedings is in effect, and notwithstanding any other law, no creditor shall enforce any remedy against the property of the farmer or shall commence or continue any proceedings or any action, execution or other proceeding for the recovery of a debt, the realization of any security or the taking of any property of the farmer. FDMA s.12. *The phrase "any other law" would include the commencement of a petition for receiving order under the* Bankruptcy and Insolvency Act *by a creditor of the farmer. North 40 Farms, Re* (1999), 11 C.B.R. (4th) 82 (Man. Q.B.)

- The stay of proceedings can be extended by the administrator for three additional 30-day periods where the administrator considers it to be essential to the formulation of a plan between a farmer and the creditors. FDMA s.13(1)

- Even though the administrator has a discretionary authority to extend the stay of proceedings, the stay can only be extended if:

    - the value of the farmer's assets will not significantly diminish during the period of the extension;
    - the majority of the farmer's creditors will not be unduly prejudiced by the extension; and
    - there is no indication of bad faith by the farmer. FDMR s.3

7.1.3 DETERMINING WHEN DEFAULT HAS OCCURRED

- To determine what acts would constitute "default" under a power of sale proceeding, check the language of the mortgage document. Principal and interest due under the mortgage are, of course, most common; however, most mortgage documents include a right of power of sale in case the mortgagor fails to pay other amounts, such as taxes, insurance and condominium common expenses, or fails to keep up maintenance on the property to a reasonable standard. In other cases, mortgage documents can exclude certain defaults from giving the right to power of sale.

Practice Tip: If the default is other than a monetary fault, a letter of demand should be made to the mortgagor indicating that there has been a default under the mortgage and that the mortgagee is accelerating its debt. At the same time, include a *Bankruptcy and Insolvency Act* section 244 notice.

Practice Tip: In the event that a mortgage has matured, and a power of sale notice is issued, the mortgagor is not entitled to bring the mortgage arrears into good standing, because the mortgage has matured. In such a case, the mortgagor must pay off the full amount due and owing under the mortgage.

- Default on failure to pay monetary amounts is relatively straightforward: either the payments have been received by the required date and time, or they haven't. *Note that this is in contrast to a matured mortgage, where the monetary amounts for the full amount of the mortgage have to be paid.*

- Default on other grounds, such as failure to maintain the property, can be open to interpretation, however. If you plan on pursuing a power of sale based on failure to make repairs, for example, be prepared to prove that the failure is significant and substantial, that it has continued for some time, and/or that it is decreasing the value of the property. *A report from an accredited appraiser will be helpful, together with any outstanding work orders and written complaints from tenants or other occupants of the premises.*

- If you suspect that you have grounds for default, you may also wish to bolster your case by checking with the mortgagor's insurance company to verify whether the insurance policy is still current. *Assuming that your client has been noted as the mortgagee on the insurance policy, check with the insurance company to see if there is a history of late payments or if the insurance policy is in default and is about to be cancelled. If the insurance policy is about to be cancelled, the mortgagee can pay the outstanding premiums and then has evidence to show that there has been default and can start the power of sale proceedings.*

- Defaults can also be reversed: if, for example, the mortgagor makes good the repairs or pays the arrears before the mortgagee launches power of sale proceedings, the mortgagee may not be able to claim rights to power of sale or acceleration of the mortgage. *Tijoe v. Holman* (1975), 8 O.R. (2d) 425 (H.C.)

- Under both Parts II and III of the *Mortgages Act*, you may issue a notice of sale only after the mortgagor has been in default of payments for at least 15 days. *Mortgages Act,* s.26(2), 32

Practice Tip: In times of high interest rates and locked-in mortgages, mortgagors have been known to go into default under their mortgages, and then wait until the mortgagee has issued a power of sale notice. The mortgagor would then refinance the property at a lower interest rate and pay off the higher mortgage. (Remember, once the mortgagee issues a power of sale, no prepayment penalty can be claimed.) Mortgagees have become wise to this tactic, however, and now may choose to sue on the covenant, obtain judgment against the mortgagor, and attempt to realize on the judgment by various means, including garnishment of wages or bank accounts, and sheriff's sale. This tactic could have a negative effect on the mortgagor's credit record, because there would now be a lower credit rating from the mortgagee, which could limit the mortgagor's ability to obtain credit in the future either with the mortgagee or other creditors. This approach would be taken mostly in the case where there are private mortgagees. The cost to institutional mortgagees can be prohibitive.

7.1.4 POWER OF SALE AND THE *BANKRUPTCY AND INSOLVENCY ACT*

- Power of sale proceedings may be restricted under the *Bankruptcy and Insolvency Act* automatic stay of proceedings ("the stay") that ensues when a mortgagor has filed a notice of intention to make a proposal or the proposal itself, or becomes bankrupt. In the case of a notice of intention to make a proposal or a proposal, the stay remains in force until the mortgagor completes the proposal or becomes bankrupt. BIA, s.69(1), 69.1(1), 69.2(1) and 69.3(1). *This applies irrespective of whether the proposal is a Division I - Commercial Proposal or a Division II - Consumer Proposal.*

- If a mortgagor has filed a notice of intention to make a proposal or has filed for bankruptcy, the mortgagee can continue to enforce the terms of the mortgage and the collateral security in accordance with the provisions of the BIA. BIA, s.69(2), 69.1(2), 69.2(4) and 69.3(2). The stay does not apply:

- to prevent a secured creditor who took possession of the secured assets of the insolvent person for the purpose of realizing before the notice of intention to make a proposal under section 50.4 was filed from dealing with those assets;
- to prevent a secured creditor who gave notice of intention under section 244(1) to enforce that creditor's security against the insolvent person more than 10 days before the notice of intention to make a proposal under section 50.4 was filed, from enforcing that security, unless the secured creditor consented to the stay; or
- to prevent a secured creditor who gave notice of intention under section 244 to enforce the creditor's security, from enforcing the security if the insolvent person has, under section 244(2) consented to the enforcement action. BIA s.69(2)

- If none of the aforesaid conditions are applicable and the mortgagor has filed a notice of intention to make a proposal, the mortgagee may not take enforcement proceedings under the mortgage until the proposal has been made. BIA s.50.4(1), 69(1)(a) and (b)

- If the debtor's proposal does not include the mortgagee, the stay does not apply. BIA s.69.1(5)

- If the proposal was not accepted by the secured creditors in the mortgagee's class of creditors, the stay does not apply. BIA s. 69.1(6)

- The mortgagee may also apply to the court for a declaration that the stay does not apply to them, thus allowing them to exercise the power of sale. To show that the stay should not apply, the mortgagee must be able to prove that the stay materially prejudices them, or that it is equitable on other grounds for the stay to be lifted. BIA s.69.4. *Cumberland Trading Inc. Re* (1994), 23 C.B.R. (3d) 225 (Ont. Gen. Div. [Commercial List])

- If the debtor becomes bankrupt because it has filed an assignment for the general benefit of creditors, or did not file the proposal within the appropriate period of time, or the proposal is defeated by the creditors or is not ratified by the court, the mortgagee can proceed and will not have to lift the stay of proceedings. BIA s.69.3(2). *In these cases, there is no requirement to lift the stay of proceedings in order to start the power of sale process. If you wish to obtain possession of the property, however, you will have to consider obtaining an order lifting the stay of proceedings to continue as against the bankrupt mortgagor. At this point, you should also obtain an order under rule 11.02 of the Rules of Civil Procedure to add the trustee as a party to the action.*

- Be aware that if the mortgagee enforces its security under a power of sale by taking possession of the rents of a property, and those rents constitute all or substantially all of the business accounts receivable of an individual who is insolvent (but not bankrupt), the mortgagee can be considered a receiver under the BIA. Duties of a receiver include notifying all known creditors and the Superintendent of Bankruptcy of the receivership within 10 days, preparing a statement with information relating to the receivership, preparing interim reports and preparing a final report and statement of accounts. Ostroff, Percy. *Mortgage Enforcement and the Bankruptcy and Insolvency Act*, p. 10-13, BIA s.245 and 246

Practice Tip: In the perfect world, documents should be served in the following order:

(i) Demand letter and BIA section 244 notice;

(ii) Wait for 10 days;

(iii) Appointment of receiver, if applicable;

(iv) Attorn rents, if applicable;

(v) Issue and serve a Statement of Claim for payment on the covenant and for possession; and

(vi) Issue power of sale notice.

7.2 NOTICE OF SALE

7.2.1 CONTENTS OF THE NOTICE OF SALE

- Use the Notice of Sale Under Mortgage form contained at the end of the *Mortgages Act* to create the notice of sale under both Part II and Part III. *Mortgages Act* s.26(1), 31(1)

- Complete the Form with the following information:

  - mortgage date;
  - names of the mortgagor and mortgagee;
  - the property's full legal description, including the property identifier number (PIN), if any;
  - mortgage registration number;
  - date the mortgage was registered on title to the property;
  - name of the registry office where the mortgage was registered;
  - details of any mortgage assignment;
  - details of any mortgage renewals or amendments;
  - whether the power of sale is being exercised under Part II or Part III of the *Mortgages Act*;
  - the total amount due on the mortgage, and a breakdown that explains how that figure was arrived at (e.g. principal, interest, taxes, insurance premiums, legal costs as provided for in the mortgage document and associated GST); and
  - the date after which the property will be sold if the amount due is not paid. (The notice period under Part II of the *Mortgages Act* is at least 45 clear days; under Part III of the *Mortgages Act*, it is at least 35 clear days). *Mortgages Act* s.26(1),32, *Mortgages Act*, Notice of Sale Form

> **Practice Tip:** To avoid any possibility of confusion, you should use the property's legal description for completing the Power of Sale Form, even though the Form itself simply asks you to "describe mortgaged property." If for some reason this is not possible or practical, ensure that you describe the property in such a way that the mortgagor cannot later claim that the Form did not allow them to identify the property that would be subject to the power of sale. *Koutoulakis v. Aaron* (1980), 4 A.C.W.S. (2d) 336 (Ont. H.C.)

- Follow the form as much as possible. *Being creative and redesigning the form can lead to problems, which potentially can result in defects leading to the proceedings being a nullity.*

- The mortgagee or the mortgagee's solicitor must sign the Form; if it is the solicitor, they must be clearly identified as such. *It is also good practice to type the individual's name below the actual signature to ensure that no confusion arises as to who has issued the notice of sale. Salciccia v. Reid* (1978), 21 O.R. (2d) 10 (H.C.)

- Despite careful attention to the information required by the Form, it is possible that errors, in amounts or dates, for example, could occur. These errors can be used by the mortgagor as a basis for applying to the court to invalidate the notice of sale - which would, of course, effectively cease the power of sale proceedings.

- If errors do occur, you may be able to argue that the error in question should not invalidate the notice of sale, because the error was minor, did not affect the Form's substance, and would not confuse or mislead other parties such as the mortgagor. *Interpretation Act,* s.27; *Smith v. Cobham* (1988), 65 O.R. (2d) 211 (H.C.) at 212, 213. *The test to determine whether an error is an irregularity or an error in substance is whether or not the person receiving the form would likely be misled by the misstatement to their detriment.* Munro v. Pago Developments Ltd. *(1979), 26 O.R. (2d) 37 (H.C.)*

> **Practice Tip:** If you discover an error in the Form after it has been issued, such as in the amounts calculated as owing, or in dates, re-issue the Form immediately and re-start the proceedings to ensure that the mortgagor cannot later use the error as a means to have the court invalidate the notice of sale. This is more cost-efficient, and reduces the potential stress and possibility of an errors and omissions claim, than if you wait to see if the mortgagor or some other party notices the error. If you are a gambler and decide not to re-issue the notice of sale, be prepared to accept the consequences of having to start over or get a court order, and of having to explain the extra time and expense to your client.

- Situations that have resulted in the invalidation of the notice of sale include:
  - amounts for principal and interest improperly combined. *Morgan v. Canada Trust Co.* (1983), 42 O.R. (2d) 246 (H.C.)
  - an arithmetical error of 4.65 percent. *Roth v. 340529 Ontario Ltd.* (1982), 24 R.P.R. 198 (Ont. H.C.);
  - claiming unpaid taxes when the taxes had been paid by the receiver. *Grenville Goodwin Ltd. et al v. MacDonald* (1988), 65 O.R. (2d) 381 (C.A.);
  - claiming interest where the mortgage document shows no interest rate. *Sleightholme Estates Ltd. v. Bank of Montreal* (1984), 48 O.R. (2d) 217 (H.C.);
  - an insufficient notice period. *371802 Ontario Ltd. v. Schramm* (1979), 26 O.R. (2d) 550 (H.C.);
  - the solicitor's signature was not identified as such. *Salciccia v. Reid* (1978), 21 O.R. (2d) 10 (H.C.); and
  - discrepancies between the amount claimed due and the principal amounts due under the specified mortgages. *Munro v. Pago Developments Ltd.* (1979), 26 O.R. (2d) 37 (H.C.)

Practice Tip: If you discover that the power of sale notice is defective and it is too late to re-serve it, consider the following:

- Apply to court under section 39 of the *Mortgages Act* to dispense with service of the power of sale notice. If you do this on a without notice basis, you must serve the order together with the motion material on all of the other parties involved. This could result in one of the parties moving to set aside the order obtained on a without notice basis. If you must resort to obtaining a court order, consider serving the motion materials on all of the affected parties, prior to appearing in court.
- Obtain a release or quit claim deed from the parties who were either not served or were served with a defective notice. You will have to show these parties that the proceedings that have been taken, including the price for which the property has been sold, is proper under the circumstances. If subsequent encumbrancers balk at signing, consider whether some form of "sweetener" may be required to obtain the required signatures, e.g. paying reasonable solicitor's fees to the solicitor obtaining the release or quit claim deed.

7.2.2 SERVING THE NOTICE OF SALE

- Many mortgagees will send demand letters to the mortgagor as part of their standard collection procedures if payments have fallen behind. A demand letter is not required prior to a notice of sale unless the default involves non-payment of amounts other than principal or interest (such as taxes). *National Trust Co. v. Maxwell* (1989), 3 R.P.R. (2d) 263 (Ont. H.C.) at 269; *Boyer v. Fox* (1980), 29 O.R. (2d) 330 (H.C.)

- If the mortgagor gives the mortgagee a written demand for a statement under section 22 of the *Mortgages Act*, ensure that the statement is prepared and given to the mortgagor within 15 days as required under that section, and prior to serving the notice of power of sale.

Mortgages Act, s.22(2); *Counsel Trust Co. v. Whitelaw* (1985), 1 W.D.C.P. 366 (Ont. Master). *The preparation and forwarding of the statement will not invalidate the power of sale notice.*

- Under both Parts II and III of the *Mortgages Act*, you may issue a notice of sale once the mortgagor has been in default of payments for 15 days. *Mortgages Act*, s.26(2),32

- Serve the notice of sale on the following parties:

  - all mortgagors to the property including present and past;
  - spouse of the mortgagor, present and past;
  - guarantors; and
  - execution creditors.

- Note that under the *Registry Act,* the registered owner of the property must be served with the notice. If the current owner is not the original mortgagor, the mortgagee does not need to serve the original mortgagor with the notice, because the original mortgagor has assigned its equity of redemption and ceases to be entitled to redeem it. *HomePlan Realty Ltd. v. Adair* (1982), 13 A.C.W.S. (2d) 227 (Ont. Co. Ct.)

- Also serve the notice of sale on statutory lien claimants in favour of the Crown and other public authorities who have liens against the property where the mortgagee has been provided with "written notice of the lien," e.g., liens under the *Corporations Tax Act. Mortgages Act, s.*31(1)

- The notice of sale must also be served on every execution creditor who has filed a writ of seizure and sale with the sheriff or the Land Registrar before the mortgagee serves the notice of sale. *Mortgages Act*, s.31(1). *Execution creditors required to be served are those that would be listed on an execution certificate issued by a sheriff's office on the day prior to the day that the power of sale notice is issued. If an execution is filed with the sheriff's office on the date of issue of the power of sale notice, that execution creditor does not need to be served with the power of sale notice because it will not be recorded on the sheriff's abstract until the following business day. The execution creditor may be served either directly with the notice of sale or by serving the lawyer who filed the writ of seizure and sale.* Mortgages Act, s.33(2*). Any party that has filed a construction lien claim against the property should be served with the notice of sale by serving the lawyer who filed the claim for lien.* Mortgages Act, *s.31(3). In the event that there is no lawyer's name or address for service listed on the claim for lien, the lien should be served on the construction lien claimant directly.*

- Persons under a disability may be served with the notice of sale. *Mortgages Act,* s.33(4) and Rules of Civil Procedure 1.03.10

- Deceased persons should also be served with the power of sale notice. *Mortgages Act,* s.33(1) and 33(5). *If the mortgagee has actual notice in writing of the interest of any person in the deceased person's estate prior to service of the notice, such persons should also be served with the notice as well.*

- The mortgagee should also consider serving tenants of the premises. The decision as to whether to serve tenants must be made very cautiously as the mortgagee may wish to sell the property subject to the existing tenancy because there may be more value created in the property with the current tenant in place. If there is a notice of lease registered on title, the mortgagee should decide whether to serve the tenant. If there is no lease or notice of lease registered on title, the notice does not have to be served: the tenant does not have to be given notice, because they do not come within any of the categories set out in the *Mortgages Act,* s.31(1). *433414 Ontario Ltd. v. Lehndorff Property Management Ltd.* (1981), 31 O.R. (2d) 769 (H.C.)

- Conduct a corporations search to see if the mortgagor is a dissolved corporation. In the event that the corporation has been dissolved under the *Ontario Business Corporations Act,* service of the notice may be made on the director or officer of the corporation as recorded in the Ministry of Consumer and Business Services. *Ontario Business Corporations Act,* s.242(2). In addition, a copy of the notice of sale should also be served on the Public Guardian and Trustee. OBCA s.242(3). *Failure to serve the notice of sale on the Public Guardian and Trustee may result in the escheated mortgage property not being available for the mortgagee to sell under power of sale.* OBCA s.242(2)

- If the dissolved corporation is a federal corporation governed by the *Canada Business Corporations Act,* the notice of sale may be served on a director of the dissolved corporation shown on the notices filed under the *Canada Business Corporations Act* under section 106 or 113. CBCA s.226(3)

- In the event that a corporation was dissolved under section 261(8) of the *Canada Business Corporations Act,* service of the notice can be made on the director named in the last annual summary filed by the corporation under the Act.

- A notice of sale should be served on any person that has registered a notice of security interest against the title to the mortgaged property under the *Personal Property Security Act.*

Where the mortgagee has actual written notice of any other interest in the property, such persons should also be served with the notice of sale under mortgage. *Mortgages Act,* s.31(1)

Practice Tip: Ensure that you have verified the addresses for all of the parties. Note that the mortgagee may have a different address for service of either the mortgagor, or spouse of the mortgagor, in their file that may not appear on the mortgage document. Check with your client to see if they have any alternate addresses. In addition, subsequent mortgagees may have moved their offices, and execution creditors' solicitors may have amalgamated their firms or have moved their offices.

Practice Tip: You will only need to obtain an execution certificate against the mortgagor. No execution certificate is required against the spouse of the mortgagor or any guarantors. The reason for obtaining the execution certificate is to ensure that if there are any execution creditors against the mortgagor, they will have been notified of the notice of sale proceedings and will be entitled to any surplus sale proceedings in priority to the mortgagor.

Practice Tip: In the event that you act for the first mortgagee, the second mortgagee and an execution creditor, or any of them, technically, you may not need to serve the notice of sale on your client for the subsequent encumbrances. However, as a practical point, you will save a lot of time if you serve them at the appropriate addresses notwithstanding the fact that they may be your client. Solicitors may attempt to advance the point that the power of sale is deficient because you have not served the subsequent encumbrancers who may well be your client. By actually serving the subsequent encumbrancers, that argument will not be valid.

- You should also serve any guarantors and the original mortgagor in order to be able to maintain an action against them for any deficiency after the sale, if there is one.

- Your subsearches of the register of title and abstract index must include up to 4:30 p.m. on the day immediately prior to the day you issue the notice of sale. *However, you may wish to subsearch on the day after issue as well, in order to further protect the notice of sale from being invalidated due to its not being served on all applicable parties.* Mortgages Act, *s.31(2). This further search will allow you to serve other applicable parties that have either registered on title or filed writs of seizure and sale from the date of your original search to the date of the serving of the notice of sale.*

- Ensure that you serve the notice of sale on the mortgagor's spouse if the property in question is a matrimonial home. Family Law Act, s. 22(1). *To be on the safe side, serve the spouse whether it is the matrimonial home or not. What was once an income property may now be the matrimonial home. If you know the name of the spouse, serve that person. If you do not know the name of the spouse, serve it on "Spouse of A (mortgagor)" at the address of the property and any other address that the mortgagee is aware of.*

Practice Tip: Even if you think you know the name of the spouse, still serve the notice of sale on "Spouse of A (mortgagor)," because it is possible that the mortgagor may have acquired a new spouse.

If the property is owned by A and C who are the spouses of one another, still serve the "Spouse of A" and the "Spouse of C" to cover the situation where one or both of the original mortgagors have obtained different spouses, either through marriage or common law.

If you do not serve the spouse of the mortgagor, one way of dealing with this is to satisfy yourself as to the spousal

Practice Tip Cont'd: status of the mortgagor as of the date of service of the power of sale notice and execute an affidavit setting out the information in order to comply with the *Family Law Act.*

- If the current property owner is not the original mortgagor, you are not required to serve the original mortgagor in order to proceed with a valid power of sale. However, if you anticipate that there will be a deficiency of funds once the sale is completed, and you expect to proceed against the original mortgagor to make up the deficiency, you should also serve the original mortgagor with the notice of sale. *Baresyd Enterprises Ltd. v. Csizmadia,* [1981] O.J. No. 2257, 23 R.P.R. 60 (Co. Ct.)

Practice Tip: Time taken to verify all parties with an interest in the property will be well spent. If you fail to serve the notice of sale on a party, that party's interest will survive the sale, and as a mortgagee selling under power of sale, you may not be able to provide clear title to a purchaser. This will mean that you either have to start the whole power of sale process over again or go to court to obtain an order either allowing short service on the party you originally failed to serve or an order dispensing with service on that party.

- Service methods include personal service, registered mail to the usual or last known address, leaving the notice at that address, or as required by the mortgage itself. *Mortgages Act,* s.33(1). *Always check the wording of the mortgage document, as the required method of service is often set out there.*

Practice Tip: While it may not be required by the *Mortgages Act,* be careful to ensure that you have up-to-date addresses for the parties being served. The mortgage may have been registered 10 or 15 years ago and

Practice Tip Cont'd: your client may have a new address for service on the affected party, e.g. the mortgagor. To be on the safe side, use both the old address and the new address.

Once the power of sale notice is served, prepare an affidavit of service immediately. This should be done to ensure that the person who served the notice signs the affidavit while they are still with the firm. If the affidavit of service is done at a later date, the person who served the notice may no longer be with the firm or worse, no one may have any recollection of who served the notice.

Note that if the mortgagor does redeem during the redemption period, you cannot charge back to the mortgagor the costs of the affidavit of service or other sale papers that you have prepared: presumably, you will not be able to charge these costs to the mortgagee, and these costs will therefore be lost.

7.2.3 WHEN NO NOTICE IS REQUIRED

- Where the mortgage secures bonds or debentures for a corporation, and the document contains a corporate promise to pay and a pledge of the property, Part III of the *Mortgages Act* does not apply, and no notice of sale is required. *Mortgages Act,* s.41; *Kimberly Steel Ltd. v. K-W Navroz Investments Inc.* (1987), 3 A.C.W.S. (3d) 407 (Ont. Dist. Ct.)

- You may also apply to the court to commence sale proceedings without the notice of sale. *Mortgages Act,* s.39. *The general practice in Ontario is to proceed by way of notice of application and affidavit evidence. Rules of Civil Procedure, Rule 14.05(2). The application can be made either to a judge or a Master.*

- Be prepared to show evidence justifying the elimination of notice, such as where the mortgagor has abandoned the property, or cannot be found.

7.2.4 NOTICE REQUIREMENTS AND THE *BANKRUPTCY AND INSOLVENCY ACT*

- If the mortgagee has written notice that the mortgagor is bankrupt, the notice of sale should be served on both the mortgagor and their trustee in bankruptcy. *Also serve the spouse of the mortgagor at the address of the property, care of the trustee in bankruptcy and at any other address where the mortgagee has reason to believe the spouse may be residing.*

> **Practice Tip:** A bankruptcy search should be conducted to see if the mortgagor is bankrupt. If the answer is yes, the trustee should be served whether they have registered their interest on title to the property or not.

- If the mortgagee intends to enforce its security on a property that constitutes all or substantially all of the business property or accounts receivable (i.e., rents collected from tenants of the property) of an insolvent person, they must serve notice of their intention to enforce the security on that person at least 10 days before proceeding with the enforcement. BIA 244(1) and (2). *Note that the definition of insolvent person specifically excludes those who are bankrupt, but would include those who are operating under a notice of intention to file a proposal, or proposal proceedings. BIA s.2(1), Josephine V. Wilson Family Trust v. Swartz* (1993), 23 C.B.R. (3d) 88 (Ont. Gen. Div.)

- The form of notice is Form 86 of the Bankruptcy Rules.

- If the notice of intention to enforce security is not sent, the court can order the mortgagee to send the appropriate notice, or to stop the power of sale process until the notice has been sent and the notice period elapsed. BIA s.248(1)

Practice Tip:

(i) Serve the *Farm Debt Mediation Act* notice first;

(ii) Wait the appropriate time period;

(iii) Serve the demand letter together with the *Bankruptcy and Insolvency Act* section 244 notice; and

(iv) Lastly, serve the power of sale notice.

- In the case of rents, the mortgagee can request that the insolvent person agree to waive the 10-day notice period in order to ensure that procedures can be put into place to have the following month's rents collected by the mortgagee. Ostroff, Percy. *Mortgage Enforcement and the Bankruptcy and Insolvency Act*, p.5

- If the insolvent person does not agree to the waiver, the mortgagee can apply to the court to appoint an interim receiver who can then collect the rents before the 10-day period elapses. BIA 47(1)

7.3 NOTICE PERIOD

7.3.1 DURING THE NOTICE PERIOD

- Once you have served the notice of sale, a notice (redemption) period commences before the mortgagee can actually sell the property. The notice period under Part II of the *Mortgages Act* is at least 45 clear days; under Part III of the *Mortgages Act*, it is at least 35 clear days. *Mortgages Act,* s.26(1),32. *From a practice perspective, to be on the safe side, consider adding an addition seven working days to the notice period in the power of sale form. If there are rents to be attorned, serve the attornment notice before serving the notice of sale under mortgage.*

- Under Part II proceedings (where the mortgage document does not include a specific provision regarding power of sale), the mortgagee is stayed from proceeding with any action that could be construed as taking steps to sell the property during the 45-day notice period and during the three months from the date of default. *Mortgages Act,* 42(1). Such actions include:

- taking possession of and changing the locks on mortgaged property. *Bank of Nova Scotia v. Barnard* (1984), 46 O.R. (2d) 409 (H.C.) at 411;
- attorning rents. *Bank of Nova Scotia v. Barnard,* supra. *If the mortgagee wants to attorn the rents, service of the notice of attornment of rents on all of the tenants should be done after serving the BIA section 244 notice and one or two days prior to starting the power of sale proceedings;*
- issuing, serving the originating process and signing judgment during the notice of sale period. Lee v. Guettler (1975), 10 O.R. (2d) 257 (C.A.) at 261. If you want to proceed to judgment on the covenant and possession, and this is more important to your client than starting the power of sale proceedings, issue, serve and file the statement of claim first. If no defence is filed, obtain your judgment and then obtain the writ of possession. After that, you can issue the power of sale proceedings. If a defence is filed, issue the power of sale proceedings after the defence is filed and take no action with respect to the statement of claim until the notice period under the power of sale proceedings has expired. Then you can then proceed to deal with the defence;
- placing newspaper advertisements about the sale of the property. *Smith v. Brown* (1890), 20 O.R. 165 (Ch.); and
- entering into an agreement of purchase and sale*; Hal Wright Motor Sales Ltd. v. Industrial Development Bank* (1975), 8 O.R. (2d) 76 (Dist. Ct.)

Dunn and Gray, *Marriott & Dunn Practice in Mortgage Remedies in Ontario, Fifth Edition,* s.31.2

- The following proceedings are permitted during the redemption period:
  - assignment of the mortgage. *490352 Ontario Inc. v. ASAAPV Financial Corp.* (1985), 1 C.P.C. (2d) 36 (Ont. H.C.);
  - serving the notice of intention to enforce security under section 244(1) of the *Bankruptcy and Insolvency Act* and a notice of intention to realize security under section 22(1) of the *Farm Debt Mediation Act. Prudential Assurance (Trustee of) v. 90 Eglington Ltd. Partnership* (1994), 18 O.R. (3d) 201 (Gen. Div. [Commercial List]); *Farm Credit Corp. v. Wade* (1994), 28 C.B.R. (3d) 203 (Ont. Gen. Div.); however, it is a better practice to serve notices and let them expire prior to serving the power of sale notice; and
  - commencement of a power of sale proceeding under another encumbrance, even if the owner of the other encumbrance is the same as the mortgagee who has commenced the power of sale proceedings. *Bread and Roses Credit Union Ltd. v. 424043 Ontario Ltd.* (1983), 18 A.C.W.S. (3d) 517 (Ont. Gen. Div.)

- In some circumstances, negotiations between the mortgagor and the mortgagee will be allowed during the redemption period. For example, if partial payment is made by the mortgagor of the arrears due under the mortgage. *Aloi v. Spencer* (1980), 114 D.L.R. (3d) 485 (Ont. H.C.)

Practice Tip: Be very careful about accepting partial payments. If your client is prepared to accept partial payments, do not provide the party paying with any type of acknowledgment that this will stop the mortgage proceedings. In fact, when giving a receipt for partial

> **Practice Tip Cont'd:** payment, have the party paying acknowledge at the bottom of the receipt indicating that this will not stop any of the existing mortgage proceedings and will not stop the mortgagee from taking any further proceedings.

7.3.2 MORTGAGOR'S RIGHTS

- Because the power of sale proceeding gives the mortgagee the right to accelerate the mortgage, the mortgagor has the right to redeem the mortgage (i.e., to pay out the amount in arrears, thus preventing the sale from proceeding); *Municipal Savings & Loan Corp. v. Wilson* (1981), 127 D.L.R. (3d) 127 (Ont. C.A.). *This applies only to the situation where the mortgage has not matured. In the event that the mortgage has matured, the full amount of the mortgage must be paid.*

- The mortgagor may also trigger a stay of sale proceedings at any time before the property is sold or before the mortgagee commences an action to enforce its rights under the mortgage by paying the arrears only and not the accelerated balance. *Mortgages Act,* s.22(1)

- The mortgagor can also determine the amount required to bring the mortgage into good standing (including the mortgagee's expenses incurred as a result of the default), and request that the mortgagee furnish information as to the nature of the default under the mortgage. The mortgagee must respond to the mortgagor's request within 15 days, or face losing its right to enforce its security, and in any case cannot proceed with enforcing its security until it responds to the mortgagor. *Mortgages Act,* s.22(2) and (3).

- This right to redeem also applies to a party who has received an interest in the mortgage from the mortgagor. *Martin v. Miles* (1883), 5 O.R. 404 (C.A.)

- If a mortgagee wants to avoid triggering a right to redeem, they should pursue a course of action other than a power of sale, such as an action for the arrears, with or without a claim for possession, an action for the full amount of the mortgage together with a claim for possession, the remedy of attornment (attorning the property's rents if tenanted and pursuant to the mortgage), or asking the court or using the mortgage terms to appoint a receiver. Davis et al., *Strategies in Mortgage Disputes*, p.27-28

- An agreement of purchase and sale signed between the mortgagee and a purchaser after the notice period has elapsed may extinguish the mortgagor's right to redeem, unless the agreement includes a provision to allow the mortgagor to redeem until the sale's closing date, or unless the sale was fraudulent or improper, or other special circumstances apply. *Montreal Trust Co. of Canada v. Raptis* (1994), 42 R.P.R. (2d) 283 (Ont. Gen. Div.); *Hal Wright Motor Sales Ltd. v. Industrial Development Bank* (1975), 8 O.R. (2d) 76 (Dist. Ct.) at 82; *Weiss v. Standard Trust Co.* (1993), 42 A.C.W.S. (3d) 146 (Ont. Gen. Div.). *If there is no provision in the agreement about terminating the agreement of purchase and sale upon the mortgagor's redeeming, the agreement of purchase and sale may be binding. In such a case, where the mortgagee is obliged to close and cannot terminate the agreement of purchase and sale, a technical non-compliance with the notice of sale under the mortgage will prevent the mortgagee from completing the agreement of purchase and sale. The mortgagee cannot comply with the* Mortgages Act, *and is therefore not compelled to close the transaction.*

- In situations where the mortgagor's rights have been severely affected, the court may agree to set aside a sale that has already taken place. For example, a sale was set aside where the mortgagor did not receive an auction notice and the sale would cause considerable hardship. A sale was also set aside where the mortgagor intended to redeem the mortgage, but the mortgagee sold the property conditionally on the failure to redeem. *Sarlis v.*

Canadian Imperial Bank of Commerce, [1984] 1 W.W.R. 160 (Man. Q.B.), subsequently reversed [1984] 3 W.W.R. 561 (Man. C.A.), leave to appeal refused (1984), 29 Man. R. (2d) 320 (S.C.C.); *Camp-Wee-Gee-Wa for Boys Ltd. v. Clark*, [1972] 1 O.R. 374 (H.C.J.)

- If, during the process of the mortgagor asserting their rights, the mortgagee becomes concerned that the property could be deteriorating or otherwise be adversely affected, the mortgagee should appoint a receiver, either under the terms of the mortgage or by applying to the court. *Ryder Truck Rentals Canada Ltd. v. 568907 Ontario Ltd.* (1987), 16 C.P.C. (2d) 130 (Ont. H.C.J.) and *Courts of Justice Act*, s. 101(4). *In a court-appointed receivership, the mortgagee does not go into possession of the property or assume management and control of the property. Furthermore, the mortgagee will not be liable if there is an improvident sale. In a private appointed receivership, the receiver is empowered to realize on the property. If the private appointment includes an appointment as receiver and manager, the receiver and manager has the additional powers of managing the business of the mortgagor. Bayhold Financial Corp. v. Clarkson Co.* (1991), 86 D.L.R. (4th) 127 (N.S. C.A.) *Powers of the privately appointed receiver are as set out in the mortgage. Ostrander v. Niagara Helicopters Ltd. (1973), 1 O.R. (2d) 281 (H.C.). These powers would be subject to any statutory restraints that are contained in the* Mortgages Act, *the* Bankruptcy and Insolvency Act, *the* Land Titles Act *and the* Farm Debt Mediation Act.

7.3.3 NEGOTIATING WITH THE MORTGAGOR

- Taking the step of serving the mortgagor with a notice of sale may encourage a previously uncommunicative or uncooperative mortgagor to attempt to settle the default. If the mortgagee's preference is to have the mortgage continue, rather than to proceed with a sale, it will be to the mortgagor's advantage to bring the defaulted mortgage into good standing or to negotiate new terms for the mortgage.

- If the mortgagee does negotiate with the mortgagor, the rights of other parties with an interest in the mortgage must be taken into account. *Paul Horvat Investments Ltd. v. Goldcrown Holdings Ltd.* (1982), 26 R.P.R. 36 (Ont. H.C.)

- Negotiations with the mortgagor may prevent the mortgagee from continuing the sale proceeding under the existing notice of sale and may require the mortgagee to issue a new power of sale notice. *Hotel California Holdings Ltd. v. Grossman* (1980), 11 R.P.R. 66 (Ont. H.C.) at 72

- If the negotiations lead to an agreement, and the mortgagor subsequently defaults on the agreement's terms, the mortgagee must issue a new notice of sale in order to exercise the right to power of sale.

- If a spouse has a right to possession to the matrimonial home under section 19 of the *Family Law Reform Act,* R.S.O. 1990, c.F-3, the spouse has a right to redeem or to seek injunctive relief. *Family Law Reform Act,* s.22(1). *Therefore, even a non-titled spouse has the right to redeem. Be careful to ensure that you have complied with service on the spouse to ensure that there is no defect or irregularity in the power of sale notice which could invalidate the sale and cause embarrassment to the mortgagee.*

- If the non-titled spouse brings the mortgage into good standing, this will terminate the power of sale proceedings. *Family Law Reform Act,* s.22(4). *From the mortgagee's perspective, there is no concern if the non-titled spouse brings the mortgage into good standing. Presumably, the non-titled spouse will then have an action against the titled spouse for the payment made to the mortgagee, including a claim for any costs paid to the mortgagee.*

7.3.4 INJUNCTIVE RELIEF APPLICATION BY THE MORTGAGOR

- The mortgagor has the right to apply to the court for an injunction to halt the power of sale. To succeed, they must meet the test set out by the Supreme Court of Canada, which includes assessing:
  - the merits of the case;
  - whether the applicant would suffer irreparable harm if the application were refused; and
  - which of the parties would suffer greater harm from the granting or refusal of the remedy pending a decision on the merits.

RJR-Macdonald v. Canada (Attorney General), [1994] 1 S.C.R. 311 (S.C.C.)

- Injunctions have been denied where, for example:
  - errors contained in the notice of sale were minor, insubstantial, and did not mislead or confuse the parties involved, such as errors in the date of the mortgage and registration, or partial descriptions of the property. *Kenney v. Barnard* (1910), 2 O.W.N. 470 (H.C.); *Koutoulakis v. Aaron* (1980), 4 A.C.W.S. (2d) 336 (Ont. H.C.);
  - the mortgagor had been given reasonable opportunities to make arrangements, had a poor payment record, tax arrears and previous unsuccessful refinancing attempts. *Arnold v. Bronstein* (1970), [1971] 1 O.R. 467 (H.C.); and
  - the mortgagor was in default, and had allowed the property to fall into serious disrepair. *Campus Downs Developments Ltd. v. Grimwood* (1982), 15 A.C.W.S. (2d) 192 (Ont. H.C.).

- Injunctions have been or could be granted where, for example:
  - there were significant and substantial errors in the notice of sale, such as a failure to explain the mort-

gage account in adequate detail, or the inclusion of more than one date for redemption due to the failure to delete reference to the applicable Part of the *Mortgages Act*. *Morgan v. Canada Trust Co.* (1983), 42 O.R. (2d) 246 (H.C.); *Comrie Lumber Co. v. Tomlinson Construction Services Ltd.* (1977), 15 O.R. (2d) 613 (H.C.);

- the mortgagor had an oral agreement with the mortgagee, in which the mortgagee had agreed not to enforce its security while re-financing attempts were ongoing. *Hotel California Holdings Ltd. v. Grossman* (1980), 11 R.P.R. 66 (Ont. H.C.);
- the mortgagor's claim was neither frivolous nor vexatious. *American Cyanamid Co. v. Ethicon Ltd.*, [1975] 1 All E.R. 504 (H.L.);
- the mortgagee was acting in bad faith, or willfully and recklessly, thus harming the mortgagor's interests. *Yepremian v. National Trust Company Limited* (1981), 12 A.C.W.S. (2d) 234 (Ont. H.C.);
- the mortgagee took steps to enforce its security during the notice period. *Mortgages Act,* s. 42;
- the mortgagee exercised a power of sale without notice to the mortgagor. *Steffen v. Toronto Dominion Bank* (1980), 5 A.C.W.S. (2d) 296 (Ont. H.C.); and
- the mortgagee was selling the property for significantly less than its market value. *Couch v. National Bank of Canada* (1984), 28 Man. R. (2d) 60 (Q.B.)

> **Practice Tip:** If you are dealing with an application for an injunction by a mortgagor, and you believe the application may be granted, you may be able to mitigate the effects of the injunction for your client by requesting that the court impose terms on the mortgagor as part of granting the injunction. Such terms could include the mortgagor paying amounts in arrears, or making regular payments of principal and interest as set out in the mortgage. If the mortgagor does not meet the terms of the order, the mortgagee can bring a motion to set aside the injunction because the terms agreed by the mortgagor were not satisfied.

7.4 GOING AHEAD WITH THE SALE

7.4.1 PREPARING FOR THE SALE

- In dealing with a power of sale, the mortgagee must be able to show that it has acted in good faith, and that the sale price of the property was a true market value. *Siskind v. Bank of Nova Scotia* (1984), 46 O.R. (2d) 575 (H.C.)

- The three accepted methods of selling the property are: listing the property with a realtor; selling it by auction; or selling it by public tender. The method that is chosen will depend on the type of property and its use. *If the mortgagee decides to sell by any other means, e.g. private sale, they run the risk that any interested party may bring an action against the mortgagee for improvident sale and for damages.*

- The sale price should be the best price available given the economic conditions and the real estate market in the property's area at the time. The "good faith" requirement does not mean that the mortgagee must wait until real estate values increase in order to sell the property; the mortgagee has the right to sell at any time after the notice period has elapsed. *Siskind v. Bank of Nova Scotia*, supra

- To demonstrate that the mortgagee is attempting to sell the property in good faith and for fair market value, the property should be adequately advertised (including the use of multiple listing services and placing a "for sale" sign on the property) for a reasonable length of time, and qualified appraisal(s) sought. *Wood v. Bank of Nova Scotia* (1979), 10 R.P.R. 156 (Ont. S.C.), affirmed (1980), 29 O.R. (2d) 35 (C.A.); *Canadian Imperial Bank of Commerce v. Income Trust Co.* (1990), 17 A.C.W.S. (3d) 222 (Ont. H.C.), varied (November 30, 1992), Doc. CA 663/89 (Ont. C.A.)

- Ensure that one appraisal is obtained from an individual who is not only qualified as an appraiser, but also experienced in the type of property involved. The more prudent practice is to obtain two appraisals; however, reality is such that it would be too expensive to obtain two appraisals. Accordingly, one appraisal is usually obtained and in addition, a Certified Market Analysis that recommends a sale price is obtained through a real estate agent. Note: If there is a large discrepancy between the appraisal and the certified market analysis, this should alert you to the fact that a second appraisal may be necessary. *This will afford some protection to the mortgagee should the eventual sale price be questioned by any of the interested parties.*

- Instruct the appraiser not to factor the power of sale into the appraisal, to avoid an appraisal being below fair market value. *Canadian Imperial Bank of Commerce v. Income Trust Co.* (1990), 17 A.C.W.S. (3d) 222 (Ont. H.C.), varied (November 30, 1992), Doc. CA 663/89 (Ont. C.A.)

- The mortgagee does not have to accept any offer that is less than the amount of the mortgage debt. *Crown Trust Co. v. River Town Developments Ltd.* (1986), 1 A.C.W.S. (3d) 290 (Ont. H.C.)

- Note that a mortgagee may only purchase the property if the court approves it. *Annis v. Annis* (1984), 27 A.C.W.S. (2d) 293 (Ont. H.C.), affirmed (1986), 4 A.C.W.S. (3d)

287 (Ont. C.A.). *If the mortgagee wants to own the property, they should consider foreclosure proceedings instead of power of sale proceedings, which are discussed in Chapter 8.*

7.4.2 THE AGREEMENT OF PURCHASE AND SALE

- Because the mortgagee may have limited or restricted knowledge as to the condition of the property, certain warranties that usually appear in an agreement of purchase and sale should be avoided or modified. There should be an acknowledgment that the sale is being made by the mortgagee in accordance with the rights contained in the mortgage to exercise the power of sale. For an excellent and detailed discussion of these terms, which is summarized below, please consult Dunn and Gray, *Marriott & Dunn Practice in Mortgage Remedies in Ontario, Fifth Edition*, s.35.1 to 35.13

- There should be no agreement to discharge the claims of those with an interest in the mortgaged property that is subordinate to the mortgagee's claim, such as subsequent encumbrances or execution creditors.

- There should be a restricted agreement to discharge the claims of those with an interest in the mortgaged property that ranks in priority to the mortgagee's claim (prior encumbrancers), such as construction liens. *Scarbim Realty Ltd. v. Toronto* (1978), 90 D.L.R. (3d) 747 (Ont. H.C.)

- There should be no warranty that the property does not contain urea formaldehyde foam (UFFI) insulation, asbestos or polychlorinated biphenyls (PCBs). *Post v. Dundas* (1993), 30 R.P.R. (2d) 214 (Gen.Div.)

- Ensure that if the property is a new home that falls under the *Ontario New Home Warranties Plan Act*, the mortgagee registers properly under that plan as a vendor. *Ontario New Home Warranty Program v. Crown Trust Co.* (1984), 50 O.R. (2d) 588 (Co. Ct.), affirmed (1985), 50 O.R. (2d) 593 (C.A.)

- If the purchaser requires vacant possession and the property is vacant, there should be no problem.

- If the premises are occupied by the owner and family who refuse to leave the premises, it will be necessary to start an action for possession, obtain a judgment for possession and then obtain a writ of possession. (See 8.6 for further details). *If the owner and family still refuse to leave the premises, after obtaining the writ of possession, the sheriff can serve a Notice to Vacate and if they have still not left after the appointed time, the sheriff, with the assistance of a locksmith and possibly the police, will simply change the locks and hand over the keys to the mortgagee. If the sheriff is required to take this action, a representative of the mortgagee will have to attend at the premises to receive the keys and to take possession of the property.*

- If the premises are occupied by residential tenants, the mortgagee at any time after default and before taking steps to enforce the mortgage, can request particulars from the mortgagor or the tenant about the tenancy agreement and can require the mortgagor to provide a list of tenants for the property. *Mortgages Act,* s. 50

- Where tenants are currently living in the property, and the purchaser demands vacant possession, include a provision in the agreement that makes the sale conditional on the mortgagee being able to remove the tenants and obtain vacant possession.

- If the mortgage does not contain provisions for the assignment of tenants' leases to the mortgagee, ensure that the agreement states that the leases are not assignable. *Property & Bloodstock Ltd. v. Emerton* (1967), [1968] Ch. 94 (C.A.)

- Include a provision that the property is being sold "as is, where is."

- Where other property belonging to the mortgagor is located in or on the mortgaged property, and is not part of the mortgagee's security, the agreement must make clear that the property, or chattels, of the mortgagor are not included in the transaction. *If you can't get the mortgagor to remove the items prior to the closing of the transaction, it may be necessary for the mortgagee to remove and store the items and seek a further order of the court as to the disposition of this property.*

- The agreement of purchase and sale should indicate that the mortgagee is only selling whatever interest it has in the chattels and fixtures located on the property without any warranty as to title and that they are being sold on an "as is, where is" basis. The mortgagee should not be required to provide any bill of sale, warranty or any other title document for these items.

- Ensure that any property that could be considered a fixture (items that are normally sold with a property, such as standard light fixtures) is a true fixture, and not property of the mortgagor, before including it as a fixture in the agreement.

- Include a provision that the mortgagee selling under power of sale has taken all of the necessary steps required to be taken in exercise of the power of sale proceedings to the date of the agreement of purchase and sale.

- The agreement of purchase and sale should state that the mortgagee is making no representations, warranties or conditions as to the zoning, condition, legal use or fitness of the property.

- Include a provision that the mortgagee is allowing the mortgagor the right of redemption up to the date of the actual sale. *Such a clause will allow the mortgagee an "out" from an obligation under the agreement of purchase and sale if a mortgagor does redeem.*

- Include provisions that explain that this is a power of sale proceeding and therefore could be restrained either judicially or through the mortgagor's redemption. The provision should state that the mortgagee is not liable to the purchaser for damages or expenses as a result of the transaction not being completed.

- Exclude the normal provision that the purchaser can assume the mortgage or any subsequent encumbrance. *665456 Ontario Ltd. v. Barelan Management Inc.* (1990), 72 O.R. (2d) 705 (C.A.)

- Once the agreement of purchase and sale is signed, transfer the property as prescribed in the *Land Registration Reform Act*, the *Registry Act* or the *Land Titles Act*, depending on the applicable Act.

7.4.3 CLOSING THE SALE

- The letters of requisition will be forwarded by the purchaser's solicitors. A lot of requisitions are not valid in relationship to a power of sale. For example, the mortgage that is being used to sell under the power of sale cannot be discharged on or after closing, because it is the route from which the power of sale is being conducted. Since the property is sold on an "as is, where is" basis, there can be no requirement for representations or warranties.

- The only real requisitions can relate to the power of sale notice and the validity thereof. In the event that the power of sale notice is valid, the ability of the purchaser's solicitor to make requisitions is extremely narrow.

- In order to close the transaction, certain documents will be required.

- When the property is governed by the *Registry Act,* R.S.O. 1990, c.R.20, it will be necessary to include in the Transfer/Deed of Land various recitals, which will include the particulars of the mortgage, registration date and number, the date of default and the particulars of the power of sale notice issued, together with the notice period having expired and the default still continues.

- In addition to the Transfer/Deed of Land, the mortgagee will have to register a Document General pursuant to section 99 of the *Registry Act* that includes the following:

  - an affidavit of service of the power of sale notice by whoever served it. The affidavit of service must contain the method of service, a copy of the notice of sale, and the evidence of how it was served: e.g., the post office registration information if sent by registered mail;
  - a declaration by the mortgagee or person having authority to bind the corporation. This declaration will include the date of the default, that the default still continues, the amount due and owing under the mortgage, and that no monies have been paid; and
  - a solicitor's declaration that there has been compliance with the *Mortgages Act.* This declaration is made by the solicitor acting for the mortgagee and will include particulars of the searches made prior to issuing the notice of sale under mortgage and who was served with the notice and an acknowledgment that the proceedings comply with either Part II or Part III of the *Mortgages Act.*

- The aforesaid documents registered in the Document General will be conclusive evidence of compliance with Part II or Part III of the *Mortgages Act* (whichever is applicable) and is sufficient to provide good title to the purchaser. *Mortgages Act,* s.35

- When the property is governed by the *Land Titles Act,* R.S.O. 1990, c.L.5, the mortgagee must provide:

  - a Transfer/Deed of Land, which will contain a recital that the transferor is the registered owner of the charge and that the transfer is being made pursuant to either Part II or Part III of the *Mortgages Act*; and
  - a series of declarations, similar to the declarations made under the Registry System, R.R.O. 1990, Reg. 690, s.30 and Form 30.

- The declarations will be attached to the Transfer. LTA *s*.30(3)

- The Transfer/Deed of Land must be executed by either the mortgagee or, if the mortgagee is a corporation, by a person who has authority to bind the corporation.

Practice Tip: Check with your Registry Office/Land Titles Office to see if the documents need to be pre-approved prior to registration. Note that in some Registry Offices/Land Titles Offices, 48 hours is required for pre-approval of the documents. *There has been a recent change in various Registry/Land Titles Offices with respect to pre-approval. In certain cases, pre-approval is no longer required. Check with the appropriate Registry/Land Titles Office to see if your documents need to be pre-approved.*

- Land Transfer Tax is payable by a purchaser who is buying from a mortgagee. No Land Transfer Tax is payable by a mortgagee when they sell the property to the purchaser, because they are not the owners. The mortgagee only acquires a right to sell the mortgagor's interest free and clear from that mortgage.

- A statement of adjustments should be prepared similar to a statement of adjustments in ordinary residential real estate sales. The statement of adjustments will include information with respect to the deposit, particulars of any prior mortgages being assumed (after confirmation that they are assumable) and any adjustment for fuel oil, condominium fees and common element expenses, or any other items, if applicable.

- The mortgagee will not have to provide an undertaking to discharge the mortgage under which the power of sale proceedings are taking place. That mortgage will remain on title because it is the root of title under which the mortgagee is selling.

- The mortgagee will have to provide an undertaking to discharge any previous encumbrances that are not being assumed by the purchaser. *If the previous encumbrancer is not a financial institution, in accordance with the Law Society requirements, a validly executed discharge of mortgage must be tendered on closing in exchange for the mortgage proceeds and immediately registered on title. If the prior mortgagee is an institutional lender, the mortgagee can provide an undertaking to discharge the mortgage within a reasonable time after closing. In reality, an institutional lender will rarely provide an executed discharge on the actual closing date.*

- In order to comply with the *Income Tax Act,* the mortgagee may be required to provide a statutory declaration that it is not a non-resident of Canada within the meaning of section 116 of the *Income Tax Act,* or, in the alternative, provide a clearance certificate from the Canada Customs and Revenue Agency

- Include a provision that excludes the covenants normally required by the *Land Registration Reform Act* as to encumbrances and claims. *Land Registration Reform Act,* s.5(1)3,5(4) *The covenants that will be included are that the mortgagee:*

  - has done no act to encumber the property;
  - will provide further assurances; and
  - will release all existing claims.

Practice Tip: The closing of the transaction may be a bit out of the ordinary. If the solicitor handling the file is sending the closing to a clerk, ensure that there is a solicitor in the office who can deal with any problems that might arise on closing. This will ensure a smooth closing and will reduce stress levels for all concerned.

7.5 AFTER THE SALE

7.5.1 ACCOUNTING FOR THE SALE AND DISTRIBUTION OF THE SURPLUS

- The sale proceeds do not belong solely to the mortgagee. Instead, they must be paid out in the following general priority:

  - the expenses incident to the sale or incurred in any attempted sale;
  - payment of all interest and costs due with respect to the mortgage;
  - payment of the principal money due under the mortgage;
  - payment of the amounts due to subsequent encumbrancers according to their priorities;
  - payment to any tenants of the mortgagor of security deposits under the Tenant Protection Act where the security deposit was not applied in payment of the last month's rent; and
  - the mortgagor.

  Mortgages Act, s.27 and *Mortgages Amendment Act,* 1991, c.6, s.1

> **Practice Tip:** In most cases there will not be any surplus. Accounting for the surplus will only be required when there is one.

- Prior to disbursing any funds from the surplus, the mortgagee (or their solicitor) must prepare a full accounting of the proceeds. The accounting is basically a summary of the funds received from the sale, the expenses that have been paid or must be paid as a result of the sale process, and the claims against the proceeds.

> **Practice Tip:** While there is no legal obligation to send a report to the mortgagor and to the subsequent encumbrancers, they do have the right to ask for the report. To avoid potential litigation, prepare and forward the report as a matter of course, rather than waiting for a request. Remember that under the provisions of the *Bankruptcy and Insolvency Act* section 244 notice, you are required as a receiver to prepare and serve the necessary reports as set out therein.

- The mortgagor has the right to require an accounting from the mortgagee. If the mortgagor's right to redeem still exists, an offer to redeem must be made in order to request the accounting; if the right to redeem has expired, such an offer is not required. *Northern Heights (Sault) Ltd. v. Belgrand Investment Ltd.*, [1968] 2 O.R. 266 (H.C.); *Equitas Investment Corp. v. Goodman* (1987), 57 O.R. (2d) 795 (H.C.) at 798

- Calculate interest to the date that the sale actually took place. *West v. Diprose* [1900] 1 Ch. 337 at 340. *That is the date up to which the mortgagee is entitled to interest.*

- Where the mortgagee has taken a mortgage back as part of the transaction, it will be obliged to treat the whole of the mortgage back as if it were cash, and credit the mortgage account with the amount of the mortgage back. *Beatty v. O'Connor,* (1884), 5 O.R. 731 (H.C.). An exception to this is when the mortgage specifically provides that the mortgagee is only accountable for monies actually received in payment of the mortgage. *Sauder v. Gnanapandithen* (1995), 25 O.R. (3d) 379 (Gen. Div.)

- In conducting the accounting, subsearch title to the property (to ensure that any new claims against the property will be included in the distribution plan), make any financial transactions necessary to complete the mortgagee's responsibilities, and determine what expenses and claims are due against the property.

- An execution creditor who files a writ of seizure and sale after the closing of the sale by the mortgagee does not have a right to share in any of the surplus, because only the property in which the mortgagor (the judgment debtor) had a beneficial interest is subject to the seizure. *La Rose v. White Packing Co.*, [1937] O.R. 470 (S.C.C.). *In such a case, the execution creditor can issue a notice of garnishment, and garnishee the mortgagee to the extent of any surplus that will be payable by it to the mortgagor, and to the extent of the amount claimed in the writ of seizure and sale. If the mortgagor has already received the funds, consider issuing a notice of garnishment to the mortgagor's bank account (or if the money was paid to the mortgagor's solicitor, a garnishment to the mortgagor's solicitor).*

- For legal costs, allowable costs have included the mortgagee's travel and accommodation costs necessary for sale negotiations, professional management fees where the property management was troublesome; real estate commissions in accordance with the mortgage and costs of a motions and service. Dunn and Gray, *Marriott and Dunn Practice in Mortgage Remedies in Ontario, Fifth Edition*, s.39.5

- The time allowed for the accounting depends on the complexity of the property and the situation; however, ensure that it is conducted as quickly as is reasonable. *It should take between 30 and 60 days to provide an accounting to the mortgagor and the subsequent mortgagees.*

- Any surplus proceedings should be placed immediately after closing in an interest-bearing trust account, and the surplus when paid should also include the interest accrued in the interest-bearing trust account.

- The mortgagee will have incurred costs in connection with the maintenance of the property. These are to be paid out in the priority as set out above. These costs include realty taxes (*Traders Realty Ltd. v. Huron Heights Shopping Plaza Ltd.*, [1967] 2 O.R. 522 (Master)); repairs to the premises (*Federal Life Assurance Co. v. Siddall* (1910), 1 O.W.N. 796; and insurance premiums (*Traders Realty Ltd. v. Huron Heights Shopping Plaza Ltd.*, [1967] 2 O.R. 522 (Master)). *Ensure that the mortgagee only maintains the property, and does not carry out any capital improvements. If there are out of the ordinary repairs that must be done, get a written expert report that this work is required maintenance. This will counter what could become a potential defence from a mortgagor.*

- Because a situation where a power of sale has been required often involves a mortgagor who has significant other creditors, the distribution of proceeds often does not fully meet the claims of those creditors, and can be challenged by them in an attempt at full restitution. *To protect yourself against subsequent challenges, ensure that you have effectively searched and subsearched the property to find all of the claimants who could be involved. Then, ensure that you have documentation that shows the claims are valid and the amount fairly arrived at. If the documentation is not sufficient, request a statutory declaration from the claimant as to the nature of the claim and its amount.*

- Report on the sale to all claimants, with documentation, clearly showing:

    - sale details, including how the listing price was arrived at (appraisals), method of sale, sale price (agreement of purchase and sale), and the mortgagee's account (mortgage statement), legal costs and costs of sale (with copies of bills);
    - the surplus amount;
    - the proposed distribution scheme by priority;
    - any action required by the claimant to obtain a share;
    - a copy of a final release and indemnity to be signed by the claimant (the claimant is not required to sign these documents, but they should be included as potential protection for the mortgagee in the case of future challenges to the distribution).

Dunn and Gray, *Marriott and Dunn Practice in Mortgage Remedies in Ontario, Fifth Edition*, s.37.10 and 37.12

- If you cannot reasonably determine the priority of claimants, you should apply to the court for an order for payment into court, allowing you to deposit the surplus funds into court. *Samuel Keller (Holdings) v. Martin's Bank Ltd.*, [1970] 3 All E.R. 950 (C.A.). *This will provide protection to the mortgagee from either the mortgagor or any subsequent encumbrancers who have competing claims to the funds.*

- The claimants whose priority or claim is not clear will likely launch court action to have the priority or claim determined. Once the court action is complete, you should then be able to distribute the surplus in accordance with the court order.

7.5.2 DEALING WITH A DEFICIENCY

- Once the property has been sold under a power of sale, the mortgagee has exhausted its rights under the mortgage. *Brigden v. Bank of Montreal* (1982), 49 O.R. (2d) 502 (Co. Ct.)

- However, if the sale does not provide sufficient proceeds to pay the mortgage debt, the mortgagee can bring an action against the mortgagor for the deficiency. *Pegg v. Hobson* (1887), 14 O.R. 272 (Ch.)

- Such an action will be reduced by any amount the court finds was improperly charged against the mortgagee's accounting, or for which the mortgagee is found liable as a result of mismanagement or negligence. *Beber (Trustee of) v. Romko Investments Ltd.* (1992), 32 A.C.W.S. (3d) 1171 (Ont. Gen. Div.), affirmed (January 22, 1997), Doc. CA C12166 (Ont. C.A.)

7.6 ACTION FOR PAYMENT ON THE COVENANT AND POSSESSION

7.6.1 ACTION FOR PAYMENT ON THE COVENANT

- The mortgagee's right to sue arises once there is a default in payment on the covenant contained in the mortgage.

- The mortgagee can choose when to start the action. The choices are:

  - after default in payment and prior to commencing any power of sale proceedings. *Price v. Letros* (1973), 2 O.R. (2d) 292 (C.A.); or
  - after expiry of the power of sale notice and before sale of the property;
  - after default and after the sale is completed, assuming there is a deficiency. *Gordon Grant & Co. v. Boos*, [1926] A.C. 781 (West Indies P.C.)

- If the mortgagee decides to sue prior to commencing power of sale proceedings, they should also claim for possession of the premises. This will ensure that once a judgment is obtained for payment, at the same time, the mortgagee can obtain possession as well.

Practice Tip: If the mortgagee starts the action prior to power of sale proceedings, it can be for the arrears due under the mortgage, but a much better practice is to sue for the arrears due and the accelerated balance together with any costs incurred to date.

- The action will be started by way of statement of claim. *In Ontario, where cases are managed under case management, consider proceeding on a fast track as opposed to the standard track so that the matter will proceed relatively quickly.*

- The mortgagee has the choice of either:

  - suing the original mortgagor on the covenant. *Pegg v. Hobson* (1887), 14 O.R. 272 (Ch.); or
  - suing the present owner of the property (owner of the equity of redemption). Mortgages Act, s.20(1)

- The mortgagee cannot sue both the original owner and the present owner of the property, and must choose which one to proceed against. *Mortgages Act,* s.20(3). *If there is more than one original mortgagor, the mortgagee does have the right to sue all of the original mortgagors.*

- If the mortgagee does bring an action against both the original mortgagor and the current owner, the last judgment signed will be set aside as a nullity. *Moscarelli v. Vosgerichian* (1981), 32 O.R. (2d) 532 (H.C.). *Ensure that you obtain instructions from the mortgagee as to whom you should proceed against. That decision will have to be based on a number of factors, including the ability to locate the parties, the anticipated ability of the parties to pay and the ease with which the judgment can be realized upon. In the event that power of sale proceedings are commenced and completed and you are then trying to collect on the deficiency, failure to serve the power of sale notice on the party you are suing may prove to be a fatal defect to the action on the covenant and judgment may be refused. Bareysyd Enterprises Ltd. v. Cszimadia,* [1981] O.J. No. 2257, 23 R.P.R. 60 (Co. Ct.). *This will also be the case if you are attempting to sue a guarantor and have failed to serve the power of sale notice on the guarantor. If the current owner of the property has signed an assumption agreement whereby the original owner of the property is relieved of liability on the mortgage, the mortgagor will not be able to successfully sue the original owner of the property. G & B Properties (Morrisberg) Ltd. v. Hopkins* (1981), 8 A.C.W.S. (2d) 48 (H.C.)

- If an action is commenced on the covenant prior to issuing the power of sale notice and a defence is entered, wait until the power of sale notice time has expired, and then proceed to obtain judgment on the covenant. *It is not necessary to wait for the sale to be completed prior to obtaining the judgment. Doing it in this way will ensure that there is no further delay that would incur further costs.*

- In the event that judgment is obtained on the covenant, once the property is sold and an accounting is made, the mortgagee will have to reduce the amount of the judgment obtained by the amount of any monies paid on the mortgage account. *Rules of Civil Procedure,* Rule 60.16(1). *A letter to the Sheriff where the writ of seizure and sale is filed indicating the amount that the judgment should be reduced by is satisfactory. The decision as to when to sue on the covenant, either before or after power of sale proceedings are commenced, will depend on various factors, which include the following:*
  - Is there sufficient equity in the property to cover payment of the mortgage debt?
  - Is the mortgagor financially viable or is the mortgagor running into financial difficulty?
  - Will more cooperation be obtained by the mortgagor if an action on the covenant is not commenced?
  - Are there any potential defences to an action on the covenant?

- The aforesaid factors will assist in determining how the mortgagee best wishes to proceed.

- In the event that an action is brought on the covenant after sale, defences may be raised that include a claim for improvident sale, failure to take reasonable steps in the way the property was sold, fraud or that the mortgagee was not acting in good faith.

7.6.2 ACTION FOR POSSESSION

- The mortgagee must decide whether it wishes to obtain possession of the mortgaged property.

- If the property is vacant or abandoned, the mortgagee should consider using a self-help remedy, entering into possession of the property, changing the locks and starting to manage the property. In doing so, the mortgagee will have to ensure that there is insurance in place, the property is inspected on a regular basis and that it is heated and repaired. If the property is a multi-tenant building, the mortgagee may wish to obtain the services of a property management company to ensure the smooth operation and management of the property. *Tenants who know that the property is under power of sale sometimes take great liberties with the property and cause considerable damage, and also fail to pay rent as it becomes due.*

- Either the mortgage document or the standard charge terms that govern the mortgage set out the express provisions that deal with the question of the mortgagee obtaining possession once there is default. The usual provision is that upon default, the mortgagee is entitled to quiet possession of the property.

- The spouse of the mortgagor has the same right of possession as does a mortgagor, provided that it is the matrimonial home. *Family Law Act,* s.19(1)

- The essential requirement in order to obtain possession is that there must be an act of default by the mortgagor. Acts of default include the following:

  - failure to make payments. Land Registration Reform Act, s.7(1)1 i, v;
  - failure to insure the property. Land Registration Reform Act, s.7(1) 1(iv); and
  - non-payment of condominium fees. Condominium Act, R.S.O. 1990, c.C.26, s.33(3)(b).

- In the event of a default, the mortgagee is not required to take possession of the property. *Schantz v. Hallman,* [1928] S.C.R. 213.

- The statement of claim in an action for possession must set out the terms for payment and that a mortgagee has the right of possession as set out in the mortgage.

- The defendants to a mortgage action for possession may include the following:

  - all mortgagors if there is more than one, Kinross Mortgage Corp. v. Balfour (1981), 33 O.R. (2d) 213 (H.C.);
  - spouse of the mortgagor, Family Law Act, s.19(1); and
  - tenants in actual possession of the mortgaged property whose interest is subsequent to that of the mortgagee, Rule 60.10(2). *In certain circumstances, you may not want to obtain vacant possession from the tenant, instead preferring to keep that tenant in possession. In such a case, especially if their tenancy brings increased value to the property, do not serve them with the notice of sale under mortgage, as this will allow them a chance to get out of the tenancy.*

- Once the statement of claim for possession has issued and the time period has expired for filing a statement of defence, the defendants should be noted in default and judgment for possession or for possession and payment can be signed. Rules of Civil Procedure, 19.04(1)(a) and (b).

- If a defence has been filed and the defence does not appear to have merit or is frivolous, a motion can be made pursuant to the Rules of Civil Procedure, Rule 20, for summary judgment. A motion for summary judgment will succeed where the defendant cannot produce an organized set of facts with evidence to show that there is a genuine triable issue based on admissible evidence. *Pizza Pizza Ltd. v. Gillespie* (1990), 75 O.R. (2d) 225 (Gen. Div.)

- In the event that the mortgagee obtains a judgment for possession, that judgment for possession must be served on all persons who are in actual possession of the property in question. *Central Guaranty Trust Co. v. McRae* (1993), 13 O.R. (3d) 295 (Gen. Div.). *In the event that certain persons in possession do not receive written notice of the judgment, a writ of possession should not be granted by the court. Therefore, it would be prudent to have a representative of the mortgagee attend at the premises to make the proper inquiries to see who is in possession of the premises and under what circumstances they are in possession. That information should then be included in the affidavit evidence before the court.*

- After obtaining the judgment for possession, the mortgagee must apply for a writ of possession. If the judgment for possession was obtained by default, the writ of possession is made on a without notice basis for an order granting the mortgagee leave to issue a writ of possession. *If the action for possession was defended, the motion for the writ of possession must be made on all parties who filed a Notice to Defend. Rules of Civil Procedure, Rule 60.01(1). The motion can be made to either a Master or a Judge.*

- In order to succeed on the motion, the court must be satisfied that all persons in actual possession of the property have received sufficient notice of the proceedings when the judgment for possession was obtained. Rules of Civil Procedure, 60.10(2). When bringing the motion to issue the writ of possession, the mortgagee must include in the affidavit material a clear statement as to whether the mortgaged property is a residential rental property.

- The court does have discretion to impose a stay of proceedings before the issuance of the writ of possession if the court is satisfied that the mortgagor's difficulties can be overcome. *Farm Credit Corp. v. Bale* (1994), 49 A.C.W.S. (3d) 1156 (Ont. Gen. Div.).

- Once a writ of possession is issued, it will be served by the sheriff on all of the necessary parties, together with a Sheriff's Notice to Vacate. The Notice to Vacate will provide a certain date and time within which the people on the premises must vacate the property.

- A defendant can apply to set aside the writ of possession; however it will not be set aside where the sheriff has taken possession of the premises pursuant to the writ of possession. *Beedell v. Pritchard* (1991), 29 A.C.W.S. (3d) 996 (Ont. Gen. Div.)

- A writ of possession will remain in force for a period of one year from the date of the order. The writ can subsequently be renewed before the expiry of the one-year period by further order of the court. Rules of Civil Procedure, 60.10(3)

8

FORECLOSURE PROCEEDINGS

Table of Contents

8.1 A STRATEGIC CHOICE

- A foreclosure action allows the mortgagee to obtain title to the mortgaged property (as opposed to a power of sale action, under which the property is sold and proceeds distributed to the mortgagee and other creditors without the mortgagee ever obtaining title to the property).

- If the foreclosure is successful, the interests of subsequent encumbrancers on the mortgage are also foreclosed upon.

- If the mortgagee wants to own the property, consider foreclosure proceedings instead of power of sale proceedings. Situations where the mortgagee would gain an advantage in owning the property include those where the real estate market is not good, or where the property requires significant repairs or improvements in order to attract buyers. In both cases, power of sale proceedings - where the property is sold immediately at fair market value - would likely result in a shortfall in proceeds. The mortgagee would therefore realize a better result by foreclosing, and waiting to sell until the market rebounds or the repairs have been carried out (assuming that the expenses associated with maintaining or repairing the property would not outstrip any increase in the property's value).

- Prior to proceeding with foreclosure proceedings, the mortgagee who wants title to the property could request that the mortgagor sign a quit claim deed. This would allow the mortgagee to obtain title to the property without having to incur the time and legal expense that a foreclosure action would require. In some cases, a debtor who knows that they are in financial difficulty and cannot continue mortgage payments will sign a quit claim deed rather than face being foreclosed upon. *The quit claim deed will only work where there are no subsequent encumbrancers or if the mortgagee is prepared to assume the subsequent encumbrances. Be careful to ensure that you get a written acknowledgment from the mortgagee should they choose to take this route, so that in the event that the picture in relationship to the subsequent encumbrancers changes, you have something on file that indicates that you advised them of the pitfalls of proceeding in this way.*

- A foreclosure does have certain advantages over a power of sale:

  - the court supervises the proceedings, which takes some responsibilities off the mortgagee's shoulders for conducting the sale process (which is open to scrutiny and challenge by the mortgagor in a power of sale) and for accounting for any surplus accruing from a sale;

- any surplus realized on a sale of the property after a final order of foreclosure belongs solely to the mortgagee - not to any subsequent encumbrancers;
- court-supervised references provided for in the Rules of Civil Procedure allow the parties quick access to a neutral forum for resolving disputes that may arise during the foreclosure process; and
- mortgagees may combine the foreclosure action with claims for possession and for recovery of the mortgage debt.

• On the flip side of the coin, disadvantages of foreclosure include:

- timelines are lengthier in foreclosure actions than in power of sale actions;
- no action against another party may be taken if a sale of the property after a final order of foreclosure results in a deficiency (although if a defendant to a foreclosure action requests a judicial sale that subsequently results in a deficiency, the mortgagee does have the right to pursue the defendant for the amount of the deficiency) ;
- court supervision of the foreclosure means that attending court for motions or hearings may be necessary, thus increasing legal expenses (although these expenses can be added to the statement of claim and thus the mortgage debt);
- court supervision also allows the mortgagor to bring motions that could delay the action;
- personal service of the statement of claim is necessary;
- the mortgagee is responsible for paying the land transfer tax;
- the mortgagee cannot abandon a defended foreclosure action without seeking the court's leave; and
- the mortgagee cannot abandon a foreclosure action and then commence a power of sale action without seeking the court's leave.

Practice Tip: The common thought is that a foreclosure allows the mortgagee to take the property in satisfaction of the mortgage debt. Although this is true, a claim on the covenant to pay contained in the mortgage can also be joined with the claim for foreclosure. Usually, the judgment for foreclosure will grant judgment on the covenant, for foreclosure and possession. Notwithstanding the registration of a judgment for foreclosure, the mortgagee is still entitled to enforce the monetary judgment as long as they remain in a position to return the mortgaged property. Accordingly, if the mortgagee attempts to enforce collection of the judgment, the defendant's right to redeem is revived. If the mortgagee has disposed of the property, they will no longer be entitled to enforce the monetary judgment.

8.2 PREPARATION

- Discuss the situation with the mortgagee to verify what, if any, action or correspondence has been undertaken to date with respect to the mortgagor and any claims that may have been made against the property to date. At this point, you should try to obtain a current address for the mortgagor, since personal service of the statement of claim will be required. This will not, of course, always be the same address as the property itself. It is also good practice to determine at this time whether or not there is a spouse involved, either of the mortgagor or of a guarantor, as service of the statement of claim should be made on spouses who have potential claims on the property under the *Family Law Act*.

Practice Tip: Review the security documents under which you are going to foreclose to ensure that they are properly drafted, executed and registered.

- To determine what acts would constitute "default" under a foreclosure proceeding, check the language of the mortgage document to ascertain which defaults allow the mortgagee to accelerate the payment of principal and/or to foreclose. Principal and interest due under the mortgage are, of course, most common; however, most mortgage documents include a right to foreclose in case the mortgagor fails to pay other amounts, such as taxes, insurance and condominium common expenses, or fails to keep up maintenance on the property to a reasonable standard. In other cases, mortgage documents can exclude certain defaults from giving the right to foreclose.

Practice Tip: If the default is other than a monetary fault, a letter of demand should be made to the mortgagor indicating that there has been a default under the mortgage and that the mortgagee is accelerating its debt. At the same time, if applicable, include a *Bankruptcy and Insolvency Act* section 244 notice. See Chapter 7.1.3.

- Default on failure to pay monetary amounts is relatively straightforward: either the payments have been received by the required date and time, or they haven't. *Note that this is in contrast to a matured mortgage, where the monetary amounts for the full amount of the mortgage have to be paid.*

- Default on other grounds, such as failure to maintain the property, can be open to interpretation, however. If you plan on pursuing a foreclosure based on failure to make repairs, for example, be prepared to prove that the failure is significant and substantial, that it has continued for some time, and/or that it is decreasing the value of the property. *A report from an accredited appraiser will be helpful, together with any outstanding work orders and written complaints from tenants or other occupants of the premises.*

- In certain cases, the mortgagee may wish to pay amounts that should be paid by the mortgagor. These include taxes, to prevent a municipality from being entitled to seize the property for unpaid taxes; insurance premiums, to protect the property from loss or damage; and repair costs to maintain the property's safety and value (non-monetary default). Payment of these amounts gives the mortgagee the right to foreclose; however, it is important to notify the mortgagor that the mortgagee has paid the amounts, and to give the mortgagor the opportunity to repay the amounts by a certain date. If the amounts are not thus repaid, the mortgagee then has the right to foreclose. *Boyer v. Fox* (1980), 29 O.R. (2d) 330 (H.C.); *Royal Trust Corp. of Canada v. Filoso* (1994), 5 W.D.C.P. (2d) 433 (Ont. Gen. Div.)

- If you suspect that you have grounds for default, you may also wish to bolster your case by checking with the mortgagor's insurance company to verify whether the insurance policy is still current. *Assuming that your client has been noted as the mortgagee on the insurance policy, check with the insurance company to see if there is a history of late payments or if the insurance policy is in default and is about to be cancelled. If the insurance policy is about to be cancelled, the mortgagee can pay the outstanding premiums and then has evidence to show that there has been default and can start the foreclosure proceedings.*

- When the mortgage is in default, prior to issuing a statement of claim, it is usual for the mortgagee, through its solicitor, to send a demand letter, and, if applicable, a *Bankruptcy and Insolvency Act* notice ("BIA section 244 notice") to the mortgagor and guarantor, to notify them of the default and to require that they cure the default within a specific period of time. The usual default is in the payment of principal and/or interest. *Out of an abundance of caution, you may wish to provide the letter of demand and the BIA section 244 notice to the spouse of the mortgagor, if any, to defuse any potential problems in the future.*

- If you are dealing with the property of a farmer, ensure that you are in compliance with the *Farm Debt Mediation Act*. For a more detailed treatment of this statute, see chapter 7.1.2.

- Subsearch the title of the property. This will allow you to ensure that the mortgagor is still registered as the property's owner, and may assist you with finding the mortgagor's current address and a spouse with a potential claim. It will also reveal any encumbrances that have been registered subsequent to the mortgage.

- Search executions filed with the sheriff against the property's registered owner. This will reveal any executions registered subsequent to the mortgage.

- If the mortgagee holds several mortgages on the defendant's property or properties and wishes to consolidate them, or where the mortgagee is claiming priority over a prior encumbrancer, note that you will need to bring a motion for judgment in the matter, with a separate statement of claim. Motions and summary judgments are covered in detail in chapter 3.

8.3 INITIATING FORECLOSURE PROCEEDINGS

8.3.1 THE STATEMENT OF CLAIM

- The statement of claim in a foreclosure action is Form 14B. Rule 64.03(4). *For a detailed description of how to complete and serve the statement of claim, see chapter 3.2.1.*

- In addition to claiming for foreclosure, you may also claim for payment of the mortgage debt by any party personally liable for it, and for possession of the mortgaged property. Rule 64.03(5)

Note that the right to possession has been held as a prima facie right of the mortgagee, available when there is a breach of any covenant in the mortgage. *Prudential Assurance Co. (Trustee of) v. 90 Eglinton Ltd. Partnership* (1994), 18 O.R. (2d) 201 (Gen. Div. [Commercial List]) at 207

Practice Tip: In order to save time and expense, the mortgagee should consider combining the claim for foreclosure, the claim for payment on the mortgage debt and for possession of the mortgaged property into one action; however, this is not required by the regulations. *Hay v. McArthur* (1880), 8 P.R. 321; *Holt v. Chaplin* (1982), 14 A.C.W.S. (2d) 418, Rule 64.03(5)

- You must name all persons interested in the equity of redemption (including subsequent encumbrancers) as defendants in the statement of claim. Rule 64.03(1). This may include construction lien claimants, those who have registered a certificate of pending litigation against the property, and spouses of the owners who are not registered on title to the property.

Practice Tip: If you believe that the property's registered owner has a spouse, include the spouse of the current owner as a party on the statement of claim. *Family Law Act*, s.22(1)

- Note that a "subsequent encumbrancer" is a person who has a lien, charge or encumbrance on the mortgaged property subsequent to the mortgage in question in the action. Rule 64.01. *This includes those who hold mortgages on the property that were registered after the mortgage you are dealing with, and those who have filed writs of seizure and sale on the property.*

- Tenants are not considered parties interested in the equity of redemption, so they do not have to be named on the statement of claim. Their interest is not foreclosed upon, but rather terminated on foreclosure. *Mortgages Act*, Part V

- Where there are numerous subsequent encumbrancers, and it is not expedient to name them in the statement of claim, you may commence the foreclosure action without naming them as defendants. You would then make a motion without notice on a reference after judgment to add them as defendants. Rule 64.03(2). *From a practical perspective, you should include all parties as defendants in the statement of claim, if possible.*

- Serve the statement of claim on the parties named. Personal service is required, unless you can establish to the court that a party or parties are not available and that substitutional service is justified. Rule 16 and 17

- Note that on a reference, where the referee considers that subsequent encumbrancers should have been named as defendants in the statement of claim, the referee may refuse to allow the additional costs of adding them on the reference. Rule 64.03(3). *If the only reason for holding a reference is to add subsequent encumbrancers, the referee may decide that the extra time and expense incurred for the reference is to be at the expense of the plaintiff.*

- If the mortgagee wishes to stop foreclosure proceedings and proceed with a power of sale, after the statement of claim has been issued, they must apply to the court for leave to do so. To obtain the court's leave, the mortgagee must establish that there is virtually no chance that any of the defendants in the foreclosure action would be able to derive any benefit from a foreclosure, judgment *nisi*, the test being on a balance of convenience. *Roebuck v. Syndicated Shopping Centres Inc.* (1985), 52 O.R. (2d) 265 (H.C.); *Petranik v. Dale* (1976), [1977] 2 S.C.R. 959

- Stays of proceedings can be ordered in mortgage actions, but follow the usual requirements to be ordered sparingly, and only when required to deal with an action that is vexatious or frivolous, or that abuses the process of the court. *Elipro Holdings Inc. v. Shenkman* (1975), 8 O.R. (2d) 433 (C.A.)

8.3.2 DEALING WITH BANKRUPTCY OR INSOLVENCY

- Foreclosure proceedings may be curtailed under the *Bankruptcy and Insolvency Act* automatic stay of proceedings ("the stay") that ensues when a mortgagor has filed a notice of intention to make a proposal or the proposal itself, or becomes bankrupt. In the case of a notice of intention to make a proposal or a proposal, the stay remains in force until the mortgagor completes the proposal or becomes bankrupt. BIA s.69(1), 69.1(1), 69.2(1) and 69.3(1) *This applies irrespective of whether the proposal is a Division I - Commercial Proposal or a Division II - Consumer Proposal.*

- If a mortgagor has filed a notice of intention to make a proposal or has filed for bankruptcy, the mortgagee can continue to enforce the terms of the mortgage and the collateral security in accordance with the provisions of the BIA. BIA, s.69(2), 69.1(2), 69.2(4) and 69.3(2) The stay does not apply:

  - to prevent a secured creditor who took possession of the secured assets of the insolvent person for the purpose of realizing before the notice of intention to make a proposal under section 50.4 was filed, from dealing with those assets;
  - to prevent a secured creditor who gave notice of intention under section 244(1) to enforce that creditor's security against the insolvent person more than 10 days before the notice of intention to make a proposal under section 50.4 was filed, from enforcing that security, unless the secured creditor consented to the stay; or
  - to prevent a secured creditor who gave notice of intention under section 244 to enforce the creditor's security, from enforcing the security if the insolvent person has, under section 244(2) consented to the enforcement action. BIA s.69(2)

- If none of the aforesaid conditions are applicable and the mortgagor has filed a notice of intention to make a proposal, the mortgagee may not take enforcement proceedings under the mortgage until the proposal has been made. BIA s.50.4(1), 69(1)(a) and (b)

- If the debtor's proposal does not include the mortgagee, the stay does not apply. BIA s.69.1(5)

- If the proposal was not accepted by the secured creditors in the mortgagee's class of creditors, the stay does not apply. BIA s. 69.1(6)

- The mortgagee may also apply to the court for a declaration that the stay does not apply to them, thus allowing them to proceed with the foreclosure. To show that the stay should not apply, the mortgagee must be able to prove that the stay materially prejudices them, or that it is equitable on other grounds for the stay to be lifted. BIA s.69.4; *Cumberland Trading Inc., Re* (1994), 23 C.B.R. (3d) 225 (Ont. Gen. Div. [Commercial List])

- If the debtor becomes bankrupt because it has filed an assignment for the general benefit of creditors, or did not file the proposal within the appropriate period of time, or the proposal is defeated by the creditors or is not ratified by the court, the mortgagee can proceed and will not have to lift the stay of proceedings. BIA s.69.3(2) *In these cases, there is no requirement to lift the stay of proceedings in order to start the foreclosure process. If you wish to obtain possession of the property, however, you will have to consider obtaining an order lifting the stay of proceedings to continue as against the bankrupt mortgagor. At this point, you should also obtain an order under Rule 11.02 of the Rules of Civil Procedure to add the trustee as a party to the action.*

- If the mortgagor is insolvent, you must serve on them a BIA section 244(1) notice of intention to enforce security. This notice must be served prior to the issuance of the statement of claim as required by the *Bankruptcy and Insolvency Act*. BIA s. 244(1). The notice only needs to be served where the mortgagee intends to enforce security on all or substantially all of the inventory, accounts receivable or other property of the insolvent person that was acquired for or is used in connection to a business carried on by that insolvent person.

8.3.3 DEALING WITH DEFENCES

- There are three possible responses by a defendant to a statement of claim for foreclosure:
  - defend the action on its merits;
  - obtain time to redeem; or
  - convert the proceeding to a judicial sale.
- If the defendant is defending the action on the merits, they must deliver a statement of defence within 20 days after the service of statement of claim if served in Ontario, 40 days if served in Canada or the U.S., and 60 days if served elsewhere. Rule 18.01

- You may be required to deal with a defence that challenges the validity or provisions of the mortgage. Such defences must be raised in a pleading (i.e., a statement of defence), rather than at the reference, because the master or registrar would not have jurisdiction at the reference to decide such questions. *Bickford v. Grand Junction Railway* (1878), 1 S.C.R. 696 at 726; *Dacres v. 354008 Ontario Ltd.* (1987), 4 A.C.W.S. (3d) 161 (Ont. H.C.)

- The principles of both legal and equitable set-off applies: if the mortgagee owes the defendant a sum of money, this may be applied against the amount owed by the defendant with respect to the mortgage, thus reducing the amount required to redeem the mortgage. *Hanak v. Green,* [1958] All E.R. 141 (C.A.); *Coba Industries Ltd. v. Millie's Holdings (Canada) Ltd.* (1985), 65 B.C.L.R. 31 (C.A.). A defendant can, therefore, raise set-off as a defence. *Courts of Justice Act*, s.111. *Equitable set off cannot be pleaded as a defence. It can only be pleaded as a counterclaim. 459017 Ontario Ltd. v. Braithwaite* (April 12, 2000), Doc. 99-CV-167793, [2000] O.J. No. 1300 (S.C.J.)

- A motion for summary judgment for foreclosure was dismissed where the plaintiffs were not entitled to proceed without permitting set-off: the defendants' claims for fraudulent misrepresentation, breach of warranty and breach of non-competition contract were part of the same contract that required the defendants to execute the mortgage that the plaintiffs were attempting to foreclose. *Johnson v. Boyle* (1994), 48 A.C.W.S. (3d) 50 (Ont. Gen. Div.)

- A defendant who disagrees with the amount of the mortgagee's claim has the option to use it as a basis for a statement of defence (particularly if the discrepancy is substantial enough that it threatens the mortgagee's ability to obtain judgment). If the defendant wishes to redeem the mortgage, however, any disagreement over the amount of the claim can be handled by a motion for summary judgment. Rule 20.01, 20.03.

- As set out in Dunn & Gray's *Marriott & Dunn Practice in Mortgage Remedies in Ontario, Fifth Edition,* chapter 6.4, defences and counterclaims that have been successful include:

  - fraud in the original mortgage transaction. *Soloman v. Ming Sun Holdings Inc.* (1993), 41 A.C.W.S. (3d) 737 (Ont. Gen. Div.);
  - lack of default. *Morguard Trust Co. v. Moore* (1981), 6 A.C.W.S. (2d) 328 (Ont. Master);
  - failure to give statutory notices;
  - unconscionable transactions based on the debtor's incapacity or position. *Morrison v. Coast Finance Ltd.* (1965), 55 D.L.R. (2d) 710 (B.C. C.A.);
  - undue influence. *Russell v. S.W. Mifflin Ltd.* (1991), 89 Nfld. & P.E.I.R. 168 (Nfld. T.D.);
  - unequal bargaining position. *Premier Trust Co. v. Beaton* (1990), 14 R.P.R. (2d) 280 (Ont. Gen. Div.); additional reasons at (January 8, 1991), Doc. Toronto 33485/88 (Ont. Gen. Div.);
  - *non est factum. Duca Community Credit Union Ltd. v. Fulco Automotive Ltd.* (1993), 39 A.C.W.S. (3d) 187 (Ont. Master);
  - an issued and unexpired notice of sale. *Mortgages Act,* s. 42;

- lack of independent legal advice. *Premier Trust Co. v. Beaton* (1990), 14 R.P.R. 280 (Ont. Gen. Div.) at 298;
- novation. *National Trust Co. v. Mead* (1990), 71 D.L.R. (4th) 488 (S.C.C.);
- lack of consideration;
- the mortgagee's failure to use reasonable care and diligence in their duties to the mortgagor. *C.I.B.C. Mortgage Corp. v. Harding* (1993), 39 A.C.W.S. (3d) 190 (Ont. Gen. Div.);
- expiry of limitation periods under the *Limitations Act*;
- failure of the mortgagee to mitigate. *165852 Ontario Inc. v. Les Gestions Koliba Inc.* (1994), 45 A.C.W.S. (3d) 753 (Ont. Gen. Div.);
- the plaintiff's incapacity;
- promissory estoppel;
- criminal rate of interest. *William E. Thomson Associates Inc. v. Carpenter* (1989), 69 O.R. (2d) 545 (C.A.), leave to appeal refused (1990), 37 O.A.C. 398 (note) (S.C.C.);
- forgery. *767648 Ontario Ltd. v. Engel* (1993), 33 R.P.R. (2d) 221(Ont. Gen. Div.), additional reasons at (June 8, 1993), Doc. Milton C7575/91, 92/56841 C.U. (Ont. Gen. Div.), affirmed (1994), 1 R.F.L. (4th) 144 (Ont. C.A.)
- misrepresentation. *Royal Trust Corp. of Canada v. Mpampas* (November 16, 1995), Doc. 95-CQ-64220CM (Ont. Gen. Div.), affirmed (May 24, 1996), Doc. CA C23385 (Ont. C.A.)
- invalid mortgage. *Royal Bank v. Mayhew*, (July 12, 1995), Doc. 04607/90U (Ont. Gen. Div.);
- contrary to the Statute of Frauds; and
- the mortgagee's failure to give notice of assignment of the mortgage. *Toronto Dominion Bank v. Eichelberger* (1996), 5 R.P.R. (3d) 149 (Ont. Gen. Div.) at 156

• On the other hand, certain difficulties with the mortgagee's actions in granting the mortgage have been found not to invalidate the mortgage and thus not establish a valid defence, including:

  - the mortgagee's contravention of a statute or regulation such as the *Bank Act's* loan-to-capital ratios. *Swiss Bank Corp. (Can.) v. Odyssey Industries Inc.* (1995), 30 C.B.R. (3d) 49 (Ont. Gen. Div. [Commercial List]) at 59; and
  - the mortgage being in excess of 75 percent of the mortgaged property's value contrary to the *Loan and Trust Corporations Act* s. 162(1). *Lamarche v. Mastercraft Development Corp.*, (March 9, 1995), Doc. Ottawa 75320/93 (Ont. Gen. Div.)

- In a case where mortgagors opposed an application made after default for possession and summary judgment, judgment was granted to the mortgagee, because the court found there were no triable issues in respect of the mortgagors' allegations of absence of independent legal advice, conflict of interest, *non est factum* or duress. *Municipal Savings and Loan Corp. v. Gagnon* (1991), 30 A.C.W.S. (3d) 597 (Ont. Gen. Div.)

8.3.4 OBTAINING AND REGISTERING JUDGMENT

- Depending on the defence raised, you then need to proceed through the applicable process to obtain judgment for the outstanding amount on the mortgage. (See chapter 3 for a discussion of both Simplified and Ordinary Procedures for obtaining judgment).

- If you are dealing with a mortgaged property that is registered under the *Land Titles Act*, and which has a certificate of pending litigation registered on title after the mortgage, consider adding a clause to the judgment specifically deleting the certificate, even if the person who registered the certificate is a defendant and would be foreclosed upon once judgment for foreclosure is signed. Dunn & Gray, *Marriott & Dunn Practice in Mortgage Remedies in Ontario, Fifth Edition,* chapter 7.1

- To register the judgment on title to the property in question, file the judgment in the appropriate registry office or land titles office, together with a land transfer tax affidavit signed by the mortgagee or their representative and pay the necessary registration fee and land transfer tax. *Check with the registry office/land titles office to see if the documents need to be pre-approved prior to registration. It would be helpful to have the judgment for foreclosure reviewed by the registry office/land titles office prior to having it signed to ensure that it complies with their requirements. Ensure that the property identifier number (PIN), if any, is included in the legal description.*

- The land transfer tax is calculated on the value of the mortgages foreclosed, which may exceed the fair market value of the property. In such a case, contact the Ministry of Revenue, Land Transfer Tax Section at 1-800-263-7965 or 1-905-433-6443 to determine the procedure to calculate the proper amount of land transfer tax payable.

> **Practice Tip:** After the writ of foreclosure is issued, subsearch title of the property again for subsequent encumbrancers who may have filed their claims after you began proceedings. The court has held the mortgagee has an onus to search the title, and must bear the consequence of failing to bring lienholders into the action. *Tessier (in Trust) v. Federal Trust Co. Ltd.,* [1978] A.C.W.S. 232 (Ont. Co. Ct.)

- If the property's tenants do not leave the property once the judgment for foreclosure has been registered, obtain a writ of possession (see section 8.11.2).

8.4 DEFAULT JUDGMENT FOR FORECLOSURE

- The defendant must deliver the statement of defence within 20 days after the service of statement of claim if served in Ontario, 40 days if served in Canada or the U.S., and 60 days if served elsewhere. Rule 18.01

- Once the time limit has passed for the defendants to file a defence or a notice of intent to defend, check the court file to ensure that no request for redemption or sale has been filed.

- If no such request has been filed, have the defendants noted in default. For details on this process, see chapter 3.2.3. Note that default judgments can be set aside if the defendant is able to show the court why the judgment should not have been given, or why no defence was filed in the appropriate time periods. Rule 19.09.

- In the case where you have had a defendant in a foreclosure action noted in default, and that defendant has not filed a request to redeem, you have a choice to make. If you wish a reference concerning subsequent encumbrancers to be held, you can require the registrar to sign judgment for foreclosure with a reference (Form 64B). If you do not wish a reference to be held, you can require the registrar to sign judgment for immediate foreclosure (Form 64C, which includes claims both for the money owed and for possession). Rule 64.03(9)

- To obtain the judgment for immediate foreclosure, file your statement of claim with affidavit of service, a requisition for default judgment, the judgment itself, and your bill of costs. In the judgment's first paragraph, ensure that you include the mortgage date, parties, registration date and the mortgage's registered instrument number. This will ensure that the mortgage can be identified clearly.

- Where a second mortgagor obtained judgment for immediate foreclosure, but failed to register judgment on title, the foreclosed mortgagor subsequently entered into an agreement for purchase and sale, which was registered on title. The court held that the earlier, unregistered judgment had priority over the agreement. *1224948 Ontario Ltd. v. 448332 Ontario Ltd.* (1998) 85 A.C.W.S. (3d) 440. *Although this would indicate that failure to register is not fatal to the mortgagee's priority, it is certainly not good practice. The best practice is to register the judgment on title as soon as is practical.*

- If you have had the defendant noted in default, but the defendant has filed a request to redeem, you again have a choice to make regarding a reference concerning subsequent encumbrancers. If you wish a reference to be held, require the registrar to sign judgment for foreclosure with a reference (Form 64B). If you do not wish a reference to be held, require the registrar to take an account of the amount due to you, determine the priority of those parties who are entitled to redeem, and sign judgment for foreclosure. Rule 64.03(10)

- Where you direct the registrar to take the account, they will require notice to be given to the parties and will require the account to be proven. If the registrar is in doubt or if a dispute arises between the parties on the taking of the account or in determining priorities, the registrar may sign judgment for foreclosure with a reference (Form 64B). Rule 64.03(11)

- A reference directed by a default judgment in a mortgage action shall be directed to a judge or master sitting in the county where the action was commenced or to the registrar in that county. Rule 64.02. *A registrar for a judicial region that legally and geographically includes a particular regional municipality is considered to be the "registrar for that county" for the purposes of Rule 64.02. National Trustco v. Hill* (1993), 13 O.R. (3d) 62 (Gen. Div.)

8.5 REFERENCES

- Note that Rule 64.06 applies specifically to references in actions for foreclosure, sale or redemption; Rule 55 applies to all references. This means that Rule 55 procedures are followed unless otherwise noted in Rule 64.06. Rule 64.06(1)

8.5.1 PREPARING FOR THE REFERENCE

- Basically, a reference is a mechanism by which to decide certain matters in the simplest, least expensive and most expeditious manner. Subject to any directions contained in the order directing the reference, the referee may therefore give such directions as are necessary, and may either dispense with any procedure ordinarily taken that the referee considers to be unnecessary, or adopt a procedure different from that ordinarily taken. Rule 55.01(1)

- A "referee" means the person to whom a reference in a proceeding is directed. Rule 1.03

- A referee must include in their report any special circumstances relating to the reference and must generally inquire into, decide and report on all matters relating to the reference as fully as if they had been specifically referred. Rule 55.01(2). *Thus, a referee can deal with whatever matters are necessary to the issue at hand, even if they have not specifically been referred to in the order for the reference.*

- The referee may grant leave to make any necessary amendments to the pleadings that are not inconsistent with the order of reference. Rule 55.02(10)

- The referee may not, however, deal with matters that are beyond its powers, including amending the judgment itself or considering whether the mortgage is invalid. *Olympia & York Developments Ltd. v. Chicquen* (1978), 6 C.P.C. 221 (Ont. H.C.)

- A registrar who believes that a mortgage reference directed to him or her ought to be dealt with by a judge may request directions from a judge. Rule 64.06(20)

- The judgment or order that provides the grounds for the reference must have been signed by the registrar or judge involved, and entered, in order for the reference to be held. *400091 British Columbia Ltd. v. Copper Beach Estates Ltd.* (1994), 49 A.C.W.S. (3d) 1150 (B.C. S.C. [In Chambers])

- Once the order directing the reference is issued, the party having carriage of the reference initiates the reference by immediately having the order signed and entered. Within 10 days after entry, the party then requests an appointment with the referee for a hearing to consider directions for the reference. Should the party having carriage of the reference fail to do so, any other party having an interest in the reference may assume carriage of it. Rule 55.02(1).

- Be prepared to produce all documentation that the referee will require, including the original judgment and a copy of that judgment to be filed with the referee, a solicitor's affidavit listing any new parties to be added to the action, and draft notices of reference for the referee to sign. *In practice, file the order in advance and bring everything else to the hearing. If the issue is particularly complex, send over a draft of the order giving directions and a draft of the terms of reference.*

- The party having carriage of the reference must serve a notice of hearing for directions (Form 55A) and a copy of the order directing the reference on every other party to the proceeding at least five days before the hearing, unless the referee directs or the Rules of Civil Procedure provide otherwise. Rule 55.02(2)

- At the hearing for directions, the referee shall give appropriate directions for the conduct of the reference, including the time and place for the reference, any special directions concerning the parties who are to attend, and any special directions concerning what evidence is to be received and how documents are to be proved. These directions can be varied or supplemented during the course of the reference. Rule 55.02(3)(4)

- The party having carriage of the reference must then serve the notices of reference on all parties. Rule 55.02(2). Proof of service must be filed at the reference.

- If the referee believes that any other person should be added as a party to the proceeding, they may order that the person be added as a defendant or respondent, and that the person be served with the order directing the reference and a notice to party added on reference (Form 55B). On being served, the person becomes a party to the proceeding. Rule 55.02(5). As with adding subsequent encumbrancers, such parties have 10 days after service (or more, if served outside Ontario), to bring a motion to set aside or vary the referee's order. Rule 55.02(6)

- A party who is served with notice of a reference and does not appear at the reference is not entitled to notice of any step in the reference and need not be served with any document in the reference, unless the referee orders otherwise. Rule 55.02(7)

- Subject to Rule 64.05(2) (subsequent encumbrancers in redemption action), the referee shall direct that all persons who appear to have a lien, charge or encumbrance on the mortgaged property subsequent to the mortgage in question, and who were not named as defendants in the statement of claim, be added as defendants and served with a notice of reference to subsequent encumbrancer added on reference (Form 64N). Rule 64.06(4)

- A subsequent encumbrancer added on reference may be served with documents on the reference as follows:

  - in the case of an execution creditor, by mail at the address shown on the writ of execution or the most recent request to renew it or, if the creditor's address is not shown, by serving the creditor's solicitor in a manner authorized by Rule 16.05(1);
  - in the case of a person who has registered a claim for lien under the *Construction Lien Act*, by mail at the address for service shown on the claim for lien; or
  - in any other case, personally or by an alternative to personal service under Rule 16.03.

  Rule 64.06(5)

- A subsequent encumbrancer added on reference and served with Form 64N has 10 days after service (or further time as the referee directs where the person is served outside Ontario) to set aside or vary the judgment in the action or the order adding the person as a defendant. Rule 64.06(6)

- Where it appears to the referee that a person who was named as a defendant in the statement of claim may have a lien, charge or encumbrance on the mortgaged property subsequent to the mortgage in question, although the person was not alleged to be a subsequent encumbrancer in the statement of claim, the referee shall direct that defendant to be served with a notice of reference to subsequent encumbrancer named as original party (Form 64O). Rule 64.06(7)

- All persons who were named as defendants in the statement of claim shall be served with a notice of reference to original defendants (Form 64P), stating the names and nature of the claims of all those appearing to have a lien, charge or encumbrance on the mortgaged property. Rule 64.06(8). *The only exception to this is a subsequent encumbrancer named as a defendant in the statement of claim who has not filed a request to redeem or a request for sale: they are not entitled to notice of a reference for foreclosure. Rule 64.06(10)*

- Any person named as a defendant in the statement of claim who is not a subsequent encumbrancer and who has not filed a request to redeem or a request for sale may be served with the notice of reference by mail at the person's last known address. Rule 64.06(9)

- Where on a reference it appears that there are persons interested in the equity of redemption, other than subsequent encumbrancers, who are not already defendants to the action, the referee may order that they be added as defendants on the reference on such terms as are just. The person having carriage of the reference then serves the order on them, along with the judgment in the action and a notice to added party (Form 64Q), personally or by an alternative to personal service under Rule 16.03. Rule 64.06(11). *This party then has 10 days after service (or further time as directed by the referee where service was outside Ontario) to set aside or vary the judgment in the action or the order adding the person as a defendant. Rule 64.06(12)*

- Where it appears to the referee that two or more parties have substantially similar interests and can be adequately represented as a class, the referee can require them to be represented by the same solicitor and, where they cannot agree on a solicitor to represent them, the referee may designate a solicitor on such terms as are just. Rule 55.02(8). *This is designed to further expedite the proceedings and reduce legal costs.*

- A party whom the referee believes should be represented as a class may insist on being represented by a different solicitor. If they do so, however, they cannot recover the costs of the separate representation and, unless the referee orders otherwise, they must pay all costs incurred by the other parties as a result of the separate representation. Rule 55.02(9)

- Where the party having carriage of the reference does not proceed with reasonable diligence, the referee may, on the motion of any other interested party, transfer carriage of the reference to another party. Rule 55.02(12)

8.5.2 WITNESSES AND EVIDENCE AT THE REFERENCE

- Although most claims are proved in a reference via affidavit and documentary evidence, the referee can call witnesses and request additional documents where necessary to determine an issue.

- Witnesses on a reference shall be examined orally unless the referee directs otherwise, and evidence taken orally shall be recorded. Rule 55.02(13)

- The attendance of a person to be examined on a reference may be compelled in the same manner as provided in Rule 53.04 for a witness at a trial. Rule 55.02(14)

- The referee may require any party to be examined and to produce such documents as the referee thinks fit and may give directions for their inspection by any other party. Rule 55.02(15)

- While a reference is pending, all documents relating to it shall be filed with the referee and, on completion of the reference, the documents shall be returned to the office in which the proceeding was commenced. Rule 55.02(16)

- Where a person refuses or neglects to execute or deliver an instrument that becomes necessary under an order directing the reference, the referee may give directions for its execution or delivery. Rule 55.02(17)

- Where the referee has made a ruling on the admissibility of evidence or any other matter relating to the conduct of the reference, the referee shall, on the request of any party, set out the ruling and the reasons for it in the report or, in the discretion of the referee, in an interim report on the reference. Rule 55.02(18). *Particularly where the referee has not ruled in your favour, requesting that the ruling and the referee's reasons for it be included in the report can provide you with a basis for an argument against the ruling.*

- On a reference in an action for foreclosure, sale or redemption, the plaintiff must file sufficient evidence to enable the referee to determine which parties appear to have a lien, charge or encumbrance on the mortgaged property subsequent to the mortgage in question. Rule 64.06(2).

8.5.3 MOTIONS ON A REFERENCE

- A referee shall hear and dispose of any motion made in connection with the reference; however, a judge or master may hear and dispose of the motion if the referee is absent or consents. Rule 54.05 (1)

- Note that Rule 37.03 (place of hearing of motions) does not apply to a motion made in connection with a reference and heard by the referee. Rule 54.05(2)

- Where a referee has made an order on a motion in the reference, a person who is affected by the order may make a motion to a judge to set aside or vary the order. To do so, they must serve a notice of motion within seven days after the order is made, naming the first available hearing date that is at least three days after service of the notice of motion. Rule 54.05(3). *The notice of motion will also require a motion record, including the affidavit evidence to be relied upon and the necessary factums.*

8.5.4 PROVING CLAIMS AND ATTENDING THE REFERENCE

- On the reference, the referee's duties and powers include:
  - adding subsequent encumbrancers as defendants as appropriate;
  - fixing a time and place for determining the validity of the claims of subsequent encumbrancers;
  - determining who has a lien, charge or encumbrance on the mortgaged property subsequent to the mortgage in question;
  - taking an account of what is due on the mortgage and what is due to subsequent encumbrancers who prove a claim;
  - fixing or assessing the costs of the parties;
  - fixing a time and place for payment, where applicable;
  - where the reference is for immediate sale, giving directions for the sale and deferring taking accounts until after the sale is held or proves abortive;
  - where a sale is being conducted on the request of a subsequent encumbrancer, determining that the encumbrancer has a valid claim before giving directions for the sale;
  - taking all necessary steps for redemption by or foreclosure of the parties entitled to redeem the mortgaged property and, where applicable, for sale of the mortgaged property; and
  - taking subsequent accounts and fixing or assessing subsequent costs as required.

  Rule 64.06(3)

- To make a claim, prepare an affidavit of proof of account, with an account in itemized, numbered debit and credit form verified by affidavit. The referee may also direct the form that the claim should take. Rule 55.03(2)(3)(4)(5). *The mortgagee should also include the duplicate registered copy of the mortgage or a certified copy of it and any amendments, assignments or renewals pertaining to the mortgage. Keep in mind that your job here is to make the referee's approval of your claim as straightforward as possible: including all of the required information in a clear and organized manner will greatly assist the referee.*

> **Practice Tip:** When taking an account, include the principal amount of monies, interest and disbursements made by the plaintiff (mortgagee); e.g. taxes, insurance premiums and any other items related to the management of the property.

- In an action for foreclosure or sale by, or for redemption against, an assignee of a mortgagee, a statement of the mortgage account, verified by the assignee's affidavit may be taken as proof of the state of the account. However, the mortgagor, the mortgagor's assignee, or any party entitled to redeem can dispute the statement of account by affidavit. If this occurs, then an affidavit as to the state of the account must be completed by the mortgagee, any intermediate assignee denying any payment to the mortgagee, or intermediate assignee. Rule 64.06(15)

- In determining claims, the referee may take accounts with rests or otherwise; take into account amounts received or amounts that might have been received had the mortgagor not wilfully defaulted or neglected their responsibilities; determine and make allowances for occupation rent; take into account all necessary repairs, lasting improvements, costs and expenses properly incurred; and make such other allowances as are just. Rule 55.04(1). *This means that the referee can consider amounts for principal and interest, insurance premiums, repairs, taxes and property management as applicable under the circumstances.*

- As per Dunn & Gray's *Marriott & Dunn Practice in Mortgage Remedies in Ontario, Fifth Edition,* chapter 10.9, "just allowances" have been found to include amounts paid by the mortgagee in the following circumstances:

  - to enforce the mortgage;
  - to appoint a receiver and/or manager;
  - to protect the property and defend the mortgagor's title;
  - to care for and sell chattels;
  - realtor's commissions for the property sale;
  - rental and leasing commissions;
  - appraisal and valuation fees;
  - taxes;
  - property insurance premiums;
  - water and sewer rates;
  - repairs and improvements;
  - payments to vacate construction lien claims;
  - tinsurance premiums on a life policy that is part of the mortgage security;
  - to obtain the release of a prior charge;
  - the reasonable costs of taking care of the property where the mortgagee mistakenly believed it had ownership; and
  - costs.

- Once all the claims have been determined, the referee can then decide who has the right to redeem the property. If more than one party is entitled to redeem, the referee determines the priority in which they are entitled to redeem, and fixes one day for payment by all of those parties. Rule 64.06(13)

- If more than one of the parties makes the payment required to redeem, any of those parties can bring a motion on the reference for further directions. Rule 64.06(14)

- The referee maintains a procedure book in which they note all steps taken and all directions given in respect of the reference. Note that these directions are binding on the parties whether or not they are included in a formal order or report. Rule 55.02(11)

8.5.5 REFEREE'S REPORT

- The referee's findings as to claims, priorities and other issues that were referred are contained in the referee's report, which is drafted by the party who has carriage of the reference, and signed by the referee. Once signed, and if not successfully opposed, the report stands as confirmed.

- On a straightforward reference, during which all issues and claims are settled during the reference, the report may also be drafted and settled at the reference itself.

- Otherwise, when the hearing of the reference is completed, the referee sets a date to settle the report. The party having carriage of the reference serves notice of this date on all parties who appeared on the reference, unless the referee dispenses with notice. Rule 55.02(19*). If the referee does not dispense with notice, and the notice is not given, the report can be set aside. Situations where the referee may dispense with notice include where all parties who would be entitled to notice are present at the reference, at which a date and time for settling the report is given.*

- The party having carriage of the reference prepares a draft report and presents it to the referee on the day fixed for settling the report. Rule 55.02(20)

- The referee's report includes:

    - the names of all persons who were parties on the reference, all subsequent encumbrancers who were

served with notice of the reference, and all subsequent encumbrancers who failed to attend on the reference and prove their claims;
  - the amount and priority of the claims of the parties who attended and proved their claims on the reference (the report shows these parties as the only encumbrancers of the property);
  - the date on which the report was settled;
  - the time and place for redemption of the mortgage; and
  - if the judgment directed payment on the covenant, the amount due to the mortgagee on the covenant as of the report's date.

  Rule 64.06(13)(16)

- Once the referee settles the report and signs it, the plaintiff (the party having carriage of the reference) then serves the report on all parties who attended on the reference and on any defendant who filed a request to redeem or a request for sale, and files it with proof of service. Rule 64.06(17)

- A party who opposes the referee's report has 15 days after the date that notice of the report's filing was served, or (if no defendant required service) the date on which the report was filed to serve a notice of motion to oppose the report's confirmation. If no such motion is received during this time, the report is automatically confirmed. Rule 54.09(1).

- If the mortgagee is concerned that this 15-day delay could cause serious difficulties with respect to the mortgaged property, such as the need to conduct extensive repairs, you may bring a motion for the report's immediate confirmation. Rule 54.09(4)

- A motion that opposes the report's confirmation acts as an appeal of the report, and thus will only be approved under the usual test for appeal, which requires an error in law (including jurisdiction) to have been made. *Thompson v. Hermon* (1988), 65 O.R. (2d) 538 (H.C.);

Jordan v. McKenzie (1987), 26 C.P.C. (2d) 179 (Ont. H.C.), affirmed (1989), 39 C.P.C. (2d) 217 (Ont. C.A.)

8.6 CHANGE OF ACCOUNT

- Given the time periods in which procedures such as references take place, it is likely that the statement of account prepared for the reference will change, as interest and unpaid payments continue to accumulate.

- Where any period fixed for payment expires within 15 days after confirmation of the referee's report, a new account must be taken. Rule 64.06(18)

- Additionally, where the state of account contained in an order or report changes before the day fixed for payment, the mortgagee may, at least 15 days before that day, serve notice of the change of account on the person required to pay, giving particulars of the change of account and of the sum to be paid. Rule 64.06(21). *Doing so will ensure that additional interest charges, for example, will be paid when the mortgaged property is redeemed. Providing a notice of change of account after the redemption date can potentially result in the final order of foreclosure being set aside. Cameron v. D'Estrada,* [1939] O.W.N. 399 (H.C.)

> **Practice Tip:** Service of the notice of change of account is made on the defendant's solicitor of record. If the defendant has either filed a request to redeem or is self-represented, service is made on the defendant personally or as provided in Rule 16.01(4)(b) of the Rules of Civil Procedure.

- Where notice of a change of account has been served and the sums mentioned in it are correct, the court may make a final order without further notice or, on the motion for a final order, may fix a new day for payment and may require notice to be served. Rule 64.06(22)

- A party served with notice of change of account who is dissatisfied may make a motion to the court to determine the amount to be paid and to fix a new day for payment. Rule 64.06(23)

- If notice of the change has not been served, and the amount payable for redemption has decreased before the day fixed for payment, a new day must be fixed for payment, on notice to the persons entitled to redeem. If the amount payable has increased, the mortgagee may move for a final order after the day fixed for payment, without the fixing of a new day. Rule 64.06(24)

- Where the state of the new account has changed after the day fixed for payment, it is not necessary to fix a new day, unless the court so directs on the motion for a final order. Rule 64.06(25)

- Where it becomes necessary to fix a new day for payment after the expiration of the original period, the further time allowed shall be 30 days. The court also has the power to extend or abridge the time for redemption as they see fit on the motion of any party. for such time and on such terms as are just to orders otherwise. Rule 64.07(26) (27)

8.7 DEALING WITH A REQUEST TO REDEEM ON A FORECLOSURE

- A defendant in a foreclosure action, whether the mortgagor or a subsequent encumbrancer, has the right to redeem the mortgaged property. Rule 64.03(6).

- To redeem, the money is generally paid into a financial institution to the credit of the entitled party, or to the joint credit of the entitled party and the Accountant of the Superior Court of Justice or local registrar. Rule 55.05(1). *Where the money is paid into a financial institution of the party entitled, obtain a receipt from the financial institution that the money was in fact paid.*

- The mortgagee's statement of claim triggers the right of redemption, so although the regulations stipulate that the defendant has, for example, the right to redeem for 60 days after accounts are taken on a reference (which is, of course, after judgment for the claim has been issued), the defendant can redeem the mortgage at any point prior to this as well. If the defendant is the only party with the right to redeem, this effectively ends the action. If, however, there are other parties who still have a right to redeem based on their equity, the action continues to judgment and foreclosure after the mortgagee obtains an order to proceed. Dunn & Gray, *Marriott & Dunn Practice in Mortgage Remedies in Ontario, Fifth Edition,* chapter 14.5

- A defendant who is a subsequent encumbrancer is entitled to redeem only if the claim is proved on a reference or is not disputed. Rule 64.03(8)

- A request to redeem (Form 64A) must be served by the defendant mortgagor on the plaintiff, and filed with proof of service within the time prescribed by Rule 18.01 for delivery of a statement of defence, or at any time before being noted in default, whether or not the defendant delivers a statement of defence. Rule 64.03(6)

- A subsequent encumbrancer who files a request to redeem must include particulars, verified by affidavit, of the claim and the amount owing. Rule 64.03(7)

- defendant who has filed a request to redeem is entitled to seven days notice of the taking of the accounts of the amount due to the plaintiff; and sixty days after the taking of the accounts of the amount due to the plaintiff, to redeem the mortgaged property. Rule 64.03(8). *The taking of accounts is, of course, carried out by the referee on the reference itself.*

- The courts can extend the time for redemption, and have taken into consideration factors such as whether the mortgagor has a reasonable prospect of paying the amount owed, and whether the property itself has sufficient value to secure the outstanding amount. *Canada Permanent Mortgage Corp. v. Dan-al Construction Co. Ltd.* (1982), 16 A.C.W.S. (2d) 224 (B.C. C.A.)

- Caselaw also shows extensions approved where the mortgage account was significantly reduced by rent collection by the mortgagee-in-possession, and where the mortgagee would make a considerable profit on the mortgage. *Ontario Mortgage Corp. v. 296216 Ontario Ltd.* (1980), 3 A.C.W.S. (2d) 55 (Ont. Master); *Sovereign Life Insurance Co. v. Swanham Investments Inc.* (1991), 25 A.C.W.S. (3d) 1129 (B.C. S.C.)

- On the other hand, the court rarely allows the time for redemption to be abridged. A pre-condition for court approval of a request for immediate foreclosure is that the property's value is less than the amount owed on the mortgage. *Wiarton (Town) v. Canada Casket Co.* (1918), 14 O.W.N. 321 (H.C.)

- A defendant who has filed a request to redeem (and, if a subsequent encumbrancer, whose claim is proved or not disputed on a reference) may redeem the mortgage by paying - within the time fixed either by the judgment or by a report on a reference - the amount, including costs, that was found to be due to the plaintiff (the mortgagee). Rule 64.03(12)

- A subsequent encumbrancer added on a reference who attends on the reference and whose claim is proved or is not disputed is entitled to redeem the mortgaged property within the time fixed by the report on the reference. Rule 64.03(13)

- If a subsequent encumbrancer whom you served with a notice of reference fails to attend and prove their claim, the referee includes that fact in their report. Upon confirmation of the report, the encumbrancer's claim is foreclosed, and you may then bring a motion without notice to obtain a final order of foreclosure (Form 64E) against that encumbrancer. Rule 64.03(14)

- Where no defendant other than a subsequent encumbrancer has filed a request to redeem, and where no subsequent encumbrancer has attended and proved a claim on the reference, the referee includes that fact in their report. Upon confirmation of the report, you may then bring a motion without notice to obtain a final order of foreclosure against all defendants. Rule 64.03(15)

- If the defendant defaults on the payment required by the judgment or report on a reference, you may bring a motion without notice to obtain a final order of foreclosure against the party in default, or an order dismissing their redemption action with costs. Rule 64.03(16), 64.05(6)

8.8 ACTION TO REDEEM

- The borrower always has a right to bring an action to redeem where the lender is refusing to accept payment or where there is a dispute as to the amount to pay off the mortgage. *This commonly occurred where borrowers were trying to reopen a closed mortgage that had a term of more than five years.*

- In a redemption action by the mortgagor, where the defendant (in this case, the mortgagee) has been noted in default, the plaintiff (the party wishing to redeem the mortgage) may require the registrar to sign judgment for redemption (Form 64M). Rule 64.05(4)

- A person interested in the equity of redemption may also claim possession of the mortgaged property. Rule 64.05(4)

- Every judgment for redemption shall direct a reference, whether or not there are any subsequent encumbrancers. Rule 64.05(5)

- Where the plaintiff is declared foreclosed, directions may be given, in the final order foreclosing the plaintiff or by a subsequent order, that the reference be continued for redemption or foreclosure, or for redemption or sale, against any subsequent encumbrancers, or for the adjustment of the respective rights and liabilities of the original defendants. Rule 64.05(7)

- In such a case, where the reference is continued for redemption or foreclosure, the reference proceeds as in a foreclosure action; where it is continued for redemption or sale, it proceeds as in a sale action. The last encumbrancer is treated as the owner of the equity of redemption. Rule 64.05(8)

- Where the plaintiff is declared foreclosed, a subsequent encumbrancer who proves their claim at the reference has 30 days to redeem the mortgaged property. Rule 64.05(9)

- Where, on a reference in a redemption action, nothing is found due to the defendant (in this case, the mortgagee), the defendant is liable for the costs of the action and must pay any balance due to the plaintiff (the party who requested the right to redeem) forthwith after confirmation of the report on the reference. Rule 64.05(10)

- Subject to the *Mortgages Act*, where a party pays the amount found due on the mortgage, the mortgagee must, unless the judgment directs otherwise, transfer the mortgaged property to the party making the payment or the party's nominee, free and clear of all encumbrances incurred by the mortgagee. The mortgagee must also deliver up all instruments (documents) in the mortgagee's possession, control or power that relate to the mortgaged property. Rule 64.06(19)

8.9 FINAL ORDER OF FORECLOSURE

- The mortgagee is entitled to move for a final order of foreclosure in several circumstances, including:

    - where no statement of defence or request to redeem was filed within the appropriate time limits. Rule 64.03(9);

  - where a request to redeem was filed, but no redemption was made;
  - on confirmation of a referee's report that includes a notation that no defendant other than a subsequent encumbrancer filed a request to redeem and no subsequent encumbrancer attended the reference and proved a claim. Rule 64.03(15); and
  - where the referee fixed a redemption period and no redemption was made. Rule 64.03(16)

- To obtain a final order of foreclosure, produce the original judgment, and file the mortgagee's affidavit of non-payment, plus a written certification that redemption monies have not been paid into court (obtained through the local registrar's office or, in Toronto, through the Office of the Accountant of the Superior Court of Justice). If a notice of change of account was served, file a copy with proof of service. If a reference was held, produce the confirmed report instead of the judgment, and file (or produce if you have already filed) the proof of service of notice of filing the report. Dunn & Gray, *Marriott & Dunn Practice in Mortgage Remedies in Ontario, Fifth Edition,* chapter 15.2

- To register the final order of foreclosure, first ensure that it is entered and issued by the court, and request a certificate of the order for title registration purposes. Rule 4.05(1) and 4.03.

- Then register on title the certificate of the foreclosure order and a statutory declaration on the order's status (Form 96). If the property is registered under the *Registry Act*, ensure that the certificate includes a legal description of the land. *Registry Act*, s.40(2)

- An affidavit of land transfer tax signed by the mortgagee and the land transfer tax payment is also required. *Land Transfer Tax Act*, s.2

- The land transfer tax is based on the lesser of the gross sale price and the value of any liability assumed under the mortgage, plus amounts owing under the mortgage, plus all prior encumbrances, or on the fair market value on the date of the final order of foreclosure. *Land Transfer Tax Act*, s.1(1)

- The land transfer tax is calculated on the value of the mortgages foreclosed, which may exceed the fair market value of the property. In such a case, contact the Ministry of Revenue, Land Transfer Tax Section at 1-800-263-7965 or 1-905-433-6443 to determine the procedure to calculate the proper amount of land transfer tax payable.

- If the property's tenants do not leave the property once the immediate judgment for foreclosure has been registered, obtain a writ of possession (see Chapter 7.6.2).

- Once the final order of foreclosure is in hand, the mortgagee is considered the owner of the property, and has no right to pursue any further action against the mortgagor, including claims for costs. *Ruhl v. Royal Bank* (1993), 31 R.P.R. (2d) 71 (Ont. Gen. Div.). *As set out above, if the lender tries to enforce its judgment on the covenant, then it re-opens the foreclosure proceedings and allows the mortgagee a new right to redeem.*

- A judgment for either an immediate foreclosure or a final order of foreclosure can be reopened by the court, even if the mortgagee has sold the property involved. *Dovercourt Land Building & Savings Co. v. Dunvegan Heights Land Co.* (1920), 47 O.L.R. 105 (H.C.) at 108

- Re-opening a foreclosure should only be done where severe hardship would result to the mortgagor, and where the mortgagor is not attempting to take advantage of the mortgagee. *Canada Deposit Insurance Corp. v. Greymac Mortgage Corp.* (1991), 2 O.R. (3d) 446 (Gen. Div.), affirmed (1991), 4 O.R. (3d) 608 (C.A.)

- To set aside a final order of foreclosure, the following tests are applied:

  - the application must be made reasonably promptly;

  - there must be a reasonable prospect of immediate or prompt payment;
  - the applicant must have been active in trying to raise the money to redeem, and that unforeseen circumstances prevented the redemption within the required time;
  - the applicant must have a significant interest in the property; and
  - if the property has been sold, the rights of the purchaser must not be unduly prejudiced.

    Rennie v. Canada Trustco Mortgage Co. (1991), 27 A.C.W.S. (3d) 1056 (Ont. Gen. Div.); *Royal Bank of Canada v. Swan* (1980), 3 A.C.W.S. (2d) 341 (Ont. Div. Ct.)

- The court did not set aside a final order for foreclosure where a second mortgagee had not acted reasonably to protect its interests after the foreclosure action was commenced. *737371 Ontario Inc. v. 810139 Ontario Ltd.* (1992), 34 A.C.W.S. (3d) 149 (Ont. Gen. Div.)

- The court has set aside an order of foreclosure where special circumstances exist, for example:

  - where default judgment was obtained while the mortgagors were out of the country. *Ontario Housing Corp. v. Ong* (1987), 58 O.R. (2d) 125, 15 C.P.C. (2d) 279 (H.C.), affirmed (1988), 26 C.P.C. (2d) 139 (Ont. C.A.); and
  - where default judgment for immediate foreclosure was signed, but a request for sale had been made. *Beber v. Davis* (1987), 22 C.P.C. (2d) 25 (Ont. Master)

- The court has refused to set aside an order for foreclosure where there was no evidence that the mortgagee tried to arrange for redemption of a mortgage during the proceedings. *Banbury v. Tahir* (1993), 13 O.R. (3d) 609 (Gen. Div.)

8.10 DEALING WITH A REQUEST FOR SALE

- A foreclosure can be converted to a sale in three situations:
  - when a defendant in a foreclosure action who is not a subsequent encumbrancer wishes a sale but does not wish to defend the action. Rule 64.03(17);
  - when a subsequent encumbrancer named as a defendant in the statement of defence wishes a sale but does not wish to defend the action and redeem the property. Rule 64.03(18); and
  - on a motion of any party, a sale may be directed instead of a foreclosure. Rule 64.03(22).

- A defendant who is not a subsequent encumbrancer, and who wishes a sale but does not wish to defend the action, must serve on the plaintiff (the mortgagee), and file with proof of service, a request for sale (Form 64F) (within the time prescribed by rule 18.01 for delivery of a statement of defence), or at any time before being noted in default. Upon receiving the request for sale, you may then require the registrar to sign judgment for sale (Form 64G or 64H). Rule 64.03(17)

- A subsequent encumbrancer named as a defendant in your statement of claim who wishes a sale, but does not wish to defend the action or redeem the mortgaged property, may serve a request for sale on the plaintiff within (the time prescribed by rule 18.01 for delivery of a statement of defence), or at any time before being noted in default. In this case, the defendant must pay $250 into court as security for costs, and must serve on the plaintiff, and file with proof of service, a request for sale (Form 64F), together with particulars, verified by affidavit, of the claim and the amount owing. Upon receiving the request for sale, you may then require the registrar to sign judgment for sale (Form 64I) conditional on proof of the subsequent encumbrancer's claim. Rule 64.03(18)

- If the subsequent encumbrancer who was added on a reference, rather than on the statement of claim, wishes to request a sale, they have 10 days after they were served with notice of the reference (or further time allowed by the referee if they were served outside Ontario) to make that request. They must pay $250 into court as security, and must serve on the plaintiff, and file with proof of service, a request for sale (Form 64F), together with particulars, verified by affidavit, of the claim and the amount owing. Assuming that they prove a claim at the reference, the referee will then amend the judgment to create a judgment for sale. Rule 64.03(19)

- Note that on the reference, the referee may require the subsequent encumbrancer to pay an additional sum of money into court as security for costs. Rule 64.03(20).

- Any party may bring a motion - to the court before judgment or to the referee after judgment - asking that a sale be directed instead of foreclosure. The referee has the power to direct an immediate sale without previously determining the priorities of encumbrancers or giving the usual or any time to redeem. Rule 64.03(22). If a final order of foreclosure has been granted, this rule cannot be used to direct a sale. *Silver Tam Enterprises Ltd. v. Seavy* (1986), 56 O.R. (2d) 793 (C.A.). *Anyone can apply to court at any time to direct a sale instead of a foreclosure. This would only need to be done if a party has not filed a request for sale under rule 64.3(17 or 18).*

- Where judgment for foreclosure has been granted and the time for redemption has expired, the defendants may still apply for a sale; however, there must be a reasonable possibility of a profitable sale. *Coronation Credit (Ontario) Ltd. v. Franklin Motel (North Bay) Ltd.,* [1966] 2 O.R. 300 (S.C.)

- Where a plaintiff claimed against a defendant for improper dealings regarding property, the plaintiff brought a motion for summary judgment seeking a transfer of the defendant's interest in property to the plaintiff pursuant to foreclosure. In this case, the court awarded the plaintiff damages claimed, but ordered that the defendant's interest be offered for sale, as sale was a more accurate method of measuring the liability of the defendant. *Dufferin-Finch Investments Ltd. v. J.D.S. Investments Ltd.* (1994), 51 A.C.W.S. (3d) 614 (Ont. Gen. Div.)

- Where a first mortgagee sought foreclosure, and where a trustee in bankruptcy opposed this on the grounds of entitlement to an equitable mortgage in priority to a second mortgagee, the court ordered that proceedings be by way of sale, rather than foreclosure. The value of the property was likely to exceed the first mortgagee's claim. *Montreal Trust Co. of Canada v. Olympia & York Developments Ltd. (Trustee of)* (1998), 79 A.C.W.S. (3d) 826 (Ont. Gen. Div.)

- Where property equity exceeded the value of two mortgages, an application for foreclosure was dismissed, and an order for sale granted. *Knudsen v. Knudsen* (1998), 37 O.R. (3d) 676 (Gen. Div.), additional reasons at (1998), 40 R.F.L. (4th) 82 (Ont. Gen. Div.)

- In a foreclosure action that has been converted into a sale action, any party may bring a motion - to the court before judgment or to the referee after judgment - requesting that the action be converted back into a foreclosure action on the grounds that the property's value will not likely satisfy the plaintiff's claim. Rule 64.03(23).

- Where a property's value meant that reconverting back to a foreclosure would provide the plaintiff with a significant profit, the court ordered an extended period of time for redemption (four months) as relief. *426034 Ontario Ltd. v. Pasquale Marra Enterprises Inc.* (1993), 16 O.R. (3d) 285, 23 C.P.C. (3d) 43 (Gen. Div.), additional reasons at (1994), 23 C.P.C. (3d) 43 (Ont. Gen. Div.) at 48, affirmed (1994), 41 R.P.R. (2d) 1 (Ont. C.A.)

- Where a judgment for sale has been obtained in a foreclosure action, a subsequent encumbrancer is entitled to notice of the hearing for directions on the reference for sale, whether the encumbrancer has filed a request to redeem the mortgaged property or not. Rule 64.03(24)

- If a judicial sale has been ordered and if the plaintiff (the mortgagee) does not want to handle the sale themselves, you may transfer the carriage of the sale to the defendant by serving on the defendant a notice of election to transfer carriage of the sale and filing it with proof of service. The defendant then has carriage of the sale, and is entitled to the return of the deposits they paid into court as security. Rule 64.03(25)

Where a foreclosure action is converted to a sale action, the reference shall proceed in the same manner as in a sale action. Rule 64.03(26)

8.11 ACTION FOR JUDICIAL SALE (SALE ACTION)

- The procedure that follows is the same for a foreclosure that is converted into a sale or an action for judicial sale. *Once a foreclosure has been converted into a judicial sale, it is the same as an action for a judicial sale.*

- In an action for sale of a mortgaged property, all persons interested in the equity of redemption, other than subsequent encumbrancers, must be named as defendants in the statement of claim. Subsequent encumbrancers shall be added as parties on a reference after judgment. Rule 64.04 (1)(2)

- The statement of claim in a sale action is Form 14B. Rule 64.04(3)

- In a sale action, a mortgagee may also claim payment of the mortgage debt by any party personally liable for it; and possession of the mortgaged property. Rule 64.04(4)

- A defendant in a sale action who wishes to redeem the mortgaged property shall serve on the plaintiff, and file with proof of service, a request to redeem (Form 64A) within the time prescribed by Rule 18.01 for delivery of a statement of defence, or at any time before being noted in default, whether the defendant delivers a statement of defence or not. Rule 64.04(5)

- In a sale action, a subsequent encumbrancer is not entitled to file a request to redeem. If the foreclosure action is converted to a sale action, a subsequent encumbrancer is not entitled to redeem in the sale action even if they have filed a request to redeem in the foreclosure action. Rule 64.04(6)

- A defendant who has filed a request to redeem is entitled to:

    - seven days notice of the taking of the account of the amount due to the plaintiff; and
    - 60 days after the taking of the account of the amount due to the plaintiff to redeem the mortgaged property. Rule 64.04(7)

- Where a defendant in a sale action has been noted in default and has not filed a request to redeem, the plaintiff may require the registrar to sign judgment for immediate sale with a reference (Form 64J). If they have filed a request to redeem, the plaintiff may require the registrar to sign judgment for sale with a reference (Form 64K). Rule 64.04(8)

- A defendant named in the statement of claim who has filed a request to redeem may redeem the mortgaged property on paying, within the time fixed by the report on the reference, the amount, including costs, found due to the plaintiff. Rule 64.04(9)

- Where no defendant has filed a request to redeem and where no subsequent encumbrancer has attended and proven a claim on the reference, the referee shall so report and, on confirmation of the report, a final order for sale (Form 64L) may be obtained on motion to the court without notice. Rule 64.04(10)

- On default of payment according to the judgment or a report on a reference in a sale action, a final order for sale may be obtained on motion to the court without notice. Rule 64.04(11)

8.12 CONDUCT OF THE SALE

- Where an order for sale has been obtained, the property shall be sold under the referee's direction, and the purchaser shall pay the purchase money into court unless the referee directs otherwise. Rule 64.04(12)

- The sale is conducted as per the referee's instructions: this can include sale by public auction, private contract or tender, or by a combination of these methods. Rule 55.06(1). *The most common method of sale is private sale through a licenced real estate broker.*

- Form 55F sets out the conditions of sale for auction or tender methods, subject to the referee's directions. Rule 55.06(3). *A clause should be included in the agreement of purchase and sale that contains the conditions of sale. An additional clause should also be included that the agreement of purchase and sale is conditional upon approval of the sale by the referee. Then apply to the referee for approval of the agreement of purchase and sale. Once the referee has granted the order approving the sale, attend at the office of the Accountant of the Superior Court of Justice, deposit the monies into court, then return to the referee and obtain a vesting order, which will be registered on title to the subject property.*

- At the hearing for directions (Rule 55.02(3)), the referee:

    - settles the form of the advertisement;
    - fixes the time and place of sale;
    - names an auctioneer, where one is to be employed;
    - gives directions for publication of the advertisement;
    - gives directions for obtaining appraisals;
    - fixes a reserve bid, if any; and
    - makes all other arrangements necessary for the sale. Rule 55.06(4)

- Where property is being sold by auction or tender, the party having carriage of the sale (usually the mortgagee) prepares a draft advertisement according to the referee's instructions. The advertisement must include:

- the short title of the proceeding;
- that the sale is by order of the court;
- the time and place of the sale;
- a short description of the property to be sold;
- whether the property is to be sold in one lot or several and, if in several, in how many, and in what lots;
- the terms of payment;
- that the sale is subject to a reserve bid, if that is the case; and
- any conditions of sale different from those set out in Form 55F.
  Rule 55.06(2)

- Any party may bid on the property, with the exception of the party having carriage of the sale and any trustee or agent for that party or other person in a fiduciary relationship to that party. Note that if the party having carriage of the sale wishes to bid, the referee may transfer carriage of the sale to another party or to any other person. Rule 55.06(5)(6)

- Where no auctioneer is employed, the referee or a person designated by the referee conducts the sale. Rule 55.06(7)

- The purchaser shall enter into an agreement of purchase and sale at the time of sale. Rule 55.06(8)

Practice Tip: The agreement of purchase and sale will be entered into similarly to an agreement of purchase and sale in a power of sale action; however ,it will have to be amended to reflect the fact that the sale is being conducted by the court instead of being a private power of sale.

- Consider adding the following provisions to the agreement of purchase and sale:

  - recognition that the sale is being made pursuant to a judicial sale;
  - recognition that the sale may be susceptible to judicial restraint;
  - that the agreement of purchase and sale would become null and void in the event that the mortgagee is unable to complete the sale by reason of such judicial restraint;
  - that the property is being sold on an 'as is where is' basis; and
  - that the title will be transferred by way of vesting order.

- The deposit required by the conditions of sale shall be paid to the party having carriage of the sale or the party's solicitor at the time of sale, and the party or solicitor then immediately pays the money into court in the purchaser's name. Rule 55.06(9)

- Where a sale is made through an auctioneer, the auctioneer makes an affidavit concerning the result of the sale. Where no auctioneer is employed, the referee shall enter the result in the procedure book. In both cases, the referee may make an interim report on the sale in Form 55G. Rule 55.06(10)

- A party may object to a sale by making a motion to the referee to set it aside. Notice of the motion must be served on all parties to the reference and on the purchaser, who shall be deemed to be a party for the purpose of the motion. Rule 55.06(11)

- The purchaser may pay the purchase money or the balance of it into court without order and, after the confirmation of the report on the sale, on notice to the party having carriage of the sale, the purchaser may obtain a vesting order. Rule 55.06(12)

- Where possession is wrongfully withheld from the purchaser, either the purchaser or the party having carriage of the sale may move for a writ of possession. Rule 55.06(13). *It may be easier for the person having car-*

riage of the sale to obtain the writ of possession because of their previous involvement in the matter.

- The purchase money may be paid out of court in accordance with the report, on either the purchaser's or their solicitor's consent, or on proof to the Accountant or registrar that the purchaser has received a transfer or vesting order of the property for which the money in question was paid into court. Rule 55.06(14)

- No transfer shall be approved until the referee is satisfied that the purchase money has been paid into court and, where a mortgage is taken for part of the purchase money, that the mortgage has been registered and deposited with the Accountant or registrar. Rule 55.06(15). *In the event that there is a mortgage, the mortgagee would be the original mortgagee that brought the foreclosure action.*

- The purchase money shall be applied in payment of what has been found due to the plaintiff and the other encumbrancers, if any, according to their priorities, together with subsequent interest and subsequent costs. Rule 64.04(13)

- Where the purchase money is not sufficient to pay what has been found due to the plaintiff, the plaintiff is entitled, on motion to the court without notice, to an order for payment of the deficiency by any defendant liable for the mortgage debt. Rule 64.04(14)

8.13 ACTION FOR POSSESSION

- The mortgagee must decide whether they wish to obtain possession of the mortgaged property, either by actual possession or by assuming control of the property and collecting rents from the property's tenants. *Noyes v. Pollock* (1886), 32 Ch. D. 53 (Eng. C.A.)

- If the property is vacant or abandoned, the mortgagee should consider using a self-help remedy, entering into possession of the property, changing the locks and starting to manage the property. In doing so, the mortgagee will have to ensure that there is insurance in place, the property is inspected on a regular basis and that it is heated and repaired. If the property is a multi-tenant building, the mortgagee may wish to obtain the services of a property management company to ensure the smooth operation and management of the property. *Tenants who know that the property is under foreclosure sometimes take great liberties with the property and cause considerable damage, and also fail to pay rent as it becomes due.*

- If the mortgagee assumes control of the property, they are responsible to collect monies due from the property, such as rent from tenants. They must account to the mortgagor for any amounts received, and can be held accountable for the failure to collect the proper amounts due. *Synod of Toronto v. De Blaquiere* (1880), 27 Gr. 536 at 549 (Ont. Ch.), affirmed (1880), 27 Gr. 550n; *Beber (Trustee of) v. Romko Investments Ltd.* (January 22, 1997), Doc. CA C12166, [1997] O.J. No. 236 (C.A.)

- Either the mortgage document or the standard charge terms that govern the mortgage set out the express provisions that deal with the question of the mortgagee obtaining possession once there is default. The usual provision is that upon default, the mortgagee is entitled to quiet possession of the property.

- The spouse of the mortgagor has the same right of possession as does a mortgagor, provided that it is the matrimonial home. *Family Law Act,* s.19(1).

The essential requirement in order to obtain possession is that there must be an act of default by the mortgagor. Acts of default include the following:

  - failure to make payments. *Land Registration Reform Act,* s.7(1)1 i, v;
  - failure to insure the property. *Land Registration Reform Act,* s.7(1) 1(iv); and

  - non-payment of condominium fees. *Condominium Act,* R.S.O. 1990, c.C.26, s.33(3)(b).

- *For a further discussion of what constitutes default, see* section 8.2.

- In the event of a default, the mortgagee is not required to take possession of the property. *Schantz v. Hallman,* [1928] S.C.R. 213.

- The statement of claim in an action for possession must set out the terms for payment and that a mortgagee has the right of possession as set out in the mortgage.

- The defendants to a mortgage action for possession may include the following:

  - all mortgagors if there is more than one, *Kinross Mortgage Corp. v. Balfour* (1981), 33 O.R. (2d) 213 (H.C.);
  - spouse of the mortgagor, *Family Law Act,* s.19(1); and
  - tenants in actual possession of the mortgaged property whose interest in subsequent to that of the mortgagee, Rule 60.10(2). *In certain circumstances, you may not want to obtain vacant possession from the tenant, instead preferring to keep that tenant in possession. In such a case, especially if their tenancy brings increased value to the property, do not serve them with the notice of foreclosure, as this will allow them a chance to get out of the tenancy.*

- Once the statement of claim for possession has issued and the time period has expired for filing a statement of defence, the defendants should be noted in default and judgment for possession or for possession and payment can be signed. Rules of Civil Procedure*,* 19.04(1)(a) and (b).

- If a defence has been filed and the defence does not appear to have merit or is frivolous, a motion can be made pursuant to the Rules of Civil Procedure*,* Rule 20, for summary judgment. A motion for summary judgment will succeed where the defendant cannot produce an organized set of facts with evidence to show that there is a genuine triable issue based on admissible evidence. *Irving Ungerman Ltd. v. Galanis* (1991), 83 D.L.R. (4th) 734 (Ont. C.A.); *Dawson v. Rexcraft Storage & Warehouse Inc.* (1988), 164 D.L.R. (4th) 257 (Ont. C.A.); *Aguoinie v. Galion Solid Waste Material Inc.* (1998), 156 D.L.R. (4th) 222 (Ont. C.A.)

- In the event that the mortgagee obtains a judgment for possession, the judgment for possession must be served on all persons who are in actual possession of the property in question. *Central Guaranty Trust Co. v. McRae* (1993), 13 O.R. (3d) 295 (Gen. Div.). *Ensure that everyone in actual possession has notice of the proceedings. If there is someone else living in the premises who does not get notice of the proceedings, it will be necessary to serve the judgment on such persons in order to get vacant possession. Therefore, it would be prudent to have a representative of the mortgagee attend at the premises to make the proper inquiries to see who is in possession of the premises and under what circumstances they are in possession. That information should then be included in the affidavit evidence before the court. Without this information, a writ of possession will not be issued.*

- After obtaining the judgment for possession, the mortgagee must apply for a writ of possession. If the judgment for possession was obtained by default, the writ of possession is made on a without notice basis for an order granting the mortgagee leave to issue a writ of possession. *You can either obtain the writ of possession at the time that you get your judgment for possession when you bring your motion for summary judgment, or you can apply ex parte at a subsequent time. It would be preferable to provide the necessary information at the time that you are obtaining summary judgment and obtain leave to issue the writ of possession, thereby avoiding going back to court on an ex parte basis to get the writ of possession. The danger of going back on an ex parte basis may be that someone could attempt to set aside the ex parte order. The motion can be made to either a Master or a Judge. A mortgagee cannot obtain vacant possession from a tenant unless they comply with the provisions of the* Tenant Protection Act, *1997,* S.O. 1997, c.24.

- In order to succeed on the motion, the court must be satisfied that all persons in actual possession of the property have received sufficient notice of the proceedings when the judgment for possession was obtained. Rules of Civil Procedure, 60.10(2). When bringing the motion to issue the writ of possession, the mortgagee must include in the affidavit material a clear statement as to whether the mortgaged property is a residential rental property.

- In a case where the mortgagee was entitled to judgment for foreclosure with reference, other persons who were not mortgagors were in actual possession of part of the mortgaged premises. The court would not issue a writ of possession until those persons received sufficient notice of proceedings as required by Rule 60.10(2) of the Rules of Civil Procedure. *Madill v. Haas* (1992), 34 A.C.W.S. (3d) 150 (Ont. Gen. Div.)

- The court does have discretion to impose a stay of proceedings before the issuance of the writ of possession if the court is satisfied that the mortgagor's difficulties can be overcome. *Farm Credit Corp. v. Bale* (1994), 49 A.C.W.S. (3d) 1156 (Ont. Gen. Div.).

- Once a writ of possession is issued, it will be served by the sheriff on all of the necessary parties, together with a Sheriff's Notice to Vacate. The Notice to Vacate will provide a certain date and time within which the people on the premises must vacate the property.

- A defendant can apply to set aside the writ of possession; however it will not be set aside where the sheriff has taken possession of the premises pursuant to the writ of possession. *Beedell v. Pritchard* (1991), 29 A.C.W.S. (3d) 996 (Ont. Gen. Div.)

- A writ of possession will remain in force for a period of one year from the date of the order. The writ can subsequently be renewed before the expiry of the one-year period by further order of the court. Rules of Civil Procedure, 60.10(3)

9

BANKRUPTCY PROCEEDINGS

Table of Contents

Over the last ten years, the *Bankruptcy and Insolvency Act* (BIA) has undergone substantial review and significant revision. The result has encouraged debtors to make proposals rather than declare bankruptcy, and has further balanced the need to provide honest but unfortunate debtors the opportunity for a fresh start while protecting the interests of their creditors.

Creditors often believe that when debtors become bankrupts, their debt is beyond recovery. Although, clearly, this is often the case, bankruptcy is not necessarily an automatic loss for creditors: with careful attention to the process, it is possible to have at least some of the debt recovered, particularly if you are able to identify hidden or improperly transferred assets that constitute property of the bankrupt.

9.1 WHO CAN FILE FOR BANKRUPTCY?

9.1.1 CONSUMER BANKRUPTCY

- In order to file for bankruptcy, an individual must be an insolvent person, which means that:

  - the individual resides, carries on business or has property in Canada;
  - has unsecured debt of at least $1,000.00; and
  - is unable to meet their obligations generally as they become due. BIA s. 2

- Once the debtor has consulted a trustee in bankruptcy, and has determined that the only appropriate solution is to file an assignment in bankruptcy, the debtor provides the trustee with specific information, including a list of all assets, broken down by categories, and a list of debts.

- The debtor completes a Statement of Affairs and an Assignment for the General Benefit of Creditors, whereby the debtor assigns him or herself into bankruptcy and specifies a trustee in bankruptcy to file the assignment and subsequently administer the estate.

- The Assignment and Statement of Affairs are filed with the official receiver's office. The official receiver then appoints the trustee in bankruptcy who filed the bankruptcy to administer the estate.

9.1.2 COMMERCIAL BANKRUPTCY

- In order to file for bankruptcy, a corporation must be an insolvent person, which means that:

  - it has unsecured debt of at least $1000.00;
  - it has its head office or carries on business in Canada; and
  - it is either unable to pay its current obligations in the ordinary course as they become due, or its realizable value of assets is insufficient to pay its obligations that are due and owing. BIA s.2

- A majority of the corporation's Board of Directors must pass a resolution authorizing the assignment into bankruptcy. A copy of this resolution is provided to the trustee in bankruptcy, whereupon the trustee will prepare an Assignment for the General Benefit of Creditors and a Statement of Affairs, including all assets owned by the corporation and a list of debtors, including their names, addresses and amounts due and owing.

- The trustee files the Assignment and Statement of Affairs with the official receiver, in the jurisdiction where the debtor has carried on business in the year immediately preceding the bankruptcy, or, where that is inapplicable, where the greater portion of the debtor's property is located. Upon this filing, the bankruptcy begins. BIA s.2 and 3

9.1.3 PETITIONING AN INDIVIDUAL OR COMMERCIAL ENTITY INTO BANKRUPTCY

The decision to petition an individual or business into bankruptcy must be carefully considered, as it encompasses both risks and benefits. Bankruptcy creates its own priorities amongst the various classes of creditors, which may or may not supercede your client's priority. The downside is that your client will have to bear the costs of engaging the trustee in bankruptcy and will have to sign an indemnity for those costs. Furthermore, if the bankrupt's property includes any environmental problems, the trustee, and indirectly your client, may be responsible for paying to clean up the environmental damage. *Lamford Forest Products Ltd., Re* (1991), 10 C.B.R. (3d) 137 (B.C. S.C.). *A trustee is not personally liable nor is the client who appointed the trustee for any environmental damage that occurred before the trustee's appointment or after the trustee's appointment unless it can be shown that the condition arose or the damage occurred as a result of the trustee's gross negligence or willful misconduct.* BIA s.14.06(2)

(a) Who Can Petition Whom?

- One or more creditors having provable claims against the debtor totalling at least $1,000.00 can file a petition for a receiving order if the debtor has committed an act of bankruptcy in the six months preceding the petition. BIA s.43(1)

- If you are acting for a secured creditor who wishes to petition for a receiving order, they must place a reasonable value on their security, with the unsecured part of their claim being at least $1,000.00. Exercise caution in valuing the security, as future dividends for the unsecured part of the claim will be based on it. *Columbia Properties Ltd. v. Commonwealth Mortgage Corp.* (1963), 5 C.B.R. (N.S.) 258 (B.C. S.C.), affirmed (1964), 6 C.B.R. (N.S.) 321 (B.C. C.A.) and *Button, Re* [1905] 1 K.B. 602 (C.A.). *Note that a secured creditor can also give up their security and become an unsecured creditor for the full amount.*

- The BIA defines the debtor as an insolvent person, or a person who has committed an act of bankruptcy. The "person" can include an individual and most forms of businesses; however, those who cannot be petitioned into bankruptcy include farmers, fishers, certain types of cooperatives, banks, trust companies and insurance companies. BIA s.2 and Houlden and Morawetz, *Bankruptcy Law of Canada, Third Edition,* pp. 2-14.2 to 2-20

- Acts of bankruptcy include where the debtor has:

  - assigned property to the trustee in bankruptcy for the benefit of creditors generally, whether authorized by the BIA or not;
  - made a fraudulent conveyance or transfer of property;
  - made a conveyance or transfer constituting a fraudulent preference;
  - absented themselves out of Canada with the intent to defeat or delay creditors;
  - permitted an execution returned by the sheriff indicating that there is nothing to seize;
  - shown creditors a statement of assets and liabilities that indicates insolvency, or admits in writing to being unable to pay debts;
  - disposed of property with the intent to defraud, defeat or delay creditors;
  - notified creditors that debt payments are, or will be, suspended;
  - defaulted in a proposal to creditors under the BIA; or
  - ceased to meet their liabilities generally as they become due. BIA s.42(1)

- To prove that the debtor has ceased to meet their liabilities as they became due, you must show the court that there are at least two other unpaid debts. *Joyce, Re* (1984), 51 C.B.R. (N.S.) 152 (Ont. Bktcy.). *However, special circumstances can apply. If your client is a significant creditor - such that the claims of other creditors are of so little significance that there is only really one major creditor - the court can find an act of bankruptcy in the non-payment of your client's debt. Global Marketing Franchise Ltd., Re* (1982), 40 C.B.R. (N.S.) 269 (Ont. S.C.); *Dixie Market (Nurseries) Ltd., Re* (1971), 14 C.B.R. (N.S.) 281 (Ont. S.C.); *Mendzigall v. Albrecht Enterprises Inc.,* [2000] O.J. 4056 , 20 C.B.R. (4th) 269 (Bktcy.)

- Note that a petition will not be accepted by the court if the creditor is using it:

    - to get rid of a business competitor;
    - to use the bankruptcy system as a collection agency or to obtain a payment solely for the benefit of the petitioning creditor;
    - to extort a payment beyond what is legally due; or
    - to harass a debtor. Howell, Richard D. *Bankruptcy Petitions.* p. 11

- The court may, however, approve petitions that:

    - although filed for spite or revenge, are otherwise well-founded;
    - are filed to obtain remedies available only under the BIA; or
    - are filed to change priorities among creditors. Ibid.

(b) How to File a Petition

- The petitioning creditor, or an authorized representative who knows the circumstances involved in the petition, must sign the petition and the accompanying affidavit of truth. BIA s.43(3). *The affidavit of truth should not be signed by the solicitor, because that solicitor would be compellable as a witness based on the affidavit and would thus not be able to act. If the petition and the affidavit are signed by an authorized representative, ensure that the affidavit contains a provision that the individual is authorized and does have knowledge of the facts involved.*

Practice Tip: The petition can be signed by the solicitor for the petitioning creditor *Flora Lane Frocks Ltd., Re* (1952), 32 C.B.R. 154 (Ont. S.C.)

Practice Tip: A petition by a limited company is not required to have the company seal on it. *Croteau, Re* (1945), 27 C.B.R. 32 (Ont. S.C.). No resolution of a board of directors is required from the petitioning creditor if the petition is signed by an officer of such creditor under its corporate seal. *Batini Construction Co., Re* (1979), 29 C.B.R. (N.S.) 215 (Ont. S.C.) Furthermore, it is not necessary to have a meeting of the board of directors to approve the execution of the petition. *Glanzer, Re* (1973), 18 C.B.R. (N.S.) 266 (Ont. S.C.)

- File the petition in duplicate in the judicial district corresponding to the locality of the debtor. This means the place where the debtor carried on business or resided in the year prior to bankruptcy, or where the debtor's property is principally located. BIA s.2 and s.43(5)

- Obtain a hearing date that is at least 10 days later to ensure that you have enough time to serve the documents.

- Serve the petition, the notice of hearing, and the affidavit of truth on the debtor, on the trustee named in the petition and on the Division Office of the Superintendent of Bankruptcy at least 10 days before the hearing date. Bankruptcy Rules, Rule 70(1).

Practice Tip: The petition must be filed in court before it is served on the debtor. If the petition is served before it is filed, the petition is a nullity: *Chanteclerc de Ste-Rose Ltée v. Racz* (1962), 10 C.B.R. (N.S.) 298 (Que. S.C.)

- After the petition has been served, file a copy forthwith at the office of the Registrar in Bankruptcy and at the Division Office of the Superintendent in Bankruptcy. Bankruptcy Rules, Rule 70(2)

- The affidavit of service and the original petition must be filed in court at least two days before the petition is to be heard. Bankruptcy Rules, Rule 72

- If the debtor dies before the petition is served, service can be made on the deceased's legal representative. Bankruptcy Rules, Rule 73.

Practice Tip: Where the petition is against a debtor who is outside of the jurisdiction, service will be made in accordance with the Rules of Civil Procedure. Rule 3. In Ontario, an application should be made to the Registrar in Bankruptcy granting leave to serve the petition outside of Ontario.

- An application can be made to the court to obtain an order for substituted service of the petition for the receiving order. Bankruptcy Rules, Rules 70 and 71(1) and Forms 20 and 89

- Where an order is made for substitutional service, the documents are served as directed in the order together with a copy of the order. Bankruptcy Rules, Rule 70(2)

- Prepare a consent for the trustee in bankruptcy to sign, consenting to the appointment as trustee in the bankrupt estate if the receiving order is granted.

- Be prepared to provide the trustee with an indemnity to cover the costs of administering the estate, particularly if the estate contains few assets. The indemnity requested will vary with the complexity of the estate.

- The court has power to permit amendments to be made to the petition. Bankruptcy Rules, Rule 187(9)

- If a debtor intends to dispute a petition, they must file in court a notice setting out the statements in the petition that they intend to dispute and the grounds of the dispute. They must serve a copy of the notice on the petitioning creditor or their solicitor at least two clear days before the day appointed for hearing. Bankruptcy Rules, Rule 74. *A simple appearance is not sufficient. The notice of dispute must contain the information as required by Rule 74. Imbeault v. Petroles Irving Inc.* (1968), 13 C.B.R. (N.S.) 123 (Que. Q.B.)

- If the debtor has filed a notice of dispute but does not appear at the hearing, the court may make an order based on the allegations contained in the petition if the court considers the allegations to be sufficient. Bankruptcy Rules, Rule 75.

- The BIA includes a definition for "date of the initial bankruptcy event" which means that the bankruptcy relates back to the date the petition was filed. Previously, s. 71(1) BIA provided for the dating back of the bankruptcy to the date when the petition was filed. This section has now been repealed. *This relating back is very important because it is designed to prevent fraudulent conveyances or preferences from occurring between the date of the issuing of the petition for the receiving order and the signing of the receiving order.*

- A receiving order has the effect of transferring to the trustee in bankruptcy all of the property of the bankrupt. BIA s. 71(2)

(c) Dealing with Defences

- If a dispute is filed within eight days of the date you served the petition, the Registrar in Bankruptcy places the petition on the Judge's list to await a hearing. If your client's situation is urgent, you may apply to the court to obtain an earlier hearing date than that of the list.

- You should receive the notice of dispute at least two days before the hearing. Review the notice of dispute to ensure that the debtor has clearly listed the statements that they are disputing, the grounds for the dispute, and their address for service. *Bankruptcy Rules,* Rule 74

- Also review the notice of dispute to ascertain whether the debtor in fact denies having committed the alleged acts of bankruptcy. *Elar Construction Ltd., Re* (1961), 3 C.B.R. (N.S.) 249, 38 W.W.R. 85 (Man. Q.B.). *If the debtor does not deny at least one of these points, you can argue that the dispute is not valid.*

- The court can, at its discretion, stay a petition if it is disputed or for other sufficient reasons. BIA s. 43(10) and (11). *You should ensure that your case is as thorough as possible, and clearly outlines the benefit to the creditors in general, to reduce the risk that the court will grant a stay.*

- The court can stay a petition even if the petitioning creditor has proven all of the essential facts for the making of a receiving order: BIA s. 43(11). *The stay can be either absolute or for a limited time.*

- The onus is on the debtor to satisfy the court that there is sufficient reason for staying the petition. BIA s. 43(11), *Re Mediacoat Inc.* (1990), 80 C.B.R. (N.S.) 39 (Ont. S.C.)

- If the debtor files a notice of dispute, be prepared for them to cross-examine your client (or their authorized representative) on the affidavit of truth that was filed with the petition.

- The onus is on the petitioning creditor to prove the facts alleged in the petition and to satisfy that a receiving order should be made. *R. v. Yasmanicki* (1946), 27 C.B.R. 269 (Ont. S.C.)

- The petitioning creditor, if it believes it is appropriate, can call the debtor as a witness. *Freedman, Re* (1982), 50 C.B.R. (N.S.) 106 (Ont. S.C.). Furthermore, the petitioning creditor can call an officer of the debtor company as a witness. *Baker-Martin Ltd., Re* (1978), 27 C.B.R. (N.S.) 293 (Ont. H.C.)

- If the debtor appeals a receiving order that has been granted on the basis of a petition, the receiving order is automatically stayed; however, you may apply to the Court of Appeal to lift the stay if, for example, the appeal is not being prosecuted diligently. BIA s.195

(d) Interim Receivers

- If your client, as the petitioning creditor, is concerned that the debtor's estate is in need of protection, you should, perhaps, apply ex parte to a Registrar in Bankruptcy or Judge to have an interim receiver appointed. BIA s.46, s.192(1)(e) and (f) and Bankruptcy Rules, Rule 77 *It is better to give the debtor some notice of the application, even it is short notice. This will reduce the risk that the Interim Receivership Order will be overturned once the debtor has notice of it.*

- The onus is on your client as the applicant to show that a strong enough case for bankruptcy exists for a receiving order to be issued, and that the debtor's estate requires immediate protection. *Big Eddy Shops Ltd., Re* (1977), 24 C.B.R. (N.S.) 90 (Ont. S.C.) *This is particularly important in light of* Re Imperial Broadloom, *which found that the court should exercise greater caution in issuing an interim receiving order than would be exercised in granting an interim injunction. Imperial Broadloom Co., Re* (1978) 29 C.B.R. (N.S.) 113 (Ont. Bktcy.)

- You should apply for an interim receiver when the risks of not having the debtor's estate protected outweigh the costs involved in employing a receiver.

- The function of an interim receiver is to act as a monitor of the debtor's estate until the petition is heard. *Big Eddy Shops Ltd., Re,* supra; *Austroquip Manufacturing Ltd., Re* (1988), 68 C.B.R. (N.S.) 161 (Ont. S.C.)

- In addition, the interim receiver can, if authorized by the court, take conservatory measures and summarily dispose of property that is perishable or likely to depreciate in value. BIA s. 46(2)

(e) Withdrawing or Dismissing a Petition

- If you need to terminate a petition by way of dismissal, the order of dismissal ends the matter.

- If you want to withdraw the petition, you need to apply for an order giving you leave to withdraw the petition, and also serve and file the notice of withdrawal. Assuming that there are no assets, that the petition was not filed for an improper use, and that withdrawing the petition will not prejudice the other creditors or the BIA, the court will allow the withdrawal. *Host Restaurateurs Ltd. Re* (1991), 8 C.B.R. (3d) 15 (N.S. T.D.)

- Note that the court has held that an agreement between the debtor and the petitioning creditor does not constitute grounds for withdrawal of the petition. *Abu-Hatoum, Re* (1987), 63 C.B.R. (N.S.) 60 (Ont. S.C.)

9.2 STAY OF PROCEEDINGS

- Once the assignment into bankruptcy is filed, there is an automatic stay of proceedings against actions by creditors who have claims that are "provable in bankruptcy." This means that in most circumstances, unsecured creditors will be unable to take further steps outside the bankruptcy process to collect their outstanding debts from the bankrupt. BIA s.69.3(1) and s.195.

- However, you can apply to the court for an order granting leave to proceed with collecting the debt if the creditor can show:

    - that the creditor is likely to be materially prejudiced by continuing the stay; or
    - that it is equitable on other grounds for the stay to be lifted. BIA s.69(4). *This section gives the court a wide discretion.*

- Note that the test of "material prejudice" is an objective test, not a subjective test. It refers to the degree of prejudice suffered vis-à-vis the indebtedness and the security in question and not to the extent that such prejudice may affect the creditor as a person, organization or entity. *Cumberland Trading Inc., Re* (1994), 23 C.B.R. (3d) 225 (Ont. Gen. Div. [Commercial List]).

- A secured creditor's rights to enforce its security are not affected by a bankruptcy unless the trustee obtains an order postponing that right. BIA s.69.3

- The trustee does have the opportunity to consider whether anything can be realized on the security for the benefit of the estate over and above the amount due to secured creditors. BIA s. 69.3(2)

9.3 NOTICE TO CREDITORS

- After filing for the debtor's bankruptcy, the trustee will mail to all of the creditors disclosed by the bankrupt, or of which the trustee has knowledge, a copy of the Statement of Affairs, plus a Proof of Claim form, a Proxy form and a Notice of the First Meeting of Creditors.

- Although the bankrupt is required under BIA section 158(d) to give the names of all creditors to the trustee, there are numerous cases where this does not happen. Of major concern to you is that even if your client's name is not given to the trustee and your client does not therefore receive notice of the bankruptcy, in the case of an individual, an order of discharge from bankruptcy will still release your client's claim. *Scotia Mortgage Corp. v. Winchester* (1997), 46 C.B.R. (3d) 314 (Alta. Master). *Note that there is no mechanism for a corporation to be discharged. The only way that a corporation can be discharged is if it pays 100 cents on the dollar to all of its creditors and then it can obtain a discharge from bankruptcy.*

> **Practice Tip:** If you suspect that, given the debtor's financial situation as you know it, an assignment into bankruptcy is likely, it is worthwhile to monitor the bankruptcies filed in the jurisdiction where the debtor does business. In this way, you may be able to identify the need to file a proof of claim.

- If you discover after the bankrupt has obtained their discharge that your client should have been identified as a creditor (and assuming that the debt was a claim provable in bankruptcy and that a dividend was paid to other creditors), you should apply to the court to require the bankrupt to pay your client the equivalent amount of dividend that the other creditors received. BIA s.178(1)(f). *However, if your client was not disclosed as a creditor, yet knew about the bankruptcy and did not take reasonable steps to prove their claim, the bankrupt would not be liable to pay the dividend. Hall v. New Breton Homes Ltd.* (1994) 25 C.B.R. (3d) 307 (N.S. S.C.)

9.4 PROOFS OF CLAIM

9.4.1 PROVABLE CLAIMS

- Ensure that your client has a claim provable in bankruptcy: i.e., a debt that the debtor would be liable for either at the time of bankruptcy, or at the time of discharge because of an obligation incurred prior to bankruptcy. BIA s.121 to 123.

- To be a provable claim, the debt or liability must be due either at law or in equity from the bankrupt to the person seeking to prove the claim: *Excelsior Electric Dairy Machinery Ltd., Re* (1922), 2 C.B.R. 599 (Ont. S.C.). The claim must be one that is recoverable by legal process. *Central Capital Corp., Re* (1996), 38 C.B.R. (3d) 1 (Ont. C.A.)

- If your client has property that is in the debtor's possession, you need to file a Proof of Claim with the trustee giving the grounds on which your claim is based, and identifying the property with sufficient detail to allow it to be identified. BIA s.81(1). *The trustee then has 15 days after receiving the Proof of Claim, or after the first meeting of creditors, whichever is later, to either admit the claim and deliver the property to the creditor or give notice that the claim is disputed. BIA s.81(2). If the creditor does not appeal a disputed claim or respond to a trustee's request to prove his claim within 15 days, the property vests in the trustee. BIA s.81(4)*

9.4.2 FILING THE PROOF OF CLAIM

- The Proof of Claim form (Form 31) must be delivered to the trustee in order for the creditor to establish their claim in the bankruptcy. If it is not filed, the creditor loses their right to vote at any meeting of creditors and their entitlement to any dividend in the estate. BIA s.124(1)(2) and 129(1). *Wright v. Schwalm* (1926), 7 C.B.R. 465 (Ont. S.C.)

- Complete the proof of claim as fully and accurately as possible, and ensure that you provide all information requested by the trustee in bankruptcy. Note whether or not the creditor is unsecured, secured or preferred. BIA s.124(5). *Failure to do so can lead to the trustee disallowing the creditor's claim.*

Practice Tip: To complete the Proof of Claim form:

- The creditor must state their full and complete legal name;
- If an individual is completing a proof of claim and is not a creditor themselves, they must state their position or title;
- Give the complete address for forwarding all notices or correspondence;
- Ensure that the amount on the statement of account corresponds to the amount indicated on the proof of claim;
- Ensure that the statement of account is complete. A detailed statement of account for the last three months must be attached to the proof of claim, and must show the date plus the number and the amount of all of the invoices or charges, together with the date, the number and the amount of all credits or payments;
- All claimants must indicate whether or not they are related to the debtor;
- The claimant must attach a detailed list of payments or credits received within three months preceding the bankruptcy if the claimant and the debtor are not related, or within twelve months preceding the bankruptcy if the claimant and the debtor are related;
- The individual completing the declaration must personally sign the document; and
- The witness must sign the document.

- The proof of claim must be signed by the creditor or by their authorized representative who is familiar with the facts of the case (and must state the authority and how the representative has knowledge of the case). BIA s.124(3)

> **Practice Tip:** *The signature must be witnessed. Lack of a witness can lead to the claim being disallowed.*

- Attach statements of account or other documentation to back up the claim as required. Ensure that this documentation clearly shows the amount being claimed. BIA s.124(4)

- If your client is a secured creditor who wishes to receive a dividend, a proof of claim must be filed. BIA s.128(2). *The secured creditor will only be entitled to a dividend with respect to the balance due after deducting the value of the security from the debt.*

- File the proof of claim prior to the commencement of the first meeting of creditors (in order to allow your client to vote as a creditor at the meeting). *Failure to file by this time may allow your client's claim, but will not allow your client to vote at that crucial first meeting. You can file your proof of claim in person, by mail, courier or fax.*

- The trustee will review the proof of claim and either accept or disallow it. The trustee may also request further information of the creditor. BIA s.135(2)

- If the proof of claim is accepted, the creditor is now entitled to vote at meetings of creditors and to receive any dividends paid out of the bankrupt's assets.

> **Practice Tip:** In the case of the bankruptcy of an individual, you can request the following information by checking the boxes near the bottom of the proof of claim: (i) advice of any material change in the financial situation of the bankrupt; (ii) advice regarding the amount that the bankrupt is required to pay for surplus income; (iii) a copy of the section 170 trustee's report regarding the bankrupt's application for discharge.

Practice Tip: If you have concerns about your client's statements in the Proof of Claim, you may wish to remind them that a willfully false statement or willful misrepresentation can result in the court disallowing the proof of claim in whole or in part. BIA s.125 In addition, it is a bankruptcy offence to make a willfully false statement or misrepresentation. This can result in a fine of up to $5,000.00 and/or one year in prison. BIA s.201

9.4.3 DISALLOWANCE OF PROOF OF CLAIM

- A trustee can disallow, in whole or in part, a creditor's claim if the trustee finds that the claim is not entitled to be included in the estate, if it exceeds the creditor's entitlement, or if the creditors or inspectors have passed a resolution directing the disallowance of the claim. BIA s.135(2)

- The notice of disallowance must be sent by registered mail or courier. Bankruptcy Rules, Rule 113.

- A creditor can also ask the trustee to disallow or reduce the claim of another creditor, and may apply to court if the trustee does not agree. *The creditor must take proceedings for this under section 38. Only the creditors who have joined in the proceedings under section 38 are entitled to the benefit of the disallowance. The benefit to those creditors would be the dividend that would have been paid to the creditor whose claim was disallowed. Newman, Re* (1990), 77 C.B.R. (N.S.) 296 (Ont. S.C.)

- If the trustee disallows a creditor's claim, the trustee must serve on the creditor (NOT on you as their solicitor) a Notice of Disallowance as per Form 77, which must contain the reasons for the disallowance. BIA s.135(3), Bankruptcy Rules, Rule 113 and *Dominion Pegasus Helicopters Ltd., Re* (1976), 21 C.B.R. (N.S.) 238 (Ont. Bktcy.)

- There is no time set out for serving the Notice of Disallowance. It is, however, usual for a trustee to defer service until it is clear whether any dividends are to be paid. BIA s. 135(2), *Proprietary Mines Ltd. v. MacKay,* [1939] O.R. 461 (C.A.), affirmed [1941] 1 D.L.R. 240 (S.C.C.)

- If you believe the trustee has erred, you can appeal the disallowance, either to the Registrar in Bankruptcy or to a Judge sitting in Bankruptcy Court. The appeal must be filed within 30 days after service; if this time is insufficient, you must apply to the court for an extension within the 30 days. BIA s.135(4). *If the trustee in bankruptcy will consent, you can informally agree to extend the time for filing the appeal. Ensure that you obtain the consent of the trustee in writing.*

- Since the onus to prove the claim is on the party appealing, you must ensure that you have the necessary documentation to clearly satisfy the court that the trustee made an error in disallowing your client's claim.

- You must make the appeal by way of motion to the court. The notice of motion must specify the relief claimed in very precise terms. It is not acceptable to commence the appeal by sending a letter to the trustee with a copy to the Bankruptcy office. *Clarke Road Building Supplies Ltd., Re* (1983) 48 C.B.R. (N.S.) 220 (Ont. S.C.)

- You must also file affidavit evidence setting out the reasons why the trustee made an error in disallowing your client's claim, including the appropriate documents to back up this assertion.

- Serve the notice of motion and supporting affidavits on the trustee by personal service, mail, courier, facsimile or electronic transmission.

- File the notice of motion with the court prior to the hearing, along with every affidavit to be used in support of the motion, plus proof of service of the motion and supporting affidavits.

9.4.4 RECONCILIATION OF CLAIMS

- After the first meeting of creditors, the trustee will attempt to reconcile the claims filed by the creditors against the debts on the bankrupt's account books. In doing so, the trustee will also identify rights of set-off on behalf of the bankrupt. Creditors' claims can therefore be disallowed in whole or in part at this stage of the process as well.

9.5 EXAMINATIONS

9.5.1 OFFICIAL RECEIVER'S EXAMINATION

- In the case of a consumer bankruptcy, the bankrupt may be required to attend at an examination conducted by the official receiver to determine the causes of the bankruptcy and to see what assets (if any) were transferred by the bankrupt, and when. BIA s.163(1), Form 27

- In the case of a commercial bankruptcy, at least one of the officers and directors of the corporation will be required to attend at an examination conducted by the official receiver to determine if property has been disposed of, and how, within three months, one year and five years of the bankruptcy. BIA s.164, Form 28

- Note that the examination covers time periods prior to the bankruptcy, as well as the bankruptcy itself, and is usually only conducted where the estate is large or complex enough that improper transactions could have been made in the time period leading up to bankruptcy.

- If you suspect that property has been transferred by the bankrupt improperly, or if you need further information in order to prove your claim, submit your questions to the official receiver, who will then ask them of the bankrupt at the examination.

- If examination transcripts are not automatically sent to you, they can be viewed in the applicable bankruptcy file. BIA s.163(3)

9.5.2 EXAMINATION BY THE TRUSTEE

- The trustee is permitted to examine under oath the bankrupt, any person reasonably thought to have knowledge of the affairs of the bankrupt, or any person who is or has been an agent, clerk, servant, officer, director or employee of the bankrupt. BIA s.163(1)

- The purpose of examination is to obtain information that will assist the trustee in carrying out his duties to administer the bankrupt estate. The trustee must determine the extent of the property interests of the bankrupt and whether there have been any dispositions or dealings with the properties that could be challenged. *303687 Ontario Ltd.* (1986), 58 C.B.R. (N.S.) 198 (Ont. S.C.)

- Courts have allowed individuals such as the bankrupt's solicitor, accountant and spouse to be examined. *Clarkson Co. v. Chilcott* (1984), 53 C.B.R. (N.S.) 251 (Ont. C.A.)

- A solicitor must answer questions regarding the transfer of funds in and out of a bankrupt's trust account. *Lauzier, Re* (1996), 43 C.B.R. (3d) 207 (Ont. Bktcy.)

- A client's trust account ledger is not privileged and must be produced on a section 163 examination. *Lauzier Re,* supra

- A prima facie case of fraud must be established in order to examine a solicitor under section 163(1) with respect to communications made with a client. This will also be the case if a solicitor is required to make production of documents on the basis that the communications were made for or in furtherance of fraud. *Canbook Distributing Corp. v. Borins* (1999), 7 C.B.R. (4th) 121 (Ont. Gen. Div. [Commercial List]).

- Any person being examined is required to answer all questions relating to business or property of the bankrupt, the causes of bankruptcy and the dispositions of the bankrupt's property. BIA s.167. *The scope of the examination is therefore very wide. 303687 Ontario Ltd., Re* supra

- The trustee is authorized to order any person to be examined to produce any books, records, documents, correspondence or papers in their possession or power relating to the bankrupt and the bankrupt's dealings with property. BIA s.163(1)

- The trustee can demand the production of the documents before conducting the examination. *S.P. Paint Factory Ltd. Re* (1980), 39 C.B.R. (N.S.) 12 (Man. Q.B.) *The usual practice in Ontario is to serve the person to be examined with an appointment and serve a notice with the appointment that the witness is to produce all books, documents, correspondence and papers in the witness's possession or power relating all or in part to the bankrupt, his dealings or property. Trend International Tool Ltd. (Trustee of) v. Wayne Forge Ltd.* (1986), 59 C.B.R. (N.S.) 164 (Ont. S.C.)

9.5.3 EXAMINATION BY THE CREDITOR

- If the creditor is unsatisfied with the official receiver's examination (or the trustee's examination if one has been held), or if they have additional questions to ask, they can apply to the court to conduct their own examination of the bankrupt and/or those associated with the bankruptcy, including the trustee, an inspector or another creditor. BIA s.163(2) *The cost of the examination will be paid for by your client.*

- The examination is held with a court stenographer present, taking a transcript of the evidence. The party being examined is placed under oath or is allowed to affirm the evidence. *This enables you, as the client's solicitor, to actually meet the debtor and form a firsthand impression of their attitude, and to examine the debtor's assets and liabilities. Depending on whom you are permitted to examine, it may also uncover assets and debts that you were not previously aware of.*

- As a creditor, your client can also review, and take copies of, the books, records and documents that relate to the administration of the bankrupt's estate. BIA s.26(3)

9.6 FIRST MEETING OF CREDITORS

- The trustee calls a First Meeting of Creditors, notice of which must be sent to all known creditors and the Superintendent of Bankruptcy within five days after the assignment is filed or the receiving order is made. The meeting itself must be held within 21 days after the filing of the assignment or the making of the receiving order. BIA s.102(1). *Through the meetings of creditors, the creditors control the decisions that must be made in the course of the bankruptcy.*

> **Practice Tip:** Since the trustee must advertise the meeting of creditors in a local newspaper at least five days before the date of the meeting, it may be wise to monitor such listings. You may be able to identify debtors with whom your clients have dealings, and be prepared to act proactively to have your client's claims filed even if they have not been identified by the bankrupt as creditors. BIA s.102(4)

- The first meeting is held for the purpose of affirming the appointment of a trustee or substituting a different trustee. In addition, inspectors must be appointed and general directives must be given for the administration of the estate.

- The meeting is usually chaired by the official receiver or its nominee (usually the trustee in bankruptcy). The bankrupt individual, or a representative from the bankrupt company (both of whom are entitled to be represented by counsel at the meeting) also attend. BIA s.105

- The chair will certify which of the creditors attending have filed a proof of claim and are therefore entitled to vote. BIA s.108(1) and 109(1). *The chair may briefly adjourn the meeting to consider proofs of claim filed before the meeting but not yet reviewed.*

- A quorum is met if at least one of the creditors attends the meeting. BIA s.106(1). *If no creditors attend the meeting, the trustee's appointment is deemed to be confirmed without further need to consult creditors. BIA s.106(2)*

- Creditors who have filed provable claims in bankruptcy are entitled to vote on the basis of one vote for each dollar of a creditor's claim. All questions are decided by resolutions, which are carried by a majority of votes. BIA s.115.

- If the chair or another creditor raise doubts about whether a certain claim is, in fact, provable, the creditor with the questioned claim should be allowed to vote. If the claim is later confirmed not to be provable, the vote can then be discounted. BIA s.108(3). *Wholesale Grocery Ltd., Re* (1923), 3 C.B.R. 650 (Ont. S.C.)

- Each class of creditors votes separately. BIA s.107

- If a creditor cannot attend the meeting, they can assign someone else (as long as it is not the debtor) a proxy via a letter, fax or electronic communication. BIA s.109(2)(3)(4)

- Note that if the creditor was not dealing with the debtor at arm's length in the year prior to the debtor's bankruptcy, that creditor cannot vote at meetings. The only exception to this occurs by leave of the court when the creditors who were dealing at arm's length do not constitute at least 20 percent in value of the total claims against the debtor. BIA s. 109(6)(7)

- The appointment of a trustee under an assignment or a receiving order is only effective until the first meeting of creditors. The appointment must be affirmed at the first meeting of creditors or a substitute trustee appointed.

Reliable Specialties Ltd., Re (1960), 1 C.B.R. (N.S.) 56 (Ont. S.C.). If there is no quorum at the meeting of creditors, the appointment of the trustee is deemed to be affirmed. BIA s.106(2)(a)

- Creditors either affirm the trustee's appointment, or substitute a trustee of their own choosing via a special resolution, which requires a majority in number and three-quarters of the value of the proven claims present, personally or by proxy, and voting on the resolution. BIA s.2(1), 14; *Windsor Home Furniture Co., Re* (1954), 34 C.B.R. 53 (Ont. S.C.). *If the creditors wish to successfully substitute the trustee, they should ensure prior to the first meeting of creditors that they have sufficient votes to substitute the trustee, and that the substituted trustee is waiting outside the meeting to step in should the vote for substitution be successful.*

- Creditors may also elect up to five inspectors, who have the role of supervising the trustee, instructing the trustee to take whatever steps are considered appropriate to protect the estate and the creditors. BIA s.116 and 120; *Fishman, Re* (1985), 56 C.B.R. (N.S.) 316 (Ont. S.C.). The only people not eligible to be inspectors are the bankrupt or someone who is a party to an action or proceeding against the bankrupt's estate. BIA s.116(2)

- The inspectors will, among other duties, be responsible for verifying the estate's bank balance, examining the trustee's accounts, inquiring into the adequacy of the security filed by the trustee, and approving the final statement of receipts and disbursements, dividend sheet and disposition of unrealized property. BIA s.120(3). Care should therefore be taken to elect inspectors who have experience or knowledge in these matters. However, in case of conflict between the creditors and the inspectors, the creditors' directions override the inspectors'. In addition, the court can review the inspectors' decisions as it deems proper. BIA s.119(1)(2)

- Expect documents including the Statement of Affairs, the Assignment and the official receiver's examination (if applicable) to be tabled at the meeting. The trustee will either read the report prepared with respect to the bankrupt's affairs, or allow the creditors time to review the report and ask questions of the trustee, the bankrupt (who, of course, must attend) or a representative of the bankrupt corporation. This will allow the creditors attending the meeting to make decisions and give directions to the trustee and the inspectors on matters such as how to realize the property of the bankrupt.

- In more complex bankruptcies, more than one meeting of creditors is required. The trustee can call such a meeting at any time, and must call a meeting when directed to do so by the court, by a majority of inspectors (in writing), or by 25 percent of the creditors holding 25 percent of the value of proved claims. BIA s.103(1)

9.7 SURPLUS INCOME

- At the beginning of a bankruptcy, the Trustee determines the amount, if any, that the bankrupt will be required to pay to the creditors. This amount is called "surplus income".

- The bankrupt's surplus income is considered in two situations:

  - on setting the amounts the bankrupt is to pay the trustee during the period of bankruptcy for distribution to creditors; and
  - on considering the amounts the bankrupt is to pay the trustee for distribution to creditors as a condition of discharge.

- An understanding of how surplus income is calculated will assist you in determining whether to oppose the amount decided upon by the trustee. The trustee calculates a bankrupt's surplus income by first subtracting from their total income the expenses associated with personal and family situations - such as statutory payments of income tax and pension deductions, child or spousal support, child care, medical care, court fines, and debts not subject to a stay of proceedings. BIA s. 68(3). *Section 4(1) of the Office of the Superintendent of Bankruptcy's Directive No. 11 details the expenses that may be deducted from the bankrupt's total income to arrive at net income. The trustee must obtain from the bankrupt proof of income and a completed Income and Expense Statement. Section 6, Directive No. 11.*

- Once the bankrupt's net monthly income has thus been determined, the trustee uses the standards as set out in Appendix A to Directive No. 11 to calculate the portion of this income that must be paid to creditors.

- A bankrupt is required to inform the trustee of any material change in his or her financial situation. BIA s.158(n.1)

- If there is a material change in the personal or family situation of the bankrupt, the trustee may amend the amount that the bankrupt is required to pay. BIA s.68(4).

- If you or another creditor, or the bankrupt, oppose the amount calculated by the trustee, the trustee files a mediation request. BIA s 170.1(5)

- Only if there is a failure to reach an agreement at the mediation does the trustee need to apply to court for a hearing. *Landry, Re* (1999), 14. C.B.R. (4th) 112 (Ont. Bktcy.), reversed (2000), 3 C.C.E.L. (3d) 1 (Ont. C.A.). *Directive 11.*

- Until the trustee takes action under section 68(3), the bankrupt is free to receive their income and use it as they see fit. *Chisick, Re* (1967), 10 C.B.R. (N.S.) 240 (Man. Q.B.) aff'd (1967), 11. C.B.R. (N.S.) 161 (Man. C.A.)

- If the official receiver recommends an alteration in the amount payable by the bankrupt, the trustee may amend the amount that the bankrupt is required to pay. BIA s.68(5)

- The trustee will be permitted to attach after-acquired earnings of the bankrupt having regards to the needs of the bankrupt and their dependents. *Sihler, Re* (1982), 43 C.B.R. (N.S.) 49 (Ont. Bktcy.).

9.8 PROPERTY OF THE BANKRUPT

9.8.1 WHAT CONSTITUTES PROPERTY?

- After the first meeting of creditors, the trustee will dispose of the assets (selling them by tender, public auction or private contract) and place the net proceeds in the trustee's trust account until they can be disbursed to the creditors.

- Prior to the first meeting of creditors, the trustee may have found a buyer for the assets, which may or may not be perishable. In the event that the transaction cannot wait until the first meeting of creditors for the creditors' approval, the trustee can apply to court for directions to sell the assets prior to the first meeting. BIA s.34(1). *The trustee must be able to show that the amount being paid is reasonable under the circumstances, and must provide copies of any relevant appraisals. National Capital Region, Ottawa Rough Riders Professional Football Club Ltd., Re* (1995), 31 C.B.R. (3d) 136 (Ont. Bktcy.)

- If the trustee proceeds with the sale of assets prior to the appointment of inspectors and no court approval is obtained, the sale will be void and the trustee will be liable in damages to the purchaser. *Johnstone Fabricators Ltd. v. Canadian Credit Men's Trust Assn.* (1964), 7 C.B.R. (N.S.) 22 (B.C.S.C.)

- Other powers of the trustee include (in a commercial bankruptcy): leasing real property; carrying on the bankrupt's business; bringing, instituting or defending any action or legal proceedings relating to the bankrupt's property; and retaining, assigning or disclaiming any lease made by the bankrupt. BIA s.30

- Certain assets are not considered property of the bankrupt for the purposes of the estate: these include property held in trust and property exempt from execution under provincial law. BIA s.67. *Provincial exemptions vary across the country; however, in Ontario, they include: wearing apparel of the debtor and family not exceeding $1,000.00; household effects of the debtor not exceeding $2,000.00; and tools of the debtor's trade not exceeding $2,000.00.* Execution Act, s.2. *In addition, personal injury awards and certain life insurance contracts and pensions are exempt.*

- Property that is subject to the rights of secured creditors will also not be divisible among the creditors, provided that the security is valid and there is no equity in the property. If there is equity in the property, the secured creditor is obligated to account to the trustee for any surplus, whether they have been asked to or not.

- Transactions made by the bankrupt prior to the assignment into bankruptcy should come under scrutiny by the trustee to determine if they are reviewable. As counsel for a creditor, you must monitor the trustee's actions to ensure that the scrutiny is sufficient.

- Property that the bankrupt acquires after the date of bankruptcy and before the date of discharge may also be considered "after-acquired property" that must be deposited to the estate for distribution to creditors. Such property includes earnings relating to pre-bankruptcy employment, inheritances and lottery winnings. BIA s.99. *Wages, however, are not considered after-acquired property. Instead, wages are taken into consideration in the calculation of surplus income payments.*

Practice Tip: The trustee's disposition of assets can often be a lengthy process. However, as A. Duncan Grace notes in "Special Procedures and Rights in Bankruptcy," a strategy used in some situations to speed up the process involves the debtor's negotiation and execution of an Agreement of Purchase and Sale. When

Practice Tip Cont'd: pre-conditions are close to being fulfilled, the commercial debtor makes an assignment into bankruptcy, and the trustee applies to the court to complete the transaction. In this way, assets are disposed of even before the first meeting of creditors. Secured creditors of the debtor would be well advised to monitor the process leading to the Agreement of Purchase and Sale to ensure their rights are protected. Grace, A. Duncan. "Special Procedures and Rights in Bankruptcy," *Insolvency From Petition to Discharge: Getting Results in Bankruptcy*

9.8.2 SETTING ASIDE TRANSACTIONS

For a guide to setting aside transactions outside the BIA, please see Chapter 6.

(a) Reviewable Transactions Under the BIA

- A reviewable transaction is one where the transaction takes place between a bankrupt and a person not dealing at arms length with the bankrupt. BIA s.3(1). *Persons related to each other as defined in BIA s. 4 are deemed not to be dealing at arms length.*

- A reviewable transaction that occurs within the 12 months prior to bankruptcy can be reviewed by the court as to whether the consideration given was at fair market value for the goods or services involved. BIA s.100(1)

- Where the consideration for the transaction is conspicuously greater or lesser than fair market value, the court can give judgment to the trustee for the difference between the actual consideration and the fair market value of the property. BIA s.100(2)

- The test as to whether or not the difference in consideration is conspicuous is whether it is conspicuous to the court having regard to the particular circumstances of the case. *Skalbania (Trustee of) v. Wedgewood Village Estates Ltd.* (1988), 70 C.B.R. (N.S.) 232 (B.C. S.C.), aff'd (1989), 74 C.B.R. (N.S.) 97 (B.C. C.A.), leave to appeal refused (1989), 40 B.C.L.R. (2d) xxxiii (note) (S.C.C.)

Practice Tip: To be successful on a reviewable application, you must prove the existence of three factors:

1. The transaction is reviewable: i.e., where the participants were not at arm's length;
2. The transaction between the parties not at arm's length took place within the 12 months preceding the bankruptcy; and
3. The price of the goods or services given or received was far greater or far less than their fair market value. BIA s. 100

- If a corporation paid a dividend (other than a stock dividend) or redeemed or purchased its own shares in the 12 months prior to bankruptcy, it may be considered a reviewable transaction. The court can investigate whether the dividend was paid or the shares redeemed or purchased at a time when the corporation was insolvent, or whether the dividend/share action rendered the corporation insolvent. BIA s.101(1). *In this case, the court can give judgment to the trustee against the corporation's directors and against shareholders related to the directors, for the amount of the dividend or redemption plus interest, unless that director properly protested the dividend or share redemption/purchase. BIA s.101(2) and (3)*

(b) Settlements Under the BIA

- Settlements are defined as transfers or gifts that the bankrupt has made gratuitously or for nominal consideration. BIA s.1 and s.91

- If the bankrupt has made any settlement of property within one year prior to bankruptcy, the settlement is void. BIA s.91(1)

- If the bankrupt has made any settlement of property within five years prior to bankruptcy, which is the earliest of an assignment filed by the person, a proposal made in respect of the person, a notice of intention to make a proposal filed by the person or a petition in respect of which a receiving order is made, and it can be proved that the bankrupt, at the time of the settlement, was unable to pay their debts without the property involved in the settlement or that the bankrupt's interest in the property did not pass on, the settlement is void. BIA s.91(2)

- Note that this section does not apply to settlements made before or in consideration of marriage, in favour of a purchaser in good faith and for valuable consideration, or in the interests of the bankrupt's spouse or children. BIA s.91(3)

- Until a court sets aside a settlement, the transaction is considered to be valid. Therefore, the trustee must bring an application to declare that the transaction is a settlement. Failure to do so means that the transaction is not affected by the bankruptcy. *Cox v. R.* (1995), 31 C.B.R. (3d) 266 (T.C.C.)

- In the event that a settlement is declared void as against the trustee, then the settled property reverts to the trustee of the bankrupt's estate, who holds it for the benefit of the creditors. *Ramgotra (Trustee of) v. North American Life Assurance Co.* (1996) 37 C.B.R. (3d) 141 (S.C.C.)

Practice Tip: Where a trustee applies to a court to set aside or avoid any settlement, the court may: (i) proceed in a summary manner to try the question or issue in the case; (ii) adjourn the hearing; (iii) direct or settle any issue to be tried; (iv) give directions for the preparation of the filing of pleadings for the trial of the issue or question; or (v) make such further order as the court otherwise considers desirable. Houlden & Morawetz, *Bankruptcy Law of Canada, Third Edition, 4-19*

(c) Fraudulent Preferences Under the BIA

- A conveyance or transfer of property made by the bankrupt to a creditor within the three months prior to bankruptcy, if done while the debtor was insolvent and with the intent to prefer certain creditors over others, is a fraudulent preference and is void. BIA s.95(1) Fraudulent preferences can only involve property that would otherwise be available for distribution to creditors: transactions dealing with exempt property that is not part of the bankrupt's estate cannot be set aside.

- Where such a conveyance or transfer was done in favour of a person related to the bankrupt, the period is extended to 12 months. BIA s.96

- The object of section 95 is to prevent the debtor from making a distribution of their property that would defeat the purpose of the BIA, which is that all ordinary creditors should share equally. *Hudson v. Benallack* (1975), 21 C.B.R. (N.S.) 111 (S.C.C.)

- Fraudulent preferences appear in five types of transaction:

  - conveyances or transfers of property;
  - charges on property;
  - payments made; or
  - obligations incurred; and
  - judicial proceedings taken or suffered.

    BIA s.95(1)

- The usual method for attacking a transaction alleged to be a fraudulent preference is by way of notice of motion. Houlden & Morawetz, *Bankruptcy Law of Canada, Third Edition,* Precedents 30 to 35.

- The court will use the procedure provided for by the ordinary *Rules of Civil Procedure. Pratchler Agro Services Inc. (Trustee of) v. Cargill Ltd.* (1999), 11 C.B.R. (4th) 107 (Sask. Q.B.). A fraudulent preference action will usually be tried by way of trial of an issue. At a trial of an issue, the court will hear viva voce evidence and appraise the witnesses and determine the matter, largely on a factual basis. *Candie Maid Ltd., Re* (1975), 20 C.B.R. (N.S.) 106 (Ont. S.C.). *There have been exceptions where the court has decided the matter on the basis of affidavit evidence and examinations and did not direct the trial of an issue. Townson, Re* (1990), 80 C.B.R. (N.S.) 216 (Ont. Bktcy.)

- If a section 95 motion is contested and a respondent files affidavit evidence, the courts will normally direct the trial of an issue so that the decision can be based on viva voce evidence, rather than on affidavits and attached exhibits. *Craig (Trustee of) v. Devlin Estate* (1989), 76 C.B.R. (N.S.) 256 (Man. C.A.). *In Ontario, if a trustee applies for an order declaring certain transactions to be a fraudulent preference, where the intent is a decisive criteria, a trial of an issue will be directed. In such cases, the practice has not been to require the respondent to file an affidavit, because such an affidavit would only delay the process and, as a rule, would not eliminate the necessity of having a trial of an issue. Jolie Femme Ltd., Re* (1977), 26 C.B.R. (N.S.) 108 (Ont. S.C.), leave to appeal refused by Martin, J.A. (1978), 26 C.B.R. (N.S.) 108 (Ont. C.A.)

- You must be able to prove that the effect of the transfer was to prefer a certain creditor or creditors: the court will then presume intent on the part of the bankrupt, even if the bankrupt made the transfer under pressure from that creditor or creditors. BIA s.95(2)

9.8.3 WHEN THE TRUSTEE REFUSES TO ACT

- Even when property has been improperly transferred or payments improperly made, a trustee may not wish to pursue an action, particularly if the estate does not contain enough assets to cover the cost of that action. You, on behalf of the creditor, can apply to the court for an order to take over the trustee's cause of action (on any matter, not just on a property transfer matter), on the proviso that the action would benefit the estate in general: i.e., the creditors as a whole. BIA s.38. *Note that you can do this regardless of whether or not the cause of the action relates to your client's claim. Toronto Dominion Bank v. Alex L. Clark Ltd.* (1993), 22 C.B.R. (3d) 6 (Ont. Gen. Div.)

- In order to take over the right of action from the trustee, your client must be a creditor with a claim provable in bankruptcy.

- Before making the section 38 application, ensure that the trustee has been asked to take action, and that the trustee has refused to do so. If needed, you should request that the trustee take the proceedings and the trustee must either refuse or neglect to do so. BIA s.38 and *Points of Call Airlines Ltd., Re* (1990), 80 C.B.R. (N.S.) 157 (B.C. S.C.) *The action brought by the creditor is based on the trustee's right to bring the action, so the creditor using the section 38 order is taking the action as if the creditor were the trustee. The section 38 action does not create a cause of action in the creditor; it merely allows the creditor to stand in the place of the trustee to advance a cause of action vested in the trustee that the trustee has refused to take. Zammit, Re* (1998), 3 C.B.R. (4th) 193 (Ont. Bktcy.) *Before bringing the application under section 38 and the resulting action, the creditor would be prudent to investigate the matter by an examination under section 163(2). This way, the creditor can consider the suitability of the section 38 action.*

> **Practice Tip:** When filing the section 38 notice of motion, you should include a supporting affidavit showing that the statutory prerequisites have been complied with. This should include:
>
> - the date of the bankruptcy;
> - evidence of the creditor's request to the trustee to bring the action; and
> - the trustee's refusal to proceed. *Dominion Trustco Corp., Re* (1997), 45 C.B.R. (3d) 25 (Ont. Bktcy.) aff'd (1997), 50 C.B.R. (3d) 84 (Ont. C.A.)

- In the event that a trustee has been discharged, it does not affect the operation of section 38: a creditor can still apply under BIA section 41(10) to obtain the section 38 order. *Coulter, Re* (1968), 11 C.B.R. (N.S.) 250 (Ont. S.C.); *Gladstone v. Bronson Granite & Marble Ltd.* (1998), 4 C.B.R. (4th) 265 (Ont. Bktcy.)

- The only party that you need to serve with the notice of application is the trustee *Swerdlow, Re* (1985), 57 C.B.R. (N.S.) 180 (Ont. S.C.). In particular, you do not have to serve the defendant with the section 38 notice of application. *Caisse populaire Vanier Ltée v. Bales* (1991), 3 C.B.R. (3d) 264 (Ont. Gen. Div.); *Coroban Plastics Ltd., Re* (1994), 28 C.B.R. (3d) 260 (B.C. S.C.), leave to appeal refused (1994), 34 C.B.R. (3d) 50 (B.C. C.A.)

- Even where a proposed defendant does receive notice of the section 38 application, they have no standing to cross-examine on the affidavit in support of the section 38 application, nor are they entitled to appear at the application hearing. *Nesi Energy Marketing Canada Inc., Re* (1998), 8 C.B.R. (4th) 76 (Alta. Q.B.)

- You do not need to notify the estate's other creditors before applying for the section 38 order. If you are successful in obtaining the order, however, you must give those creditors a reasonable opportunity to decide whether or not to participate in the action. The section 38 order will generally include provisions for notifying the other creditors, including the need to make the notification by registered mail. BIA s.38(3); *Toyota Canada Inc. v. Imperial Richmond Holdings Ltd.* (1993), 20 C.B.R. (3d) 102 (Q.B.), aff'd (1994) 27 C.B.R. (3d) 1 (Alta. C.A.), leave to appeal to S.C.C. refused (1994), 29 C.B.R. (3d) 153 (S.C.C.); *Hord, Re* 27 C.B.R. 229; [1946] O.W.N. 580 (S.C.)

- Just as other creditors can opt to join your action, you can choose to join an action that they have brought. Creditors must share pro rata the expenses associated with the action; however, they of course share the fruits of the action on the same basis. If no other creditors join your action, for example, any benefits from the action belong exclusively to your client, to the extent of your client's claim. BIA s.38(3)

- If creditors decide to join the proceedings, they should not be made a party plaintiff in the action. *Waffle's Electric Ltd. v. Davis* (1988), 70 C.B.R. (N.S.) 316 (Ont. H.C.)

Practice Tip: If your creditor's claim is of a low priority in relation to other claims, joining an action by another creditor where the trustee has refused to act may be a strategic way to increase the monies your client stands to receive. The fruits of such a creditor action do not become the property of the bankrupt: they belong solely to the creditors who participated in the action. (If the action provides a surplus after the creditors' claims have been satisfied in full, that surplus then belongs to the estate. BIA s.38(3)) You'll need to assess the costs your client may incur in the action, the strength of the case, the likelihood of success and the potential distribution of assets in order to advise your client.

- Once the creditor has obtained the order under section 38, a summary application can be made in bankruptcy court if appropriate. The section 38 application, if unopposed, can be dealt with by the registrar in bankruptcy.

BIA s.192(1)(f); *Wagon Stop Inc., Re* (1979), 30 C.B.R. (N.S.) 63 (Ont. S.C.)

- If the trustee opposes the section 38 application, the matter will have to be dealt with by a judge sitting in bankruptcy court, as the registrar will not have jurisdiction. BIA s.192(1)(f)

9.9 PRIORITIES

- In order to assess the likelihood of your client receiving dividends from a bankrupt's estate (and thus the course of action to follow and its associated expenses), you need to assess the priorities ahead of your client's claim.

- The priorities in a bankruptcy fall thus:

  - secured claims;
  - trust claims;
  - if the bankrupt is deceased, reasonable funeral and testamentary expenses incurred by the legal representatives;
  - the costs of administration of the bankrupt estate and any associated legal costs;
  - the levy payable to the Superintendent of Bankruptcy, which is calculated to be five percent of each dividend (this levy reduces the costs of administering the bankruptcy system);
  - wages and salaries of employees for services rendered within six months immediately before the date of bankruptcy to a maximum of $2,000.00 per employee, or, in the case of a travelling salesperson, a further $1,000 for disbursements within that six-month period;
  - a claim for spousal or child support, whether for periodic payments or a lump sum under an order or agreement made before the initial bankruptcy event and a time when the spouse or child was living apart from the bankrupt;
  - municipal taxes levied within the two years immediately preceding the date of bankruptcy that do not

constitute a preferential lien or charge against the real property to the maximum of the value of the bankrupt's interest in the property;

- any arrears to a landlord for rent for the three months immediately preceding the date of bankruptcy, and accelerated rent for the three months following the date of bankruptcy to a maximum of the value of any distrainable goods on the premises as at the date of bankruptcy;
- fees and expenses of the first creditor who enforced an execution. *The priority is limited to the extent of the realization from the property seizable under the writ of seizure and sale.*
- claims resulting from injuries to the bankrupt's employees that are not covered by any Worker's Compensation Act, to the extent of monies received from persons or companies guaranteeing the bankrupt against damages resulting from injury; and
- the unsecured creditors, who are paid on a pro rata basis. BIA s.136(1)

9.10 DISCHARGE

9.10.1 ENTITLEMENT TO DISCHARGE

- A key part of the bankruptcy and discharge process is the trustee's filing of the Section 170 Trustee's Report with the Superintendent's office and with those creditors who have requested a copy of the report. This report indicates several essential points, including whether the bankrupt has performed their duties satisfactorily, the bankrupt's conduct, whether or not the trustee is recommending a conditional discharge, and the amount of assets that have been or are to be realized in the estate. The trustee also recommends whether the bankrupt should be discharged subject to conditions, based on whether the bankrupt has made the required surplus payments during the bankruptcy, the total amount paid by the bankrupt and the fact that the bankrupt chose bankruptcy over making a proposal to resolve their indebtedness. In addition, in the case of a corporate bankruptcy, the report also includes a resolution of the inspectors as to whether or not they agree with the report. BIA s.170

- A first-time individual bankrupt is entitled to an automatic discharge nine months from the date of the filing of the assignment in bankruptcy, assuming that no one has opposed the bankrupt's discharge and that the trustee's report is favourable. BIA s.168.1(1)(f). *The practice has evolved that, for a first-time bankrupt, the trustee includes with the initial notice of the first meeting of creditors a Notice of Impending Automatic Discharge.*

- In the case of a second-time or subsequent bankrupt, or where the bankrupt has failed to meet their responsibilities (such as refusing to attend required counselling sessions), a court hearing is set to determine whether sanctions should be imposed on the bankrupt. These may include:

    - suspending the bankrupt's discharge;
    - refusing the bankrupt's discharge (which is rarely done, and generally only when rehabilitation seems very unlikely); or
    - imposing conditions on the bankrupt that must be performed in order for the bankrupt to obtain an absolute discharge. BIA s.172.

9.10.2 OPPOSING THE DISCHARGE

- The discharge can be opposed, within the nine-month period, by creditors with a claim provable in bankruptcy, the trustee or the official receiver. The matter will then go to either mediation, depending on the circumstances, or to a hearing by a Registrar in Bankruptcy or a Bankruptcy Judge. BIA s. 170.1(4)

- To oppose the discharge of a first-time bankrupt, prepare and serve a notice of opposition, clearly stating your grounds for opposition, to the bankrupt, the trustee and the Superintendent of Bankruptcy any time prior to when the nine-month period of bankruptcy expires. *Williams Re,* [2000] B.C.J. No. 1851, 21 C.B.R. (4th) 139 (S.C.)

- The notice of opposition to discharge must be in accordance with section 173(1). *Please note that many cases have been dismissed by the court where the notice of opposition was defective because it was not in accordance with section 173(1). If you have additional grounds, other than those set out in section 173, include those grounds together with the section 173 grounds to ensure that you will have standing at the hearing.*

- Ordinarily, a secured creditor who is not claiming as an unsecured creditor has no right to object to the discharge. The courts have provided an exception, however, if you can show that the bankrupt's conduct has been inappropriate, and you bring it to the court's attention in order to protect the integrity of the BIA and its administration or the interests of unsecured creditors. *Goldman, Re* (1982), 43 C.B.R. (N.S.) 30 (Ont. S.C.).

> **Practice Tip:** Maintain in your diary the deadlines to oppose discharges to ensure that you do not miss a key date. *The latest date that you should file the notice of oppostion to discharge is aftee the eighth month, once you receieve the section 170 trustee's report.*

- The trustee files its section 170 report with the court and the creditors at least 10 days before the discharge hearing. BIA s.170(2). *In Toronto's Commercial List cases, the trustee is also required to, at least 14 days before the hearing, file with the court and any creditors opposing the discharge a supplementary report that includes information on the facts relating to the creditor's objection, outstanding matters in the estate, the bankrupt's income statement, assets available for distribution to the creditors, voluntary payments made by the bankrupt and any other appropriate information. Superintendent of Bankruptcy Directive. Houlden & Morawetz, Bankruptcy Law of Canada, Third Edition,* pp. 6-44 to 6-45.

- The BIA says that you are only required to give notice of your opposition if it is based on grounds other than those contained in the trustee's section 170 report. BIA s.170(7). *However, the better and safer practice is to file notice of your opposition to discharge anyway, so that you will be given notice of the hearing and when the hearing proceeds, your submissions will be allowed. This will also ensure that you receive notice of the discharge hearing, at which time you can appear and argue your case.*

> **Practice Tip:** Do not fall into the trap of thinking that the trustee's opposition to the discharge will deal with your client's grounds for opposing the discharge, or that you will be able to present your grounds at the discharge hearing without filing your own opposition. Once the trustee's grounds of opposition to discharge have been dealt with, a trustee can withdraw the opposition, allowing the matter to go forward on an unopposed basis. You cannot rely on the trustee's notice of opposition to discharge to deal with your client's concerns.

- If your client does not agree with the statements contained in the section 170 trustee's report, they can contest them. The creditor can also raise additional grounds other than those found in the trustee's report to oppose the discharge. BIA s. 170(7)

- If the Trustee's section 170 report was favourable, but you are opposing the discharge, the onus is on you as a creditor to prove the misconduct or facts under section 173(1). *Kemper, Re,* (1961), 2 C.B.R. (N.S.) 130 (Ont. S.C.)

> **Practice Tip:** If the debtor made an assignment into bankruptcy in order to avoid paying a judgment for damages obtained by your client arising out of negligent or wrongful conduct, you should oppose the discharge and request that conditions placed on the discharge include payments toward the judgment. Provided that the bankrupt has the capacity to make payments, the court will make a conditional order of discharge. *Kozack v. Ritter* (1974) 20 C.B.R. (N.S.) 223. *This also applies to cases where the debtor filed for bankruptcy prior to your creditor obtaining a judgment for damages.*

- If the bankrupt with whom you are dealing also owes Canadian Customs and Revenue Agency (CCRA) a significant debt for income tax arrears, or debts owing to CCRA for GST or source deductions, it is likely that CCRA will oppose the discharge. *Prior to the 1992 BIA amendments, Revenue Canada had preferred creditor status; however, its successor, CCRA, now shares on a pro rata basis with other unsecured creditors. The trend has been for CCRA to continue to oppose discharges, even though the dividend to CCRA is not as great as it would have been under pre-1992 legislation.*

- If the trustee has also filed an opposition, your opposition will be heard at the same time as the trustee's. The trustee automatically sends a notice of the hearing date, place and time to all creditors with provable claims at least 14 days before the hearing. Bankruptcy Rules, Rule 5.1.

- You will be able to cross-examine the bankrupt at the hearing, as they are required to be present. If the bankrupt fails to appear, the matter is usually adjourned *sine die*, and the onus will be on the trustee or the bankrupt to bring a motion to hear the discharge.

- Your questions to the bankrupt should focus on the bankrupt's circumstances and present financial situation. In drafting your opposition and your questions, the factors that preclude an automatic discharge may be helpful, as follows:

- the bankrupt's assets do not total at least 50 cents on the dollar due to circumstances for which the bankrupt is responsible;
- the bankrupt has not kept proper books and records;
- the bankrupt continued to trade after knowing they were insolvent;
- the bankrupt failed to account satisfactorily for any loss or deficiency of assets;
- the bankrupt contributed to the bankruptcy by unjustifiable extravagance; and
- the bankrupt put any of the creditors to unnecessary expense by frivolous or vexatious defence to any action brought against the bankrupt. BIA s.173

- If you can prove any of the following facts, the court cannot grant an absolute discharge but must either suspend the discharge or make the discharge conditional. BIA s.173

    - the bankrupt's assets do not total at least 50 cents on the dollar due to circumstances for which the bankrupt is responsible;
    - the bankrupt has not kept proper books and records;
    - the bankrupt continued to trade after knowing they were insolvent;
    - the bankrupt failed to account satisfactorily for any loss or deficiency of assets;
    - the bankrupt contributed to the bankruptcy by unjustifiable extravagance; and
    - the bankrupt put any of the creditors to unnecessary expense by frivolous or vexatious defence to any action brought against the bankrupt. BIA s.173

- In considering conditions to be placed on a bankrupt's discharge, the court will ask "why" the person became bankrupt. This may provide you with an important line of questioning to support your opposition. The courts can also consider various factors such as the lifestyle that professional people may need to maintain, the bankrupt's earning capacity and probable expenses, the effect of denying a discharge, the bankrupt's age and health, the bankrupt's efforts to meet their obligations before and during bankruptcy, and the income of a spouse or live-in partner. *MacKenzie, Re* (1990), 78 C.B.R. (N.S.) 46 (B.C. S.C.); *Lambert, Re* (1962), 3 C.B.R. (N.S.) 216 (Ont. S.C.); *Taylor, Re* (1991), 6 C.B.R. (3d) 66 (N.S. T.D.); and *Kierdorf, Re* (1990), 80 C.B.R. (N.S.) 6 (Ont. S.C.)

- The court may impose conditions such as the continued payment of monies to the trustee for distribution to creditors, volunteer work, a consent to judgment in favour of the trustee to pay a certain amount of money over a certain period of time, and the provision of monthly income and expense reports to the trustee. BIA s.172(2)(c)

- The court will also consider the amount of the bankrupt's surplus income in setting any monetary conditions on discharge: i.e., how much money is left after the bankrupt pays their personal and family living expenses. (See 9.7 in this chapter for a discussion of surplus income.) *Policy Statement 11 - Surplus Income*

> **Practice Tip:** You may wish to ensure that the creditor's expectations of the discharge hearing or mediation are realistic. The discharge is designed to balance the rehabilitation of the debtor with the creditors receiving a fair dividend, and the judge or mediator should ensure that both factors are considered.

- Regardless of who opposed the discharge, any monies ordered to be paid at the discharge hearing are payable to the trustee, who then divides them on a pro rata basis among all of the creditors with proven claims. BIA s.176(3); *Milad, Re* (1984), 50 C.B.R. (N.S.) 113 (Ont. C.A.). *The court cannot order that monies be paid by the debtor to a specific creditor or creditors.*

- If you have opposed the bankrupt's discharge, and a discharge conditional on the bankrupt paying or consenting to judgment to pay an amount of money is subsequently granted, the court may award your client costs. These will not exceed the amount realized by the estate under the conditional order. BIA s.197(6.1). *Your opposition to discharge should therefore include a request for costs, if not on the written notice of opposition to discharge, then at least when you make submissions.*

- If the bankrupt does not appear at the discharge hearing, after a period of time, the trustee can apply for and receive their discharge. BIA s.41

- Once the trustee has been discharged and the bankrupt remains undischarged, a creditor with a provable claim may be able to take proceedings against the undischarged bankrupt without the requirement of obtaining leave of the court. BIA s.69.3(1); *Canada (Attorney General) v. Ramjag* (1995), 33 C.B.R. (3d) 89 (Alta. Q.B.); *Fraser, Re* (1996), 41 C.B.R. (3d) 33 (Sask. Q.B.). Note that in *Morgan, Re* (1999), 12 C.B.R. (4th) 48 (Man. Q.B.) the court refused to follow the *Ramjag and Fraser* cases and held that the creditor still had to obtain leave of the court prior to proceeding against the bankrupt.

9.10.3 DEBTS THAT SURVIVE BANKRUPTCY

- The following nine classes of debt are not discharged by bankruptcy:

  - court-imposed fines or restitution orders;
  - damages in civil proceedings for bodily harm intentionally inflicted, sexual assault, or wrongful death resulting therefrom;
  - debts for alimony;
  - liability to a creditor for a dividend where the bankrupt failed to properly identify that creditor to the trustee;
  - debts for support and maintenance;

- debts arising out of fraud, embezzlement, misappropriation or defalcation while acting in a fiduciary capacity;
- debts for obtaining property by false pretenses or fraudulent misrepresentation;
- debts for student loans where the date of bankruptcy occurred: (a) before the date on which the bankrupt ceased to be a full-time or part-time student, or (b) within 10 years after the date on which the bankrupt ceased to be a full-time or part-time student; and
- any debt for interest owed in relation to the previous eight classes.

BIA s.178(1).

- If your client's claim falls within one of these classes, you need to bring an action in the ordinary Civil Courts in order to pursue recovery. *Beneficial Finance v. Durward* (1961), 2 C.B.R. (N.S.) 173 (Ont. Bktcy.)

- To proceed with such a claim in Civil Court, both the bankrupt and the trustee must be discharged. However, if one or neither of them is discharged, you can apply in Bankruptcy Court for leave to take proceedings to enforce the claim. BIA s.69.4

- If the claim is not a provable claim, for example a claim for support, the leave of the Bankruptcy Court is not required. *Simon v. Simon* (1984), 50 C.B.R. (N.S.) 161 (Ont. Div. Ct.)

- If the claim is based on a judgment, obtained prior to the bankruptcy, that falls into the nine classes at BIA section 178(1), the court can consider the judgment's preamble as well as the evidence to determine whether the claim falls within one of the classes. *Morgan v. Demers* (1986) 60 C.B.R. (N.S.) 241 (C.A.)

- If the judgment's preamble and evidence are insufficient to determine whether the claim falls within one of the nine classes, the court can direct a trial of an issue to determine the question. Be prepared to prove that the claim falls within one of the nine classes: the onus is on the creditor to show that this is the case. *Kushnir v. Voshall* (1989), 77 C.B.R. (N.S.) 181 (Alta. Master)

- Student loans include loans under the *Canada Student Loan Act*, under the *Canada Student Financial Assistance Act* or any enactments of a province for loans or guarantees of loans to students. *If a loan is granted by a school, check whether or not the loan was granted under any of these statutes. If the loan is not granted under any of these statutes, it could be argued that the loan does not survive bankruptcy as set out in BIAs 178(1)(g).*

- Ten years after the bankrupt ceases to be a full-time or part-time student, the bankrupt can ask the court to order that section 178(1)(g) does not apply. The court must be satisfied that the bankrupt has acted in good faith in connection with their liabilities under the loan, and that the bankrupt has and will continue to experience financial difficulty to such an extent that they will be unable to pay the liabilities under the loan. BIA s.178(1.1) *BIA s.178(1)(g)(ii) and s. 178(1.1) apply only to bankruptcies that commenced after June 1998. These sections formerly imposed a two-year limitation period. The two-year limitation period applies to bankruptcies that were commenced after September 30, 1997 and prior to January 18, 1998.*

Practice Tip: If the bankrupt wishes to apply under section 178(1.1) to discharge their student loan, they can obtain the assistance of the trustee in making the application. In such a case, the court has found that the trustee can make the application, but the onus remains on the bankrupt to prove that the conditions for approving the discharge exist. The trustee's role is simply to bring to court, in an objective manner, information relating to the administration of the bankrupt's estate, and in particular, to represent fairly the interests of both the bankrupt and the creditors. *Wood, Re* (1998), 7 C.B.R. (4th) 23 (Man. Q.B.)

- If, when your client extended credit to the debtor, the debtor certified that they had certain assets and liabilities, and subsequently declared bankruptcy, your client may be able to show that the debtor's certification was false. If this is the case, and your client can prove that the debtor made the certification with the intent of inducing them to extend credit (which was then extended), the debt will survive bankruptcy. You should, therefore, bring an action for judgment on the full debt. BIA s.178(1)(e)

9.10.4 AFTER THE DISCHARGE

- The court issues the order for discharge 10 days after it makes the order, to allow for any appeals that might flow from the order. Rules 30(2) and 31(1)

- The trustee prepares a final statement of receipts and disbursements, including the result of the discharge application and any failure of the bankrupt to pay conditional discharge amounts, and forwards the statement to the Superintendent of Bankruptcy and all creditors. Superintendent of Bankruptcy Directive No. 18.

- Once the bankrupt has been discharged, the trustee will pass its accounts, distribute dividends to the creditors that have proven claims, and apply for its discharge from the estate. BIA s.41

- If a bankrupt had property prior to filing for bankruptcy, the order of discharge does not revest the property in the bankrupt, nor does it give the bankrupt any power to dispose of or deal with such property. The trustee can, however, divest itself of its interest in the property of the bankrupt by providing a quit claim or disclaimer, at which point the property will revest in the bankrupt. BIA s.20 and *Canadian Imperial Bank of Commerce v. Woodgrove Hills Developments Ltd.* (1982) 43 C.B.R. (N.S.) 239 (Ont. H.C.), affirmed (1983), 48 C.B.R. (N.S.) 223 (Ont. Div. Ct.)

9.11 BANKRUPTCY MEDIATION

As a creditor, your client can expect to participate in a bankruptcy mediation triggered on the following specific consumer bankruptcy situations:

- where the amount of a bankrupt's surplus income is in dispute; and
- where the bankrupt's discharge is opposed.

9.11.1 REQUESTING MEDIATION

- If your client disagrees with the surplus income payment amount that the trustee has recommended be paid by the bankrupt into the bankrupt's estate, you should trigger mediation by requesting it within the 30-day period after either the date of bankruptcy, or the date that the payment amount was amended. The trustee, within five days after the end of this 30-day period, requests mediation via the official receiver and sends a copy of this request to the bankrupt and the creditor(s) requesting the mediation. BIA s. 68(7)

- The trustee would also file a mediation request in the case where either a creditor or the trustee opposes the bankrupt's discharge at least in part because the bankrupt has failed to pay surplus income amounts, or because bankruptcy was chosen over a viable proposal. Such an opposition to discharge is automatically deemed a request for mediation. BIA s 170.1(5) and 173(1)(m) and (n)

9.11.2 WHO ATTENDS THE MEDIATION?

- When mediation is requested, the official receiver appoints a mediator, either an employee from a Division Office (including Division Offices outside the bankruptcy division where the proceedings began) or a mediation-trained or experienced individual whom the Superintendent considers qualified.

- The bankrupt, the trustee or trustee's representative, and any creditors who requested the mediation are also parties to the mediation. In a case where several creditors have requested the mediation, having at least one of them attend will prevent the mediation from being adjourned or cancelled. Bankruptcy Rules, Rule 105(13)

> **Practice Tip:** If you have a client who is an individual, as opposed to a corporation, it can be useful to include someone your client relies upon for moral support - a spouse, friend or colleague, for example - in the mediation session. Their role would be one of passive observer during the mediation, with the possibility of more direct assistance during caucusing. Their attendance can have a positive effect on the mediation through their ability help your client deal with personal, cultural, emotional or other matters that you as counsel may not even be aware of. Of course, their attendance must not be a surprise: the other designated parties must be notified and must give their consent.

- For the mediation to succeed, it is essential that the parties in attendance have authority to settle the matters in dispute. If a designated party needs someone else's approval of their agreement to settle, they must arrange for that individual to be immediately and continuously available by telephone throughout the mediation session.

9.11.3 THE MEDIATION TIME AND LOCATION

- Whether or not the mediator chooses to conduct the mediation with all parties physically present in the same location, the locations in question are either Division Offices, or sites specified by the mediator. It is important to note at this stage that the mediator will choose locations that give a "home-turf" advantage to no-one: the atmosphere of a mediation is one of equality, with no party having a real or perceived benefit over the other.

> **Practice Tip:** Find out from the mediator if refreshments such as coffee are available; if they're not, ask how they can be brought in, particularly if you expect the mediation to last longer than a couple of hours. Also ensure you're satisfied with mediation location's neutrality. For example, you don't want your client to be intimidated by walking into an expensively furnished boardroom at an opposing party's legal firm. In this case, the location can send a message before the mediation even begins.

- Regardless of how, when and where the mediator decides to conduct the mediation, the date for mediation to take place must be set for no later than 45 days after the official receiver received the trustee's mediation request. Bankruptcy Rules, Rule 105(4)

- To ensure that the parties are as prepared as possible for the mediation, the mediator sends the bankrupt, the trustee, and any creditors requesting mediation, a copy of the notice of mediation. This needs to be sent at least 15 days prior to the mediation date (unless all the parties have agreed to a different deadline).

- The mediator has a degree of flexibility to allow for unavoidable circumstances that preclude a party's attendance at mediation. At any time before the mediation has begun, the mediator can reschedule the mediation if he or she believes that the process cannot go ahead at the scheduled time. The new time must be set for within 10 days after the date on which the rescheduling occurs. The mediator may also adjourn or cancel the mediation if necessary. Bankruptcy Rules, Rule 105(8) and 105(10)

9.11.4 THE MEDIATION PROCESS

- The process encompasses four progressive stages, each of which reinforces the positive nature of mediation, moves the parties forward, and lays the groundwork for the next stage:
  - Introducing the Process;

- Identifying the Issues;
- Exploring and Resolving the Issues; and
- Finalizing the Settlement.

- Mediation requires committed effort on the part of both client and counsel prior to the mediation session. Your role as counsel is to work with your client to encourage productive, cooperative discussions during the mediation, and will include:

  - determining and discussing the consequences of proceeding to court and the subsequent implications of either winning or losing the case;
  - estimating the costs of proceeding to a court hearing;
  - analyzing what elements would create the best possible mediated settlement, what elements would be essential for an acceptable mediated settlement, and what elements or solutions your client is prepared to propose;
  - analyzing the other parties' positions and their issues;
  - deciding whether a court precedent needs to be set;
  - factoring in whether publicity or maintaining an ongoing relationship with other parties is an issue; and
  - identifying and understanding the emotional issues that need to be voiced.

- You will also need to assemble all applicable documentation in advance, including the breakdown of financial figures to their constituent parts, on paper. Present this to your client prior to the mediation, to ensure that your client agrees on the figures and issues that are documented. (Waiting until the mediation to present it can create a situation where your client doesn't agree with your figures, requiring you to deal with that issue before you can even begin to deal with the mediation.) Not only is this preparation necessary for the mediation to reach a concrete settlement, but it will also prove helpful in case mediation fails and the matter proceeds to a court hearing.

- Another key element in your preparation is preparing your client to speak for themselves, possibly as early as the mediation session's opening statement. The client needs to understand the active and essential role that mediation requires of them. Your role as counsel during the mediation session itself becomes much more passive than in litigation: you are an observer, a strategist and an advisor on legal areas, protecting your client's interests in the settlement agreement, but keeping in mind that the client's interests and emotions can be as important in mediation as the legal issues of right and wrong.

Practice Tips:

- Discuss the settlement options with your client prior to the mediation, so that you're on the same page when negotiating begins in earnest.

- The client has to be prepared to be an active participant in the process: they can't expect to hide behind you as their lawyer. They are the best representative for their issues and concerns during mediation, and may even have information or documents that they don't realize are important until they're discussing their position with you. That's why it's important to talk to your client in depth prior to the mediation, rehearsing if necessary their opening statements and their responses to statements likely to be made by the other parties.

Practice Tips Cont'd:

- Bring to the mediation all documents and files relating to the matter, including auxiliary files that may contain references to the matter. At the time of the mediation, there may not have been a disclosure of documents, so what you think is important may not be what the other parties think is important. You therefore need to have all available information on hand to enable you to deal effectively with changes in direction.

- Come to the mediation prepared to settle. Mediation is a reality, not an inconvenient stop on the way to court. Even if you or your client don't like the concept of mediation, you still have to be there, and you still have to participate.

- The lawyer who prepares the pleading should be the counsel at the mediation as well. Counsel participating in mediation need to know the file, so it's important that the lawyer who is familiar with the file doesn't send a substitute or junior who has a poor grasp on the matters in dispute: this reflects badly on both lawyers.

9.11.5 MEDIATION RESULTS

- If the mediation is unresolved for any other reason than cancellation, the mediator notifies the Division Office and the parties involved that the issues submitted to mediation were not resolved, and an agreement was not reached. Bankruptcy Rules, Rule 105(19)

- With surplus income cases, the trustee may apply to the court for a hearing; however, if a creditor, the official receiver or an inspector has requested a court hearing, the trustee must apply to the court. BIA s. 68(10)

- Where the mediation involves bankruptcy discharge, the trustee must immediately apply to the court for a hearing. BIA s. 170.1(7)

- Note that although the mediation settlement agreement is not confidential, the process, from referral to the mediator until the end of the mediation, is. (The only exceptions to this are where certain information is required by law to be open to the public, or where the people involved have authorized the release of the information.) Bankruptcy Rules, Rule 105(16)

- If the mediation results in an agreement, it is considered binding on the parties, although it is, of course, subject to any subsequent court order that applies to the bankrupt's situation. Bankruptcy Rules, Rule 105(17)

- Payments decided upon as part of the mediation settlement agreement must be made by the bankrupt to the trustee, at which time they are deposited into the estate for distribution to the creditors. Bankruptcy Rules, Rule 105(18)

- Should the bankrupt not comply with the mediation settlement agreement, either in the case of surplus income payments or bankruptcy discharge, the trustee requests a court hearing. BIA s. 68(10) and 170.1(7)

- Compliance with surplus income payment orders is taken into account in determining whether the subsequent discharge should be absolute or conditional, while compliance with bankruptcy discharge conditions means that the bankruptcy can be discharged as agreed upon with no requirement for a court hearing. BIA s. 170.1(1), (2a) and (8)

10

CONSUMER PROPOSALS

Table of Contents

The 1992 amendments to the *Bankruptcy and Insolvency Act* (BIA) were intended to encourage consumers to file proposals instead of opting for bankruptcy. A consumer proposal can be made for the purpose of seeking a composition, extension of time or scheme of arrangement between a debtor and their creditors. Your client, as the creditor, may be asked to consider stopping the interest, reducing the amount of the debt, extending the time allowed for payment of the debt, or some combination of these measures. At all times, your advice will be essential in helping your client balance their need to recoup as much of their debt as possible with the debtor's ability to repay the debt.

10.1 WHO CAN MAKE A PROPOSAL?

- In order to file a consumer (Division II) proposal, an insolvent person must have debts that are less than $75,000.00 excluding any home mortgage. BIA s.2, 66.12(1) and 66.32(1). *A company cannot make a consumer proposal; however a partner in a business may be able to, depending on the specific circumstances.*

- A bankrupt may file a consumer proposal, which, if approved, has the effect of annulling the bankruptcy and revesting the debtor's property in the debtor or in third parties as the proposal or the court directs. BIA s.66.4

- In certain cases where it makes sense for two or more consumer proposals to be dealt with together due to the close financial relationship between the individuals (in the case of a husband and wife, for example), the proposals can be dealt with as if they were one proposal, i.e. a joint proposal. BIA s.66.12(1.1)

- If the debtor has filed a notice of intention or lodged a proposal under Division I (commercial proposals), they cannot make a consumer proposal until the trustee who was dealing with the Division I proceedings is discharged. BIA s.66.12(2)

- If a proposal is filed, and it is later found that the debtor was not eligible to make a consumer proposal, this fact alone is not enough to invalidate the proposal. BIA s.66.13(4). *In this case, the administrator will inform the creditors and the official receiver of the debtor's ineligibility as soon as it is known. It will be up to the official receiver or creditors to decide if they want to bring a motion to invalidate the proposal.*

- The debtor can withdraw the proposal at any time before it is accepted, deemed accepted or refused by the court. BIA s.66.25. *The administrator will notify all known creditors and the official receiver of the withdrawal within five days. BIA s.66.27. Once a proposal is withdrawn, all stays of proceedings previously in place are lifted and creditors can resume or start any legal proceedings against the debtor. It is important to monitor the progress of the proposal, because if it is withdrawn, you must advise your client, the creditor, on how to proceed. Failure to proceed may cost your client more money or may result in a larger write-off.*

- If the debtor files an assignment into bankruptcy before the proposal is approved or deemed approved by the court, the date of the assignment is the earlier of the filing date of either the consumer proposal or a petition for a receiving order, if any. BIA s.66.33

10.2 CONTENTS OF THE PROPOSAL

- A debtor makes the proposal to their creditors generally. BIA s.66.12(3). *The debtor cannot selectively choose which creditors they wish to make the proposal to.*

- Proposals can be paid in a lump sum, over a period of time, or by way of a combination of both.

- A consumer proposal cannot be spread out over a period of greater than five years. *If a five-year proposal goes into default and is rectified, however, it may in fact take longer than five years to complete.*

- Certain claims and fees take priority over other creditors, as follows:

  - preferred claims; and then
  - fees and expenses for the administrator in respect of the proposal, for any counsellors who provided financial counselling to the debtor under BIA 66.13(2)(b), and for distributing dividends to creditors. BIA s.66.12(6). Bankruptcy Rule 129.

- If a claim would not be released under a bankruptcy, it would also not be released under a completed proposal unless the creditor consents to the proposal. BIA s.66.28(2) and 178. *Your client therefore has a decision to make regarding such a claim (one that, for example, you believe you can prove to have been obtained by fraudulent misrepresentation*). If the claim is included in the proposal and your client votes to accept the proposal's terms, the dividends will be limited to those set out in the proposal. Your client cannot vote in favour of the proposal and then claim that the debt survives bankruptcy.

- If your client chooses to vote against the proposal, however, you can take action against the debtor for the amount that was not repaid under the proposal, once the proposal has been completed. Alternatively, you can bring a motion under section 69.4 to lift the stay of proceedings such that your client will be able to continue to proceed against the debtor during the term of the proposal. Note that under section 69.4 your client must be prepared to show that:
  - Your client is likely to be materially prejudiced by the continuing stay; or
  - It is equitable on other grounds that the stay be lifted.
- You will need to advise your client on the appropriate voting strategy: if the proposal would be rejected on the basis of your client's vote against it, for example, you'll need to weigh the benefits that the proposal offers against the cost of not being able to pursue the balance of the claim.

10.3 RESPONDING TO THE PROPOSAL

- To begin the proposal process, the debtor meets with an administrator (a trustee or an individual appointed by the Superintendent of Bankruptcy), who determines whether a proposal is appropriate, counsels the debtor, and prepares the proposal with the debtor's approval. BIA s.45 and 66.13(1)(2). *Be prepared to be flexible when dealing with a proposal: its design is limited only by the imagination of the person drafting it. If your client is not prepared to vote in favour of the proposal, your challenge is to find common ground where the debtor will agree to increase the amount paid under the proposal to a level that is acceptable to the creditors.*
- The administrator files the proposal with the Official receiver's office. Within 10 days after filing the proposal, the administrator also sends a report to the Official receiver containing their opinion about whether the proposal is fair and reasonable, and whether the debtor will

be able to fulfill the proposal's conditions. The report also lists the debtor's assets, liabilities, income and expenses, plus the names, addresses and account numbers, if any, of the creditors whose claims exceed $250.00. BIA s.66.14(a)

- At the same time, the administrator sends a notice to all known creditors advising of the proposal. This includes copies of the proposal and the report to the Official receiver, a Proof of Claim form, a voting letter and an explanation of whether a First Meeting of Creditors needs to be held. BIA s.66.14(b). *In most cases, a first meeting of creditors will not be held, because neither the Official receiver nor the creditors will request one.*

> **Practice Tip:** In some cases, the debtor with whom your client is dealing may also be an employee of your client. Since an employer may not dismiss, suspend or discipline in any way an employee solely because a proposal was filed, you may wish to caution your client to be particularly careful when dealing with the employee. If your client's situation requires that employees be laid off, for example, or if the employee's conduct requires disciplinary action, the reasons for such action must be clearly documented to avoid future litigation by the employee. BIA s.66.36

- File a proof of claim within 45 days of the administrator's notice of the proposal to ensure that your client is included in the proposal approval process and the potential distribution of dividends. *See section 10.5 below for a detailed description of proofs of claim.*

- The date that the proposal was filed is the date on which to value the creditor's claim. BIA s.66.28(1)

- Once you have proved the claim, your client can either agree or disagree with the proposal's terms. You should indicate assent or dissent to the administrator within the 45-day period after receiving the notice of proposal. If the administrator receives dissents from creditors representing at least 25 percent of the total claims, a first meeting of creditors must be called. BIA s.66.17. *See section 10.6 below for a detailed treatment of meetings of creditors.*

> **Practice Tip:** In order to advise your client on whether or not to accept the proposal, you should take into consideration the following:
>
> - Is your client's debt a debt that would survive bankruptcy? If so, consider whether or not you wish to be included in the proposal.
> - Do you believe the debtor can meet the proposal's terms?
> - Does the proposal give your client more than they would receive under a bankruptcy's liquidation of the debtor's assets?
> - What caused the debtor's insolvency, and are those causes likely to recur?
> - Has the debtor dealt with your client in good faith?
> - Is the documentation (the debtor's statements of assets, liabilities, income and expenses) reasonable?
> - Is the administrator acting within the provisions of the BIA?
> - Does the proposal conform to the BIA?

- If you have not already indicated assent or dissent, you can do so at or prior to the first meeting of creditors. BIA s.66.17(1). *Whether or not your client attends the meeting, such assent or dissent is considered to be a vote cast at the meeting, and will thus contribute to the approval or refusal of the debtor's proposal. BIA s.66.17(2)*

- The filing of a proposal means that creditors cannot terminate or amend existing agreements, or claim any accelerated payments, solely on the grounds that the debtor is insolvent or that a proposal has been filed. If the creditor is a leaseholder, this applies even if the debtor is in arrears for rent owing prior to the proposal's filing; if the creditor is a public utility, this applies even if the debtor is in arrears for services or utilities provided prior to the proposal. However, the creditor is not prevented from demanding that goods, services, leased property or other items be paid for in cash after the proposal is filed. The creditor is also under no obligation to advance any further money or credit. BIA s.66.34

> **Practice Tip:** Even if your client's agreement with the debtor contains a clause that allows for the termination or amendment of an agreement if the debtor files a proposal, that clause is void under BIA s.66.34(5). If your client believes, however, that they will suffer significant financial hardship if the agreement is not terminated or amended, you can apply to the court for a declaration that s.66.34 does not apply.

10.4 STAY OF PROCEEDINGS

- Once a consumer proposal is filed, an automatic stay of proceedings applies against unsecured creditors. This means that your client will be prevented from taking legal steps to recover their debts, including seizing of property or garnisheeing of wages, unless or until the proposal is either rejected or annulled.

- The stay of proceedings suspends all of the creditors' remedies against the insolvent person or their property, including the right to commence an action for recovery of a claim provable in bankruptcy. BIA s.69.2(1)

- If your client is adversely affected by the stay of proceedings, you may apply to the court to lift the stay. Be prepared to show that:

  - your client is likely to be materially prejudiced by the continuance of the stay; or
  - it is equitable on other grounds that the stay be lifted. BIA s.69.4 *This section gives the court a wide discretion.*

- The court can lift the stay, with or without conditions. Note that in proving prejudice, "material prejudice" refers to the degree of prejudice suffered by the creditor in relation to the indebtedness and the security held by the creditor, and not to the extent that such prejudice may affect the creditor as an organization, person or entity. The test is one of objective prejudice, not subjective prejudice. *Cumberland Trading Inc., Re* (1994), 23 C.B.R. (3d) 225 (Ont. Gen. Div. [Commercial List]).

- The stay of proceedings does not prevent a secured creditor from enforcing their security, as long as the court has not ordered that the security cannot be enforced. BIA s.69.2(4). *If the court has so ordered, the enforcement with respect to a claim that is due on or within six months of the proposal approval cannot be postponed more than six months from that date. If the claim is due later than six months from the proposal approval, enforcement cannot be postponed more than six months from the date unless all interest and arrears of more than six months' standing are paid in full, and even then, cannot be postponed beyond the date at which the claim becomes payable under the terms of its agreement.*

- A stay of proceedings will not prevent a spouse from seeking support payments during the term of the proposal. *No order to lift the stay of proceedings will be required. BIA s.69.41(1) and 121(4)*

- For further information on stay of proceedings, see Chapter 9.2

10.5 PROOFS OF CLAIM

10.5.1 PROVABLE CLAIMS

- Ensure that your client has a claim that would be provable in bankruptcy: i.e., a debt that the debtor would be liable for either at the time of the proposal's filing, or due to an obligation incurred prior to the proposal. BIA s.121 to 123.

- To be a provable claim, the debt or liability must be due either at law or in equity by the debtor to the person seeking to prove the claim: *Excelsior Electric Dairy Machine Ltd., Re* (1922), 2 C.B.R. 599 (Ont. S.C.). The claim must be recoverable by legal process. *Central Capital Corp., Re* (1996) 38 C.B.R. (3d) 1 (C.A.)

10.5.2 FILING THE PROOF OF CLAIM

- The Proof of Claim form (Form 31) must be filed in order for the creditor to establish their claim for the proposal. If it is not filed, the creditor loses their right to vote at any meeting of creditors and their entitlement to any dividends under the proposal. BIA s.66.12(4),124(1) and 129(1). *Wright v. Schwalm* (1926), 7 C.B.R. 465 (Ont. S.C.)

- Complete the proof of claim as fully and accurately as possible, and ensure that you provide all information requested by the administrator. Note whether or not the creditor is unsecured, secured or preferred. BIA s.124(5) *Failure to do so can lead to the administrator disallowing the creditor's claim.*

Practice Tip: To complete the Proof of Claim form:

- The creditor must state their full and complete legal name;
- If an individual is completing a proof of claim and is not a creditor themselves, they must state their position or title;

Practice Tip Cont'd:

- Give the complete address for forwarding all notices or correspondence;
- Ensure that the amount on the statement of account corresponds to the amount indicated on the proof of claim;
- Ensure that the statement of account is complete. A detailed statement of account for the last three months must be attached to the proof of claim, and must show the date plus the number and the amount of all of the invoices or charges, together with the date, the number and the amount of all credits or payments;
- All claimants must indicate whether or not they are related to the debtor;
- The claimant must attach a detailed list of payments or credits received within three months preceding the proposal if the claimant and the debtor are not related, or within twelve months preceding the proposal if the claimant and the debtor are related;
- The individual completing the declaration must personally sign the document; and
- The witness must sign the document.

- The proof of claim must be signed by the creditor or by their authorized representative who is familiar with the facts of the case (and must state the authority and how the representative has knowledge of the case). BIA s.124(3)

Practice Tip: *The signature must be witnessed. Lack of a witness can lead to the claim being disallowed.*

- Attach statements of account or other documentation to back up the claim as required. Ensure that this documentation clearly shows the amount being claimed. BIA s.124(4)

- If your client is a secured creditor who wishes to receive a dividend, a proof of claim must be filed. BIA s.128(2). *The secured creditor will only be entitled to a dividend with respect to the balance due after deducting the value of the security from the debt.*

- File the proof of claim prior to the commencement of the first meeting of creditors (in order to allow your client to vote as a creditor at the meeting). *Failure to file by this time may allow your client's claim, but will not allow your client to vote at that crucial first meeting. You can file your proof of claim in person, by mail, courier or fax.*

- The administrator will review the proof of claim and either accept or disallow it. The administrator may also request further information of the creditor. BIA s.135(2)

- If the proof of claim is accepted, the creditor is now entitled to vote at meetings of creditors and to receive any dividends paid out under the proposal.

> **Practice Tip:** If you have concerns about your client's statements in the proof of claim, you may wish to remind them that a willfully false statement or willful misrepresentation can result in the court disallowing the proof of claim in whole or in part. BIA s.125

10.5.3 DISALLOWANCE OF PROOF OF CLAIM

- A administrator can disallow, in whole or in part, a creditor's claim if the administrator finds that the claim is not entitled to be included in the estate, if it exceeds the creditor's entitlement, or if the creditors or inspectors have passed a resolution directing the disallowance of the claim. BIA s.135(2)

- The notice of disallowance must be sent by registered mail or courier. Bankruptcy Rules, Rule 113.

- A creditor can also ask the administrator to disallow or reduce the claim of another creditor, and may apply to court if the administrator does not agree. *The creditor must take proceedings for this under section 38. Only the creditors who have joined in the proceedings under section 38 are entitled to the benefit of the disallowance. The benefit to those creditors would be the dividend that would have been paid to the creditor whose claim was disallowed. Newman, Re* (1990), 77 C.B.R. (N.S.) 296 (Ont. S.C.)

- If the administrator disallows a creditor's claim, the administrator must serve on the creditor (NOT on you as their solicitor) a Notice of Disallowance as per Form 77, which must contain the reasons for the disallowance. BIA s.135(3), Bankruptcy Rules, Rule 113 and *Dominion Pegasus Helicopters Ltd., Re* (1976), 21 C.B.R. (N.S.) 238 (Ont. Bktcy.)

- There is no time set out for serving the Notice of Disallowance. It is, however, usual for an administrator to defer service until it is clear whether any dividends are to be paid. *Proprietary Mines Ltd. v. MacKay,* [1939] O.R. 461 (C.A.), aff'd [1941] 1 D.L.R. 240 (S.C.C.)

- If you believe the administrator has erred, you can appeal the disallowance, either to the Registrar in Bankruptcy or to a Judge sitting in Bankruptcy Court. The appeal must be filed within 30 days after service; if this time is insufficient, you must apply to the court for an extension within the 30 days. BIA s.135(4). *If the administrator will consent, you can informally agree to extend the time for filing the appeal. Ensure that you obtain the consent of the administrator in writing.*

- Since the onus to prove the claim is on the party appealing, you must ensure that you have the necessary documentation to clearly satisfy the court that the administrator made an error in disallowing your client's claim.

- You must make the appeal by way of motion to the court. The notice of motion must specify the relief claimed in very precise terms. It is not acceptable to commence the appeal by sending a letter to the administrator with a copy to the Bankruptcy office. *Clarke Road Building Supplies Ltd., Re* (1983), 48 C.B.R. (N.S.) 220 (Ont. S.C.)

- You must also file affidavit evidence setting out the reasons why the administrator made an error in disallowing your client's claim, including the appropriate documents to back up this assertion.

- Serve the notice of motion and supporting affidavits on the administrator by personal service, mail, courier, facsimile or electronic transmission.

- File the notice of motion with the court prior to the hearing, along with every affidavit to be used in support of the motion, plus proof of service of the motion and supporting affidavits.

10.5.4 RECONCILIATION OF CLAIMS

- After the first meeting of creditors, the administrator will attempt to reconcile the claims filed by the creditors against the debts on the debtor's account books. In doing so, the administrator will also identify rights of set-off on behalf of the debtor. Creditors' claims can therefore be disallowed in whole or in part at this stage of the process as well.

10.6 MEETINGS OF CREDITORS

- The First Meeting of Creditors can be requested within 45 days of the notice of proposal by either the Official receiver or by creditors who represent at least 25 percent in value of the proven claims. BIA s.66.15(1)(2). *In dealing with consumer proposals, there is often no requirement for a meeting of creditors, if there is no request for one from either the requisite number of creditors or the Official receiver.*

- If the Official receiver requests the meeting, the administrator calls the meeting forthwith. BIA s.66.15(2)(a)

- If the creditors request the meeting, the administrator calls the meeting at the expiration of the 45-day waiting period. BIA s.66.15(2)(b)

- In both cases, the meeting must be held within 21 days after being called. At least 10 days before the meeting, the administrator must send notice of the meeting with a proxy and voting letter to the debtor, every known creditor and the Official receiver. BIA s.66.15(2)(3)

- Expect other creditors, the debtor and the administrator to attend the meeting. *Although the meeting is chaired by either the Official receiver or its nominee, the practice in the Ottawa area has been to allow the administrator to chair the meeting. BIA s.66.16(1)*

- If further investigation of the debtor's affairs or property is needed, or if the situation calls for the examination of the debtor or another individual who is familiar with the debtor's affairs, the meeting can be adjourned. BIA s.66.16(2). *For information on examinations, please see chapter 10.5.*

Practice Tip: If you believe that more information is needed about the debtor's affairs, the best way to obtain that information is to request the meeting of creditors. If the information presented or available at that meeting is still not sufficient, creditors can vote to adjourn the meeting in order to obtain that information. *Sutherland, Re* (1995), 34 Alta. L.R. (3d) 356, [1996] 2 W.W.R. 379 (Q.B.). If you foresee this being necessary, it may be prudent to discuss it beforehand with other creditors to ensure the majority needed for the vote within the meeting.

- The proposal will be explained to the creditors, who may then ask questions of the debtor, or the administrator in the debtor's absence, to allow them to render their opinion on whether or not to approve the proposal. *In voting on the proposal, your client must be prepared to weigh the ability of the debtor to fulfill their conditions against the potential for bankruptcy if the proposal is refused, as well as weighing the potential payments under the proposal against the total debt owed.*

- During the course of the meeting, the proposal may be amended in order to address concerns of the creditors, thus increasing the chances of its approval. This includes adding provisions for the supervising the debtor's affairs. BIA s.66.20

- In order to supervise the debtor's affairs, creditors can appoint up to three inspectors, who will be responsible for guiding the administrator in completing the proposal's terms, including realizing on the debtor's property and distributing dividends to creditors. BIA s. 66.21

- Creditors vote as one class by ordinary resolution whether to accept or refuse the consumer proposal. A creditor related to the debtor may vote against, but not for, the proposal; the administrator, as a creditor, may not vote on the proposal. BIA s.66.19. *The proposal's terms are, of course, subject to the rights of secured creditors.*

- Creditors vote on the basis of one vote for each dollar of their claim. BIA s.115

- Creditors can vote either in person or by proxy. The proxy can be a printed letter or any form of telecommunication, and must authorize the designated individual to vote either according to their judgment or as directed specifically by the proxy. Note that you cannot assign a debtor as proxy. BIA s.109(2)(3)(4). *If you or your client cannot attend the meeting of creditors, the person you designate as proxy must fully understand the case and the implications of voting to approve or refuse the proposal. In many cases, the administrator is given the proxy by creditors and will usually vote all of the proxies in the same way, i.e. in favour or against the proposal, depending on what instructions they have been given by the creditors.*

- In order for a consumer proposal to pass, it must receive the approval of 50.1 percent (a simple majority) of the creditors voting in person or by proxy within the 45 days following the filing of the proposal.

- If a meeting of creditors is held, the proposal must be passed by a simple majority. *What is really important is not how many creditors there are listed on the statement of affairs, but rather, how many creditors vote either in person or by proxy. Those creditors will determine whether the proposal passes or is refused.*

10.7 REFUSAL OF PROPOSAL

- If the creditors refuse the proposal, the debtor must then decide how to proceed: there is no automatic bankruptcy. *The debtor has choices. The debtor can (a) do nothing so that the creditors will then proceed with legal action against the debtor; or (b) the debtor can file for bankruptcy.*

- The refusal of a proposal lifts the stay of proceedings, and revives the rights of creditors so that further action can be taken. You may wish to proceed by way of garnishment of wages, or by starting or continuing a collection action. BIA s.69.2(1)

- The administrator must, within five days, send notice of the proposal's refusal to the debtor, all creditors and the Official receiver. BIA s.66.27. *The form of notice is Form 52.*

10.8 ACCEPTANCE OF PROPOSAL

- If a first meeting of creditors is not triggered by dissents or requests from at least 25 percent of the value of creditors' claims, there is deemed to be a creditor acceptance of the proposal 45 days after the proposal was served. The administrator will then notify the debtor, creditors and Official receiver of the deemed acceptance. BIA s.66.18(1)

- The proposal is also deemed to be accepted if there is no quorum at the first meeting of creditors. BIA s.66.18(2). *A quorum is the attendance of at least one creditor. BIA s.106(1)*

- In the 15 days after the proposal's acceptance or deemed acceptance, the Official receiver or any interested party - including a creditor - can ask the administrator to have the court review the proposal. If no such request is received, the proposal is deemed to be approved by the court. BIA s.66.22

- If a review request is received, the administrator sends a notice of hearing to the debtor, all creditors with proven claims and the official receiver at least 15 days before the hearing date. In addition, the administrator prepares and files with the court a report describing the consumer proposal and the conduct of the debtor. BIA s.66.23

- The court will consider the administrator's report, along with arguments and evidence from the official receiver, the debtor and any opposing creditor or other interested party. BIA s.66.24. *If the court finds that the proposal does not comply with the BIA in that the time period for the proposal's completion exceeds five years or that it does not follow the required priorities, the court will refuse the proposal. The court may also refuse the proposal if it finds that the terms are not reasonable or fair for either the debtor or the creditors, if the debtor committed a bankruptcy offence (BIA s.198 to 200), or if the debtor was not eligible to make a consumer proposal.*

10.9 WORKING WITH THE PROPOSAL

- The court-accepted proposal is binding on all unsecured creditors, and on secured creditors who have filed proofs of claim for any unsecured portion of their claims. BIA s.66.28(2)

- The debtor must make the specified payments under the proposal to the administrator, who then distributes them as per the proposal to the creditors. BIA s.66.26. *Many proposals are drafted to have payments distributed by the administrator every six months. Creditors may prefer to have payments made every three months. You can request that the proposal be amended to have the payments made by the administrator every three months. In many cases, the administrator will agree to do so in order to get the proposal approved.*

- If the proposal doesn't specify that payments must be distributed to creditors at least every three months, the administrator must carefully monitor the debtor's financial situation. If a change in the debtor's circumstances jeopardizes the debtor's ability to fulfill the proposal's terms, the administrator will notify the official receiver and all known creditors, alerting them to the problem. BIA s.66.25(1)

- If the debtor must amend the proposal after it has been approved by the court, the administrator calls a meeting of creditors within 21 days of the amendment's filing so that the creditors can approve or refuse the amended proposal. BIA s.66.37(1)

- If the proposal is approved or deemed approved and the administrator believes that the debtor owns valuable property or land, they can issue a certificate under the proposal that has the effect of a certificate of judgment or writ of execution. BIA s.66.29 *The certificate is filed with the enforcement office in the judicial district where the property is located. It will only be lifted once the proposal is completed. If the property is sold prior to the completion of the proposal, an arrangement will have to be made to pay the equity in the property to the administrator to the extent of the balance outstanding under the proposal. This may have the effect of completing the proposal prior to the expected completion date.*

- The purpose of filing the certificate as set out above is to ensure that the debtor does not dispose of property that would otherwise fall into a bankruptcy, until the proposal is completed.

- Any knowledge or evidence that your client has about potential property or land owned by the debtor should be given to the administrator, so that the administrator can file the required certificate and thus protect the creditors' interests in general.

- You should note that any assignment of wages made by a debtor before the filing of a consumer proposal does not apply to wages earned after the proposal. BIA s.66.35(1). *In other words, an assignment of wages is stayed by the filing of a proposal. If the proposal is refused or annulled, the assignment of wages comes back into force.*

10.10 ANNULMENT OF THE PROPOSAL

- If the debtor defaults in the terms of the proposal and does not remedy the default, the proposal is deemed annulled once it has been in default for three months. BIA s.66.31. *There is no discretion in the administrator or the court to provide relief as against the annulment. Schrader, Re* (1999), 13 C.B.R. (4th) 256 (N.S. S.C.)

- If the debtor files an amendment to the proposal prior to or while in default, the amendment's refusal by creditors or withdrawal by the debtor annuls the proposal. BIA s.66.31(2)

- The proposal can also be annulled if a court finds that the debtor was not eligible to make a consumer proposal, if the proposal will cause injustice or undue delay, if the court's original approval of the proposal was obtained by fraud or if the debtor has committed an offence under the BIA. If your client believes that any of these factors are applicable, you can apply to the court for the proposal's annulment. BIA s.66.3. *To be successful in annulling the proposal, you have to provide evidence by way of affidavit as to why the proposal should be annulled. The court can proceed on the basis of the affidavit or evidence, or by way of trial of an issue.*

- The annulment means that the stay of proceedings is lifted, and creditors rights revived; you and your client can therefore proceed, or continue, with any appropriate action against the debtor for the amount of the claim less any dividends received during the proposal. BIA s.66.32(2). *Note that a consumer proposal annulment does not result in an automatic bankruptcy: the debtor must decide how to proceed to deal with their financial situation.*

> **Practice Tip:** The annulment of a proposal does not invalidate any sale, realization of property or payment already made under the proposal's terms. *For example, if the debtor, during the term of the proposal, sold a vehicle that had no lien against it and the administrator did not register a certificate under section 66.29, the sale by the debtor would be valid and could not be overturned provided that the vehicle had been sold for valuable consideration.* BIA s.66.3(2) and 66.31(3)

- Any guarantees given under the proposal also remain in force. BIA s.66.3(2) and 66.31(3). *Any person giving a guarantee will still be liable for the payment, even if the proposal is annulled.*

- Once the proposal has been annulled, the administrator notifies forthwith the official receiver and all known creditors. BIA s.66.3(4) and 66.31(1)

- The debtor cannot make another proposal until all claims under the annulled proposal are either paid in full or extinguished by BIA s.178(2). BIA s.66.32(1)

- If the debtor made the proposal while they were bankrupt, the annulment of the proposal is deemed to be an assignment into bankruptcy, and the administrator must then send a notice of a meeting of creditors to all known creditors. BIA s.66.3(5)

10.11 COMPLETION OF THE PROPOSAL

- If the debtor complies with the terms of the proposal, a certificate of compliance is issued. At this point, the debt to your client is considered extinguished; no action can be brought to recover the difference between the original debt and the revised debt paid under the proposal's terms. BIA s.66.38

- If the debtor defaults in the terms of the proposal, but remedies the default, the terms of the proposal are considered met, and a certificate of compliance is issued.

11

COMMERCIAL PROPOSALS

Table of Contents

Amendments to the *Bankruptcy and Insolvency Act* (BIA) in 1992 were intended to encourage insolvent individuals and businesses or corporate entities to file proposals instead of opting for bankruptcy, thus promoting financial rehabilitation as opposed to promoting or facilitating the liquidation of a business. A commercial proposal can be made for the purpose of seeking a composition, extension of time or scheme of arrangement between a debtor and his or her creditors. Your client, as the creditor, may be asked to consider reducing or stopping the interest, reducing the amount of the debt, extending the time allowed for payment of the debt, or some combination of these options. At all times, your advice will be essential in helping your client balance their need to recoup as much of their debt as possible with the debtor's ability to repay the debt.

11.1 WHO CAN FILE A COMMERCIAL PROPOSAL?

- In order to file a commercial, or Division I, proposal, the person must have debts that, excluding a home mortgage, total $75,000.00 or more. BIA s.2, s.66.11. *In reality, a corporation or a partnership must file a Division I proposal notwithstanding the fact that the debts may not be $75,000.00. Neither a partnership nor a corporation can file a consumer proposal however, a sole proprietor can. The definition of "person" would also exclude incorporated banks to which the* Bank Act *applies, savings banks, insurance companies, trust companies, loan companies or railway companies.*

- In some cases, a debtor may not qualify to file a Division I proposal but may decide to do so if there are related debtors making a Division I proposal.

- The proposal may be made by an insolvent person, or a receiver, liquidator or trustee dealing with that person's affairs. BIA s.50(1). *We refer in this chapter to the insolvent person as the debtor.*

- A bankrupt may file a commercial proposal, which, if approved has the affect of annulling the bankruptcy and revesting the debtor's property in the debtor or in third parties as the proposal or the court directs. BIA s.50(1)(d)(e)

- If the debtor has filed a proposal under Division II (consumer proposal), that debtor cannot make a Division I proposal (commercial proposal) until the trustee who was dealing with the Division II proceedings is discharged. BIA s.50(1.1)

- If the debtor has commenced proceedings under the *Companies' Creditors Arrangement Act* (CCAA), those proceedings cannot be continued under the BIA; similarly, if a proposal under the CCAA has been filed and is either rejected by the creditors or does not receive court ratification, the debtor cannot file a proposal under the BIA. BIA s.66

- If the bankrupt files a Notice of Intention to make a proposal under the BIA, it can continue those proceedings under the CCAA, assuming that no proposal has been filed under the BIA. s.11.6 CCAA

11.2 HOW A COMMERCIAL PROPOSAL IS COMMENCED

- In order to advise your client on how to respond to a commercial proposal, it is helpful to understand how it is commenced. Proceedings commence when the debtor files with the official receiver either a Notice of Intention to Make a Proposal ("Notice of Intention") or the Proposal itself.

- In the case where the debtor files a Notice of Intention, the Notice of Intention must contain the name and address of a licensed trustee in bankruptcy who has consented in writing to act as the trustee in the proposal. BIA s.50.4(i)(v). The Notice of Intention is filed in the locality of the debtor. BIA s.50.4(1)

- The form of the Notice of Intention is Form 33.

11.3 DEALING WITH CLASSES OF CREDITORS

11.3.1 GENERALLY

- A debtor makes a commercial proposal to their creditors generally, either as a whole or separated into classes. BIA s.50(1.2)

11.3.2 SECURED CREDITORS

- The debtor may include secured creditors in the proposal; however, if they make a proposal to one or more secured creditors in a particular class, they must include all secured creditors in that class in the proposal. BIA s.50(1.2)(1.3). *The debtor may choose not to make a proposal to the secured creditors because the debtor may try to negotiate separately with the secured credi-*

tors and have them on side in advance of filing the proposal.

- Secured creditors may be included in the same class if they have a "commonality of interest", considering:
  - the nature of the debts;
  - the nature and priority of the security involved;
  - the remedies available to the creditors if the proposal was not filed;
  - the extent to which those remedies would provide recovery;
  - the treatment of claims under the proposal
  - the extent to which the proposal would provide recovery; and
  - other such interests as the court deems fit to take into account. BIA s.50(1.4); *Nova Metal Products Inc. v. Cominskey (Trustee of)* (1990), 1 C.B.R. (3d) 101 (Ont. C.A.)

- If you are not satisfied with the proposed separation of secured claims into classes, or with which class your client (secured creditor) has been assigned, you can apply to the court for a determination as to whether the classes or your client's designation should be changed. BIA s.50(1.5). *This application may be made any time after a notice of intention or proposal is filed.*

11.3.3 UNSECURED CREDITORS

- Although the BIA is not specific as to how unsecured claims should be separated into classes, practice would follow a similar rationale as to that which the BIA provides for secured claims to be divided into classes. Honsberger, John D. *Debt Restructuring Principles and Practice*, p. 8-16.

11.3.4 CASH FLOW STATEMENTS

- If the debtor files a Notice of Intention, within 10 days after filing a Notice of Intention, the trustee must file with the official receiver a projected cash flow statement that the trustee has reviewed for reasonableness; the trustee's report on the statement's reasonableness; and the debtor's report containing prescribed representations regarding the cash flow statement's preparation. BIA s.50.4(2) and Forms 42.2 and 42.3. *If the cash flow statements are not filed within the 10 days, the debtor is deemed to have made an assignment in bankruptcy. BIA s.50.4(8) and IDG Environmental Solutions Inc., Re,* [1993] O.J. No. 771, 16 C.B.R. (3d) 317 (Bktcy.). *There is no allowance under the BIA for an extension of time to file the cash flow statements. However, in the case of Casa v. Verde Health Centre Inc.* (1993) 22 C.B.R. (3d) 24 (Ont. Gen. Div.), *the court did grant an extension of time for filing of the cash flow statements and the related reports, nunc pro tunc, and also set aside the deemed assignment for the general benefit of creditors. While the case does not state under what basis the court allowed for the extension of time, it is presumed to be pursuant to BIA section 187(11).*

- If the debtor files a proposal, they must file a statement showing their financial position (verified by affidavit), a cash-flow statement that includes the trustee's report on its reasonableness and any representations made by the debtor in its regard, plus particulars of any sureties or securities they have signed. BIA s.50(2)(6). *Note that if the debtor is a bankrupt, the proposal must include a Statement of Affairs approved by the inspectors. BIA s.50(2), Form 74 and s.50(3)*

- Unless the court orders otherwise, creditors have the right to request the trustee to provide a copy of the cash-flow statement. BIA s.50(7) and 50.4(7). *If the debtor did not file the cash flow statements with a Notice of Intention to make a proposal, but filed them within the 10-day period afterwards, the creditor should request the cash flow statements from the trustee so that they can see what the debtor is projecting for their business in the future. This should be done as soon as possible so that, as a creditor, you can have a good handle on the debtor's situation. Failure to do so may allow the debtor to remain in the suspended state between the commencement of the proceedings and when the proceedings are voted on for a longer period of time.*

> **Practice Tip:** You may want to put the debtor on notice that you will be opposing either a request to extend the time for filing the proposal and/or the proposal itself, and request that as creditor, you be served on reasonable notice with any request for an extension of time to file the proposal so that representations can be made to the court of your concerns with respect to the matter.

- You should exercise caution when dealing with the cash-flow statement. Assuming that the trustee acted in good faith and with reasonable care in reviewing it, you cannot hold it responsible for any loss or damage incurred based on your reliance on the statement. *Sections 50(9) and 50.4(5) BIA. The trustee is, however, required to report any material adverse changes in the cash-flow statements or financial circumstances of the debtor to the official receiver and to the creditors after becoming aware of such material adverse changes. BIA s.50(9)(10) and 50.4(5)(6)(7). A copy must be filed with the court. Bankruptcy Rule 90(1)(i)*

11.3.5 EXTENSIONS OF THE TIME FOR FILING OF THE PROPOSAL

- The trustee has 30 days from the filing of the Notice of Intention (or from any extension granted by the court) to file a proposal with the official receiver. BIA s.50.4(8). *If the trustee fails to file a proposal within the required time, the debtor is deemed to have made an assignment into bankruptcy as of the expiration of the allowed time period. BIA s.50.4(8)*

- The court can grant extensions not exceeding 45 days for each individual extension, and not exceeding an aggregate of five months. BIA s.50.4(9). *The request for extensions is made by the debtor by way of motion to the court.*

- The prerequisites for obtaining an extension of time to file a proposal are as follows:

  - the debtor is acting in good faith and with due diligence. *Air Atlantic Ltd., Re* (1994) 27 C.B.R. (3d) 225 (Nfld. T.D.), additional reasons at (July 28, 1994), Doc. NF 6725/94, Estate No. 049454 (Nfld. T.D.);
  - the debtor would likely be able to make a viable proposal if the extension were granted. *High Street Construction Ltd., Re* (1993) 19 C.B.R. (3d) 213 (Ont. Bktcy.); *St. Isidore Meats Inc./Viande St. Isidore Inc. v. Paquette Fine Foods Inc.* (1997), 46 C.B.R. (3d) 280 (Ont. Gen. Div.); and
  - no creditor would be materially prejudiced if the extension were granted. *St. Isidore Meats Inc./Viande St. Isidore Inc. v. Paquette Fine Foods Inc., supra.*

- On granting the extension, the court may impose conditions as it sees fit. *Air Atlantic Inc., supra*

- The court can also refuse to extend the time to file a proposal: see section 11.5, Terminating a Proposal.

11.3.6 MISCELLANEOUS

- Once the proposal itself has been filed, you must file a proof of claim with the trustee in order for your client to be included in the proposal. BIA s.50(1.6)

- The proposal cannot be withdrawn until the creditors and the court have made their decision; however, the debtor can make an assignment into bankruptcy prior to the rendering of a decision on the proposal. BIA s.50(4)(4.1)

- The trustee has a duty to both the debtor and the creditors. In reviewing the affairs and property of the debtor, the trustee is attempting to determine the cause of the debtor's financial difficulty and the financial situation: this information must then be reported to the meeting of creditors. BIA s.50(5) and Directive 20 of the Superintendent of Bankruptcy, Ottawa. *For a detailed treatment of meetings of creditors, please see section 9.6.*

- The trustee must also send a report on the state of the debtor's business and financial affairs to all creditors at least 10 days before the meeting of creditors. BIA s.50(10)(b)

- The filing of a proposal means that creditors cannot terminate or amend existing agreements (including leases and licensing agreements), or claim any accelerated payments, solely on the grounds that the debtor is insolvent or that a proposal has been filed. If the creditor is a public utility, this applies even if the debtor is in arrears for services or utilities provided prior to the proposal. However, the creditor is not prevented from demanding that goods, services, leased property or other items be paid for in cash after the proposal is filed. The creditor is also under no obligation to advance any further money or credit. BIA s.65.1. *Note that this does not apply to eligible financial contracts or to a member of the Canadian Payments Association acting as a clearing agent for the debtor. An eligible financial contract such as a commodity swap, where it was entered into before the notice of intention (or the proposal if there was no notice) was filed, can be terminated and the setting off of obligations between the parties can be undertaken. If the creditor has a net amount owing after the setoff, that amount is considered a claim provable in bankruptcy. BIA s.65.1(8)(9)*

> **Practice Tip:** Even if your client's agreement with the debtor contains a clause that allows for the termination or amendment of an agreement if the debtor files a proposal, that clause is void under BIA s.65.1(5). If your client believes, however, that they will suffer significant financial hardship if the agreement is not terminated or amended, you can apply to the court for a declaration that this section does not apply, or applies only to a limited extent. BIA s.65.1(6)

11.3.7 DISCLAIMERS OF COMMERCIAL LEASES

- The debtor can disclaim a commercial lease for real property where they are a tenant at any time between the filing of a notice of intention and the proposal, or on the filing of the proposal, giving the landlord 30 days notice. If your client is a landlord, the disclaimer will mean they cannot claim for accelerated rent, and the proposal must then indicate whether the landlord's proof of claim will be permitted for the full amount of the actual losses from the disclaimed lease, or for the lesser of three years' rent or the aggregate of the first year's rent dated from the disclaimer plus 15 percent of the rent under the remainder of the lease. The proposal will also classify the landlord's claim either as a separate class of similar landlord claims, or as a class of unsecured claims that do not involve landlord claims. If you disagree with the classification, you can apply to the court to determine the correct class. BIA s.65.2(1)(4)(7)

- To challenge the disclaimer, you must within 15 days after being notified of the disclaimer, apply to the court for a declaration that BIA s.65.2(1) does not apply to that particular lease. You must be prepared to show the court that the debtor would be able to make a viable proposal if the lease was not disclaimed; if the court believes that the debtor's proposal would not be viable without the disclaimer of your lease and all other disclaimed leases, the court will not make the declaration. BIA s.65.2(3). *In such a case, it may be prudent to consult with other creditors whose leases have been disclaimed, in order to present a united case to the court.*

11.4 CONTENTS OF THE PROPOSAL

Proposals can be paid in a lump sum, over a period of time, or by way of a combination of both.

11.4.1 PRIORITIES

- Certain claims and fees take priority over other creditors, as follows;
  - preferred claims as set out in section 136 of the BIA, e.g. wages, landlord's priority claim; and then
  - fees and expenses for the trustee arising out of the proposal. BIA s.60(1)

- The proposal must include payment in full within six months of the court approving the proposal for amounts owed to the federal or provincial governments under the *Income Tax Act* subsection 224(1.2) or similar provincial legislation (i.e., for the employee's share of source deductions, such as income tax, employment insurance and Canada Pension Plan) when the notice of intention was filed or, if no notice was filed, when the proposal itself was filed. BIA s.60(1.1). *The crown does have the right to extend the six-month time frame if consensus can be reached with the debtor.*

- If the debtor is an employer, the proposal must include payment to employees and former employees of wages, salaries or commissions due for the six months previous to the filing of the earlier of the notice of intention or the proposal, to a maximum of $2,000.00. Travelling sales representatives are also entitled to a maximum of $1,000.00 for expenses during the same period. The proposal must also provide for payment of the full amount of wages, etc. during the period between the earlier of the filing of the notice of intention or the proposal and the court approval of the proposal. BIA s.60(1.3) and 136(1)(d).

- The proposal may contain provisions to prefer the claims of creditors who extend credit after the proposal has been filed: subsequent creditors may require this protection in order to extend credit to a debtor who is already experiencing financial difficulty. *Lipson, Re,* [1924] 3 D.L.R. 761 (Ont. C.A.)

11.4.2 CLAIMS AGAINST DIRECTORS

- The proposal may include provisions for creditors to compromise, or forgive either partially or completely, their claims against the company's directors, as long as those claims arose before proceedings began under the BIA, and involve responsibilities that the directors would, in their positions, be liable for. BIA s.50(13). *Provisions that can be compromised are statutory responsibilities but not claims for misrepresentation, contractual or obligations related to wrongful conduct. This allows the creditors to accept a lessening in responsibility by the directors in return for the directors' continued guidance and reorganization of the company. Before 1997, there was no provision for such a compromise, and thus there was no incentive for the directors to stay on board. This made it much more difficult to put an effective reorganization in place.*

- Review the proposal's suggestion for compromising claims against directors to ensure that they do not involve misrepresentations or wrongful or oppressive conduct from the directors with respect to creditors, and that where the creditor has a contract with a director, the proposal does not interfere with them. BIA s.50(14). If you believe s.50(14) applies, you can apply to the court to lift the stay of proceedings with respect to the claims against directors, or to have the court refuse the compromise of the claims.

- You can also apply to have the court refuse the compromise of the claims against directors where you can show that the compromise would not be just and equitable. BIA s.50(15)

- If you have a claim against a director, and you prove your claim as a creditor normally would as against the corporation, you are considered a creditor of the corporation: you can vote for or against the proposal; receive dividends from the proposal, and if the proposal eventually leads to bankruptcy, you can file a proof of claim for the full amount owing less any dividends you receive under the proposal. BIA s.50(16) and s.122(1)

- If you have a claim against a director that falls within section 178 of the BIA, i.e. that the debt survives bankruptcy, such a claim will not be released by the acceptance by the creditors of the proposal and subsequent court ratification. BIA s.50(16) and s.62(2)

- If you are unsatisfied with the class you have been assigned into, you can apply to the court for a determination of the appropriate class. BIA s.50(17)

11.5 TERMINATING A PROPOSAL

- As a creditor, your client (along with either a trustee or interim receiver) has the right to apply to court to terminate the proposal prior to the expiry of the initial 30-day time limit for filing the proposal or the expiry of any subsequent extension of that time limit in the case a notice of intention is filed, or prior to the first meeting of creditors in the case of a filed proposal. You must be able to show that:

    - the debtor has not acted, or is not acting, in good faith and with due diligence;
    - a viable proposal is unlikely to be forthcoming before the expiry of the time period in question;
    - the debtors will not likely be able to make a proposal acceptable to creditors before the expiry of the time period; or
    - the creditors as a whole would be materially prejudiced. BIA s.50(12) and 50.4(11)

- The onus is on you, as the applicant, to satisfy the court that one of the above conditions applies to the debtor. *N.T.W. Management Group Ltd., Re* (1993), 19 C.B.R. (3d) 162 (Ont. Bktcy.)

- Where a creditor applying for a termination order holds sufficient votes to defeat a proposal and has indicated that it would vote against the proposal, this may be sufficient to satisfy the court that the debtor will not likely be able to make a proposal acceptable to the creditors. *Cumberland Trading Inc., Re* (1994), 23 C.B.R. (3d) 225 (Ont. Gen. Div. [Commercial List])

- In addition, you should note that if it is clear that a debtor cannot make a proposal acceptable to the creditors, the court can declare that the proposal has been terminated, and that the debtor has made a deemed assignment in bankruptcy. *Triangle Drugs Inc., Re* (1993), 16 C.B.R. (3d) 1 (Ont. Bktcy.)

Practice Tip: In a situation where your client holds sufficient votes to defeat the proposal and intends to defeat the proposal, or where a successful proposal is unlikely, you should assess how a continued proposal process would affect your client. For example, if assets could be dissipated while the process continues, thus adversely affecting your client's eventual recovery of its debt, you may wish to apply to the court for a declaration that the proposal has been terminated. This, of course, will force the debtor into bankruptcy, at which time the debtor's property will be turned over to the trustee for the general benefit of the creditors. By moving the proceedings ahead more quickly, you may be able to preserve more of the debtor's assets for the creditors – including your client.

11.6 STAY OF PROCEEDINGS

- Once a Notice of Intention to Make a Proposal is filed, a stay of proceedings takes effect in order to allow the debtor the time to negotiate with creditors and prepare a proposal without having to concern themselves with those creditors taking action against them. The stay of proceedings continues until the proposal has been fully performed or until the debtor becomes bankrupt. BIA s.69.1(1)

- If a proposal is filed at the outset, a similar stay of proceedings takes effect until the proposal has been fully performed or the debtor becomes bankrupt. BIA s.69.1(1)(b)

- The stay of proceedings suspends all of the creditors' remedies against the debtor or their property, including the right to commence an action for recovery of a claim provable in bankruptcy. BIA s.69 and 69.1. *This includes suspending the right of the Crown to exercise its rights under section 224(1.2) of the* Income Tax Act *and similar provincial legislation until either a proposal is filed or a bankruptcy occurs. BIA s.69(1). Once the proposal is filed, the stay of proceedings remains in effect during the first six months of the proposal provided that current source deductions are remitted as they become due. BIA s.69(1)(c), 69(3), 69.1(c) and 69.1(3)*

- The stay of proceedings applies to unsecured and secured creditors. However, if the proposal does not deal with the secured creditor's claim, there is no stay under BIA section 69.1(1)(b) against that secured creditor. BIA s.69.1(5)

- Similarly, if a particular class of secured creditors rejects the proposal, there is no stay against that class of secured creditors. BIA s.69.1(6)

- If a secured creditor took possession of the security held by it for the purpose of realization before the Notice of Intention was filed, that creditor is exempted from the stay of proceedings. BIA s. 69(2)(a)

- If a secured creditor served a Notice of Intention to Enforce Security under BIA Section 244(1) more than 10 days before the filing of the Notice of Intention to Make a

Proposal, the stay of proceedings does not apply to that creditor. BIA s.69(2)(b)

- If a secured creditor has served a Notice of Intention to Enforce Security under BIA s.244(1) and the debtor under Section 244(2) consented to an earlier enforcement, the stay of proceedings does not apply to that creditor. BIA s.69(2)(c)

- If your client is adversely affected by the stay of proceedings, you may apply to the court to lift the stay. Be prepared to show that:

  - your client is likely to be materially prejudiced by the continuance of the stay; or
  - it is equitable on other grounds that the stay be lifted.

  BIA s.69.4. *This section gives the court a wide discretion.*

- The court can lift the stay, with or without conditions. Note that in proving prejudice, "material prejudice" refers to the degree of prejudice suffered by the creditor in relation to the indebtedness and the security held by the creditor, and not to the extent that such prejudice may affect the creditor as an organization, person or entity. The test is one of objective prejudice, not subjective prejudice. *Cumberland Trading Inc., Re* (1994), 23 C.B.R. (3d) 225 (Ont. Gen. Div. [Commercial List]).

- The following jurisprudence principles have been considered by the court in deciding to lift a stay of proceedings:

  - exemptions should be made only where compelling reasons exist;
  - material prejudice will result if the stay continues;
  - the claim is one that would survive discharge;
  - the claim is one that could succeed (not whether it will succeed, but only whether it could); and
  - success would result in recovery against the bankrupt.

Maple Homes Canada, Re, [2000] B.C.J. No. 1958, 21 C.B.R. (4th) 87 (S.C.).

- The courts have lifted stays of proceeding under the following circumstances:

  - where the debt is one for which a discharge would not be a defence;
  - where a contingent or unliquidated debt is so complex to prove and value that the summary procedure at BIA section 95(2) is not adequate;
  - where the debtor is a necessary party in actions involving other parties;
  - where the action is brought to establish judgment against the debtor so that the creditor can recover under a contract of insurance or indemnity or under compensatory legislation; and
  - where the actions have progressed to the point where it is logical to permit them to continue to judgment.

  Advocate Mines Ltd., Re (1984), 52 C.B.R. (N.S.) 277 (Ont. S.C.)

Practice Tip: A stay of proceedings will not prevent a spouse from seeking support payments from a debtor during the term of the proposal. *No order to lift the stay of proceedings will be required. BIA s.69.41(1) and 121(4). The spouse can resort to ordinary collection procedures to collect the arrears or any current payments.*

11.7 PROOFS OF CLAIM

11.7.1 PROVABLE CLAIMS

- A provable claim in a bankruptcy means all debts, liabilities, present or future, to which the bankrupt is subject on the day on which the debtor becomes bankrupt or to which the bankrupt may become subject before his/her discharge by reason of any obligation incurred before the date on which they became bankrupt.

- Ensure that your client has a claim that would be provable in bankruptcy: i.e., a debt that the debtor would be liable for either at the time of the proposal's filing, or due to an obligation incurred prior to the proposal. BIA s.121 to 123. *If it is a claim after the filing of the proposal and if that claim is not paid, that creditor is not stayed from proceeding to collect the debt and does not require a court order lifting the stay of proceedings.*

- To be a provable claim, the debt or liability must be due either at law or in equity by the debtor to the person seeking to prove the claim: *Excelsior Electric Dairy Machinery Ltd., Re* (1922), 2 C.B.R. 599 (Ont. S.C.). The claim must be recoverable by legal process. *Central Capital Corp., Re* (1996), 38 C.B.R. (3d) 1 (Ont. C.A.)

- An employee who is owed wages, salaries or commissions by the debtor and which fall into the range that would be paid pursuant to section 60(1.3)(a) does not have a claim and cannot vote on the proposal. BIA s.60(1.4). *In the event that an employee is owed wages, salaries or commissions in excess of the amounts set out in BIA s.60(1.3)(a), such creditor can file a claim and can vote on the proposal for such excess amount.*

- In determining the amount of your claim, use the date the notice of intention was filed or, if no notice of intention was filed, the date that the proposal was filed. In the case of a bankrupt who is making a proposal, your claim should be valued as of the date of bankruptcy. BIA s.62(1.1)(1.2)

11.7.2 FILING THE PROOF OF CLAIM

- The Proof of Claim form (Form 31) must be filed in order for the creditor to establish their claim for the proposal. If it is not filed, the creditor loses their right to vote at any meeting of creditors and their entitlement to any dividends under the proposal. BIA s.66.12(4),124(1) and 129(1). *Wright v. Schwalm* (1926), 7 C.B.R. 465 (Ont. S.C.)

- Complete the proof of claim as fully and accurately as possible, and ensure that you provide all information requested by the trustee. Note whether or not the creditor is unsecured, secured or preferred. BIA s.124(5). *Failure to do so can lead to the trustee disallowing the creditor's claim. The work to correct the error can be onerous, so spend a few extra minutes to ensure that the proof of claim is complete and accurate.*

Practice Tip: To complete the Proof of Claim form:

- The creditor must state their full and complete legal name;
- If an individual is completing a proof of claim and is not a creditor themselves, they must state their position or title;
- Give the complete address for forwarding all notices or correspondence;
- Ensure that the amount on the statement of account corresponds to the amount indicated on the proof of claim;
- Ensure that the statement of account is complete. A detailed statement of account for the last three months must be attached to the proof of claim, and must show the date plus the number and the amount of all of the invoices or charges, together with the date, the number and the amount of all credits or payments;
- All claimants must indicate whether or not they are related to the debtor;

Practice Tip Cont'd:

- The claimant must attach a detailed list of payments or credits received within three months preceding the proposal if the claimant and the debtor are not related, or within twelve months preceding the proposal if the claimant and the debtor are related;
- The individual completing the declaration must personally sign the document; and
- The witness must sign the document.

- The proof of claim must be signed by the creditor or by their authorized representative who is familiar with the facts of the case (and must state the authority and how the representative has knowledge of the case). BIA s.124(3)

Practice Tip: *The signature must be witnessed. Lack of a witness can lead to the claim being disallowed.*

- Attach statements of account or other documentation to back up the claim as required. Ensure that this documentation clearly shows the amount being claimed. BIA s.124(4)

- If your client is a secured creditor to whom the proposal applies and who wishes to receive a dividend, a proof of claim must be filed. BIA s.50.1, 50.2 and 128(2). *The secured creditor will only be entitled to a dividend with respect to the balance due after deducting the value of the security from the debt, so the determination of that value is an important consideration. If you are not satisfied with the proposed assessment of the security by the debtor and/or trustee, you must apply to the court for an assessment within 15 days of the proposal being sent to the creditors. Of course, if the assessed value is less than your claim, you can file a proof of claim as an unsecured creditor for the balance. You will then vote as a secured creditor for the assessed value of the security, and as an unsecured creditor for the balance. Note that if the debtor declares bankruptcy, the proof of claim for the secured portion becomes invalid. BIA s.50.1 and 50.3*

- A secured creditor is allowed to amend their status to become an unsecured creditor after the proposal has been filed, as long as they had a provable claim *at the date of the proposal. Protective Plastics Ltd., Re,* [1995] O.J. No. 4264, 36 C.B.R. (3d) 212 (Bktcy.).

- File the proof of claim prior to the commencement of the first meeting of creditors (in order to allow your client to vote as a creditor at the meeting). *Failure to file prior to the meeting may allow your client's claim at a later date, but will not allow your client to vote at that crucial first meeting and will not allow your client to request amendments to the proposal. You can file your proof of claim in person, by mail, courier or fax.*

- The trustee will review the proof of claim and either accept or disallow it. The trustee may also request further information from the creditor. BIA s.135(2)

- If the proof of claim is accepted, the creditor is now entitled to vote at meetings of creditors and to receive any dividends paid out under the proposal.

Practice Tip: If you have concerns about your client's statements in the proof of claim, you may wish to remind them that a willfully false statement or willful misrepresentation can result in the court disallowing the proof of claim in whole or in part. BIA s.125 In addition, it is a bankruptcy offence to make a willfully false statement or misrepresentation which can result in a fine of up to $5,000.00 and/or one year in prison. BIA s.201

11.7.3 DISALLOWANCE OF PROOF OF CLAIM

- A trustee can disallow, in whole or in part, a creditor's claim if the trustee finds that the claim is not entitled to be included in the estate, if it exceeds the creditor's entitlement, or if the creditors or inspectors have passed a resolution directing the disallowance of the claim. BIA s.135(2)

- The notice of disallowance must be sent by registered mail or courier. Bankruptcy Rules, Rule 113.

- A creditor can also ask the trustee to disallow or reduce the claim of another creditor, and may apply to court if the trustee does not agree. *The creditor must take proceedings for this under BIA section 38. Only the creditors who have joined in the proceedings under section 38 are entitled to the benefit of the disallowance. The benefit to those creditors would be the dividend that would have been paid to the creditor whose claim was disallowed. Newman, Re* (1990), 77 C.B.R. (N.S.) 296 (Ont. S.C.)

- In the event that the trustee declines to disallow a proof of claim, a creditor or debtor can apply to the court to expunge or reduce the proof of claim. BIA s.135(5). *Before a creditor or debtor moves under this section, it is important to confirm that the trustee has disallowed the claim. Light's Travel Service Ltd., Re* (1985), 56 C.B.R. (N.S.) 175 (B.C. S.C.)

> **Practice Tip:** Prior to a creditor or debtor bringing a motion under section 135(5), the interested party should confirm that the trustee has disallowed the claim and if not, request that the trustee disallow the claim and obtain in writing the trustee's acknowledgement that it has refused to do so. *Darabaner v. Banque Imperiale du Canada* (1961), 2 C.B.R. (N.S.) 88 (Que. Q.B.)

- If the trustee disallows a creditor's claim, the trustee must serve on the creditor (NOT on you as their solicitor) a Notice of Disallowance as per Form 77, which must contain the reasons for the disallowance. BIA s.135(3), Bankruptcy Rules, Rule 113 and *Dominion Pegasus Helicopters Ltd., Re* (1976), 21 C.B.R. (N.S.) 238 (Ont. Bktcy.)

- There is no time set out for serving the Notice of Disallowance. It is, however, usual for a trustee to defer service until it is clear whether any dividends are to be paid. *Proprietary Mines Ltd. v. MacKay,* [1939] O.R. 461 (C.A.), aff'd [1941] 1 D.L.R. 240 (S.C.C.). *In the case of a proposal, since dividends will be paid, the time for the trustee to review the proofs of claim will usually be after court ratification of the proposal.*

- If you believe the trustee has erred, you can appeal the disallowance, either to the Registrar in Bankruptcy or to a Judge sitting in Bankruptcy Court. The appeal must be filed within 30 days after service; if this time is insufficient, you must apply to the court for an extension within the 30 days. BIA s.135(4). *If the trustee will consent, you can informally agree to extend the time for filing the appeal. Ensure that you obtain the consent of the trustee in writing.*

- Since the onus to prove the claim is on the party appealing, you must ensure that you have the necessary documentation to clearly satisfy the court that the trustee made an error in disallowing your client's claim.

- You must make the appeal by way of motion to the court. The notice of motion must specify the relief claimed in very precise terms. It is not acceptable to simply send a letter to the trustee. *Clarke Road Building Supplies Ltd., Re* (1983), 48 C.B.R. (N.S.) 220 (Ont. S.C.)

- You must also file affidavit evidence setting out the reasons why the trustee made an error in disallowing your client's claim, including the appropriate documents to back up this assertion.

- Serve the notice of motion and supporting affidavits on the trustee by personal service, mail, courier, facsimile or electronic transmission.

- File the notice of motion with the court prior to the hearing, along with every affidavit to be used in support of the motion, plus proof of service of the motion and supporting affidavits.

Practice Tip: The trustee's role in allowing or disallowing claims is to supervise proceedings under the proposal. For example, in a proposal (approved by the creditors and the court) where there was one class of secured creditors, who were to be paid out of proceeds from the sale of equipment, the trustee attempted to disallow a secured claim because the creditor had failed to register the conditional sales contract pursuant to the *Conditional Sales Act*, R.S.N.S. 1989 c.84. It was later found that this was incorrect under the proposal, and the claim was allowed: the proposal did not direct the trustee to assess the validity of the security, so the trustee had no authority to disallow the claim. *Bruncor Leasing Inc. v. Zutphen Brothers Construction Ltd. (Trustee of),* [1994] N.S.J. No. 321, 26 C.B.R. (3d) 258 (N.S. C.A.), leave to appeal to S.C.C. refused (1995), 29 C.B.R. (3d) 154n (S.C.C.)

- Note that proceedings dealing with such issues as the disallowance or valuation of claims do not affect the creditors and court approvals of the proposal itself. Notwithstanding that the claim proceedings may have an effect on the proposal, the courts have found that to delay a proposal's approval pending the resolution of claim proceedings would make proposals very difficult to obtain, something that is not at all within the intent of the BIA. *Claude Resources Inc., Re,* [1993] S.J. No. 452, 22 C.B.R. (3d) 272 (Q.B.).

11.7.4 RECONCILIATION OF CLAIMS

- After the first meeting of creditors, the trustee will attempt to reconcile the claims filed by the creditors against the debts on the debtor's account books. In doing so, the trustee will also identify rights of set-off on behalf of the debtor. Creditors' claims can therefore be disallowed in whole or in part at this stage of the process as well.

11.8 MEETINGS OF CREDITORS

11.8.1 HOLDING THE MEETINGS

- A meeting of creditors must be held within 21 days after the proposal was filed with the Official Receiver. The trustee will, at least 10 days before the meeting, send all known creditors a notice of the time, date and place of the meeting, a condensed asset and liability statement, a list of all creditors with claims of $250 or more plus the claim amounts, the proposal, forms for making a proof of claim and a voting proxy, and a voting letter (if not already sent.) BIA s.51(1). If a meeting to consider the debtor's financial situation was held earlier, and the debtor's financial situation has not changed significantly, the financial information does not need to be sent again. BIA s.51(2). *Carefully study this material, because it will form the basis of your analysis as to whether or not the proposal is viable. Consider the type of assets (e.g. inventory: is it subject to unpaid suppliers' protection?), and the ability to sell these assets should the proposal be refused and bankruptcy occur. Who are the other creditors, and what is the value of their claims? Where does your claim fall in terms of priority? You will have to take the time necessary to analyze the proposal and understand what the debtor is attempting to do in the reorganization. If you have questions, confer with your lawyer and, if necessary, call the trustee or the debtor, or both, to obtain answers. You may wish to consult with other creditors and get their perspective, to see what they are planning to do. It is recommended that speaking with other creditors should be done far enough in advance of the first meeting of creditors so that if you want to propose changes to the proposal, they can be made in an orderly fashion with the potential of being accepted. This course of action may also avoid the requirement for an adjournment of the meeting to consider the amendments.*

- The official receiver or their nominee chairs the meeting. BIA s.51(3). *If the nominee chairs the meeting, it is usually the trustee. If you believe that the meeting will be contentious, write to the official receiver and the trustee, and request that the official receiver chair the meeting. This will take the onus off the trustee to deal with potential problems at the meeting.*

- If further investigation of the debtor's affairs or property is needed, or if the situation calls for the examination of the debtor, or another individual who is familiar with the debtor's affairs, the creditors may, by ordinary resolution, vote to adjourn the meeting. The time, place and location of the subsequent meeting will be set by the chair. BIA s.52. *For information on examinations, please see Chapter 10.5*

> **Practice Tip:** If you believe that still more information is needed about the debtor's affairs, the best way to obtain that information is to attend the meeting of creditors, and to vote to adjourn the meeting to obtain further information if the necessary details are not forthcoming within the meeting. If you believe the adjournment will be necessary, it may be prudent to discuss it beforehand with other creditors to ensure the majority needed for the vote within the meeting.

11.8.2 VOTING

- Unsecured and secured creditors who have proven their claims vote by class as determined either by the proposal or the court, or by BIA s.50(1.4) in the case of secured creditors.

- Creditors vote on the basis of one vote for each dollar of their claim. BIA s.115

- Creditors can vote either in person or by proxy. The proxy can be a printed letter or any form of telecommunication, and must authorize the designated individual to vote either according to their judgment or as directed specifically by the proxy. Note that the debtor cannot be a proxy. BIA s.109(2)(3)(4). *If you or your client cannot attend the meeting of creditors, the person you designate as proxy must fully understand the issues and the implications of voting to approve or refuse the proposal. In many cases, the trustee is given a proxy by creditors and will usually vote the proxies either in favour of or against the proposal, depending on what instructions they have been given by the creditors. If the creditors have provided no instructions to the trustee, the trustee will vote the proxies as it wishes.*

- If you do not wish to attend the meeting, you can indicate your acceptance or refusal of the proposal by ensuring that the trustee receives your vote prior to the meeting of creditors. Your vote will count at the meeting as if you were there. BIA s.53.

- In order for secured creditors to vote on the proposal, they must file a proof of security and satisfy the requirements of BIA section 124 to 134. BIA s.50(1.6)

- The voting of the secured creditors in respect of their secured claims does not count towards the approval or refusal of the proposal, but rather towards whether or not the proposal, if accepted, will be binding on their particular class of secured creditor. BIA s.54(2)(c) and 62(2)

- Secured creditors of a particular class can refuse the proposal. They can then realize or otherwise deal with their security, notwithstanding that the unsecured creditors or other classes of secured creditors have accepted the proposal. BIA s.69.1(6)

> **Practice Tip:** If your client is one of the debtor's major secured creditors, be prepared to discuss the proposal with the debtor or their counsel prior to it being filed. If the major secured creditors are likely to refuse the proposal, it greatly reduces the chance of the proposal being accepted. If the proposal is advantageous to your client, you may wish to consent in principle with the proposal: this may help the debtor demonstrate to other creditors that the proposal is viable.

- To be accepted, the proposal must receive affirmative votes from a majority in number and two-thirds in value of the unsecured creditors voting, either personally or by proxy, at the meeting. BIA s.54(2)(d). *What is really important is not how many creditors there are listed on the statement of affairs filed with the proposal, but rather, how many creditors vote either in person or by proxy. Those creditors will determine whether the proposal passes or is refused.*

- Voting on all other issues is carried out on the basis of an ordinary resolution of the creditors to whom the proposal applies. BIA s.50(1.8). *An ordinary resolution is a resolution passed by a majority in number holding two-thirds in value of the claims either present in person or by proxy.* BIA s.2(1)

- If there is no quorum (meaning at least one of the creditors) of a particular class of secured creditors, that class is deemed to have refused the proposal. BIA s.54(2.2) and 106(1)

- Creditors who are related to the debtor can vote against, but not for, the proposal. BIA s.54(3)

- The trustee cannot vote in its capacity as creditor in the proposal. BIA s.54(4)

- Note that creditors who have motives other than the simple recovery of their claim can be prevented from voting on their claims. For example, a debtor's competitor cannot use the proposal acceptance/rejection voting process to reject the proposal and thus force the debtor into bankruptcy: this would be an improper use of the BIA. *Laserworks Computer Services Inc., Re,* [1998] N.S.J. No. 60, 165 N.S.R. (2d) 297 (C.A.)

11.8.3 THE CREDITOR'S ROLE

- Within the limits of both the BIA and fairness to the debtor, the creditors can vote to make amendments to the proposal that will increase its chances of acceptance by the creditors. BIA s.54(1). *Of course, the debtor must agree to the amendments.*

- The creditors may also, with the approval of the debtor, add to the proposal their instructions and guidance for the supervision of the debtor's affairs. BIA s.55. *These instructions may, for example, involve periodic independent financial reviews of the debtor's accounts, the requirement to liquidate certain assets, or the assurance that the debtor will take on no further debts out of the ordinary course unless they are approved by the creditors.*

- Unlike a consumer proposal, where there is an automatic annulment of a proposal if the debtor is in default for more than three months, a commercial proposal has no set time limit for default. In addition, the annulment has to be applied for, rather than being given automatically. *Creditors should therefore ensure that the terms of the proposal are as clear as possible as to when payments are expected, to make it easier if it becomes necessary to show the court that default has occurred.* BIA s.62.1 and 63(1), Bankruptcy Rule 93

- Creditors should monitor the proposal carefully to ensure that the terms of the proposal are being complied with. If they are not, creditors should request that the trustee issue a report to inform all creditors and the official receiver of the non-compliance. BIA s.62.1

- The creditors may vote to appoint between one and five inspectors, whose role is to supervise the debtor's affairs. The inspectors will be responsible for guiding the trustee in completing the proposal's terms, including realizing on the debtor's property and distributing dividends to creditors. BIA s. 56.

- Note that subsequent creditors - those who become creditors after the proposal has been filed - should determine how their claims will be treated according to the proposal. If the proposal does not contain instructions as to how subsequent creditors' claims should be treated if the proposal is later annulled and the debtor is deemed bankrupt, those creditors rank equally with other creditors. The proposal may, however, contain a clause to prefer subsequent creditors over pre-proposal creditors, especially as subsequent creditors may require this protection in order to extend credit. *Lipson, Re,* [1924] 3 D.L.R. 761 (Ont. C.A.)

11.9 APPROVAL OF THE PROPOSAL

- A proposal requires the acceptance of both the debtor's creditors and the court.

- If the unsecured creditors vote to accept the proposal, the trustee must, within five days, apply for the court's ratification of the proposal. BIA s.58(a)

- The trustee must, at least 15 days before the court hearing on the matter, send a notice of the hearing date and place to the debtor, the official receiver and all creditors who have proven their claims. BIA s.58(b). *The trustee also sends a report on the proposal to the official receiver at least 10 days before the hearing, and files that report with the court at least 2 days before the meeting. BIA s.58(c)(d)*

11.10 REFUSAL OF THE PROPOSAL

- In approving a proposal, rather than refusing it with the result that the debtor is deemed to be bankrupt, the court takes into consideration the best interests of all creditors. The court has found that where a proposal (approved by the creditors) would provide all creditors with at least a small return on their debts, and a bankruptcy would benefit only one creditor, the proposal was in the best interests of the creditors and was thus approved. *Slavik, Re,* [1993] B.C.J. No. 1504, 21 C.B.R. (3d) 278 (S.C.).

- If the court rejects a proposal, the debtor is deemed to have made an assignment into bankruptcy. The trustee serves a Notice of the First Meeting of Creditors on all known creditors within five days of issuing the certificate of assignment. BIA s.61(2) and s.102.

- If the creditors defeat a proposal, the debtor is automatically deemed to have made an assignment into bankruptcy. The trustee must call a meeting of creditors to consider the affairs of the now-bankrupt person and to affirm the existing trustee's appointment or appoint a new one. BIA s.57(a) and s.102

- If the debtor has defaulted on any such amount that became due after the notice of intention or proposal was filed, as applicable, the court will automatically refuse the proposal.

- The court must also be satisfied that the employer can and will make these payments. If the court is not satisfied, it must refuse to ratify the proposal.

- Even if the creditors accept a proposal, the court may still refuse to ratify it.

- The court will review the trustee's report on the proposal, which covers such issues as the conduct of the debtor and the terms of the proposal, and will also hear submissions from the debtor, the trustee, the individual making the proposal (if it's not the debtor themselves) and any opposing creditor. BIA s.59(1). *If you have voted against the proposal, this is an opportunity for you to submit to the court evidence that the proposal's terms are not, for example, reasonable, or that the proposal is not in the best interests of the creditors.*

- The court reviews the terms of the proposal to determine whether they are reasonable and intended to benefit the general body of creditors. In doing so, the court considers the wishes and interests of the creditors, the conduct of the debtor, and the interests of the public and of future creditors. *Sumner Co. (1984), Re* (1987), 64 C.B.R. (N.S.) 218 (N.B. Q.B.)

- If you intend to oppose the court's approval of the proposal on the grounds that it is unreasonable or will not benefit the general body of creditors, you must be able to show that the creditors would receive a greater benefit if the debtor became bankrupt and the assets were sold, rather than if the proposal was allowed. *518906 Alberta Ltd., Re,* [2000] A.J. No. 777, 19 C.B.R. (4th) 147 (Q.B.)

- If the court finds that the proposal's terms are not reasonable, or that they do not benefit the general body of creditors, the court will refuse the proposal. BIA s.59(2). The court has refused proposals in the following situations:

  - where the proposal intentionally served the interests of individuals who were not the debtor's creditors. *Sumner Co. (1984), Re,* supra;

  - where the amount offered to unsecured creditors was minimal, and the shares being transferred to unsecured creditors in a limited company to settle their claims were considered worthless. *First Toronto Mining Corp., Re* (1991), 3 C.B.R. (3d) 246 (Ont. Bktcy.);
  - where the proposal was considered unreasonable due to lack of evidence provided by the debtor to demonstrate that the proposal's cash flow predictions could be viable (e.g. tax statements, asset analyses,

and marketing plans). *McNamara v. McNamara,* [1984] O.J. No. 2345, 53 C.B.R. (N.S.) 240 (Ont. Bktcy.);

- where the trustee prevented large creditors who would have voted against the proposal from voting their claims. *Muller, Re* (1986), 62 C.B.R. (N.S.) 194 (B.C. S.C.); and

- where the debtor, shortly before filing the proposal, had fraudulently disposed of their property, thus attempting to place it beyond the reach of the creditors. *Sumner Co. (1984) Ltd., Re, supra; Grobstein v. Brock Mills Ltd.* (1961), 2 C.B.R. (N.S.) 103 (Que. S.C.)

> **Practice Tip:** A proposal must also meet certain requirements under the wording of BIA section 60 for the court to approve it. If the creditors have approved the proposal, but your client voted against it, it may be worthwhile to review the proposal with regard to section 60, and bring to the court's attention any deficiencies.

- The court may also refuse to approve the proposal unless the proposal provides reasonable security for the payment of creditors claims to at least 50 cents on the dollar. BIA s.58(3), 173(1) and 177. *This situation arises where the debtor's conduct has already been questionable, and is designed to protect the creditors while encouraging the debtor to choose a proposal over bankruptcy. Such questionable conduct includes where the debtor is responsible for their assets not totaling at least 50 cents on the dollar of their unsecured claims, poor bookkeeping, trading when knowingly insolvent, contributing to the bankruptcy by unjustifiable spending, fraud, previously making a proposal or being a bankrupt, failing to account for a loss of assets, bringing frivolous actions or putting the creditors to unnecessary expense, unduly preferring a creditor, committing an offence under the BIA, and making fraudulent settlements.*

- When the court refuses the proposal, the only costs allowed in the proceedings will be the trustee's. BIA s.61(4). *However, the court has held that the fees of a solicitor for providing services rendered to the trustee with respect to the proposal are payable out of the estate even if the proposal does not receive court approval and the debtor is subsequently bankrupt. This is by reason of the combined effects of sections 49, 61(2)(b) and 197(6). Mastrogiovanni, Re* (1971), 16 C.B.R. (N.S.) 261 (Ont. S.C.)

11.11 WORKING WITH THE PROPOSAL

- The accepted proposal is binding on all unsecured creditors, and on all secured creditors where their claims were dealt with in the proposal and that class voted to accept the proposal's terms. BIA s.62(2). *Claims for debts that would not be released by a bankrupt's discharge are not released by the proposal - including those due to fines or awards from the court, alimony or child support, fraud or misappropriation, fraudulent misrepresentation, undisclosed debts and certain student loans - are only released with the consent of the creditor.*

- The debtor pays amounts payable under the proposal to the trustee, who distributes the monies to the creditors after paying the appropriate trustee's fees and expenses. BIA s.60(2). To the extent possible, this also applies to promissory notes and stock that are to be distributed under the terms of the proposal. BIA s.60(3). *Note that payments are not made directly from the debtor to the creditor.*

- In order to defray the costs of supervising the process, the Superintendent of Bankruptcy imposes a levy on all payments to creditors, which the trustee deducts from the payment to creditors. BIA s.60(4) and 147. *The payments are made by the debtor to the trustee who then, after deduction of its fees, disbursements, GST and the Superintendent's levy, distributes the net proceeds to the creditors on a pro-rata basis.*

- If the proposal was made by a bankrupt, the court's approval of the proposal annuls the bankruptcy and revests the debtor's property either in the debtor or in an individual appointed by the court, and as set out in the proposal. BIA s.61(1) *The proposal must be approved of by the bankrupt estate before any further action can be taken.* BIA s.50(3) *If the inspectors arbitrarily refuse to consider a proposal, the court has a discretion to overturn the decision of the inspectors and authorize the trustee to forward the proposal to all of the creditors. Henry v. Grobstein* (1947), 28 C.B.R. 101 (Que. S.C.)

- The trustee must file a report with the court on the state of the insolvent person's business and financial affairs as soon as any material adverse changes in the company's cash flow or financial circumstances are noticed, as well as at least ten days before any meeting of creditors and whenever the court orders such a report. When the creditors are advised of the meeting of creditors, they are also advised of the filing of this report. BIA s.50(10). *Examples of an adverse change would include destruction of all or part of the company's place of business or loss of a major client.*

11.12 ANNULMENT OF THE PROPOSAL

- If the debtor defaults on any term of the proposal, and does not remedy those defaults within 30 days after the date of default, the trustee informs both the official receiver and the creditors. BIA s.62.1, Bankruptcy Rule 93(a) and *Gavex, A Resource Corp., Re* (1989), 77 C.B.R. (N.S.) 102 (B.C. S.C.). *To facilitate the determination of when the proposal is in default, the proposal's terms should be as specific as possible as to when payments are expected.*

- The trustee must inform the creditors and the official receiver within 30 days after the 30-day period set out in Bankruptcy Rule 93(a) of the default in the proposal by the debtor. Bankruptcy Rule 93(b)

- The inspectors, or the creditors if there are no inspectors, may waive the default. BIA s.62.1. *If you believe that the default is unintentional, or that the debtor intends and is capable of remedying the default, it may be in your best interests to waive the default in order to let the proposal proceed and thus avoid the debtor's bankruptcy.*

- If the inspectors or creditors do not waive the default, the trustee or the creditors may then apply to the court for the proposal's annulment. *In practice, the trustee will not usually do it on their own without costs.*

  BIA s.63(1)

- The court may also annul the proposal where:

  - the proposal cannot continue without injustice or undue delay;
  - the court's approval of the proposal was obtained by fraud; or
  - the debtor is convicted of an offence under the BIA. BIA s.63(1)(3)

- Proposals in default have been annulled by the court where it was found that the debtor could not prove its position that unsecured creditors would gain nothing by the bankruptcy that would result from the annulment, there was no evidence of forthcoming funds, and the proceedings had already taken place over 11 months, with 18 court appearances. *No. 289 Taurus Ventures Ltd., Re,* [2000] B.C.J. No. 578, 16 C.B.R. (4th) 112 (S.C.).

- The court has also used its discretion to adjourn an application for annulment to allow the debtor to either fulfill the proposal's terms or provide proof of financing to do so within a specified period of time. In *544553 B.C. Ltd., Re,* [2000] B.C.J. 323, 16 C.B.R. (4th) 153 (S.C. [In Chambers]), for example, the application was adjourned for 30 days, on the grounds that the debtor had not abused the process of the court and the adjournment was not of great length.

- The annulment of a proposal results in an automatic assignment into bankruptcy for the debtor, as if the debtor had assigned himself into bankruptcy. Within five days of the annulment being ordered, the trustee sends all creditors a notice of the first meeting of creditors, at which the creditors can vote to either retain or replace the trustee. BIA s.63(4)(5)(6*). Note that a commercial proposal's annulment does not, therefore, result in a lifting of the stay of proceedings. The bankruptcy process takes over from the proposal process. Once the bankruptcy process starts, the secured creditor is no longer stayed from taking any action.*

- The annulment of a proposal does not invalidate any sale, realization of property or payment already made under the proposal's terms. Any guarantees given under the proposal also remain in force. BIA s.63(2)

- However, when a proposal is annulled, the creditors are no longer bound by its terms, and their obligations under the proposal cease. For example, creditors who became shareholders under a proposal that was later defaulted on and annulled reverted to creditor status upon the annulment. *Gavex, A Resource Corp., Re,* supra.

11.13 COMPLETION OF THE PROPOSAL

- If the debtor complies with the terms of the proposal, a certificate of compliance is issued. At this point, the debt to your client is considered extinguished; no action can be brought to recover the difference between the original debt and the revised debt paid under the proposal's terms. BIA s.65.3

- If the debtor defaults in the terms of the proposal, but remedies the default, and otherwise meets the terms of the proposal, a certificate of compliance is issued.

12

THE COMPANIES' CREDITORS ARRANGEMENT ACT

Table of Contents

The *Companies' Creditors Arrangement Act* (CCAA) is designed to facilitate compromises and arrangements between companies owing at least five million dollars and their creditors. It is more flexible than the *Bankruptcy and Insolvency Act* (BIA) with respect to the proposals that may be made under it, and in general is less prescriptive than the BIA: the courts tend to interpret the legislation quite liberally. While its purpose is to provide a period of "protected" time, during which the company can restructure its operations, thus helping the company to avoid bankruptcy and its associated economic and financial impacts, the CCAA's intent is also to balance the debtor company's interests with those of the company's creditors. Creditors are well advised to take an active and participatory interest in proceedings affecting them under the CCAA, in order to ensure that their rights and interests are indeed protected.

12.1 WHO CAN USE THE CCAA?

- To make an application for proceedings under the CCAA, the debtor company that is either bankrupt or insolvent, and must have creditor claims exceeding $5 million. CCAA s.3(1). *Debtor company includes corporations or legal persons incorporated either federally or provincially, and companies that do business or have assets in Canada. The definition also encompasses affiliated companies, where one is the subsidiary of the other, they are subsidiaries of the same company, or each of them is controlled by the same entity. It specifically excludes banks, railway, telegraph and insurance companies, and companies subject to the* Trust and Loan Companies Act. *CCAA s.3(2)(3)(4). These entities are also excluded under the BIA as well.*

- The application to propose a compromise or an arrangement between a debtor company and its creditors may be made by the company, any of its creditors, its trustee in bankruptcy or its liquidator. CCAA s.4 and 5. *Generally, however, the debtor company makes the proposal.*

- If the debtor has filed a Notice of Intention to make a proposal under the *Bankruptcy and Insolvency Act* (Division 1) those proceedings can be continued under the CCAA only if the BIA proposal has not yet been filed. CCAA s.11.6(a). *If the proposal has been filed, the debtor is barred by statute from continuing the proceedings under the CCAA and must continue by filing a proposal under the BIA.*

- A CCAA application by a bankrupt must be consented to by the inspectors of the bankrupt's estate. CCAA s.11.6(b)

- A bankrupt whose BIA proposal has been refused by either the creditors or the court, or who has been deemed to have made an assignment into bankruptcy because they failed to file the required financial statements or proposal within the appropriate time limits, cannot make an application under the CCAA. CCAA s.11.6(b)(i)(ii)

- Many insolvent companies with claims in excess of $5 million are multinational in operation. Under the CCAA, the court can make any appropriate orders to assist in coordinating proceedings between the CCAA and any foreign proceeding. As long as the court's action is not inconsistent with the CCAA's intent, foreign insolvency orders may be recognized, orders may be made conditional on compliance by foreign representatives, and assistance may be sought from a foreign tribunal. CCAA s.18.6. *Antwerp Bulkcarriers N.V., Re* (1996), 43 C.B.R. (3d) 284 (Que. S.C.), subsequently reversed (March 14, 2000), Doc. C.A. Montréal 500-09-002978-963 (Que. C.A.), leave to appeal allowed (2000), 261 N.R. 199 (note) (S.C.C.)

12.2 DEALING WITH CLASSES OF CREDITORS

- A debtor company may make a CCAA proposal to their unsecured and secured creditors, either as a whole or separated into classes of creditors. CCAA s.4 and 5.

- Creditors are separated into classes on the basis of a commonality of interest, usually following the separation described in the BIA. Thus, secured creditors may be included in the same class if their interests provide adequate common ground, considering:

    - the nature of the debts;
    - the nature and priority of the security involved;
    - the remedies available to the creditors if the proposal was not filed;
    - the extent to which those remedies would provide recovery;
    - the treatment of claims under the proposal
    - the extent to which the proposal would provide recovery; and
    - other such interests as the court deems fit to take into account. BIA s.50(1.4); *Sovereign Life*

Assurance Co. v. Dodd, [1892] 2 Q.B. 573 (C.A.); *Savage v. Amoco Acquisition Co.* (1988), 68 C.B.R. (N.S.) 154, 87 A.R. 321 (C.A.), leave to appeal refused (1988), 60 Alta. L.R. (2d) lv (S.C.C.)

- If you are not satisfied with the proposed separation of claims into classes, or with which class your client has been assigned, you can apply to the court for a determination as to whether the classes or your client's designation should be changed. *Northland Properties Ltd., Re* (1988), 73 C.B.R. (N.S.) 175 (B.C. S.C.), affirmed (1989), 34 B.C.L.R. (2d) 122 (C.A.)

- A secured creditor whose security does not cover their claim amount would file a secured claim for the amount of the security, and an unsecured claim for the balance, and would therefore fall into two separate classes of creditor: both secured and unsecured. *The creditor would then have the right to vote the applicable amount in each class.*

- Although the BIA does not refer specifically to the grounds for separating unsecured creditors into classes, the practice generally follows the "commonality of interest" test as for secured creditors. *Canadian Airlines Corp., Re,* [2000] A.J. No. 610, 80 Alta. L.R. (3d) 213 (C.A. [In Chambers]).

12.3 HOW A CCAA APPLICATION IS COMMENCED

- In order to advise your client on how to respond when a debtor company applies to file a plan under the CCAA, it is helpful to understand how the application is commenced. Prior to the CCAA's 1997 amendments, the Act envisioned that the company would file its compromise or arrangement plan, then request a meeting of creditors and perhaps a stay of proceedings. However, increasingly complex insolvencies during the 1980s and early 1990s created a need for extra time between when the company recognized the need to file a plan, and when it could actually draft a plan that would stand a good chance of being approved by the creditors. The court and the 1997 amendments to the CCAA recognized this need by allowing a period of time between the application to file a plan and the filing of the plan itself.

- The debtor company files a notice of application to the court to propose a compromise or arrangement plan. At this time, the debtor company may either file the plan, or as is more usual, request a stay of proceedings until the plan can be filed (usually several months in the future). This first application to the court is called an "initial application," and must be accompanied by the debtor company's projected cash flow statement, all financial statements prepared during the previous year, or, where no such statements are available, the most recent financial statement. The company may also request that certain financing terms be contained in the initial order, to allow the company enough funds to operate during the stay of proceedings period. CCAA s.4, 5,10 and 11(2).

- Initial applications are usually made on a without notice basis. The initial application is usually made by way of petition, originating summons or notice of motion in accordance with the practice of the court in which the application is made. CCAA s.10. *In Ontario, the practice is to commence the matter by way of a notice of application pursuant to Rule 38 of the Rules of Civil Procedure. In addition, affidavit evidence should be filed.*

- The affidavit should contain the following information about the debtor: the name under which the debtor carries on business; its head office address; a history of the company; how the company got into financial difficulty; a list of creditors and the approximate amount owed to each (to show the court that the company owes more than $5 million); and a statement that the company wishes to make a compromise or arrangements with its creditors. *The initial application is usually made on a without notice basis, together with a request that a stay of proceedings be put in place. The court can only grant up to 30 days in the initial stage order. If further time is required, a new request for an extension for the stay of proceedings would have to be on notice to the creditors.*

- The CCAA application is made in the province in which the debtor company has its head office or chief place of business, or if this is not the case, in the province where the company has assets. CCAA s.9(1). Proceedings are heard by a single judge. CCAA s.9(2)

- If the company is requesting a stay of proceedings, the court will usually set a date for the plan to be filed.

- If the stay of proceedings is approved, the court will appoint a monitor to oversee the business and financial affairs of the debtor company during the stay. CCAA s. 11.7(1). *The monitor's role was added in the CCAA's 1997 amendments to recognize the need for an independent overview of the debtor company's actions during the time when the stay prevents creditors from exercising or continuing to exercise their rights. The Act is not specific as to who can be a monitor. It is usually a trustee in bankruptcy or a chartered accountant. In certain unusual cases, the monitor could be a lawyer, or if the debtor operates a specialized business, it could be someone who is retired from the business or is not in competition with the debtor company.*

- Once the proposed plan has been filed, the court, at its discretion, may then order a meeting of creditors (and of shareholders if deemed necessary) to be held, and in the same order may also set a date for the court to consider sanctioning the plan. The court determines the method of notifying the creditors of the meeting, and also lists the material that should accompany the notice, including the plan, proof of claim and proxy forms, and explanatory documents such as information circulars from the company to help describe the plan's benefits. CCAA s.4 and 5. *Compromises and arrangements worked out between a company and its creditors often necessitate that the company also work out compromises and arrangements with its shareholders, in the event that plan would affect the shareholders (e.g. where a restructuring would require shareholder approval). The provisions of the CCAA work together with the provisions of Acts, such as the* Ontario Business Corporations Act, *that govern and sanction such plans. CCAA s.20*

- The monitor must file a report with the court on the state of the debtor company's business and financial affairs as soon as any material adverse changes in the company's projected cash-flow or financial circumstances are noticed, as well as at least seven days before any meeting of creditors, and whenever the court orders such a report. When the creditors are advised of the meeting of creditors, they are also advised of the filing of this report. CCAA s.3(b)(c). *Examples of an adverse change would include the loss of a major client, or large, uncollectable accounts receivable.*

> **Practice Tip:** You must view the monitor's report, and the financial statements on which it is based, with caution. As long as the monitor is acting in good faith and took reasonable care in preparing their report, they are not liable for any loss or damages that you incur if you rely on their report. Be prepared to question the report and its assumptions. Examples of such questions include whether the sales projections are realistic in relation to the company's past sales records, and whether the accounts receivable are comparable to previous years. CCAA 11.7(4)

- The court can dismiss the application, and has done so in the past, on the following grounds:
  - where the proposed plan did not suffice as either an arrangement or a compromise under the CCAA, and where it could not succeed as it excluded the principal creditor. *Ursel Investments Ltd., Re* (1990), 2 C.B.R. (3d) 260 (Sask. Q.B.), subsquently reversed [1992] 3 W.W.R. 106 (Sask. C.A.);
  - where the plan clearly will not succeed, due to sufficient numbers or dollar values of creditors indicating that they will not accept it (although this was later

overturned on appeal because the creditor did not sufficiently prove that the plan was doomed to failure). *Philip's Manufacturing Ltd., Re* (1992), 9 C.B.R. (3d) 25 (B.C. C.A.), leave to appeal refused (1992), 15 C.B.R. (3d) 57 (note) (S.C.C.);

  - where the company's major creditor refuses to accept the plan. *Diemaster Tool Inc. v. Skvortsoff (Trustee of)* (1991), 3 C.B.R. (3d) 133 (Ont. Gen. Div.);
  - where the company does not provide sufficient financial information to justify its request for proceedings under the CCAA. *Montreal Trust Co. of Canada v. Timber Lodge Ltd.* (1992), 15 C.B.R. (3d) 14, 101 Nfld. & P.E.I.R. 73 (P.E.I. C.A.)

- The court has also ordered the sale and transfer of a company's assets prior to the plan being presented to creditors: in this case, this option was the only realistic way forward for the company. *Canadian Red Cross Society/ Société Canadienne de la Croix-Rouge, Re* (1998), 5 C.B.R. (4th) 299 (Ont. Gen. Div. [Commercial List]), additional reasons at (1998), 5 C.B.R. (4th) 321 (Ont. Gen. Div. [Commercial List]), additional reasons at (1998), 5 C.B.R. (4th) 319 (Ont. Gen. Div. [Commercial List])

- Although the CCAA envisions that debtor companies and their creditors will work together to formulate a plan that is acceptable to both, in practice, the court is frequently asked to intervene on an ongoing basis where there are issues that parties are interpreting differently. For example, the courts have been asked to address:

  - classes of creditors. *Canadian Airlines Corp., Re,* [2000] A.J. No. 610, 80 Alta. L.R. (3d) 213 (C.A. [In Chambers]);
  - claims bar orders. *Blue Range Resources Corp., Re,* [2000] A.J. No. 1232, 193 D.L.R. (4th) 314 (C.A.);
  - the priority of unpaid suppliers. *Agro-Pacific Industries Ltd., Re,* [2000] B.C.J. No. 1069, 76 B.C.L.R. (3d) 364 (S.C.); and

  ° set-offs. *Blue Range Resources Corp., Re,* [2000] A.J. No. 830, 261 A.R. 162 (C.A.).

12.4 CONTENTS OF THE PLAN

12.4.1 GENERAL

- The CCAA mandates very little in terms of what a plan of compromise or arrangement must contain. Thus, the plan is limited only by the imagination and flexibility of the debtor company and its creditors. Creditors may be asked to accept partial instead of full payment of the debt, accept payments over a period of time, accept returned goods, cancel or amend existing contracts, terminate or amend leases, sell existing inventory and equipment out of the ordinary course, compromise their claims against the company's directors, stop or eliminate interest charges, conversion of part of the debt to equity, or a combination of the above.

- Unless agreed to by the government involved, the plan must include payment in full within six months of the court sanctioning the plan for amounts owed to the federal or provincial governments under the *Income Tax Act* subsection 224(1.2) or similar provincial legislation (i.e., for amounts related to personal income tax owed by individuals to federal or provincial governments) when the initial application was filed. CCAA s.18.2(1). *If the debtor has defaulted on any such amount that became due after the initial application was filed the court will automatically refuse the plan. CCAA s. 18.2(2)*

- The court can sanction a plan that includes terminating leases. *Ambro Enterprises, Inc., Re* (1993), 22 C.B.R. (3d) 80 (Ont. Bktcy.)

- The law of set-off applies to all creditors' claims against the debtor company. CCAA s.18.1. *Cam-Net Communications v. Vancouver Telephone Co.* (1999), 182 D.L.R. (4th) 436 (B.C. C.A.); *Blue Range Resource Corp., Re,* [2000] A.J. No. 830, 261 A.R. 162 (C.A.)

- All deemed trusts are considered invalid, except those amounts deemed held in trust under subsection 227(4) or (4.1) of the *Income Tax Act*, subsection 23(3) or (4) of the *Canada Pension Plan* of subsection 86(2) or (2.1) of the *Employment Insurance Act*, or similar provincial legislation. CCAA s.18.3

- Other Crown claims or Worker's Compensation Claims are considered unsecured claims, unless the claims are secured by a security interest that was obtained before the initial application was made. CCAA s.18.4 and 18.5. *These provisions were designed to put the Crown and workers' compensation bodies on an equal footing with other creditors.*

- A plan that proposes an orderly liquidation of the company's assets, rather than the continued operation of the business, can be sanctioned by the Court. *Associated Investors of Canada Ltd., Re* (1987), 67 C.B.R. (N.S.) 237 (Alta. Q.B.), subsquently reversed (1988), 60 Alta. L.R. (2d) 242 (C.A.)

12.4.2 PRIORITIES

- Although the CCAA does not set a priority for preferred claims, as does the BIA, certain priorities are allowed for.

- For example, subsequent creditors - those who extend credit after the initial application is made (DIP financing) - may be given priority over creditors whose claims originated prior to the application. This is designed to protect those creditors who extend credit that may well be essential to the company's continued viability during the vulnerable restructuring period. *Westar Mining Ltd., Re* (1992), 14 C.B.R. (3d) 88 (B.C. S.C.)

- In addition, claims by the Crown for the costs of cleaning up environmental damage affecting a company's real property are secured by a charge on that property (and any property next to it that is related to the cause of the damage). That charge acts like a mortgage or other security on real property, and ranks above any other claim against the property. CCAA s.11.8(8)

- The monitor has no personal liability for any environmental condition that arose or any environmental damage that occurred prior to the appointment of the monitor. CCAA s. 11.8(3)(a)

- An Ontario court has held that monitor's fees should be paid before the claims of subsequent creditors; however, caselaw regarding the priority of such fees has not always agreed, even when provisions were made for such payment in the plan itself. *Canadian Asbestos Services Ltd. v. Bank of Montreal* (1992), 16 C.B.R. (3d) 114 (Ont. Gen. Div.), additional reasons at (1993), 13 O.R. (3d) 291 (Gen. Div.). *A monitor's application for fee payment was dismissed, for example, on the grounds that the company would be unable to meet the requirements of the plan of compromise if the fees were paid. Peat Marwick Thorne Inc. v. Kinalea Development Corp.* (1993), 16 C.B.R. (3d) 141 (Ont. Gen. Div.)

- In British Columbia, the court found that it was permitted under the CCAA to order a super-priority, or priority ahead of secured creditors without the consent of those creditors, for a monitor's fees and expenses in appropriate circumstances and for the debtor's legal expenses related to a restructuring plan. *United Used Auto & Truck Parts Ltd., Re*, [2000] B.C.J. No. 409, 73 B.C.L.R. (3d) 236 (C.A.), leave to appeal allowed (2000), 261 N.R. 196 (S.C.C.)

- The court has found that a requirement to pay issued by Canada Customs and Revenue Agency under section 224 (1.2) of the *Income Tax Act* had priority over a purchase money security agreement. *United Used Auto & Truck Parts Ltd., Re,* [2000] B.C.J. No. 2367, 83 B.C.L.R. (3d) 191 (S.C. [In Chambers])

12.4.3 CLAIMS AGAINST DIRECTORS

- The proposed plan may include provisions for creditors to compromise, or forgive either partially or completely, their claims against the company's directors, as long as those claims arose before proceedings began under the CCAA, and involve responsibilities that the directors would, in their positions, be liable for. CCAA s.5.1(1). *The claims against directors which can be compromised are only statutory responsibilities and do not relate to misrepresentation or contractual or wrongful conduct. This allows the creditors to accept a lessening in responsibility by the directors in return for the directors' continued guidance and reorganization of the company. Before 1997, there was no provision for such a compromise, and thus there was no incentive for the directors to stay on board. This made it much more difficult to put in place an effective reorganization.*

- Review the proposed plan's terms for compromising claims against directors to ensure that they do not involve misrepresentations or wrongful or oppressive conduct from the directors with respect to creditors, and that where the creditor has a contract with a director, the plan does not interfere with them. CCAA s.5.1(2). If you believe s.5.1(2) applies, you can apply to the court to refuse the compromise of the claims.

- You can also apply to have the court refuse the compromise of the claims against directors where you can show that the compromise would not be fair and reasonable. CCAA s.5.1(3)

12.5 STAY OF PROCEEDINGS

12.5.1 GENERAL

- A stay of proceedings is not automatic under the CCAA; the debtor company must apply to the court for the stay, and must show that the stay is appropriate under the circumstances, and that the debtor company has acted, and is acting, in good faith and with due diligence. CCAA s.11(3)(4)(6). *Inducon Development Corp., Re* (1991), 8 C.B.R. (3d) 306 (Ont. Gen. Div.). *The onus is on the debtor to show the court that it is entitled to a stay of proceedings. Campeau v. Olympia & York Developments Ltd.,* (1992), 14 C.B.R. (3d) 303 (Ont. Gen. Div.). *The application of the stay will vary depending on the specific wording of the order. Therefore it is important to carefully review the order to determine the particulars of the stay.*

- It therefore follows that if notice is given to the creditors, you can oppose the stay or any request to extend the stay by showing that the stay is not appropriate.

- The court has said, for example, that a stay could be lifted for reasons of "necessity of payment" where a creditor could show that non-payment of its claim would force the creditor to cease a service that was essential to the debtor company's continued operations. *Quintette Coal Ltd. v. Nippon Steel Corp.* (1990), 80 C.B.R. (N.S.) 98 (B.C. S.C.)

- On an initial application under the CCAA, the court may impose a stay of up to 30 days that:

    - stays proceedings that could be launched against the debtor company under the BIA or the *Winding-Up and Restructuring Act*;
    - restrains further proceedings in any action against the company; and
    - prohibits the commencement of proceedings against the company. CCAA s.11(3)

- If the court approves a stay of proceedings as a result of an initial application, the monitor must within 10 days send a copy of the order to every known creditor who is owed more than $250.00. CCAA s.11(5)

- On an application other than initial under the CCAA, the court determines the appropriate length of the stay of proceedings. CCAA s.11(4)

- A stay order under the CCAA made in one province also stays proceedings in other provinces. *Gray v. Wentworth Canning Co.* (1950), 31 C.B.R. 182 (Man. K.B.)

- The stay does not affect those who are obligated to a creditor company under a letter of credit or guarantee. CCAA s.11.2. *This means that you can, for example, pursue actions against guarantors.*

- The stay does not prevent a creditor from requiring that additional goods, services or use of leased property be paid for immediately and in cash, nor does it require a creditor to advance further cash or credit to the debtor company. CCAA s. 11.3

- A stay order has been found to apply in the following cases:

  - to prevent a utility from cutting off service. *Gaz metropolitan Inc. v. Wynden Canada Inc.* (1982), 44 C.B.R. (N.S.) 285 (Que. S.C.), affirmed (1982), 45 C.B.R. (N.S.) 11 (Que. C.A.);
  - to prevent a landlord from terminating a lease. *Feifer v. Frame Manufacturing Corp.* (1947), 28 C.B.R. 124 (Que. C.A.);
  - to prevent a creditor from setting-off a debt. *United Co-operatives of Ontario (Re)* (order dated August 27, 1984, Ont. C.A., Houlden J.A.); and
  - to prevent a mortgagee from foreclosing. *Northland Properties Ltd., Re* (1988), 73 C.B.R. (N.S.) 141 (B.C. S.C.).

Note that these cases were decided before the 1997 amendments and should be read in that light.

Honsberger, John D. *Debt Restructuring Principles and Practice.* p.9-54 & 9-56.

- The court has also upheld a stay order where the Toronto Stock Exchange wanted it lifted in order to consider the suspension of trading in a company's listed shares. *Versatech Group Inc., Re* (September 22, 2000), Doc.

00-CL-3738, [2000] O.J. No. 3785 (Ont. S.C.J. [Commercial List])

Practice Tip: Make your application to set aside or vary a stay order to the judge who made the orginial order. *Philip's Manufacturing Ltd.* (1992), 9 C.B.R. (3d) 25 (B.C. C.A.), leave to appeal refused (1992), 15 C.B.R. (3d) 57 (note) (S.C.C.)

Practice Tip: To appeal a stay order, be prepared to show that the judge made an error either in fact or in principle. *Northland Properties Ltd. v. Guardian Trust Co.* (1988), 73 C.B.R. (N.S.) 163 (B.C. C.A.)

Practice Tip: To object to an application for a stay order, or to set one aside, be prepared to show similar justifications as you would to object to the plan itself: the debtor company is not operating in good faith; major creditors such as yourself do not support the plan; or the plan cannot succeed. Also be prepared to show that there would be material prejudice to you as a creditor, or to the debtor's assets that would eventually be available in the restructuring, if the stay were continued.

12.5.2 ELIGIBLE FINANCIAL CONTRACTS

- A stay of proceedings does not apply to the right to terminate, amend or claim any accelerated payment under an eligible financial contract such as a currency or interest rate swap agreement, a commodity swap, a forward rate agreement or a cap, collar or floor arrangement. CCAA s.11.1(2)

- In fact, the CCAA permits the setting-off of obligations under eligible financial contracts that were entered into before a stay of proceedings under the CCAA was ordered. Any net termination values owed by the debtor company under the contract will become creditors' claims. CCAA s.11.17(3)

- The court has found that a long-term natural gas supply contract was a forward commodity contract and thus an eligible financial contract under the CCAA. *Blue Range Resource Corp., Re,* [2000] A.J. No. 1032, 192 D.L.R. (4th) 281 (C.A.)

12.5.3 THE INCOME TAX ACT

- A stay of proceedings under the CCAA also stays the Crown from exercising its rights under subsection 224(1.2) under the *Income Tax Act* or similar provincial legislation. The length of the stay is at the court's discretion, but must end not later than:

    - when the stay order expires;
    - when creditors or the court refuse the proposed plan;
    - six months after the court sanctions a plan;
    - when the company defaults on any term of the plan; or
    - when the company has performed the plan. CCAA s.11.4(1)

- However, if the debtor company defaults on any payments under section 224(1.2) of the *Income Tax Act* (or similar provincial legislation) that would apply to the period after the stay order was made, the stay regarding previous amounts due is lifted. CCAA s.11.4(2)(a)

- The stay regarding these previous amounts is also lifted if any other creditor becomes entitled to realized a security on any property that the Crown could claim in exercising its rights. CCAA s.11.4(2)(b)

12.5.4 STAYING CLAIMS AGAINST DIRECTORS

- The stay order may also stay proceedings involving a claim against the company's directors (one that is eligible to be compromised) until a plan is either sanctioned by the court, or refused by either the creditors or the court. CCAA s.11.5(1)

- Such a stay does not apply to a claim based on a guarantee given by the director relating to the company's obligations, or an action seeking injunctive relief against a director in relation to the company. CCAA s.11.5(2)

12.6 CLAIMS

- A claim under the CCAA is a claim that, if unsecured, would be provable under the BIA. CCAA s.12(1). Ensure that your client has a claim that would be provable in bankruptcy: i.e., a debt that the debtor would be liable for either at the time of the initial application, or due to an obligation incurred prior to the initial application. BIA s.121 to 123.

- To be a provable claim, the debt or liability must be due either at law or in equity by the debtor to the creditor. *Excelsior Electric Dairy Machine Ltd., Re* (1922), 2 C.B.R. 599 (Ont. S.C.). The claim must be recoverable by legal process. *Central Capital Corp., Re* (1996), 38 C.B.R. (3d) 1 (Ont. C.A.). It must also be capable of being valued; thus, unliquidated or contingent claims are not provable. BIA s.121(2)

- Calculate the amount of an unsecured claim as follows:

  - in the case of a company under the *Winding-up and Restructuring Act*, the amount provable under that Act;
  - in the case of a company under the BIA, the amount provable under that Act; or
  - in any other case, the amount that would be provable under the BIA, or, if that is not agreed to by the company, the amount that the court determines upon summary application to it by either the company or the creditor. CCAA s.12(2)(a)

- Calculate the amount of a secured claim as the amount provable under the BIA as if the claim were unsecured. If the company does not agree to that amount, calculate the amount as follows:

- in the case of a company under the *Winding-up and Restructuring Act*, the amount provable under that Act as if the claim were unsecured;
- in the case of a company under the BIA, the amount provable under that Act as if the claim were unsecured; or
- in any other case, the amount that the court determines upon summary application to it by either the company or the creditor. CCAA s.12(2)(b)

- Prove your claim by returning the proof of claim form to the monitor with all appropriate documentation to back up your valuations, including a statement of account, prior to the meeting of creditors, in order to allow your vote at the meeting. See section 9.4 for further discussion on proofs of claim.

- In some cases, the court will make a claims bar order, setting out the date by which all claims must be filed. However, you may apply to the court to file after this date. Where no relevant prejudice to other creditors was found, the late filing has been allowed. *Blue Range Resource Corp., Re,* [2000] A.J. No. 1232, 193 D.L.R. (4th) 314 (C.A.). *If you apply to the court after the claims bar date, you will have to show valid reasons why the claim was not filed prior to the claims bar date.*

12.7 MEETINGS OF CREDITORS

12.7.1 WHEN MEETINGS ARE HELD

- Under the CCAA, a meeting of creditors is not automatic. If the court decides that such a meeting is necessary, it directs when the meeting will take place, who will chair it, which classes of creditors will participate, and how those creditors are to be notified of the meeting. *The date and time of the meeting are usually determined at the time that the debtor company files its plan of compromise.* CCAA s.4 and 5, *Northland Properties Ltd., Re* (1988), 73 C.B.R. (N.S.) 175 (B.C. S.C.), affirmed (1989), 34 B.C.L.R. (2d) 122 (C.A.)

- The monitor must notify the creditors of its report on the company's state of affairs, both business and financial, which it must file with the court at least seven days prior to the meeting of creditors. CCAA s.11.7(3)(b)(ii) and (c)(iii)

- The court may adjourn the meeting of creditors if specific amendments to the proposed plan are filed after the court orders the meeting and before it sanctions the plan. If the court considers that the amendments do not adversely affect any class of creditors, it may find that the meeting does not need to be adjourned or that a subsequent meeting of those creditors is not necessary. CCAA s.7

12.7.2 VOTING

- Unsecured and secured creditors who have proven their claims vote by class as determined either by the proposed plan or the court.

- To be accepted, the plan must receive affirmative votes by every class of creditors from a majority in number and two-thirds in value of the creditors voting in that class, either personally or by proxy, at the meeting. CCAA s.6. *This mirrors the requirement under the BIA. What is really important is not how many creditors there are listed on the statements filed with the plan, but rather, how many creditors vote either in person or by proxy. Those creditors will determine whether the plan passes or is refused. The threshold here is greater than under the BIA because here every class of creditors must accept the plan of compromise, whereas under the BIA acceptance of the proposal is required by the unsecured creditors only.*

- Creditors vote on the basis of one vote for each dollar of their claim. CCAA s.6 and BIA s.115

- Creditors can vote either in person or by proxy. CCAA s.6. *The proxy can be a printed letter or any form of telecommunication, and must authorize the designated individual to vote either according to their judgment or as directed specifically by the proxy. If you or your client cannot attend the meeting of creditors, the person you designate as proxy must fully understand the case and the implications of voting to approve or refuse the plan*

- If you do not wish to attend the meeting, you can indicate your acceptance or refusal of the proposal by ensuring that the chair receives your vote prior to the meeting of creditors. Your vote will count at the meeting as if you were there. CCAA s.6

- Usually, creditors are only entitled to vote on claims that have been valued and proven. However, the CCAA permits the debtor company to accept for voting purposes a claim that is otherwise unproven or disputed. CCAA s.12(3)

- The plan must be accepted by each class of creditors.

> **Practice Tip:** If the creditors vote against the plan, there is no automatic bankruptcy. This is very different than under the *Bankruptcy and Insolvency Act* where, if the plan is voted down, there is an automatic bankruptcy. If the plan is voted down under the CCAA, the company must decide what steps it will take next, because the stay of proceedings will be lifted once the plan is defeated, assuming there is no immediate appeal. Some debtor companies prefer the CCAA to the BIA because there is no automatic bankruptcy if the plan is defeated.

12.7.3 THE CREDITOR'S ROLE

- Within the limits of both the CCAA and fairness to the debtor company, the creditors can vote to make amendments to the proposal that will increase its chances of acceptance by the creditors. CCAA s.6. *Of course, the debtor company must agree to the amendments.*

- In most plans, since there are so many creditors, the practice has evolved to set up creditors' committees that represent the interests of all of the creditors in that class before the court. Their purpose is to provide consultation and facilitation of issues that may arise within these classes of creditors. The committees may retain counsel and other professionals to act on the classes' behalf; the cost of the creditors' committees is usually paid for by the debtor.

- Note that subsequent creditors - those who become creditors after the initial application has been filed - should determine how their claims will be treated according to the plan. If the plan does not contain instructions as to how subsequent creditors' claims should be treated if the plan is later annulled, those creditors rank equally with other creditors. The plan may, however, contain a clause to prefer subsequent creditors over pre-proposal creditors, especially as subsequent creditors may require this protection in order to extend credit or additional credit. *Westar Mining Ltd.,* Re (1992),14 C.B.R. (3d) 88 (B.C. S.C.)

12.8 APPROVAL OF THE PLAN

- A proposed plan requires the acceptance of both the debtor company's creditors and the court.

- The proper way to obtain court sanction of the plan is to make an application to the court, either by way of petition, by originating summons or notice of motion in accordance with the practice of the court where the original application was made. CCAA s.10. *In Ontario, this would be by way of notice of motion.*

- The debtor applies to the court to obtain approval of the plan. *In the event that the debtor does not apply to approve the plan, the creditors can apply to approve it.*

- As noted in section 12.7.2 above, the plan requires the votes of a majority in number and two-thirds in value of each class of creditors to be approved by the creditors.

- Once the creditors have voted to accept the plan, the court may also sanction it. CCAA s.6

- The court has recognized that a proposed plan does not have to be perfect in order to be sanctioned; it simply has to be fair and reasonable, equitably balancing the various competing interests and the available resources. It also noted in sanctioning the plan that the creditors would not receive any better distribution if the assets were liquidated. *Canadian Red Cross Society/ Société Canadienne de la Croix Rouge,* [2000] O.J. No. 3421, 19 C.B.R. (4th) 158 (S.C.J.)

- If the court decides that technical amendments to the creditor-approved plan are required, it may make them at the same time that it sanctions the plan. If the amendments are substantive, however, it should direct additional meetings of creditors so that creditors can approve or refuse the amended plan. *Wandlyn Inns Ltd., Re* (1992), 15 C.B.R. (3d) 316 (N.B. Q.B.)

- The court may also amend a plan where no prejudice would result and it is necessary for justice to be done. *Algoma Steel Corp. v. Royal Bank* (1992), 11 C.B.R. (3d) 11 (Ont. C.A.), leave to appeal refused (1992), 94 D.L.R. (4th) vii (S.C.C.)

12.9 REFUSAL OF THE PLAN

- Even if the creditors accept a proposed plan, the court may still refuse it. CCAA s.6

- The court will review the monitor's report on the plan, which covers such issues as the conduct of the debtor and the terms of the plan, and will also hear submissions from the debtor, the monitor and any opposing creditors. CCAA s.6. *If you have voted against the plan, this is an opportunity for you to submit to the court evidence that the plan's terms are not, for example, reasonable.*

- The court reviews the plan to ensure that all statutory requirements have been met, that all actions have been in accordance with the CCAA, and that the plan is fair and reasonable. *Northland Properties Ltd. v. Excelsior Life Insurance Co. of Canada* (1989), 73 C.B.R. (N.S.) 195 (B.C. C.A.)

- The court has refused to sanction a plan where the plan was not economically feasible. *229531 B.C. Ltd., Re* (1989), 72 C.B.R. (N.S.) 310 (B.C. S.C.)

- If the creditors or the court refuse the plan, there is no automatic bankruptcy, which is in contrast to the BIA, which states that there is an automatic bankruptcy; the debtor company must decide how best to proceed, although at this point it would be possible for a creditor to petition the company into bankruptcy.

12.10 DEALING WITH THE PLAN

- The accepted plan is binding on all unsecured and secured creditors where their class of creditors voted to accept the plan's terms. CCAA s.6(a). *Because the CCAA uses the BIA's definition of provable claims, claims for debts that would not be released by a bankrupt's discharge are not released by the plan. In addition, claims arising out of BIA section 178 - including those due to fines or awards from the court, fraud or misappropriation, fraudulent misrepresentation and undisclosed creditors - are only released with the consent of the creditor.*

- If the debtor company is a bankrupt, or is being wound up under the *Winding-Up and Restructuring Act*, the plan is also binding on the trustee in bankruptcy or liquidator and contributories of the company. CCAA s.6(b)

- The CCAA also binds federal and provincial Crowns. CCAA s.21

- The court may alter or modify the plan after it has been sanctioned by the court, for example, to rectify a mistake. *Northland Properties Ltd., Re* (1989), 74 C.B.R. (N.S.) 231 (B.C. S.C. [In Chambers])

- You may also apply to the court for directions if there is a point of contention or confusion within the plan. *Horizon Village Corp., Canada, Re* (1991), 8 C.B.R. (3d) 25, 182 Alta. L.R. (2d) 152 (Q.B.)

12.11 APPEALS

- You may appeal any decision made by the Court under the CCAA by applying for leave to appeal either to the judge who made the decision or to the court (or a judge of the court) to which the appeal lies. CCAA s.13

- You must apply for leave to appeal within 21 days of the decision being appealed, or such further time as is sanctioned by the court, and you must comply with the court or jurisdiction's time limits for perfecting your appeal and giving any security or a deposit required. CCAA s.14

- The courts do not interfere lightly in CCAA orders or decisions. It is well recognized that proceedings under the CCAA are a supervisory process, where one judge is generally responsible for balancing the needs of all parties concerned, including the debtor company and the differing classes of creditors. To overturn a decision of that judge may well upset that balance, so you must be prepared to show that the judge erred in either fact or principle. If the judge did not make such a mistake, the courts are likely to respect the judge's discretion in making the decision. *Pacific National Lease Holding Corp., Re* (1992), 15 C.B.R. (3d) 265 (B.C. C.A. [In Chambers]); *Blue Range Resources Corp., Re* (1999), 244 A.R. 103 (C.A.); *Sharp-Rite Technologies Ltd., Re,* [2000] B.C.J. No. 1260, 19 C.B.R. (4th) 135 (C.A. [In Chambers]).

- A decision made under the CCAA can also be varied under the *Rules of Civil Procedure* by the judge that made it. *Rules of Civil Procedure,* Rule 37.14(4)

13

WHEN THE SOLICITOR BECOMES THE CREDITOR

Table of Contents

The agreement between client and solicitor, either implicit or explicit, is that your client must pay you for your time, your advice and your action. Unfortunately, you may encounter situations in which clients either cannot or will not settle their accounts for the services that you have rendered. In these cases, you must be prepared to take action to collect on the debt: in effect, you are now a creditor.

13.1 PREVENTING PAYMENT PROBLEMS

13.1.1 THE INITIAL CLIENT INTERVIEW

- Be clear about fees, and the basis on which they are calculated, with the client during the initial interview. Use a written retainer to set out the obligations of the client, the cost that the client will be responsible for and the method of payment.
- Request a financial retainer.
- If the client's financial situation precludes providing a financial retainer, your other options include:
  - drawing up a written agreement that details the amount the client owes (or will owe), and the manner and timing of payment required. *Note that if the agreement deals with matters handled in court, except for Small Claims Court, the agreement must be assessed for fairness and reasonableness before*

the client pays you. Solicitors Act, R.S.O. 1990, c. S.15, s. 16 and 17;
- ° accepting payment by way of credit card or debit card;
- ° setting up a regular, periodic payment schedule. *This will quickly alert you to a client's financial difficulties, allowing you to take early remedial action*;
- ° asking the client to provide some form of security; and
- ° having the client sign an irrevocable direction for fee payment out of the proceeds of your action. *Before signing such a declaration, the client should obtain independent legal advice.*

- If, based on the initial interview, you feel that there is little likelihood of receiving fee payment, and there is no justification for pro bono work, you should consider declining to take on the matter. *This is primarily a business decision: you have a responsibility to the well-being of your practice to exercise good financial, as well as legal, judgment.*

13.1.2 ENSURE THE ACCOUNT CONFORMS TO THE *SOLICITOR'S ACT*

- You (as the solicitor), or one of your firm's partners, must sign the account, which should clearly show your name, the partner's name under which the account is billed (if applicable), and your firm's name.

- The account must be either mailed or delivered to your client at their office or home.

- Describe the services you have rendered in reasonable detail.

> **Practice Tip:** If you later proceed to Court with your claim, the clerk can enter a default judgment against your client only if your claim is liquidated: i.e., the monetary amount claimed is clear. Your account must show a fixed or hourly amount agreed to by your client and hours worked. If your claim is considered unliquidated, court attendance will be required to determine if the amount claimed is appropriate.

- List in detail the disbursements made on behalf of your client. *Solicitors Act* s. 2

- To encourage prompt payment of the account, you may charge interest once accounts are past 30 days due. Obtain the current quarterly interest rate from *The Ontario Gazette* or your local court office. The following statement must appear at the bottom of the account: "In accordance with Section 33 of the *Solicitors Act*, interest will be charged at the rate of ____ per annum on unpaid fees, charges or disbursements calculated from a date that is one month after this statement is delivered." *Courts of Justice Act,* s. 127, 128. *Solicitors Act* s. 33

- If your client has provided you with security against your costs, interest is not to commence until the amount due is ascertained by agreement or by assessment. *Solicitors Act* s. 32

13.1.3 TIME DELAY

- Under normal circumstances, no action to recover the monies due can be taken before one month has elapsed from when the account was delivered to the client. *Solicitors Act* s. 3. *This allows the client one month in which to request assessment of the account.*

- If, however, you can prove that your client is about to leave the province, you can request permission from the Superior Court of Justice to start collection action before the one-month time delay expires. *Solicitors Act* s. 8

13.1.4 ACCOUNT FREQUENCY

- Billing frequency should be discussed with the client during the initial interview. *Where the action may be prolonged, it is beneficial to you to bill, and be paid, on a regular basis, rather than at the completion of the matter. Expecting payment at the end of a lengthy matter may not be advisable, as it can create a sudden and significant debt for the client.*

- You should regularly review the age of your accounts receivable. Depending on each particular client, a reminder letter and, later, a warning of collection action, may be warranted.

- In Ontario, the time delays at 13.1.3 above apply only to the final account, which means that if the client does not pay on receipt of the interim billing, you must wait to take recovery action until the final billing's time delay is complete. *Lipsett, Re* (1976), 15 O.R. (2d) 35 (Master), affirmed (1976), 15 O.R. (2d) 35n (H.C.). *If you do not do any further work, the interim bill becomes the final bill and you only have to wait for the 30 days in order to bring the assessment. However, if you continue to work on the client's behalf, one possible way to enforce payment of the interim billing may be to request assessment of the interim accounts following the procedure at 13.2.1 below. If you believe this will be necessary, you should let the client know at the initial interview that you intend to do this. If it becomes necessary as a result of non-payment, let the client know that you will now be assessing the interim accounts.*

13.2 RECOVERING THE MONIES DUE

13.2.1 ASSESSMENT

(a) Who Requests the Assessment and When

- Both the solicitor and the client have the right to have the account assessed, or reviewed to determine its fairness, by the court. *Solicitors Act* s. 3. *This can be an effective way to resolve a dispute where a client is questioning the amount of your bill and therefore refusing to pay it. Note as well that where a third party is liable to pay your client's bill, or where they* have *paid the bill, they also have the right to request an assessment. Solicitors Act s. 9.(1)*

- You should note that you cannot commence or prosecute any action against your client with regard to the matters awaiting assessment without the court's permission. *Solicitors Act* s. 6.(4)

- The client may request the assessment before the bill's delivery, and within one month after the bill's delivery. *Solicitors Act* s. 3(a),(b)

- If you have not yet delivered the account, you must do so within 14 days of the client's request for delivery and assessment.

- If the client has paid the account, they may still apply for an order for assessment up to 12 months after that payment, if they can show that circumstances warrant the assessment. *Solicitors Act* s. 11

- The solicitor may request the assessment after the one month time delay and within a year of the bill's delivery. *Solicitors Act* s. 3(c)

- Ensure that you maintain adequate case and billing records for at least six years: the court can assess your account within a six-year statutory limitation period (the limitation period that applies to the recovery of money on a contract), dated from when you completed your last services on the account.

(b) How to Request an Assessment

- If your retainer is not in dispute, and if no other special circumstances exist, request an assessment through the local registrar of the Superior Court of Justice (stating in your requisition that the retainer is undisputed and that no special circumstances exist). *This request must be made after the one-month time delay but before twelve months have elapsed from the bill's delivery. Solicitors Act* s. 3

- You must apply for an order referring the account to assessment if the retainer or the work you did is in dispute, or if other special circumstances exist. *Such circumstances include the following: a request for assessment before the one-month time delay or after the twelve-month period has elapsed; and the assessment of a bill that has already been assessed or on which a verdict or judgment has been obtained. Solicitors Act* s. 4

- File with the court a requisition, an order for assessment (with the date and time left blank, of course) and copies of each account to be assessed. Upon payment of the required fee, you will be given a date for the assessment. *Depending on your jurisdiction, you may also need to file an affidavit regarding service of documents by mail, in which you confirm that you or your firm have recently corresponded with your client at this address, and that service by mail will therefore be effective.*

- Serve the order for assessment on your client as set out in the order: at least 15 days before the assessment date if served personally, or 20 days if service is by mail. Include copies of all accounts being assessed, along with a statement of accounts, any payments received to date, interest calculations to date and balance due.

- File with the court an affidavit of service.

(c) Who Attends the Assessment

- If the assessment is uncontested, the lawyer seeking the assessment may send an articling student or law clerk to the assessment; however, you must file an affidavit detailing the work that was done, who did it, how long it took, disbursements, interest due, payments received to date and any other information (such as documentation like time dockets) that would justify the account.

- If the assessment is contested, those who worked on the account should attend the assessment wherever possible. This includes you (as the solicitor rendering the account), other lawyers, articling students, law clerks and investigators. Ensure that all appropriate documentation, plus account records and interest calculations, are available at the assessment.

The assessment officer can be a master, but more often than not is a civil servant. They are appointed by Order in Council by the authority under s. 77(2) C.J.A. Their powers are directed to them by the Regional Director of Court Operations. Assessment officers are generally former local registrars or deputy local registrars and are considered to have the knowledge to enable them to perform assessments by virtue of their past experience in the Court system.

(d) Trial and Pre-Trial

- The first attendance at an assessment, if the client is present, will become a pre-trial. The purpose of the pre-trial is to attempt to resolve the disputed issues, or in the alternative, to identify the disputed issues and, if possible, narrow them and set a reasonable time for a hearing.

- If your client does not attend the assessment, evidence will be given under oath, and the account may then be assessed in their absence and without further notice to them. *Solicitors Act* s. 5

- You should expect to give evidence as to the year of your call to the Bar, hourly rate and scope of work, including a brief, accurate description of the services rendered, and all information required in order to prove the bill.

- You should expect to be cross-examined by the client and you are entitled to cross-examine the client if they give evidence.

- You must also declare any money that the client has paid you to date, and be prepared to account for those funds. *Solicitors Act* s. 6.(2)

- The factors that have been held through the years to constitute the framework within which a solicitor's fee should be assessed are (in no particular order):

  - the time expended by the solicitor;
  - the legal complexity of the matters dealt with;
  - the degree of responsibility assumed by the solicitor;
  - the monetary value of the matters to the client;
  - the importance of the matters to the client;
  - the degree of skill and competence demonstrated by the solicitor;
  - the results achieved;
  - the ability of the client to pay; and
  - the reasonable expectation of the client as to the amount of the fee.

  Cohen v. Kealey & Blaney (1985), 26 C.P.C. (2d) 211 (Ont. C.A.)

- In the case of a bill for an instrument that you may have prepared for the client, the assessment officer will consider the skill, labour and responsibility involved in the work, rather than simply looking at the length of the instrument. *Solicitors Act* s. 14. *Thus, even a short document that may give the client the impression of minimal effort on your part may be assessed to your benefit if you can show the work that was required to prepare that document.*

- If the assessment deals with a written agreement between you and your client, where your client has switched from your services to those of another solicitor before the matter agreed upon was concluded, the court will examine the circumstances of the change in solicitors. You may be entitled to the full amount agreed upon, as long as there was no default, negligence, improper delay or other conduct on your part that would have given your client grounds to change solicitors. You must, therefore, be prepared to demonstrate that your conduct was reasonable. *Solicitors Act* s. 30

Practice Tip: For further discussion about the factors used to assess solicitors' accounts, see *Cohen v. Kealey & Blaney* (1985), 26 C.P.C. (2d) 211 (Ont. C.A.). In this case, the solicitor and client had agreed that fees and disbursements payable would not exceed $50,000 after a successful trial, or $20,000 after an unsuccessful trial. When the solicitor demanded some $40,000 in retainers, the client switched solicitors, and the action was settled prior to trial. The client's appeal of an assessment of costs at $40,000 plus disbursements was upheld, and the amount reduced to $25,000 plus disbursements. It was found that sufficient weight had not been given to the solicitor-client agreement, with the result that the amount originally allowed was unfairly high when compared to the maximum fee agreed upon.

- The onus is always on the solicitor to prove the bill. *Ensure that you have reviewed the file, and that you are prepared.*

- If the bill includes costs for steps in the proceedings that, in hindsight, could be considered unnecessary, the assessment officer can still allow them. You'll need to show that you took those steps because they were in your client's best interests at the time. If, on the other hand, those steps were taken because your client insisted on them, you will need to show that you advised your client, at the time, that they were unnecessary or would not advance the client's best interests. *Solicitors Act,* s. 7.(1). This requirement does not apply to costs payable out of a fund not wholly belonging to the client, or by a third party. *Solicitors Act* s. 7(2)

- Costs may be assessed at the court's discretion. *Solicitors Act,* s. 4

- The court or assessment officer may also disallow interest or fix a lesser rate of interest than that charged, if they feel that it is reasonable to do so under the circumstances. *Solicitors Act,* s. 33.(5)

(e) The Certificate of Assessment

- Once the assessment is complete, the assessment officer will issue a report: a certificate of assessment. This summarizes the total account, how much it has been assessed for, whether any payments have been received to date, interest, costs allowed on the assessment, and the amount that the client must now pay. *Solicitors Act,* s. 6(5)

- Serve the client with the notice of the filing of the assessment officer's report, and a copy of the assessment officer's report, as soon as possible.

- File with the court an affidavit of service.

- The report is confirmed by the court automatically 15 days after you serve the client in person with the notice of the filing of the assessment officer's report. (The certificate requires the same confirmation steps as a referee's report under Rule 54 of the Rules of Civil Procedure.)

- If you are concerned that the client will take steps to "creditor-proof" their assets, such as selling property that you might otherwise seize, you may file an affidavit explaining the situation and bring a motion requesting an order confirming the report immediately.

- If the assessment finds that your client has overpaid you, the client is entitled to interest on that overpayment, calculated from the date the overpayment was made. The maximum interest rate is that set out for the purposes of section 128 of the *Courts of Justice Act*; *Solicitors Act,* s. 33.(2)

- If you or your client oppose the confirmation, the opposing party must bring a motion to oppose confirmation before the Superior Court of Justice, whereupon the judge can confirm the certificate in whole or in part, or make another order. *Solicitors Act* s. 6(9); *Rules of Civil Procedure* R. 54.09

- The assessment can also be appealed: amounts in excess of $25,000 go to the Court of Appeal; at $25,000 or less, the matter goes to the Divisional Court. *Courts of Justice Act* s. 6(1)(b) and s. 19(1)(a)

- Once the assessment has been confirmed, the amount is due immediately, and enforceable through normal collection procedures, such as writs of seizure and sale or garnishment. *Solicitors Act* s. 6(5) and s.13

- Postjudgment interest should be calculated from the date the account was assessed. Prejudgment interest is accounted for in the assessment itself, up to the date of the assessment.

13.2.2 SOLICITOR'S LIEN

A solicitor's lien occurs in two ways. First, you may retain the documents or funds belonging to your client that are in your possession (although with some exceptions, noted below). *Solicitors Act* s. 6(6)

Second, you may request to have the client's personal property, recovered through a judgment based on your action, act as security against the costs you incurred in obtaining that judgment. (The lien attaches to the specific judgment, rather than to your full account or to the cause of the action.)

(a) Property and Circumstances Covered by a Solicitor's Lien

- The lien on documents only extends to the client's rightful property that you received while you were acting as the client's solicitor. *Halsbury*, 4th ed., vol. 44, para. 227, p. 170, Butterworths: London, 1983

- If the papers or funds that the client has provided to you belong to a third party, you have no right to retain them. This would be also be the case where a client has provided you with a company's accounts: where the company's directors must retain possession of the accounts, you have no lien against them. *Alpha Mortgage & Investment Co., Re* (1916), 10 W.W.R. 652 (B.C. S.C.). Similarly, you have no lien against property that you received when not acting as your client's solicitor, but as a mortgagee or trustee, for example.

- You have the right to refuse your client permission to inspect or receive copies of the documents that you have retained; however, as detailed in 13.2.2.(b) below, you must forward the papers to the client's new solicitor if requested, or by order of the court. *In addition, you should ensure that your conduct does not unduly prejudice your client's case.*

- Apart from a lien on documentation, you may also ask the court to intervene to assist you in recovering the specific costs that you occurred in achieving a judgment as a result of litigation or arbitration: a lien on fruits of action. You may request the court's assistance through an action, a petition, a stop order on funds in court, a charging order or restraining your client from receiving the money until your bill is paid. *Iwanczuk v. Nachweski,* [1950] 2 W.W.R. 241 (Man. K.B.)

- In the case of a lien against the results of a monetary judgment that you were instrumental in obtaining, the lien can only be enforced against money that is paid to you in trust or the court as a direct result of the judgment. *Home Assurance Co. of Canada, Re* (1949), [1950] 1 W.W.R. 337 (Alta. T.D.), affirmed [1950] 2 W.W.R. 1169 (Alta. C.A.)

> **Practice Tip:** If, for example, you obtained a judgment for your client involving the payment of a debt, and the monies were paid into court or to you in trust, you have the right to a lien on those monies for the costs of obtaining the judgment. If, however, you were only able to obtain the monies through a subsequent garnishment request, your lien on those monies only extends to the costs you incurred in obtaining the garnishment - not the costs you incurred in the original judgment. This is because a creditor who attaches the monies is deemed to do so for the benefit of all creditors, as well as himself. *Creditor's Relief Act*, R.S.O. 1990, s.3(1) and 6(6).

- Where your client is the plaintiff, and you believe he or she may attempt to avoid paying your fees by settling direct with the defendant, you should send a letter to the defendant's counsel, if requested, or to the defendant directly if unrepresented, letting them know that you have not been paid, and that you expect to receive payment out of the proceeds of the action. If the defendant then goes ahead and settles with your client without your knowledge, you will be in a position to bring a motion in court requesting that the defendant pay your costs. *Brown v. Conant* (1856), 2 P.R. 208. *Where your client is the defendant, you would give the plaintiff notice only if there is a counterclaim and your client might expect to receive money.*

(b) Liens and the Severing of the Client/Solicitor Relationship

- Where the client has discharged you, you have the right to retain possession of the client's property until the client pays your account, either direct to you or into court. *Gladstone Re* (1971), [1972] 2 O.R. 127 (C.A.). *You should, however, consider the effect of your retention of the documents on your client's case: if it will prejudice your client's situation, you should not retain them, as per Rule 11 of the Rules of Professional Conduct.*

- Where you have discharged the client, whether for non-payment of fees or other reasons, you must, on request, provide the client's papers to the new solicitors pursuing the case. The new solicitors must return these papers to you when the matter is complete. *Collison v. Hurst*, [1946] O.W.N. 668 (C.A.). *This ensures that the client's new lawyers can represent the matter to the full extent of their abilities, and that the client's case is not prejudiced by the client's failure to pay your fees.*

(c) The Priority of a Solicitor's Lien

- Where you have been replaced by a new solicitor, your lien takes priority if it was your action that was instrumental in preserving or recovering the client's property. The new solicitor's lien takes priority if the litigation bears fruit under his or her action. *Ford v. Mason* (1893), 15 P.R. 392 (Ont. H.C.)

- Where you have successfully obtained a judgment for the client, your lien on the proceeds of the judgment takes precedence over all other creditors, whether the proceeds have been delivered directly to you or to the court. *Bell v. Wright* (1895), 24 S.C.R. 656

- However, in a bankruptcy scenario, the only proceeds available for the lien will be those directly related to the action in which monies were recovered. These monies are not available to pay costs incurred in other matters. *Broadloom Warehouse (Edmonton.) Ltd., Re* (1980), 37 C.B.R. (N.S.) 142 (Alta. Q.B.)

- If a client becomes bankrupt before paying your account, your solicitor's lien is considered a secured claim provided that the fund was created from your labour in the litigation. This is called a "charging lien." *Tots & Teens Sault Ste. Marie Ltd., Re* (1975), 21 C.B.R. (N.S.) 1 (Ont. Bktcy)

(d) Discharging a Lien

- The lien is considered discharged when the client pays the account, when you voluntarily give up possession of the liened property (excluding handing over the files to your client's new solicitor, and reserving your rights in the liened property) or if you waive further rights to the lien. *David Q.C., Rodica, Liening on Your Client and Getting a Charge Out of It, Chapter K, Unsecured Creditors, How to Get Paid, Law Society of Upper Canada, p. K-9*

13.2.3 CHARGING ORDERS

Where your action has resulted in the client being able to recover or retain property, you have the right to a charge on that property in respect of your fees. The amount of the charge is the costs of the specific action in which you were instrumental in protecting the client's property. *Solicitors Act* s. 34.(1)

(a) Property and Circumstances Covered by a Charging Order

- The property in question must be capable of being charged: property designated for personal maintenance, for example, or involving an easement, is not chargeable. *David Q.C., Rodica, Liening on Your Client and Getting a Charge Out of It, Chapter K, Unsecured Creditors, How to Get Paid, Law Society of Upper Canada, p. K-22*

- Property recovered as a result of an arbitration proceeding is not chargeable, because arbitration is not a cause or matter. *Bulmer, Re* (1926), 30 O.W.N. 71 (H.C.)

- A conveyance intended to defeat your charge is void, unless the person who purchased the property for value did so in good faith and without knowing about the charge. *Solicitors Act* s. 34(2)

(b) Obtaining the Charging Order

- Where the property is chargeable, and where you were instrumental in obtaining the judgment that protected or obtained the property, you can request a charging order. Although section 34 of the *Solicitors Act* notes that you must bring a motion to the court for the charging order, in practice, you cannot start an action for a charging order by way of a notice of motion, it must be by way of a notice of application.

- If the court agrees with you, it issues a charging order.

(c) Priorities and Charging Orders

- The charging order gives your account priority over competing claims on the property, including other creditors, the defendant's set-off of recovered costs, a subsequent attachment, a garnishment or, in the case of bankruptcy, a receiver or trustee. *Kushner v. Macdonald* (1976), 14 O.R. (2d) 385 (H.C.); *Walker v. Saunders* (1984), [1985] 1 W.W.R. 743 (B.C. C.A.)

- If your client's case has been taken over by a new solicitor, your charging order takes precedence over the new solicitor's right to a charging order only if it was your action that was instrumental in obtaining the judgment. Otherwise, the new solicitor's charging order takes precedence over yours.

13.2.4 SUING THE CLIENT

Because a number of options for recovering your fees exist, and because those options are less costly and time consuming for both you and the court, suing the client should be viewed as a last resort. In fact, proceeding directly to a suit may be viewed negatively by the court.

- If you do proceed to a suit, you should include a claim for a charging order, assuming that you can be specific as to property or funds that you were instrumental in recovering or preserving for the client.

- Depending on the amount involved, you may choose to pursue the matter either in Superior Court of Justice (see Chapter 3) or Small Claims Court (see Chapter 4).

Appendix 1

Precedents Relating to

Chapter 1

First Contact with the Secured or Unsecured Creditor and the Initial Interview

App 1-1
Collection Intake Sheet

A: CLIENT INFORMATION

Name of Opposing Counsel . . . .
Address. . . . .
Telephone number . . . .
Fax number . . . .
E-mail address . . . .
Opposing lawyer . . . .
Date

1. Defendants/debtors . . . .
2. Amount of Claim . . . .
   [*attach copies of invoices, notes, cheques or documents supporting the claim*]
3. Particulars of Claim . . . .
4. Opinions . . . .
5. Legal fees for conduct of file . . . .
6. Actions commenced:
   date: . . . .
   court: . . . .
7. Sequence of events . . . .
8. Date of Reports sent . . . .

B: DEBTOR INFORMATION

ACCOUNT DEBTOR

1. Full Name including middle names and any nicknames or alias names . . . .
2. Last Known Address . . . .
3. Telephone/Fax . . . .
4. E-mail address . . . .
5. Web Address . . . .
6. Birth date . . . .
7. Marital Status . . . .
8. Spouse's Name . . . .
9. Spouse's Place of Employment . . . .
10. Employment Record . . . .
11. Assets: House (location) . . . .
    Other Real Estate (location) . . . .
    Vehicle (licence no., description) . . . .
    Securities (list) . . . .
    Other (list) . . . .

GUARANTOR(S)

1. Full Name including middle name . . . .
2. Last known address . . . .

3. Telephone/Fax ....
4. E-mail address ....
5. Web address ....
6. Date of Birth ....
7. Marital Status ....
8. Spouse's name ....
9. Spouse's Place of Employment ....
10. Employment Record ....
11. Assets: House (location) ....
    Other Real Estate (location) ....
    Vehicle (licence no., description) ....
    Securities (list) ....
    Other (list) ....

DEBT (Attach Statements of Account)
1. Original Amount of Debt ....
2. Describe History of Debt (particulars of defaults) ....
3. Evidence of Debt ....
4. Calculation of Amount Owed ....
5. Has Demand Been Made (date) ....
6. Agreement to:
   (a) postpone ....
   (b) not enforce security ....
   (c) not pursue guarantees ....
7. Name, Addresses and Telephone Numbers of all client personnel who have been involved in:
   (a) the original transaction ....
   (b) collection action ....
8. Security Held (types of security and registration particulars) ....
9. Relevant Documents:
   (a) invoices ....
   (b) statements of account ....
   (c) contracts ....
   (d) promissory notes ....
   (e) guarantees ....
   (f) security documents ....
   (g) demand letters ....
   (h) legal opinions relating to the debt ....
10. Searches conducted by the client ....

INSTRUCTIONS
1. Reporting Cycle ....
2. Billing Cycle ....
3. Authorization Needed:
   (a) to commence litigation ....

(b) to discuss settlement . . . .
(c) to settle the matter . . . .
(d) to retain experts . . . .
(e) to retain counsel outside the jurisdiction . . . .
(f) other . . . .

4. Security Review Required . . . .
5. Opinions Required . . . .
6. Basis of Fee . . . .

Appendix 2

Precedents Relating to

Chapter 2

Searches

App 2-1

Execution Certificate

CERTIFICATE #:
NO. DE CERTIFICAT:
00421974-228470B

EXECUTION

CERTIFICATE/CERTIFICAT

SHERIFF AT: OTTAWA (LRO #4)
SHERIF A:

DATE OF CERTIFICATE: 2001-06-28
DATE DU CERTIFICAT :

THIS CERTIFIES THAT LISTED BELOW ARE ALL WRITS OF EXECUTION, EXTENT OR CERTIFICATES OF LIEN IN MY HANDS AT THE TIME OF SEARCHING AGAINST THE REAL AND PERSONAL PROPERTY OF:

J'ATTESTE PAR LA PRESENTE QU'ENUMERES CI-APRES SONT TOUS LES BREFS DE . SAISIE-EXECUTION, DE SAISIE OU CERTIFICATS DE PRIVILEGE DONT JE DISPOSAIS AU MOMENT DE LA RECHERCHE FAITE SUR LES BIENS MEUBLES ET IMMEUBLES DE:

	SURNAME /NOM	GIVEN NAMES / PRENOM(S)
(PERSON/PERSONNE)	JOHNSON	TIMOTHY
	JOHNSON	TIMOTHY J.

EXECUTION: 99-18496

CAUTION TO PARTY REQUESTING SEARCH:
ENSURE THAT THE ABOVE INDICATED NAME IS THE SAME AS THE NAME SEARCHED.
WRITS AND CERTIFICATES MAY BE REMOVED FROM THE SHERIFF'S FILES SUBSEQUENT TO THIS SEARCH AND MAY BE SHOWN AS CLEAR LATER THIS DATE.
AVERTISSEMENT A LA PARTIE QUI DEMANDE LA RECHERCHE:

ASSUREZ-VOUS QUE LE NOM INDIQUE CI-DESSUS EST LE MEME QUE CELUI QUI EST RECHERCHE. IL SE PEUT QUE DES MANDATS

ET DES CERTIFICIATS SOIENT RETIRES DES DOSSIERS DU SHERIF APRES CETTE RECHERCHE ET PURGES DANS LA JOURNEE.

App 2-2

NOTICE - BANKRUPTCY SEARCHES

By virtue of the Bankruptcy and Insolvency Act, the Superintendent of Bankruptcy is required to maintain public records of bankruptcies. A name search service is provided by the Office of the Superintendent of Bankruptcy and the information can be obtained from that Office, upon payment of the prescribed fee (currently $8.00 per name search).

For information contact:

The National Bankruptcy Search Office
Office of the Superintendent of Bankruptcy
365 Laurier Avenue West
Ottawa, Ontario
K1A 0C8

(Hours: 8:00 a.m. - 5:00 p.m. Monday - Friday)
Telephone: (613) 941-2863
Fax: (613) 941-9490

App 2-3

Bankruptcy Search Request Letter

January 11, 2001

Industry Canada
Bankruptcy Searches
365 Laurier Avenue West
8th Floor
Ottawa, Ontario
K1A 0C8
tel: (613) 941-2863
fax: (613) 941-9490
(Hours: 8:00 a.m. - 5:00 p.m. Monday - Friday)

Dear Sirs:

Re: Bankruptcy Search Request - Fantastic Restaurant Ltd.

Please conduct a search of your records and advise if Fantastic Restaurant Ltd. has made an assignment into bankruptcy or there has been a receiving order made against this corporation. Enclosed please find our cheque in the amount of $8.00 to cover your fees in this matter.

Thank you for your assistancein this regard.

Yours very truly,

ADAM & ZENA

Per: Joe Adam

App 2-4

Credit Bureau Search Request

August 21, 2001

Credit Bureau
P.O. Box 7495
Station "A"
Ottawa, Ontario
K2P 9K2

Dear Sirs:

Re: Credit Bureau Check
Fantastic Restaurant Ltd.

Would you please conduct a Credit Bureau check on the above named company. Their address is 865 Carleton Street, Ottawa, Ontario K2B 1X9, and their telephone number is (613) 233-8094.

We look forward to receipt of your report and bill for same.

Yours very truly,

ADAM & ZENA

Per: Joe Adam

Appendix 3

Precedents Relating to

Chapter 3

Collections and Enforcement of the Debt - Unsecured Precedents

NOTE: For forms dealing with mediation, see Chapter 5.

App 3-1

Demand Letter to Debtor

WITHOUT PREJUDICE
Personal & Confidential

May 14, 2001
Utopia Distribution Inc.
457 Jones Road
Ottawa, Ontario K4M 1T5

Attention: John Michael Bennett

Dear Sir:

Re: Balance Due and Owing to Naimark Novelties Ltd.

We are the solicitors for Naimark Novelties Ltd. We have been asked to collect the sum of $240,000.00 owing by you as of April 30, 2001 in respect of goods sold and delivered. Interest is accruing on this debt at the rate of 12% per cent per annum.

In order to avoid court action, would you kindly forward a certified cheque payable to Naimark Novelties Ltd., c/o our office, within ten days from the date of this letter. If it is not received, we shall have no alternative but to commence court action against you. If we are obliged to commence court proceedings, you will likely be required to pay court costs, legal fees and additional interest over the sum now owing. In addition, this action may affect your credit rating.

If you wish to discuss this matter or clarify this matter, please contact Sam Naimark, at 912 Halter Road, Ottawa, Ontario, (613) 555-5555.

Your prompt attention to this matter will save you considerable expense and inconvenience.

Yours very truly,

ADAM & ZENA

per:
Joe Adam

App 3-2

Demand Letter to Guarantor

WITHOUT PREJUDICE
Personal & Confidential
May 14, 2001

John Michael Bennett
c/o Utopia Distribution Inc.
473 Union Street
Ottawa, Ontario
K4P 1Z2

Dear Sir:

Re: Guarantee to Naimark Novelties Ltd.

We are the solicitors for Naimark Novelties Ltd. We have been asked to collect the sum of $240,000.00 owing by you personally to Naimark Novelties Ltd. This sum is owed by you personally pursuant to a guarantee that you executed agreeing to guarantee the debt of Utopia Distribution Inc. to Naimark Novelties Ltd. Utopia Distribution Inc. has defaulted in its obligations and you are now being called upon to honour your obligation.

In order to avoid court action, would you kindly forward a certified cheque to Naimark Novelties Ltd., c/o our offices, within ten days from the date of this letter. In the event that payment is not received, we shall have no alternative but to commence a court proceeding against you. If we are obliged to commence court proceedings, you will likely be required to pay court costs, legal fees and additional interest, in addition to the sum now owing. This may also have an adverse effect on your credit rating at the Credit Bureau.

If you wish to discuss this matter or clarify this matter, please contact the writer.

Your prompt attention will save you considerable expense, inconvenience and embarrassment.

Yours very truly,

ADAM & ZENA

per:
Joe Adam

App 3-3

Notice of Commencement of Proceeding

FORM 77A

Courts of Justice Act

(Title of Proceeding)

NOTICE OF COMMENCEMENT OF PROCEEDING

This action ❑ or application ❑ is for:

(*Select one only that describes the main claim*)

collection	❑	construction lien	❑
motor vehicle	❑	negligence	❑
real property	❑	landlord/tenant	❑
contract/commercial	❑	trust/fiduciary duty	❑
wrongful dismissal	❑	medical malpractice	❑
estates	❑	other professional malpractice	❑
bankruptcy	❑	other	❑

The simplified procedure (Rule 76) applies ❑ yes ❑ no

Choice of Track ❑ Fast ❑Standard

Plaintiff's Lawyer:
(or plaintiff if unrepresented)

Defendant's Lawyer:
(or defendant if unrepresented)

Name:	(1) Name:	(2) Name:
Address:	Address:	Address:
Phone:	Phone:	Phone:
Fax:	Fax:	Fax:

Plaintiff's lawyer's Law Society Registration No.

Defendant's lawyer's Law Society Registration No. (if known)

WARNING: In accordance with rule 77.08, where no notice of defence has been filed and the proceeding has not been disposed of by final order or judgment, the registrar will, 180 days after the date of issue of the originating process, dismiss the proceeding as abandoned.

WARNING: In accordance with rule 77.06 (2), this form must be given to the plaintiff.

Filed on

Signature of Registrar

O. Reg. 118/97, s. 13.

App 3-4

Claim for Monies Advanced and for Guarantee

Court File No:

SUPERIOR COURT OF JUSTICE

BETWEEN:

OMNI BANK OF CANADA

Plaintiff

- and -

MARK JOHNSON AND HANNAH JOHNSON

Defendants

STATEMENT OF CLAIM

TO THE DEFENDANT

A LEGAL PROCEEDING HAS BEEN COMMENCED AGAINST YOU by the plaintiff. The claim made against you is set out in the following pages.

IF YOU WISH TO DEFEND THIS PROCEEDING, you or an Ontario lawyer acting for you must prepare a statement of defence in Form 18A prescribed by the Rules of Civil Procedure, serve it on the plaintiff's lawyer or, where the plaintiff does not have a lawyer, serve it on the plaintiff, and file it, with proof of service in this court office, WITHIN TWENTY DAYS after this statement of claim is served on you, if you are served in Ontario.

If you are served in another province or territory of Canada or in the United States of America, the period for serving and filing your statement of defence is forty days. If you are served outside Canada and the United States of America, the period is sixty days.

Instead of serving and filing a statement of defence, you may serve and file a notice of intent to defend in Form 18B prescribed by the Rules of Civil Procedure. This will entitle you to ten more days within which to serve and file your statement of defence.

IF YOU FAIL TO DEFEND THIS PROCEEDING, JUDGMENT MAY BE GIVEN AGAINST YOU IN YOUR ABSENCE AND WITHOUT FURTHER NOTICE TO YOU. IF YOU WISH TO DEFEND THIS PROCEEDING BUT ARE UNABLE TO PAY LEGAL FEES, LEGAL AID MAY BE AVAILABLE TO YOU BY CONTACTING A LOCAL LEGAL AID OFFICE.

IF YOU PAY THE PLAINTIFF'S CLAIM, and $____ for costs, within the time for serving and filing your statement of defence you may move to have this proceeding dismissed by the court. If you believe the amount claimed for costs is excessive, you may pay the plaintiff's claim and $100 for costs and have the costs assessed by the court.

Date______________________ Issued by __________________________

Local Registrar

Address of court office: 361 University Avenue
Toronto, Ontario
M5G 1T3

TO: (Name and address of each defendant)

CLAIM

1. **The plaintiff claims as against the defendants for:**
(a) The debt owed by the defendants in the sum of $68,500.00;
(b) Prejudgment interest on the sum claimed at the rate of 13% per annum from October 15, 2001 pursuant the promissory note described below;
(c) Postjudgment interest pursuant to the *Courts of Justice Act*; R.S.O. 1990 c. C-43;
(d) Costs of this action;
(e) Such further or other relief as this Honourable Court deems just and the circumstances require.

2. The plaintiff is a chartered bank and carries on the business of banking including the granting of loans in the Province of Ontario.

3. The plaintiff's claim as against the defendant Mark Johnson is for the amount of the balance due and owing to the plaintiff as a result of a loan from the plaintiff to the defendant Mark Johnson. Details of the loan have been set out in a demand promissory note executed by the defendant dated December 23, 2000.

4. The defendant Hannah Johnson is liable for the debts of Mark Johnson as a result of a written guarantee dated December 23, 2000, guaranteeing payment of the debts of Mark Johnson to the plaintiff.

5. Full particulars of the account between the parties have been set out in statements of account sent with full particularity to the defendants.

6. The plaintiff has demanded payment of the balance owing from the defendants but the defendants have refused or otherwise neglected to pay the amount owing and the loan is in default now and the full balance is due and owing.

7. The total amount due on the account from the defendants to the plaintiff as of October 15, 2001 is $68,500.00.

8. The plaintiff claims from the defendants interest on the amount claimed at the rate of 13% per year pursuant to the Courts of Justice Act, and pursuant to the terms of the promissory note which stipulates interest accrues on overdue accounts at the rate of 13% per annum.

9. Attached hereto is Schedule "A" which is a detailed statement of account showing how the balance claimed was calculated.

10. The plaintiff proposes that this action be tried in the City of Toronto, in the Province of Ontario.

DATED at Toronto, this 16th day of October, 2001.

ADAM & ZENA
Barristers and Solicitors
281 McLeod Street
Toronto, Ontario
M5C 3C5
tel: (416) 995-9595
fax: (416) 995-9696
Attention: Sarah Zena
Solicitor for the Plaintiff

App 3-5

Claim for Balance on Credit Card

Court File No:

SUPERIOR COURT OF JUSTICE

BETWEEN:

OMNI BANK OF CANADA

Plaintiff

- and -

LAURENT GAGNON

Defendant

STATEMENT OF CLAIM

TO THE DEFENDANT

A LEGAL PROCEEDING HAS BEEN COMMENCED AGAINST YOU by the plaintiff. The claim made against you is set out in the following pages.

IF YOU WISH TO DEFEND THIS PROCEEDING, you or an Ontario lawyer acting for you must prepare a statement of defence in Form 18A prescribed by the Rules of Civil Procedure, serve it on the plaintiff's lawyer or, where the plaintiff does not have a lawyer, serve it on the plaintiff, and file it, with proof of service in this court office, WITHIN TWENTY DAYS after this statement of claim is served on you, if you are served in Ontario.

If you are served in another province or territory of Canada or in the United States of America, the period for serving and filing your statement of defence is forty days. If you are served outside Canada and the United States of America, the period is sixty days.

Instead of serving and filing a statement of defence, you may serve and file a notice of intent to defend in Form 18B prescribed by the Rules of Civil Procedure. This will entitle you to ten more days within which to serve and file your statement of defence.

IF YOU FAIL TO DEFEND THIS PROCEEDING, JUDGMENT MAY BE GIVEN AGAINST YOU IN YOUR ABSENCE AND WITHOUT FURTHER NOTICE TO YOU. IF YOU WISH TO DEFEND THIS PROCEEDING BUT ARE UNABLE TO PAY LEGAL FEES, LEGAL AID MAY BE AVAILABLE TO YOU BY CONTACTING A LOCAL LEGAL AID OFFICE.

IF YOU PAY THE PLAINTIFF'S CLAIM, and $ ______ for costs, within the time for serving and filing your statement of defence you may move to have this proceeding dismissed by the court. If you believe the amount claimed for costs is excessive, you may pay the plaintiff's claim and $100 for costs and have the costs assessed by the court.

Date ______________________ Issued by ________________________

Local Registrar

Address of court office: 161 Elgin Street
Ottawa, Ontario
K2P 2K1

TO: (Name and address of each defendant)

CLAIM

1. The plaintiff claims as against the defendant Laurent Gagnon for:

(a) The debt owed by the defendant Laurent Gagnon to the plaintiff in the sum of $14,725.11

(b) Prejudgment interest on the sum claimed at the rate of 18.99% per annum from June 15, 2001 pursuant to the agreement described below;

(c) Postjudgment interest pursuant to the Courts of Justice Act, R.S.O. 1990, c. C-43;

(d) Costs of this action;

(e) Such further or other relief as this Honourable Court deems just and the circumstances require.

2. The plaintiff is a chartered bank and carries on the business of banking and the extending of credit in the Province of Ontario. At all material times the plaintiff carried on business under the name style of OMNI BANK OF CANADA (MASTERCARD) (hereinafter referred to as "MASTERCARD") and extended credit to the defendant through the use of a "MASTERCARD" credit card.

3. The defendant applied for a "MASTERCARD" credit account with the plaintiff The plaintiff opened a "MASTERCARD" credit account for the defendant and the plaintiff issued a "MASTERCARD" credit card to the defendant. The defendant received the credit card from the plaintiff subject to the terms and conditions of the "MASTERCARD CARDHOLDER AGREEMENT". The "MASTERCARD CARDHOLDER AGREEMENT" was set out in the application for the "MASTERCARD" credit card and the "CARDHOLDER AGREEMENT" was also delivered to the defendant at the time of the delivery of the "MASTERCARD" credit card. The defendant's card account number is 8711 244 089 673.

4. The defendant agreed to abide and be bound by the terms of the "MASTERCARD CARDHOLDER AGREEMENT". The "MASTERCARD CARDHOLDER AGREEMENT" permitted the defendant to purchase goods and services on credit and to obtain cash advances on credit by the use of the "MASTERCARD" credit card. Under the terms of the "MASTERCARD CARDHOLDER AGREEMENT" the defendant agreed to be responsible to the plaintiff for all

debt on the "MASTERCARD" account resulting from the use of the "MASTERCARD" credit card.

5. The defendant used the said "MASTERCARD" credit card to purchase various goods and services on credit and/or to receive cash advances on credit, which transactions were all charged against the "MASTERCARD" credit account of the defendant.

6. As a result of the balance of the account being unpaid from time to time, interest charges were incurred on the account pursuant to the terms of the "MASTERCARD CARDHOLDER AGREEMENT" at the rate in effect from time to time, as notified to the cardholder in the monthly statement of account. At present, the rate of interest charged and accruing on the account pursuant to the notices sent to the defendant and pursuant to the terms of the "MASTERCARD CARDHOLDER AGREEMENT" is 18.99% per annum.

7. Full particulars of the goods and services and cash advances received by the defendant and of the transactions relating to the account of the defendant have been set out and delivered to the defendant in regular monthly statements.

8. The balance of the account outstanding and due and owing by the defendant to the plaintiff is $14,725.11 as of July 15, 2001. The defendant has defaulted in the payment terms and the account is in arrears. The plaintiff has demanded that the full balance owing on the account be paid. Despite repeated demands by the plaintiff, there has been no payment on the balance owing by the defendant.

9. The Plaintiff proposes that this action be tried in the City of Ottawa, in the Province of Ontario.

DATED at Ottawa, this 15th day of September, 2001

ADAM & ZENA
Barristers and Solicitors
281 McLeod Street
Ottawa, Ontario
K2P 1A1
tel: (613) 237-0000
fax: (613) 237-1111
Attention: Sarah Zena
Solicitor for the Plaintiff

App 3-6

Claim for Balance of Price for Goods Sold and Delivered and as a Guarantor

Court File No:

SUPERIOR COURT OF JUSTICE

BETWEEN:

PARADIS RESTAURANT SUPPLIES INC.

Plaintiff

- and -

FANTASTIC RESTAURANT INC. and JOHNNY FANTASTIC

Defendants

STATEMENT OF CLAIM

TO THE DEFENDANT

A LEGAL PROCEEDING HAS BEEN COMMENCED AGAINST YOU by the plaintiff. The claim made against you is set out in the following pages.

IF YOU WISH TO DEFEND THIS PROCEEDING, you or an Ontario lawyer acting for you must prepare a statement of defence in Form 18A prescribed by the Rules of Civil Procedure, serve it on the plaintiff's lawyer or, where the plaintiff does not have a lawyer, serve it on the plaintiff, and file it, with proof of service in this court office, WITHIN TWENTY DAYS after this statement of claim is served on you, if you are served in Ontario.

If you are served in another province or territory of Canada or in the United States of America, the period for serving and filing your statement of defence is forty days. If you are served outside Canada and the United States of America, the period is sixty days.

Instead of serving and filing a statement of defence, you may serve and file a notice of intent to defend in Form 18B prescribed by the Rules of Civil Procedure. This will entitle you to ten more days within which to serve and file your statement of defence.

IF YOU FAIL TO DEFEND THIS PROCEEDING, JUDGMENT MAY BE GIVEN AGAINST YOU IN YOUR ABSENCE AND WITHOUT FURTHER NOTICE TO YOU. IF YOU WISH TO DEFEND THIS PROCEEDING BUT ARE UNABLE TO PAY LEGAL FEES, LEGAL AID MAY BE AVAILABLE TO YOU BY CONTACTING A LOCAL LEGAL AID OFFICE.

IF YOU PAY THE PLAINTIFF'S CLAIM, and $__ for costs, within the time for serving and filing your statement of defence you may move to have this proceeding dismissed by the court. If you believe the amount claimed for costs is excessive, you may pay the plaintiff's claim and $100 for costs and have the costs assessed by the court.

Date______________________ Issued by________________________
Local Registrar

Address of
court office: 161 Elgin Street
Ottawa, Ontario
K2P 2K1

TO: (Name and address of each defendant)

[Where the action is brought under the simplified procedure, insert the following:

THIS ACTION IS BROUGHT AGAINST YOU UNDER THE SIMPLIFIED PROCEDURE PROVIDED IN RULE 76 OF THE RULES OF CIVIL PROCEDURE]

CLAIM

1. The plaintiff claims as against the defendants for:

(a) The liquidated debt owed by the defendants in the sum of $25,000.00;
(b) Prejudgment interest and postjudgment interest pursuant to the provisions of s. 128 and 129 of the *Court of Justice Act,* R.S.O. 1990, c. C-43 on the sum claimed from May 25, 2001 until payment;
(c) Costs of this action;
(d) Such further or other relief as this Honourable Court deems just and the circumstances require.

2. The plaintiff is a corporation and carries on business in the Province of Ontario as a supplier of restaurant equipment

3. The plaintiff's claim is for the balance of monies owing from the defendants to the plaintiff for restaurant supplies and equipment sold and delivered by the plaintiff to the defendant Fantastic Restaurant Inc. Full details and particulars of the account have been set out in invoices and statements of account and have been sent to that defendant. The plaintiff's claim against the defendant Johnny Fantastic is pursuant to a guarantee in writing dated October 8, 1993 whereby the said Johnny Fantastic agreed to guarantee the debts of Fantastic Restaurant Inc. to Paradis Restaurant Supplies Inc.

4. Despite repeated demands, the defendants have refused or otherwise neglected to pay the balance due and owing.

5. The balance due and owing as of May 25, 2001 is $25,000.00. The plaintiff also claims interest on the amount claimed at the rate of 12% per year pursuant to the terms of the purchase order signed by the defendant Fantastic Restaurant Inc. which stipulated that interest accrues on overdue accounts at the rate of 12% per year.

6. The defendant Fantastic Restaurant Inc. acknowledged its debt to the plaintiff by forwarding a cheque in the sum of $25,000.00 to the plaintiff dated April 10, 2001 payable to the plaintiff and drawn on the Argent Bank, 11 Rideau Street, Ottawa, Ontario, K1B 1X4, which cheque was duly presented by the plaintiff for payment and was dishonoured.

7. Attached hereto as Schedule "A" is a Statement of Account showing how the balance claimed was calculated.

8. The plaintiff proposes that this action be tried in the City of Ottawa.

DATE: May 28, 2001

ADAM & ZENA
Barristers and Solicitors
281 McLeod Street
Ottawa, Ontario
K2P 1A1
tel: (613) 237-0000
fax: (613) 237-1111
Attention: Sarah Zena
Solicitor for the Plaintiff

App 3-7

Claim Against Drawer of a Cheque (N.S.F.)

Court File No:

SUPERIOR COURT OF JUSTICE

BETWEEN:

HAROLD LEIKIN

Plaintiff

- and -

ALFRED BIGSHOT

Defendant

STATEMENT OF CLAIM

TO THE DEFENDANT

A LEGAL PROCEEDING HAS BEEN COMMENCED AGAINST YOU by the plaintiff. The claim made against you is set out in the following pages.

IF YOU WISH TO DEFEND THIS PROCEEDING, you or an Ontario lawyer acting for you must prepare a statement of defence in Form 18A prescribed by the Rules of Civil Procedure, serve it on the plaintiff's lawyer or, where the plaintiff does not have a lawyer, serve it on the plaintiff, and file it, with proof of service in this court office, WITHIN TWENTY DAYS after this statement of claim is served on you, if you are served in Ontario.

If you are served in another province or territory of Canada or in the United States of America, the period for serving and filing your statement of defence is forty days. If you are served outside Canada and the United States of America, the period is sixty days.

Instead of serving and filing a statement of defence, you may serve and file a notice of intent to defend in Form 18B prescribed by the Rules of Civil Procedure. This will entitle you to ten more days within which to serve and file your statement of defence.

IF YOU FAIL TO DEFEND THIS PROCEEDING, JUDGMENT MAY BE GIVEN AGAINST YOU IN YOUR ABSENCE AND WITHOUT FURTHER NOTICE TO YOU.

IF YOU WISH TO DEFEND THIS PROCEEDING BUT ARE UNABLE TO PAY LEGAL FEES, LEGAL AID MAY BE AVAILABLE TO YOU BY CONTACTING A LOCAL LEGAL AID OFFICE.

IF YOU PAY THE PLAINTIFF'S CLAIM, and $__ for costs, within the time for serving and filing your statement of defence you may move to have this proceeding dismissed by the court. If you believe the amount claimed for costs is excessive, you may pay the plaintiff's claim and $100 for costs and have the costs assessed by the court.

Date________________________ Issued by__________________________
Local Registrar

Address of
court office: 161 Elgin Street
Ottawa, Ontario
K2P 2K1

TO: (Name and address of each defendant)

[Where the action is brought under the simplified procedure, insert the following:

THIS ACTION IS BROUGHT AGAINST YOU UNDER THE SIMPLIFIED PROCEDURE PROVIDED IN RULE 76 OF THE RULES OF CIVIL PROCEDURE]

CLAIM

1. **The Plaintiff claims from the Defendant:**

(a) The sum of $50,000.00;
(b) Prejudgment interest on the sum of $50,000.00 from January 5, 2001 pursuant to the provisions of Section 128 of the *Courts of Justice Act,* R.S.O. 1990, c. C-43;
(c) Postjudgment interest on the sums set out in (a) and (b) above pursuant to the provisions of Section 129 of the *Courts of Justice Act,* R.S.O. 1990, c. C-43;
(d) Costs of this action;
(e) Such further and other relief as this Honourable Court may deem just and the circumstances require.

2. The Plaintiff Harry Leikin, at all material times resided in the City of Ottawa, in the Province of Ontario.

3. The Defendant, Alfred Bigshot, at all material times resided in the City of Ottawa, in the Province of Ontario.

4. The Plaintiff's claim is against the Defendant as drawer of a cheque. The following are the particulars:

(a) Cheque for $50,000.00 dated January 5, 2001 drawn by the Defendant upon the Argent Bank payable to the plaintiff which cheque was duly presented on January 5, 2001, but was dishonoured.

5. The Plaintiff claims interest on the sum of $50,000.00 from January 5, 2001 to the date of payment or Judgment pursuant to the provisions of Section 128 of the *Courts of Justice act,* R.S.O. 1990, c. C-43.

6. The Plaintiff proposes that this action be tried at the City of Ottawa, in the Province of Ontario.

DATE: February 10, 2001

ADAM & ZENA
Barristers and Solicitors
281 McLeod Street
Ottawa, Ontario
K2P 1A1
tel: (613) 237-0000
fax: (613) 237-1111
Attention: Sarah Zena
Solicitor for the Plaintiff

App 3-8

Summons to Witness (at Hearing)

Court File No:

SUPERIOR COURT OF JUSTICE

BETWEEN:

OMNI BANK OF CANADA

Plaintiff

- and -

MARK JOHNSON and HANNAH JOHNSON

Defendant

SUMMONS TO WITNESS

TO: Jessie James
516 Roosevelt Avenue
Toronto, Ontario

YOU ARE REQUIRED TO ATTEND TO GIVE EVIDENCE IN COURT at the hearing of this proceeding on (*day*), (*date*), at (*time*), at (*address of court house*), and to remain until your attendance is no longer required.

YOU ARE REQUIRED TO BRING WITH YOU and produce at the hearing the following documents and things: (*Set out the nature and date of each document and give particulars sufficient to identify each document and thing.*)

ATTENDANCE MONEY for __________ day(s) of attendance is served with this summons, calculated in accordance with Tariff A of the Rules of Civil Procedure, as follows:

Attendance allowance of $ ______ daily	$ ____
Travel allowance	$ ____
Overnight accommodation and meal allowance	$ ____
TOTAL	$ ____

If further attendance is required, you will be entitled to additional attendance money.

IF YOU FAIL TO ATTEND OR TO REMAIN IN ATTENDANCE AS REQUIRED BY THIS SUMMONS, A WARRANT MAY BE ISSUED FOR YOUR ARREST.

Date ________________________ Issued by ________________________
Local Registrar

Address of
court office: 361 University Avenue
Toronto, Ontario
M5G 1T3

CREDIT SOLUTIONS

This summons was issued at the request of, and inquiries may be directed to:

ADAM & ZENA
Barristers & Solicitors
281 McLeod Street
Toronto, Ontario
M5C 3C5
tel: (416) 995-9595
fax: (416) 995-9696
Solicitors for the Plaintiff

R.R.O. 1990, Reg. 194, Form 53A.

App 3-9

Warrant for Arrest (Defaulting Witness)

FORM 53B
Courts of Justice Act

Court File No:

SUPERIOR COURT OF JUSTICE

(*Name of judge*) (*Day and date*)

BETWEEN:

OMNI BANK OF CANADA

Plaintiff

- and -

MARK JOHNSON and HANNAH JOHNSON

Defendants

WARRANT FOR ARREST

TO ALL POLICE OFFICERS in Ontario

AND TO the officers of all correctional institutions in Ontario

WHEREAS the witness, Jessie James, of 516 Roosevelt Avenue, Toronto, Ontario, was served with a summons to witness to give evidence at the hearing of this proceeding, and the proper attendance money was paid or tendered,

WHEREAS the witness failed to obey the summons, and I am satisfied that the evidence of the witness is material to this proceeding,

YOU ARE ORDERED TO ARREST and bring the witness, Jessie James, before the court to give evidence in this proceeding, and if the court is not then sitting or if the witness cannot be brought forthwith before the court, to deliver the witness to a provincial correctional institution or other secure facility, to be admitted and detained there until the witness can be brought before the court.

(*Signature of judge*)

R.R.O. 1990, Reg. 194, Form 53B; O. Reg. 351/94, s. 12.

App 3-10

Requisition for Default Judgment

Court File No:

SUPERIOR COURT OF JUSTICE

BETWEEN:

OMNI BANK OF CANADA

Plaintiff

- and -

MARK JOHNSON and HANNAH JOHNSON

Defendants

REQUISITION FOR DEFAULT JUDGMENT

TO THE REGISTRAR AT TORONTO

I REQUIRE you to note the defendants Mark Johnson and Hannah Johnson in default in this action on the ground that they have failed to failed a Statement of Defence or a Notice of Intent to Defend.

I REQUIRE default judgment to be signed against the defendants Mark Johnson and Hannah Johnson.

Default judgment may properly be signed in this action because the claim is for

[x] a debt or liquidated demand in money

[ ] recovery of possession of land

[ ] recovery of personal property

[ ] foreclosure, sale or redemption of a mortgage

[x] There has been no payment on account of the claim since the statement of claim was issued.

PART A - PAYMENT(S) RECEIVED BY PLAINTIFF

1. Principal

Principal sum claimed in statement of claim (without interest) $ ....

Date of Payment	Amount of Payment	Payment Amount Principal	Applied to Interest	Principal Sum Owing
TOTAL:	$	$	$	$

2. Prejudgment interest

Date of which statement of claim was issued: ....

The plaintiff is entitled to prejudgment interest on the claim, calculated as follows:

Principal Sum Owing	Start Date	End Date (Date of Judgment)	Number of Days	Rate	Interest Amount)
				TOTAL B:	$..................

Principal Sum Owing (Total A above)	$ ....
Total Interest Amount (Total B above)	$ ....
SIGNED JUDGMENT FOR	$..................

PART B - NO PAYMENT RECEIVED BY PLAINTIFF

1. Principal
   Principal sum claimed in statement of claim (without interest) A $24,965.73

2. Prejudgment interest

Date on which statement of claim was issued: June 1, 2001

Date from which prejudgment interest is claimed: June 1, 2001

The plaintiff is entitled to prejudgment interest on the claim calculated as follows:

Principal Sum Owing	Start Date	End Date (Date of Judgment)	Number of Days	Rate	Interest Amount)
$24,965.72	June 1, 2001	July 5, 2001	35		$ 287.28

Principal Sum Owing (Total A above)	$24,965.72
Total Interest Amount (Total B above)	$ 287.28
SIGN JUDGMENT FOR:	$ 25,253.00

PART C - POSTJUDGMENT INTEREST AND COSTS

1. Postjudgment interest

   The plaintiff is entitled to postjudgment interest at the rate of 12 % per cent per year.

   [ ] under the *Court of Justice Act,* as claimed in the statement of claim.

   [x] in accordance with the claim made in the statement of claim.

2. The plaintiff wishes costs to be,

   [x] fixed by the local registrar
   or
   [ ] assessed by an assessment officer.

CREDIT SOLUTIONS

Date: July , 2001

....

ADAM & ZENA
281 McLeod Street
Toronto, Ontario
M5C 3C5
(416) 995-9595
(416) 995-9696
Joe Adam
Solicitors for the Plaintiff.

App 3-11

Default Judgment

Court File No:

SUPERIOR COURT OF JUSTICE

BETWEEN:

OMNI BANK OF CANADA

Plaintiff

- and -

MARK JOHNSON and HANNAH JOHNSON

Defendants

JUDGMENT

On reading the Statement of Claim in this action and the proof of service of the Statement of Claim on the Defendants, Mark Johnson and Hannah Johnson, and the Defendants, Mark Johnson and Hannah Johnson, having been noted in default,

1. **IT IS ORDERED AND ADJUDGED** that the Defendants pay to the Plaintiff the sum of $25,253.00 and the sum of $474.50 for the costs of this action.

This Judgment bears interest at the rate of 12 % per year from its date.

July 5, 2001

____
Registrar
Superior Court of Justice
361 University Avenue
Toronto, Ontario
M5G 1T3

App 3-12

Case Management Motion Form

SUPERIOR COURT OF JUSTICE No. .... Court file no.

SHORT TITLE OF CASE

....

CASE MANAGEMENT MOTION FORM

THIS FORM FILED BY *(Check appropriate boxes to* identify *the party filing this form as a moving/responding party on this motion AND to identify this party as plaintiff; defendant, etc. in the action.)*
[ ] moving party [ ] plaintiff/petitioner/applicant
[ ] responding party [ ] defendant/respondent – name ....
[ ] other - specify kind of party and name ....

MOTION MADE
[ ] on consent of all parties [ ] on notice to all parties and unopposed*
[ ] on notice to all parties and expected to be opposed [ ] without notice
Notice of this motion was served on (date) .... by means of ....

METHOD OF DISPOSITION REQUESTED
[ ] in writing only, no appearance [ ] conference telephone call – see below
[ ] telephone call (motion without notice) – see below [ ] appearance – see below
Proposed date and time for conference call, telephone call or appearance *(Must be confirmed with case management judge in advance.)*

....

ORDER SOUGHT BY THIS PARTY *(Responding party is presumed to request dismissal of motion and costs.)*
[ ] extension of time - specify what time period and how long an extension

....

[ ] service claim/application [ ] file or deliver defence [ ] complete discoveries
[ ] other – specify ....

....

....

MATERIAL RELIED ON BY THIS PARTY
[ ] this form [ ] pleadings [ ] affidavits - specify
[ ] transcript – specify [ ] other - specify
....

GROUNDS IN SUPPORT OF/IN OPPOSITION TO MOTION (INCLUDING RULE AND STATUTORY PROVISIONS)
(See Over.)
* filing fee required

CASE MANAGEMENT MOTION FORM, page 2
....
....
....
....

CERTIFICATION
I certify that the above information is correct, to the best of my knowledge.
Signature of solicitor
(If no lawyer, party must sign) ....Date ....

THIS PARTY'S LAWYER *(!f no lawyer, give party's address for service, telephone and fax number.)*	OTHER LAWYER *(if no lawyer, give other party's name, address for service, telephone and fax number.)*
Name and firm	Name and Firm ....
....	....
Address	Address ....
....	....
Telephone .... Fax	Telephone ....Fax ....

DISPOSITION BY CASE MANAGEMENT JUDGE/MASTER
[ ] order to go as asked [ ] adjourned to
[ ] order refused [ ] order to go as follows:
....
....
....
....

REASONS
....
....
....

Hearing Method .... Hearing duration .... min. Heard in [ ] courtroom [ ] office

[ ] No formal order need be prepared or signed
[ ] Registrar to send copy of disposition to parties
[ ] Other directions – specify

[ ] Successful party to prepare formal order for signature
[ ] No copy of disposition to be sent to parties

....
....

Date.................Judge's name...Judge's Signature..................................

App 3-13

Requisition for Writ of Seizure and Sale

Court File No:

SUPERIOR COURT OF JUSTICE

BETWEEN:

OMNI BANK OF CANADA

Plaintiff

- and -

MARK JOHNSON and HANNAH JOHNSON

Defendants

REQUISITION FOR WRIT OF SEIZURE AND SALE

TO THE REGISTRAR at Toronto, Ontario

I REQUIRE a Writ of Seizure and Sale pursuant to an order of this Court, made on July 5, 2001 in favour of Plaintiff, directed to the Sheriff of the City of Toronto, to seize and sell the real and personal property within his county or district of the Defendants, Mark Johnson and Hannah Johnson, and to realize from the seizure and sale the following sums:

a) $25,253.00 and interest at 12.00 percent per year, commencing on July 5, 2001;

b) $474.50 for costs together with interest at 12.00 percent per year, commencing on July 5, 2001; and

c) your fees and expenses in enforcing this Writ.

Date: July , 2001

ADAM & ZENA
Barristers & Solicitors
281 McLeod Street
Toronto, Ontario
M5C 3C5
tel: (416) 995-9595
fax: (416) 995-9696
Solicitors for the Plaintiff

App 3-14

Writ of Seizure and Sale

Court File No:

SUPERIOR COURT OF JUSTICE

BETWEEN:

OMNI BANK OF CANADA

Plaintiff

- and -

MARK JOHNSON and HANNAH JOHNSON

Defendants

WRIT OF SEIZURE AND SALE

TO THE SHERIFF OF THE CITY OF TORONTO,

Under an order of this court made on July 5, 2001 in favour of Omni Bank of Canada

YOU ARE DIRECTED to seize and sell the real and personal property within your county or district of

Surname of individual or name of corporation/firm etc.

JOHNSON
JOHNSON

First given name (individual only)	*Second given name (individual only) if applicable*	*Third given name (individual only) if applicable*

MARK
HANNAH

and to realize from the seizure and sale the following sums:
(a) $25,253.00 and interest at 12.00 percent per year, commencing on July 5, 2001

(Where the writ is for two or more periodic or installment payments substitute):

(a) Amount of payment Due date

____

$ _______ and interest at _______ per cent per year on the payments in default commencing on the date of default;

(b) $474.50 for costs, together with interest at 12.00 percent per year, commencing on July 5, 2001; and

(c) your fees and expenses in enforcing this writ

YOU ARE DIRECTED to pay out the proceeds according to law and to report on the execution of this writ if required by the party or solicitor who filed it.

Dated at Toronto

On ___________

Issued by ___________________________
Registrar

Address of Court Office:

361 University Avenue
Toronto, Ontario
M5G 1T3

App 3-15

Direction to Enforce Writ of Seizure and Sale

Court File No:

SUPERIOR COURT OF JUSTICE

BETWEEN:

OMNI BANK OF CANADA

Plaintiff

- and -

MARK JOHNSON and HANNAH JOHNSON

Defendants

DIRECTION TO ENFORCE WRIT

TO the Sheriff of the City of Toronto

Under an Order of this Court in favour of Omni Bank of Canada made on July 5, 2001, Mark Johnson and Hannah Johnson were ordered to pay the sum of $25,253.00 with interest at the rate of 12% per year commencing on July 5, 2001 and costs of $474.50 with interest at the rate of 12% per year commencing on July 5, 2001. Since the Order was made, the Creditor has received the following payments:

DATE OF PAYMENT	PAYMENT
Nil	Nil

Under rule 60.19 of the Rules of Civil Procedure, the Creditor is entitled to costs in the amount of,

(a) $148.00 in accordance with the regulations under the Administration of Justice Act and Tariff A, for issuing, renewing and filing with the Sheriff a Writ of Execution or Notice of Garnishment;
(b) N/A for disbursements paid to a Sheriff, Registrar, Official Examiner, Court Reporter or other public officer and to which the creditor is entitled under subrule 60.19(1); (Attach copy of all receipt)
(c) N/A for the minimum amount prescribed in Tariff A for conducting an Examination in Aid of Execution; (Attach Affidavit confirming that examination *was conducted)*
(d) $ N/A for any other costs to which the creditor is entitled under subrule 60.19(1). (Attach Certificate of Assessment)

YOU ARE DIRECTED to enforce the Writ of Seizure and Sale issued on July 5, 2001 and filed in your office for a sum sufficient to satisfy the total of the amount set out above, together with subsequent interest, and your fees and expenses.

August 4, 2001

ADAM & ZENA
Barristers & Solicitors
281 McLeod Street
Toronto, Ontario
M5C 3C5
tel: (416) 995 9595
fax: (416) 995-9696
Attention: Joe Adam
Solicitors for the Plaintiff

App 3-16

Letter to Client re Renewal of Writ of Seizure and Sale

July 20, 2001

Omni Bank of Canada
727 Richmond Street
Ottawa, Ontario
K2B 9M7

Attention: Mr. Howard Borthwick

Dear Sir.

Re: Omni Bank of Canada v. Smith

This letter will confirm that we represent the Omni Bank of Canada who obtained a Writ of Seizure and Sale against Mr. Smith on September 1, 1995. The writ is due to expire on August 31, 2001.

The amount of the writ of seizure and sale is for $22,353.00 together with assessed costs of $454.50. In order for the writ of Seizure and Sale to remain active, it must be renewed prior to August 31, 2001, together with a filing fee of $100.00 The renewal will be valid for a period of 6 years from the date it is renewed.

Would you kindly confirm on or before August 10, 2001 whether or not you wish us to renew the writ of seizure and sale. The cost of the renewal including our fees would be $233.75.

We look forward to receiving your instructions regarding the above.

Yours very truly,

ADAM & ZENA

Per: Peggy Saxe
Law Clerk

App 3-17

Request to Renew Writ of Seizure and Sale

Court File No:

SUPERIOR COURT OF JUSTICE

BETWEEN:

OMNI BANK OF CANADA

Plaintiff

- and -

JEFF SMITH

Defendant

REQUEST TO RENEW

TO THE SHERIFF of the City of Ottawa

YOU ARE REQUESTED TO RENEW the writ of seizure and sale issued on September 1, 1995 in this proceeding and filed in your office for a period of six years from the date of renewal.

August 28, 2001

____
(signature)

ADAM & ZENA
Barristers & Solicitors
281 McLeod Street
Ottawa, Ontario
K2P 1A1
Joe Adam
Solicitors for the Plaintiff

App 3-18

Notice of Motion to Vary Debtor's Name in Writ of Seizure and Sale

Court File No:

SUPERIOR COURT OF JUSTICE

BETWEEN:

OMNI BANK OF CANADA

Plaintiff

- and -

JEFF SMITH

Defendant

NOTICE OF MOTION

THE PLAINTIFF will make a motion to a Judge on the day of , 2001, at 10:00 o'clock in the forenoon, or as soon after that time as the motion can be heard, at the Court House, 161 Elgin Street, Ottawa, Ontario.

PROPOSED METHOD OF HEARING: The motion is to be heard

__x__ in writing under subrule 37.12.1(1) because it is made without notice;

_____ in writing as an opposed motion under subrule 37.12.1(4);

_____ orally.

THE MOTION IS FOR:

(a) an Order to vary the debtor's name on a Writ of Seizure and Sale to Jeff Smith a.k.a. John Smith a.k.a. Jon Smith;

THE GROUNDS FOR THE MOTION ARE:

(a) the writ of seizure and sale in respect of the judgment of the Honourable Justice A.B. Stirling dated May 25, 2001 and issued by the registrar on May 26, 2001.

(b) Rule 60.07(10)(11).

THE FOLLOWING DOCUMENTARY EVIDENCE will be used at the hearing of the motion:

(a) the Affidavit of William Kesler, filed.

DATE:

ADAM & ZENA
Barristers & Solicitors
281 McLeod Street
Ottawa, Ontario
K2P 1A1
tel: (613) 237-0000
fax: (613) 237-1111
Joe Adam
Solicitors for the Plaintiff

App 3-19

Affidavit in Support of Motion to Vary Debtor's Name in Writ of Seizure and Sale

Court File No:

SUPERIOR COURT OF JUSTICE

BETWEEN:

OMNI BANK OF CANADA

Plaintiff

- and -

JEFF SMITH

Defendant

AFFIDAVIT

I, WILLIAM KESLER, of the City of Ottawa, in the Province of Ontario, make oath and say:

1. That I am the loans manager for the Plaintiff herein and as such have personal knowledge of the matters herein deposed to, except where stated to be based on information and belief.

2. That the Plaintiff obtained judgment against the Defendant for the sum of $ and costs in the amount of $ on the day of , 2001. Annexed hereto as Exhibit "A" is a true copy of the Judgment dated the day of , 2001.

3. That on the day of , 2001 a Writ of Seizure and Sale was issued by the Registrar and was subsequently filed with the Sheriff of the City of Ottawa.

4. That I have done some further research into the location of the said Defendant and have been advised by his accountant, Alfred Books, that he uses the name John Smith and also Jon Smith.

5. That I make this Affidavit in support of a Motion to amend the Defendant's name on the Writ of Seizure and Sale to read Jeff Smith also known as John Smith also known as Jon Smith.

SWORN BEFORE ME at the City of	)	
Ottawa, in the Province of Ontario	)	
this day of , 2001	)	
	)	________________________
	)	WILLIAM KESLER
A Commissioner, etc.	)	

App 3-20

Order to Vary Debtor's Name in Writ of Seizure and Sale

Court File No:

SUPERIOR COURT OF JUSTICE

THE HONOURABLE JUSTICE	)	**DAY, THE DAY OF**
	)	
A.B. STIRLING	)	**, 2001**

BETWEEN:

OMNI BANK OF CANADA

Plaintiff

- and -

JEFF SMITH

Defendant

ORDER

THIS MOTION made by the plaintiff for an order to vary the debtor's name in the Writ of Seizure and Sale in respect of the judgment of the Honourable Justice A.B. Stirling dated May 25, 2001 was heard this day at the Court House, 161 Elgin Street, Ottawa, Ontario.

ON READING the affidavit of William Kesler filed, and on hearing the submissions of counsel for the plaintiff:

1. **THIS COURT ORDERS** that the plaintiff is granted leave to vary the name of the debtor on the Writ of Seizure and Sale in respect of the judgment of the Honourable Justice A.B. Stirling dated May 25, 2001 to include the names Jeff Smith also known as John Smith also known as Jon Smith.

____

App 3-21

Requisition for Garnishment

Court File No. 00-CV-88888

SUPERIOR COURT OF JUSTICE

BETWEEN:

OMNI BANK OF CANADA

Creditor

and

ARCHIE BUNKER

Debtor

and

ALL-RIGHT BAR & GRILL LTD.

Garnishee

REQUISITION FOR GARNISHMENT

TO: the Registrar at Ottawa:

I REQUIRE a notice of garnishment to be issued in this proceeding, in accordance with the attached draft Form 60H. The total amount to be shown in the notice of garnishment is $57,984.33 , made up as follows:

1. $54,634.62 for principal owing under the judgment or order, including prejudgment interest.

2. $125.00 for the costs of the action.

3. $100.00 in accordance with the regulations under the *Administration of Justice Act* and Tariff A, for issuing, renewing and filing with the sheriff a writ of execution or notice of garnishment.

4. $_______ for disbursements paid to a sheriff, registrar, official examiner, court reporter or other public officer and to which the creditor is entitled under subrule 60.19 (1). (*Attach copies of all receipts.*)

5. $_______ for the minimum amount prescribed in Tariff A for conducting an examination in aid of execution. (*Attach affidavit confirming that examination was conducted.*)

6. $_______ for any other costs to which the creditor is entitled under subrule 60.19 (1). (*Attach certificate of assessment.*)

7. $ 3,124.71 for postjudgment interest to today's date.

Date: June , 2001

Signature ______________________

Adam & Zena
281 McLeod Street
Ottawa, Ontario
K6V 9Y1
tel: (613) 237-0000
Solicitors for the creditor

App 3-22

Affidavit in Support of Notice of Garnishment

Court File No. 00-CV-88888

SUPERIOR COURT OF JUSTICE

BETWEEN:

OMNI BANK OF CANADA

Creditor

and

ARCHIE BUNKER

Debtor

and

ALL-RIGHT BAR & GRILL LTD.

Garnishee

AFFIDAVIT

I, ZITA JONES, of the City of Ottawa, in the Province of Ontario, **MAKE OATH AND SAY AS FOLLOWS:**

1. I am a legal assistant in the office of Adam & Zena, the solicitor for the Creditor herein, and as such have knowledge of the matters hereinafter deposed to.

2. That a Writ of Seizure and Sale was filed against the Debtor, ARCHIE BUNKER, on September 5, 2000 in the amount of $54,634.62 and $125.00 for assessed costs. The Judgment bears interest at the rate of 7% per annum. Annexed hereto and marked as Exhibit "A" is a copy of the said Writ of Seizure and Sale.

3. Annexed hereto as Exhibit "B" is a copy of the Calculation of the amounts owing together with postjudgment interest.

4. It is our information that the Debtor, ARCHIE BUNKER, will be receiving monies from ALL-RIGHT BAR & GRILL LTD., 4 Main Street, Ottawa, Ontario, K2B 1L2.

5. That ALL-RIGHT BAR & GRILL LTD. is being served with the Notice of Garnishment at 51 Main Street, Ottawa, Ontario, K2B 1L2.

6. That it is my information and belief that ALL-RIGHTBAR & GRILL LTD., is or will become indebted to the Debtor because the Debtor is employed by the Garnishee.

7. As of June 28, 2001 no monies were paid.

8. The total remaining on the payment of the Judgment inclusive of costs and interest to June 28, 2001 is $57,884.33.

9. I make this Affidavit in support of an Application for Garnishment and for no improper purpose.

SWORN BEFORE ME at the City of Ottawa	)	
in the Regional Municipality of Ottawa-	)	
Carleton, this 28th day of June, 2001	)	
	)	______________________
	)	ZITA JONES
A Commissioner for taking Affidavits, etc.	)	

App 3-23

Notice of Garnishment

Court File No. 00-CV-88888

SUPERIOR COURT OF JUSTICE

BETWEEN:

OMNI BANK OF CANADA

Creditor

and

ARCHIE BUNKER

Debtor

and

ALL-RIGHT BAR & GRILL LTD.

Garnishee

NOTICE OF GARNISHMENT

TO: ALL-RIGHT BAR & GRILL LTD.
51 Main Street
Ottawa, Ontario
K2B 1L2

A LEGAL PROCEEDING in this court between the creditor and the debtor has resulted in an order that the debtor pay a sum of money to the creditor. The creditor claims that you owe a debt to the debtor. A debt to the debtor includes both a debt payable to the debtor and a debt payable to the debtor and one or more co-owners. The creditor has had this notice of garnishment directed to you as garnishee in order to seize any debt that you owe or will owe to the debtor. Where the debt is payable to the debtor and to one or more co-owners, you must pay one-half of the indebtedness or the greater or lesser amount specified in an order made under subrule 60.08 (16).

YOU ARE REQUIRED TO PAY to the Sheriff of the City of Ottawa

(a) within 10 days after this notice is served on you, all debts now payable by you to the debtor; and

(b) within 10 days after they become payable, all debts that become payable by you to the debtor within 6 years after this notice is served on you,

subject to the exemptions provided by section 7 of the *Wages Act*. The total amount of all your payments to the sheriff is not to exceed $57,984.33 less $10 for your costs of making each payment.

EACH PAYMENT MUST BE SENT with a copy of the attached garnishee's payment notice to the sheriff at the address shown below.

CREDIT SOLUTIONS

IF YOU DO NOT PAY THE TOTAL AMOUNT OF $57,984.33 LESS $10 FOR YOUR COSTS OF MAKING EACH PAYMENT WITHIN 10 DAYS after this notice is served on you, because the debt is owed to the debtor and to one or more co-owners or for any other reason, you must within that time serve on the creditor and the debtor and file with the court a garnishee's statement in Form 60I attached to this notice.

IF YOU FAIL TO OBEY THIS NOTICE, THE COURT MAY MAKE AND ENFORCE AN ORDER AGAINST YOU for payment of the amount set out above and the costs of the creditor.

IF YOU MAKE PAYMENT TO ANYONE OTHER THAN THE SHERIFF, YOU MAY BE LIABLE TO PAY AGAIN.

TO THE CREDITOR, THE DEBTOR AND THE GARNISHEE.

Any party may make a motion to the court to determine any matter in relation to this notice of garnishment.

Date ______________________

Issued by ______________________
Local Registrar

Address of court office 161 Elgin Street
Ottawa, Ontario
K2P 2K1

Creditor's address	**Debtor's address**	**Sheriff's address**
c/o Adam & Zena 281 McLeod Street Ottawa, Ontario K2P 1A1 tel: (613) 237-0000	2 Walkerton Court Ottawa, Ontario K6V 9Y1	161 Elgin Street Ottawa, Ontario K2P 2K1

Garnishee's Payment Notice

Make payment by cheque or money order payable to the Sheriff of the City of Ottawa and send it, along with a copy of this payment notice, to the Court House, 161 Elgin Street, Ottawa, Ontario, K2P 2K1

Court Superior Court of Justice File no. 00-CV-88888
Office at 161 Elgin Street, Ottawa, Ontario K2P 2K1
Creditor Omni Bank of Canada
Debtor Archie Bunker
Garnishee All-Right Bar & Grill Ltd.
TO BE COMPLETED BY GARNISHEE FOR EACH PAYMENT
Date of payment ________________
Amount enclosed $ ______________

App 3-24

Garnishee's Statement

Court File No. 00-CV-88888

SUPERIOR COURT OF JUSTICE

BETWEEN:

OMNI BANK OF CANADA

Creditor

and

ARCHIE BUNKER

Debtor

and

ALL-RIGHT BAR & GRILL LTD.

Garnishee

GARNISHEE'S STATEMENT

1. I/We acknowledge that I/we owe or will owe the debtor or the debtor and one or more co-owners the sum of $ __, payable on (*date*) because (*Give reasons why you owe the debtor or the debtor and one or more co-owners money. If you are making payment of less than the amount stated in line 2 of this paragraph because the debt is owed to the debtor and to one or more co-owners or for any other reason, give a full explanation of the reason. If you owe the debtor wages, state how often the debtor is paid. State the gross amount of the debtor's wages before any deductions and the net amount after all deductions and attach a copy of a pay slip.*)

1.1 (*If debt owed to debtor and one or more co-owners, check here* ❑ *and complete the following:*)

Co-owner(s) of the Debt (*name, address*) ______________________________

2. (*If you do not owe the debtor money, explain why. Give any other information that will explain your financial relationship with the debtor.*)

3. (*If you have been served with any other notice of garnishment or a writ of execution against the debtor, give particulars.*)

Name of creditor *Location of Sheriff* *Date of notice or writ* *Date of service on you*

4. (*If you have been served outside Ontario and you wish to object on the ground that service outside Ontario was improper, give particulars of your objection.*)

Date ________________

Signature of or for garnishee	______________________
Name of garnishee	All Right Bar & Grill Ltd.
Address	51 Main Street Ottawa, Ontario K2B 1L2
Telephone number	(613) 822-8222

App 3-25

Letter to Debtor Serving Notice of Garnishment

July 22, 2001

Mr. Archie Bunker
12 Walkerton Court
Ottawa, Ontario
K6V 9Y1

Dear Sir:

Re: Omni Bank of Canada v. Archie Bunker

Please be advised that we are the solicitors for Omni Bank of Canada who obtained a Judgment against you on September 5, 2000 for the sum of $54,634.62 and taxed costs of $300.00.

Enclosed herein please find a copy of a Notice of Garnishment, and the Affidavit In Support of the Notice of Garnishment, served upon you pursuant to the Rules of Civil Procedure. A copy of the Notice of Garnishment has also been served upon your employer All-Right Bar & Grill Ltd.

Should you have any questions, please contact our offices.

Yours truly,

ADAM & ZENA

Per:
Joe Adam

App 3-26

Letter to Garnishee Serving Notice of Garnishment

July 22, 2001

All-Right Bar & Grill Ltd.
14 Main Street
Ottawa, Ontario
K2B 1L2.

Attention: Personnel Department

Dear Sirs:

Re: Omni Bank of Canada v. Bunker

Enclosed herewith please find a Notice of Garnishment which is served upon you pursuant to the *Rules of Civil Procedure*.

This letter will confirm that all monies owing to the debtor are subject to garnishment. As an example, salary, commissions, draws, dividends, bonuses and retroactive pay increases, repayment of loans, overtime, vacation pay, Director's fees, lump-sum payments, patronage payments, retiring allowances, retirement compensation arrangements, salary deferral arrangements, wage loss replacement plans, etc. (hereinafter referred to as "monies due to the debtor").

In relation to salary or commissions, this letter will confirm that in our opinion when you are calculating the amount to be remitted to the Sheriff pursuant to the garnishment will be 20% of the monies due to the debtor after deduction of Employment Insurance Premiums, Canada Pension Plan Premiums and Income Tax. Any other amounts can be deducted after garnishment deduction. Should you have any questions contact your local Sheriff's office for confirmation of the application of garnishment procedures.

The ***Rules of Civil Procedure*** *require* you as Garnishee to forward the Garnishee Statement to the Court office at 161 Elgin Street, Ottawa, Ontario, K2P 2K1 within ten (10) days after receipt of the same. If you do not comply with this requirement, a motion for judgment can be brought against you as the Garnishee. Please ensure that a copy of the Garnishee statement is forwarded to the Sheriff's office as well as our office at:

> 281 McLeod Street
> Ottawa, Ontario
> K2B 7L2

This letter shall also advise that the Garnishment is effective for a period of six (6) years. Therefore, should any monies be due to the debtor during the period of six (6) years, the Garnishment is in full force and effect and you are required under the *Rules of Civil Procedure* to comply with the same.

Should you have any questions, please do not hesitate to contact the undersigned.

Yours very truly,

ADAM & ZENA

Per: Joe Adam

App 3-27

Affidavit of Service of Notice of Garnishment on Debtor

Court File No. 00-CV-88888

SUPERIOR COURT OF JUSTICE

BETWEEN:

OMNI BANK OF CANADA

Creditor

and

ARCHIE BUNKER

Debtor

and

ALL-RIGHT BAR & GRILL LTD.

Garnishee

AFFIDAVIT

I, **ZITA JONES**, of the City of Ottawa, in the Province of Ontario, MAKE OATH AND SAY:

1. On July 22, 2001, I served Archie Bunker with the Notice of Garnishment, and Affidavit in Support of the Notice of Garnishment by mailing a copy of same to Mr. Archie Bunker, 12 Walkerton Court, Ottawa, Ontario, K6V 9Y1.

SWORN BEFORE ME at the City	)	
of Ottawa, in the Province of	)	
Ontario, this day of July, 2001	)	______________________
	)	**ZITA JONES**
	)	
A Commissioner, etc.	)	

App 3-28

Affidavit of Service of Notice of Garnishment on Garnishee

Court File No. 00-CV-88888

SUPERIOR COURT OF JUSTICE

BETWEEN:

OMNI BANK OF CANADA

Creditor

and

ARCHIE BUNKER

Debtor

and

ALL-RIGHT BAR & GRILL LTD.

Garnishee

AFFIDAVIT

I, **ZITA JONES**, of the City of Ottawa, in the Province of Ontario, MAKE OATH AND SAY:

1. On July 22, 2001, I served All-Right Bar & Grill with the Notice of Garnishment, and Garnishee's Statement by mailing a copy of same to 51 Main Street, Ottawa, Ontario, K2B 1L2.

SWORN BEFORE ME at the City	)	
of Ottawa, in the Province of	)	
Ontario, this day of July, 2001	)	______________________________
	)	**ZITA JONES**
	)	
A Commissioner, etc.	)	

App 3-29

Garnishment of Federal Public Servant

See *Garnishment, Attachment and Pension Diversion Act*, and Regulations including 16/4/97 Canada Gazette Part II, Vol. 131, No. 8, SOR/DORS/97-177 including Form.

1. Serve Application under *Garnishment, Attachment and Pension Diversion Act* and Regulations to Her Majesty the Queen in Right of Canada as represented by (name of department), together with a copy of the Order or Judgment.

2. These documents must be served in duplicate by registered mail on Her Majesty the Queen in Right of Canada. Consult *Garnishment and Attachment Regulations* for address for service.

App 3-30

Statement of Particulars to be Served with Notice of Garnishment of Provincial Government Employee *Proceedings Against the Crown Act*

STATEMENT OF PARTICULARS

Creditor - (name)
Debtor - (name)
Debtor's social insurance number, if available:
This statement of particulars must be served with the notice of garnishment in accordance with the regulations made under the Act.
Address of place of service:

1. Where the moneys payable to the debtor is salary, state:

(a) Occupation, profession, job classification or title of the debtor
(b) Name of employer (i.e. ministry, board, commission or agency)
(c) Section, division or branch of employer on behalf of which salary is payable to the debtor
(d) Street address of debtor's place of employment

2. Where the money payable to the debtor is remuneration for goods or services (other than wages), state:

(a) General description of the goods or services
(b) Approximate date of delivery or performance
(c) Location of delivery or performance

3. Is the attached notice of garnishment to enforce an order for support or maintenance?

Yes No

Date: Signature of Creditor

(Note: The regulation under the Proceedings Against the Crown Act provides that a notice of garnishment issued against the Crown shall be deemed to be served on the thirtieth day after the actual date of service or on the thirtieth day after the effective date of service under the rules of the relevant court.)

App 3-31

Notice of Motion for Judgment Against Garnishee

Court File No. 00-CV-88888

SUPERIOR COURT OF JUSTICE

BETWEEN:

OMNI BANK OF CANADA

Creditor

and

ARCHIE BUNKER

Debtor

and

ALL-RIGHT BAR & GRILL LTD.

Garnishee

NOTICE OF MOTION

THE CREDITOR will make a motion to a Judge on Tuesday, the 17th day of September, 2001 at 9:45 o'clock in the forenoon, or as soon after that time as the motion can be heard, at the Court House, 161 Elgin Street, Ottawa, Ontario.

PROPOSED METHOD OF HEARING: The motion is to be heard

___ in writing under subrule 37.12(1) because it is made without notice;
___ in writing as opposed motion under subrule 37.12.1(4);
_X_ orally.

THE MOTION IS FOR an Order against the Garnishee, All-Right Bar & Grill Ltd. for payment of the amount claimed in the Notice of Garnishment due from Archie Bunker to Omni Bank of Canada.

THE GROUNDS FOR THE MOTION ARE rule 60.08(11), (12) and (17) of the Rules of Civil Procedure.

THE FOLLOWING DOCUMENTARY EVIDENCE will be used at the hearing of the motion:

(a) the pleadings and proceedings herein;
(b) the Affidavit of Mary Neill, filed.

September , 2001

ADAM & ZENA
281 McLeod Street
Ottawa, Ontario
K2K 3B3
tel: (613) 237-0000
fax: (613) 237-1111
Solicitors for the Creditor

CREDIT SOLUTIONS

TO:	ARCHIE BUNKER 2 Walkerton Court Ottawa, Ontario K6V 9Y1
AND TO:	ALL-RIGHT BAR & GRILL LTD. 51 Main Street Ottawa, Ontario K2B 1L2
AND TO:	SHERIFF, CITY OF OTTAWA Court House 161 Elgin Street Ottawa, Ontario K2P 2K1

App 3-32

Affidavit in Support of Motion for Judgment Against Garnishee

Court File No. 00-CV-88888

SUPERIOR COURT OF JUSTICE

BETWEEN:

OMNI BANK OF CANADA

Creditor

and

ARCHIE BUNKER

Debtor

and

ALL-RIGHT BAR & GRILL LTD.

Garnishee

AFFIDAVIT

I, **MARY NEILL,** of the City of Ottawa, in the Province of Ontario, make oath and say as follows:

1. That I am a Clerk at Law employed with Adam & Zena, solicitors for the Creditor, Omni Bank of Canada and as such have knowledge of the matters hereinafter deposed to.

2. A Judgment was obtained on behalf of Omni Bank of Canada against Archie Bunker on the _____________ for the sum of $_______and $_________ for costs.

3. On ___________, a Notice of Garnishment was issued wherein All-Right Bar & Grill Ltd. was named as the Garnishee.

4. The Notice of Garnishment and Garnishee's Statement were served upon All-Right Bar & Grill Ltd. on the 22nd day of July, 2001 as is evidenced by an Affidavit of service of Zita Jones, attached hereto as Exhibit "A" to this my Affidavit.

5. The Notice of Garnishment and Garnishee's Statement were served upon Archie Bunker on the 22nd day of July, 2001, as is evidenced by an Affidavit of service of Zita Jones, attached hereto as Exhibit "B" to this my Affidavit.

6. On the _______ day of ___________, 2001 I spoke with Diana Woodward of the Sheriff's Office for the City of Ottawa, at which time I was advised that no moneys had been received from All-Right Bar & Grill Ltd. in respect of the Notice of Garnishment on Archie Bunker's wages.

7. To date, All-Right Bar & Grill Ltd. has not filed a Garnishee's Statement setting out any reasons for not making payment under the Notice of Garnishment.

8. I was advised by the Plaintiff and verily believe that he spoke to Archie Bunker and was advised that Archie Bunker was an employee of All-Right Bar & Grill Ltd. On __________, I spoke with Edith Bunker, the wife of Archie Bunker, who confirmed that he is still employed by All-Right Bar & Grill Ltd.

9. It would appear that the Garnishee, All-Right Bar & Grill Ltd., is indebted to Archie Bunker at this time for his salary.

10. This Affidavit is made by me in support of an Order against the Garnishee, All-Right Bar & Grill Ltd., for payment of the amount set out in the Notice of Garnishment, and is made for no improper purpose.

SWORN BEFORE ME at the City of Ottawa	)	
in the Province of Ontario, this day of	)	
, 2001	)	
	)	______________________
	)	MARY NEILL
A Commissioner, etc.	)	

App 3-33

Questions to be Asked on Examination in Aid of Execution of Personal Debtor

PERSONAL INFORMATION - Obtain the personal details of person being examined: name, address, telephone number, date of birth, marital status, if there are any dependents, etc., and confirm that they are the person who owes the money to the creditor according to the judgment.

Obtain the employment details of the person being examined: occupation, name and address of employer, position, how long employed, present wages, when paid, any bonus schemes, commissions, are they related to their employer and previous employment information, have they ever been in business on their own, if so, when and where, have they ever carried on business under any trade or business name, if so, what name, was there any inventory, what was it and where was it kept. Are they an Officer or Director of any corporation? If so, which corporation(s)? If they are unemployed, are they subject to recall?

PARTICULARS OF PLACE OF RESIDENCE - What kind of accommodation do they live in and do they rent or own. If owned, how is title taken (absolute, beneficial, joint tenant or tenant in common), when was it purchased, is there a reporting letter, how much was paid, what is the present value, number of square feet, number of bedrooms/bathrooms, are there any other amenities, i.e. central air, pool or sauna. Obtain the particulars of the mortgage including the amount, balance owing and the terms of the mortgage.

If residence is not owned, who owns the building, name of landlord, address, amount of rent, when is rent due, are they related to the landlord, is the rent paid up to date, to whom is the rent paid to, do they pay by cash or cheque, who signs the cheque, is there a lease, who signed the lease.

PARTICULARS OF SPOUSE - name, (maiden name if wife), address, age, telephone number, employment status, name of employer, address of employer, position, how long has he/she worked there, salary, when paid, is support paid to any other person.

PARTICULARS OF CHILDREN - obtain the names, ages, addresses and whether or not they are employed.

PARTICULARS OF PERSONAL BUDGET - obtain all sources of income (pensions, employment insurance, workers' compensation, room and board from others, family allowances, annuities, inheritances etc.) and determine what their expenses are such as food, clothing, housing costs including rent or mortgage, taxes, transportation costs, insurance, education and recreation, medical and dental, bank loans, etc.

ASSETS OTHER THAN INCOME - Determine if there are any other assets, either owned personally, by the spouse or by the children, ie. other real estate, vehicles, bank accounts and obtain full disclosure as to the details - what, where located, etc. Any specific assets such as mortgages, I.O.U.'s, promissory notes, loan agreements, other security for payment of money, government or other bonds, common stock and/or preferred stock in public and private corporations, R.R.S.P.'s, R.H.O.S.P., television set, refrigerator, stove, washer and dryer, furniture, fur coats, jewellery, silver or gold ware, works of arts, horses, boats, any interest in any patent, copyright, process, formula, invention or royalties, pensions, lottery tickets, coins and stamps, liquor. Do they carry life insurance on themself. If so, is it term, group or whole life, and get the particulars of the name of the insurance company, policy number, amount of policy, beneficiary, who pays premium, surrender premium, cash value. Do they carry life insurance on any other person in which they have an interest. If so, obtain the same details. Determine if there are any moneys owing to the defendant - if so, from whom, their address, the amount and security held.

In addition, you may wish to ask questions such as how much money are they carrying right now, have they any income from any other source whatsoever, have they made a will, have they an interest as beneficiary, remainderman, right of reversion, executor, administrator, trustee, guardian or otherwise under any will or *inter vivos* of trust or in any estate, have they ever been a party to a trust agreement or other trust instrument, did they at any time put any money or property of any kind in trust for themselves or anyone else, have they received any money or property of any kind under any will or by inheritance or from any estate, are there any business dealings pending which will likely provide money, do they hold property in trust for anyone else, if so, obtain particulars, during the past year did they guarantee any indebtedness for anyone, during the past year did they make or endorse any paper for anyone, when did they last apply for or obtain a loan at any bank, finance company, or other lending institution or from any non-lender, or any corporation, or person whatsoever, are they holding in their name or possession for the benefit of anyone else any property of any kind whether real property, personal property or otherwise, is anyone holding your property in trust for them.

DISPOSITION OF ASSETS - obtain information as to whether they have sold or transferred any of the assets disclosed above from the debt date to the present. A debtor should be able to account for every asset that he had at the debt date and every asset he acquired from that date to the present.

Do they own any judgment or have an interest in any judgment, do they have a claim of any kind against anyone, do they have any interest of any kind in any mortgage or any lease or interest in any leasehold on any real or personal property, are they a party to any agreement of any kind with anyone, are they a party to any action now pending in the courts, have they filed their income tax return for the last two years? (Obtain a copy), were there any tax refunds, have you ever been bankrupt - If so, obtain particulars. When did they take their last vacation, if recently, obtain particulars. What did they give their spouse for Christmas

If some other person or corporation is in possession of the judgment debtor's property, examine that person or corporation. Therefore, ask questions seeking to get such information.

LIST OF CREDITORS - what are their present debts, name of creditor, address, amount, security held, if there is a judgment. Have there been payments made to other creditors. If so, who, how much, when, why. What is the cause of their financial difficulty.

PROPOSED SETTLEMENT

Determine if there is any possibility that the debtor may be able to get the money to pay debt. If so, determine when, what terms, suggested payment amount per week or month, date of start of payments.

App 3-34

Questions to ask an Officer of a Corporate Judgment Debtor in an Examination in Aid of Execution

INTRODUCTION

1. Name of the officer.
2. Officer's address.
3. Is this the notice of appointment that was served upon you?
4. Are you aware of the amount owing to this creditor as a result of judgment?
5. What is your position with the Company?
6. How long have you been with the Company?

MINUTE BOOK

1. Location of minute book.
2. Would you please make minute book available to me if I want to examine them.

FINANCIAL STATEMENTS

1. For present period: Books of Accounting, General Ledger, etc.
2. For five years prior.
3. Particulars of revenues.
4. Particulars of expenses.
5. Particulars of loans, advances or dividends to shareholders.
6. Salaries paid to officers and directors.
7. Any extraordinary expenses or revenues during period.
8. Has the Company during the past five years returned any goods to creditors or paid creditors out of the normal course of business?
9. Copy of bank statements.
10. Who are the Company's auditors/accountants/solicitors?

PARTICULARS OF CORPORATION

1. Date of incorporation.
2. What kinds of shares were originally issued by the Company? What was their original value? How many shares were originally issued?
3. Who were the original shareholders?
4. Who are the present shareholders?
5. Could you please give me the particulars of the transfer of shares?
6. Were the shares paid for in full?
7. Who were the original directors?
8. Who are the present directors?
9. Who were the original officers?
10. Who are the present officers'?
11. Where is the Company's Head Office?
12. Are the premises owned or leased?
13. Were premises ever owned by the Company?
14. Could you please describe the type of business?
15. What was the cause for financial difficulties?

CREDITORS OF THE COMPANY

1. Are there any other creditors?
2. What is the status of their claims, i.e., do they have secured claims or judgments?
3. Do any creditors have any form of security upon the Company's assets?
4. If so what type. when given, and circumstances at time when given?
5. Please provide a list of all the creditors.

6. Does the Company owe the Bank any money either on a loan or overdraft?
7. How does the Bank secure its indebtedness, i.e., assignment of accounts receivable. Section 178 security personal guarantees, or security agreement?
8. Are there any mortgages or liens against automobiles, equipment, furniture, trade fixtures or general equipment or inventory of the Company?
9. Are any of the Company's goods taken on consignment or sold on consignment?

ASSETS OF THE COMPANY

1. Furniture.
2. Office and plant equipment.
3. Vehicles - type. when acquired. how used.
4. Trade fixtures.
5. Inventory
6. Accounts receivable - obtain list.
7. Lease for office or other leases owned by Company.
8. Any holdings outside Canada.
9. If so with whom did the Company deal?
10. Did the Company own any bonds?
11. Are any mortgages payable to the Company?
12. Are any loan agreements payable to the Company?
13. Are any securities payable to the Company?
14. Did the Company own any common stock in other Corporations'?
15. Does the Company own any other personal property, i.e., TV or refrigerator?
16. Does the Company own any real property?
17. Does the Company own any other property?

App 3-35

Notice of Termination of Garnishment

Court File No. 00-CV-88888

SUPERIOR COURT OF JUSTICE

BETWEEN:

OMNI BANK OF CANADA

Creditor

and

ARCHIE BUNKER

Debtor

and

ALL-RIGHT BAR & GRILL LTD.

Garnishee

NOTICE OF TERMINATION OF GARNISHMENT

TO: ALL-RIGHT BAR & GRILL LTD.

AND TO: Sheriff, City of Ottawa

THE NOTICE OF GARNISHMENT dated July , 2001 SERVED ON YOU IS TERMINATED and you are not to make any further payments under it.

November, 2001.

ADAM & ZENA
281 McLeod Street
Ottawa, Ontario
K2K 3B3
tel: (613) 237-0000
fax: (613) 237-1111
Solicitors for the Creditor

App 3-36

Notice of Appointment for Examination in Aid of Execution

Court File No. 00-CV-88888

SUPERIOR COURT OF JUSTICE

BETWEEN:

OMNI BANK OF CANADA

Plaintiff

and

ARCHIE BUNKER

Defendant

NOTICE OF EXAMINATION

TO: ARCHIE BUNKER

YOU ARE REQUIRED TO ATTEND FOR AN EXAMINATION in aid of execution of yourself on [*date*], at [*time*] at the office of the Official Examiner, [*address*]

YOU ARE REQUIRED TO BRING WITH YOU and produce at the examination the documents mentioned in subrule 30.04(4) of the Rules of Civil Procedure, and the following documents and things:

All and any books of account, letter books, bills of exchange, promissory notes, bills of sale, chattel mortgages, mortgages, assignment of mortgages and all other securities for money of any kind and all evidence of indebtedness of any person to you, and all ledgers, books, and documents or paper writings of any kind whatsoever showing your financial position since the debt or liability, on which this judgment was obtained, was incurred.

Date:

ADAM & ZENA
281 McLeod Street
Ottawa, Ontario
K2K 3B3
tel: (613) 237-0000
fax: (613) 237-1111
Solicitors for the Plaintiff

TO: ARCHIE BUNKER
2 Walkerton Court
Ottawa, Ontario
K6V 9Y1

App 3-37

Affidavit of Service of Notice of Adjournment of Assessment

Court File No:

SUPERIOR COURT OF JUSTICE

BETWEEN:

ADAM & ZENA

Solicitor

- and -

JOAN JEFFRY

Client

AFFIDAVIT OF SERVICE

I, **MARY NEILL**, Law Clerk, of the City of Toronto, in the Regional Municipality of Toronto, MAKE OATH AND SAY AS FOLLOWS:

1. That I did on or about the 11th day of June, 2001, serve the above-named client with the Notice of Adjournment of Assessment, by sending such copy by prepaid ordinary mail in an envelope bearing a return address thereon to Joan Jeffrey, 75 Southpark Drive, Toronto, Ontario, M4X 5V5

SWORN BEFORE ME at the City	)	
of Toronto, in the Regional Municipality	)	
of Toronto, this day of	)	______________________
June, 2001	)	**MARY NEILL**
	)	
	)	
A Commissioner, etc.	)	

App 3-38

Certificate of Non-Attendance

Court File No. 00-CV-88888

SUPERIOR COURT OF JUSTICE

BETWEEN:

OMNI BANK OF CANADA

Plaintiff

and

ARCHIE BUNKER

Defendant

CERTIFICATE OF NON-ATTENDANCE

I, Fred Ayers, HEREBY CERTIFY that an appointment was made by me for an Examination in Aid of Execution of Archie Bunker, at the hour of 9:00 o'clock in the forenoon, at my office at Suite 400-275 Elgin Street, Ottawa, Ontario, for the Examination in Aid of Execution of Archie Bunker and although proof of service of the notice of appointment has been filed, the said Defendant, Archie Bunker, did not appear before me.

Counsel for the Plaintiff attended and waited the necessary fifteen minutes after the appointed time.

Dated at Ottawa, Ontario this   day of August, 2001

Ayers and Boyd Reporting Service

Per: ______________________________
400-275 Elgin Street
Ottawa, Ontario

App 3-39

Notice of Motion for Order Compelling Attendance at an Examination in Aid of Execution

Court File No. 00-CV-88888

SUPERIOR COURT OF JUSTICE

BETWEEN:

OMNI BANK OF CANADA

Plaintiff

and

ARCHIE BUNKER

Defendant

NOTICE OF MOTION

THE PLAINTIFF will make a motion to a Judge on , the day of , at o'clock in the noon, or as soon after that time as the Motion can be heard, at the Court House, 161 Elgin Street, Ottawa, Ontario.

PROPOSED METHOD OF HEARING: The motion is to be heard:

___ in writing under subrule 37.12.1(1) because it is made without notice
___ in writing as an opposed motion under subrule 37.12.1(4)
_X_ orally

THE MOTION IS FOR an Order pursuant to rule 34.15 compelling the Defendant, Archie Bunker, to attend at an Examination in Aid of Execution, to be held before Ayers and Boyd at 400-275 Elgin St., Ottawa, Ontario, or for such other Order as may seem just.

THE GROUNDS FOR THE MOTION ARE:

1. Rule 34.15 of the Rules of Civil Procedure.

THE FOLLOWING DOCUMENTARY EVIDENCE will be used at the hearing of the motion:

(a) the pleadings and proceedings herein; and
(b) the Affidavit of Mary Neill.

Date:

ADAM & ZENA
281 McLeod Street
Ottawa, Ontario
K2K 3B3
tel: (613) 237-0000
fax: (613) 237-1111
Solicitors for the Creditor

TO: ARCHIE BUNKER
2 Walkerton Court
Ottawa, Ontario
K6V 9Y1

App 3-40

Affidavit in Support of Motion for Order Compelling Attendance at Examination in Aid of Execution

Court File No. 00-CV-88888

SUPERIOR COURT OF JUSTICE

BETWEEN:

OMNI BANK OF CANADA

Plaintiff

and

ARCHIE BUNKER

Defendant

AFFIDAVIT

I, **MARY NEILL**, of the City of Ottawa, in the Province of Ontario, MAKE OATH AND SAY AS FOLLOWS:

1. I am a Clerk-at-Law employed with Adam & Zena, solicitors for the Plaintiff herein, and as such have knowledge of the maters hereinafter deposed to.

2. That an Appointment for an Examination in Aid of Execution of Archie Bunker was taken out for   and was served upon Archie Bunker on   , as is evidenced by the Affidavit of Service of Ken Bouchard, attached hereto as Exhibit "A" to this my affidavit.

3. That I attended on   to conduct the Examination in Aid of Execution of Archie Bunker, however, he failed to appear as is evidenced by the Certificate of Non-Attendance of the Official Examiner, attached hereto as Exhibit "B" to this my Affidavit.

4. That at no time prior to the scheduled appointment of Archie Bunker did Archie Bunker contact me to advise that he would not be in attendance.

5. This Affidavit is sworn in support of a Motion for an Order compelling the attendance of Archie Bunker at an Examination in Aid of Execution and for no other or improper purpose.

SWORN BEFORE ME at the City of	)	
Ottawa, in the Province of Ontario	)	
this day of , 2001	)	
	)	______________________________
	)	**MARY NEILL**
A Commissioner, etc.	)	

App 3-41

Order Compelling Attendance at Examination in Aid of Execution

Court File No. 00-CV-88888

SUPERIOR COURT OF JUSTICE

THE HONOURABLE JUDGE	)	**, THE**	**DAY OF**
	)		
A.B. STIRLING	)	**, 2001**	

BETWEEN:

OMNI BANK OF CANADA

Plaintiff

and

ARCHIE BUNKER

Defendant

ORDER

THIS MOTION made by the Plaintiff for an Order pursuant to Rule 34.15 compelling the Defendant Archie Bunker, to attend at an examination in Aid of Execution, to be held before Ayers and Boyd, 400-275 Elgin Street, Ottawa, Ontario, or for such other Order as may seem must, was heard this day, at the Court House, 161 Elgin Street, Ottawa, Ontario.

ON READING THE pleadings and proceedings herein and the Affidavit of Mary Neill, and upon hearing counsel for the Plaintiff, no one appearing for the Defendant, although properly served as appears from the Affidavit of service of Ken Bouchard;

1. **THIS COURT ORDERS** that the Defendant Archie Bunker attend at an Examination in Aid of Execution, to be held before Ayers and Boyd, 400-275 Elgin Street, Ottawa, Ontario, after being served with notice of such appointment and a copy of this Order.

2. **THIS COURT ORDERS** that the Plaintiff shall have its costs of this motion in the amount of $250.00.

____

App 3-42

Notice of Motion for Order for Re-examination to Answer Undertakings

Court File No:

SUPERIOR COURT OF JUSTICE

BETWEEN:

OMNI BANK OF CANADA

Plaintiff

- and -

ARCHIE BUNKER

Defendant

NOTICE OF MOTION

THE Plaintiff will make a motion to a Judge on Tuesday, the 13th day of March, 2001, at 10:00 a.m., or as soon after that time as the Motion can be heard, at the Court House, 161 Elgin Street, Ottawa, Ontario.

PROPOSED METHOD OF HEARING: The motion is to be heard
_____ in writing under subrule 37.12.1(1) because it is made without notice;
__X__ in writing as an opposed motion under subrule 37.12.1(4);
_____ orally.

THE MOTION IS FOR an Order pursuant to Rule 34.15 requiring the Defendant, Archie Bunker, to attend for Re-examination in Aid of Execution to answer the undertakings given by him at his Examination in Aid of Execution on February 18, 2001, and for an Order allowing service of the Notice of Appointment for Examination in Aid of Execution by mail at 12 Walkerton Court, Ottawa, Ontario K6V 9Y1, or for such other Order as may seem just.

THE GROUNDS FOR THE MOTION ARE:
(a) Rule 34.15(1) of the Rules of Civil Procedure.

THE FOLLOWING DOCUMENTARY EVIDENCE will be used at the hearing of the motion:
(a) the Affidavit of Mary Neill.

February 23rd, 2001

ADAM & ZENA
Barristers & Solicitors
281 McLeod Street
Ottawa, Ontario
K2P 1A1
tel: (613) 237-0000
fax: (613) 237-1111
Solicitors for the Plaintiff

TO: ARCHIE BUNKER
12 Walkerton Court
Ottawa, Ontario
K6V 9Y1

(NOTE: If this motion is to be heard in writing as an opposed motion, a factum must be served with the motion.)

App 3-43

Affidavit in Support of Motion for Order for Re-examination to Answer Undertakings

Court File No:

SUPERIOR COURT OF JUSTICE

BETWEEN:

OMNI BANK OF CANADA

Plaintiff

- and -

ARCHIE BUNKER

Defendant

AFFIDAVIT

I, MARY NEILL, of the City of Ottawa, in the Province of Ontario, **MAKE OATH AND SAY**:

1. I am a Clerk-at-Law with the firm of Adam & Zena, Solicitors for the Plaintiff herein, and as such have knowledge of the matters hereinafter deposed to.

2. That Judgment was obtained on behalf of the Plaintiff against the Defendant on March 15th, 2000 for the sum of $54,634.62 and $300.00 for taxed costs.

3. That an Examination in Aid of Execution was conducted upon the Defendant, Archie Bunker, on the 15th day of February, 2001 at which time Archie Bunker was in attendance.

4. Archie Bunker undertook to provide the following information on the Examination in Aid of Execution:

(a) the number of his bank account at Bank of Not Negotiable in Ottawa, Ontario;
(b) the serial number and particulars of registration of a 1992 Honda Civic;
(c) a copy of a reporting letter to him concerning the sale of 12 Walkerton Court, Ottawa from himself to his wife, Edith Bunker, and copies of all documents evidencing the transfer of the property;
(d) particulars of all guaranteed investment certificates held by Archie Bunker.

5. At the conclusion of the Examination in Aid of Execution I requested that Archie Bunker provide the answers to these undertakings to me within ten days.

6. On February 16th, 2001, I corresponded with Archie Bunker at 12 Walkerton Court, Ottawa, Ontario, requesting that he provide the answers to the undertakings given on his Examination in Aid of Execution no later than February 25th, 2001. Attached hereto as Exhibit "A" to this my Affidavit is a copy of my letter of February 16th, 2001.

7. To date I have not received the answers to the undertakings given by Archie Bunker, and although I have attempted to contact him by telephone and have left messages for him to call me on several occasions, he has not returned my calls. The Defendant was served personally with the Appointment for Examination in Aid of Execution at 12 Walkerton Court, Ottawa, Ontario, and I verily believe Notice of the Appointment for Re-examination in Aid of Execution would come to his attention if he was served by mail at that address.

8. This Affidavit is made in support of a motion for an Order compelling the Defendant, Archie Bunker, to attend for Re-examination in Aid of Execution to answer the undertakings given by him on his Examination in Aid of Execution February 18, 2001 and for service of the Appointment by mail and is made for no improper purpose.

SWORN BEFORE ME at the City	)	
of Ottawa, in the Province of Ontario	)	
this day of February, 2001	)	
	)	______________________________
	)	**MARY NEILL**

A Commissioner, etc.

App 3-44

Order for Re-examination to Answer Undertakings

Court File No:

SUPERIOR COURT OF JUSTICE

THE HONOURABLE	)	**TUESDAY, THE 13TH DAY OF**
	)	
JUSTICE A.B. STIRLING	)	**MARCH, 2001**
	)	

BETWEEN:

OMNI BANK OF CANADA

Plaintiff

- and -

ARCHIE BUNKER

Defendant

ORDER

THIS MOTION, made by the Plaintiff for an Order pursuant to Rule 34.15 requiring the Defendant, Archie Bunker, to attend for Re-examination in Aid of Execution to answer the undertakings given by him at his Examination in Aid of Execution on February 18, 2001 and for an Order allowing service of the Notice of Appointment for Examination in Aid of Execution by mail at 12 Walkerton Court, Ottawa, Ontario, or for such other Order as may seem just, was heard this day, at Ottawa, Ontario.

ON READING THE pleadings and proceedings herein and the Affidavit of Mary Neill, and on hearing submissions of counsel for the Plaintiff, no one appearing for the Defendant, although properly served as appears from the Affidavit of Service of Ken Bouchard:

1. **THIS COURT ORDERS** that the Defendant shall attend for an Examination in Aid of Execution to answer the following undertakings:
(a) the number of his bank account at Bank of Not Negotiable, Ottawa, Ontario;
(b) the serial number and particulars of registration of a 1992 Mercedes Benz 450 SEL;
(c) a copy of a reporting letter to him concerning the sale of 12 Walkerton Court, Ottawa, Ontario from himself to his wife, Edith Bunker, and copies of all documents evidencing the transfer of the property;
(d) particulars of all guaranteed investment certificates held by Archie Bunker.

2. **THIS COURT ORDERS** that a copy of this Order and Appointment for Examination in Aid of Execution may be served upon the said Defendant by ordinary mail at the following address:

12 Walkerton Court, Ottawa, Ontario, K6V 9Y1

3. **THIS COURT ORDERS** that the Plaintiff shall have its costs of the Motion in the amount of $250.00.

____

App 3-45

Notice of Motion for Order for Committal to Jail for Contempt of Court

Court File No:

SUPERIOR COURT OF JUSTICE

BETWEEN:

OMNI BANK OF CANADA

Plaintiff

- and -

ARCHIE BUNKER

Defendant

NOTICE OF MOTION

THE PLAINTIFF will make a Motion to a Judge on Thursday, the 26th day of April, 2001 at 10:00 o'clock in the forenoon, or as soon after that time as the Motion can be heard, at the Court House, 161 Elgin Street, Ottawa, Ontario.

PROPOSED METHOD OF HEARING: The motion is to be heard

_____ in writing under subrule 37.12.1(1) because it is made without notice;

_____ in writing as opposed motion under subrule 37.12.1(4);

__X__ orally.

THE MOTION IS FOR a Contempt Order committing the Defendant, Archie Bunker, to the common jail of the County or District in which he resides, or for such other Order as may seem just.

THE GROUNDS FOR THE MOTION ARE:
(a) Rule 34.15 of the Rules of Civil Procedure.
(b) Rule 60.11 of the Rules of Civil Procedure

THE FOLLOWING DOCUMENTARY EVIDENCE will be used at the hearing of the motion:
(a) the pleadings and proceedings herein;
(b) the Affidavit of Mary Neill.

April 12, 2001

ADAM & ZENA
Barristers & Solicitors
281 McLeod Street
Ottawa, Ontario
K2P 1A1
tel: (613) 237-0000
fax: (613) 237-1111
Solicitors for the Plaintiff

TO: ARCHIE BUNKER
12 Walkerton Court
Ottawa, Ontario
K6V 9Y1

App 3-46

Affidavit in Support of Motion for Committal to Jail for Contempt of Court

Court File No:

SUPERIOR COURT OF JUSTICE

BETWEEN:

OMNI BANK OF CANADA

Plaintiff

- and -

ARCHIE BUNKER

Defendant

AFFIDAVIT

I, MARY NEILL, a Clerk-at-Law with the firm of Adam & Zena, Solicitors for the Plaintiff herein, MAKE OATH AND SAY:

1. That pursuant to the Order of A.B. Stirling of March 15th, 2000, the Defendant, Archie Bunker, was ordered to attend for Examination in Aid of Execution. Attached hereto as Exhibit "A" to this my Affidavit is a copy of the Order of The Honourable A.B. Stirling of March 15th, 2001.

2. That an Appointment for Examination in Aid of Execution of the Defendant was arranged for April 20th, 2001 and the said Defendant was served with a copy of the Order compelling his attendance, along with the Appointment for April the 20th, 2001 for Examination in Aid of Execution, on April the 7th, 2001, as is evidenced by the Affidavit of Service of Ken Bouchard attached hereto as Exhibit "B" to this my Affidavit.

3. That I attended to conduct an Examination in Aid of Execution of the Defendant, Archie Bunker, on April 20th, 2001, however, he failed to be in attendance at the examination. At no time prior to the appointment did Archie Bunker contact me to advise me he would not be in attendance at the examination. Attached hereto as Exhibit "C" to this my Affidavit is a copy of a Certificate of Non-Attendance evidencing that Archie Bunker was not in attendance for the examination on April 20th, 2001.

4. This Affidavit is made in support of a motion for an Order committing the Defendant, Archie Bunker, to jail for his contempt of the Order of The Honourable A.B. Stirling and is made for no improper purpose.

SWORN BEFORE ME at the City	)	
of Ottawa, in the Province of	)	
Ontario, this day of April, 2001	)	
	)	______________________
	)	**MARY NEILL**
A Commissioner, etc.	)	

App 3-47

Order for Committal to Jail for Contempt of Court

Court File No.

SUPERIOR COURT OF JUSTICE

THE HONOURABLE JUSTICE	)	**THURSDAY, THE 26th DAY OF**
	)	
A.B. STIRLING	)	**APRIL, A.D. 2001**

BETWEEN:

OMNI BANK OF CANADA

Plaintiff

- and -

ARCHIE BUNKER

Defendant

ORDER

THIS MOTION, made by the Plaintiff for a Contempt Order committing the Defendant, Archie Bunker, to the common jail of the county or district in which he resides was heard this day, at the Court House, 161 Elgin Street, Ottawa, Ontario.

ON READING the pleadings and proceedings herein and the Affidavit of Mary Neill, filed, and on hearing submissions of counsel for the Plaintiff, no one appearing for the Defendant, although properly served as appears from the Affidavit of Service of Ken Bouchard,

1. **THIS COURT ORDERS** that a Contempt Order be and is hereby made against the Defendant, Archie Bunker.

2. **THIS COURT ORDERS** that a Warrant for Committal shall be issued to All Police Officers in the Province of Ontario, and to the Officers of all Correctional Institutions in Ontario, ordering that Archie Bunker be arrested wherever he may be found and delivered directly to a provincial correction institution and be detained there for two days, unless before that time the said Defendant should deliver payment to the Sheriff by cash or certified cheque made payable to the Plaintiff, the sum of $54,934.62, being the amount of the Judgment and costs of the Judgment, together with interest at the rate of 12% per annum and the costs of the subsequent Examination in Aid of Execution fixed in the amount of $60.00 and the costs of the Order of March 1, 2001 in the amount of $75.00, together with any costs incurred in carrying out the warrant of committal.

3. **THIS COURT ORDERS** that the Plaintiff shall have his costs of this motion fixed in the sum of $500.00.

____

App 3-48

Warrant of Committal

Court File No.

SUPERIOR COURT OF JUSTICE

THE HONOURABLE JUSTICE	)	**THURSDAY, THE 26th DAY OF**
	)	
A.B. STIRLING	)	**APRIL, A.D. 2001**

BETWEEN:

OMNI BANK OF CANADA

Plaintiff

- and -

ARCHIE BUNKER

Defendant

ORDER

WARRANT OF COMMITTAL

TO ALL POLICE OFFICERS IN ONTARIO

AND TO THE OFFICERS OF THE OTTAWA DETENTION CENTRE

WHEREAS I have found that Archie Bunker is in contempt of this court and have ordered imprisonment as punishment for the contempt,

YOU ARE ORDERED TO ARREST Archie Bunker, and deliver him to a provincial correction institution, to be detained there for two days, unless the said Archie Bunker delivers payment to the Sheriff by cash or certified cheque made payable to the Plaintiff, in the sum of $54,934.62.

____

App 3-49

Letter to Chief of Police re Warrant of Committal

April 27, 2001

Office of the Chief of Police
P.O. Box 1234
Ottawa, Ontario
K2B 1P4

Attention: Inspector George Miller

Dear Sir.

Re: Omni Bank of Canada v. Archie Bunker

Please find enclosed a copy of the Order of the Honourable Justice A.B. Stirling and an original warrant of committal ordering that Mr. Archie Bunker be arrested and detained at the Ottawa Detention Centre for a period of 2 days. Mr. Bunker's last known place of residence is 12 Walkerton Court, Ottawa, Ontario.

Mr. Bunker is presently employed by All-Right Bar & Grill Ltd., 51 Main Street, Ottawa, Ontario, K2B 1L2. The Defendant's birthdate is January 11, 1957.

Could you kindly confirm that Mr. Bunker has, in fact, been detained pursuant to the Order of the Honourable Justice A.B. Stirling.

If we can be of any further assistance in this matter, please contact our offices.

Yours truly,

ADAM & ZENA

Per: Mary Neill
Law Clerk

App 3-50

Writ of Delivery

Court File No:

SUPERIOR COURT OF JUSTICE

BETWEEN:

OMNI BANK OF CANADA

Plaintiff

- and -

ARCHIE BUNKER

Defendant

WRIT OF DELIVERY

TO the Sheriff of the City of Ottawa:

Under an Order of this Court made on July 5, 2001

YOU ARE DIRECTED to seize from Archie Bunker and to deliver without delay to Omni Bank of Canada possession of the following personal property:

1992 Mercedes Benz Sport 450 SEL, VIN #92837465VRM

Date: July , 2001

Issued by: ____________________________
Local Registrar

Address of Court Office: 161 Elgin Street
Ottawa, Ontario
K2P 2K1

App 3-51

Writ of Sequestration

Court File No:

SUPERIOR COURT OF JUSTICE

BETWEEN:

OMNI BANK OF CANADA

Plaintiff

- and -

ARCHIE BUNKER

Defendant

WRIT OF SEQUESTRATION

TO the Sheriff of the City of Ottawa:

Under an Order of this Court made on July 5, 2001 on motion of Omni Bank of Canada,

YOU ARE DIRECTED to take possession of and hold the following property within your county or district of Archie Bunker:

One 1992 Mercedes Benz Sport 450 SEL, VIN #92837465VRM

Date: July , 2001

Issued by: ______________________________
Local Registrar

Address of
Court Office: 161 Elgin Street
Ottawa, Ontario
K2P 2K1

App 3-52

Release

TO: **ARCHIE BUNKER** (herein called the "Releasee")

KNOW ALL PERSONS BY THESE PRESENTS THAT WE, OMNI BANK OF CANADA, (hereinafter called the "Releasor" which term includes my successors and assigns) in consideration of the payment of the sum of $54,934.62 and other good and valuable consideration, the receipt and sufficiency whereof is hereby acknowledged by me, do hereby remise, release and forever discharge the Releasee of and from all actions, causes of action, damages, claims and demands whatsoever, whether in law or in equity, which the Releasor had, and has, or which the Releasor shall or may have by reason of, or arising out of, any other cause, matter or thing whatsoever existing up to the present time, and in particular without limiting the generality of the foregoing, all matters in regard to the Releasor's claim for goods sold and delivered to the Releasees referred to in action Court file no. .

Dated this 20th day of July, 2001, at the City of Ottawa.

OMNI BANK OF CANADA

______________________________ Per: ______________________________

Witness **HARRY FREEDMAN**

I have authority to bind the within Corporation.

App 3-53

Satisfaction Piece

Court file no.

SUPERIOR COURT OF JUSTICE

BETWEEN:

OMNI BANK OF CANADA

Plaintiff

- and -

ARCHIE BUNKER

Defendant

SATISFACTION PIECE

Satisfaction is hereby acknowledged of the Judgment bearing date the 1st day of May, 2001, in an action in this Honourable Court wherein Omni Bank of Canada was the Plaintiff and Archie Bunker was the Defendant, whereby it was adjudged that the Plaintiff should recover against the Defendant the sum of $54,934.62 for debt and the sum of $300.00 for costs.

And the said Omni Bank of Canada hereby expressly nominates and appoints Joe Adam, its solicitor, to witness and attest its acknowledgment of satisfaction.

OMNI BANK OF CANADA	)	Signed by a duly authorized officer of Omni
	)	Bank of Canada Inc. in the presence of
	)	Joe Adam, solicitor, of the Superior Court of
	)	Justice, this 27th day of August, 2001, at the City
Per: ______________________	)	of Ottawa, in the Province of Ontario
	)	
	)	And I, the said Joe Adam, hereby declare that
	)	I am the solicitor for the said Omni Bank of
	)	Canada expressly named by it and attending at
	)	its request to inform its duly authorized officer
	)	of the nature and effect of this
	)	acknowledgment and of this satisfaction, which
	)	I accordingly did before the same was
	)	executed by it.
	)	
	)	In testimony whereof I subscribe
	)	my name as such solicitor.
	)	
	)	
______________________	)	Joe Adam

This satisfaction piece has been noted and recorded in the margin of the entry of the Judgment referred to this ________ day of August, 2001.

____

Registrar

Appendix 4

Precedents Relating to

Chapter 4

Using Small Claims Court to Your Client's Advantage

App 4-1
Small Claims Court
Letter to Court to Issue Claim

June 4, 2001

Superior Court of Justice
Toronto Small Claims Court
Court House
47 Sheppard Avenue East
Toronto, Ontario
M2N 5X5

Dear Sir/Madam:

Re: Omni Bank of Canada v. Smith

We are the solicitors for the Plaintiff in this matter.

Enclosed please find the original and two copies of the Plaintiff's claim. Would you please issue the claim, retain a copy for your file, and return the original and one copy to our office for service upon the defendant. Enclosed is the sum of [fee] for your filing fee.

Thank you for your assistance in this matter.

Yours truly,

ADAM & ZENA

Per:
Mary Neill
Law Clerk

Encl.

App 4-2
Form 7A
Plaintiff's Claim

SUPERIOR COURT OF JUSTICE
TORONTO SMALL CLAIMS COURT

BETWEEN:

OMNI BANK OF CANADA

Plaintiff

- and -

JEFF SMITH

Defendant

PLAINTIFF'S CLAIM

TO THE DEFENDANT:

JEFF SMITH
454 Westmount Drive
Toronto, Ontario
M4V 3P3
(416) 869-5324

The Plaintiff claims from you $9,500.00 and costs for the reason(s) set out below.

IF YOU DO NOT FILE A DEFENCE WITH THE COURT WITHIN TWENTY (20) DAYS AFTER YOU HAVE RECEIVED THIS CLAIM, JUDGMENT MAY BE ENTERED AGAINST YOU.

TYPE OF CLAIM

Unpaid Account __X__	Contract________	Motor Vehicle Accident________
Promissory Note ________	Services Rendered ________	N.S.F cheque_______
Damage to Property________	Lease________	Other ________

REASONS FOR CLAIM AND DETAILS
(Explain what happened, where and when and the amounts of money involved.)

The plaintiff's claim is against the defendant for the balance outstanding on a credit card issued by the Plaintiff to the Defendant in the amount of $9,500.00. The plaintiff claims interest from the defendant at the rate of 18% per annum pursuant to the terms of a credit card agreement between the plaintiff and the defendant from January 24, 2001, to the date of payment or Judgment at the rate of $4.6849 per day. A copy of the credit card agreement and last statement are attached.

If the claim is based in whole or in part on a document, attach a copy of the document to the claim, or if the document is lost or unavailable, explain why it is not attached.

....

(Date) (Clerk's signature)

App 4-3

Affidavit of Jurisdiction / Forum

Court File No.

SUPERIOR COURT OF JUSTICE
TORONTO SMALL CLAIMS COURT

BETWEEN:

OMNI BANK OF CANADA

Plaintiff

- and -

JEFF SMITH

Defendant

AFFIDAVIT OF JURISDICTION / FORUM

I, JOE ADAM, of the City of Toronto, in the Regional Municipality of Toronto

MAKE OATH AND SAY (or AFFIRM):

(Give facts in support of the motion. If the facts are not within your own personal knowledge, give the source of your information or the grounds for your belief.)

1. I am the solicitor for the Plaintiff, Omni Bank of Canada, in this action.

2. The Plaintiff is entitled to enter this action in this territorial division because the plaintiff's claim is for the balance due and owing on a credit card and the defendant resides in this jurisdiction.

SWORN BEFORE ME at the City of	)	
Toronto, in the Regional Municipality	)	
of Toronto, this day of June, 2001	)	
	)	______________________________
	)	**JOE ADAM**
A Commisssioner, etc.	)	

App 4-4

Form 8A

Certificate of Service

Court File No.

SUPERIOR COURT OF JUSTICE
TORONTO SMALL CLAIMS COURT

BETWEEN:

OMNI BANK OF CANADA

Plaintiff

- and -

JEFF SMITH

Defendant

BAILIFF OR BAILIFF'S OFFICER

I, Tom Rogers, bailiff (or bailiff's officer) of the Toronto Small Claims Court, certify

that I have served the Claim
(name of document)

X Personally on Jeff Smith,
(Name of Person Served)

on April 15, 2001

OR

by leaving a copy of document in a sealed envelope addressed to the defendant with:

.... at ....
(Name of Person document was left with) (Address)

and by mailing another copy of the document addressed to the defendant at:

on ....
(Date)

....
(Date) (Signature of bailiff/deputy bailiff)

App 4-5
Form 8B
Affidavit of Service

Court File No.

SUPERIOR COURT OF JUSTICE
TORONTO SMALL CLAIMS COURT

BETWEEN:

OMNI BANK OF CANADA

Plaintiff

- and -

JEFF SMITH

Defendant

AFFIDAVIT OF SERVICE

I, Ken Bouchard, Process Server of the City
(full name) (City, Town, etc.)
of Toronto, in the Regional Municipality of Toronto

(Name of City/Town)(County/Regional Municipality, etc.) (Name of County/Regional Municipality)

MAKE OATH AND SAY (or AFFIRM):

I have served the Claim on Jeff Smith
(Name of document) (Name of person)

personally on April 15, 2001 by leaving a copy with him/her
(Date)

at 454 Westmount Drive
Toronto, Ontario
M4V 3P3

I was able to identify the person by means of (state the means by which the person's identity was ascertained.) his identity to me.

OR

by leaving a copy of the .... in a sealed envelope addressed
(Name of document)

to .... with ....
(Name of party to be served) (Identify person served, if known)

who appeared to be an adult member of the same household in which

....
(Name of person to be served)

resides at ....
(Address where service was made)

and by sending another copy of the ....
(Name of Document)

by regular lettermail addressed to .... at the same address
(Name of party to be served)

on .... ;
(Date)

SWORN (AFFIRMED) BEFORE ME	)
at the City of Toronto, in the Regional	)
Municipality of Toronto, this day	)
of April , 2001	)
	) ______________________________
	) KEN BOUCHARD
A Commissioner, etc.	)

App 4-6

Form 9A

Defence

Court File No.

SUPERIOR COURT OF JUSTICE
TORONTO SMALL CLAIMS COURT

BETWEEN:

OMNI BANK OF CANADA

Plaintiff

- and -

JEFF SMITH

Defendant

DEFENCE

_X_ I/We dispute the full claim made by the plaintiff.

____ I/We admit the plaintiff's full claim and propose the following terms of payment.

____ $ .... per .... commencing ....

____ I/We admit part of the plaintiff's claim amounting to $ .... and propose the following terms of payment: $ ...... per .... commencing ....

____ I/we dispute the balance of the claim.

REASONS FOR DISPUTING THE CLAIM AND DETAILS:

(set out grounds for disputing the claim)

If the defence is based in whole or in part on a document, attach a copy of the document to the defence, or if the document is lost or unavailable, explain why it is not attached.

NOTE:

If the defence contains a proposal for terms of payment, the plaintiff is deemed to have accepted the terms unless the plaintiff, in writing to the clerk, disputes the proposal and requests a hearing within 20 days of service of a copy of the DEFENCE.

IF THE DEFENDANT FAILS TO MAKE PAYMENT IN ACCORDANCE WITH THE TERMS OF PAYMENT PROPOSED, THE CLERK MAY SIGN JUDGMENT FOR THE UNPAID BALANCE WITHOUT A HEARING.

....	....
(Date)	(Defendant's Signature or Solicitor/Agent's Name)

App 4-7

Form 9B

Dispute of Proposal of Terms of Payment

Court File No:

SUPERIOR COURT OF JUSTICE
TORONTO SMALL CLAIMS COURT

BETWEEN:

OMNI BANK OF CANADA

Plaintiff

- and -

JEFF SMITH

Defendant

REQUEST FOR A HEARING

TO THE COURT:

I, _______________, dispute the defendant's proposal to terms of payments to the claim filed, and request that a hearing be held in this proceeding for the following reasons:

(Give reasons for request).

The offer for payment is not acceptable because it is too low.

....
(Signature of party, solicitor or agent)

App 4-8

Form 9C

Order as to Terms of Payment

Court File No:

SUPERIOR COURT OF JUSTICE
TORONTO SMALL CLAIMS COURT

BETWEEN:

OMNI BANK OF CANADA

Plaintiff

- and -

JEFF SMITH

Defendant

ORDER AS TO TERMS OF PAYMENT

At a hearing held on July 9, 2001 the following terms of payment for a total of
(Date)
$6,750.00 and $250.00 were ordered.
(claim) (costs)

The Defendant Jeff Smith shall pay the sum of $350.00 per month to the Plaintiff Omni Bank of Canada, commencing August 1, 2001 and each and every month thereafter up to and including March 1, 2003.

July 11, 2001 ______________
(Date order made) Signature of referee/designated person

NOTE:

If the defendant fails to make payment in accordance with this order, the clerk shall sign judgment for the balance without a hearing.

App 4-9

Defence Admitting Liability And Proposing Terms For Repayment

Court File No.

SUPERIOR COURT OF JUSTICE
TORONTO SMALL CLAIMS COURT

BETWEEN:

OMNI BANK OF CANADA

Plaintiff

- and -

JEFF SMITH

Defendant

____ I/We dispute the full claim made by the plaintiff.

_X_ I/We admit the plaintiff's full claim and propose the following terms of payment.

____ $ 100.00 per month commencing June 1, 2001

____ I/We admit part of the plaintiff's claim amounting to $ and propose the following terms
of payment: $ .... per .... commencing ....

____ I/we dispute the balance of the claim.

REASONS FOR DISPUTING THE CLAIM AND DETAILS:

I do not dispute the claim of the Plaintiff, however I wish to make arrangements for payment of the amount claimed by way of monthly payments in the amount of $100.00 per month to commence June 1, 2001.

If the defence is based in whole or in part on a document, attach a copy of the document to the defence, or if the document is lost or unavailable, explain why it is not attached.

NOTE:

If the defence contains a proposal for terms of payment, the plaintiff is deemed to have accepted the terms unless the plaintiff, in writing to the clerk, disputes the proposal and requests a hearing within 20 days of service of a copy of the DEFENCE.

IF THE DEFENDANT FAILS TO MAKE PAYMENT IN ACCORDANCE WITH THE TERMS OF PAYMENT PROPOSED, THE CLERK MAY SIGN JUDGMENT FOR THE UNPAID BALANCE WITHOUT A HEARING.

....	....
(Date)	(Defendant's Signature or Solicitor/Agent's Name)

App 4-10

Form 11A

Notice of Default Judgment

Court File No:

SUPERIOR COURT OF JUSTICE
TORONTO SMALL CLAIMS COURT

BETWEEN:

OMNI BANK OF CANADA

Plaintiff

- and -

JEFF SMITH

Defendant

NOTICE OF DEFAULT JUDGMENT

NOTE: Take notice that default judgment has been entered in this action as against Jeff Smith for the following sums:

Debt	$ ______________________
Pre-judgment Interest	$ ______________________
Costs	$ ______________________
Sub-Total	$ ______________________

Post-judgment Interest at ____________ per cent per annum commencing this date.

______________________ (Date)

______________________ (Clerk)

App 4-11

Form 13A

Request for Pre-Trial Conference

Court File No:

SUPERIOR COURT OF JUSTICE
TORONTO SMALL CLAIMS COURT

BETWEEN:

OMNI BANK OF CANADA

Plaintiff

- and -

JEFF SMITH

Defendant

REQUEST FOR PRE-TRIAL CONFERENCE

TO THE COURT:

Omni Bank of Canada ______________________________

requests that a pre-trial conference be held in this proceeding.

____

(Signature of party, solicitor or agent)

App 4-12

Offer to Settle

Court File No:

SUPERIOR COURT OF JUSTICE
TORONTO SMALL CLAIMS COURT

BETWEEN:

OMNI BANK OF CANADA

Plaintiff

- and -

JEFF SMITH

Defendant

OFFER TO SETTLE

The Plaintiff offers to settle this proceeding on the following terms:

1. The Defendant pays to the plaintiff $7,000.00 in satisfaction of the Plaintiff's claim and the Plaintiff's costs of the action.

This offer will expire one minute after the commencement of trial.

Date: June 23, 2001

ADAM & ZENA
281 McLeod Street
Toronto, Ontario
M5C 3C5
tel: (416) 995-9595
fax: (416) 995-9696
Joe Adam
Solicitors for the Plaintiff

TO: JEFF SMITH
454 Westmount Drive
Toronto, Ontario
M4V 3P3

App 4-13

Form 20A

Certificate of Judgment

Court File No:

SUPERIOR COURT OF JUSTICE

TORONTO SMALL CLAIMS COURT

BETWEEN:

OMNI BANK OF CANADA

Plaintiff

- and -

JEFF SMITH

Defendant

CERTIFICATE OF JUDGMENT

TO THE CLERK OF THE TORONTO SMALL CLAIMS COURT

Person requesting Certificate is ____
(Name of person requesting Certificate)

of ____
(Address)

A Judgment was recovered in this action against ______________________
(Name of person against whom judgment was recovered)

on _______ **in the** __________ **Small Claims Court** _____________________
(Date)

for the following:

Debt	$ ______________________
Pre-Judgment Interest	$ ______________________
Costs	$ ______________________
Subtotal	$ ______________________
Amount paid	$ ______________________
Balance Due	$ ______________________
Additional Cost	$ ______________________
Total	$ ______________________

The amount unpaid on the judgment is $ __________ **as stated in this certificate**
(Total)

and the rate of postjudgment interest is _____ **per cent.**

________________________ ________________________
(Date) (Signature of Clerk)

App 4-14

Consent for Payment

Court File No:

SUPERIOR COURT OF JUSTICE
TORONTO SMALL CLAIMS COURT

BETWEEN:

OMNI BANK OF CANADA

Plaintiff

- and -

JEFF SMITH

Defendant

CONSENT FOR PAYMENT

I, **JEFF SMITH,** the Defendant in this action, hereby consent to an Order being made for payment of the above Judgment at the rate of $250.00 per month, commencing October 15, 2001 and continuing until the full amount of the claim together with costs are paid.

DATED at Toronto, Ontario, this 15th day of September, 2001.

"Sally Roberts" "Jeff Smith""

WITNESS SIGNATURE

App 4-15

Affidavit in Support of Request for a Notice of Examination

Court File No:

SUPERIOR COURT OF JUSTICE
TORONTO SMALL CLAIMS COURT

BETWEEN:

OMNI BANK OF CANADA

Plaintiff

- and -

JEFF SMITH

Defendant

AFFIDAVIT

I, **JOE ADAM**, of the City of Toronto, in the Regional Municipality of Toronto,
(full name) (City, Town, etc.) (County, Regional Municipality, etc.)

MAKE OATH AND SAY (or AFFIRM):

1. I am the solicitor for the Plaintiff Omni Bank of Canada, in this action.

2. Judgment was recovered on behalf of the plaintiff Omni Bank of Canada against the defendant Jeff Smith on July 30, 2000 in the Toronto Small Claims Court as follows:

Claim	$9,500.00
Pre-Judgment Interest	175.00
Costs	150.00
Post-Judgment Interest	292.06
Amount paid	nil
Additional Cost	45.00
Total	$10,162.06

3. Post-Judgment interest accrues on this judgment at the rate of 7 % per annum. There have been no payments on the Judgment and the balance of $10,162.06 remains owing. Additional costs will be incurred for the Notice of Examination.

4. This affidavit is made in support of a request for a Notice of Examination and is made for no improper purpose.

SWORN (or AFFIRMED) BEFORE ME)
at the City of Toronto, in the Regional)
Municipality of Toronto, this day of)
January, 2001)
) ______________________________
) **JOE ADAM**

A COMMISSIONER FOR TAKING AFFIDAVITS (or as may be)

WARNING IT IS A CRIMINAL OFFENCE TO KNOWINGLY SWEAR A FALSE AFFIDAVIT

App 4-16

Form 20C

Writ of Seizure and Sale of Personal Property

Court File No:

SUPERIOR COURT OF JUSTICE
TORONTO SMALL CLAIMS COURT

BETWEEN:

OMNI BANK OF CANADA

Plaintiff

- and -

JEFF SMITH

Defendant

WRIT OF SEIZURE AND SALE OF PERSONAL PROPERTY

TO: BAILIFF OF TORONTO SMALL CLAIMS COURT

Under an order of this court made on July 30th, 2001 (date) in favour of Omni Bank of Canada (name of creditor)

YOU ARE DIRECTED to seize and sell the personal property of Jeff Smith (name of debtor)

situate within your jurisdiction and to realize from the seizure and sale the following sums:

(A)	Debt	$ 9,500.00
	Pre-Judgment Interest at 18% per cent	$ 885.45
	per annum commencing January 24, 2001	
(B)	Costs	$ 150.00
	Post-Judgment Interest at 7% per cent	$ 75.00
	per annum commencing July 30, 2001	
	Subsequent costs incurred after judgment	$ 45.00
	This Execution	$ ____
		$ ____
(C)	Your fees and expenses in enforcing this writ	$ 40.00

YOU ARE DIRECTED to pay the proceeds over to the clerk of this court for the creditor.

______________________ (Date)

______________________ (Signature of Clerk)

THIS WRIT REMAINS IN FORCE FOR SIX (6) MONTHS FROM THE DATE OF ITS ISSUE.

App 4-17

Form 20D

Writ of Seizure and Sale of Land

Court File No:

SUPERIOR COURT OF JUSTICE
TORONTO SMALL CLAIMS COURT

BETWEEN:

OMNI BANK OF CANADA

Plaintiff

- and -

JEFF SMITH

Defendant

WRIT OF SEIZURE AND SALE OF LAND

TO: THE SHERIFF OF Regional Municipality of Toronto
(name of area)

Under an order of this court made on July 30, 2001 in favour of Omni Bank of Canada
(date) (name of creditor)

YOU ARE DIRECTED to seize and sell the personal property of Jeff Smith
(name of debtor)

situate within your jurisdiction and to realize from the seizure and sale the following sums:

(A)	Debt	$ 9,500.00
	Pre-Judgment Interest at 18% per cent	$ 885.45
	per annum commencing January 24, 2001	
(B)	Costs	$ 150.00
	Post-Judgment Interest at 7% per cent	$ 75.00
	per annum commencing July 30, 2001	
	Subsequent costs incurred after Judgment	$ 45.00
	This Execution	$ ____
		$ ____
(C)	Your fees and expenses in enforcing this writ	$ 40.00

YOU ARE DIRECTED to pay out the proceeds according to law and to report on the execution of this writ if required by the party or solicitor who filed it.

______________________ Issued by ______________________
(Date) (Clerk)

Court office: 2 Richmond Street
Toronto, Ontario
M2C 3B6

App 4-18

Form 20E

Notice of Garnishment

Superior Court of Justice
Toronto Small Claims Court

Refer to No. /
Amount Unsatisfied $ ____

Creditor

Full name OMNI BANK OF CANADA
Address for Service (*street and number, city, postal code*)
Phone No. Fax No. (If any)
Creditor's Lawyer/Agent (Full Name) ADAM & ZENA
Lawyer/Agent's Address for Service 281 McLeod Street Toronto, Ontario M5C 3C5
Lawyer/Agent's Phone No. (416) 995-9595 Fax No. (If any) (416) 995-9696

Debtor

Full name JEFF SMITH
Address for Service (*street and number, city, postal code*) 454 Westmount Drive Toronto, Ontario M4V 3P3
Phone No. (416) 869-5234 Fax No. (If any)
Debtor's Lawyer/Agent (Full Name)
Lawyer/Agent's Address for Service
Lawyer/Agent's Phone No. Fax No. (If any)

Garnishee

Full name ABC COMPANY LTD.
Address for Service (*street and number, city, postal code*) 5454 Birch Street Richmond Hill, Ontario M6K 2B4
Phone No. (416) 889-8324 Fax No. (If any)

TO: GARNISHEE

A LEGAL PROCEEDING in this court between the creditor and the debtor has resulted in an order that the debtor pay a sum of money to the creditor. The creditor claims that you owe a debt to the debtor. A debt to the debtor includes both a debt payable to the debtor and a debt payable to the debtor and one or more co-owners. The creditor has had this notice of garnishment directed to you as garnishee in order to seize any debt that you owe or will owe to the debtor. Where the debt is payble to the debtor and to one or more co-owners, you must pay one-half of the indebtedness or a greater or lesser amount specified in an order made under subrule 20.08(15).

Subject to the exemptions provided by section 7 of the *Wages Act*.

YOU ARE REQUIRED TO PAY to the clerk of the Toronto Small Claims Court
(Issuing Court)

(a) within ten days after this notice is served on you, all debts now payable by you to the debtor; and

(b) within ten days after they become payable, all debts that become payable by you to the debtor within twenty-four (24) months after this notice is served on you.

The total amount of all your payments to the clerk is not to exceed $ 9,985.00

IF YOU DO NOT PAY THE TOTAL AMOUNT OR SUCH LESSER AMOUNT AS YOU ARE LIABLE TO PAY UNDER THIS NOTICE WITHIN TEN DAYS after this notice is served on you, you must file with the clerk a statement signed by you setting out the particulars of why you have not done so. **EACH PAYMENT MUST BE SENT** to the clerk at the address shown below.

IF YOU FAIL TO OBEY THIS NOTICE, AN ORDER MAY BE OBTAINED AGAINST YOU BY THE CREDITOR for payment of the amount set out above and the costs of the creditor as may be ordered by the court.

IF YOU MAKE PAYMENT TO ANYONE OTHER THAN THE CLERK, YOU MAY BE LIABLE TO PAY AGAIN.

TO THE CREDITOR, THE DEBTOR AND THE GARNISHEE:

Any party may make a motion to determine any matter in relation to this notice of garnishment.

____
(Date)

____
(Signature of Clerk)

____
(Address of court office)

THIS NOTICE SHALL BE SERVED TOGETHER WITH THE NOTICE TO GARNISHEE.

O. Reg. 295/99, s. 1.

App 4-19

Form 20H

Notice of Examination

Superior Court of Justice
Toronto Small Claims Court

Claim No. /

Creditor

Full name OMNI BANK OF CANADA
Address for Service (*street and number, city, postal code*)
Phone No. Fax No. (If any)
Creditor's Lawyer/Agent (Full Name) ADAM & ZENA
Lawyer/Agent's Address for Service 281 McLeod Street, Toronto, Ontario M5C 3C5
Lawyer/Agent's Phone No. (416) 995-9595 Fax No. (If any) (416) 995-9696

Debtor

Full name JEFF SMITH
Address for Service (*street and number, city, postal code*) 454 Westmount Drive Toronto, Ontario M4V 3P3
Phone No. (416) 869-5324 Fax No. (If any)
Debtor's Lawyer/Agent (Full Name)
Lawyer/Agent's Address for Service
Lawyer/Agent's Phone No. Fax No. (If any)

TO: Jeff Smith
(name of person to be summoned)

On July 30, 2001, the plaintiff recovered judgment against Jeff Smith
(Date) (name of person/ party against whom judgment was made)

in the Toronto Small Claims Court for $ 9,675.00 and $ 150.00 costs.
(name of court)

The judgment remains outstanding.

YOU ARE REQUIRED TO ATTEND AN EXAMINATION to determine the means
Jeff Smith
(name of defendant)

has to satisfy this judgment and whether Jeff Smith
intends to satisfy it or *has* any reason for not doing so.

THE EXAMINATION WILL BE HELD at the next sitting of this court at _____
(location of court)

on ____________________ at ____________________
(Date) (Time)

TAKE NOTICE THAT IF YOU DO NOT ATTEND AS REQUIRED BY THIS NOTICE OR YOU REFUSE TO ANSWER QUESTIONS, THE COURT MAY FIND YOU IN CONTEMPT OF COURT AND ORDER YOU TO ATTEND FOR A CONTEMPT HEARING.

____________________ ____________________
(Date) (Signature of Clerk)

App 4-20

Form 20I

Notice of Contempt Hearing

Court File No:

SUPERIOR COURT OF JUSTICE
TORONTO SMALL CLAIMS COURT

BETWEEN:

OMNI BANK OF CANADA

Plaintiff

- and -

JEFF SMITH

Defendant

NOTICE OF CONTEMPT HEARING

TAKE NOTICE:

That an order for a contempt hearing has been made against you for:

(a) failure to attend as required by the notice of examination; or

(b) refusal to answer questions at the examination

The contempt hearing is to be held at ____________________ on _____________
(Address) (Date)

on ___ beginning at _______________
(Date) (Time)

If you fail to attend this contempt hearing, the court may:

(a) order that you attend at an examination;

(b) make an order as to payment; or

(c) order that you be jailed for a period not exceeding 40 days.

__________________________ __________________________________
(Date) (Signature of Clerk)

App 4-21

Form 20J

Warrant of Commital

Court File No:

SUPERIOR COURT OF JUSTICE
TORONTO SMALL CLAIMS COURT

BETWEEN:

OMNI BANK OF CANADA

Plaintiff

- and -

JEFF SMITH

Defendant

WARRANT OF COMMITTAL

TO ALL POLICE OFFICERS IN ONTARIO

AND TO THE OFFICERS OF ALL CORRECTIONAL INSTITUTIONS IN ONTARIO:

A NOTICE OF CONTEMPT HEARING was issued from this court by which

JEFF SMITH

(Name of person required to attend Contempt Hearing)

was required to attend the sittings of this court at 10:00 o'clock in the forenoon
(time)

on September 4, 2001
(date)

WHEREAS it has been duly proved that the notice of contempt hearing has been

properly served on JEFF SMITH
(name)

WHEREAS (state facts relating to failure to attend or refusal to answer questions)

JEFF SMITH failed to attend at the hearing at 10:00 o'clock in the forenoon on September 4, 2001

WHEREAS a judge of this court thereupon ordered JEFF SMITH to be committed.
(name)

YOU ARE ORDERED to take the person named above to the nearest correctional

institution and admit and detain him or her there for 2 days.

This Warrant expires twelve (12) months from the date of issue, unless renewed by court order.

______________________ ______________________
(Date) (Signature of Clerk)

App 4-22

Notice of Motion for Consolidation Order

Court File No:

SUPERIOR COURT OF JUSTICE
TORONTO SMALL CLAIMS COURT

BETWEEN:

OMNI BANK OF CANADA

Plaintiff

- and -

JEFF SMITH

Defendant

NOTICE OF MOTION

TAKE NOTICE:

A motion will be made to the court by the defendant,Jeff Smith at
(Name of party)
the Court House, 2 Richmond Street, Toronto, Ontario on September 20, 2001
(Name and location of court) (Date)

at 10:00 o'clock in the forenoon (or so soon thereafter as the motion can be heard)
(Time)

for the following order: (Specify)

For a Consolidation Order, consolidating the orders for payment obtained against me in this court.

The following material will be relied on at the hearing of the motion: (Specify, and where an affidavit is to be relied on, attach a copy.)

The Affidavit of Jeff Smith

TAKE NOTICE: If you fail to appear at the hearing of this motion, an order may be made in your absence.

______________________ ______________________________
(Date) (Signature of party or party's lawyer/agent)

App 4-23

Affidavit in Support of Motion for Consolidation Order

Court File No:

SUPERIOR COURT OF JUSTICE
TORONTO SMALL CLAIMS COURT

BETWEEN:

OMNI BANK OF CANADA

Plaintiff

- and -

JEFF SMITH

Defendant

AFFIDAVIT

I, Jeff Smith, **of theCity of Toronto, in the Regional Municipality of Toronto**
(full name) (City, Town, etc.) (County, Regional Municipality)

MAKE OATH AND SAY (or AFFIRM)

(Give facts in support of the motion. If the facts are not within your own personal knowledge, give the source of your information or the grounds for your belief.)

1. Judgment was obtained against me by the Plaintiff, Omni Bank of Canada, in action number 6543/2000 in the Small Claims Court at Toronto on July 30, 2000. The amount that remains owing under that Judgment is $10,162.06. A Notice of Garnishment was issued against my wages.

2. Judgment was also obtained against me in action number 1032/99 in the Small Claims Court at London on April 22, 199 on behalf of Roy Wright & Associates Inc. and the balance outstanding on that Judgment is $2,432.00.

3. I am employed by Albert's Meat Market in the City of London. My take-home pay is $325.00 per week and I have no other source of income.

4. My monthly expenses are as follows:

Rent	$300.00
Food	400.00
Car Payment	175.00
Clothing, gas, insurance	100.00
Entertainment	75.00
Proposed payment under Consolidation Order	150.00
TOTAL MONTHLY EXPENSES	$1200.00

5. I request that an Order be made for Consolidation of the Debts, ordering that I am to make a payment in the amount of $150.00 per month to the Small Claims Court.

SWORN (or AFFIRMED) BEFORE ME)
at the City of Toronto, in the Regional)
Municipality of Toronto, this day of)
September, 2001)
) ______________________________
) JEFF SMITH

A COMMISSIONER FOR TAKING AFFIDAVITS (or as may be)

WARNING IT IS A CRIMINAL OFFENCE TO KNOWINGLY SWEAR A FALSE AFFIDAVIT

Appendix 5

Precedents Relating to

Chapter 5

Collection from Deceased Estates
Precedents

App 5-1

Notice of Motion to Appoint an Estate Trustee During Litigation

Court file no.

ONTARIO
SUPERIOR COURT OF JUSTICE

IN THE ESTATE OF JEFF SMITH
LATE OF THE CITY OF TORONTO, IN THE MUNICIPALITY OF METROPOLITAN TORONTO
SALES MANAGER, DECEASED.

NOTICE OF MOTION

OMNI BANK OF CANADA will make a motion to a Judge of the Superior Court of Justice on Wednesday, the 18th day of July, 2001 at 10:00 o'clock in the forenoon, or as soon after that time as the motion can be heard, at the Court House, 361 University Avenue, Toronto, Ontario.

THE MOTION is for an order appointing Snyder Trust Company or such other person as this court deems appropriate as estate trustee during litigation of the estate of the late Jeff Smith.

THE GROUNDS FOR THE MOTION ARE that Susan Smith, appointed as estate trustee under certificate of appointment issued by the Superior Court of Justice for the Municipality of Metropolitan Toronto on the 25th day of March, 2001, has passed away and the last will and testament of Jeff Smith made no provision for the appointment of an alternate estate trustee. As a result, there is no estate trustee able to administer this estate pending the outcome of these proceedings.

THE FOLLOWING DOCUMENTARY EVIDENCE will be used at the hearing of the motion:

1. the affidavit of Zita Jones sworn on the 4th day of July, 2001
2. the consent of Snyder Trust Company

Date: July 4, 2001

ADAM & ZENA
Barristers & Solicitors
281 McLeod Street
Toronto, Ontario
M5C 3C5
tel: (416) 995-9595
fax: (416) 995-9696
Solicitors for the Plaintiff

To: CHILDS & ELLIOTT
1992 Kingfisher Avenue
Toronto, Ontario
M4L 9S2
(416) 596-9674
Jordan F. Childs
Solicitors for the estate of Jeff Smith

App 5-2

Consent of Proposed Estate Trustee

Court File No:

ONTARIO

SUPERIOR COURT OF JUSTICE

BETWEEN:

OMNI BANK OF CANADA

Plaintiff

- and -

JEFF SMITH

Defendant

CONSENT

SNYDER TRUST COMPANY, having no interest adverse to Jeff Smith, deceased, or his estate, hereby consents to act as estate trustee during litigation of the estate of Jeff Smith, in the above action.

DATED at Toronto this 18th day of May, 2001

SNYDER TRUST COMPANY

Per:______________________________
Harold Lobb

App 5-3

Consent of Beneficiary

Court File No.

ONTARIO
SUPERIOR COURT OF JUSTICE

IN THE ESTATE OF JEFF SMITH
LATE OF THE CITY OF TORONTO, IN THE MUNICIPALITY OF METROPOLITAN TORONTO
SALES MANAGER, DECEASED.

CONSENT OF BENEFICIARY

I, **JUDY J. SMITH**, hereby consent to the appointment of Snyder Trust Company to act as estate trustee during litigation of the estate of Jeff Smith.

DATED at Toronto this 13th day of May, 2001

____
JUDY SMITH

App 5-4

Order Appointing Estate Trustee during Litigation

Court File No.

ONTARIO
SUPERIOR COURT OF JUSTICE

THE HONOURABLE JUDGE	)	**WEDNESDAY, THE 18TH DAY OF**
	)	
A.B. STIRLING	)	**JULY, 2001**

IN THE ESTATE OF JEFF SMITH
LATE OF THE CITY OF TORONTO, IN THE MUNICIPALITY OF METROPOLITAN TORONTO
SALES MANAGER, DECEASED.

ORDER

THIS MOTION, made by Omni Bank of Canada, for the appointment of an estate trustee during litigation, was heard this day, at the Court House, 361 University Avenue, Toronto, Ontario.

ON READING the affidavit of George Goodman sworn on the 30th day of June, 2001, filed, and on reading the Consent of Snyder Trust Company, filed, and on hearing submission of counsel for the applicant,

1. **THIS COURT ORDERS** that Snyder Trust Company be and is here by appointed estate trustee during litigation of the property of the deceased, Jeff Smith, pending the disposition or settlement of the proceedings now pending in this court considering the validity of the Last Will and Testament of the deceased, Jeff Smith, dated August 27, 1994.

2. **THIS COURT ORDERS** that Snyder Trust Company, as estate trustee during litigation of the estate of Jeff Smith, is hereby authorized to exercise those powers provided to the executors and trustees under the following Last Will and Testament of the late Jeff Smith, dated the 27th day of August, 1994 namely:

[Set Out Powers]

3. **THIS COURT DECLARES** that attached as schedule "A" to this Order is the Last Will and Testament of the deceased, Jeff Smith, dated the 27th day of August, 1994.

4. **THIS COURT ORDERS** that Snyder Trust Company be at liberty to appoint an agent or agents and obtain such assistance from time to time as it may consider necessary for the purpose of performing its duties as estate trustee during litigation of the estate of the late Jeff Smith.

5. **THIS COURT ORDERS** that the costs of all parties to this motion be assessed on a solicitor and client basis out of the estate of Jeff Smith, deceased.

____

App 5-5

Notice of Motion for Appointment of a Litigation Administrator

Court File No:

SUPERIOR COURT OF JUSTICE

BETWEEN:

OMNI BANK OF CANADA

Plaintiff

- and -

JEFF SMITH

Defendant

NOTICE OF MOTION

OMNI BANK OF CANADA. will make a motion to a Judge on Wednesday, the 11th day of July, 2001 or as soon after that time as the motion can be heard at 361 University Avenue, Toronto, Ontario.

THE MOTION IS FOR:

1. an order appointing Snyder Trust Company as litigation administrator representing the estate of the defendant, Jeff Smith, now deceased, for the purposes of the proceeding herein;

2. such other relief as this Honourable Court deems just.

THE GROUNDS FOR THE MOTION ARE:

1. the defendant, Jeff Smith, died during the course of this proceeding on or about January 6, 2001;

2. a certificate of appointment of estate trustee has been granted by the Superior Court of Justice in the Municipality of Metropolitan Toronto, in the estate of Jeff Smith, deceased, in favour of Susan Smith, who passed away on the 16th day of March, 2001 prior to the estate being fully administered.

3. Rule 9.02(1) of the Rules of Civil Procedure.

THE FOLLOWING DOCUMENTARY EVIDENCE will be heard at the hearing of the motion:

1. the affidavit of Rita Haydon and the exhibits attached thereto, sworn the 30th day of June, 2001.

2. such further and other material as counsel may advise.

Date: July 4, 2001

ADAM & ZENA
Barristers & Solicitors
281 McLeod Street
Toronto, Ontario
M5C 3C5
tel: (416) 995-9595
fax: (416) 995-9696
Solicitors for the Plaintiff

TO: CHILDS & ELLIOTT
1992 Kingfisher Avenue
Toronto, Ontario
M4L 9S2
(416) 596-9674
Jordan F. Childs
Solicitors for the estate of Jeff Smith

App 5-6

Order Appointing Litigation Administrator

SUPERIOR COURT OF JUSTICE

THE HONOURABLE JUDGE	)	**WEDNESDAY, THE 11TH DAY OF**
	)	
A.B. STIRLING	)	**JULY, 2001**

BETWEEN:

OMNI BANK OF CANADA

Plaintiff

- and -

JEFF SMITH

Defendant

ORDER

THIS MOTION, made by Omni Bank of Canada for the appointment of a litigation administrator, was heard this day, at 361 University Avenue, Toronto, Ontario.;

ON READING the affidavit of Rita Haydon sworn on the 30th day of June, 2001, filed, and on hearing the submissions of counsel for the plaintiff and the defendant,

1. **THIS COURT ORDERS** that Snyder Trust Company be and is hereby appointed litigation administrator representing the estate of the defendant, Jeff Smith, deceased, for the purposes of the proceeding herein.

2. **THIS COURT ORDERS** that Snyder Trust Company be at liberty to appoint an agent or agents and obtain such assistance from time to time as it may consider necessary for the purpose of performing its duties as litigation administrator for the purposes of the proceeding against the late Jeff Smith.

3. **THIS COURT ORDERS** that the costs of all parties to this motion be assessed on a solicitor and client basis out of the estate of Jeff Smith, deceased.

____

App 5-7
Requistion for an Order Transferring Liability to the Deceased Estate

Court File No:

SUPERIOR COURT OF JUSTICE

BETWEEN:

OMNI BANK OF CANADA

Plaintiff

- and -

JEFF SMITH

Defendant

REQUISITION

TO THE REGISTRAR at Toronto

I REQUIRE:

An order to continue the above proceeding originally commenced in this Court amending the title of proceedings to name Omni Bank of Canada, as plaintiff and Snyder Trust Company, litigation administrator of the estate of Jeff Smith, deceased, as defendant

THE GROUNDS FOR THIS REQUEST ARE:

1. The affidavit of Zita Jones and

2. The order of The Honourable Justice A.B. Stirling of the Superior Court of Justice dated the 11th day of July, 2001 appointing Snyder Trust Company as the litigation administrator for the estate of Jeff Smith, deceased, in the within proceeding.

3. Rule 11.02(1) of the Rules of Civil Procedure.

Date: July 4, 2001

ADAM & ZENA
Barristers & Solicitors
281 McLeod Street
Toronto, Ontario
M5C 3C5
tel: (416) 995-9595
fax: (416) 995-9696
Solicitors for the Plaintiff

App 5-8

Affidavit Verifying the Transmission of Interest

Court File No:

SUPERIOR COURT OF JUSTICE

BETWEEN:

OMNI BANK OF CANADA

Plaintiff

- and -

JEFF SMITH

Defendant

AFFIDAVIT

I, **ZITA JONES**, of the City of Toronto, in the Province of Ontario, solicitor, MAKE OATH AND SAY:

1. I am a solicitor in the law firm of Messrs. Adam & Zena, solicitors for the plaintiff in the above action and as such have knowledge of the matters hereinafter deposed to.

2. On or about the 14th day of January, 2000, Adam & Zena commenced the within action on behalf of the plaintiff against the defendant, now deceased.

3. On or about the __________ day of ________________. the defendant passed away.

4. On the _______ day of _____________. 2001, this Court heard a motion for an order requesting that Snyder Trust Company be appointed litigation administrator to represent the deceased's estate in this proceeding. The order was granted by the Honourable Justice A.B. Stirling of this court. Attached hereto and marked as Exhibit "A" is a true copy of the above order issued and entered.

5. The solicitors now request that the registrar grant an order continuing this proceeding naming Snyder Trust Company, litigation administrator of the estate of Jeff Smith, as defendant.

SWORN BEFORE ME at the	)	
City of Toronto, in the	)	
Province of Ontario, this	)	
day of , 2001	)	
	)	______________________________
	)	**ZITA JONES**
A Commissioner, etc.	)	

App 5-9

Order Transferring Liability to the Deceased Estate

Court File No:

SUPERIOR COURT OF JUSTICE

BETWEEN:

OMNI BANK OF CANADA

Plaintiff

- and -

JEFF SMITH

Defendant

ORDER TRANSFERRING LIABILITY

ON THE REQUISITION of the plaintiff and on reading the affidavit of Zita Jones, filed, and on reading the order of the Honourable Justice A.B. Stirling, filed, dated ______________________ whereby this Court ordered that Snyder Trust Company be appointed litigation administrator of the estate of Jeff Smith, deceased, for the purposes of the proceeding herein.

IT IS ORDERED that this proceeding continue with Omni Bank of Canada as plaintiff and Snyder Trust Company, as litigation administrator for the estate of Jeff Smith and that the title of proceeding be amended accordingly in all documents issued, served or filed after the date of this order.

Dated: _________________________

____
Local Registrar

App 5-10

Notice of Contestation

Court File No.

ONTARIO
SUPERIOR COURT OF JUSTICE

IN THE ESTATE OF JEFF SMITH
LATE OF THE CITY OF TORONTO, IN THE MUNICIPALITY OF METROPOLITAN TORONTO
SALES MANAGER, DECEASED

B E T W E E N :

SNYDER TRUST COMPANY

Estate Trustee

– and –

WALTER REID HOSPITAL

Claimant

NOTICE OF CONTESTATION

Pursuant to section 44 or 45 of the *Estates Act*, the estate trustee of the estate contests the claim made by you against the estate, on the following grounds:

(*state grounds*)

You may apply to this court at (*insert address of court office*) for an order allowing your claim and determining its amount. If you do not apply within 30 days after receiving this notice, or within 3 months after that date if the judge on application so allows, you shall be deemed to have abandoned your claim and your claim shall be forever barred.

DATE:

(*Name, address and telephone number of estate trustee or solicitor for estate trustee*)

TO: (*Name and address of person submitting claim*)

O. Reg. 484/94, s. 13; O. Reg. 292/99, s. 1(3, 4).

App 5-11

Claim Against Estate

Court File No.

ONTARIO
SUPERIOR COURT OF JUSTICE

**IN THE ESTATE OF JEFF SMITH
LATE OF THE CITY OF TORONTO, IN THE MUNICIPALITY
OF METROPOLITAN TORONTO
SALES MANAGER, DECEASED**

BETWEEN:

SAM'S ABC MUSIC LTD.

Claimant

– and –

**SNYDER TRUST COMPANY, ESTATE TRUSTEE OF
THE ESTATE OF JEFF SMITH, DECEASED**

Estate Trustee

CLAIM AGAINST ESTATE

1. The claim against the estate is for:

(a) $11,500.00 being the cost of the goods as set out in the purchase agreement between the claimant and the deceased;

(b) Pre- and post-judgment interest pursuant to sections 128 and 129 of the *Courts of Justice Act,* R.S.O. 1990, c. C.43;

(c) Its costs in this action; and

(d) Such further and other relief as this Honourable Court may deem just.

2. The claimant is a company duly incorporated pursuant to the laws of the Province of Ontario and carries on business as a supplier of musical instruments in the City of Toronto.

3. Snyder Trust Company is the estate trustee of the late Jeff Smith, of the City of Toronto, in the Province of Ontario, deceased.

4. By agreement dated the 20th day of January, 2001 the late Jeff Smith ("the deceased") agreed to purchase from Sam's ABC Music Ltd. two Stratocastrer Guitars ("the goods") at a total cost of $11,500.00.

5. Sam's ABC Music Ltd. delivered the goods to the deceased on or about the 25th day of January, 2001.

6. Sam's ABC Music Ltd. has not received any payment for the goods and the entire balance of $11,500.00 remains outstanding.

The claimant proposes this action to be tried at Toronto.

February 28, 2001

PHILIPS & WYNN
Barristers & Solicitors
1112 Broad Street
Toronto, Ontario
M8C 3Z5
tel: (416) 995-1212
Attention: Harry Philips

App 5-12

Affidavit in Support of Claim

Court File No.

ONTARIO
SUPERIOR COURT OF JUSTICE

IN THE ESTATE OF JEFF SMITH
LATE OF THE CITY OF TORONTO, IN THE MUNICIPALITY
OF METROPOLITAN TORONTO
SALES MANAGER, DECEASED.

BETWEEN:

SAM'S ABC MUSIC LTD.

Claimant

– and –

SNYDER TRUST COMPANY, ESTATE TRUSTEE OF
THE ESTATE OF JEFF SMITH, DECEASED

Estate Trustee

AFFIDAVIT

I, **GEORGE GOODMAN**, of the City of Toronto, in the Province of Ontario, make oath and say:

1. I am an office manager of Sam's ABC Music Ltd., the claimant in the within action, and as such have knowledge of the matters hereinafter deposed to.

2. The grounds set out in this claim are true.

SWORN BEFORE ME at the City of)
Toronto, in the Province of Ontario)
this day of , 2001)
)
) _______________________________
) **GEORGE GOODMAN**
A Commissioner, etc.)

App 5-13

Request for Assignment of Mediator

FORM 75.1A

Courts of Justice Act

Court File No:

ONTARIO

SUPERIOR COURT OF JUSTICE

IN THE ESTATE OF JEFF SMTIH, deceased,
late of the City of Toronto, in the Province of Ontario,
general contractor, occupation
who died on March 25, 2001

REQUEST FOR ASSIGNMENT OF MEDIATOR

TO: Mediation co-ordinator for Toronto

An order giving directions was made under rule 75.1.05 on (*date of order*). A copy of the order is attached to this request.

The designated parties have not chosen a mediator under subrule 75.1.06 (1). The 30-day period mentioned in subrule 75.1.07 (1) has expired.

This is a request that you assign a mediator from the list for the county.

(*Date*)

(Name, address, telephone number and fax number, if any, of lawyer or party filing request, or of party)

O. Reg. 290/99, s. 5.

App 5-14

Notice by Mediator

FORM 75.1B
Courts of Justice Act

Court file no.

ONTARIO
SUPERIOR COURT OF JUSTICE

IN THE ESTATE OF JEFF SMITH deceased,
late of the City of Toronto, in the Province of Ontario,
general contractor, occupation,
who died on March 25, 2001

NOTICE BY MEDIATOR

TO:

AND TO:

I am the mediator whom the mediation co-ordinator has appointed to conduct the mediation session under Rule 75.1. (*Delete this paragraph if mediator was chosen by designated parties under clause 75.1.06 (1) (a) or (c).*)

The mediation session will take place on (*date*), from (*time*) to (*time*), at (*place*).

You are required to attend this mediation session. If you have a lawyer representing you in this proceeding, he or she is also required to attend.

You are required to file a statement of issues (Form 75.1C) by (*date*) (seven days before the mediation session). A blank copy of the form is attached.

When you attend the mediation session, you should bring with you any documents that you consider of central importance in the proceeding. You should plan to remain throughout the scheduled time. If you need another person's approval before agreeing to a settlement, you should make arrangements before the mediation session to ensure that you have ready telephone access to that person throughout the session, even outside regular business hours.

YOU MAYBE PENALIZED UNDER RULE 75.1.10 IF YOU FAIL TO FILE A STATEMENT OF ISSUES OR FAIL TO ATTEND THE MEDIATION SESSION.
(*Date*) (*Name, address, telephone number and fax number, if any, of mediator*)

O. Reg. 290/99, s. 5.

App 5-15

Statement of Issues

Court file no.

ONTARIO
SUPERIOR COURT OF JUSTICE

IN THE ESTATE OF JEFF SMTIH, deceased,
late of the City of Toronto, in the Province of Ontario,
general contractor, occupation
who died on March 25, 2001

STATEMENT OF ISSUES

(*To be provided to mediator and designated parties at least seven days before the mediation session*)

1. Factual and legal issues in dispute

The undersigned designated party states that the following factual and legal issues are in dispute and remain to be resolved.

(*Issues should be stated briefly and numbered consecutively.*)

2. Party's position and interests (what the party hopes to achieve)

(*Brief summary.*)

3. Attached documents

Attached to this form are the following documents that the designated party considers of central importance in the proceeding: (*list*)

(*date*)

(*party's signature*)
(*Name, address, telephone number and fax number, if any, of lawyer of party filing statement of issues, or of party*)

NOTE: Rule 75.1.11 provides as follows:

All communications at a mediation session and the mediator's notes and records shall be deemed to be without prejudice settlement discussions.

O. Reg. 290/99, s. 5.

Appendix 6

Precedents Relating to Chapter 6

Statutory Remedies Precedents

App 6-1

Statement of Claim for Fradulent Conveyance Action

Court File No.

SUPERIOR COURT OF JUSTICE

BETWEEN:

ALBERT HOLMES

Plaintiff

- and -

576 ONTARIO INC., ROBERT SMITH and ALBERTA SMITH

Defendants

STATEMENT OF CLAIM

TO THE DEFENDANTS

A LEGAL PROCEEDING HAS BEEN COMMENCED AGAINST YOU by the Plaintiff. The claim made against you is set out in the following pages.

IF YOU WISH TO DEFEND THIS PROCEEDING, you or an Ontario Lawyer acting for you must prepare a statement of defence in Form 18A prescribed by the Rules of Civil Procedure, serve it on the plaintiff's lawyer or, where the plaintiff does not have a lawyer, serve it on the plaintiff, and file it, with proof of service, in the Court Office, WITHIN TWENTY DAYS after this statement of claim is served on you, if you are served in Ontario.

If you are served in another province or territory of Canada or in the United States of America, the period for serving and filing your statement of defence is forty days. If you are served outside Canada and the United States of America, the period is sixty days.

Instead of serving and filing a statement of defence, you may serve and file a notice of intent to defend in Form 18B prescribed by the Rules of Civil Procedure. This will entitle you to ten more days within which to serve and file your statement of defence.

IF YOU FAIL TO DEFEND THIS PROCEEDING, JUDGMENT MAY BE GIVEN AGAINST YOU IN YOUR ABSENCE AND WITHOUT FURTHER NOTICE TO YOU. IF YOU WISH TO DEFEND THIS PROCEEDING BUT ARE UNABLE TO PAY LEGAL FEES, LEGAL AID MAY BE AVAILABLE TO YOU BY CONTACTING A LOCAL LEGAL AID OFFICE.

Date:

Issued by ______________________
Local Registrar

Address of Court Office:
80 Dundas Street
London, Ontario

TO: 576 Ontario Inc.
(address)

AND TO: ROBERT SMITH
(address)

AND TO: ALBERTA SMITH
(address)

CLAIM

1. The Plaintiff claims:

(a) A declaration that the conveyance of the lands from 576 Ontario Inc. to Alberta Smith under Instrument No. 12457 in the Land Registry Division of Middlesex East (No. 33) is fraudulent and void as against the Plaintiff and other creditors of 576 Ontario Inc., pursuant to the *Fraudulent Conveyances Act,* R.S.O. 1990, c. F.29;

(b) A declaration that the lands as described in Instrument No. 12457 are subject to execution at the instance of the Plaintiff as a creditor of 576 Ontario Inc.;

(c) That a Certificate of Pending Litigation be issued and registered against the lands set out in Instrument No. 12457;

(d) Cost of this action on a solicitor and client basis;

(e) Such further and other relief as this Honourable Court deems just.

2. The Plaintiff, Albert Holmes, at all material times resided in the City of London, in the County of Middlesex, in the Province of Ontario.

3. The Defendants, Robert Smith and Alberta Smith, at all material times resided in the City of London, in the County of Middlesex in the Province of Ontario.

4. The Defendant, 576 Ontario Inc., is a company incorporated pursuant to the laws of the Province of Ontario having its head office in the City of London, in the Province of Ontario.

5. The Defendant, 576 Ontario Inc., mortgaged property in the City of London, in the County of Middlesex, to the Plaintiff, Albert Holmes, under a mortgage dated the 25th day of March, 1999. The mortgage was guaranteed by Robert Smith.

6. The said mortgage went into default on or about the 25th day of February, 2000 and the Plaintiff issued a Statement of Claim for payment of the amounts due under the covenant contained in the mortgage on the 1st day of March, 2000.

7. Judgment was obtained by the Plaintiff against the Defendant, 576 Ontario Inc., on the 1st day of April, 2000 for the sum of $85,271.50 and $785.00 for taxed costs. Judgment was obtained against Robert Smith as a Guarantor on the 1st day of April, 2000 for the sum of $85,271.50 and $785.00 for taxed costs.

8. Writs of Seizure and Sale were filed with the Sheriff of the County of Middlesex in respect of both judgments.

9. The Defendant, 576 Ontario Inc., was until the 21st day of March, 2000, the sole registered owner of certain lands and premises described below subject only to a first mortgage in favour of Grant Mortgage Company and a second mortgage in favour of Jackson Investments Ltd. The following is a description of the lands as set out in Instrument No. 12457 in the Land Registry Division of Middlesex East (No. 33):

> Those lands and premises located in the following municipality, namely in the City of London, in the County of Middlesex, in the Province of Ontario and being composed of the whole of Lot #22 according to Registered Plan No. 468 for the said City of London. Property Identifier No. 12345-6789.

10. By Deed dated the 21st day of March, 2000 and registered as Instrument No. 12457 in the Land Registry Division of Middlesex East (No. 33) the Defendant, 576 Ontario Inc., transferred the lands described above to Alberta Smith. The Affidavit of Value and Consideration in Instrument No. 12457 indicates that the purchaser Alberta Smith assumed the first mortgage in the amount of $44,000.00 and the second mortgage in the amount of $28,500.00.

11. The property in question is a 5 unit apartment building located at 1750 Bank Street, London, Ontario, at the time that 576 Ontario Inc. owned the property the Defendants, Robert Smith and Alberta Smith, resided in one unit of the building. All of the other units were rented. After the transfer of the property from 576 Ontario Inc. to Alberta Smith, the Defendants, Robert Smith and Alberta Smith, continued to reside in their unit. The defendants, Robert Smith and Alberta Smith continue to manage the property and collect the rents from the tenants.

12. The Plaintiff states and the fact is that the said conveyance had the effect of removing the property described above out of the reach of the Plaintiff and other creditors by way of execution, and that the said conveyance was made with the intent of defeating, hindering, delaying or defrauding the Plaintiff and as such is void against the Plaintiff and all other creditors of the Defendant, 576 Ontario Inc. Further, the Plaintiff states and the fact is that the conveyance was not bona fide to a person without notice and knowledge of the said intention of the Defendant, 576 Ontario Inc., and there was no consideration or inadequate consideration for the said conveyance.

13. The Plaintiff states and the fact is that the Defendant, Robert Smith, was residing on the premises known as 1750 Bank Street, London, Ontario when the said lands were owned by 576 Ontario Inc., and the said Defendant, Robert Smith, is an officer, director and shareholder of the Defendant corporation, 576 Ontario Inc. The Defendant, Robert Smith, is also indebted to the Plaintiff under a Judgment and this Defendant has continued to enjoy this asset, previously owned by the Defendant, 576 Ontario Inc., while ensuring that the asset was out of the reach of the creditors of 576 Ontario Inc.

14. The Plaintiff states and the fact is that the property is presently listed for sale with ABC Realty Ltd. for the sum of $425,00.00 while the two outstanding mortgages total $72,500.00.

15. The Plaintiff's Judgment remains outstanding as of this date.

16. The Plaintiff pleads and relies on the provisions of the *Fraudulent Conveyances* Act, R.S.O. 1990, c. F:29.

The Plaintiff proposes that this action be tried in the City of London.

DATED: May 10th, 2000

ADAM & ZENA
Barristers and Solicitors
281 McLeod Street
London, Ontario
N6P 9X4

Joe Adam
(519) 666-0000

App 6-2

Notice of Motion for Certificate of Pending Litigation

Court File No.

SUPERIOR COURT OF JUSTICE

BETWEEN:

ALBERT HOLMES

Plaintiff

- and -

576 ONTARIO INC., ROBERT SMITH and ALBERTA SMITH

Defendants

NOTICE OF MOTION

THE PLAINTIFF will make a motion to a Judge on Monday, the 1st day of June, 2001, at 10:00 o'clock in the forenoon, or as soon after that time as the motion can be heard, at the Court House, 80 Dundas Street, London, Ontario.

PROPOSED METHOD OF HEARING: The motion is to be heard
__X__ in writing under subrule 37.12.1(1) because it is made without notice;
_____ in writing as an opposed motion under subrule 37.12.1(4);
_____ orally.

THE MOTION IS FOR an Order granting leave to the Plaintiff to issue and register a Certificate of Pending Litigation against the title of the lands described as follows:

> "Those lands and premises located in the following municipality, in the City of London, in the County of Middlesex, and being composed of the whole of Lot #22 according to Registered Plan No. 468 for the said City of London, Property Identifier Number 12345-6789."

THE GROUNDS FOR THE MOTION ARE:
(a) the *Fraudulent Conveyances Act,* R.S.O. 1990, c. F.29;
(b) the *Assignments and Preferences Act,* R.S.O. 1990, c. A.33.

THE FOLLOWING DOCUMENTARY EVIDENCE will be used at the hearing of the motion:
(a) the pleadings and proceedings herein;
(b) the Affidavit of Zita Jones, filed;
(c) such further and other material as counsel may advise and this Honourable Court permit

DATED: May 18, 2001

ADAMS & ZENA
281 McLeod Street
London, Ontario
N5P 1L8
Joe Adam
(519) 666-6666

App 6-3

Order re Certificate of Pending Litigation

Court File No.

SUPERIOR COURT OF JUSTICE

THE HONOURABLE JUSTICE	)	**TUESDAY, THE 18TH DAY OF**
	)	
A.B. STIRLING	)	**OF JUNE, 2000**

BETWEEN:

ALBERT HOLMES

Plaintiff

- and -

576 ONTARIO INC., ROBERT SMITH and ALBERTA SMITH

Defendants

ORDER

THIS MOTION made by the Plaintiff for an Order granting leave to the Plaintiff to issue and register a Certificate of Pending Litigation against the title to the lands described below was heard this day, at London.

ON READING the pleadings and proceedings herein, the Affidavit of Zita Jones, filed, and on healing the submissions of counsel for the Plaintiff:

1. **THIS COURT ORDERS** that the Plaintiff shall have leave to issue and register a Certificate of Pending Litigation against the title of the property described as follows:

> "Those lands and premises located in the following municipality, in the City of London, in the County of Middlesex, and being composed of the whole of Lot # 22, according to Registered Plan No. 468, for the said City of London, Property Identifier Number 12345-6789.

____

App 6-4

Certificate of Pending Litigation

Court File No.

SUPERIOR COURT OF JUSTICE

BETWEEN:

ALBERT HOLMES

Plaintiff

- and -

576 ONTARIO INC., ROBERT SMITH and ALBERTA SMITH

Defendants

CERTIFICATE OF PENDING LITIGATION

I CERTIFY that in this proceeding an interest in the following lands is in question:

> Those lands and premises located in the following municipality, namely in the City of London, in the County of Middlesex, Province of Ontario, and being composed of the whole of Lot # 22 according to Registered Plan No. 468, for the said City of London, Property Identifier Number 12345-6789.

This Certificate is issued under an Order of the Court made on Tuesday, the 18th day of June, 2000.

DATED: June 29, 2000 Issued by: ______________________________

Local Registrar

Address of
Court Office: 80 Dundas Street
London, Ontario
N6A 1E7

App 6-5

Notice of Application for Exemption Order under Bulk Sales Act

Court File No:

SUPERIOR COURT OF JUSTICE

IN THE MATTER OF THE SALE IN BULK OF THE ASSETS OF WORMAN MENSWARE LTD. (THE "VENDOR") TO HARRY AGULNIK HABERDASHERY LTD. (THE "PURCHASER")

AND IN THE MATTER OF THE BULK SALES ACT, R.S.O. 1990, c. B-14.

BETWEEN:

WORMAN MENSWARE LTD.

Applicant

- and -

THE CREDITORS OF WORMAN MENSWARE LTTD.

Respondents

NOTICE OF APPLICATION

TO THE RESPONDENT:

A LEGAL PROCEEDING HAS BEEN COMMENCED by the Applicant. The claim made by the Applicant appears on the following page.

THIS APPLICATION will come on for a hearing before a Judge on , the day of , 2001, at 10:00 o'clock in the forenoon, or as soon after that time as the Application can be heard, at the Court House, 361 University Avenue, Toronto, Ontario.

IF YOU WISH TO OPPOSE THIS APPLICATION, you or an Ontario lawyer acting for you must forthwith prepare a notice of appearance in Form 38C prescribed by the Rules of Civil Procedure, serve it on the Applicant's lawyer or, where the Applicant does not have a lawyer, serve it on the Applicant, and file it, with proof of service, in this court office, and you or your lawyer must appear at the hearing.

IF YOU WISH TO PRESENT AFFIDAVIT OR OTHER DOCUMENTARY EVIDENCE TO THE COURT OR TO EXAMINE OR CROSS-EXAMINE WITNESSES ON THE APPLICATION, you or your lawyer must, in addition to serving your notice of appearance, serve a copy of the evidence on the Applicant's lawyer or, where the Applicant does not have a lawyer, serve it on the Applicant, and file it, with proof of service, in the court office where the application is to be heard as soon as possible, but not later than 2.00 p.m. on the day before the hearing.

IF YOU FAIL TO APPEAR AT THE HEARING, JUDGMENT MAY BE GIVEN IN YOUR ABSENCE AND WITHOUT FURTHER NOTICE TO YOU.

IF YOU WISH TO OPPOSE THIS APPLICATION but are unable to pay legal fees, legal aid may be available to you by contacting a local Legal Aid office.

Date: , 2001 Issued by ______________________

Local Registrar

Address of
court office: 361 University Avenue
Toronto, Ontario
M5G 1T3

TO: (Name and address of each creditor of the Applicant)

APPLICATION

1. The Applicant makes application for:

(a) an order exempting a sale in bulk from Worman Mensware Ltd. to Harry Agulnik Haberdashery Ltd. from the provisions of the Bulk Sales Act, R.S.O. 1990, c. B.14 (the "Act"), save section 7 thereof.

2. The grounds for the application are:

(a) The sale is advantageous to the seller, Worman Mensware Ltd. and will not impair the seller's ability to pay creditors in full.

(b) Section 3 of the Act.

3. The following documentary evidence will be used at the hearing of the application:

(a) the Affidavit of Bert Worman, filed, and the exhibits thereto.

(b) such further and other material as counsel may advise and this Honourable Court permit.

Date:

Christie & Harris
160 Parkway Drive
Toronto, Ontario
M9B 2L2
tel: (416) 922-5995
fax: (416) 992-6996
Ken Christie
Solicitors for the Applicant

App 6-6

Judgment Giving Exemption Order

Court File No:

SUPERIOR COURT OF JUSTICE

THE HONOURABLE JUSTICE	)	**DAY, THE DAY OF**
	)	
A.B. STIRLING	)	**, 2001**

IN THE MATTER OF THE SALE IN BULK OF THE ASSETS OF WORMAN MENSWARE LTD. (THE "VENDOR") TO HARRY AGULNIK HABERDASHERY LTD. (THE "PURCHASER")

AND IN THE MATTER OF THE BULK SALES ACT, R.S.O. 1990, c. B-14.

BETWEEN:

WORMAN MENSWARE LTD.

Applicant

- and -

THE CREDITORS OF WORMAN MENSWARE LTD.

Respondents

JUDGMENT

THIS APPLICATION was heard this day with notice in the presence of counsel for the Applicant, and the following Respondents, being creditors of Worman Mensware Ltd., no one opposing for the following creditors although served as evidenced by the Affidavit of Service of Ginette Bouchard on (name of creditors served)

ON READING the Notice of Application and the evidence filed by the parties, including the Affidavit of Bert Worman, filed, and on hearing the submissions of counsel for the Applicant, and Respondents in attendance:

1. **THIS COURT ORDERS** that the sale in bulk by Worman Mensware Ltd. to Harry Agulnik Haberdashery Ltd. be, and the same is hereby exempted from the application of the Bulk Sales Act, save Section 7 thereof.

____

App 6-7

Waiver of Creditor of Bulk Sales Act

Bulk Sales Act
(Section 8(1)(c))

Court File No:

SUPERIOR COURT OF JUSTICE

IN THE MATTER OF THE SALE IN BULK OF THE ASSETS OF WORMAN MENSWARE LTD. (THE "VENDOR") TO HARRY AGULNIK HABERDASHERY LTD. (THE "PURCHASER")

AND IN THE MATTER OF THE BULK SALES ACCT, R.S.O. 1990, c. B-14.

WAIVER

MORGAN ZIPPERS LTD., an unsecured trade creditor of the above-named Seller hereby waives the provisions of the Bulk Sales Act that requires that adequate provisions be made for the immediate payment in full of my claim forthwith after the completion of the sale, and I hereby acknowledge and agree that the Buyer may pay or deliver the proceeds of the sale to the Seller and thereupon acquire the property of the Seller in the stock without making provision for the immediate payment of my claim and that any right to recover payment of my claim may, unless otherwise agreed, be asserted against the Seller only.

DATED at Toronto, this 25th day of September, 2001.

MORGAN ZIPPERS LTD.

Per: ______________________________
HENRY MORGAN
I have authority to bind the corporation

App 6-8

Creditor's Consent to Sale and Appointment of Trustee

Bulk Sales Act
Section 8(2)(a) and 9(1)(a))

Court File No:

SUPERIOR COURT OF JUSTICE

IN THE MATTER OF THE SALE IN BULK OF THE ASSETS OF WORMAN MENSWARE LTD. (THE "VENDOR") TO HARRY AGULNIK HABERDASHERY LTD. (THE "PURCHASER")

AND IN THE MATTER OF THE BULK SALES ACT, R.S.O. 1990, c. B-14.

BETWEEN:

HARRY AGULNIK HABERDASHERY LTD.

(hereinafter called the "Purchaser")

- and -

WORMAN MENSWARE LTD.

(hereinafter called the "Vendor")

CONSENT

I, **LEON CURTIS**, of the City of Toronto, in the Province of Ontario, President of Sonia Linen Supplies Ltd., an unsecured trade creditor of the above-named Vendor, hereby acknowledge and agree:

1. That I have received,

(a) a copy of the statement showing the names and addresses of the unsecured trade creditors and the amount of the indebtedness or liability due, owing, payable or accruing due or to become due and payable by the Vendor, and showing the names and addresses of the secured trade creditors, the nature of their security and whether their claims are or, in the event of sale, become due on the date fixed for the completion of the sale, and the amount of the indebtedness or liability due, or owing, payable or accruing due or to become due and payable by the Vendor;

(b) a statement of the affairs of the Vendor; and

(c) a copy of the agreement of the sale in bulk.

2. That I consent to the sale; and

3. That I consent to the appointment of R. Martindale & Co. Ltd. as trustee.

DATED at Toronto, this 20th day of September, 2001.

WITNESS **SONIA LINEN SUPPLIES LTD.**

Per: ______________________________
LEON CURTIS
I have authority to bind the corporation

App 6-9

Bulk Sales Act

STATEMENT AS TO SELLER'S CREDITORS

Statement showing names and addresses of all unsecured trade creditors and secured trade creditors of Worman Mensware Ltd. of the City of Toronto, and the amount of the indebtedness or liability due, owing, payable or accruing due, or to become due by Worman Mensware Ltd. to each of them.

UNSECURED TRADE CREDITORS

NAME OF CREDITOR	ADDRESS	AMOUNT
NIL		NIL

SECURED TRADE CREDITORS

Name of Creditor	Address	Amount	Nature of Security	Due or becoming due on the date fixed for the completion of the sale
NIL				NIL

I, **BERT WORMAN**, of the City of Toronto, in the Province of Ontario make oath and say:

1. That the foregoing statement is a true and correct statement

(a) of the names and addresses of all the unsecured trade creditors of the said owing, payable or accruing due or to become due and payable by the said Worman Mensware Ltd. to each of the said unsecured trade creditors; and

(b) of the names and addresses of all the secured trade creditors of the said Worman Mensware Ltd. and of the amount of the indebtedness or liability due, owing, payable or accruing due or to become due and payable by the said Worman Mensware Ltd. to each of the said secured creditors, the nature of their security and whether they are or in the event of sale will become due and payable on the date fixed for the completion of the sale.

Sworn before me at the City of Toronto	)	
in the Province of Ontario, this	)	
day of September, 2001	)	
	)	______________________________
	)	**BERT WORMAN**
A Commissioner, etc.	)	

App 6-10

Buyer's Affidavit under the Bulk Sales Act

Court File No:

SUPERIOR COURT OF JUSTICE

IN THE MATTER OF THE SALE IN BULK OF THE ASSETS OF WORMAN MENSWARE LTD. (THE "VENDOR") TO HARRY AGULNIK HABERDASHERY LTD. (THE "PURCHASER")

AND IN THE MATTER OF THE BULK SALES ACT, R.S.O. 1990, c. B-14.

AFFIDAVIT

I, **RALPH ALTSON**, of the City of Toronto, in the Province of Ontario

DO SOLEMNLY DECLARE THAT:

1. I am a solicitor with the firm Altson, Harris, Barristers and Solicitors, which firm represented the Purchaser in the above-named transaction and as such have knowledge of the matters hereinafter set forth;

2. The Purchaser is Harry Agulnik Haberdashery Ltd., of _______________, Toronto, Ontario.

3. The Vendor is Bert Worman Mensware Ltd. of _______________, Toronto, Ontario, which formerly operated a menswear store at _______________, Toronto, Ontario.

4. The Purchaser has purchased from the Vendor's certain chattels and equipment situated in the Vendor's former place of business at _______________, Toronto, Ontario.

5. The sale was completed on the 30th day of September, 2001.

6. Annexed hereto and marked as Exhibit "A" to my affidavit is a true copy of the statement as to the Vendor's creditors prescribed by section 4 of the Bulk Sales Act, R.S.O. 1990, c. B.14, executed by the Vendor.

7. This affidavit is made pursuant to the Bulk Sales Act, R.S.O. 1990, c. B.14, and is made for no improper purpose.

AND I make this solemn Declaration conscientiously believing it to be true and knowing that it is of the same force and effect as if made under oath.

SWORN BEFORE ME at the City of Toronto in the Province of Ontario, this day of October, 2001	))))	
	)	________________________
	)	**RALPH ALTSON**
A Commissioner, etc.	)	

App 6-11

Notice of Application, on Notice for Registration, of a Non-Ontario Provincial Judgment

Court File No:

SUPERIOR COURT OF JUSTICE

BETWEEN:

LYNDON TERRACE INVESTMENTS LTD.

Applicant

- and -

HAROLD LINCOLN

Respondent

NOTICE OF APPLICATION

TO THE RESPONDENTS:

A LEGAL PROCEEDING HAS BEEN COMMENCED by the applicant. The claim made by the applicant appears on the following pages.

THIS APPLICATION will come on for a hearing on , the day of , 2001 at 10:00 o'clock in the forenoon, at the Court House, 161 Elgin Street, Ottawa, Ontario.

IF YOU WISH TO OPPOSE THIS APPLICATION, to receive notice of any step in the application or to be served with any documents in the application, you or an Ontario lawyer acting for you must forthwith prepare a notice of appearance in Form 38A prescribed by the Rules of Civil Procedure, serve it on the applicant's lawyer or, where the applicant does not have a lawyer, serve it on the applicant, and file it, with proof of service, in this court office, and you or your lawyer must appear at the hearing.

IF YOU WISH TO PRESENT AFFIDAVIT OR OTHER DOCUMENTARY EVIDENCE TO THE COURT OR TO EXAMINE OR CROSS-EXAMINE WITNESSES ON THE APPLICATION, you or your lawyer must, in addition to serving your notice of appearance, serve a copy of the evidence on the applicant's lawyer or, where the applicant does not have a lawyer, serve it on the applicant, and file it, with proof of service, in the court office where the application is to be heard as soon as possible, but not later than 2 p.m. on the day before the hearing.

IF YOU FAIL TO APPEAR AT THE HEARING, JUDGMENT MAY BE GIVEN IN YOUR ABSENCE AND WITHOUT FURTHER NOTICE TO YOU. IF YOU WISH TO OPPOSE THIS APPLICATION BUT ARE UNABLE TO PAY LEGAL FEES, LEGAL AID MAY BE AVAILABLE TO YOU BY CONTACTING A LOCAL LEGAL AID OFFICE.

Dated: , 2001 Issued by ______________________________

Local Registrar

Address of the Court House:

161 Elgin Street
Ottawa, Ontario
K2P 2K1

APPLICATION

1. The Applicant makes application for:

(a) an Order pursuant to Section 2(1) of the *Reciprocal Enforcement of Judgments Act*, R.S.O. 1990, c. R-5, that the judgment of Lyndon Terrace Investments Ltd. against Harold Lincoln which was obtained in the Alberta Court of Queen's Bench on July 5, 2001 be registered in the Superior Court of Justice;

(b) the reasonable costs of and incidental to the registration of the judgment pursuant to Section 4(c) of the *Reciprocal Enforcement of Judgments Act.*

2. The grounds for the Application are:

(a) the *Reciprocal Enforcement of Judgments Act*;
(b) the *Rules of Civil Procedure*;
(c) the Applicant obtained a judgment against Harold Lincoln which was obtained in the Alberta Court of Queen's Bench on July 5, 2001;
(d) the Respondent has not satisfied the outstanding judgment;
(e) the Province of Alberta is a reciprocating jurisdiction pursuant to the *Reciprocal Enforcement of Judgments Act*, (cite the relevant registration).

3. The following documentary evidence will be used at the hearing of the Application:

(a) the judgment against Harold Lincoln which was obtained in the Alberta Court of Queen's Bench on July 5, 2001;

(b) the Affidavit of Harry Freedman.

(where the Notice of Application is to be served outside Ontario without a court order, state the facts and the specific provisions of Rule 17 relied on in support of such service).

Date: 2001

ADAM & ZENA
281 McLeod Street
Ottawa, Ontario
K2K 3B3
tel: (613) 237-0000
fax: (613) 237-1111
Attention: Joe Adam
Solicitors for the Applicant

App 6-12

Order Registering a Non-Ontario Judgment

Court File No:

SUPERIOR COURT OF JUSTICE

THE HONOURABLE JUSTICE	)	**DAY, THE DAY OF**
	)	
A.B. STIRLING	)	**, 2001**

BETWEEN:

LYNDON TERRACE INVESTMENTS LTD.

Applicant

- and -

HAROLD LINCOLN

Respondent

ORDER

THIS MOTION made by the Applicant for an Order to register a judgment from the Province of Alberta in the Ontario Superior Court of Justice:

ON READING the Judgment and on reading the Affidavit of Harry Freedman:

1 **THIS COURT ORDERS** that the judgment in the action Lyndon Terrace Investments Ltd. against Harold Lincoln, Court File No. 7234/01 obtained in the Alberta Court of Queen's Bench, shall be registered in the Superior Court of Justice at 161 Elgin Street, Ottawa, Ontario, pursuant to the Reciprocal Enforcement of Judgments Act, R.S.O. 1990, c. R-5.

2. **THIS COURT ORDERS** that the costs of this application be paid by the Respondent to the Applicant forthwith after assessment.

THIS ORDER BEARS INTEREST AT THE RATE OF 8% per cent per year.

____

(Signature of Judge or Registrar)

Appendix 7

Precedents Relating to

Chapter 7

Residential Power of Sale Proceedings Precedents

App 7-1

Notice of Power of Sale

NOTICE OF POWER OF SALE UNDER CHARGE

TAKE NOTICE that default has been made in payments of the monies due under a certain mortgage dated the 20th day of January, 2001,

made between:

PETER NODAY

Mortgagor

- and -

OMNI BANK OF CANADA

Mortgagee

on the security of all and singular that certain parcel or tract of land and premises situate, lying and being in the City of Ottawa, being Parcel 54-1, Plan 4M-540, Property Identifier Number 12345-6789, which Mortgage was registered on the 20th day of January, 2001, in the Land Titles Division of Ottawa (No. 4) as No. 200152.

AND OMNI BANK OF CANADA HEREBY GIVES YOU NOTICE that the amount now due under the mortgage for principal money, interest, taxes, insurance premium, and costs, respectively are made up as follows:

-	for principal	$175,000.00
-	for interest to July 15, 2001	1,750.00
-	for taxes	1,000.00
-	for insurance premium	0.00
-	for costs on a solicitor and client basis inclusive of GST	1,610.00
TOTAL:		$179,360.00

(such amount for costs being up to and including the service of this notice only, and thereafter such further costs and disbursements will be charged as may be proper), together with interest at the mortgage rate and in accordance with the terms of the mortgage from the date hereof to the date of payment.

AND UNLESS the said sums are paid on or before the 10th day of August, 2001, OMNI BANK OF CANADA SHALL SELL THE PROPERTY covered by the said mortgage under the provisions contained in it. This notice is given to you as you appear to have an interest in the mortgaged property and may be entitled to redeem the same.

DATED at Ottawa, this 20th day of July, 2001.

OMNI BANK OF CANADA by its solicitors
Attention: Jay Stanley
STANLEY & JOHN
496 Wilson Court
Ottawa, Ontario
K9B 2L2
tel: (613) 965-9595
fax: (613) 965-9696

App 7-2

Notice of Intention to Enforce Security under Bankruptcy and Insolvency Act Form 86

(Rule 124)

NOTICE OF INTENTION TO ENFORCE SECURITY
(Subsection 244(1))

TO: PEPPERPIKE PINOCHLE FARMS LIMITED, an insolvent person

Take notice that:

1. OMNI BANK OF CANADA, a secured creditor, intends to enforce its security on the insolvent person's property described below:

All of the assets of Pepperpike Pinochle Farms Limited

2. The security that is to be enforced is in the form of a General Security Agreement, Assignment of Book Debts and a first charge on the real property owned by Pepperpike Pinochle Farms Limited located at R.R. 5, Lindsay, Ontario and being more particularly described as Lot 26, Concession 2, Township of Lindsay, Property Identifier Number 12345-6789.

3. The total amount of indebtedness secured by the security is $250,000.00.

4. The secured creditor will not have the right to enforce the security until after the expiry of the 10-day period after this notice is sent unless the insolvent person consents to an earlier enforcement.

Dated at Ottawa, this 17th day of July, 2001

OMNI BANK OF CANADA

Per: ________________________________
William Kesler
I have authority to bind the within corporation

NOTE: If the debtor consents to an earlier enforcement of the security before the expiry of the 10-day period, the debtor should execute the following consent.

Pepperpike Pinochle Farms Limited hereby consents to an immediate enforcement of the Notice of Intention to Enforce Security.

Dated at Lindsay, Ontario, this 18th day of July, 2001

PEPPERPIKE PINOCHLE FARMS LIMITED

Per: ________________________________
Amram Singh
I have authority to bind the within corporation

App 7-3

Conditions of Sale in an Auction

CONDITIONS OF SALE IN AN AUCTION

1. The property is sold on an "as is" basis. It is understood that there are no representations or warranties made as to the condition of the property. No furniture, broadloom, fixtures, or appliances are included in the purchase price, except as otherwise may be indicated by the Auctioneer at the auction.

2. The auction is subject to postponement, or to withdrawal of the property from sale at any time or times, as the selling mortgagee and/or the Auctioneer shall deem proper in their absolute discretion.

3. The property is offered for sale subject to a reserve bid set by the selling mortgagee.

4. The Auctioneer shall have the right to receive sealed bids in writing accompanied by a certified cheque for 10% of the purchase price as a deposit payable to the solicitors in trust for the selling mortgagee prior to the sale and may include such bids in the sale in such manner as he may deem proper.

5. No person shall advance less than $500.00 per bid over the prior bid and no person shall retract his/her bid once made.

6. If the highest bid for the property is not equal to or greater in amount than the reserve bid, the Auctioneer shall announce that the reserve bid has not been reached and shall call for higher bids. If no higher bid is then received or if a higher bid is then received not equal to or greater than the reserve bid, the Auctioneer, at the discretion of the selling mortgagee, shall then declare the sale to be aborted.

7. The highest bidder above the reserve bid stipulated for the property shall be the purchaser thereof and if any dispute arises as to the last or highest bidder, the property may be put up for rebidding at a former bidding at the option of the Auctioneer.

8. The purchaser, at the end of the auction sale, is to subscribe his/her name and address to the within conditions of sale thereby constituting an agreement for the purchase of the property with respect to which he/she is the successful bidder, and he/she is to indicate the name of the solicitor acting for him/her in which case all notices and communications shall be deemed properly served upon his/her solicitor, and tender, if necessary, may be made upon his/her solicitor.

9. The purchaser shall pay a deposit of ten percent (10%) on the amount of his purchase price to the solicitors for the selling mortgagee by cash or certified cheque.

10. The purchaser will agree to pay the balance of the purchase price, subject to the usual adjustments, by certified cheque to the selling mortgagee on closing.

11. If the purchaser shall fail to comply with the conditions herein or any of them, the deposit, and all other payments made hereunder shall be forfeited, and the premises may be resold and the deficiency, if any, occasioned by such resale, together with all charges attending the same or occasioned by the default, are to be made good by the purchaser.

12. The selling mortgagee shall not be required to furnish any abstract of title and shall produce only such deeds, surveys, copies thereof, or other evidences of title as are in his possession or control.

13. The purchaser shall be allowed fifteen (15) days from the date of execution hereof, to investigate the title as his/her own expense, and if within that time he/she shall furnish the selling mortgagee or his/her solicitor in writing with any objection to the title which the selling mortgagee shall be unable or unwilling to remove, the selling mortgagee may by notice in writing to the purchaser rescind the sale, in which case the selling mortgagee shall not be liable for any compensation, costs, damages or expenses incurred by the purchaser. If within the said fifteen (15) days the purchaser shall not have furnished any objection to title as aforesaid, he/she shall be deemed to have accepted same.

14. The sale is to be closed on the first day that the Registry Office is open after 30 days from the date of sale, with adjustments as of the date of closing.

15. The selling mortgagee shall have the right to terminate this agreement by notice in writing delivered to the purchaser or his/her solicitor at any time prior to closing if the mortgage has been redeemed or if an injunction has been issued by a court of competent jurisdiction, restraining this sale. If the agreement is terminated, the deposit shall be returned to the purchaser without interest or deduction and the selling mortgagee shall not have any further liability to the purchaser hereunder.

16. Time shall be of the essence of the transaction hereby contemplated.

17. These conditions of sale are subject to amendment, deletion, or addition prior to the actual sale.

DATED at Ottawa this day of , 2001.

ADAM & ZENA
Barristers & Solicitors
281 McLeod Street
Ottawa, Ontario
K2K 3B3
tel: (613) 237-0000
fax: (613) 237-1111
Attention: Joe Adam
Solicitors for the
Selling Mortgagee

The undersigned hereby agree to purchase the property municipally known as 17 Armstrong Street, Ottawa, Ontario accordance with the terms of the advertisement of this sale and the conditions of sale aforesaid for the total purchase price of $ ________

Witness: ____________________ Purchaser: ____________________

Address: ____________________

Solicitor: ____________________

Closing Date: ____________________

App 7-4

Clauses to be included in Agreement of Purchase and Sale

SCHEDULE "A"
forming an integral part of the Agreement of
Purchase and Sale
between Omni Bank of Canada as Vendor under Power of Sale
and Kevin Kerr as Purchaser

1. The Purchaser acknowledges that the Vendor is selling the property in exercise of a power sale contained in the Vendor's mortgage registered May 30, 1993 as No. CT 987654 and agrees that the Vendor shall have the right to terminate this agreement by notice in writing delivered to the Purchaser or the Purchaser's solicitor at any time prior to closing if the mortgage has been redeemed or if the within sale has been restrained by an injunction issued by a court of competent jurisdiction. If the agreement is so terminated, the deposit shall be returned to the Purchaser without interest or deduction.

2. The Vendor warrants to the Purchaser that all steps required to be taken by the Vendor in the exercise of the power of sale have been properly taken in the exercise of the power of sale to the date of this agreement.

Suggested additional or alternative clauses

3. The Purchaser acknowledges that no representations or warranties have been made by the Vendor, or anyone acting on its behalf, to the Purchaser as to the condition of the Property or any buildings located thereon or as to the performance of any parts thereof. The Purchaser acknowledges that the Property is sold on an "as is, where is" basis including, without limitation, outstanding work orders, zoning and building code violations. No representation, warranty, or condition is expressed or can be implied as to title, description, fitness for purpose, quantity, condition or quality thereof or in respect of any other thing whatsoever and the Purchaser shall complete the purchase and take possession of the Property as it exists on the date of closing.

4. The Purchaser and Vendor agree that only existing fixtures and chattels which the Vendor has authority to sell are included in the purchase price. All fixtures and chattels are on an "as is, where is" basis with no representation as to title, quality or quantity. The Vendor will deliver possession of the said fixtures and chattels as found on the Property on closing without a Bill of Sale, warranty or other title documentation and shall make no adjustment in the purchase price with respect thereto.

5. The description of the Property is believed by the Vendor to be correct but if any statement, error or omission shall be found in the particulars thereof the same shall not annul the sale nor entitle the Purchaser to be relieved of any obligation hereunder, nor shall any compensation be allowed to either the Vendor or the Purchaser in respect thereof.

6. Notwithstanding anything to the contrary in this Agreement, the Vendor may, if a certificate of pending litigation is registered against the Property, or if the Purchaser submits a valid title requisition which the Vendor is unable to satisfy prior to closing or if the sale of Property is restrained at any time by a court of competent jurisdiction, at its option, elect by written notice to the Purchaser to:

(a) terminate this Agreement whereupon the deposit will be returned to the Purchaser with interest earned thereon and neither party will have any further rights or liabilities hereunder; or

(b) extend the date of closing otherwise established pursuant to paragraph • hereof for up to 90 days to enable the Vendor to obtain an order vacating such restraining order or such certificate or to satisfy such title requisitions, as the case may be.

7. (a) The Purchaser agrees that if there are tenants in possession of the premises at the time this offer is being made and the tenants remain in possession on the date of closing, the Vendor shall not be responsible for providing vacant possession.

(b) In the event the Purchaser requires vacant possession and vacant possession cannot be provided by the closing date, the Vendor may, at its option, extend the closing date for a period or periods of time not exceeding 45 days in total. If vacant possession cannot be provided by the expiry of such extension periods the Purchaser may accept title subject to such tenancies or this agreement will terminate without any further liability on the part of either party. The Purchaser agrees to execute any documentation required to assist the Vendor in obtaining possession on the Purchaser's behalf.

8. The Vendor has no knowledge and makes no representations or warranties whatsoever as to the existence of urea formaldehyde foam insulation or any hazardous or toxic substances whatsoever.

App 7-5

Declaration by Chargee as to Default - Land Titles Act

STATUTORY DECLARATION OF CHARGEE

CANADA	)	IN THE MATTER of the Land Titles Act, R.S.O. 1990, c.L-5
PROVINCE OF ONTARIO	)	
	)	IN THE MATTER of the Mortgages Act, R.S.O. 1990, c. M-40
	)	IN THE MATTER of mortgage number LT56789 registered on title to the lands and premises described as Lot 526-1, Plan 4M-635, City of Ottawa, Province of Ontario
	)	AND IN THE MATTER of the exercise of a power of sale in respect of the said lands and premises by Jack Kelly dated November 10, 2001
TO WIT:		

I, JACK KELLY, of the City of Ottawa, in the Province of Ontario, solemnly declare that:

1. I am the registered owner of charge no. LT56789 and as such have personal knowledge of the facts herein declared.

2. To the best of my knowledge and belief, money or moneys worth was actually advanced or supplied under the said charge without the chargee having actual notice of any encumbrance registered or filed subsequent to the said charge.

(Where assignee of mortgage makes declaration, insert instead:)

2. To the best of my knowledge and belief, money or moneys worth was actually advanced or supplied under the said charge without the original chargee, *(original mortgagee's name),* having actual notice of any encumbrance registered subsequent to the said charge.

(Where the charge was registered on or after April 2, 1983, add:)

3. To the best of my knowledge and belief, subsections 78(2) and (5) of the Construction Lien Act do not give priority to any lien claimant under that Act over the said charge.

4. Default entitling me to sell the charged land was made in respect of payment of the said charge on October 1, 2001 and the said charge remained in default at the time a sale under the said charge was made.

5. The said charge remains in default as of the date hereof.

(Where the chargor is an individual, choose the appropriate paragraph from the following:)

6. The registered owner of the charged land was not a spouse within the meaning of the Family Law Act at the time that the notice of sale was served under the said charge.

6. The registered owner of the charged land is a spouse who is not separated from his *(or her)* spouse and the charged land is not ordinarily occupied by the spouses as their family residence.

6. The registered owner of the charged land is a spouse who is separated from his *(or her)* spouse and the charged land was not, at the time of their separation, ordinarily occupied by the spouses as their family residence.

6. The charged land is not designated by both spouses as a matrimonial home and another property is designated as a matrimonial home by both spouses and such designation is registered and not cancelled.

6. The registered owners were spouses of one another at the time that the notice of sale was served under the said charge.

7. The said charge has priority over the following subsequent encumbrances affecting the charged land:

(a) *(recite all subsequent encumbrances)*

I MAKE THIS SOLEMN DECLARATION conscientiously believing it to be true, and knowing that it is of the same force and effect as if made under oath.

DECLARED BEFORE ME at the City	)	
of Ottawa, in the Province of Ontario	)	
this day of November, 2001	)	
	)	______________________________
	)	JACK KELLY
A Commissioner, etc.	)	

App 7-6

Declaration of Service of Notice of Sale - Land Titles Act

STATUTORY DECLARATION OF SERVICE OF NOTICE OF SALE UNDER CHARGE

CANADA	)	IN THE MATTER of the Land Titles Act,
	)	R.S.O. 1990, c.L-5
PROVINCE OF ONTARIO	)	
	)	IN THE MATTER of the Mortgages
	)	Act, R.S.O. 1990, c. M-40
	)	
	)	IN THE MATTER of mortgage number
	)	LT56789 registered on title to
	)	the lands and premises described as
	)	Lot 526-1, Plan 4M-635, City of Ottawa,
	)	Province of Ontario
	)	
	)	AND IN THE MATTER of the exercise of
	)	a power of sale in respect of the said lands
	)	and premises by Jack Kelly dated November
	)	10, 2001
TO WIT:		

I, DONA STETHEM, of the City of Ottawa, in the Province of Ontario, solemnly declare that:

1. I am secretary with David White, the solicitor for Jack Kelly (the "Chargee"), the registered owner of a charge or mortgage registered as instrument no. LT56789, and as such have personal knowledge of the facts herein declared.

2. On November 10, 2001 I caused the following persons named in the notice of sale under charge annexed hereto as Exhibit "A" to be served with a true copy thereof by sending the same to each of the said parties by prepaid registered mail in accordance with Part III of the Mortgages Act:

   (a) *(list names and capacities of persons served)*

3. The original Canada Post Registration Receipt in support thereof is annexed hereto as Exhibit "B".

I MAKE THIS SOLEMN DECLARATION conscientiously believing it to be true, and knowing that it is of the same force and effect as if made under oath.

DECLARED BEFORE ME at the City	)	
of Ottawa, in the Province of Ontario	)	
this day of November, 2001	)	
	)	_______________________
	)	DONA STETHEM
A Commissioner, etc.	)	

App 7-7

Declaration by Solicitor for Compliance and Persons Served - Land Titles Act

STATUTORY DECLARATION OF SOLICITOR

CANADA	)	IN THE MATTER of the Land Titles Act, R.S.O. 1990, c.L-5
PROVINCE OF ONTARIO	)	IN THE MATTER of the Mortgages Act, R.S.O. 1990, c. M-40
	)	IN THE MATTER of mortgage number LT56789 registered on title to the lands and premises described as Lot 526-1, Plan 4M-635, City of Ottawa, Province of Ontario
	)	AND IN THE MATTER of the exercise of a power of sale in respect of the said lands and premises by Jack Kelly dated November 10, 2001

TO WIT:

I, DAVID WHITE, of the City of Ottawa, in the Province of Ontario, solicitor, solemnly declare that:

1. I am the solicitor for Jack Kelly (the "Chargee"), the registered owner of a charge or mortgage registered as instrument no. LT56789 (the "Charge"), and as such have personal knowledge of the facts herein declared.

2. I have made or caused to be made a thorough search in the Land Titles Office for the Land Titles Division of Ottawa (No. 4) and found no persons entitled to notice of the exercise of a power of sale other than the following who were served with the notice of sale as required by Part III of the Mortgages Act:

   (a) *(list names and capacities of persons served)*

3. In my opinion the sale proceedings carried out by Jack Kelly in exercise of the power of sale contained in the said charge are in compliance with the terms of the said charge, Part III (*or:* Part II) of the Mortgages Act, section 50(18) of the Planning Act, where applicable and the Farm Debt Mediation Act and other relevant requirements of law.

I MAKE THIS SOLEMN DECLARATION conscientiously believing it to be true, and knowing that it is of the same force and effect as if made under oath.

DECLARED BEFORE ME at the City of Ottawa, in the Province of Ontario this day of November, 2001	)	
	)	____________________
	)	DAVID WHITE
A Commissioner, etc.	)	

App 7-8

Declaration by Solicitor for Compliance and Persons Served - Registry Act

STATUTORY DECLARATION OF SOLICITOR

CANADA	)	IN THE MATTER of the Mortgages
	)	Act, R.S.O. 1990, c. M-40
PROVINCE OF ONTARIO	)	
	)	IN THE MATTER of mortgage number
	)	N576542 registered on title to
	)	the lands and premises described as
	)	Lot 452, Plan 857, City of Ottawa,
	)	Province of Ontario
	)	
	)	AND IN THE MATTER of the exercise of
	)	a power of sale in respect of the said lands
	)	and premises by Jack Kelly dated November
	)	10, 2001

TO WIT:

I, DAVID WHITE, of the City of Ottawa, in the Province of Ontario, solicitor, solemnly declare that:

1. I am the solicitor for Jack Kelly, the registered owner of a charge or mortgage registered as instrument no. N576542 and as such, have personal knowledge of the facts herein declared.

2. The said mortgage contains a provisions that:

(set forth the sale provisions contained in the mortgage or charge or standard charge terms which apply).

2. I am advised by Jack Kelly and believe that default occurred under the said mortgage on October 11, 2001.

2. I made or caused to be made a search of the abstract index for the mortgaged property subject to the said mortgage in the Land Registry Office for the Land Registry Division of Ottawa and inquiry to be made with the Sheriff of the City of Ottawa, which searches disclosed that as at 4:30 p.m. of the day immediately prior to the date on which the notice of sale was served, the following persons were entitled to notice of the exercise of a power of sale:

(a) (List names and capacities of persons served).

which said persons, and the spouses of the present registered owners of the mortgaged property, in accordance with the requirements of s. 22(1) of the Family Law Act, 1986, were each given notice of the mortgagee's intention to exercise a power of sale by prepaid registered mail addressed to each person at their respective usual or last known place of address or addresses as set forth in Schedule "A" to the said notice of sale, a true copy of which is attached to the declaration of Dona Stethem.

3. I am advised by the said mortgagee, and believe, as at the date of this declaration, that no mortgage, Part III *(or:* Part II) of the Mortgages Act, section 50(18) of the Planning Act where applicable, and the Farm Debt Mediation Act.

I MAKE THIS SOLEMN DECLARATION conscientiously believing it to be true, and knowing that it is of the same force and effect as if made under oath.

DECLARED BEFORE ME at the City	)	
of Ottawa, in the Province of Ontario	)	
this day of November, 2001	)	
	)	______________________________
	)	DAVID WHITE
A Commissioner, etc.	)	

App 7-9

Declaration by Chargee as to Default - Registry Act

STATUTORY DECLARATION OF CHARGEE

CANADA	)	IN THE MATTER of the Mortgages
	)	Act, R.S.O. 1990, c. M-40
PROVINCE OF ONTARIO	)	
	)	IN THE MATTER of mortgage number
	)	N576542 registered on title to
	)	the lands and premises described as
	)	Lot 452, Plan 857, City of Ottawa,
	)	Province of Ontario
	)	
	)	AND IN THE MATTER of the exercise of
	)	a power of sale in respect of the said lands
	)	and premises by Jack Kelly dated November
	)	10, 2001

TO WIT:

I. JACK KELLY, of the City of Ottawa, in the Province of Ontario, solemnly declare that:

1. I am the registered owner of a mortgage or charge registered in the Land Registry Office for the Land Registry Division of Ottawa (No. 4) on February 1, 2000 as Instrument No. N576542 and as such, I have personal knowledge of the facts herein declared.

2. By said mortgage or charge is the first mortgage or charge of the mortgaged property described therein.

3. Default occurred under the said mortgage on October 1, 2001.

4. The amount due under the said mortgage on the date that the notice of sale was served was $175,325.00.

5. Neither I, nor any person for or on my behalf, has received the above said sum nor any part thereof, or any security for the same except the said mortgage.

6. Prior to the service of the notice of sale, I did not receive actual written notice from or on behalf of any person claiming any other interest in the mortgaged property.

7. Default under the said mortgage has continued to the date of this declaration and continues.

8. I am not a non-resident of Canada within the meaning of section 116 of the Income Tax Act (Canada).

(Where the charge was registered on or after April 2, 1983, add:)

9. To the best of my knowledge and belief, subsections 78(2) and (5) of the Construction Lien Act do not give priority to any lien claimant under that Act over the said mortgage.

(Where the chargor is an individual, choose the appropriate paragraph from the following:)

10. The registered owner of the mortgaged property was not a spouse within the meaning of the Family Law Act at the time that the notice of sale was served under the said charge.

10. The registered owner of the mortgaged property is a spouse who is not separated from his *(or her)* spouse and the mortgaged property is not ordinarily occupied by the spouses as their family residence.

10. The registered owner of the mortgaged property is a spouse who is separated from his *(or her)* spouse and the mortgaged property was not, at the time of their separation, ordinarily occupied by the spouses as their family residence.

10. The mortgaged property is not designated by both spouses as a matrimonial home and another property is designated as a matrimonial home by both spouses and such designation is registered and not cancelled.

10. The spouse of the registered owner of the mortgaged property has released all rights under Part II of the Family law Act by a separation agreement.

10. The registered owners were spouses of one another at the time that the notice of sale was served under the said mortgage.

I MAKE THIS SOLEMN DECLARATION conscientiously believing it to be true, and knowing that it is of the same force and effect as if made under oath.

DECLARED BEFORE ME at the City)
of Ottawa, in the Province of Ontario)
this day of November, 2001)
) ______________________________
) JACK KELLY

A Commissioner, etc.

App 7-10

Declaration of Service of Notice of Sale - Registry Act

STATUTORY DECLARLATION OF SERVICE OF NOTICE OF SALE UNDER CHARGE

CANADA	)	IN THE MATTER of the Mortgages
	)	Act, R.S.O. 1990, c. M-40
PROVINCE OF ONTARIO	)	
	)	IN THE MATTER of mortgage number
	)	N576542 registered on title to
	)	the lands and premises described as
	)	Lot 452, Plan 857, City of Ottawa,
	)	Province of Ontario
	)	
	)	AND IN THE MATTER of the exercise of
	)	a power of sale in respect of the said lands
	)	and premises by Jack Kelly dated Novembe
	)	10, 2001

TO WIT:

I, DONA STETHEM, of the City of Ottawa, in the Province of Ontario, solemnly declare that:

1. I am a secretary with David White, the solicitor for Jack Kelly, the registered owner of a mortgage registered as instrument no. N576542 and as such, have personal knowledge of the facts herein declare.

2. On November 10, 2001 I caused the following persons named in the notice of sale under Charge annexed hereto as Exhibit "A" to be served with a true copy thereof by sending the same to each of the said parties by prepaid registered mail in accordance with Part III of the Mortgages Act.

(a) (list names and capacities of persons served).

3. The original Canada Post Registration Receipt in support thereof is annexed hereto as Exhibit "B".

I MAKE THIS SOLEMN DECLARATION conscientiously believing it to be true, and knowing that it is of the same force and effect as if made under oath.

DECLARED BEFORE ME at the City	)	
of Ottawa, in the Province of Ontario	)	
this day of November, 2001	)	
	)	______________________
A Commissioner, etc.	)	DONA STETHEM

App 7-11

Recitals for Deed Under Power of Sale (Registry)

WHEREAS:

1. By a Mortgage dated the 20th day of January, 2001 and registered in the Land Registry Office for the Registry Division of Ottawa (No. 4) as Instrument No. 200152 on the 20th day of January, 2001

PETER NODAY

as Mortgagor

did mortgage the lands herein to

OMNI BANK OF CANADA

as Mortgagee

for securing payment of the sum of ($175,000.00) Dollars and interest as therein mentioned.

2. The Mortgagee on default of payment under the said Mortgage for fifteen (15) days is entitled on thirty-five (35) days notice to sell the said lands.

3. A default has been made in payment of the principal and interest secured by the said Mortgage and notice of exercising the power to sell the said lands has been duly given by the Mortgagee to all persons entitled thereto.

4. A default has not been remedied and the time set forth in the notice of sale has expired.

5. Statutory Declarations setting forth the particulars of such default, the service of notice of sale and the sale proceedings have been deposited and registered in the said Land Registry Office as Instrument No. .

AND THEREFORE under and by virtue of the powers of sale contained in the said Mortgage, the said lands were sold to the Transferee.

App 7-12

Notice to Tenant to Vacate Premises

Court File No:

SUPERIOR COURT OF JUSTICE

BETWEEN:

OMNI BANK OF CANADA

Plaintiff

- and -

PETER NODAY

Defendant

NOTICE

TAKE NOTICE that Omni Bank of Canada, the above-named Plaintiff, has obtained Judgment in an action in this Court against the Defendant Peter Noday, entitling them to immediate possession of the lands and premises described as:

> "All and singular that certain parcel or tract of land and premises situate, lying and being in the City of Ottawa, and being composed of all of Parcel 54-1, Plan 4M-540, Property Identifier Number 12345-6789.

A copy of the Judgment being attached hereto.

The said action was commenced in the Superior Court of Justice as Number 01-CV-81325.

It appears that you may be in actual possession of all or part of the lands and premises in question in this action. You are therefore advised to vacate and deliver up possession of the said lands and premises to the said Plaintiff; Omni Bank of Canada. If you have not quit the property by the 5th day of December, 2001 next, an application will be made to the Court without further notice to you for an Order permitting the issue of a Writ of Possession directing the Sheriff of the City of Ottawa to deliver the possession of the said lands and premises to the Plaintiff, Omni Bank of Canada.

DATED at Ottawa, Ontario, this 15th day of October, 2001.

OMNI BANK OF CANADA, by its solicitors,
STANLEY & JOHN

Per. ______________________________
Jay Stanley
(613) 965-9595

App 7-13

Statement of Claim for Payment on the Covenant Contained in a Mortgage and for Possession of the Property

Court File No:

SUPERIOR COURT OF JUSTICE

BETWEEN:

OMNI BANK OF CANADA

Plaintiff

- and -

PETER NODAY and SHARON NODAY

Defendants

STATEMENT OF CLAIM

TO THE DEFENDANT

A LEGAL PROCEEDING HAS BEEN COMMENCED AGAINST YOU by the plaintiff. The claim made against you is set out in the following pages.

IF YOU WISH TO DEFEND THIS PROCEEDING, you or an Ontario lawyer acting for you must prepare a statement of defence in Form 18A prescribed by the Rules of Civil Procedure, serve it on the plaintiff's lawyer or, where the plaintiff does not have a lawyer, serve it on the plaintiff, and file it, with proof of service in this court office, WITHIN TWENTY DAYS after this statement of claim is served on you, if you are served in Ontario.

If you are served in another province or territory of Canada or in the United States of America, the period for serving and filing your statement of defence is forty days. If you are served outside Canada and the United States of America, the period is sixty days.

Instead of serving and filing a statement of defence, you may serve and file a notice of intent to defend in Form 18B prescribed by the Rules of Civil Procedure. This will entitle you to ten more days within which to serve and file your statement of defence.

IF YOU FAIL TO DEFEND THIS PROCEEDING, JUDGMENT MAY BE GIVEN AGAINST YOU IN YOUR ABSENCE AND WITHOUT FURTHER NOTICE TO YOU. IF YOU WISH TO DEFEND THIS PROCEEDING BUT ARE UNABLE TO PAY LEGAL FEES, LEGAL AID MAY BE AVAILABLE TO YOU BY CONTACTING A LOCAL LEGAL AID OFFICE.

Date____________________ Issued by____________________
Local Registrar

Address of
court office: 161 Elgin Street
Ottawa, Ontario
K2P 2K1

TO: PETER NODAY
17 Armstrong Street
Ottawa, Ontario

AND TO: SHARON NODAY
17 Armstrong Street
Ottawa, Ontario

CLAIM

1. The Plaintiff claims:

(a) Possession of the mortgaged property more particularly described in Schedule "A" hereto (hereinafter referred to as "the property");

(b) Payment by the defendants, or either of them, of the sum of $178,532.00 now due and owing under the mortgage together with interest from the 9th day of December, 2001 at the rate of 9% per annum calculated semi-annually, not in advance, until judgment;

(c) Post-judgment interest in accordance with the mortgage at the rate of 9% per annum calculated semi-annually, not in advance;

(d) Costs of this action on a solicitor and client basis; and

(e) Such further and other relief as to this Honourable Court seems just.

2. The Plaintiff Omni Bank of Canada is a bank carrying on business in Canada, with a branch in the City of Ottawa, Province of Ontario.

3. The Defendants, Peter Noday and Sharon Noday reside in the City of Ottawa, in the Province of Ontario.

4. The Defendant Sharon Noday is the spouse of the Defendant Peter Noday.

5. The Plaintiff's claim is on a mortgage dated the 20th day of January, 2001 made between Omni Bank of Canada as mortgagee and Peter Noday as mortgagor and registered on the 20th day of January, 2001 as Instrument No. 200152 in the Land Registry Office for the Land Titles Division of Ottawa (No. 4) under which the Defendant mortgaged the property described for a term of one (1) year. The principal amount of the Mortgage was $175,000.00 and bears interest at the rate of 9% per annum, calculated semi-annually, not in advance. The mortgage is governed by Standard Charge Terms 852. The interest adjustment date is February 1, 2001. Monthly payments of principal and interest, each in the amount of $1,112.50 are due and payable on the first day of each and every month from and including the 1st day of March 2001 to and including February 1, 2002 at which time the outstanding balance, together with accrued interest would become due and payable.

6. The said mortgage and Standard Charge Terms 852 provide, inter alia, that in the event of any default, the mortgagee shall be entitled to all costs incurred on a solicitor and client basis and that the mortgagee shall be entitled to charge interest at the rate set forth in the within Charge.

7. Default in payment of principal and interest occurred on or about the 15th day of July, 2001 and still continues.

8. There is now due and owing as at the 9th day of December, 2001, under the said mortgage, the sum of $178,532.20. The defendant, Peter Noday, is liable to pay these sums and subsequent interest at the rate of 9% per annum compounded semi-annually.

9. The terms of the mortgage and/or Standard Charge Terms 852 provide that in the event of default the Plaintiff would be entitled to possession of the mortgaged premises.

10. The following is a description of the mortgaged property:

> ALL AND SINGULAR that certain parcel or tract of land and premises situate, lying and being in the City of Ottawa, being Parcel 54-1, Plan 4M-540, Property Identifier Number 12345-6789

10. The Plaintiff proposes that this action be tried at the City of Ottawa, Province of Ontario.

Date of Issue: __________________, 2001

STANLEY & IRVING
496 Wilson Court
Ottawa, Ontario
K9B 2L2
tel: (613) 965-9595
fax: (613) 965-9696
Attention: Jay Stanley
Solicitors for the Plaintiff

SCHEDULE "A"

ALL AND SINGULAR that certain parcel or tract of land and premises situate, lying and being in the City of Ottawa, being Parcel 54-1, Plan 4M-540, Property Identifier Number 12345-6789

App 7-14

Judgment for Monetary Amount and Possession

Court File No.

SUPERIOR COURT OF JUSTICE

BETWEEN:

OMNI BANK OF CANADA

Plaintiff

- and -

PETER NODAY

Defendant

JUDGMENT

ON READING THE Statement of Claim in this action and the proof of service of the Statement of Claim on the Defendants, filed, and the Defendants having been noted in default:

1. **IT IS ORDERED AND ADJUDGED** that the Defendant Peter Noday pay to the Plaintiff the sum of $178,941.23.

2. **IT IS ORDERED AND ADJUDGED** that the Defendants Peter Noday and Sharon Noday deliver to the Plaintiff possession of the following land:

> "All and singular that certain parcel or tract of land and premises situate, lying and being in the City of Ottawa, and being composed of all of Parcel 54-1, Plan 4M-540, Property Identifier Number 12345-6789".

3. **IT IS ORDERED AND ADJUDGED** that the Defendant Peter Noday pay to the Plaintiff costs in accordance with the mortgage to be assessed on a solicitor and client basis.

4. This Judgment bears interest at the rate of 9% per cent per year from its date.

DATE: September 10, 2001

____

Local Registrar
Superior Court of Justice

Address of
Court Office: Court House
161 Elgin Street
Ottawa, Ontario
K2P 2K1

App 7-15

Notice of Motion for Order to Issue Writ of Possession

Court File No.

SUPERIOR COURT OF JUSTICE

BETWEEN:

OMNI BANK OF CANADA

Plaintiff

- and -

PETER NODAY

Defendant

NOTICE OF MOTION

THE PLAINTIFF will make a motion to a Judge on Wednesday, the 20th day of September, 2001 at 10:00 o'clock in the forenoon, or as soon after that time as the Motion can be heard, at the Court House, 161 Elgin Street, Ottawa, Ontario.

PROPOSED METHOD OF HEARING: The motion is to be heard

_X_ in writing under subrule 37.12.1(1) because it is made without notice;
___ in writing as an opposed motion under subrule 37.12.1(4);
___ orally.

THE MOTION IS FOR an Order to issue a Writ of Possession.

THE GROUNDS FOR THE MOTION ARE:

(a) Rule 60.10 of the Rules of Civil Procedure.

THE FOLLOWING DOCUMENTARY EVIDENCE will be used at the hearing of the motion:

(a) the pleadings and proceedings herein;
(b) the Affidavit of Sylvia Henry.

DATE: September 10, 2001

STANLEY & JOHN
496 Wilson Court
Ottawa, Ontario
K9B 2L2
tel: (613) 965-9595
fax: (613) 965-9696
Attention: Jay Stanley

App 7-16

Order to Issue Writ of Possession

Court File No:

SUPERIOR COURT OF JUSTICE

THE HONOURABLE JUSTICE	)	**WEDNESDAY, THE 20TH DAY OF**
	)	
A.B. STIRLING	)	**SEPTEMBER, 2001**

BETWEEN:

OMNI BANK OF CANADA

Plaintiff

- and -

PETER NODAY

Defendant

ORDER

THIS MOTION, made by the Plaintiff; for an Order to issue a Writ of Possession, was heard this day, at Ottawa, Ontario.

ON READING the pleadings and proceedings herein, and the Affidavit of Sylvia Henry filed, and on hearing the submissions of counsel for the Plaintiff:

1. **THIS COURT ORDERS** that the Plaintiff be at liberty to issue a Writ of Possession forthwith against the lands known municipally as 17 Armstrong St. Ottawa, Ontario and more particularly described as:

> "All and singular that certain parcel or tract of land and premises situate, lying and being in the City of Ottawa, and being composed of all of Parcel 54-1, Plan 4M-540, Property Identifier Number 12345-6789".

2. **THIS COURT ORDERS** that the Plaintiff shall have its costs of this Motion to be assessed by the Registrar on a solicitor-and-client basis.

THIS ORDER BEARS INTEREST at the rate of 12 per cent per year, commencing on September 20, 2001.

____

App 7-17

Requisition for Writ of Possession

Court File No:

SUPERIOR COURT OF JUSTICE

BETWEEN:

OMNI BANK OF CANADA

Plaintiff

- and -

PETER NODAY

Defendant

REQUISITION

TO THE LOCAL REGISTRAR AT OTTAWA

I REQUIRE a Writ of Possession directed to the Sheriff of the City of Ottawa for possession of the lands and premises described as:

> "All and singular that certain parcel or tract of land and premises situate, lying and being in the City of Ottawa, and being composed of all of Parcel 54-1 Plan 4M-540, Property Identifier Number 12345-6789. The property is municipally known as 17 Armstrong Street, Ottawa, Ontario".

DATED at Ottawa, on September 22, 2001

STANLEY & JOHN
496 Wilson Court
Ottawa, Ontario
K9B 2L2
tel: (613) 965-9595
fax: (613) 965-9696
Attention: Jay Stanley

App 7-18

Writ of Possession

Court File No:

SUPERIOR COURT OF JUSTICE

BETWEEN:

OMNI BANK OF CANADA

Plaintiff

- and -

PETER NODAY

Defendant

WRIT OF POSSESSION

TO THE SHERIFF OF THE CITY OF OTTAWA

Under an Order of this Court made on September 20, 2001 in favour of Omni Bank of Canada, YOU ARE DIRECTED to enter and take possession of the following land and premises in your County or District:

> "All and singular that certain parcel or tract of land and premises situate, lying and being in the City of Ottawa, and being composed of all of Parcel 54-1, Plan 4M-540, Property Identifier Number 12345-6789. The property is municipally known as 17 Armstrong Street, Ottawa, Ontario".

AND YOU ARE DIRECTED to give possession of the above land and premises without delay to Omni Bank of Canada.

DATED: September 30, 2001

Issued by: ______________________
Local Registrar

Address of
Court Office:
161 Elgin Street
Ottawa, Ontario
K2P 2K1

App 7-19

Letter to Sheriff to Act on Writ of Possession

September 30, 2001

Sheriff
City of Ottawa
161 Elgin Street
Ottawa, Ontario
K2P 2K1

Dear Sir:

Re: Omni Bank of Canada v. Noday

Pursuant to the Writ of Possession enclosed, could you please attend at 17 Armstrong Street, Ottawa, Ontario and take possession of the premises. The premises are presently occupied by Peter Noday against whom the Writ of Possession was obtained.

Please advise us when possession will be taken in order that we may arrange to have a locksmith available to change the locks at that time.

Yours very truly,

STANLEY & JOHN

Per: Jay Stanley

App 7-20

Farm Debt Mediation Act - Notice of Intent to Realize on Security s.21 [Prescribed Form AAFC/AAC4805 (97/110)]

Form unable to be included. Please check Statutes of Canada.

App 7-21

General Differences Between Foreclosure and Power of Sale

	FORECLOSURE	POWER OF SALE
1. METHOD	court action and motions before court	self-help remedy may be conducted without judicial interference
2. SERVICE	personal service of statement of claim	personal service or registered mail
3. SPEED	statement of claim, statement of defence, request to redeem and a time period up to 60 days	15-day default period and then a 35-day notice period before sale can take place
4. COSTS	costs are those of a solicitor and his or her own client	costs are those of a solicitor and his or her own client
5. TYPE OF SALE	sale is regulated by the Master and can be auction, tender sale or private sale	private sale, no court supervision
6. DEFICIENCY BALANCE	mortgagee takes property in lieu of debt and therefore cannot claim deficiency. If sale, mortgagee can claim deficiency	mortgagor and guarantors liable for deficiency
7. POSSESSION OF PROPERTY	action for possession is included in the foreclosure or sale action	self-help or action for possession
8. PURCHASER'S TITLE	mortgagee obtains title in a foreclosure and purchaser obtains a vesting order at a judicial sale	purchaser receives good title
9. LAND TRANSFER TAX	mortgagee pays land transfer tax on foreclosure and purchaser pays land transfer tax on the purchase	mortgagee does not pay land transfer tax
10. ACCOUNTABILITY	mortgagee is accountable throughout the court action	informal report

Appendix 8

Precedents Relating to

Chapter 8

Foreclosure Proceedings Precedents

App 8-1

Statement of Claim for Foreclosure and Possession

Court File No:

SUPERIOR COURT OF JUSTICE

BETWEEN:

OMNI BANK OF CANADA

Plaintiff

- and -

JEFF SMITH AND SUSAN SMITH and XYZ MORTGAGE CORP.

Defendants

STATEMENT OF CLAIM (MORTGAGE ACTION - FORECLOSURE)

TO THE DEFENDANTS

A LEGAL PROCEEDING HAS BEEN COMMENCED AGAINST YOU by the Plaintiff The claim made against you is set out in the following pages.

IF YOU WISH TO DEFEND THIS PROCEEDING, you or an Ontario lawyer acting for you must prepare a statement of defence in Form 18A prescribed by the Rules of Civil Procedure, serve it on the plaintiff's lawyer or, where the plaintiff does not have a lawyer, serve it on the plaintiff, and file it, with proof of service, in the Court Office, **WITHIN 20 DAYS** after this statement of claim is served on you, if you are served in Ontario.

If you are served in another province or territory of Canada or in the United States of America, the period for serving and filing your Statement of Defence is 40 days. If you are served outside Canada and the United States of America, the period is 60 days.

Instead of serving and filing a statement of defence, you may serve and file a notice of intent to defend in Form 18B prescribed by the Rules of Civil Procedure. This will entitle you to 10 more days within which to serve and file your statement of defence.

Whether or not you serve and file a statement of defence, you may request the right to redeem the mortgaged property by serving a request to redeem (Form 64A) on the plaintiff and filing it in this court office within the time for serving and filing your statement of defence or at any time before being noted in default. If you do so, you will be entitled to seven days' notice of the taking of the account of the amount due to the plaintiff and to 60 days from the taking of the account within which to redeem the mortgaged property.

If you hold a lien charge or encumbrance on the mortgaged property subsequent to the mortgage in question and you do not serve and file a request to redeem, you may file a request for sale which must contain particulars of your claim verified by an affidavit, and must be accompanied by a receipt showing that $250.00 has been paid into court as security for the costs of the plaintiffs) and of any other party having carriage of the sale.

DEFAULT JUDGMENT

IF YOU FAIL TO SERVE AND FILE A STATEMENT OF DEFENCE, JUDGMENT MAY BE GIVEN AGAINST YOU IN YOUR ABSENCE AND WITHOUT FURTHER NOTICE TO YOU. IF YOU WISH TO DEFEND THIS PROCEEDING BUT ARE UNABLE TO PAY LEGAL FEES, LEGAL AID MAY BE AVAILABLE TO YOU BY CONTACTING A LOCAL LEGAL AID OFFICE.

Date: July , 2001

Issued by: ____________________________
Registrar

Address of
Court Office: 161 Elgin Street
Ottawa, Ontario
K2P 2K1

TO: JEFF SMITH
454 Westmount Drive
Ottawa, Ontario
K3B 3K2

AND TO: SUSAN SMITH
454 Westmount Drive
Ottawa, Ontario
K3B 3K2

AND TO: XYZ Mortgage Corp. Inc.
698 Merrill Boulevard
Scarborough, Ontario
M3X 4M4

CLAIM

1. The Plaintiff claims:

(a) That the equity of redemption in the property secured by the mortgage mentioned below be foreclosed;
(b) Possession of the mortgaged property;
(c) Payment by the defendants, Jeff Smith and Susan Smith, of the sum of $121,555.20 now due under the mortgage together with interest at the rate of 12% per year from September 1, 2001 to the date of payment of Judgment:
(d) Postjudgment interest at the rate of 12% per year in accordance with the mortgage;
(e) The costs of this action on a solicitor-and client basis; and
(f) Such further and other relief as this Honourable Court may deem just.

2. The Plaintiff's claim is on a mortgage dated the 1st day of June, 1999 made between Omni Bank of Canada, as Mortgagee, and Jeff Smith and Susan Smith, as Mortgagors, and registered in the Land Titles Office for the Land Titles Division of Ottawa (No. 4) on the 1st day of June, 1999 as instrument number 38888, under which the defendants mortgaged the property described below for a term of five years securing the sum of $130,000.00 and interest on that sum at the rate of 12% per year. The mortgage provides for payment of principal and interest as follows:

"Provided this mortgage to be void on payment of $130,000.00 DOLLARS of lawful money of Canada with interest at 12 per centum per annum calculated half-yearly, not in advance, as well after as before maturity and both before and after default, as follows: Interest at the aforesaid rate on the amounts advanced from time to time, computed from the respective dates of such advances, shall become due and be paid on the 1st day of June, 1999, and thereafter, the sum of $130,000.00 with interest thereon at the aforesaid rate computed from the 1st day of June, 1999 (such installments to be applied FIRST in payment of the interest due from time to time, calculated at the said rate of 12 per centum per annum, and the BALANCE to be applied in reduction of the principal sum) and the BALANCE of the said principal sum of $130,000.00 dollars with interest thereon as aforesaid shall become due and payable on the 1st of June, 2004."

3. The mortgage further provided:

"In case default shall be made in payment of any sum to become due for interest at the time provided for payment in the Mortgage, compound interest shall be payable and the sum in arrears for interest from time to time, as well after as before maturity, shall bear interest at the rate provided for in the mortgage. In case the interest and compound interest are not paid within the interest calculation period provided in the Mortgage from the time of default a rest shall be made, and compound interest at the rate provided for in the Mortgage shall be payable on the aggregate amount then due, as well after as before maturity, and so on from time to time, and all such interest and compound interest shall be a charge upon the land."

4. The mortgage further provided:

"In default of the payment of the interest secured by the Mortgage, the principal amount secured by the Mortgage shall, at the option of the Mortgagee, immediately become payable, and upon default of payment of installments of principal promptly as the same mature, the balance of the principal and interest secured by the Mortgage shall, at the option of the Mortgagee, immediately become due and payable. The Mortgagee may in writing at any time or after default waive such default and any such waiver shall apply only to the particular default waived and shall not operate as a waiver of any future default."

5. The mortgage further provided:

"The Mortgagee may pay all premiums of insurance and all taxes, rates, levies, charges, assessments, utility and heating charges which shall from time to time fall due and be unpaid in respect of the land, and that such payments, together with all costs, charges, legal fees (as between solicitor and client) and expenses which may be incurred in taking, recovering and keeping possession of the land and of negotiating the Mortgage, investigating title, and registering the Mortgage and other necessary deeds, and generally in any other proceedings taken in connection with or to realize upon the security given in the Mortgage (including legal fees and real estate commissions and other costs incurred in leasing or selling the land or in exercising the power of entering, lease and sale contained in the Mortgage) shall be, with interest at the rate provided for in the Mortgage, a charge upon the land in favour of the Mortgagee pursuant to the terms of the Mortgage and the Mortgagee may pay or satisfy any lien, charge or encumbrance now existing or hereafter created or claimed upon the land, which payments with interest at the rate provided for in the Mortgage shall likewise be a charge upon the land in favour of the Mortgagee. Provided, and it is hereby further agreed, that all amounts paid by the Mortgagee as aforesaid shall be added to the principal amount secured by the Mortgage and shall be payable forthwith with interest at the rate provided for in the Mortgage, and on default all sums secured by the Mortgage shall immediately become due and payable at the option of the Mortgagee, and all powers in the mortgage conferred shall become exercisable."

6. The mortgage further provided:

"Where the Mortgagee enters on and takes possession of the land on default, the Mortgagee shall enter into, have, hold, use, occupy, possess and enjoy the land without the let, suit, hindrance, interruption or denial of the Mortgagor or any other person or persons whomsoever".

7. Default in payment of principal and interest occurred on August 1, 2001 and still continues.

8. There is now due on the mortgage:

(a)	For principal	117,928.30
(b)	For interest to September 1, 2001	1,201.80
(c)	For taxes paid	1,200.00
(d)	For premiums of insurance paid	750.00
(e)	For maintenance costs paid	475.00
(f)	For heating costs	0.00
(g)	For utility costs	0.00
	Balance due as of September 1, 2001	$121,555.20

9. The Defendants, Jeff Smith and Susan Smith, are liable to pay these sums and subsequent interest at the rate of 12% per year, from September 1, 2001, to the date of payment or Judgment.

10. The following is a description of the mortgaged property.

> ALL AND SINGULAR that certain parcel or tract of land and premises situate, lying and being in the City of Ottawa, being composed of all of Lot No. 26 according to Registered Plan No. 4498, Property Identifier Number 12345-6789. The property is municipally known as 454 Westmount Drive, Ottawa, Ontario.

12. The Plaintiff proposes that this action be tried at Ottawa, Ontario.

DATED: September 1, 2001

ADAM & ZENA
Barristers and Solicitors
281 McLeod Street
Ottawa, Ontario
K2P 2K1
tel: (613) 237-0000
fax: (613) 237-1111
Attention: Joe Adam
Solicitor for the Plaintiff

App 8-2

Requisition for Judgment for Immediate Foreclosure as Requested in Statement of Claim

Court File No:

SUPERIOR COURT OF JUSTICE

BETWEEN:

OMNI BANK OF CANADA

Plaintiff

- and -

JEFF SMITH, SUSAN SMITH and XYZ MORTGAGE CORP.

Defendants

REQUISITION FOR IMMEDIATE FORECLOSURE

TO THE LOCAL REGISTRAR AT OTTAWA

I require you to note the Defendants in Default on the grounds that they have failed to file a Statement of Defence or Notice of Intent to Defend and I hereby require that Default Judgment be signed against the Defendants, Jeff Smith and Susan Smith.

The Defendants have not filed a Request to Redeem or Request for Sale.

Default Judgment may be properly signed in this action because the claim is for:

A debt or liquidated demand in money;
Recovery of possession of land;
Foreclosure, sale or redemption of a mortgage.

There has been no payment on account of the claim since the statement of claim was issued.

NO PAYMENT RECEIVED BY PLAINTIFF

1. Principal

   Principal sum claimed in statement of claim $120,353.40

2. Prejudgment interest 1,201.80

   Date on which statement of claim was issued: September 1, 2001.

   Date from which prejudgment interest is claimed: September 1, 2001.

The Plaintiff is entitled to prejudgment interest on the claim calculated as follows:

PRINCIPAL SUM	START DATE	END DATE	NUMBER OF DAYS	RATE	INTEREST AMOUNT
$121,555.20 [Total A]	Sept. 1/01	Sept. 25/01	25	12%	$999.08 [Total B]

Principal Sum Owing [*Total A above*]	$121,555.20
Total Interest Amount [*Total B above*]	$999.08
SIGN JUDGMENT FOR	$122,554.28

POSTJUDGMENT INTEREST AND COSTS

1. Postjudgment Interest

The Plaintiff is entitled to postjudgment interest at the rate of 12% per year, in accordance with the claim made in the statement of claim.

2. Costs

The Plaintiff wishes costs to be assessed by an assessment officer on a solicitor-and-client basis.

DATE: September 25, 2001

ADAM & ZENA
Barristers and Solicitors
281 McLeod Street
Ottawa, Ontario
tel: (613) 237-0000
fax: (613) 237-1111
Attention: Joe Adam
Solicitors for the Plaintiff

App 8-3

Default Judgement for Immediate Foreclosure

Court File No:

SUPERIOR COURT OF JUSTICE

BETWEEN:

OMNI BANK OF CANADA

Plaintiff

- and -

JEFF SMITH, SUSAN SMITH and
XYZ MORTGAGE CORP.

Defendants

JUDGMENT

ON READING THE statement of claim in this action and the proof of service of the statement of claim on the defendants, filed, no request to redeem or request for sale having been served and filed, the defendants having been noted in default, and the plaintiff not wishing a reference,

1. **IT IS ORDERED AND ADJUDGED** that the right, title and equity of redemption of the defendants Jeff Smith, Susan Smith and XYZ Mortgage Corp. to and in the mortgaged property described in the attached schedule are foreclosed. The mortgage is dated June 1, 1999 made between Omni Bank of Canada as mortgagee and Jeff Smith and Susan Smith as mortgagors, and registered in the Land Titles Office for the Land Titles Division of Ottawa (No. 4) on June 1, 1999 as Instrument No. 38888.

2. **IT IS ORDERED AND ADJUDGED** that the defendants, Jeff Smith and Susan Smith, forthwith deliver to the plaintiffs or as the plaintiff directs, possession of the mortgaged property or of such part of it as is in the possession of the defendant. The following is the legal description of the mortgaged property: "ALL AND SINGULAR that certain parcel or tract of land and premises situate, lying and being in the City of Ottawa, being composed of all of Lot No. 26 according to Registered Plan No. 4498, Property Identifier Number 12345-6789, which property is municipally known as 454 Westmount Dr., Ottawa, Ontario."

3. **IT IS ORDERED AND ADJUDGED** that the defendants Ken Smith and Susan Smith forthwith pay to the plaintiff the sum of $122,554.28, being the amount due to the plaintiff today for principal, interest and costs.

THIS JUDGMENT BEARS INTEREST at the rate of 12% per year from its date.

DATE: September 25, 2001 Signed by:

____

Local Registrar
161 Elgin Street
Ottawa, Ontario
K2P 2K1

App 8-4
Request to Redeem

Court File No:

SUPERIOR COURT OF JUSTICE

BETWEEN:

OMNI BANK OF CANADA

Plaintiff

- and -

JEFF SMITH, SUSAN SMITH and XYZ MORTGAGE CORP.

Defendants

REQUEST TO REDEEM

THE DEFENDANT, Jeff Smith, requests an opportunity to redeem the mortgaged property.

DATE: October 25, 2001

JEFF SMITH
18 Courtland Road
Ottawa, Ontario
K6B 2X2
tel: (613) 561-0000
fax: (613) 561-1111

App 8-5

Request for Sale

Court File No:

SUPERIOR COURT OF JUSTICE

BETWEEN:

OMNI BANK OF CANADA

Plaintiff

- and -

JEFF SMITH AND SUSAN SMITH and
XYZ MORTGAGE CORP.

Defendants

REQUEST FOR SALE

The Defendant, XYZ MORTGAGE CORP., hereby requests a sale of the mortgaged property.

Attached is a certificate of the Accountant of the Superior Court of Justice stating that the Defendant, XYZ MORTAGE CORP. has paid into Court the sum of $250.00 as security for the costs of the Plaintiff and of any other party having carriage of the sale.

DATE: October 10, 2001

LEIKIN & PALMER
107 Lisgar Street
Ottawa, Ontario
K2B 4X5
Abe Palmer
(613) 234-8888
Solicitor for XYZ Mortgage Corp.

App 8-6

Affidavit Verifying Claim

Court File No:

SUPERIOR COURT OF JUSTICE

BETWEEN:

OMNI BANK OF CANADA

Plaintiff

- and -

JEFF SMITH AND SUSAN SMITH and XYZ MORTGAGE CORP.

Defendants

AFFIDAVIT VERIFYING CLAIM

I, WILLIAM BODOVSKY, of the City of Ottawa, in the Province of Ontario, Loans Manager of XYZ Mortgage Corp., MAKE OATH AND SAY:

1. There is now due to XYZ Mortgage Corp. under a second mortgage registered against the property owned by Jeff Smith:

(a)	for principal	$45,000.00
(b)	for interest	$2,175.00
(c)	for collection costs	$400.00

SWORN BEFORE ME at the City of Ottawa, in the Province of Ontario this day of October, 2001	))))	
	)	WILLIAM BODOVSKY
A Commissioner, etc.	)	

App 8-7

Notice of Hearing for Directions

FORM 55A

Courts of Justice Act

Court File No:

SUPERIOR COURT OF JUSTICE

BETWEEN:

OMNI BANK OF CANADA

Plaintiff

- and -

JEFF SMITH, SUSAN SMITH and XYZ MORTGAGE CORP.

Defendants

NOTICE OF HEARING FOR DIRECTIONS

By order of the court, a copy of which is served with this notice, a reference was directed to the Plaintiff (*person conducting reference*) for the purpose of (*set out purpose of reference*).

The Plaintiff (*identify party*) has obtained an appointment with (*name of person conducting reference*) on (*day*), (*date*), at (*time*), at (*address*) for a hearing to consider directions for the conduct of the reference in this proceeding.

IF YOU FAIL TO ATTEND, in person or by an Ontario lawyer acting for you, directions may be given and the reference may proceed in your absence and without further notice to you, and you will be bound by any order made in the proceeding.

ADAM & ZENA
Barristers & Solicitors
281 McLeod Street
Ottawa, Ontario
K2P 2K1
tel: (613) 237-0000
fax: (613) 237-1111
attention: Joe Adam
Solicitor for the Plaintiff

TO: (Name and address of solicitor or party receiving notice)

R.R.O. 1990, Reg. 194, Form 55A.

App 8-8

Notice to Party Added on Reference

FORM 55B

Courts of Justice Act

SUPERIOR COURT OF JUSTICE

BETWEEN:

OMNI BANK OF CANADA

Plaintiff

- and -

JEFF SMITH, SUSAN SMITH and XYZ MORTGAGE CORP.

Defendants

NOTICE TO PARTY ADDED ON REFERENCE

TO: (*Name of party added on reference*)

By order of the court, a copy of which is served with this notice, a reference was directed to (*person conducting reference*) for the purpose of (*set out purpose of reference*).

YOU HAVE BEEN MADE A PARTY TO THIS PROCEEDING by order of (*name of person conducting reference*), a copy of which is also served with this notice.

THE REFERENCE WILL PROCEED on (*day*), (*date*), at (*time*), at (*address*).

YOU MAKE A MOTION to a judge of this court WITHIN TEN DAYS (*or where the person is to be served outside Ontario, such further time as the referee directs*) after this notice is served on you to set aside or vary the order directing the reference or the order adding you as a party.

IF YOU FAIL TO DO SO OR IF YOU FAIL TO ATTEND ON THE REFERENCE, in person or by an Ontario lawyer acting for you, the reference may proceed in your absence and without further notice to you, and you will be bound by any order made in this proceeding.
(*Date*)

ADAM & ZENA
Barristers & Solicitors
281 McLeod Street
Ottawa, Ontario
K2P 2K1
tel: (613) 237-0000
fax: (613) 237-1111
Solicitors for the Plaintiff

TO: (*Name and address of party added on reference*)

R.R.O. 1990, Reg. 194, Form 55B.

App 8-9

Notice of Taking of Accounts in a Foreclosure Action

Court File No:

SUPERIOR COURT OF JUSTICE

BETWEEN:

OMNI BANK OF CANADA

Plaintiff

- and -

JEFF SMITH, SUSAN SMITH and XYZ MORTGAGE CORP.

Defendants

APPOINTMENT TO TAKE ACCOUNTS AND SIGN JUDGMENT BEFORE A REGISTRAR

TAKE NOTICE that the Local Registrar has appointed Thursday, the 30th day of October, 2001 at 9:30 in the forenoon at the Court House, 161 Elgin Street, in the City of Ottawa, Province of Ontario, to take the accounts and sign Judgment in this action.

This notice is given to you pursuant to the provisions of rule 64.03(8) of the Rules of Civil Procedure. If you do not attend at the said time and place, the accounts will be taken and Judgment signed in your absence.

DATED at Ottawa, Ontario this 10th day of October, 2001

ADAM & ZENA
281 McLeod Street
Ottawa, Ontario
K2P 2K1
tel: (613) 237-0000
fax: (613) 237-1111
Joe Adam
Solicitor for the Plaintiff

TO: KEN SMITH and SUSAN SMITH
[address]

AND TO: XYZ MORTGAGE CORP.
[address]

App 8-10

Default Judgment for Foreclosure Without a Reference

Court File No:

SUPERIOR COURT OF JUSTICE

BETWEEN:

OMNI BANK OF CANADA

Plaintiff

- and -

JEFF SMITH, SUSAN SMITH and XYZ MORTGAGE CORP.

Defendants

JUDGMENT

On reading the statement of claim in this action and the proof of service of the statement of claim on the defendants, filed, no request for sale having been served and filed, the defendants Jeff Smith and Susan Smith having served and filed a request to redeem and the defendants having been noted in default, and the accounts having been taken in the presence of the solicitor for the plaintiff and the solicitor for the defendants Jeff Smith and Susan Smith:

1. **I FIND** that the following sums are due to the plaintiff from the defendants Jeff Smith and Susan Smith on (redemption date), the day I have fixed for payment under the mortgage in question in this action;

(a) for principal	$117,928.30
(b) for taxes paid to September 1, 2001	1,200.00
(c) for premiums of insurance paid to September 1, 2001	750.00
(d) for maintenance costs paid	475.00
(e) for heating costs paid	00.00
(f) for utility costs paid	00.00
(g) for interest up to September 1, 2001	1,201.80
(h) for costs of this action	1,114.70
(i) for subsequent interest on the principal at the rate of 12% per year	5,075.35
making a total amount due on January 5, 2002	$126,630.55

2. **IT IS ORDERED AND ADJUDGED** that:

a) on payment of the sum of $ $126,630.55 into the Omni Bank of Canada, at 321 Rideau Street, Ottawa, Ontario to the joint credit of the plaintiff and the Accountant of the Superior Court of Justice;

b) on recovery by the plaintiff of the amount due under paragraph 5 of this judgment, together with post judgment interest,

on or before January 5th, 2002 the plaintiff shall convey the mortgaged property described in the attached schedule to the defendants Ken Smith and Susan Smith or as the defendants direct, in accordance with section 2 of the Mortgages Act, and deliver up all documents relating to the mortgaged property. The mortgage is dated June 1, 1999 and made between Omni Bank of Canada as mortgagee and Ken Smith and Susan Smith as mortgagors, and registered in the Land Titles Office for the Land Titles Division of Ottawa (No. 4) as Instrument No. 38888 on June 1, 1999.

3. **IT IS ORDERED AND ADJUDGED** that, on default in payment as required by paragraph 2, the right, title and equity of redemption of the defendants to and in the mortgaged property described in the attached schedule are foreclosed.

4. **IT IS ORDERED AND ADJUDGED** that the defendants Ken Smith and Susan Smith forthwith deliver to the plaintiff or as the plaintiff directs, possession of the mortgaged property, or of such part of it as is in the possession of the defendant.

5. **IT IS ORDERED AND ADJUDGED** that the defendants Ken Smith and Susan Smith forthwith pay to the plaintiff the sum of $123,992.96, being the amount due to the plaintiff today for principal, interest and costs.

THIS JUDGMENT BEARS INTEREST at the rate of 12% per cent per year from its date.

Date: October 30, 2001

Issued by:______________________________
Local Registrar

Address of Court Office:
161 Elgin Street
Ottawa, Ontario
K2P 2K1

SCHEDULE "A"

ALL AND SINGULAR that certain parcel or tract of land and premises situate, lying and being in the City of Ottawa, and being composed of all of Lot No. 26 according to registered Plan No. 4498, Property Identifier Number 12345-6789. The property is municipally known as 454 Westmount Drive, Ottawa, Ontario.

App 8-11

Notice of Motion for Final Order for Foreclosure

Court File No:

SUPERIOR COURT OF JUSTICE

BETWEEN:

OMNI BANK OF CANADA

Plaintiff

- and -

**JEFF SMITH, SUSAN SMITH and
XYZ MORTGAGE CORP.**

Defendants

NOTICE OF MOTION

THE PLAINTIFF will make a motion to a Judge on Wednesday, the 10th day of January, 2002 at 10:00 o'clock, or as soon after that time as the Motion can be heard, at the Court House, 161 Elgin Street, Ottawa, Ontario.

PROPOSED METHOD OF HEARING: The motion is to be heard
X in writing under subrule 37.12.1(1) because it is made without notice;
_ in writing as an opposed motion under subrule 37.12.1(4);
_ orally.

THE MOTION IS FOR a Final Order for foreclosure pursuant to rule 64.03(16) of the Rules of Civil Procedure.

THE GROUNDS FOR THE MOTION ARE:

(a) Rule 64.03(16) of the Rules of Civil Procedure.

THE FOLLOWING DOCUMENTARY EVIDENCE will be used at the hearing of the motion:

(a) the Affidavit of Sarah Zena
(b) the pleadings and proceedings herein.

January 3, 2002

ADAM & ZENA
281 McLeod Street
Ottawa, Ontario
K2P 2K1
tel: (613) 237-0000
Joe Adam
Solicitor for the Plaintiff

App 8-12

Final Order of Foreclosure

Court File No:

SUPERIOR COURT OF JUSTICE

THE HONOURABLE JUSTICE	)	**FRIDAY, THE 10TH DAY OF**
	)	
A.B. STIRLING	)	**JANUARY, 2002**

BETWEEN:

OMNI BANK OF CANADA

Plaintiff

- and -

JEFF SMITH, SUSAN SMITH and XYZ MORTGAGE CORP.

Defendants

FINAL ORDER OF FORECLOSURE

THIS MOTION, made by the plaintiff; without notice, was heard this day.

ON READING the judgment in this action dated October 30, 2001, and the affidavit of Sarah Zena, and on hearing the submissions of counsel for the plaintiff, and since the defendants entitled to redeem have not redeemed the mortgaged property.

1. **IT IS ORDERED** that the right, title and equity of redemption of the defendants Ken Smith and Susan Smith to and in the mortgaged property described in the attached Schedule "A" are foreclosed. The mortgage is dated June 1, 1999 and made between Omni Bank of Canada as mortgagee and Ken Smith and Susan Smith as mortgagors, and registered in the Land Titles Office for the Land Titles Division of Ottawa (No. 4) as Instrument No. 38888 on June 1, 1999.

____

SCHEDULE "A"

ALL AND SINGULAR that certain parcel or tract of land and premises situate, lying and being in the City of Ottawa, in the Province, and being composed of all of Lot No. 26 according to registered Plan No. 4498, Property Identifier Number 12345-6789. The property is municipally known as 454 Westmount Ave., Ottawa, Ontario.

Appendix 9

Precedents Relating to

Chapter 9

Bankruptcy Proceedings Precedents

App 9-1

Statement of Affairs—Non-Business Bankrupt

FORM 1

Statement of Affairs (Non-Business Bankruptcy)
(Paragraph 158(d) of the Act)

(*Title Form 1*)

ASSETS					
Type of assets		Description (be specific)	Exempt Property		Estimated Dollar Value
			Yes	No	
1. Cash on hand					
2. Furniture					
3. Personal effects					
4. Cash-surrender value of life insurance policies, RRSPs, etc.					
5. Securities					
6. Real Property	House				
	Cottage				
	Land				
7. Motor vehicle	Automobile				
	Motorcycle				
	Snowmobile				
	Other				
8. Recreational equipment					
9. Estimated tax refund					
10. Other assets					
TOTAL					

Date ______________________ Bankrupt ______________________

FORM 79 -- *Continued*

LIABILITIES

Creditor	Address	Postal Code	Account No.	Amount of debt		
				Unsecured	Secured	Preferred
1.						
2.						
3.						
4.						
5.						
6.						
7.						
8.						
9.						
10.						
11.						
12.						
13.						
14.						
15.						
16.						
17.						
18.						
19.						
20.						
21.						
22.						
23.						
24.						
25.						
Details of pledged assets		TOTAL	Unsecured			
		TOTAL	Secured			
		TOTAL	Preferred			
TOTAL						

Date

Bankrupt

FORM 79 -- *Continued*
INFORMATION RELATING TO THE AFFAIRS OF A BANKRUPT

A- PERSONAL DATA

1. Family name	Given names	Date of Birth ___/___/___ DD / MM / YY

2. Also known as:

3. Complete address including postal code:

4. Marital status _Married _Single _Widowed _Separated _Divorced _Common-law

5. Full name of spouse:

6. Name of present employer	Occupation (Bankrupt)

7. DEPENDENTS (*as defined by the Income Tax Act*)

Number aged 15 or less	Number from 16 to 21	Number of adults (including spouse)

Number of dependents residing with the bankrupt (excluding bankrupt):

8. Have you operated a business within the last 5 years?	Yes	No	(If yes) Type of business

B- WITHIN THE 12 MONTHS PRIOR TO THE DATE OF THE INITIAL BANKRUPTCY EVENT, HAVE YOU...

9A. Sold or disposed of any of your assets?	Yes	No
9B. Made payments in excess of the regular payments to creditor?	Yes	No
9C. Had any assets seized by a creditor?	Yes	No

C- WITHIN FIVE YEARS PRIOR TO THE DATE OF THE INITIAL BANKRUPTCY EVENT, HAVE YOU...

10A. Sold or disposed of any real estate?	Yes	No
10B. Made any gifts to relatives or others in excess of $500?	Yes	No
10C. Have you made any arrangements to continue to pay any creditors?	Yes	No

_______________ _______________
Date Bankrupt

FORM 79 -- *Concluded*

D- BUDGET INFORMATION			
11. INCOME		12. EXPENSES	
a- Total earnings		a- Fixed expenses	
b- Financial contributions of all others in the household		b- Others	
c- Other earnings (specify)		c- Payment being made to trustee	
E- TOTAL INCOME		**F- TOTAL EXPENSES**	

13. Have you been bankrupt before?	Yes No
14. If you answered Yes to question 13, when did you receive your absolute discharge? Date / / _	
15. Have you ever filed a proposal under the *Bankruptcy and Insolvency Act*?	Yes No
16. If you answered Yes to question 16, when did you file the proposal?Date / / _	
17. Give reasons for your financial difficulty.	
18. If your answer to any of questions 8, 9, 10, 13 and 15 is yes, give details:	

I, __________, of the ________ of _________________ in the Province of _____________, do swear (*or* solemnly declare) that this statement is to the best of my knowledge a full, true and complete statement of my affairs on the ___________ day of _________ ____ and fully disclose all property of every description that is in my possession or that may devolve on me in accordance with section 67 of the Act.

SWORN (or SOLEMNLY DECLARED)
before me at the ____________________
___________ of ___________in the Province
of _______________________this
________ day of _________________.

______________________________ ______________________________

Commissioner of Oaths
for the Province of
____

Bankrupt

App 9-2

Assignment—Non-Business

FORM 22

Assignment for the General Benefit of Creditors
(Natural Person)
(Section 49 of the Act)

(*Title Form 1*)

Full Legal Name of debtor (please print)

Bennett ______________________ John Michael ______________________
Family Name Given Names (*Underline name used*)

Other previous Legal Names or Aliases

____

Address Occupation

96 George Street, Ottawa Ontario general contractor

______________________ ______________________

______________________ ______________________

Name of Trustee:

R. Martindale & Co. Ltd.

I, __________ being unable to pay my debts as they become due, hereby assign and abandon all my property to the trustee, for the general benefit of my creditors pursuant to the Act.

Signed at Ottawa, in the Province of Ontario, this day of , 2001.

______________________ ______________________
Witness Debtor

App 9-3

Notice of Bankruptcy and of Impending Automatic Discharge and Request of a First Meeting of Creditors

R. Martindale & Co. Ltd. Trustee in Bankruptcy - Receiver Manager

1127 Kingsmere Road
Suite 404
Ottawa, Ontario K1P 9L3
Tel: (613) 233-3333
Fax: (613) 233-4444

NOTICE OF BANKRUPTCY AND OF IMPENDING AUTOMATIC DISCHARGE OF FIRST-TIME BANKRUPT AND REQUEST A FIRST MEETING OF CREDITORS

IN THE MATTER OF THE BANKRUPTCY OF
John Michael Bennett
of the City of Ottawa,
in the Province of Ontario

(Summary Administration)

TAKE NOTICE THAT:

1. John Michael Bennett filed an assignment in bankruptcy on October 7th, 2000, and the undersigned R. Martindale & Co. Ltd. were appointed as Trustee of the estate of the bankrupt by the Official Receiver, subject to the affirmation by the creditors of the Trustee's appointment or the substitution of another Trustee by the creditors.

2. Pursuant to paragraph 155(d.l) of the Act a first meeting of creditors will be required only if within thirty days after the date of bankruptcy, the Official Receiver or creditors who have in aggregate at least twenty five percent in value of the proven claims request a meeting to be held.

3. To request such a meeting and to vote at a meeting, a creditor must lodge with the Trustee before such request for a meeting, a proof of claim and, where necessary, a proxy.

4. Enclosed with this notice is a form of proof of claim, a form of proxy and a list of creditors with claims amounting to twenty five dollars or more, showing the amounts of their claims.

5. Also enclosed pursuant to paragraph 102(3) of the Act is information concerning the financial situation of the bankrupt and the obligation of the bankrupt to make payments to the estate of the bankrupt, as required under section 68 of the Act.

6. Creditors must prove their claims against the estate of the bankrupt in order to share in any distribution of the proceeds realized from the estate.

7. Pursuant to section 168.1 of the *Bankruptcy and Insolvency Act*, the bankrupt, being individual who has never before been bankrupt, will be given an automatic discharge on the 7th day of July, 2001 *(insert the date that is nine months after the date of the bankruptcy)*, unless the Superintendent of Bankruptcy, the Trustee of the estate of the bankrupt, or a creditor of the bankrupt gives notice of intended opposition to the discharge of the bankrupt before that date.

8. Any creditor who intends to oppose the discharge of the bankrupt shall state in writing the grounds for their opposition, and send a notice to this effect to Division Office, the Trustee of the estate of the bankrupt, and the bankrupt at any time before the 7th day of July, 2001. *(Insert the same date as in item 7).*

9. Where any creditor opposes the discharge of the bankrupt, a court fee applies.

10. Where the discharge of the bankrupt is opposed, the Trustee will apply to the Court without delay for an appointment for the hearing of the opposition in the manner prescribed by the Act unless it is a matter to be dealt with through mediation pursuant to subsection 170.1(4) of the Act.

DATED at Ottawa, Ontario this 11th day of October, 2000.

R. Martindale & Co. Ltd.

App 9-4

Income and Expense Statement

INCOME AND EXPENSE STATEMENT

NET MONTHLY INCOME

Net Salary .... $ ____________
Pension/Annuities .... ____________
Spousal Income .... ____________
Family Allowance .... ____________
Alimony/Child Support .... ____________

Employment Insurance Benefits .... ____________
Social Assistance .... ____________
Rental Income .... ____________
Other Income .... ____________

TOTAL NET MONTHLY INCOME $

MONTHLY EXPENSES

Non-discretionary expenses
Child Support Payments .... ________________
Spousal Support Payments .... ________________
Child Care .... ________________
Health-related expenses .... ________________
Fines/Penalties being paid .... ________________
Employment-related expenses .... ________________
Debts where stay has been lifted by court ________________
Sub-Total: $ ____________

Discretionary expenses
Rent/Mortgage .... ____________
Property Taxes .... ____________
Electricity .... ____________
Heating and/or Gas .... ____________
Telephone .... ____________
Cable .... ____________
Car Maintenance .... ____________
Transportation Costs .... ____________
Car Insurance .... ____________
Life Insurance .... ____________
Food and Meals .... ____________
Hygiene Products .... ____________
Clothing .... ____________
Aesthetic Services .... ____________
Other (specify: ______________________) .... ____________

TOTAL MONTHLY EXPENSES .... ____________

SURPLUS OR DEFICIT .... ____________

DATED Ottawa, this day of July, 2001.

Bankrupt ____________________________ Witness

App 9-5

Form 31

Proof of Claim

(Section 50.1, subsections 65.2(4), 81.2(1), 102(2), 124(2), 128(1), and paragraphs 51(1)(e) and 66.14(b) of the Act)

(*All notices or correspondence regarding this claim must be forwarded to the following address:*

Shulman Fruit & Vegetable Ltd. c/o Adam & Zena, 281 McLeod Street, Toronto, Ontario, M5C 3C5

In the matter of the bankruptcy (*or* the proposal, *or* the receivership) of Fantastic Restaurant Ltd. (*name of debtor*) of Ottawa, Ontario (*city and province*) and the claim of Shulman Fruit & Vegetable Ltd. creditor.

I, Irving Shulman (*name of creditor or representative of the creditor*), of Ottawa, Ontario (*city and province*), do hereby certify:

1. That I am a creditor of the above-named debtor (*or* that I am the President of (*state position or title*) of Shulman Fruit & Vegetable Ltd. (*name of creditor*)).

2. That I have knowledge of all the circumstances connected with the claim referred to below.

3. That the debtor was, at the date of bankruptcy (*or* the date of the receivership, *or in the case of a proposal,* the date of the notice of intention *or* of the proposal, *if no notice of intention was filed*), namely the 18th day of January, 2001, and still is, indebted to the creditor in the sum of $24,900.00 as specified in the statement of account (*or* affidavit *or* solemn declaration) attached and marked Schedule “A”, after deducting any counterclaims to which the debtor is entitled. (*The attached statement of account or affidavit must specify the vouchers or other evidence in support of the claim.*)

4. (*Check and complete appropriate category.*)

X A. UNSECURED CLAIM OF $24,900.00

That in respect of this debt, I do not hold any assets of the debtor as security and

(*Check appropriate description.*)

X Regarding the amount of $24,900.00, I do not claim a right to a priority.

___ Regarding the amount of $, I claim a right to a priority under section 136 of the Act.

(*Set out on an attached sheet details to support priority claim.*)

___ B. CLAIM OF LANDLORD FOR DISCLAIMER OF A LEASE $___________

That I hereby make a claim under subsection 65.2(4) of the Act, particulars of which are as follows:

(*Give full particulars of the claim, including the calculations upon which the claim is based*)

___ C. SECURED CLAIM OF $___________

That in respect of this debt, I hold assets of the debtor valued at $_____ as security, particulars of which are as follows:

(*Give full particulars of the security, including the date on which the security was given and the value at which you assess the security, and attach a copy of the security documents.*)

___ D. CLAIM BY FARMER, FISHERMAN OR AQUACULTURIST OF $_____

That I hereby make a claim under subsection 81.2(1) of the Act for the unpaid amount of $_____

(*Attach a copy of sales agreement and delivery receipts.*)

___ E. CLAIM AGAINST DIRECTOR $__________

(*To be completed when a proposal provides for the compromise of claims against directors*)

That I hereby make a claim under subsection 50(13) of the Act, particulars of which are as follows:

(*Give full particulars of the claim, including the calculations upon which the claim is based*)

5. That, to the best of my knowledge, I am (*or* the above-named creditor is) (*or* am not *or* is not) related to the debtor within the meaning of section 4 of the Act.

6. That the following are the payments that I have received from, and the credits that I have allowed to, the debtor within the three months (*or, if the creditor and the debtor are related within the meaning of section 4 of the Act,* within the 12 months) immediately before the date of the initial bankruptcy event within the meaning of Section 2 of the Act: (*Provide details of payments and credits.*)

(*Applicable only in the case of the bankruptcy of an individual.*)

___ I request to be advised of any material change in the financial situation of the bankrupt, pursuant to subparagraph 102(3)(b)(i) of the Act.

___ I request to be advised of any amendment made regarding the amount that the bankrupt is required to pay, pursuant to subsection 68(4) of the Act.

___ I request that a copy of the report filed by the trustee regarding the bankrupt's application for discharge pursuant to subsection 170(1) of the Act be sent to the above address.

Dated at Ottawa, this 15th day of April, 2001

________________________ ________________________

Witness **IRVING SHULMAN** (Creditor)

Phone Number: ________________
Fax Number : ________________
E-mail Address : ________________

NOTE: *If an affidavit is attached, it must have been made before a person qualified to take affidavits.*

WARNINGS: *A trustee may, pursuant to subsection 128(3) of the Act, redeem a security on payment to the secured creditor of the debt or the value of the security as assessed, in a proof of security, by the secured creditor.*

Subsection 201(1) of the Act provides severe penalties for making any false claim, proof, declaration or statement of account.

Directions to Complete Proof of Claim

DIRECTIONS AS TO COMPLETING PROOF OF CLAIM FORM

-

CLAIMS NOT COMPLETED CORRECTLY IN EVERY RESPECT WILL BE RETURNED. Every creditor who does not prove his or her claim is not entitled to share in any distribution.

The following checklist is provided to assist the claimant in preparing the proof of claim and where required, the proxy form in a complete and accurate manner. In completing the attached Proof of Claim, the claimant should review the following:

General

1. The declaration must be completed and signed personally by an individual.

2. There must be a witness to the signing of the proof and the witness must sign his or her name in the place provided.

3. The claimant should give the complete address where all notices or correspondence are to be sent. If the claimant moves, the claimant should notify the Trustee of the new address.

4. If the person completing the claim is acting for a corporation or other person, the person must state the capacity in which he or she is acting, such as a, "Credit Manager", "Secretary", or "Authorized Agent".

The Claim

5. The debtor's name and date of the bankruptcy must be filled in and a Statement of Account containing details of the claim must be attached and marked Schedule "A".

6. The amount on the statement of account must correspond to the amount on the proof of claim.

7. The status of the claim must be shown. The claimant should select appropriate status and delete others.

8. If the claimant is asserting a secured claim, the claimant must value the security. The claimant should attach details of each item of security being on a separate schedule together with documents.

9. The claimant must attach a detailed list of all payments or credits received or granted within 3 months preceding the bankruptcy or proposal where the bankrupt and claimant are not related, and within 12 months preceding the bankruptcy or proposal where the bankrupt and the claimant are related.

10. All claimants must indicate if he or she is or is not related to the bankrupt as defined in section 4 to the Act.

General proxy

11. If the claimant wishes to appoint a proxy, the Proxy Form must be completed and signed by the creditor and if the creditor is a corporation, it must be completed and signed in the corporate name.

App 9-6

General Proxy

GENERAL PROXY

IN THE MATTER OF THE BANKRUPTCY OF
Utopia Distribution Inc., of the City of Ottawa
in the Province of Ontario

I (or We), ____
_____(*name of creditor*), of ____ (*name of city, town or village*), a creditor in the above matter, hereby appoint ______________ _____, of ____, to be my (or our) general proxy in the above matter except as to the receipt of dividends, with (or without) power to appoint another general proxy in his or her place.

Dated at ____________ this _________day of ____________, 2001

______________________ Witness	______________________ Individual Creditor
	Name of Corporate Creditor ______________________
______________________ Witness	Per ______________________
	______________________ Name and Title of Signing Officer

App 9-7

Petition for a Receiving Order

Estate no. 33-121345

SUPERIOR COURT OF JUSTICE
IN BANKRUPTCY AND INSOLVENCY

IN THE MATTER OF A PETITION FOR A RECEIVING ORDER OF UTOPIA DISTRIBUTION INC., OF THE CITY OF OTTAWA, IN THE PROVINCE OF ONTARIO

PETITION FOR A RECEIVING ORDER

Naimark Novelties Ltd., a corporation carrying on business in the City of Ottawa, hereby petitions the Court that Utopia Distribution Inc. be adjudged bankrupt and a Receiving Order be made in respect of the property of Utopia Distribution Inc. of the City of Ottawa, in the Province of Ontario, and says:

THAT the said Utopia Distribution Inc. has at some time during the six months next preceding the filing of this Petition carried on business as a gift distributon company in the City of Ottawa and elsewhere in the Province of Ontario, within the jurisdiction of this Court.

THAT the said Utopia Distribution Inc. is justly and truly indebted to the Petitioner in the sum of $240,000.00 on account of goods sold and delivered to Utopia Distribution Inc. over the last twelve months.

3. The Petitioner does not, nor does any person on its behalf, hold any security on the property of Utopia Distribution Inc. or any part thereof, for the payment of the said supplies.

[or in the case where security is held]

[The Petitioner holds security against the assets of Utopia Distribution Inc. in the form of a General Security Agreement and values the said assets at no more than $100,000.]

4. THAT the said Utopia Distribution Inc Inc., within six months next preceding the date of the filing of the Petition has committed the following acts of bankruptcy, namely:

(a) It has permitted a Writ of Seizure and Sale issued by the Registrar at Ottawa of the Superior Court of Justice, formerly the Ontario Court of Justice (General Division), to be returned endorsed to the effect that the Sheriff of the City of Ottawa cannot levy, seize or take any property of the said Utopia Distribution Inc.;

(b) It has ceased to meet its liabilities generally as they become due in that it has failed to pay the Petitioner [and other creditors].

5. THAT R. Martindale & Co. Ltd., Trustee in Bankruptcy, of the City of Ottawa, is a person qualified to act as Trustee of the property of the said Utopia Distribution Inc., has agreed to act as such and is acceptable to the undermentioned creditor:

Creditor	Amount of Debt
Naimark Novelties Ltd.	$240,000.00

DATED at Ottawa, this 6th day of January, 2000.

Signed by the Petitioner in my presence:

______________________________	)))	______________________________
(Signature of Witness)		(Signature of Petitioner)

Issued at the City of Ottawa, in the Province of Ontario, this 6th day of January, 2000.

____
Deputy Registrar in Bankruptcy

App 9-8

Affidavit of Verification

Estate no. 33-121345

SUPERIOR COURT OF JUSTICE
IN BANKRUPTCY AND INSOLVENCY

IN THE MATTER OF A PETITION FOR A RECEIVING ORDER OF
UTOPIA DISTRIBUTION INC.,
OF THE CITY OF OTTAWA,
IN THE PROVINCE OF ONTARIO

AFFIDAVIT OF VERIFICATION

I, SAM NAIMARK, of the City of Ottawa, in the Province of Ontario, MAKE OATH AND SAY:

1. THAT I am the President of Naimark Novelties Ltd., the Petitioning Creditor herein and as such have personal knowledge of the facts deposed to in this affidavit.

2. THAT Utopia Distribution Inc., carrying on business as a chain of distributors in the City of Ottawa and elsewhere in the Province of Ontario, is justly and truly indebted to Naimark Novelties Ltd. in the sum of $240,000.00 as set out in the Petition.

3. THAT the facts alleged in the said Petition are, insofar as Naimark Novelties Ltd. is concerned, are within my own knowledge, true.

SWORN BEFORE ME at City of)
Ottawa, in the Province of)
Ontario, this 6th day of January, 2000.)
) ______________________)
SAM NAIMARK

A Commissioner for oaths in and)
for the Province of Ontario)

App 9-9

Notice of Hearing

Court File No. 33-121345

SUPERIOR COURT OF JUSTICE
IN BANKRUPTCY AND INSOLVENCY

IN THE MATTER OF A PETITION FOR A RECEIVING ORDER OF UTOPIA DISTRIBUTION INC., OF THE CITY OF OTTAWA, IN THE PROVINCE OF ONTARIO

NOTICE OF HEARING

TAKE NOTICE that a Petition that Receiving Order be made in respect of your property will be heard before a Judge sitting in Bankruptcy Court [*or if unopposed, before the Deputy Registrar in Chambers, at the Court House, Room 5022*] 161 Elgin, Ottawa, Ontario on Wednesday, the 18th day of January, 2000 at the hour of 10:00 o'clock in the forenoon or so soon thereafter as the Petition can be heard.

And further take notice that if notice of cause against the Petition is not filed in Court and a copy thereof served on the solicitor for the Petitioning Creditor at least two days before the hearing and if Utopia Distribution Inc. does not appear at the hearing the Court may make a Receiving Order on such proof of the statements in the Petition as the Court shall think sufficient.

Dated at Ottawa, this day January, 2000

TO: Utopia Distribution Inc.
[address]

ADAM & ZENA
281 McLeod Street
Ottawa, Ontario
K2K 3B3
Tel: (613) 237-0000
Fax: (613) 237-1111
Attention: Joe Adam
Solicitor for the Petitioning Creditor

App 9-10

Consent to Act as Trustee

Court File No. 33-121345

SUPERIOR COURT OF JUSTICE
IN BANKRUPTCY AND INSOLVENCY

IN THE MATTER OF A PETITION FOR A RECEIVING ORDER OF UTOPIA DISTRIBUTION INC., OF THE CITY OF OTTAWA, IN THE PROVINCE OF ONTARIO

CONSENT

The undersigned, R. Martindale & Co. Ltd., hereby consents to act as Trustee in bankruptcy with respect to the Petition to be issued against the above debtor.

Dated: January 6, 2000.

R. MARTINDALE & CO. LTD.

Per: ______________________________

App 9-11

Receiving Order

Estate no. 33-121345

SUPERIOR COURT OF JUSTICE
IN BANKRUPTCY AND INSOLVENCY

THE HONOURABLE JUSTICE)
)
A.B. STIRLING)

IN THE MATTER OF THE BANKRUPTCY OF
UTOPIA DISTRIBUTION INC.
of the City of Ottawa,
in the Province of Ontario

RECEIVING ORDER

ON the Petition of Naimark Novelties Inc., a corporation carrying on business in the City of Ottawa, in the Province of Ontario, a creditor, filed on the day , 2000;

AND HAVING HEARD the submissions of counsel for the petitioning creditor, the *viva voce* evidence of and having seen the exhibits and counsel for Utopia Distribution Inc.; [no one appearing for the debtor although duly served as appears from the affidavit of service of sworn , 2000 and no one appearing for the Superintendent of Bankruptcy although duly served as appears from the affidavit of service of sworn , 2000;]

AND IT APPEARING to the Court that the following acts of bankruptcy have been committed:

(a) The said Utopia Distribution Inc. has, within six months next preceding the date of the filing of the Petition, made a fraudulent conveyance or transfer of its property or part thereof in that it conveyed or transferred all or part of its inventory to a corporation without notice to the Petitioner; and

(b) The said Utopia Distribuiton Inc. has, within six months next preceding the date of the filing of the Petition, ceased to meet its liabilities generally as they became due in that it has failed to pay the Petitioner and other creditors.

1. **THE COURT HEREBY ORDERS** that Utopia Distribution Inc., (address), of the City of Ottawa, in the Province of Ontario, (postal code) be adjudged bankrupt by virtue of a Receiving Order hereby made on this date.

2. **THE COURT FURTHER ORDERS** that R. Martindale & Co. Ltd., of the City of Ottawa, in the Province of Ontario, be appointed trustee of the estate of the bankrupt.

3. **THE COURT FUTHER ORDERS** that the trustee give security in cash or by bond without delay, in accordance with subsections 16(1) of the Act.

4. **THE COURT FURTHER ORDERS** that the costs of the petitioner shall be paid out of the estate of the bankrupt on taxation of the estate.

DATED at Ottawa, this day of , 2000.

____

App 9-12

Notice of Examination Before the Official Receiver (Individual Bankrupt)

Estate no. 32-124356

SUPERIOR COURT OF JUSTICE

IN BANKRUPTCY AND INSOLVENCY

IN THE MATTER OF THE BANKRUPTCY OF JOHN MICHAEL BENNETT OF THE CITY OF OTTAWA, IN THE PROVINCE OF ONTARIO

TO: John Michael Bennett, the bankrupt

TAKE NOTICE that you, John Michael Bennett, of the City of Ottawa, in the Province of Ontario, the bankrupt herein, are required to perform all duties imposed on a bankrupt by section 158 of the *Bankruptcy and Insolvency Act.*

YOU ARE HEREBY REQUIRED, pursuant to section 158, to attend at the office of the Official Receiver at 473 Albert Street, 2nd Floor, Ottawa, Ontario, on Tuesday, the 24th day of January, 2001, at the hour of 10:30 in the forenoon, there to answer such questions as may be put to you by the Official Receiver with respect to your conduct, the causes of your bankruptcy and the disposition of your property.

FAILURE TO APPEAR for your examination is an offence under the *Bankruptcy and Insolvency Act*, which may have serious consequences on your application for discharge from bankruptcy.

THIS NOTICE is not to be confused with the notice to attend the first meeting of creditors you may have received from the trustee.

____
Official Receiver

____

RECEIVING ORDER

____

ADAM & ZENA
281 McLeod Street
Ottawa, Ontario
K2K 3B3
Attention: Joe Adam
Tel: (613) 237-0000
Fax: (613) 237-1111
Solicitor for the Petitioning Creditor

App 9-13

Notice of Examination Before the Official Receiver (Corporate Bankrupt)

TO: John Michael Bennett
President of Utopia Distribution
Inc.

Estate no. 33-121345

SUPERIOR COURT OF JUSTICE

IN BANKRUPTCY AND INSOLVENCY

IN THE MATTER OF THE BANKRUPTCY OF UTOPIA DISTRIBUTION INC. OF THE CITY OF OTTAWA IN THE PROVINCE OF ONTARIO

TAKE NOTICE that you, John Michael Bennett, of the City of Ottawa, in the Province of Ontario, President of the bankrupt named herein, are required pursuant to section 159 of the *Bankruptcy and Insolvency Act*, to perform all duties imposed upon a bankrupt by section 158 of the said Act.

YOU ARE HEREBY REQUIRED, pursuant to section 158, to attend at the office of the Official Receiver at 473 Albert Street, Ottawa, Ontario, on Tuesday, the 24th day of January, 2001, at the hour of 10:30 in the forenoon, there to answer such questions as may be put to you by the Official Receiver with respect to the conduct of the said bankrupt corporation, the causes of its bankruptcy and the disposition of its property.

AND TAKE NOTICE, that if you fail to present yourself for examination, the Court may by warrant, cause you to be apprehended and brought up for examination. You may liable on conviction under indictment to imprisonment for a term not exceeding three years.

____
Official Receiver

____

RECEIVING ORDER

____

ADAM & ZENA
Barristers & Solicitors
281 McLeod Street
Ottawa, Ontario
K2K 3B3
Attention: Joe Adam
Tel: (613) 237-0000
Fax: (613) 237-1111
Solicitor for the Petitioning Creditor

App 9-14

Notice of First Meeting of Creditors

Estate no. 33-124356

SUPERIOR COURT OF JUSTICE
IN BANKRUPTCY AND INSOLVENCY

IN THE MATTER OF THE BANKRUPTCY OF
JOHN MICHAEL BENNETT
of the City of Ottawa
in the Province of Ontario

(Summary Administration)

NOTICE OF FIRST MEETING OF CREDITORS

TAKE NOTICE THAT:

1. A first meeting of creditors has been requested to be held by the Official Receiver (or creditors).

2. The first meeting of creditors of the bankrupt will be held on the 27th day of November, 2000 at 10:00 in the morning at the offices of the Trustee, (*insert place of meeting*) 1127 Kingsmere Road, Suite 404, Ottawa, Ontario.

3. To be entitled to vote at the meeting, a creditor must lodge with the trustee, before the meeting, a proof of claim and, where necessary, a proxy.

DATED at Ottawa, this 12th day of November, 2000.

R. Martindale & Co. Ltd.

____
Trustee

App 9-15

Statement of Affairs—Business Bankrupt

IN THE MATTER OF THE BANKRUPTCY OF
Utopia Distribution Inc.
of the City of Ottawa
in the Province of Ontario

To the Bankrupt:

You are required to complete carefully and accurately this Form and the applicable attachments, showing the state of your affairs on the date of your bankruptcy, viz.: the day of , 2000. When completed, this form and the applicable attached lists will constitute your Statement of Affairs and must be verified by oath or solemn declaration:

Liabilities
(as stated and estimated by debtor)

1.	Unsecured creditors as per List 'A'	$________
2.	Secured creditors as per List 'B'	$________
3.	Preferred creditors as per List 'C'	$________
4.	Contingent trusts claims or other liabilities as per	$________
	List 'D' estimated to reclaimable for	$________
	Total liabilities	$________
	Surplus	$________

Assets
(as stated and estimated by debtor)

1.	Inventory		$______
2.	Trade fixtures, etc.		$______
3.	Accounts receivable and other receivables as per List 'E'		$______
	Good_	$________	
	Doubtful	$________	
	Bad	$________	
	Estimated to produce	$________	
4.	Bills of exchange, promissory notes, etc. as per List 'F'		$______
5.	Deposits in Financial Institutions		$______
6.	Cash		$______
7.	Livestock		$______
8.	Machinery, equipment and plant		$______
9.	Real estate as per List 'G'		$______
10.	Furniture		$______
11.	RRSPs, RRIFs, Life insurance etc.		$______
12.	Securities (Shares, Bods, Debentures, etc.)		$______
13.	Interest under wills		$______
14.	Vehicles		$______
15.	Other property, as per List 'H'		$______
		________	$______
	If bankrupt is a corporation, add:		
	Amount of capital subscribed	________	
	Amount paid on capital	________	$______
	Balance subscribed and unpaid		$______
	Estimated to produce		$______
	Total Assets $____________________		
	Deficiency $____________________		

I, John Michael Bennett, President of Utopia Distribution Inc. of the City of Ottawa in the Province of Ontario do swear (or solemnly declare) that this statement and the attached lists are to the best of my knowledge a full, true and complete statement of affairs on the day of , , and fully disclose all its property of every description in its possession and or that may devolve on it in accordance with section 67 of the *Bankruptcy and Insolvency Act.*

SWORN before me at the City of Ottawa,)
in the Province of Ontario,)
this ____ day of , 2000.) ____________________________
) (Signature of bankrupt or officer)
__________________________________)
A Commissioner, etc.

IN THE MATTER OF THE BANKRUPTCY OF
Utopia Distribution Inc.
of the City of Ottawa
in the Province of Ontario

List "A"
Unsecured Creditors

(The names to be arranged in alphabetical order and numbered consecutively)

No.	Name	Address	Account Number	Amount of Claim
1.				
2.				
3.				
4.				
5.				
6.				
7.				
8.				
9.				
10.				
11.				
12.				
	TOTAL			$

Dated:

Signature of bankrupt or officer

IN THE MATTER OF THE BANKRUPTCY OF
Utopia Distribution Inc.
of the City of Ottawa
in the Province of Ontario

List "B"
Secured Creditors

No.	Name Address	Amount of Claim	Particulars of Security	When Given	Estimated Value of Security	Estimated Surplus from Security	Balance of Claim Unsecured
1.							
2.							
3.							
4.							
5.							
6.							
7.							
8.							
9.							
10.							
11.							
	TOTAL	$					

Dated:

____
Signature of bankrupt or officer

IN THE MATTER OF THE BANKRUPTCY OF
Utopia Distribution Inc.
of the City of Ottawa
in the Province of Ontario

List "C"
Preferred Creditors for Wages, Rent, Etc.

No.	Name of Creditor	Address and Occupation	Nature of Claim	Period During which Claim Accrued	Amount of Claim	Amount Payable in Full	Difference Ranking for Dividend
1.							
2.							
3.							
4.							
5.							
6.							
7.							
8.							
9.							
10.							
11.							
	TOTAL				$		

Dated:

Signature of bankrupt or officer

IN THE MATTER OF THE BANKRUPTCY OF
Utopia Distribution Inc.
of the City of Ottawa
in the Province of Ontario

List "D"
Contingent or Other Liabilities

(Full particulars of all liabilities not otherwise scheduled to be given here)

No.	Name of Creditor or Claimant	Address and Occupation	Amount of Liability or Claim	Amount expected to rank for dividend	Date Liability Incurred Month, Year	Nature of Liability
1.						
2.						
3.						
4.						
5.						
6.						
7.						
8.						
9.						
10.						
11.						
	TOTAL					

Dated:

____
Signature of bankrupt or officer

IN THE MATTER OF THE BANKRUPTCY OF
Utopia Distribution Inc.
of the City of Ottawa
in the Province of Ontario

List "E"
Debts Due to the Estate, Including Book Debts

No	Name of debtor, Address & Occupation of Debtor	Nature of Debt	Amount of Debt			Folio of Ledgers or other books where particulars are to be found	When Contracted Month Year	Estimated to Produce	Particulars of any securities held for debt
			Good	Doubtful	Bad				
1.									
2.									
3.									
4.									
5.									
6.									
7.									
8.									
9.									
10.									
11.									
	TOTAL								

Dated:

____
Signature of bankrupt or officer

IN THE MATTER OF THE BANKRUPTCY OF
Utopia Distribution Inc.
of the City of Ottawa
in the Province of Ontario

List "F"
Bills of Exchange, Promissory Notes, Lien Notes, Chattel Mortgages, etc., Available as Assets

No.	Name of all promissors, acceptors endorsers, mortgagors, and guarantors	Address	Occupations	Amount Of bill or note, etc.	Date When Due	Estimated to produce	Particulars of any property held as security for payment of bill or note etc
1.							
2.							
3.							
4.							
5.							
6.							
7.							
8.							
9.							
10.							
11.							
	TOTAL			$			

Dated:

Signature of bankrupt or officer

IN THE MATTER OF THE BANKRUPTCY OF
Utopia Distribution Inc.
of the City of Ottawa
in the Province of Ontario

List "G"
Real Estate or Immovable Property Owned by Bankrupt

No.	Description of Property	Nature of bankrupt's interest	In whose name does title stand	Total value	Particulars of mortgages, hypothecs or other encumbrances Name & Address, Amount	Equity or Surplus
1.						
2.						
3.						
4.						
5.						
6.						
7.						
8.						
9.						
10.						
11.						
	TOTAL					

Dated:

Signature of bankrupt or officer

App 9-16

Assignment—Business

ASSIGNMENT FOR GENERAL BENEFIT OF CREDITORS

THIS INDENTURE made in duplicate this 7th day of July 2000.

PURSUANT TO THE *BANKRUPTCY AND INSOLVENCY ACT*

BETWEEN

Utopia Distribution Inc.
hereinafter called "the debtor" of the first part;

and

R. Martindale & Co. Ltd.
hereinafter called "the trustee" of the second part.

WHEREAS the debtor is insolvent and desires to assign and to abandon all its property for distribution among its creditors in pursuance of the said Act.

NOW THEREFORE THIS INDENTURE WITNESSETH that the debtor does hereby assign to R. Martindale & Co. Ltd. all its property for the uses, intents and purposes provided by the said Act.

SIGNED AND SEALED at the City of	)	UTOPIA DISTRIBUTION INC.
Ottawa, in the Province of Ontario.	)	
In the presence of	)	
	)	Per: ____________________
______________________________	)	
witness		

AFFIDAVIT OF EXECUTION OF ASSIGNMENT

CANADA

Province of Ontario	I, Lillian Wilson of the City of Ottawa in the Province of Ontario

make oath and say:

1. That I was present and saw the within Indenture and the duplicate thereof duly signed, sealed and executed by John Michael Bennett, at the City of Ottawa, in the Province of Ontario.

2. That I know the said John Michael Bennett and that he is of the full age of eighteen years.

3. That I am a subscribing witness to the said Indenture and duplicate.

SWORN before me at the City of Ottawa in the Province of Ontario this 7th day of July, 2000.	____________________ Lillian Wilson

____

A Commissioner, etc., or a Notary Public in
and for the Province of Ontario

App 9-17

Form 27

Examination of Bankrupt by Official Receiver
(Non-Business)
(Section 161 of the Act)

Instructions to Official Receiver

The following questions, or questions to a like effect, are to be put to the person examined under section 161 by the official receiver. The questions should be expanded or supplemented by the official receiver in an endeavour to extract from the examination the maximum of essential information and to determine as nearly as possible the true cause of the bankruptcy, the disposition of the property and the conduct of the bankrupt.

OFFICIAL RECEIVER'S NOTES (To be completed by Official Receiver)

Previous Bankruptcy(ies):

Reviewable Transactions:

Undisclosed Assets:

Undisclosed Debts:

Preferential Payments:

Excessive Credit Use:

Settlements:

Other Matters or Concerns:

____
Official Receiver

1. Give your full legal name (and aliases) and your birthday.

2. What is your current address?

3. Have you ever been the owner, or are the current owner of the residence that you live in, or does a family member own it?

4. How much is your rent, or your mortgage payments?

5. Have you been informed of your duties, according to the Bankruptcy & Insolvency Act?

6. Approximately on what date did you become aware that you were unable to meet your debts as they became due and what made you aware of this fact?

7. Did you use or obtain credit after this date? If yes, from whom did you obtain credit?

8. Have you ever been bankrupt before, or made a proposal to your creditors? If yes, when?

9. Do you have any credit cards in your possession at this time?

10. Who is your present employer, and how much is your monthly "Take Home" pay?

11. Do you have any other source of income, other than your job? If yes, what is the source and amount of the income?

12. What bank or banks do you have accounts at, and what is your present balance?

13. Do you have any other debts that you have not disclosed on your Statement of Affairs? If yes, give details.

14. Do you have any other assets that you have not disclosed on your Statement of Affairs? If yes, give details.

15. Explain the following debts, giving the date they were started, and the reason or cause of the debt.

16. Have you sold, given away or disposed of any assets in the 12 months prior to the date of the initial bankruptcy event? If so, give details.

17. From the sale of the above assets, how much money did you receive, and what did you do with the money?

18. Did you sell or give away anything that you bought on credit before it was fully paid for? If so, give details.

19. Have you paid back any debts to family members in the 12 months prior to the date of the initial bankruptcy event? If so, give details.

20. Did you pay your trustee at the time of signing your papers? If so, how much?

21. Are you presently making payments to your trustee? If so, how much?

22. Did you consider any other formal insolvency options before you filed your bankruptcy?

23. What creditors did you make payments to in the 3 months prior to filing bankruptcy? Did you pay any of these creditors in full, or give them larger than normal payments?

24. Are you aware of anyone holding any assets in trust? If so, give details.

25. Are you preparing monthly income and expense statements for your trustee?

26. List all monthly income, including that of your spouse (including common-law), and the source of the income.

27. List all monthly expenses, with the dollar amounts beside them.

28. If your expenses are more than your income, please explain what expenses you are not paying, and what you are doing to correct this problem.

29. Who advised you in regard to your financial problems?

30. Do you own or lease a motor vehicle? If yes, give details (are you paying the trustee to keep the vehicle, or who are paying to keep it, and what amount is being paid).

31. Are you presently borrowing a motor vehicle? If yes, give details.

32. Did you obtain any cash advances on any credit cards in the 12 months prior to the date of the initial bankruptcy event? If so, list them giving cash amounts and the last date an advance was taken.

33. Did you pay for any trips with your credit cards in the 12 months prior to the date of the initial bankruptcy event? If yes, what trips did you take, and how much money was charged on the cards?

34. Please explain why and how you ran up a total credit card debt of over $x.xx on your credit cards. I.e., what type of purchases were made and over what period of time?

35. What do you believe are the causes of your bankruptcy? Please give a brief explanation.

36. Do you feel you are directly or partially responsible for your bankruptcy? Please explain your answer.

NOTE TO OFFICIAL RECEIVER

Any additional questions put by the official receiver and the answers to them should be entered in the space provided below or on a sheet to be attached to this form.

I, ____________________________, of the City of Toronto, in the Province of Ontario do swear (or solemnly declare) that to the best of my knowledge the above answers are true in every respect. I understand that this examination is being adjourned sine die and may be continued at a later date if necessary.

SWORN before me at the City of	)	
Toronto, in the Province of Ontario,	)	
this day of June, 2001	)	
	)	
	)	
____________________________	)	____________________________
Official Receiver for Bankruptcy	)	Bankrupt
Division No__________ of the		
Bankruptcy District of		
______________________		

App 9-18

Form 28

Questions To Be Put to an Officer of the Bankrupt Corporation, or a designated person, by the Official Receiver (Sections 159 and 161 of the Act)

Instructions to Official Receiver

The following questions, or questions to a like effect, are to be put to the person examined under section 159 by the official receiver. The questions should be expanded or supplemented by the official receiver in an endeavour to extract from the examination the maximum of essential information and to determine as nearly as possible the true cause of the bankruptcy, the disposition of the property and the conduct of the bankrupt corporation. The books, statements, etc., of the bankrupt corporation should be available to the official receiver for reference or for the purpose of a more detailed examination of any phase of the corporation's business or conduct which the official receiver may deem warranted.

1. Are you an officer of the corporation referred to in these proceedings?

2. Have you been made aware of your duties pursuant to sections 158 and 159 of the Act?

3. What is your full name and what position do you hold in the corporation?

4. What is the full name of the corporation and what is the address of its head office?

5. When and under what Act of Parliament or of a province was it incorporated?

6. What is the authorized capital of the corporation?

7. What amount of the capital has been subscribed and what amount of subscribed capital has been paid in full?

8. What amount of the capital was paid in cash and what was the consideration for any other issue of the share capital?

9. Did the corporation have a share register containing particulars of the allotment, issue and transfer of all shares?

10. Does it disclose the amount paid, whether by cash or otherwise, on each share of the corporation?

11. What is the total amount, if any, unpaid on the shares of the corporation and by whom is that amount owing?

12. What are the names of the principal shareholders?

13. What are the names of the directors and officers of the corporation?

14. Has the corporation any wholly-owned subsidiary corporations? If so, give particulars.

15. Has the bankrupt corporation or any of its subsidiaries ever been in bankruptcy before or made a proposal or arrangement with the creditors?

16. When did the corporation commence business?

17. What was the nature of its business?

18. Was a proper set of books kept, and are they up to date?

19. Were the books audited annually?

20. What is the name of the auditor and when was the last statement drawn up?

21. Have all proper returns been made to the various government departments requiring them?

22. When did the corporation first become aware of its insolvency?

23. Did the corporation continue to carry on business and contract liabilities after it became aware of its insolvency?

24. Did the corporation make any payments, return any goods, deliver any property or give security to any of its creditors during the three months before the date of the initial bankruptcy event or since it became aware of its insolvency, except in the ordinary course of business? If so, give particulars.

25. Did the corporation, within the 12 months before the date of the initial bankruptcy event,

    (a) execute any bill of sale or chattel mortgage or pledge any of its property?

    (b) sell, dispose of or remove any of its property, except in the ordinary course of trade? If so, give particulars.

26. Did the corporation make or was it a party to any settlement of property within the five years before the date of the initial bankruptcy event? If so, give particulars.

27. What are the causes of the bankruptcy of the corporation?

28. What were the sales for the past three years and what percentage of the sales represented the profit or mark-up?

29. When did the corporation last show a profit?

30. Did the corporation, within the last twelve months pay a cash dividend or redeem any of its shares, notes, debentures, or any other long-term liabilities? If so, when and for what amounts?

31. What was the total amount of salary and expenses for the officers and directors of the corporation during the twelve months prior to the initial bankruptcy event?

32. Did you personally keep track of the corporation's financial position?

33. Are you involved as director, officer or manager in any other business or corporation? If yes, give details.

34. In the last twelve months prior to the date of the initial bankruptcy event, has the corporation entered into any transactions with the following persons:

    (1) Employees, officers or directors
    (2) An individual related to any employee, officer or director of the corporation
    (3) Another corporation, in which you or any of the persons mentioned in (1) or (2) above, or any individual related to them, had a financial interest?

35. Did the corporation have any creditors or customers who fall within questions number 34(1), (2) or (3) above? If yes, give details.

36. Were all sales made just prior to bankruptcy recorded?

37. Was the corporation selling at a normal markup just prior to bankruptcy? If not, give details.

38. Have you ever been involved as an officer in a corporation which has previously gone bankrupt? If so, give details.

39. At the date of bankruptcy, were there any orders previously accepted but unfilled? If so, what has been the disposition of these orders?

40. Does the Corporation have any other assets other than those shown on the Statement of Affairs, or are any assets held in trust by anyone for the Corporation?

41. What Banks or other Financial Institutions did the Corporation use for banking purposes?

42. Were all business receipts deposited in these bank accounts?

43. Were all goods and services provided by the creditors solely for the corporate use and not for use by an officer, Director, or other person/business?

44. Have any other assets been disposed of or seized in the year prior to the date of the initial bankruptcy event other than as already disclosed?

45. How do you account for the deficiency created by the business? Example: How or where were the major losses incurred?

NOTE TO OFFICIAL RECEIVER

Any additional questions put by the official receiver and the answers to them should be entered in the space provided below or on a sheet to be attached to this form.

I, ______________________________, of the City of Toronto, in the Province of Ontario, do swear (*or* solemnly declare) that to the best of my knowledge the above answers are true in every respect. I understand that this examination is being adjourned *sine die* and may be continued at a later date if necessary.

SWORN (*or* SOLEMNLY DECLARED) ....)
before me at the City of Toronto, in the ....)
Province of Ontario, this day of)
June, 2001)
)
______________________________) ______________________________
Official Receiver for Bankruptcy) Signature of Individual Examined
Division No__________ of the
Bankruptcy District of
____

App 9-19

Notice of Disallowance of Claim

Estate no. 33-121345

SUPERIOR COURT OF JUSTICE
IN BANKRUPTCY AND INSOLVENCY

IN THE MATTER OF THE BANKRUPTCY OF
Utopia Distribution Inc.
of the City of Ottawa,
in the Province of Ontario

NOTICE OF DISALLOWANCE OF CLAIM,
RIGHT TO PRIORITY OR SECURITY

TAKE NOTICE THAT,

(A) as Trustee of the estate of Utopia Distribution Inc., a bankrupt, we have disallowed your claim against the estate (or your right to a priority in the estate or your security on the property of the estate) in whole (or to the extent of $____________), pursuant to subsection 135(3) of the Act for the following reasons:

(Set out the reasons for the disallowance.)

(B) as Trustee of the estate of Utopia Distribution Inc., a bankrupt, we have determined that your contingent or unliquidated claim is a provable claim and have valued it at $________________ and therefore, it is deemed a proved claim to this amount pursuant to subsection 135(1.1) of the Act.

AND TAKE NOTICE that if you are dissatisfied with our decision in disallowing your claim in whole or in part (or right to priority or your security or valuation of your claim), you may appeal to the court within the 30-day period after the day on which this notice is served or sent, or within such other period as the court may, on application made within the 30-day period, allow.

DATED at Ottawa, this 5th day of July, 2001

____
R. Martindale & Co. Ltd., Trustee of the Estate of
Utopia Distribution Inc., a bankrupt

App 9-20

Notice Disputing Trustee's Report

Estate no. 33-124356

SUPERIOR COURT OF JUSTICE
IN BANKRUPTCY AND INSOLVENCY

IN THE MATTER OF THE BANKRUPTCY OF
JOHN MICHAEL BENNETT
of the City of Ottawa
in the Province of Ontario

(Summary Administration)

NOTICE OF INTENTION TO DISPUTE

TAKE NOTICE THAT John Michael Bennett intends to dispute the statements contained in the Trustee's report prepared under subsection 170(1) on his application for discharge.

DATED at Ottawa, this _ day of April, 2001.

LONG & SHORT
Barristers & Solicitors
473 RIdeau Street
Ottawa, Ontario
K1A 2P1
Attention: Chris Long
Tel: (613) 238-4444
Fax: (613) 238-4446

TO: R. Martindale & Co. Ltd.
1127 Kingsmere Road
Suite 404
Ottawa, Ontario
K1P 9L3

Robert Martindale
Tel: (613) 233-3333
Fax: (613) 233-4444

App 9-21

Notice of Opposition to Discharge

Estate no. 33-124356

SUPERIOR COURT OF JUSTICE
IN BANKRUPTCY AND INSOLVENCY

IN THE MATTER OF THE BANKRUPTCY OF
JOHN MICHAEL BENNETT
of the City of Ottawa
in the Province of Ontario

(Summary Administration)

NOTICE OF OPPOSITION TO DISCHARGE

TAKE NOTICE that   hereby opposes the discharge of the bankrupt, pursuant to subsection 170(7) of the *Bankruptcy and Insolvency Act*, on the following among other grounds:

1. The assets of the bankrupt are not of a value equal to fifty cents on the dollar on the amount of his unsecured liabilities.

2. The bankrupt is capable of earning substantial income, some of which should be made available to ordinary creditors.

3. The bankrupt has been convicted of fraud on December 23, 1999.

DATED at Ottawa, this day of _____________, ______.

ADAMS & ZENA
281 McLeod Street
Ottawa, Ontario
K2K 3B3
Attention: Joe Adam
Tel: (613) 237-0000
Fax: (613) 237-1111
Solicitor for the Applicant

TO: John Michael Bennett [the bankrupt]

AND TO: [the Trustee]

AND TO: [the Superintendent c/o the Official Receiver]

App 9-22

Consent to Judgment

Estate no. 33-124356

SUPERIOR COURT OF JUSTICE
IN BANKRUPTCY AND INSOLVENCY

IN THE MATTER OF THE BANKRUPTCY OF
JOHN MICHAEL BENNETT
of the City of Ottawa
in the Province of Ontario

CONSENT TO JUDGMENT

I, John Michael Bennett, a bankrupt, do consent to judgment being entered against me in this Court by the Trustee, R. Martindale & Co. Ltd., for the sum of $8,400.00 with payments in the amount of $350.00 per month, payable on the first day of each month, commencing the 1st day of February, 2001, without interest unless I default on any one payment in which case interest shall become immediately due, in accordance with the *Courts of Justice Act*, on all amounts due and owing.

DATED at Ottawa this 7th day of January, 2001.

______________________________	)	______________________________
Witness	)	**JOHN MICHAEL BENNETT**

App 9-23

Judgment

Estate no. 33-124356

SUPERIOR COURT OF JUSTICE
IN BANKRUPTCY AND INSOLVENCY

R. T. SIMS, DEPUTY REGISTRAR	)	**WEDNESDAY, THE 8th**
	)	
IN BANKRUPTCY	)	**OF JULY, 2001**

IN THE MATTER OF THE BANKRUPTCY OF
JOHN MICHAEL BENNETT
of the City of Ottawa
in the Province of Ontario

BETWEEN:

R. Martindale & Co. Ltd., Trustee in Bankruptcy
in the Estate of John Michael Bennett

Applicant

- and -

John Michael Bennett

Respondent

JUDGMENT

PURSUANT to the order made herein and dated the 9th day of January, 2001 whereby it was ordered that John Michael Bennett pay to his trustee, R. Martindale & Co. Ltd., the sum of $8,400.00, payable in amounts of $350.00 per month, payable on the first day of each month, with payments commencing on the 1st day of February, 2001;

AND the consent mentioned in the said order having been given and filed;

1. **IT IS THIS DAY ADJUDGED** that the applicant recover against the said respondant the sum of $8,400.00 without interest, payable in monthly installments of $350.00 on the first day of each month commencing February 1, 2001 but interest on default at the rate provided in the *Courts of Justice Act*.

2. **AND IT IS ORDERED** that the costs of , an opposing creditor, fixed in the amount of $1,000.00 shall be paid by the applicant to out of the first moneys received in the Estate from the $8,400.00.

____

R.T. Sims, Deputy Registrar in
Bankruptcy

App 9-24

Absolute Order of Discharge

Estate no. 33-124356

SUPERIOR COURT OF JUSTICE
IN BANKRUPTCY AND INSOLVENCY

R. T. SIMS, DEPUTY REGISTRAR	)	**WEDNESDAY, THE 8th**
	)	
IN BANKRUPTCY	)	**OF JULY, 2001**

IN THE MATTER OF THE BANKRUPTCY OF
JOHN MICHAEL BENNETT
of the City of Ottawa
in the Province of Ontario

ABSOLUTE ORDER OF DISCHARGE

UPON the application for discharge of John Michael Bennett who made an assignment on the 7th day of October, 2000, and upon reading the report of the Trustee as to the bankrupt's conduct and affairs dated the 30th day of May, 2001, and upon hearing the trustee (if applicable) and the following creditors, ____________________________;

AND WHEREAS proof has not been made of any of the facts mentioned in section 173 of the *Bankruptcy and Insolvency Act*, or that the bankrupt has been guilty of any misconduct in relation to his property or affairs;

1. **IT IS ORDERED** that he be and he is hereby discharged.

____
R.T. Sims, Deputy Registrar in Bankruptcy

App 9-25

Conditional Discharge Order

Court File No. 33-124356

SUPERIOR COURT OF JUSTICE
IN BANKRUPTCY AND INSOLVENCY

R.T. SIMS, DEPUTY	)	**, THE**
	)	**DAY OF , 2000**
REGISTRAR IN BANKRUPTCY	)	

IN THE MATTER OF THE BANKRUPTCY
JOHN MICHAEL BENNETT,
of the City of Ottawa
in the Province of Ontario

BETWEEN:

R. MARTINDALE & CO. LTD., Trustee in Bankruptcy
in the Estate of John Michael Bennett

Applicant

- and -

JOHN MICHAEL BENNETT

Respondent

CONDITIONAL DISCHARGE ORDER

UPON the application of JOHN MICHAEL BENNETT, who made an Assignment for the General Benefit of Creditors on , and upon reading the report of the Trustee as to the Bankrupt's conduct and affairs;

AND WHEREAS proof has been made of the following facts mentioned in Section 173 of the *Bankruptcy and Insolvency Act*, namely:

(a) The assets of the bankrupt are not of a value equal to fifty cents on the dollar on the amount of unsecured liabilities.

1. **IT IS ORDERED** that the bankrupt shall be required to perform the following conditions:

(a) The bankrupt shall consent to the Judgment in favour of the Trustee in Bankruptcy in the amount of $8,400.00 which will be repayable by way of monthly payments of $350.00 on the 12th day of each and every month from and including February 1, 2001 until the full amount of $8,400.00 has been paid.

(b) That the bankrupt's discharge shall be suspended until such time as he has filed his 2000 income tax return, the Notice of Assessment has been delivered and the 2000 taxes are paid in full.

2. **IT IS ORDERED** that no interest will be charged on the amount payable to the Trustee unless there is a default by the bankrupt in his payments. In the event that the bankrupt is in default of his payments, the interest rate will be set in accordance with the *Courts of Justice Act.*

3. **IT IS ORDERED** that once the bankrupt has complied with the conditions in paragraph 1(a) and (b) above and has consented to Judgment in accordance with paragraph 1(a) above, that an Absolute Discharge shall issue.

____

R.T. SIMS, DEPUTY REGISTRAR
IN BANKRUPTCY

App 9-26

Absolute Order of Discharge After Conditions Satisfied

Court File No. 33-124356

SUPERIOR COURT OF JUSTICE
IN BANKRUPTCY AND INSOLVENCY

R.T. SIMS, DEPUTY	**)**	**, THE**	**DAY**
	)		
REGISTRAR IN BANKRUPTCY	**)**	**OF**	**, 2001**

IN THE MATTER OF THE BANKRUPTCY OF
JOHN MICHAEL BENNETT
of the City of Ottawa, in the Province of Ontario

ABSOLUTE ORDER OF DISCHARGE

UPON a Conditional Order of Discharge being granted by R.T. Sims, Deputy Registrar in Bankruptcy, on April , 2001.

AND WHEREAS the Bankrupt has satisfied the conditions as set out in the Conditional Discharge Order:

1. **IT IS ORDERED** that he be and he hereby is discharged.

____

R.T. Sims, Deputy Registrar in Bankruptcy

App 9-27

Request for Mediation Made by Trustee

SUPERIOR COURT OF JUSTICE
IN BANKRUPTCY AND INSOLVENCY

IN THE MATTER OF THE BANKRUPTCY OF
JOHN MICHAEL BENNETT
of the City of Ottawa
in the Province of Ontario

REQUEST FOR MEDIATION MADE BY THE TRUSTEE

I, , president of R. Martindale & Co. Ltd. Trustee of the estate of John Michael Bennett, bankrupt, who made an assignment (*or,* against whom a Receiving Order was made) on the day of , 2000, hereby apply to the Official Receiver to refer this matter to the mediator, who shall set the time and place for the mediation.

This application for mediation is being made for the following reasons:

(*Check appropriate description*)

[ ] Subsection 68(6) - There is disagreement as to the amount of surplus income to be paid by the bankrupt.

[ ] Subsection 68(7) - There is a written request from ________________, a creditor, __________________ (creditor's address), to proceed with the mediation process.

[ ] Subsection 170.1(4) - The bankrupt does not agree with the discharge recommendation of the trustee.

[ ] Subsection 170.1(5) - The trustee is opposed to the discharge of the bankrupt on a ground referred to in paragraph 173(1)(m) or (n) of the Act.

[ ] Subsection 170.1(5) - ______________________________________, a creditor, ____(creditor's address), is opposed to the discharge of the bankrupt on a ground referred to in paragraph 173(1)(m) or (n) of the Act.

An income and expense statement of the bankrupt is attached to this request.

(*Indicate name, address, phone numbers of all parties.*)

Dated at Ottawa, this ___ day of ______________.

____

R. Martindale & Co. Ltd.

Trustee

App 9-28

Notice of Mediation

Estate no. 33-124356

SUPERIOR COURT OF JUSTICE
IN BANKRUPTCY AND INSOLVENCY

IN THE MATTER OF THE BANKRUPTCY OF
JOHN MICHAEL BENNETT
of the City of Ottawa
in the Province of Ontario

(Summary Administration)

NOTICE OF MEDIATION

To:	John Michael Bennett	Bankrupt
To:	R. Martindale & Co. Ltd.	Trustee
To:	______________________	Creditor(s) (where applicable)

TAKE NOTICE that the mediation in the matter of the bankruptcy of John Michael Bennett, bankrupt, will be held on ____________, the _____ day of May, 2001 (or as soon as possible) at: ______________________

The mediation will be held for the following reasons:

(*Check appropriate description*)

[ ] Subsection 68(6) - There is disagreement as to the amount of surplus income to be paid by the bankrupt.

[ ] Subsection 68(7) - There is a written request from ______________________, a creditor, ____ (creditor's address), to proceed with the mediation process.

[ ] Subsection 170.1(4) - The bankrupt does not agree with the discharge recommendation of the trustee.

[ ] Subsection 170.1(5) - The trustee is opposed to the discharge of the bankrupt on a ground referred to in paragraph 173(1)(m) or (n) of the Act.

[ ] Subsection 170.1(5) - ______________________________, a creditor, ____ (creditor's address), is opposed to the discharge of the bankrupt on a ground referred to in paragraph 173(1)(m) or (n) of the Act.

AND TAKE NOTICE that the mediation can only be rescheduled on extraordinary grounds and that under the Bankruptcy and Insolvency Rules, only one such adjournment will be allowed. Therefore, if the mediation has already been adjourned and a second adjournment is requested, regardless of the ground for adjournment, the mediator must cancel the mediation.

DATED at Ottawa, this ______ day of May, 2001

App 9-29

Mediation Settlement Agreement

Estate no. 33-124356

SUPERIOR COURT OF JUSTICE
IN BANKRUPTCY AND INSOLVENCY

IN THE MATTER OF THE BANKRUPTCY OF
JOHN MICHAEL BENNETT
of the City of Ottawa
in the Province of Ontario

MEDIATION SETTLEMENT AGREEMENT

THE PARTIES ACKNOWLEDGE that an agreement was reached in the mediation held on ____________, the ______ day of July, 2001, and that the results of the mediation are as follows:

____

____

____

____

____

____

____

DATED at Ottawa, this ______ day of July, 2001.

______________________ Bankrupt	______________________ Bankrupt's Counsel (where applicable)
______________________ Trustee	______________________ Trustee's Counsel (where applicable)
______________________ Creditor	______________________ Creditor's Counsel (where applicable)

App 9-30

Notice of Motion for a Section 38 Order

Estate no. 33-124356

SUPERIOR COURT OF JUSTICE
IN BANKRUPTCY AND INSOLVENCY

IN THE MATTER OF THE BANKRUPTCY OF
JOHN MICHAEL BENNETT
of the City of Ottawa
in the Province of Ontario

NOTICE OF MOTION

TAKE NOTICE that a motion will be made by counsel on behalf of the Omni Bank of Canada, a creditor of John Michael Bennett, a bankrupt, before R.T. Sims, Deputy Registrar in Bankruptcy, at the Court House, 161 Elgin Street, Ottawa, Ontario on Thursday, the 28th day of January, 2001 at the hour of 10:00 o'clock in the forenoon or so soon thereafter as a motion can be heard for an Order pursuant to section 38 of the *Bankruptcy and Insolvency Act*, R.S.C. 1985, c. B-3 as amended, authorizing the said Omni Bank of Canada to take proceedings in its own name and at its own expense and risk for the purposes of bringing an application to set aside or avoid a certain settlement and, in the alternative, conveyance made by John Michael Bennett, a bankrupt, to Judith Kearns and Jack Kearns of 3 Madhatter Lane, Kanata, Ontario.

AND TAKE NOTICE that in support of such motion will be read the Affidavit of Roger Martindale, President of R. Martindale & Co. Ltd., Trustee of the Estate of John Michael Bennett, bankrupt, filed and the Affidavit of Jennifer Finch, filed, and such further and other material as counsel may advise and this Honourable Court may permit.

DATED at Ottawa this 9th day of January, 2001

ADAMS & ZENA
281 McLeod Street
Ottawa, Ontario
K2K 3B3
Attention: Joe Adam
Tel: (613) 237-0000
Fax: (613) 237-1111
Solicitor for Omni Bank of Canada

App 9-31

Section 38 Order

Court File No. 33-124356

SUPERIOR COURT OF JUSTICE
IN BANKRUPTCY AND INSOLVENCY

R.T. SIMS, DEPUTY REGISTRAR	)	**THURSDAY, THE 28TH DAY OF**
	)	
IN BANKRUPTCY	)	**JANUARY, 2001**

IN THE MATTER OF THE BANKRUPTCY OF
JOHN MICHAEL BENNETT
of the City of Ottawa
in the Province of Ontario

IN THE MATTER OF AN APPLICATION BY
OMNI BANK OF CANADA
for an Order pursuant to section 38 of the
Bankruptcy and Insolvency Act

ORDER PURSUANT TO SECTION 38

UPON the application of Omni Bank of Canada, a creditor of the above named bankrupt, upon reading the Affidavit of Roger Martindale and the Affidavit of Jennifer Finch [where the affidavit is from the creditor, obtain the consent of the Trustee], filed, and upon hearing counsel for the applicant, and it appearing that the said creditor has requested the Trustee to take proceedings to set aside a certain conveyance of the property municipally known as 3 Madhatter Lane, Kanata, Ontario, by the bankrupt to his sister, Judith Kearns and his brother-in-law, Jack Kearns, and the said Trustee, under the direction of the inspectors has refused by reason of lack of funds in the bankrupt's estate to take such proceedings:

1. **IT IS ORDERED** that the applicant may and it is hereby authorized to commence and prosecute proceedings in its own name and at its own expense and risk; for the purpose of setting aside a certain conveyance made by the bankrupt herein to his sister, Judith Kearns and his brother-in-law, Jack Kearns, of the property known as 3 Madhatter Lane, in the City of Kanata, in the Province of Ontario.

2. **AND IT IS FURTHER ORDERED** that notice of the granting of this Order upon the other creditors of the said bankrupt shall be deemed to be sufficiently served by mailing the said notice in a prepaid addressed envelope by registered mail to each of the said creditors at the address as shown in the bankrupt's statement of affairs.

3. **AND IT IS FURTHER ORDERED** that service of notice granting this Order shall be deemed to be made on the day following the date on which the same is mailed as aforesaid.

4. **AND IT IS FURTHER ORDERED** that all benefits to be derived from the proceedings authorized by this Order, together with the costs of same, shall belong exclusively to the applicant, and to such other creditors of the said bankrupt who may within [seven] days of the service upon them of the notice of the granting of this Order as hereinafter provided, agree to contribute *pro rata* according to the amount of their respective proven claims to the expense and risk of such proceedings, and who within the like time in writing directed to Adam & Zena, 281 McLeod Street, Ottawa, Ontario, K2K 3B3, attention: Joe Adam, solicitors for the applicant herein, signify their agreement.

5. **AND IT IS FURTHER ORDERED** that the costs of the applicant and of such others as may join with it in the said proceedings shall be paid first, and after paying the said costs, the balance, if any, shall be divided between the said applicant and any creditors who may contribute under paragraph 4 hereof *pro rata* according to the respective amounts of their proven claims in addition to any dividends that they may be entitled to out of the said bankrupt's other assets, but only to the extent of their said proven claims.

6. **AND IT IS FURTHER ORDERED** that in case there be a surplus after paying the applicant its said claim and costs and the costs of the bankruptcy proceedings herein and the claims of such other parties, if any, entitled to participate, according to the priority of the same respectively as determined by paragraph 5 hereof, such surplus shall be paid to the Trustee in augmentation of the said bankrupt's estate.

7. **AND IT IS FURTHER ORDERED** that if any creditor or creditors shall fail to join in the said agreement provided for in paragraph 4 hereof, within the time hereby limited, they shall be thereafter excluded from participating in the benefits to be derived from the said proceedings.

8. **AND IT IS FURTHER ORDERED** that the Trustee shall provide the applicant within four days of service of this Order upon it with a list of the names and addresses of all creditors who have proven claims against the said estate.

9. **AND IT IS FURTHER ORDERED that** the Trustee shall within four days of service of this Order upon it, execute an assignment assigning all its right, title and interest in the subject matter of the proceedings and shall transfer and make available, all books and documents in support thereof or relevant thereto and that such assignment shall vest in Omni Bank of Canada and such other creditors as may join in these proceedings all the right, title and interest which the said Trustee has, had or shall have in the subject matter of the proceedings by virtue of its office as trustee.

10. **AND IT IS FURTHER ORDERED** that the costs of this application shall be in the discretion of the Court on the hearing of the proceedings.

____

R.T. SIMS, Deputy Registrar in Bankruptcy

App 9-32

Statement of Claim After Section 38 Proceedings

Court file no.

SUPERIOR COURT OF JUSTICE
IN BANKRUPTCY AND INSOLVENCY

BETWEEN:

OMNI BANK OF CANADA

Plaintiff

- and -

JUDITH KEARNS and
JACK KEARNS

Defendants

STATEMENT OF CLAIM

TO THE DEFENDANT(S)
A LEGAL PROCEEDING HAS BEEN COMMENCED AGAINST YOU by the plaintiff(s). The claim made against you is set out in the following pages.

IF YOU WISH TO DEFEND THIS PROCEEDING, you or an Ontario lawyer acting for you must prepare a statement of defence in Form 18A prescribed by the *Rules of Civil Procedure* serve it on the plaintiff(s) lawyer(s) or, where the plaintiff(s) do(es) not have a lawyer, serve it on the plaintiff(s) and file it, with proof of service in this court office, WITHIN TWENTY DAYS after this statement of claim is served on you, if you are served in Ontario.

If you are served in another province or territory of Canada or in the United States of America, the period for serving and filing your statement of defence is forty days. If you are served outside Canada and the United States of America, the period is sixty days.

Instead of serving and filing a statement of defence, you may serve and file a notice of intent to defend in Form 18B prescribed by the *Rules of Civil Procedure*. This will entitle you to ten more days within which to serve and file your statement of defence.

IF YOU FAIL TO DEFEND THIS PROCEEDING, JUDGMENT MAY BE GIVEN AGAINST YOU IN YOUR ABSENCE AND WITHOUT FURTHER NOTICE TO YOU. IF YOU WISH TO DEFEND THIS PROCEEDING BUT ARE UNABLE TO PAY LEGAL FEES, LEGAL AID MAY BE AVAILABLE TO YOU BY CONTACTING A LOCAL LEGAL AID OFFICE.

IF YOU PAY THE PLAINTIFF(S) CLAIM, and $1000.00 for costs, within the time for serving and filing your statement of defence, you may move to have this proceeding dismissed by the court. If you believe the amount claimed for costs is excessive, you may pay the plaintiff(s) claim and $100.00 for costs and have the costs assessed by the Court.

DATE: January , 2001

Issued by: ______________________
Registrar

Address of court office:
161 Elgin Street
Ottawa, Ontario
K2P 2K1

TO: JUDITH KEARNS
3 Madhatter Lane
Kanata, Ontario

AND TO: JACK KEARNS
3 Madhatter Lane
Kanata, Ontario

CLAIM

1. The plaintiff claims against the defendants for:

(a) a declaration against John Michael Bennett, Judith Kearns and Jack Kearns setting aside and declaring fraudulent and void as against the Plaintiff and all creditors of John Michael Bennett the deed, transfer or conveyance transferring to Judith Kearns and Jack Kearns from John Michael Bennett the lands and premises described as Lot 25, Plan 5M-429, Parcel 25-2, Section 5M-429, in the City of Ottawa, in the Province of Ontario as set out in Instrument No. LT472154, registered on the 10th day of May, 2000, in the Registry Office for the Land Titles Division of Ottawa (No. 4) at Ottawa, and municipally known as 3 Madhatter Lane, Kanata, Ontario on the basis that the deed, transfer or conveyance is a settlement within the meaning of section 91 of the *Bankruptcy and Insolvency Act*, R.S.C. 1985 c. B-3 as amended and, in the alternative, a fraudulent conveyance within the meaning of sections 2 and 4 of the *Fraudulent Conveyances Act*, R.S.O. 1990, c. F-29;

(b) a declaration that the defendants Judith Kearns and Jack Kearns hold all, or part of the said lands and premises in trust for the Plaintiff and other creditors of John Michael Bennett, as the court may determine and declare;

(c) an Order pursuant to the *Partition Act*, R.S.O. 1990, c. P-4 directing the sale of the lands and premises and directing the proceeds of the sale be paid into court to the credit of this action and to be paid out as directed by the court, or in the alternative, directing that the portion of the proceeds of the sale to which John Michael Bennett would otherwise be entitled, be paid to plaintiff to the credit of the creditors of John Michael Bennett participating in the proceeding;

(d) an Order that all necessary directions be given, accounts taken, enquiries made, costs taxed and proceedings had, and such further Orders and directions as this Honourable Court may deem just and the circumstances require;

(e) an interim injunction restraining the defendants Judith Kearns and Jack Kearns from in any way granting, conveying, mortgaging, disposing of or in any way dealing with the said lands and premises, pending the final disposition of the claims herein;

(f) leave to issue and file a certificate of pending litigation in respect to the lands and premises municipally known as 3 Madhatter Lane, Kanata, Ontario, and being Lot 25, Plan 5M-429, Parcel 25-2, Section 5M-429, in the City of Ottawa, in the Province of Ontario, registered in the Land Titles Office in the City of Ottawa, and more particularly described as Instrument No. LT472154 at the said Registry Office;

(g) costs of this action on a solicitor and its own client basis.

2. The plaintiff is a chartered bank and it carries on the business of banking which includes the granting of loans and the granting of credit in the Province of Ontario and elsewhere. At all material times, the plaintiff carried on business under the name and style of Omni Band of Canada and extended credit to the defendant John Michael Bennett.

3. The defendant John Michael Bennett made an assignment in bankruptcy on the 31st day of January, 2000, appointing R. Martindale & Co. Ltd. Trustee as his Trustee in bankruptcy.

4. The defendant Judith Kearns is the sister of John Michael Bennett.

5. The defendant Jack Kearns is the brother-in-law of John Michael Bennett.

Settlement and Fraudulent Conveyance

6. Pursuant to an Order dated the 25th day of January, 2001 pursuant to section 38 of *the Bankruptcy and Insolvency Act*, R.S.C. 1985, c. B-3 as amended, the plaintiff is authorized to commence and prosecute this action in its own name and at its own expense for the purpose of setting aside a certain transfer of real property made by the defendant John Michael Bennett to his sister, Judith Kearns and to his brother-in-law Jack Kearns, which real property is municipally known as 3 Madhatter Lane, Kanata, Ontario.

7. By a deed registered on the 12th day of June, 1991 in the Registry Office for the Land Titles Division of Ottawa (No. 4) in the City of Ottawa, in the Province of Ontario as Instrument No. LT41699, the defendant John Michael Bennett became the owner of the property described in Schedule "A" attached hereto.

8. By a deed registered on the 10th day of May, 2000, in the Registry Office for the Land Titles Division of Ottawa (No. 4) in the City of Ottawa, in the province of Ontario as Instrument No. LT472154, the defendant John Michael Bennett conveyed his interest in the lands and premises referred to in paragraph 7 herein, to his sister, the defendant Judith Kearns and to his brother-in-law, the defendant Jack Kearns. The consideration for this deed as described in the Affidavit of land transfer tax was $485,000.00.

9. At the date of the conveyance referred to in paragraph 8, herein, the defendant John Michael Bennett was insolvent in that his assets were less than his liabilities and he was unable to meet his current obligations as they generally became due. The said conveyance removed the property from the defendant John Michael Bennett's name and had the effect of removing the property from his bankrupt estate which would have otherwise been available for payment to his creditors.

10. The said transfer by the defendant John Michael Bennett was made with the intent to defeat, hinder, delay or defraud the creditors or others of their just and lawful actions, suits, debts, accounts, damages, penalties or forfeitures.

11. The said transfer was made within five years of the date of the bankruptcy of John Michael Bennett, and as such, is a settlement of property by the bankrupt within the meaning of section 91 of the *Bankruptcy and Insolvency Act*, R.S.C. 1985, c. B-3 as amended.

12. The plaintiff pleads and relies upon the provisions of the *Bankruptcy and Insolvency Act*, R.S.C. 1985, c. B-3 as amended and in particular section 91 thereof, and the provisions of the *Fraudulent Conveyances Act*, R.S.O. 1990, c. F-29 and in particular sections 2 and 4 thereof.

The Plaintiff proposes that this action be tried at the City of Ottawa, in the Province of Ontario.

DATED: January 20, 2001

ADAM & ZENA
Barristers & Solicitors
281 McLeod Street
Ottawa, Ontario
K2P 1A1
Joe Adam
Solicitors for the plaintiff

App 9-33

Notice of Motion to Declare Reviewable Transaction

Estate no. 33-121345

SUPERIOR COURT OF JUSTICE
IN BANKRUPTCY AND INSOLVENCY

IN THE MATTER OF THE BANKRUPTCY OF
Utopia Distribution Inc.
of the City of Ottawa,
in the Province of Ontario

BETWEEN:

R. MARTINDALE & CO. LTD., Trustee in Bankruptcy
in the Estate of Utopia Distribution Inc.

Applicant

- and -

HOWARD BENNETT

Respondent

NOTICE OF MOTION

R. MARTINDALE & CO. LTD., Trustee of the Estate of Utopia Distribution Inc., a bankrupt, will make a motion to the Presiding Judge of this Honourable Court on Wednesday, the 14th day of July, 2001 at 10:00 in the forenoon or as soon after that time as the motion may be heard, at the Court House, 161 Elgin Street, Ottawa, Ontario.

THE MOTION IS FOR:

1. An Order pursuant to section 101 of the *Bankruptcy and Insolvency Act* directing John Michael Bennett to pay to the Trustee the amount of $67,712.84, being the amount received by the said Howard Bennett from the bankrupt by way of dividend within the twelve month period preceding the bankruptcy at a time when the bankrupt was insolvent or was rendered insolvent by such dividend payment;

2. Such further relief as this Honourable Court deems just.

THE GROUNDS FOR THIS MOTION ARE

1. Howard Bennett was a shareholder and director of the bankrupt between at least August 30, 1999 and August 7, 2000, the date of the Receiving Order.

2. The bankrupt was insolvent between at least August 30, 1999 and August 7, 2000, the date of the Receiving Order.

3. Howard Bennett received a total of $67,712.84 from the bankrupt by way of dividends within the twelve month period preceding the bankruptcy.

4. The bankrupt was insolvent at the time the dividend payments were made, or was rendered insolvent by the payments.

5. Sections 2 and 101 of the *Bankruptcy and Insolvency Act*;

6. Such further grounds as counsel may advise.

THE FOLLOWING DOCUMENTARY EVIDENCE will be used at the hearing of the motion:

1. Affidavit of George Rand sworn on the 5th day of September, 2000,

2. The transcript of the examination of Howard Bennett held on the 20th day of August, 2000;

3. Such other evidence and materials as counsel may advise and this Honourable Court may permit.

DATED September, 5 2000.

ADAMS & ZENA
281 McLeod Street
Ottawa, Ontario
K2K 3B3
Attention: Joe Adam
Tel: (613) 237-0000
Fax: (613) 237-1111
Solicitor for the Applicant

TO: HOWARD BENNETT
1234 Andrew Street
Ottawa, Ontario
K2M 3P7

App 9-34

Notice of Motion to Declare a Settlement

Estate no. 33-121345

SUPERIOR COURT OF JUSTICE
IN BANKRUPTCY AND INSOLVENCY

IN THE MATTER OF THE BANKRUPTCY OF
Utopia Distribution Inc.
of the City of Ottawa,
in the Province of Ontario

NOTICE OF MOTION TO DECLARE A SETTLEMENT

R. MARTINDALE & CO. LTD., Trustee of the Estate of Utopia Distribution Inc., a bankrupt, will make a motion before the Presiding Judge of this Honourable Court on Friday, the day of July, 2001 at the hour of 10:00 in the forenoon or so soon thereafter as the application can be heard at 161 Elgin Street, Ottawa, Ontario.

THE MOTION IS FOR:

1. An Order declaring that a deed dated the day of , , and registered on the day of , as Instrument No. in the Land Titles Office for the Land Titles Division of Ottawa (No. 4) between Utopia Distribution Inc. as Grantor and William Brady as Grantee is void as a settlement against the Trustee within the meaning of subsection 91(1) of the Bankruptcy and Insolvency Act, R.S.C. 1985, c. B-3;

2. In the alternative, an Order that the transfer in paragraph 1 aforesaid is a fraudulent conveyance within the meanings of sections 2 and 4 of the Fraudulent Conveyances Act, R.S.O., 1990, c. F-29;

3. An Order directing the issuance of a certificate of pending litigation against the lands and premises referred to in "A" hereto annexed pursuant to Rule 107 of the Bankruptcy and Insolvency Act, R.S.C. 1985, c. B-3 since the title to or an interest in the said property has been brought into question pursuant to section 103 of the Courts of Justice Act, R.S.O. 1990, c. 43 as amended, section 91 of the Bankruptcy and Insolvency Act, R.S.C. 1985, c. B-3 and sections 2 and 4 of the Fraudulent Conveyances Act, R.S.O. 1990, c. F-29; and

4. Such further and other relief as to this Honourable Court may seem just.

THE GROUNDS FOR THE MOTION ARE:

1.

2.

3.

THE FOLLOWING DOCUMENTARY EVIDENCE will be used at the hearing of the motion:

1. the Affidavit that Samuel Leonard, C.A., filed, and

2. such further and other materials counsel may advise and this Honourable Court may permit.

AND TAKE NOTICE that such application affects the property in Schedule "A" hereto annexed.

DATED , 2000.

ADAM & ZENA
281 McLeod Street
Ottawa, Ontario
K2K 3B3
Attention: Joe Adam
Tel: (613) 237-0000
Fax: (613) 237-1111
Solicitor for the Applicant

TO: William Brady
(address)

App 9-35

Notice of Motion to Declare Fraudulent Preference

Estate no. 33-121345

SUPERIOR COURT OF JUSTICE
IN BANKRUPTCY AND INSOLVENCY

IN THE MATTER OF THE BANKRUPTCY OF
Utopia Distribution Inc.
of the City of Ottawa,
in the Province of Ontario

NOTICE OF MOTION FOR A DECLARATION

R. MARTINDALE & CO. LTD., Trustee of the Estate of Utopia Distribution Inc., a bankrupt, before the presiding Judge of this Honourable Court on Tuesday, the 28th day of January, 2001 at the hour of 10:00 in the forenoon or so soon thereafter as the motion can be heard at the Court House, 161 Elgin Street, Ottawa, Ontario.

THE MOTION IS FOR:

1. A declaration that the payment of $100,000.00 by Utopia Distribution Inc. to Argent Bank is fraudulent and void as a preference within the provisions of section 95 of the *Bankruptcy and Insolvency Act*;

2. An Order that the Argent Bank be required to repay the sum of $100,000.00;

3. Such further and other relief as to this Honourable Court may seem just.

THE GROUNDS FOR THE MOTION ARE:

1. The payment by the bankrupt to the Argent Bank on December 27, 1999 constitutes a fraudulent preference within the meaning of section 95 of the *Bankruptcy and Insolvency Act*.

2. The payment was made within 3 months of the date of the initial bankruptcy event.

3. The bankrupt was insolvent at the time of the payment.

4. The payment had the effect of preferring the Argent Bank over other creditors of the bankrupt.

5. In the alternative, the payment constitutes an unjust preference within the meaning of sections 4 and 5 of the *Assignment and Preferences Act*, R.S.O. 1990, c. A.33.

THE FOLLOWING DOCUMENTARY EVIDENCE will be used at the hearing of the motion:

1. the Affidavit of George Rand, and

2. such further and other material as counsel may advise.

DATED January 14, 2001.

ADAMS & ZENA
281 McLeod Street
Ottawa, Ontario
K2K 3B3
Attention: Joe Adam
Tel: (613) 237-0000
Fax: (613) 237-1111
Solicitor for the Applicant

App 9-36
Commercial List Request Form—Continuing Matter

Commercial List Court File No.______/______

Superior Court File No.______/______

Weekly Court File No. ______/______

Date filed: ____________

SUPERIOR COURT OF JUSTICE - COMMERCIAL LIST

REQUEST FORM - CONTINUING MATTER

A. Short Title of Proceedings:

____

B. The estimated time for the hearing of this matter is . mins. _____ hours _____ days.

C. The nature of this hearing in this continuing matter is:

____

____

D. State the date(s) and time(s) for hearing the matter that has (have) been arranged with other counsel.

____________________ ____________________ ________________

E. Specify when this matter was last dealt with on the Commercial List and by what judge or other judicial official. Advise of any known judicial conflicts.

____

____

F. The following materials will be necessary for the matter to be considered. (It is the responsibility of counsel to confirm that the proper materials are available for the Court.)

____

Counsel for applicant/moving party:	**Counsel for other party:**
Party: ______________________	Party: ______________________
Counsel: ______________________ Print name and sign or initial	Counsel: ______________________ Print name and sign or initial
Address: ______________________ ______________________ ______________________	Address: ______________________ ______________________ ______________________
Phone: ______________________	Phone: ______________________
Fax: ______________________	Fax: ______________________

(If more than 2 parties involved, add additional signatures and particulars on reverse or separate page)

To be submitted to:

Commercial List/Bankruptcy Court Office
393 University Avenue, 10th Floor
Toronto, Ontario
Telephone No. (416) 327-5043
Fax No. (416) 327-6228

Endorsement / disposition

Appendix 10

Precedents Relating to

Chapter 10

Consumer Proposals Precedents

NOTE: Precedents for Proof of Claim and Proxy are contained in Chapter 9

App 10-1
Consumer Proposal

Estate no. 33-142635

**IN THE MATTER OF THE CONSUMER PROPOSAL OF
PATRICIA PHYLLIS JENNER
of the City of Ottawa
in the Province of Ontario**

CONSUMER PROPOSAL

I, **PATRICIA PHYLLIS JENNER**, a consumer debtor, hereby make the following consumer proposal under the *Bankruptcy and Insolvency Act*:

1. That payment of the claims of secured claims shall be made in the following manner: n/a

(*Set out terms of the proposal in respect of secured claims.*)

2. That payment of all claims directed by the *Bankruptcy and Insolvency Act* to be so paid in priority to other claims in the distribution of my property shall be made in the following manner: n/a

(*Set out terms of the proposal in respect of preferred claims.*)

3. That payment of the fees and expenses of the administrator of the consumer proposal, legal fees on and incidental to the proceedings arising out of this Consumer Proposal and in connection with the preparation of this Consumer Proposal, including advice to me in connection therewith, and payment of the fees and expenses of any person in respect of counseling, shall be made in the following manner:

All such fees and expenses shall be paid in priority to all claims of creditors.

(*Set out the terms of the proposal in respect of these fees and expenses.*)

4. That I shall make the following payment to R. Martindale & Co. Ltd., of the City of Ottawa, in the Province of Ontario, the administrator of the Consumer Proposal, for the benefit of the unsecured creditors:

$350.00 monthly for 36 months starting on the 1st day of the month following the date of court approval for a total of $12,600.00.

5. That the administrator of the Consumer Proposal shall distribute the moneys received from me to the unsecured creditors in accordance with the following schedule:

Proceeds, less administrative fees as noted above will be distributed on a pro rata basis by the administrator, every six (6) months, commencing on July 1, 2001.

(*Describe the manner for distributing dividends.*)

6. That the Consumer Proposal may include the following additional terms:

(a) The creditors may appoint up to three inspectors of the estate of the consumer debtor. The inspector may have, in addition to any powers of Inspectors under the *Bankruptcy and Insolvency Act*, the power to:

 (i) receive any notice of default in the performance of the Consumer Proposal and waive any such default, and

 (ii) approve any amendment to the consumer proposal without calling a meeting of creditors, where the amendment would alter the schedule for and the amount of payments to be made by the consumer debtor, but would not change the total amount to be paid, and

(b) Such other terms as may be proposed.

DATED at Ottawa this 6th day of October, 2000.

_________________________	_________________________
Witness	**PATRICIA PHYLLIS JENNER**

App 10-2

Notice to Creditors of Consumer Proposal

Estate no. 33-142635

IN THE MATTER OF THE CONSUMER PROPOSAL OF
PATRICIA PHYLLIS JENNER
of the City of Ottawa
in the Province of Ontario

NOTICE TO CREDITORS OF CONSUMER PROPOSAL

TAKE NOTICE THAT:

1. Patricia Phyllis Jenner, a consumer debtor, made a consumer proposal under section 66.13 of the Act on the day of , 2000 and a copy of it was filed with the Official Receiver by us, R. Martindale & Co. Ltd., the administrator of the consumer proposal on the day of , 2000.

2. Attached to this Notice are the following documents:

(a) a copy of the consumer proposal;

(b) a copy of our report on the consumer proposal that was filed with the Official Receiver on the day of , 2000; and

(c) a form of proof of claim.

3. As the administrator of the consumer proposal, we will be required to call a meeting of creditors only if, pursuant to section 66.15 of the Act,

(a) we are directed to do so by the Official Receiver within the 45-day period after the filing of the consumer proposal; or

(b) at the expiration of the 45-day after the filing of the consumer proposal, creditors having the aggregate at least 25 percent in value of the proven claims have so requested.

4. A creditor who has proved a claim and who indicated dissent from the consumer proposal to us before the expiration of the 45-day period after the filing of the consumer proposal should be deemed to have requested a meeting of creditors.

5. If, within that 45-day period, we are not required to call a meeting of creditors, the consumer proposal shall, by virtue of subsection 66.18(1) of the Act, be deemed to have been accepted by the creditors.

6. In the event that the consumer proposal has been accepted or has deemed to have been accepted by the creditors, we will apply to the Court to review the consumer proposal only if pursuant to section 66.22 of the Act, we are requested to do so by the Official Receiver or any other interested party within 15 days after the day of acceptance or deemed acceptance of the consumer proposal.

7. If within that 15-day period mentioned in paragraph 6, we are not requested to apply to the Court to review the consumer proposal, the consumer proposal is deemed to have been approved by the Court.

DATED at Ottawa, this ______ day of ______________, 2000.

____
R. Martindale & Co. Ltd.
Trustee to the Proposal of Patricia
Phyllis Jenner

App 10-3

Report of Administrator on Consumer Proposal

Estate no. 33-142635

IN THE MATTER OF THE CONSUMER PROPOSAL OF
PATRICIA PHYLLIS JENNER
of the City of Ottawa
in the Province of Ontario

REPORT OF ADMINISTRATOR ON CONSUMER PROPOSAL

I, , of R. Martindale & Co. Ltd., the administrator of the consumer proposal of Patricia Phyllis Jenner, a consumer debtor, hereby report to the official receiver as follows:

1. That the consumer debtor made a proposal on the day of , 2000 and that I filed a copy of it with the official receiver on day of , 2000 .

2. That I have investigated, or have had investigated, the consumer debtor's property and financial affairs so as to be able to assess with reasonable accuracy the consumer debtor's financial situation and the cause of the consumer debtor's insolvency.

3. That attached to this report is a condensed statement of the consumer debtor's assets, liabilities, income and expenses and a list of the creditors whose claims exceed $250.00.

4. That I am of the opinion that the cause or causes of the consumer debtor's insolvency are as follows:

(*Set out fully the causes of the insolvency.*)

5. That I am also of the opinion, for the following reasons, that the consumer proposal is reasonable and fair to both the consumer debtor and the creditors, and that the consumer debtor will be able to perform it (*or*, as the case may be, will not be able to perform it):

(*Set out your reasons.*)

DATED at Ottawa, this __day of , 2000.

R. Martindale & Co. Ltd.
Administrator of Consumer Proposal

App 10-4

Voting Letter

District of ONTARIO
Division No. 11
Court No. 33-142635
Estate No. 33-142635

VOTING LETTER

**IN THE MATTER OF THE CONSUMER PROPOSAL OF
PATRICIA PHYLLIS JENNER
of the City of Ottawa
in the Province of Ontario**

I, ____

of ____

a creditor in the above matter for the sum of $______________________________,

hereby request the trustee acting with respect to the proposal to record my vote FOR / AGAINST the acceptance of the consumer proposal as made on the of , 2000.

DATED at Ottawa, this day of ______, 2000.

______________________________	______________________________
Signature of witness	Signature of creditor
______________________________	______________________________
Signature of witness	Name and Title of Signing Officer

App 10-5

Report of Administrator on Consumer Proposal and Conduct of Consumer Debtor

Estate no. 33-142635

IN THE MATTER OF THE CONSUMER PROPOSAL OF
PATRICIA PHYLLIS JENNER
of the City of Ottawa
in the Province of Ontario

REPORT OF ADMINISTRATOR ON CONSUMER PROPOSAL AND CONDUCT OF CONSUMER DEBTOR

I, ...
....
of R. Martindale & Co. Ltd., the administrator of the consumer proposal of Patricia Phyllis Jenner, a consumer debtor, hereby report to the court as follows:

1. That the consumer debtor made a proposal on the day of , 2000, a copy of which is attached to this report, and that I filed a copy of it with the official receiver on day of , 2000.

2. That I filed a report on the consumer proposal with the official receiver on a copy of which is attached to this report.

3. That I sent to every known creditor of the consumer debtor a copy of the consumer proposal, a copy of the report on the consumer proposal, a form of proof of claim, a list of the creditors of the consumer debtor whose claims exceed $250.00 and the statement respecting a meeting of creditors referred to in subparagraph 66.14(b)(iv) of the Act.

4. That the consumer proposal is deemed to have been accepted by the creditors of the consumer debtor by virtue of section 66.18 of the Act (*or* the consumer proposal was accepted by the creditors of the consumer debtor at a meeting held on the day of , 2000, and a copy of the minutes of the meeting of creditors is attached to this report).

5. That the official receiver (*or* ____________________, an interested party) requested, within the 15 days after the day of deemed acceptance (or acceptance) of the consumer proposal by the creditors, that I apply to the court to have the consumer proposal reviewed, on the following grounds:

(*Set out the grounds given by the official receiver or other interested party for requesting the review.*)

6. That I have changed my opinions on the consumer proposal expressed in my report, in the following respects:

(*Set out the changes in your opinion and give the reasons for the changes.*)

7. That I am of the opinion that the conduct of the consumer debtor is (*or* is not) subject to censure in the following respects:

(*Set out the reasons for this opinion, which should be based on the conduct on the consumer debtor both before and after the filing of the consumer proposal.*)

DATED at Ottawa, this _ day of , 2000.

App 10-6

Form 52

Notice of Status of Consumer Proposal
(Section 66.27 of the Act)

Estate no. 33-142635

IN THE MATTER OF THE CONSUMER PROPOSAL OF
PATRICIA PHYLLIS JENNER
of the City of Ottawa
in the Province of Ontario

Take notice that the consumer proposal of Patricia Phyllis Jenner a consumer debtor, made on the 6th day of October, 2000, a copy of which was filed with the Official Receiver on the 7th day of October, 2000 has been

(Check appropriate description.)

☐ refused by the creditors of the consumer debtor.

☐ refused by the ______________________ Court of ______________________ *(province)* in Bankruptcy.

☐ withdrawn by the consumer debtor.

Dated at Ottawa, Ontario this ________ day of October, 2000

____
R. Martindale & Co. Ltd.,
Administrator of
Consumer Proposal

App 10-7

Certificate of Full Performance of Consumer Proposal

Estate no. 33-121345

SUPERIOR COURT OF JUSTICE
IN BANKRUPTCY AND INSOLVENCY

IN THE MATTER OF THE PROPOSAL OF
PATRICIA PHYLIS JENNER
of the City of Ottawa,
in the Province of Ontario

CERTIFICATE OF FULL PERFORMANCE OF PROPOSAL

THE UNDERSIGNED, R. Martindale & Co. Ltd., the trustee acting in the Consumer Proposal of Patricia Phylis Jenner, certifies that the proposal, as filed with the official receiver on the 7th day of October, 2000 has been fully performed as of the 1st day of July, 2001.

DATED at Ottawa, this 5th day of December 2003.

R. Martindale & Co. Ltd., Trustee
in the Common Property
P.P.J.

Appendix 11

Precedents Relating to

Chapter 11

Commercial (Division 1) Proposal Precedents

NOTE: Precedents for Proof of Claim and Proxy are contained in Chapter 9

Precedent for Voting Letter is contained in Chapter 10

App 11-1

Notice of Intention to Make a Proposal

Estate no. 33-121345

SUPERIOR COURT OF JUSTICE
IN BANKRUPTCY AND INSOLVENCY

IN THE MATTER OF THE PROPOSAL OF
KAUFFMAN KITCHENS INC.
of the City of Ottawa,
in the Province of Ontario

NOTICE OF INTENTION TO MAKE A PROPOSAL

TAKE NOTICE THAT:

1. We, Kauffman Kitchens Inc., an insolvent person, pursuant to subsection 50.4(1) of the *Bankruptcy and Insolvency Act,* intend to make a proposal to our creditors.

2. R. Martindale & Co. Ltd., a licensed Trustee, has consented to act as Trustee under the proposal and a copy of the consent is attached hereto.

3. A list of the names of the known creditors with claims amounting to $250.00 or more and the amounts of their claims is attached.

4. Pursuant to section 69 of the *Bankruptcy and Insolvency Act*, all proceedings against us are stayed as of the date of filing this notice with the Official Receiver in our locality.

DATED at Ottawa this 7th day of October, 2000.

Kauffman Kitchens Inc.

per: ______________________
Marty Kauffman
An Insolvent Person

To be completed by Official Receiver:

Filing Date: _______________ ________________________
Official Receiver

App 11-2

Division I (Commercial) Proposal

Estate no. 33-121345

SUPERIOR COURT OF JUSTICE
IN BANKRUPTCY AND INSOLVENCY

IN THE MATTER OF THE PROPOSAL OF
KAUFFMAN KITCHENS INC.
of the City of Ottawa,
in the Province of Ontario

PROPOSAL

KAUFFMAN KITCHENS INC., the above named debtor, hereinafter called the "Company", hereby submits the following Proposal under the *Bankruptcy and Insolvency Act*:

1. THAT secured claims shall be paid in accordance with the following arrangement:

(a) The Omni Bank of Canada and the Argent Bank will each continue to deal with the Company according to the present arrangements in their security agreements save and excepting that each will agree to postpone its interest to the interests of New Territory Bank.

2. THAT payment in priority to all other claims directed by the said Act to be so paid in the distribution of the property of an insolvent person shall be provided for as follows:

Preferred claims, without interest, are to be paid in full in priority to all other claims of ordinary creditors.

3. THAT provision for payment of all proper fees and expenses of the Trustee and legal fees on and incidental to the proceedings arising out of this Proposal and in connection with the preparation of this Proposal, including advice to the Company in connection therewith shall be made in the following manner:

All such fees and expenses shall be paid in priority to all claims of creditors.

4. THAT the Company shall pay and keep current Her Majesty in right of Canada or in right of Ontario during the operation under this proposal all amounts of a kind that could be subject to a demand under subsection 222(4) of the *Income Tax Act* or any substantially similar provision of Ontario legislation after the filing of the notice of intention and shall pay any arrears that were outstanding at the time of the filing of the notice of intention within six (6) months after the time of such filing.

5. THAT the Company shall pay to its employees and former employees any amount that would be payable under paragraph 136(1)(d) of the Act as if the Company became bankrupt on the date of court approval of this Proposal.

6. THAT the Company shall pay compensation to such landlords that have received notice of disclaimer within thirty (30) days following court approval of this proposal or within such other time period as may be arranged between the Company and the respective landlord.

7. THAT claims arising in respect of goods supplied, services rendered or other consideration given after October 7, 2000, the date of filing of the notice of intention, shall be paid in full in priority to the claims of ordinary creditors.

8. THAT provision for payment of all claims of ordinary creditors, being those persons with claims not referred to in paragraphs 2 to 6 of this Proposal, including claims of every nature and kind whatsoever, whether due or not due for payment as of the date of this Proposal, and including contingent or unliquidated claims arising out of any transaction entered into by the Company prior to the date of this Proposal, which creditors shall hereinafter be referred to as "ordinary creditors", shall be made as follows:

(a) The Company shall pay to the Trustee the sum of $600,000.00 which shall be paid in equal monthly payments of $100,000.00 per month, on the 15th day of each and every month following court ratification of the Proposal.

The Trustee shall pay and distribute the money referred to in paragraph (a) pro rata among the ordinary creditors of the Company referred to therein, and the ordinary creditors shall accept the money referred to in paragraph (a), as the case may be, in full and complete satisfaction of their claims.

9. THAT R. Martindale & Co. Ltd., of the City of Ottawa, in the Province of Ontario, shall be the Trustee under this Proposal and the moneys payable under this Proposal shall be paid to the Trustee who shall make distribution under this Proposal.

10. THAT the Trustee shall control all receipts and disbursements and monitor the business operations for all creditors until the Proposal is either accepted or rejected.

11. THAT at a meeting of creditors held to consider this Proposal, the creditors, if they so desire, may appoint one or more, but not exceeding five Inspectors who shall have the powers of the Inspectors under the Bankruptcy and Insolvency Act, who shall have the power to extend the dates of payments provided for herein if they are in the best interests of the creditors and who shall assist the Trustee in giving directions relative to the carrying out of the Trustees duties under this Proposal.

DATED at Ottawa this 6th day of November, 2000.

Kauffman Kitchens Inc.

Per: ____________________________

Marty Kauffman, President

App 11-3

Resolution of Board of Directors

RESOLUTION OF THE BOARD OF DIRECTORS
of
KAUFFMAN KITCHENS INC.

MINUTES OF A MEETING of the Directors of Kauffman Kitchens Inc. held in the City of Ottawa on the 7th day of October, 2000 at the hour of 11:00 in the forenoon.

PRESENT: Marty Kauffman
William Brady

BEING ALL THE DIRECTORS OF THE CORPORATION.

UPON motion duly made, seconded and carried Marty Kauffman acted as Chair and William Brady acted as Secretary of the Meeting.

ALL the Directors being present in person, the Chair declared the Meeting to be regularly constituted.

THE CHAIR reported that the corporation was in financial difficulties and was no longer able to meet its obligations generally as they became due and for this reason, Motion duly made, seconded and carried that the corporation attempt to re-structure its debt to its creditors by filing a notice of intention to make a proposal pursuant to the *Bankruptcy and Insolvency Act* and for that purpose, Kauffman Kitchens be authorized to execute such documents in connection therewith as may be required.

ON MOTION made, seconded and carried, the meeting was adjourned.

______________________________ ______________________________

Chair - Marty Kauffman Secretary - William Brady

App 11-4

Notice of Proposal to Creditors

Estate no. 33-121345

SUPERIOR COURT OF JUSTICE
IN BANKRUPTCY AND INSOLVENCY

IN THE MATTER OF THE PROPOSAL
KAUFFMAN KITCHENS INC.
of the City of Ottawa,
in the Province of Ontario

NOTICE OF PROPOSAL TO CREDITORS

TAKE NOTICE that Kauffman Kitchens Inc. of the City of Ottawa, in the Province of Ontario has lodged with us a Proposal under the *Bankruptcy and Insolvency Act*.

A COPY of the Proposal, a condensed statement of the Debtor's assets, and liabilities, a list of creditors affected by the proposal and whose claims amount to $250.00 or more are enclosed herewith.

A GENERAL MEETING of the creditors will be held at 1127 Kingsmere Road, Suite 404, Ottawa, Ontario, on the 26th day of November, 2000, at the hour of 10:00 in the forenoon.

THE CREDITORS or any class of creditors qualified to vote at the meeting made by resolution accept the proposal either as made or as altered or modified at the meeting. If so accepted and if approved by the Court, the proposal is binding on all the creditors or the class of creditors affected.

PROOFS OF CLAIM, proxys and voting letters intended to be used at the meeting must be lodged with us prior thereto.

DATED at Ottawa, this 8th day of November, 2000.

____

R. Martindale & Co. Ltd.
Trustee in the Proposal of Kauffman Kitchens Inc.
(address, telephone, fax)

(A form of Proof of Claim, a form of Proxy and a voting letter should be enclosed with each notice.)

App 11-5

Insolvent Person's Report on Cash Flow

Estate no. 33-121345

SUPERIOR COURT OF JUSTICE
IN BANKRUPTCY AND INSOLVENCY

IN THE MATTER OF THE PROPOSAL OF
KAUFFMAN KITCHENS INC.
of the City of Ottawa,
in the Province of Ontario

INSOLVENT PERSON'S REPORT ON
CASH-FLOW STATEMENT

THE MANAGEMENT of Kauffman Kitchens Inc. has developed the assumptions and prepared the attached statement of projected cash-flow of the insolvent person, as of the 7th day of January, 2001, consisting of a projected cash-flow statement for the period January 7, 2001 to June 7, 2001 and the Notes to the projected cash-flow statement.

THE HYPOTHETICAL ASSUMPTIONS are reasonable and consistent with the purpose of the projection described in Note 1, and the probable assumptions are suitably supported and consistent with the plans of the insolvent person and provide a reasonable basis for the projection. All such assumptions have been disclosed in Notes 2-7.

SINCE THE PROJECTION is based on assumptions regarding future events, actual results will vary from the information presented and the variations may be material.

THE PROJECTION has been prepared solely for the Official Receiver, the Court and the Creditors of Kauffman Kitchens Inc. for the purpose described in Note 1, using a set of probable and hypothetical assumptions set out in Notes 2-7. Consequently, readers are cautioned that it may not be appropriate for other purposes.

DATED at Ottawa, Ontario this 7th day of January, 2001.

Kauffman Kitchens Inc.

Per: ______________________________
President & Director

App 11-6

Trustee's Report on Cash-flow Statement

Estate no. 33-121345

SUPERIOR COURT OF JUSTICE
IN BANKRUPTCY AND INSOLVENCY

IN THE MATTER OF THE PROPOSAL
KAUFFMAN KITCHENS INC.
of the City of Ottawa,
in the Province of Ontario

TRUSTEE'S REPORT ON CASH-FLOW STATEMENT

THE ATTACHED STATEMENT of projected cash-flow of Kauffman Kitchens Inc. as of the 7th day of January, 2001, consisting of a projected cash-flow statement for the period January 7 2000 to July 7, 2001 and the Notes to the projected cash-flow statement has been prepared by the management of the insolvent person for the purpose described in Note 1, using probable and hypothetical assumptions set out in Notes 2-7.

OUR REVIEW consisted of inquiries, analytical procedures and discussions related to information supplied to us by the management and employees of the insolvent person. Since hypothetical assumptions need not be supported, our procedures with respect to them were limited to evaluating whether they were consistent with the purpose of the projection. We have also reviewed the support provided by management for the probable assumptions and the preparation and presentation of the projection.

BASED ON OUR REVIEW, nothing has come to our attention that causes us to believe that, in all material respects:

(a) the hypothetical assumptions are not consistent with the purpose of the projection;

(b) as at the date of this report, the probable assumptions developed by management are not suitably supported and consistent with the plans of the insolvent person or do not provide a reasonable basis for the projection, given the hypothetical assumptions; or

(c) the projection does not reflect the probable and hypothetical assumptions.

SINCE THE PROJECTION is based on assumptions regarding future events, actual results will vary from the information presented even if the hypothetical assumptions occur, and the variations may be material. Accordingly, we express no assurance as to whether the projection will be achieved.

THE PROJECTION has been prepared solely for the Official Receiver, the Court and the Creditors of Kauffman Kitchens Inc., for the purpose described in Note 1 and readers are cautioned that it may not be appropriate for other purposes.

DATED at Ottawa, Ontario this 7th day of January, 2001.

R. Martindale & Co. Ltd.
the Trustee acting in re the Proposal of
Kauffman Kitchens Inc.

App 11-7

Certificate of Full Performance of Proposal

Estate no. 33-121345

SUPERIOR COURT OF JUSTICE
IN BANKRUPTCY AND INSOLVENCY

IN THE MATTER OF THE PROPOSAL OF
KAUFFMAN KITCHENS INC.
of the City of Ottawa,
in the Province of Ontario

CERTIFICATE OF FULL PERFORMANCE OF PROPOSAL

THE UNDERSIGNED, R. Martindale & Co. Ltd., the trustee acting in the Proposal of Kauffman Kitchens Inc., certifies that the proposal, as filed with the Official Receiver on the 7th day of October, 2000 has been fully performed as of the 1st day of August, 2001.

DATED at Ottawa, this 4th day of August, 2001.

R. Martindale & Co. Ltd., Trustee

Appendix 12

Precedents Relating to

Chapter 12

The Companies' Creditors Arrangement Act Precedents

App 12-1

Resolution of Board of Directors Authorizing Proposal of a Plan of Compromise or Arrangement

GRANDACO LTD., OF THE CITY OF TORONTO, IN THE PROVINCE OF ONTARIO

RESOLVED:

1. That this Company immediately proposes under the *Companies' Creditors Arrangement Act,* R.S.C. 1985, c. C-36, to the classes of creditors described in the plan of compromise (or arrangement) dated September 20, 2001 now submitted to this meeting and initialled by the chairman for the purpose of identification;

2. That the proper officers of the Company be and they are authorized and instructed to retain and instruct counsel to apply on behalf of the Company to the Superior Court of Justice for an order authorizing the summoning under the Act of a meeting of the aforesaid classes of creditors in the manner as the Court may direct and that the officers be and are authorized and instructed on behalf of the Company to do all acts and things and sign, execute and deliver, whether under the corporate seal of the Company or otherwise, all documents and writings that may be necessary or may be deemed advisable in connection with the summoning and holding of the meetings pursuant to the order and, in the event that the plans shall be agreed to by the classes of creditors (or any or all classes), to cause application to be made to the Court for sanction; and

3. That this Company apply to the Superior Court of Justice for the appointment of an interim receiver of its (or some specified part of its) property with the power of [describe applicable powers].

4. That this Company appoints ABC Co. Ltd., Trustee in Bankrkuptcy, to be a monitor with the authority described in the draft letter to the proposed monitor now submitted to this meeting and initialled by the Chairman for the purposes of identification,

I, Albert Harris, Secretary of Grandaco Ltd., certify that this is a true and correct copy of a resolution passed by the board of directors of the Company duly called and regularly held on the 20th day of September, 2001.

WITNESS my hand and the seal of the Company, this 20th day of September, 2001.

ALBERT HARRIS
[signature and seal]

App 12-2

Petition or Notice of Motion For Directions

Court File No:

SUPERIOR COURT OF JUSTICE

IN THE MATTER OF THE COMPANIES' CREDITORS ARRANGEMENT ACT, R.S.C. 1985, c. C-36, as amended

PETITION OR ORIGINATING SUMMONS (NOTICE OF MOTION)

TO: The Honourable, Superior Court of Justice

The petition of Grandaco Ltd., (the "Petitioner") shows that:

1. The Petitioner is a company incorporated under the laws of the Province of Ontario and is a "debtor company" within the meaning of the *Companies' Creditors Arrangement Act,* R.S.C. 1985, c. C-36.

2. The arrangement proposed by the Petitioner includes a compromise or arrangement between the Petitioner and the holders of the debentures.

3. The Petitioner proposes an arrangement with its secured creditors and some of its unsecured creditors.

4. The Petitioner's creditors to be affected by this Petition fall into several classes.

5. The details of the Petitioner's proposed arrangement, including its proposed classification of its creditors, are contained in the Plan of Arrangement (the "Plan") attached as Exhibit 2 to the affidavit of Albert Harris, filed.

6. The purpose of the Plan is to permit the Petitioner to continue to carry on business in the expectation that the secured and unsecured creditors and shareholders of the Petitioner will derive a greater benefit from the continuation than from a suspension of business and forced liquidation of its business assets.

THE PETITIONER THEREFORE ASKS for an order pursuant to the *Companies' Creditors Arrangement Act:*

1. Directing that a meeting of each of the following classes of creditors be convened to consider the Plan:

(a) Class A, being the Operating Lenders, as defined in the Plan.
(b) Class B, being the Project Lenders, as defined in the Plan.
(c) Class C, being certain Unsecured Creditors, as defined in the Plan.

2. Directing the Petitioner to hold the meetings at the City of Toronto, in the Province of Ontario, on the following dates:

(a) Class A Creditors: October 1, 2001;
(b) Class B Creditors: October 2, 2001;
(c) Class C Creditors: October 3, 2001.

3. Approving the forms of notice and the instruments of proxy and various related forms to be used at the meetings.

4. Directing the manner in which notice of the meetings shall be published and served.

5. Directing that the Vice-President Finance of the Petitioner or a person or persons designated by him preside at the meetings.

6. Staying all proceedings which might be taken against the Petitioner under the *Bankruptcy and Insolvency Act,* R.S.C. 1985, c. B-3, or the *Winding-Up Act,* R.S.C. 1985, c. W-11, or either of them until October 21, 2001, or until otherwise ordered by this Honourable Court.

7. Staying all suits, actions or other proceedings of any nature against the Petitioner until October 21, 2001, or until otherwise ordered by this Honourable Court.

8. Directing that no suit, action or other proceeding of any nature shall be commenced or proceeded with against the Petitioner except with the leave of this Honourable Court until October 21, 2001, or until otherwise ordered by this Honourable Court.

9. Dispensing with notice to the creditors and shareholders of the Petitioner of the application for the stay contained in this Petition.

10. Setting a date for an application to this Honourable Court for an order sanctioning the Plan.

11 Dispensing with notice to the creditors of the Petitioner of the application to sanction the Plan, provided that the date of the application is contained in the information circular and announced at the meetings.

12. Dispensing with notice to creditors of the Petitioner not included in the Plan of the application to sanction the Plan.

ISSUED this 21st day of September, 2001, and filed by Adam & Zena, Barristers & Solicitors, solicitors for the petitioner, whose address for service is in care of its solicitors at 281 McLeod Street, Toronto, Ontario, M5C 3C5.

____

[Signature and seal of Clerk of the Court]

NOTE: Section 10 of the CCAA states that "an application shall be made by petition or by way of originating summons or notice of motion in accordance with the practice of the Court in which the application is made". In Ontario, the usual practice would be to start the application by way of Notice of Application.

App 12-3

Notice of Application to the Court to Sanction Arrangement Given with Notice Summonsing Meetings

Court File No:

SUPERIOR COURT OF JUSTICE

IN THE MATTER OF THE COMPANIES' CREDITORS ARRANGEMENT ACT, R.S.C. 1985, c. C-36, as amended

AND IN THE MATTER OF GRANDACO INC.

NOTICE CONCERNING AN APPLICATION TO SUPERIOR COURT OF JUSTICE

On December 10, 2001, the Honourable Justice A.B. Stirling, of the Superior Court of Justice, ordered as follows:

1. The Application for the Final Order approving the Plan of Arrangement under ss. 191 and 192 of the *Canada Business Corporations Act,* R.S.C. 1985, c. C-44 (the CBCA), the *Companies' Creditors Arrangement Act,* R.S.C. 1985, c. C-36 ("CCAA"), and s. 185 of the *Business Corporations Act* (Ontario) ("OBCA") (the "Final Application") shall be made on January 20, 2002 at 10:00 o'clock in the forenoon or so soon thereafter as counsel may be heard at the Court House, 361 University Avenue, Toronto, Ontario.

2. Any interested persons may make submissions on the Final Application upon matters relating to the Plan of Arrangement including the fairness of any aspects of the Plan of Arrangement and of any valuation made thereunder, the onus of proof of the fairness of which shall be upon the applicants for the Final Order, and such other matters as the court may deem appropriate if they have filed and served notice of their intention to appear, including their address for service, on [address], on or before January 10, 2002.

3. In the event that the Final Application is adjourned, only those persons who have filed and served a notice of intention to appear on the Final Application shall be served with notice of the adjourned date.

On the Final Application, the following shall be sought:

(a) a declaration that the terms and conditions of the Plan of Arrangement are fair to the persons affected thereby;

(b) an order approving the Plan of Arrangement pursuant to the provisions of ss. 191 and 192 of the CBCA, the CCAA, and s. 186 of the OBCA;

(c) a declaration that the Plan of Arrangement will, upon the filing of Articles of Arrangement under the CBCA Articles of Reorganization under the CBCA and Articles of Arrangement under the OBCA, and the issuance of the Certificate of Amendment under the CBCA, the issuance of the Certificate of Amendment under the ABCA, be effective under the CBCA, the CCAA and the OBCA in accordance with its terms; and

(d) such other and further orders, declarations and directions as the Honourable Court may deem just.

Date: December 15, 2001

ADAM & ZENA
281 McLeod Street
Toronto, Ontario
M5C 3C5
tel: (416) 995-9595
fax: (416) 995-9696
Attention: Sarah Zena
Solicitors for Grandaco Ltd.

App 12-4

Order Sanctioning Arrangement

Court File No:

SUPERIOR COURT OF JUSTICE

BEFORE THE HONOURABLE	)	**FRIDAY, THE 20TH DAY OF**
	)	
JUSTICE A.B. STIRLING	)	**JANUARY, 2002**

IN THE MATTER OF THE COMPANIES' CREDITORS ARRANGEMENT ACT, R.S.C. 1985, c. C-36, as amended

AND IN THE MATTER OF GRANDACO INC.

ORDER

UPON MOTION made this day to this Court by counsel on behalf of Grandaco Inc. in the presence of counsel for ABC Co. Ltd., Trustee for the Operating Lender of the Company, notice of this motion having been given as directed by the Honourable Justice A.B. Stirling , as appears by affidavit of Jayne Brown, filed, upon hearing read the Order filed in support of it, the affidavits of Wendy Long and Harold Peters, filed, and the exhibits referred to in them, and upon hearing what was alleged by counsel and it appearing that Grandaco Inc. is a debtor company within the meaning of the *Companies' Creditors Arrangement Act,* R.S.C. 1985, c. C-36:

1. **THIS COURT ORDERS** that the Plan of Compromise dated the 31st day of October, 2001, proposed between Grandaco Inc. and the [describe creditors], a copy of which [as so altered or modified is annexed as a schedule to and made part of this Order, be and the same is sanctioned as a compromise or arrangement under the *Companies Creditors Arrangement Act.*

____

Appendix 13

Precedents Relating to

Chapter 13

When the Solicitor Becomes the Creditor Precedents

App 13-1

Letter to Client Advising Account will be Assessed

April 16, 2001

Ms. Joan Jeffry
75 Southpark Drive
Toronto, Ontario
M4X 5V5

Dear Ms. Jeffry:

Re: Your Outstanding Account

As you are aware, our account dated December16, 2001 remains outstanding in the amount of $23,660.00 and we enclose herein a copy of the account for your reference.

Please forward payment of this sum to our office within ten (10) days of the date of this letter. If payment is not received, the account will be assessed before the Assessment Officer of the Superior Court of Justice. Once the account has been assessed, it has the same effect as that of a Judgment, and the same collection proceedings will be taken thereunder.

In the event that payment is not made within ten (10) days, you will be forwarded notice of the date of the hearing, and should you wish to dispute our account you will have an opportunity to attend at that time. If you do not dispute our account, it is not necessary for you to be in attendance at the hearing. We trust you realize that any costs incurred in taxing this account and in the collection of same will be added to the amount presently outstanding.

We trust this has merely been an oversight on your part, and that you will be forwarding payment of our account immediately, without the necessity of having it assessed.

Yours very truly,

ADAM & ZENA

Per.
Mary Neill
Law Clerk

Encl.

App 13-2

Requisition for Assessment by Solicitor

Court File No.

SUPERIOR COURT OF JUSTICE

BETWEEN:

ADAM & ZENA

Solicitor(s) of the Superior Court of Justice

- and -

JOAN JEFFRY

Client(s)

APPLICATION UNDER THE SOLICITORS ACT

REQUISITION FOR ASSESSMENT (BY SOLICITOR)

TO THE LOCAL REGISTRAR AT Toronto

I REQUIRE:

AN ORDER for the Assessment of the bill(s) of fees, charges and disbursements delivered:

TO: JOAN JEFFREY
75 Southpark Drive
Toronto, Ontario
M4X 5V5

on or about the 16th day of February, 2001, no order for the assessment of such bill(s) having been previously made, the retainer of the Solicitor(s) not being disputed, and there being no special circumstances.

Date: May 6, 2001

ADAM & ZENA
281 McLeod Street
Toronto, Ontario
M5C 3C5
tel: (416) 995-9595
fax: (416) 995-9696
Attention: Joe Adam

App 13-3

Order for Assessment

Court File No.

SUPERIOR COURT OF JUSTICE

BETWEEN:

ADAM & ZENA

Solicitor(s) of the Superior Court of Justice

- and -

JOAN JEFFRY

Client(s)

ORDER FOR ASSESSMENT
(Solicitor's Application)

On requisition of the above-named Solicitor(s), it is ordered that the bill of fees, charges and disbursements delivered by the said Solicitor(s) to

JOAN JEFFRY, 75 Southpark Drive, Toronto, Ontario, M4X 5V5

a copy of which is attached hereto be referred to the Assessment Officer at Toronto, Ontario to be assessed.

Date .... Signed by ....
Registrar

Address of Court office: 10th Floor
393 University Ave.
Toronto, Ontario
M5G 1E6

I hereby appoint Tuesday, the 3rd day of June 2001, at the hour of 9:45 o'clock in the forenoon at my chambers at the Court House, 10th Floor, 393 University Ave., Toronto, Ontario for the assessment above ordered.

WARNING TO CLIENT - The Assessment Office will certify what, if anything, is due by you to the Solicitor(s) and, upon confirmation of his certificate, payment may be enforced by execution.

App 13-4

Letter to Client Enclosing Order for Assessment

May 6, 2001

Ms. Joan Jeffry
75 Southpark Drive
Toronto, Ontario
M4X 5V5

Dear Ms. Jeffry:

Re: Your Outstanding Account

We note that we have not received payment on our outstanding account. We have now scheduled an appointment for the account to be assessed. Enclosed please find a copy of the Order for Assessment which is served upon you pursuant to the *Rules of Civil Procedure* and the *Solicitors Act*. You will note that the assessment is to be heard on Tuesday, the 3rd day of June, 2001 at 9:45 a.m. at the Court House, Toronto, Ontario. We also enclose a copy of the account to be assessed.

If you wish to consent to the assessment as requested, please contact me by phone at least 48 hours prior to the assessment.

Please notify us if you intend to appear and contest the account. In the event that you do, it will be necessary to have witnesses attend unless you intend to appear yourself or through Counsel. If you fail to notify us of your intent to appear and if you appear and as a result we do not have our witnesses present, we will be forced to ask for an adjournment which will result in an inconvenience to all parties involved. We would therefore appreciate having some statement of your intentions, and would ask that you contact the writer.

We thank you for your anticipated cooperation in this matter.

Yours very truly,

ADAM & ZENA

Per:
Mary Neill
Law Clerk

App 13-5

Report of Assessment

Court File No:

SUPERIOR COURT OF JUSTICE

IN THE MATTER OF THE *SOLICITORS ACT,*

AND IN THE MATTER OF

ADAM & ZENA

Solicitors, of the Superior Court of Justice

- and -

JOAN JEFFRY

Client

REPORT OF ASSESSMENT

Pursuant to the order dated the 5th day of April 2001, I issued my appointment for the assessment of the bill of costs delivered by the above named solicitor to the above named client and on

the 3rd day of June 2001 I was attended by the solicitor

the client appearing

and proceeded with the assessment of the said bill and I find as follows:

That the bill of costs as delivered amounted to the sum of	$23,660.00
and as assessed by me amounts to the sum of	$23.660.00
and	
has been paid on account of the said bill:	500.00
and therefore I find there is due to the solicitor by the client (or) to the client by the solicitor the sum of-.	$23,160.00
and I allow interest to the solicitor in the sum of	$ 721.30
and the costs and disbursements of the assessment are allowed to the solicitor at the sum of	$ 125.00
making a total of due (to) the solicitor (by) the client.	$24,016.30

All of which I respectfully beg to report

Dated this 1st day of June, 2001

____

ASSESSMENT OFFICER

App 13-6

Affidavit of Service of Notice of Filling of Assessment Officer's Report

Court File No:

SUPERIOR COURT OF JUSTICE

BETWEEN:

ADAM & ZENA

Solicitor

- and -

JOAN JEFFRY

Client

AFFIDAVIT

I, MARY NEILL, Law Clerk, of the City of Toronto, in the Regional Municipality of Toronto, **MAKE OATH AND SAY:**

1. On the 4th day of June, 2001, I served the above-named client with the Notice of Filing of the Assessment Officer's Report in this matter and the Certificate of Assessment hereto annexed, by sending such copy by pre-paid ordinary mail in an envelope bearing a return address thereon to Joan Jeffry, 75 Southpark Drive, Toronto, Ontario, M4X 5V5

SWORN BEFORE ME at the City of Toronto, in the Regional Municipality of Toronto, this 4th day of June, 2001	))))	
	)	**MARY NEILL**
A Commissioner, for Oaths in and for the Province of Ontario.	))	

App 13-7

Notice of Filling of Assessment Officer's Report

Court File No:

SUPERIOR COURT OF JUSTICE

BETWEEN:

ADAM & ZENA

Solicitor

- and -

JOAN JEFFRY

Client

NOTICE OF FILING OF ASSESSMENT OFFICER'S REPORT

TAKE NOTICE that pursuant to the Order dated the 6th day of April, 2001, we received the report of the Assessment Officer dated June 3rd, 2001, a copy of which is attached hereto, as Superior Court of Justice File No. 12345.

AND TAKE NOTICE that this report will be confirmed fifteen (15) days after service upon you of this notice to the report.

AND FURTHER TAKE NOTICE that should you fail to satisfy the total amount owing within that time, action will be taken to enforce the Judgment of the Assessment Officer.

ADAM & ZENA
Barristers & Solicitors
281 McLeod Street
Toronto, Ontario
M5C 3C5
tel: (416) 995-9595
fax: (416) 995-9696
Attention: Joe Adam

App 13-8

Affidavit of Service of Notice of Adjournment of Assessment

Court File No:

SUPERIOR COURT OF JUSTICE

BETWEEN:

ADAM & ZENA

Solicitor

- and -

JOAN JEFFRY

Client

AFFIDAVIT OF SERVICE

I, **MARY NEILL**, Law Clerk, of the City of Toronto, in the Regional Municipality of Toronto, MAKE OATH AND SAY AS FOLLOWS:

1. That I did on or about the 11th day of June, 2001, serve the above-named client with the Notice of Adjournment of Assessment, by sending such copy by prepaid ordinary mail in an envelope bearing a return address thereon to Joan Jeffrey, 75 Southpark Drive, Toronto, Ontario, M4X 5V5

SWORN BEFORE ME at the City)
of Toronto, in the Regional Municipality)
of Toronto, this day of) ________________________
June, 2001) **MARY NEILL**
)
)
A Commissioner, etc.)

App 13-9

Notice of Motion for Order for Confirmation of Assessment Officer's Report

Court File No:

SUPERIOR COURT OF JUSTICE

BETWEEN:

ADAM & ZENA

Solicitor

- and -

JOAN JEFFRY

Client

NOTICE OF MOTION

THE PLAINTIFF will make a motion to a Judge on Thursday, the 11th day of June, 2001, at 10:00 a.m., or as soon after that time as the Motion can be heard, at the Court House, 130 Queen Street West, Toronto, Ontario.

PROPOSED METHOD OF HEARING: The motion is to be heard

X in writing under subrule 37.12.1(1) because it is made without notice;

_ in writing as an opposed motion under subrule 37.12.1(4);

_ orally.

THE MOTION IS FOR an Order confirming the Report of the Assessment Officer given June 3, 2001.

THE GROUNDS FOR THE MOTION ARE:

(a) Rule 54.09(4) of the Rules of Civil Procedure.

THE FOLLOWING DOCUMENTARY EVIDENCE will be used at the hearing of the motion:

(a) the pleadings and proceedings herein; and

(b) the Affidavit of Joe Adam, filed;

(c) such further or other material as this Honourable Court may deem just.

June 4th, 2001

ADAM & ZENA
Barristers & Solicitors
281 McLeod Street
Toronto, Ontario
M5C 3C5
tel: (416) 995-9595
fax: (416) 995-9696
Attention: Joe Adam

App 13-10

Affidavit in Support of Order for Confirmation of Assessment Officer's Report

Court File No:

SUPERIOR COURT OF JUSTICE

BETWEEN:

ADAM & ZENA

Solicitor

- and -

JOAN JEFFRY

Client

AFFIDAVIT

I, JOE ADAM, of the City of Toronto, in the Regional Municipality of Toronto, MAKE OATH AND SAY:

1. That I am a partner in the firm of Adam & Zena, the solicitors in this action, and as such have knowledge of the matters hereinafter deposed to.

2. That I acted on behalf of Joan Jeffry with respect to litigation involving the sale of a rental property, and rendered my account to Ms. Jeffry on the 1st day of April, 2001, for the sum of $20,260.00 for fees and $3,400.00 for disbursements for a total of $23,660.00.

3. That Joan Jeffry failed to pay my account and the account was assessed before the Assessment Officer on June 3, 2001. Attached hereto and marked as Exhibit "A" to this my Affidavit is a copy of the Report on Assessment given by the Assessment Officer.

4. That I have some concern that Joan Jeffry is selling off a large part of her assets and that she has no intention of making voluntary payment of the account as taxed.

5. That Ms. Jeffry had advised me after she had received the Order for Assessment that it was her intention to sell her home at 75 Southpark Drive, Toronto, Ontario and that she would be moving to the State of Alabama in a short time and had no intention of paying my outstanding account.

6. That I have recently attempted to contact Ms. Jeffry at her place of employment; however, I was told by her employer that she was no longer working there, and that she had moved to Alabama.

7. That Ms. Jeffry's home at 75 Southpark Drive, Toronto, Ontario was advertised for sale by Hawkesbury Realty, and now has a for sale sign on it. I contacted Hawkesbury Realty; however, they refused to advise me of the particulars of the sale of the property. I have not been able to contact Ms. Jeffry at her home as her telephone has been disconnected.

8. That I am concerned that the property located at 75 Southpark Drive, Toronto, Ontario, will have been conveyed to a purchaser prior to the fifteen day time period for confirmation of the Assessment Officer's Report and that the moneys received from the sale of the property will be taken to Alabama or elsewhere, which will make collection of the account as assessed very difficult.

9. This Affidavit is made in support of a Motion for an Order confirming the Report of Assessment at this time and is made for no improper purpose.

SWORN BEFORE ME at the City	)	
of Toronto, in the Regional Municipality	)	
of Toronto, this 4th day of June, 2001	)	____________________
	)	
	)	**JOE ADAM**
A Commissioner, for Oaths in and	)	
for the Province of Onario	)	

App 13-11

Order for Confirmation of Assessment Officer's Report

Court File No:

SUPERIOR COURT OF JUSTICE

THE HONOURABLE JUSTICE	)	**THURSDAY, THE 11TH DAY OF**
	)	
A.B. JUDGE	)	**JUNE, A.D. 2001**

BETWEEN:

ADAM & ZENA

Plaintiff

- and -

JOAN JEFFRY

Defendant

ORDER

THIS MOTION, made by Adam & Zena an Order confirming the Report of the Assessment Officer dated the 1st day of June, 2001, was heard this day at Toronto.

ON READING the pleadings and proceedings herein and on hearing the submissions of counsel on behalf of Adam & Zena.

1. **THIS COURT ORDERS** that the Report of the Assessment Officer dated June 3, 2001, is hereby confirmed and Adam & Zena Firm may proceed with collection under the said Report of Assessment.

____

INDEX TO PRECEDENTS

NOTE: For forms dealing with mediation, see Chapter 5.

Appendix 4

Precedents Relating to Chapter 4

Using Small Claims Court to Your Client's Advantage

App

Appendix 5

Precedents Relating to Chapter 5

Collection from Deceased Estates

Precedents

App

Appendix 6

Precedents Relating to Chapter 6

Statutory Remedies Precedents

App

Appendix 8

Precedents Relating to Chapter 8

Foreclosure Proceedings Precedents

App

Appendix 9

Precedents Relating to Chapter 9

Bankruptcy Proceedings Precedents

App

Appendix 10

Precedents Relating to Chapter 10

Consumer Proposals Precedents

App

NOTE: Precedents for Proof of Claim and Proxy are contained in Chapter 9

Appendix 11

Precedents Relating to Chapter 11

Commercial (Division 1) Proposal Precedents

App

NOTE: Precedents for Proof of Claim and Proxy are contained in Chapter 9

Precedent for Voting Letter is contained in Chapter 10

Appendix 12

Precedents Relating to Chapter 12

The Companies' Creditors Arrangement Act Precedents

App

Appendix 13

Precedents Relating to Chapter 13

When the Solicitor Becomes the Creditor Precedents

App

INDEX

(References are to section number, or Appendix number for Precedents)